> اَحْسَنَ مِنْكَ لَمْ تَرَ قَطُّ عَيْنِيْ
> وَاَجْمَلَ مِنْكَ لَمْ تَلِدِ النِّسَاءُ
> خُلِقْتَ مُبَرَّءً مِنْ كُلِّ عَيْبٍ
> كَاَنَّكَ قَدْ خُلِقْتَ كَمَا تَشَاءُ

Better than you no eye has ever seen
More beautiful than you no woman has given birth to
You have been created free from any defect
As if you were created like how you desired

Seeratul Mustafa ﷺ

Seeratul Mustafa
ﷺ

(Abridged Version)

Biography of the Chosen Messenger of Allah,
Nabi Muhammad Mustafa ﷺ

Prepared by
Hadhrat Moulana Muhammad Idrees Kaandhlawi رحمه الله

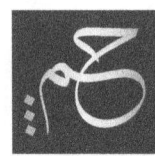

HA-MEEM PUBLICATIONS

🌐 www.hameemstore.com
📷 @hameemstore
✉ orders@hameemstore.com
💬 +1 (416) 879-2545

Permission is granted for reprinting this booklet without any alterations. A humble appeal is made to the readers to offer suggestions, corrections, etc. to improve the quality of future publications. May Allah Ta'ala reward you for this.

The author, translators, editors and typesetters humbly request your duas for them, their parents, families, asaatiza and mashaaikh.

Title: Seeratul Mustafa ﷺ
Author: Hadhrat Moulana Muhammad Idrees Kaandhlawi رحمه الله
Translated by: Mufti Muhammad Kadwa and Moulana Mahommed Mahommedy

Jamiatul Ulama (KZN)
Ta'limi Board
4 Third Avenue
P.O.Box 26024 Isipingo Beach 4115
South Africa

Tel: (+27) 31 912 2172 - Ext: 209
Fax: (+27) 31 902 9268
Mobile: (+27) 83 7500095
E-mail: info@talimiboardkzn.org
Website: www.talimiboardkzn.org

First Edition: Ramadhaan 1435 / June 2014
Second Edition: Ramadhaan 1436 / June 2015

Contents

Introduction to the Abridged version XXIII

Foreword XXV
    by Hadhrat Moulana Abdullah Amejee Saahib (daamat barakaatuhu)
.... XXV

Foreword XXVII
    by Hadhrat Maulana Ashraf 'Ali Thaanwi رحمه الله XXVII

Preface XXIX
    by Hadhrat Moulana Idrees Kaandhlawi رحمه الله XXIX

Chapter 1 1
    Untainted Family Lineage 1
        Maternal Lineage 2
        Reason for the name of Quraysh 4
        'Abdul Muttalib's Dream and the Well of Zam Zam 7
        'Abdul Muttalib's Vow 9
        Hadhrat 'Abdullah's Marriage to Hadhrat Aaminah 13
        Incident of the People of the Elephants 14

Chapter 2 17
    The Auspicious Birth 17
        The Collapse of Chosroes' Palace and the Sinking of Lake Sawah 18
        'Aqeeqah and Naming 19
        Title (Kuniyyat) 21
        Upbringing and Suckling 21
        The Splitting of the Chest 25
        In the Guardianship of 'Abdul Muttalib 26
        Death of 'Abdul Muttalib 26
        In the Guardianship of Abu Taalib 27

The First Journey to Syria and his encounter with the Monk Bahira............ 27
Participation in Hilful-Fudool.. 29
Occupation of Trade and the Title of Al-Ameen 30
Grazing Goats.. 31
Second Journey to Syria and the Encounter with Nastoora, the Monk........ 31
Marriage to Hadhrat Khadijah ﺭﺿﻲﺍﻟﻠﻪﻋﻨﻬﺎ.. 33
The Renovation of the K'abah and Rasulullah's ﺻﻠﻰﺍﻟﻠﻪﻋﻠﻴﻪﻭﺳﻠﻢ Arbitration .. 34
His Divine Aversion to Pagan Customs.. 36

Chapter 3 41

The Sunrise of Prophethood on Mount Faran...................................... 41
Date of Prophethood.. 44
Salaah - The Primary Obligation after Tauheed and Risaalat....................... 44

Chapter 4 47

The Earliest Pioneers 47
Islam of Abu Bakr Siddeeq ﺭﺿﻲﺍﻟﻠﻪﻋﻨﻪ 48
The Islam of Ja'far bin Abi Taalib ﺭﺿﻲﺍﻟﻠﻪﻋﻨﻪ 49
Islam of 'Afeef Kindi ﺭﺿﻲﺍﻟﻠﻪﻋﻨﻪ 50
Islam of Talhah ﺭﺿﻲﺍﻟﻠﻪﻋﻨﻪ 50
Islam of S'ad bin Abi Waqqaas ﺭﺿﻲﺍﻟﻠﻪﻋﻨﻪ 51
Islam of Khaalid bin Sa'eed bin Aas ﺭﺿﻲﺍﻟﻠﻪﻋﻨﻪ 51
Islam of 'Usmaan bin 'Affaan ﺭﺿﻲﺍﻟﻠﻪﻋﻨﻪ 52
Islam of 'Ammaar ﺭﺿﻲﺍﻟﻠﻪﻋﻨﻪ and Suhaib ﺭﺿﻲﺍﻟﻠﻪﻋﻨﻪ 55
Islam of 'Amr bin 'Abasah ﺭﺿﻲﺍﻟﻠﻪﻋﻨﻪ 56
Islam of Abu Zarr ﺭﺿﻲﺍﻟﻠﻪﻋﻨﻪ 57
Assembly of the Muslims in Daar-e-Arqam 58
Open Proclamation of Islam... 58
Invitation to Islam and Ta'aam (meals)... 59
Qurayshi conference for hampering the spread of Islam 62
Islam of Hamzah ﺭﺿﻲﺍﻟﻠﻪﻋﻨﻪ 64

Chapter 5 67

The Spread of Islam and the Quraysh of Makkah 67
Revelation of Qul Yaa Ayyuhal-Kaafirun 69
Pointless and absurd questions of the Makkan disbelievers 70
Quraysh of Makkah consult Jewish scholars 71
Disbelievers persecute Rasulullah ﺻﻠﻰﺍﻟﻠﻪﻋﻠﻴﻪﻭﺳﻠﻢ 73

Islam of Dimaad bin Tha'labah رضي الله عنه 76

Chapter 6 77

Arch-enemies 77
Abu Jahal bin Hishaam 78
Abu Lahab 79
Umayyah bin Khalaf Jumahi 81
Ubayy bin Khalaf 81
'Uqbah bin Abi Mu'eet 82
Waleed bin Mughirah 83
Abu Qays bin Faakihah 84
Nadr bin Haaris 84
'Aas bin Waa'il Sahmi 85
Nubaih and Munabbihah, the sons of Hajaaj 86
Aswad bin Muttalib 86
Aswad bin 'Abdi-Yaghuth 87
Haaris bin Qays Sahmi 87
Persecution of the Muslims 88
Sayyidina Bilal bin Rabaah رضي الله عنه (The Imaam of the callers to Salaah and success) 89
'Ammaar bin Yaasir رضي الله عنه 90
Suhaib bin Sinaan رضي الله عنه 91
Khabbaab bin Aratt رضي الله عنه 92
Abu Fukayhah Juhani رضي الله عنه 93
Zanirah رضي الله عنها 94
The Miracle of the Splitting of the Moon 97
The Miracle of the Return of the Sun 98
The Miracle of the Halting of the Sun 99
The First Migration to Abyssinia 99
The Second Migration to Abyssinia 101
The Inspirational Sermon of Ja'far رضي الله عنه in the Court of Negus 102
Three questions of Ja'far رضي الله عنه to the Qurayshi delegates 105
Islam of 'Umar bin Khattaab رضي الله عنه - 6th year of Prophethood 107
Boycott of Banu Haashim and the Penning of an Oppressive Decree 111
Migration of Abu Bakr رضي الله عنه 114
The Year of Anguish and Bereavement - The death of Khadijatul-Kubra رضي الله عنها and Abu Taalib 116
Journey to Taaif for the Propagation of Islam 117
Return from Taaif and Attendance of the Jinn 121
Islam of Tufail bin 'Amr Dawsi 122

Chapter 7 125

Mi'raaj 125
Wisdom behind Mi'raaj 125
Mi'raaj in Detail 126
The Marvels of this Celestial journey 127
Baitul-Muqaddas 129
Glorification of Ibraaheem عَلَيْهِ ٱلسَّلَام: 130
Glorification of Musa عَلَيْهِ ٱلسَّلَام: 130
Glorification of Dawood عَلَيْهِ ٱلسَّلَام: 131
Glorification of Sulaymaan عَلَيْهِ ٱلسَّلَام: 131
Glorification of 'Isa عَلَيْهِ ٱلسَّلَام: 131
Glorification of Rasulullah صَلَّى ٱللَّهُ عَلَيْهِ وَسَلَّم: 132
Ascension to the Heavens 133
Meeting the Ambiyaa عَلَيْهِمُ ٱلسَّلَام 133
Sidratul-Muntaha: 135
Observation of Jannah and Jahannam: 135
Sareeful-Aqlaam - The Site of the Scratching of the Pens: 135
Divine Proximity - (Celestial vision, divine conversation and the conferral of sacred edicts) 136
Stalling the Sun 139

Chapter 8 143

Invitation to Islam during the days of Haj 143
Islam of Iyaas bin Mu'aaz رَضِىَ ٱللَّهُ عَنْهُ 145
The Inception of Islam in Madinah Munawwarah – 11th Year of Prophethood 145
The First Pledge of the Ansaar – 12th year prophethood 146
Islam of Rifa'ah رَضِىَ ٱللَّهُ عَنْهُ 149
The Institution of Jumu'ah at Madinah 149
Second Pledge of the Ansaar – 13th year of prophet-hood 150
Assigning Nuqabaa (Leaders) 152
Names of the Nuqabaa 152
Bay'at – the pledge, what is it? 153
Important Note 154
Open proclamation of Islam in Madinah 155

Chapter 9 157

Migration to Madinah Munawwarah 157
Assembly of Quraysh in Daarun-Nadwah and their Resolution to Assassinate Rasulullah صَلَّى ٱللَّهُ عَلَيْهِ وَسَلَّم 160

Cave of Saur 164
Date of Departure.. 167
Story of Umm-e-Ma'bad 167
Incident of Suraaqah bin Maalik 168
Incident of Buraidah Aslami 169
Foundation of Masjidut Taqwa.. 171
Date of Hijrah... 172
The Inception of the Islamic Calendar 172
Khutbatut-Taqwa (First Khutbah and Jumu'ah) 173
The Appearance of the Rabbis before Rasulullah ﷺ 180
Islam of 'Abdullah bin Salaam ﺭﺿﻲ ﺍﻟﻠﻪ ﻋﻨﻪ 182
Islam of Maymun bin Yaameen ﺭﺿﻲ ﺍﻟﻠﻪ ﻋﻨﻪ 184
Islam of Salmaan bin Islam ﺭﺿﻲ ﺍﻟﻠﻪ ﻋﻨﻪ 185
Erection of Masjid-e-Nabawi... 189
Erection of Rooms for the Wives... 192
After the Demise of the Pure Wives 192
Expansion of the Masjid by the Khulafaa.. 193
Site of Janaazah Salaah... 194

Chapter 10 195

Brotherhood between the Muhaajireen and Ansaar........................ 195
Second Occasion of Brotherhood 196
Inception of the Azaan 199
Treaty with the Jews.. 201
Miscellaneous Incidents of the First Year of Hijrah.................................. 204
Islam of Sarumah bin Abi Anas ﺭﺿﻲ ﺍﻟﻠﻪ ﻋﻨﻪ 205
Change of Qiblah direction – 2nd Year of Hijrah 206
Suffah and As-haabus Suffah.. 207
Attributes of As-haabus Suffah 210
Names of As-haabus Suffah 210
Fasting of Ramadhaan 212
Sadaqatul-Fitr and Eid Salaah.. 212
Salaatul-Adhaa and Qurbaani.. 213
Durood Shareef 213
Zakaat on wealth.. 213

Chapter 11 215

Ghazawaat and Saraaya (Military Expeditions) 215
Sariyyah of Hadhrat Hamzah ﺭﺿﻲ ﺍﻟﻠﻪ ﻋﻨﻪ 215
Sariyyah of 'Ubaidah bin Haaris ﺭﺿﻲ ﺍﻟﻠﻪ ﻋﻨﻪ 216
Sariyyah of S'ad bin Abi Waqqaas ﺭﺿﻲ ﺍﻟﻠﻪ ﻋﻨﻪ 216
Expedition of Abwa 216

The Battle of Bawaat 217
Expedition of 'Ushayrah 217
First Battle of Badr - Also referred to as the battle of Safwaan or the minor
battle of Badr 218
Sariyyah of 'Abdullah bin Jahsh رضي الله عنه 219
The first spoils of war in Islam 220

Chapter 12 223

Battle of Badr – 2 A.H. 223

Preamble to the Battle of Badr 223
Departure 224
Mashwarah with the Sahaabah رضي الله عنهم and their Staunchly Devoted
Discourses 227
Selfless sermon of Miqdaad bin Aswad رضي الله عنه 227
The Valiant Speech of S'ad bin Mu'aaz رضي الله عنه 228
Dream of Aatikah bint 'Abdul Muttalib 230
Dream of Juhaim bin Salat 231
Preparation for War 234
Battleground speech of 'Utbah 236
Inception of the war 237
Slaying of 'Utbah, Shaybah and Waleed 238
Rasulullah's ﷺ Dua for Victory 240
Descent of the angels to assist the Muslims 243
Abu Jahal's dua and his Incitement of War 244
Slaying of Umayyah bin Khalaf and his Son 247
Slaying of Abu Jahal – Pharaoh of this Ummah 249
Searching for Abu Jahal's Body after the Victory 249
The Prisoners of Badr 252
Disposing of the Corpses in the well of Badr 253
Despatching a Messenger to Madinah with News of Victory 254
Distribution of the booty 255
Distribution of the War Captives amongst the Muslims 256
Consultation over the Captives of Badr 257
Divine Admonishment upon the Acceptance of Ransom 259
Ransom Amount 261
Back in Makkah 262
Abul 'Aas bin Rabi' رضي الله عنه 264
Abbaas bin Abdul Muttalib رضي الله عنه 267
Salaatul-Eid 270

Chapter 13 271

Virtues of the Badriyeen 271

Number of Badri Sahaabah رَضِيَٱللَّهُعَنْهُم 272
Register of the Badri Angels 272
Register of the Martyrs of Badr 272
Prisoners of Badr 276

Chapter 14 277

Other Expeditions 277
Assassination of 'Asma, the Jewess – 26th Ramadhaan 2 A.H. 277
Battle of Qarqaratul-Kudr 278
Assassination of Abu 'Afak, the Jew 279
Campaign of Qaynuqaa - Saturday 15th of Shawwaal 2 A.H. 279
Campaign of Saweeq – 5th Zul-Hijjah 2 A.H. 281
Eidul-Adhaa 281
Nikah of Hadhrat Faatimah رَضِيَٱللَّهُعَنْها 281
Campaign of Ghitfaan 3 A.H. - Also referred to as the campaign of Anmaar and the campaign of Zu Amar 282
Campaign of Buhraan 284
Assassination of K'ab bin Ashraf 284
Islam of Huwayyisah bin Mas'ood رَضِيَٱللَّهُعَنْهُ 287
Sariyyah of Zaid bin Haarisah رَضِيَٱللَّهُعَنْهُ - 3 A.H. 288
Assassination of Abu Raaf'i - Jumaadath-Thaani 3 A.H. 288

Chapter 15 291

The Battle of Uhud - Shawwaal 3 A.H. 291
Quraysh Taking the Womenfolk Along 292
'Abbaas رَضِيَٱللَّهُعَنْهُ Notifies Rasulullah صَلَّىٱللَّهُعَلَيْهِوَسَلَّم of the Quraysh's Plan .. 292
Rasulullah صَلَّىٱللَّهُعَلَيْهِوَسَلَّم Consulting the Sahaabah رَضِيَٱللَّهُعَنْهُم 292
Rasulullah's صَلَّىٱللَّهُعَلَيْهِوَسَلَّم Preparation and Donning the Armour 295
Rasulullah's صَلَّىٱللَّهُعَلَيْهِوَسَلَّم Departure and Inspection of his Forces 295
Disengagement and Return of the Hypocrites 297
Drawing up the Battle Lines 298
Condition of the Quraysh Army 298
Rasulullah صَلَّىٱللَّهُعَلَيْهِوَسَلَّم Addressing the Troops 299
The Launch of the Battle and the Killing of the Leading Qurayshi Contenders 300
The first contestant: 300
The second contestant: 300
The third contestant: 301
The fourth contestant: 301
The fifth contestant: 301
The sixth contestant: 302
The seventh contestant: 302

The eighth contestant: 302
The ninth contestant: 302
The tenth contestant: 302
The eleventh contestant: 302
The Valour of Abu Dujaanah رضي الله عنه 302
Valour and Martyrdom of Hadhrat Hamzah رضي الله عنه 303
Martyrdom of Hanzalah, Ghaseelul-Malaa'ikah رضي الله عنه 305
Muslims Archers Abandoning Positions and the Reversal of the War-Scales
.... 306
Martyrdom of 'Abdullah bin Jubair رضي الله عنه and His Ten Companions 306
Martyrdom of Mus'ab bin 'Umair رضي الله عنه 306
Huzaifah's Father is Erroneously Martyred by the Muslims.................... 307
The unexpected Attack of Khaalid bin Waleed and the Unwavering Stance
of Rasulullah صلى الله عليه وسلم 307
Bodyguards of Rasulullah صلى الله عليه وسلم 308
Unexpected Attack of the Quraysh against Rasulullah صلى الله عليه وسلم and the
Valiant Sacrifice of the Sahaabah رضي الله عنهم 308
Martyrdom of Ziyaad bin Sakan رضي الله عنه 309
Attack of 'Utbah bin Abi Waqqaas upon Rasulullah صلى الله عليه وسلم 309
Attack of 'Abdullah bin Qumayyah upon Rasulullah صلى الله عليه وسلم 309
Support of Hadhrat Ali رضي الله عنه and Hadhrat Talhah رضي الله عنه to Rasulullah
صلى الله عليه وسلم 310
The Gallant Sacrifice of Abu Dujaanah رضي الله عنه 312
Rasulullah صلى الله عليه وسلم Lamenting over the Disbelievers 312
Rasulullah صلى الله عليه وسلم Cursing Some of the Qurayshi Chieftains 312
Qataadah bin Nu'maan رضي الله عنه Loses an Eye during the Battle............. 313
Rumour of Rasulullah's صلى الله عليه وسلم Martyrdom 314
Martyrdom of Anas bin Nadr رضي الله عنه 314
Killing of Ubayy bin Khalaf 315
Hadhrat Ali رضي الله عنه and Hadhrat Faatimah رضي الله عنها bathe the wounds of
Rasulullah صلى الله عليه وسلم 316
Mutilating the Corpses of the Muslims.. 316
Abu Sufyaan's Taunts and Hadhrat 'Umar's رضي الله عنه reply 316
Martyrdom of S'ad bin Rab'i رضي الله عنه 319
The Search for the Body of Hadhrat Hamzah رضي الله عنه 320
Martyrdom of 'Abdullah bin Jahsh رضي الله عنه 321

Martyrdom of 'Abdullah bin 'Amr bin Haraam رَضِيَ اللَّهُ عَنْهُ 322
Martyrdom of 'Amr bin Jamooh رَضِيَ اللَّهُ عَنْهُ 323
Martyrdom of Khaysamah رَضِيَ اللَّهُ عَنْهُ 324
Martyrdom of Usayrim رَضِيَ اللَّهُ عَنْهُ 325
People of Madinah Scurry to Ascertain the Well-being of Rasulullah صَلَّى اللَّهُ عَلَيْهِ وَسَلَّمَ 325
A Special Favour upon the Sincere Sahaabah رَضِيَ اللَّهُ عَنْهُ during the Anxiety of Battle 326
Shrouding and Burial of the Martyrs 327
Patriotic martyrdom 327
A Synopsis of the Wisdom behind the Defeat at Uhud 328
Campaign of Hamraa ul-Asad - Sunday 16th Shawwaal 3 A.H. 330

Chapter 16 333

Miscellaneous events of 3 A.H. 333
Sariyyah (expedition) of Abu Salamah 'Abdullah bin 'Abdul-Asad رَضِيَ اللَّهُ عَنْهُ (4 A.H.) 333
Sariyyah (expedition) of 'Abdullah bin Unais رَضِيَ اللَّهُ عَنْهُ 334
Incident of Raj'i 334

Chapter 17 341

The Incident of Bi'r Ma'unah 341
Battle of Banu Nazeer - Rabi'ul-Awwal 4 A.H. 343
Prohibition of liquor 347
Expedition of Zaatur-Riqaa - Jumaadal-Awwal 4 A.H. 347
Expedition of the Badr - Sha'baan 4 A.H. 348
Miscellaneous Incidents of 4 A.H. 350
Expedition of Dawmatul Jandal 350
Expedition of Murays'i or Banu Mustaliq 350
Incident of Slander 354
Revelation of the Verses of Exoneration 360
Revelation of Tayammum 363

Chapter 18 365

Battle of Khandaq (Trench) or Ahzaab (Confederates) - Shawwaal 5 A.H. 365
Expedition of Banu Qurayzah 375
Rasulullah's صَلَّى اللَّهُ عَلَيْهِ وَسَلَّمَ Nikah with Hadhrat Zaynab رَضِيَ اللَّهُ عَنْهَا 380
Revelation of Hijaab 380

Expedition of Muhammad bin Maslamah Ansaari ﷺ towards Qurta - 10th Muharram 6 A.H. 381
Islam of Sumaamah bin Usaal 381
Expedition of Bani Lihyaan - Rabi'ul-Awwal 6 A.H. 384
Expedition of Zi Qarad - Rabi'ul-Awwal 6 A.H. 385
Expedition of 'Ukkaashah bin Mihsan ﷺ towards Ghamr 386
Expedition of Muhammad Bin Maslamah ﷺ towards Zil-Qassah 386
Expedition of Abu 'Ubaidah bin Jarrah ﷺ towards Zil-Qassah 386
Expedition of Jamum 387
Expedition of 'Is 387
Expedition of Tarif 387
Expedition of Hasma 387
Expedition of Waadiul-Quraa 388
Expedition of Dawmatul Jandal 388
Expedition of Fidak 390
Expedition of Umme Qirfah 391
Expedition of 'Abdullah bin Rawaahah ﷺ 391
Expedition of Kurz bin Jaabir Fihari towards 'Uraniyyeen 392
Expedition of 'Amr bin Umayyah Damri ﷺ 392

Chapter 19 395

'Umratul-Hudaybiyyah – 1st Zul-Q'adah 6 A.H. 395
Bay'atur-Ridwaan 397
Terms of the Treaty of Hudaybiyyah 402

Chapter 20 409

International Efforts to Spread Islam - Letters to World Leaders .. 409
(1) Letter to the Emperor of Rome 410
Hadhrat Dihyaa's ﷺ Sermon in the Emperor's court 411
(2) Letter to Chosroe Parvez, emperor of Persia 416
(3) Letter to Negus, the Emperor of Abyssinia 418
Negus' Response 419
Negus' Reply to Rasulullah's ﷺ Letter 419
(4) Letter to Muqawqis, Governor of Egypt and Alexandria 422
Lecture of Haatib ﷺ in the Court of Muqawqis 423
Response of the Governor 424
Muqawqis, Reply to Rasulullah's ﷺ Letter 424
Letter to Munzir bin Sawa, Governor of Bahrain 428
Response of Munzir bin Sawa 428
Munzir bin Sawa's Response to Rasulullah's ﷺ Letter 429
(6) Letter to the Ruler of Amman 430

(7) Letter to the Chief of Yamaamah, Huzah bin Ali 434
(8) Letter to the Ruler of Damascus Haaris Ghassaani 435

Chapter 21 437

The Battle of Khaybar 7 A.H.. 437
(1) Na'im Fort... 441
(2) Qamus Fort... 441
(3) S'ab bin Mu'aaz Fort.. 443
(4) Qullah Fort... 443
(5) Watih and Salalim... 444
Conquest of Fadak... 444
An Attempt to Poison Rasulullah ﷺ 445
Mukhaabarah – Sharecropping.. 446
The Arrival of Abu Hurayrah رضى الله عنه 447
Return of the Orchards of the Ansaar.. 447
Prohibitions at Khaybar 448
Return of the Emigrants from Abyssinia.. 448
Conquest of Wadil-Quraa and Tayma.. 448
Return Journey and the incident of Laylatut-T'aris 449
Consummation of Marriage with Umme Habibah رضى الله عنها 449
'Umratul-Qadaa – Zul Q'adah 7 A.H... 449
Nikah with Maymunah رضى الله عنها 451
Expedition of Akhram bin Abil 'Awjaa - Zul-Hijjah 7 A.H. 452
Expedition of Ghaalib bin 'Abdullah Laysi رضى الله عنه - Safar 8 A.H.... 453
Other expeditions 453
Islam of Khaalid bin Waleed رضى الله عنه, 'Usmaan bin Talhah رضى الله عنه and 'Amr bin 'Aas رضى الله عنه 453

Chapter 22 459

Expedition of Muta - Jumaadal-Ula 8 A.H... 459
Expedition of 'Amr bin 'Aas رضى الله عنه towards Zaatus-Salaasil............ 466
Expedition of Abu 'Ubaidah رضى الله عنه towards Siful-Bahr (the coastline) ... 468

Chapter 23 469

The Conquest of Makkah - Ramadhaan 8 A.H.................................. 469
Abu Sufyaan leaves Makkah in order to renew the peace treaty 472
The story of Haatib ibn Abi Balta'ah رضى الله عنه 473
The subject matter of Haatib's رضى الله عنه letter....................................... 474
Departure from Madinah 475
Stopping over at Marruz-Zahraan 478

Abu Sufyaan embraces Islam 479
Entry into Makkah 482
Entering the Sacred Masjid 484
Rasulullah ﷺ delivers a speech from the door of the Ka'bah 485
The Azaan is given at the door of the Ka'bah 486
Pledge of allegiance from men and women 489
Rasulullah's ﷺ second speech 491
The dwellings of the Muhaajireen 492
After the year of amnesty 492
Abu Quhaafah embraces Islam 499
Safwaan ibn Umayyah embraces Islam 500
Suhayl ibn 'Amr embraces Islam 501
'Utbah and Mu'tab embrace Islam 502
Mu'aawiyah embraces Islam 502
Small battalions are sent to destroy idols 503
'Uzza and Suwa' are destroyed 503
Manaat is destroyed 504

Chapter 24 505

The Battle of Hunayn - Shawwaal 8 A.H. 505
The siege of Taa'if 509
The booty of Hunayn is distributed 510
Umrah Ji'irraanah 513
The prohibition of mut'ah 513
Other incidents that took place in this year (8 A.H.) 513
The appointment of governors 514
The 9th year A.H. 514
The expedition of 'Uyaynah ibn Hisn Fazaari 514
The speech of 'Ataarid ibn Haajib 515
The expedition of Waleed ibn 'Uqbah ibn Abi Mu'eet 516
The expedition of 'Abdullah ibn 'Ausjah ؓ 517
The expedition of Qutbah ibn 'Aamir ؓ 517
The expedition of Dahhaak ibn Sufyaan ؓ 517
The expedition of 'Alqamah ibn Mujazzaz Mudlaji ؓ 517
The expedition of Ali ibn Abi Taalib ؓ 518
Ka'b ibn Zuhayr embraces Islam 519

Chapter 25 521

The Battle of Tabuk - Rajab 9 A.H. 521
Masjidud Diraar 524
Those who remained behind 526
Abu Bakr ؓ is appointed Ameer of Haj 528
Various incidents that took place in 9 A. H. 530

Chapter 26..531
   The 10th year A.H. – The year of delegations...................................... 531
      1. The delegation of Hawaazin... 532
      2. The delegation of Saqeef... 533
      3. The delegation of Banu ʿAamir ibn Saʿsaʿah 534
      4. The delegation of ʿAbd al-Qays... 535
      5. The delegation of Banu Hanifah – 9 A.H. 536
      6. The delegation of Tayy... 537
      7. The delegation of Kindah... 538
      8. The delegation of Ashʿariyyin 538
      9. The delegation of Azd 539
      10. The delegation of Banu Haaris 539
      11. The delegation of Hamdaan... 540
      12. The delegation of Muzaynah 540
      13. The delegation of Daus 541
      14. The delegation of Christians from Najraan 541
      Mubaahalah (invoking curses) 543
      15. Farwah ibn ʿAmr Juzaami 545
      16. Dimam ibn Saʿlabah comes to Madinah.................................... 546
      17. The delegation of Taariq ibn ʿAbdillah Muhaaribi and the Bani Muhaarib 547
      18. The delegation of Tujib 548
      19. The delegation of Huzaym 549
      20. The delegation of Bani Fazaarah 549
      21. The delegation of Bani Asd – 9 A.H. 550
      22. The delegation of Bahraaʾ.. 550
      23. The delegation of ʿUdhrah.. 551
      24. The delegation of Baliyy 551
      25. The delegation of Bani Murrah 552
      26. The delegation of Khaulaan 552
      27. The delegation of Muhaarib 552
      28. The delegation of Sudaʾ... 553
      29. The delegation of Ghassaan 553
      30. The delegation of Salaamaan 553
      31. The delegation of Bani ʿAbas... 554
      32. The delegation of Ghaamid 554
      33. The delegation of Azd 554
      34. The delegation of Bani al-Muntafiq 556
      35. The delegation of Nakhaʿ.. 556
      Islam is taught in Yemen... 556
      Khaalid ibn Waleed's ؓ expedition to Najraan................................... 557
      Ali's ؓ expedition towards Yemen 559

Chapter 27..560
   Hajjatul Wadaa – The Farewell Haj 560

The Farewell Sermon 561
The sermon at Ghadir Khum 562
Return to Madinah 562
Jibraa'eel عَلَيْهِ السَّلَام comes to Rasulullah ﷺ 563
The military expedition of Usaamah ibn Zaid رَضِيَ اللَّهُ عَنْهُ 563

Chapter 28 565

Preparation for the journey to the hereafter 565
Rasulullah ﷺ falls ill 567
Faatimah رَضِيَ اللَّهُ عَنْهَا cries and smiles 567
The incident of Qirtaas 568
Rasulullah's ﷺ final sermon 570
Rasulullah's ﷺ last Salaah with congregation 572
The day of Rasulullah's ﷺ demise 573
Rasulullah ﷺ in the throes of death 574
The date of Rasulullah's ﷺ demise 575
The uneasiness of the Sahaabah رَضِيَ اللَّهُ عَنْهُمْ 576
Abu Bakr's رَضِيَ اللَّهُ عَنْهُ sermon 577
The remainder of Abu Bakr's رَضِيَ اللَّهُ عَنْهُ sermon 578

Chapter 29 581

The Ansaar gather at Saqeefah Bani Saa'idah 581
The burial arrangements 582
The Janaazah Salaah 583
Burial 584

Chapter 30 585

Saqeefah Bani Saa'idah and the pledge of allegiance 585
The speech of Sa'd ibn 'Ubaadah رَضِيَ اللَّهُ عَنْهُ 586
Abu Bakr's رَضِيَ اللَّهُ عَنْهُ speech 587
Sa'd ibn 'Ubaadah's رَضِيَ اللَّهُ عَنْهُ acknowledgement 589
The general pledge after the special pledge 591
'Umar رَضِيَ اللَّهُ عَنْهُ delivers a speech before the general pledge 591
Abu Bakr's رَضِيَ اللَّهُ عَنْهُ first speech after the general pledge 592
Ali's رَضِيَ اللَّهُ عَنْهُ pledge of allegiance 593
Abu Bakr's رَضِيَ اللَّهُ عَنْهُ intention to give up the caliphate 595
An interesting incident 595

Chapter 31 597

The Pure Wives of Rasulullah ﷺ 597

The number of Rasulullah's ﷺ wives and the order in which he married them 598
Ummul-Mu'mineen Khadijah رضى الله عنها 598
Children 602
Demise 602
Virtues and merits 603
Ummul-Mu'mineen Saudah bint Zam'ah رضى الله عنها 603
Ummul-Mu'mineen Aa'ishah Siddeeqah رضى الله عنها 605
Knowledge 606
Abstinence 607
Merits and virtues 608
Ummul-Mu'mineen Hafsah bint Umar رضى الله عنها 609
Ummul-Mu'mineen Zaynab bint Khuzaymah رضى الله عنها 610
Ummul-Mu'mineen Umme Salamah bint Abi Umayyah رضى الله عنها 610
Demise 611
Virtues and merits 612
Ummul-Mu'mineen Zaynab bint Jahsh رضى الله عنها 612
Date of the marriage 616
Walimah 616
Virtues and merits 617
Piety 617
Worship 618
Abstinence 619
Demise 619
Ummul-Mu'mineen Juwayriyah bint Haaris رضى الله عنها 620
Ummul-Mu'mineen Umme Habibah bint Abi Sufyan رضى الله عنها 621
Ummul-Mu'mineen Safiyyah bint Huyayy رضى الله عنها 624
Ummul Mu'mineen Maymoonah bint Haaris رضى الله عنها 626
Slave women 626
Rasulullah's ﷺ children 627
Qaasim رضى الله عنه 627
Zaynab رضى الله عنها 628
Ruqayyah رضى الله عنها 628
Umme Kulsoom رضى الله عنها 629
Faatimah رضى الله عنها 630
Ibraaheem رضى الله عنه 631

Chapter 32 633

The blessed physical features of Rasulullah ﷺ 633
The seal of prophet-hood 633
Rasulullah's ﷺ blessed beard 634
The clothing of Rasulullah ﷺ 634

Chapter 33 637
The Miracles of Nabi Muhammad ﷺ 637
    Miracles of barakah (blessings) 637
    Acceptance of Duas 638
    Curing the sick 639
    Bringing the dead to life 641

Chapter 34 643
Khasaa'is-e-Nabawi (Special Merits of Nabi ﷺ) 643

Conclusion 645

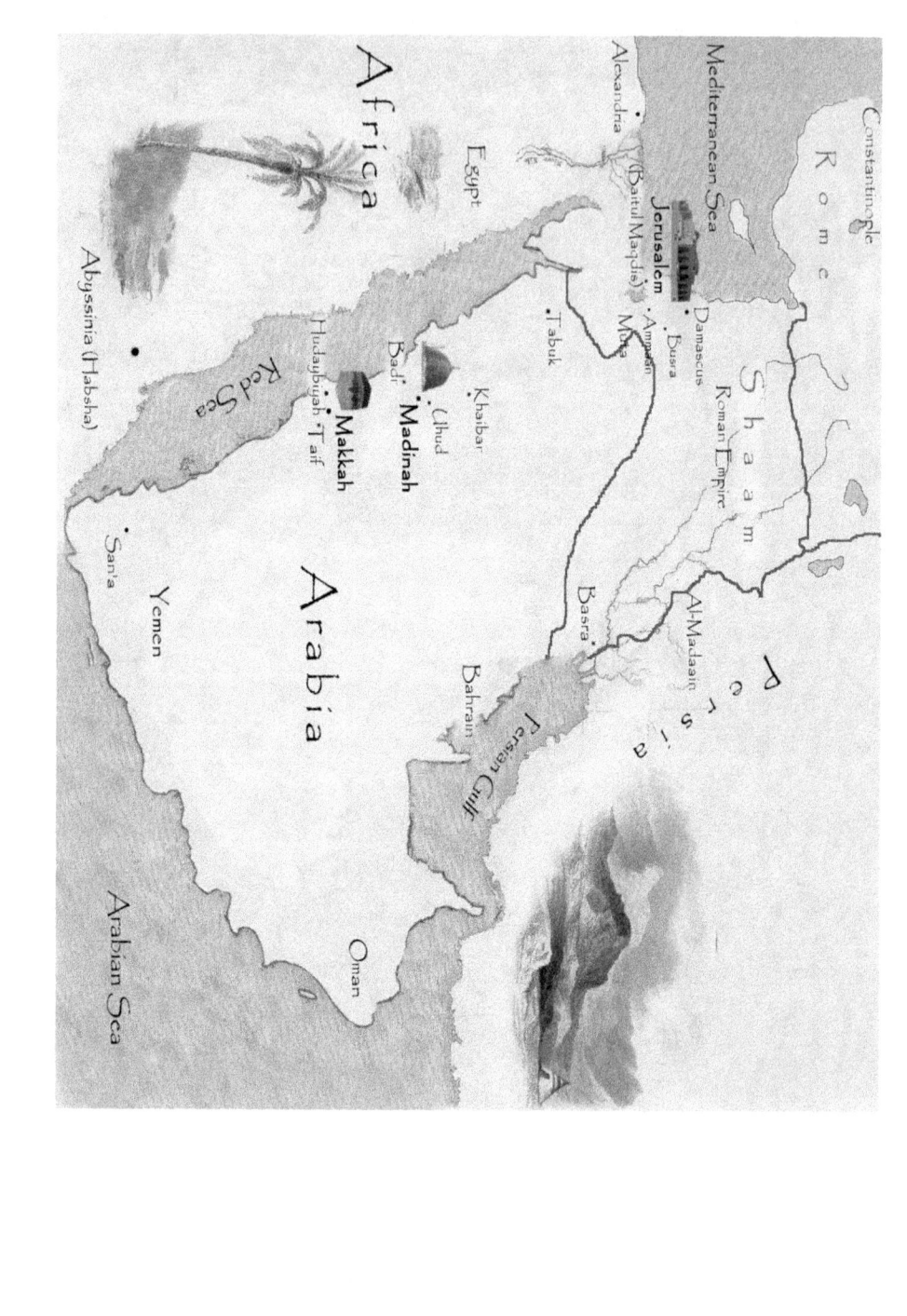

Introduction to the Abridged version

Thousands of books on the Seerah of Rasulullah ﷺ have been written and millions of books can still be written on the noble seerah of Rasulullah ﷺ, but justice can never be done to his blessed biography.

Studying and pondering over the life of Rasulullah ﷺ is the incumbent duty of every Muslim. How is it possible for one to profess the kalimah and claim to be a follower of Nabi Muhammad ﷺ, but yet not know who ones' Nabi is.

Among the many books of seerah that have been written in recent times, Allah Ta'ala has conferred great acceptance to the book titled "Seeratul Mustafa", authored by the great Muhaddith, Hadhrat Moulana Idrees Kaandhlawi رحمه الله. Great luminaries such as Hadhrat Moulana Ashraf Ali Thaanwi رحمه الله and other senior Ulama have approved this book and encouraged reading and studying it. May Allah Ta'ala reward the author abundantly and fill his grave with noor for having prepared such a masterpiece on the life of our Master ﷺ and presenting it to the Ummah.

By the grace of Allah Ta'ala this book has now been translated into English in three volumes by the Ulama of Madrasah Arabia Islamia, Azaadville. Mufti Muhammad Kadwa and Maulana Mahommed Mohammedy have done an excellent piece of work translating the book into clear, spoken English for the benefit of the English speaking public.

Many Madaaris and makaatib have been contemplating including this book into the curriculum. However, since the book is quite voluminous, (each of the three volumes consists of approximately 600 pages) including it in the curriculum of the Makaatib in its current form was difficult. Hence a need arose to abridge the original text into one volume thus making it easier for the public as well as students to benefit from.

Thus with the kind permission of Moulana Abdullah Amejee Saahib (damat barakaatuhu), the Jamiatul Ulama (KZN) Ta'limi Board took up the task, with the grace and mercy of Allah Ta'ala, as well as the duas of Hadhrat Mufti Ebraheem Salehjee Saahib (daamat barakaatuhu), to abridge the present book, focusing more on the life of our beloved Nabi ﷺ and omitting the scholarly discussions of various issues that are derived from the noble seerah. This would Insha-Allah make it easier to be used as a text book in the Madaaris as well as a handy reference book for the general public on the auspicious life of Rasulullah ﷺ.

It is only through the grace of Allah Ta'ala and the duas of our senior Ulama that this task had been accomplished. May Allah Ta'ala accept this humble effort and make it a means of attaining His pleasure as well as the closeness of our beloved and noble Master, Sayyiduna, wa Moulana Muhammadur Rasulullah ﷺ. *Aameen.*

$$\text{رَبَّنَا تَقَبَّلْ مِنَّا ۖ إِنَّكَ أَنْتَ السَّمِيعُ الْعَلِيمُ وَتُبْ عَلَيْنَا إِنَّكَ أَنْتَ التَّوَّابُ الرَّحِيمُ}$$

28 Sh'abaan 1434
At the Raudha Mubaarak
Aqdaam-e-Aaliyya of Rasulullah ﷺ
Madinah Munawwarah

Foreword

by Hadhrat Moulana Abdullah Amejee Saahib (daamat barakaatuhu)

All praise is due to Allah Ta'ala, the Rabb of the universe. Peace and salutations be upon our noble leader and master, Hadhrat Muhammad ﷺ.

As Muslim parents and teachers, we find that one of the very easy ways and means to inculcate Islam into our children and nurture them in the way of the Sunnah, is to show them the most perfect and ideal role model. This is none other than Nabi Muhammad ﷺ. The importance of teaching the Seerah to a child can never be over emphasised. In this day and age, it is of vital importance to educate every Muslim child about the life of Rasulullah ﷺ. If this is done, then Insha Allah, at every point in his/her life, the child will tend to hold onto the example of Rasulullah ﷺ. This is because at some point during a persons' life, he/she tends to look for a role model, an example, someone to hold onto.

In His infinite grace and mercy, Allah Ta'ala has given every Muslim the perfect and ideal role model, someone sent to teach us what life is about and what are our responsibilities. This particular role model has been sent as a mercy to the universe. Unlike the leaders of other religions, every aspect of his life, private or public, has been recorded and transmitted to us authentically. There is probably no other individual about whom so much has been written in such detail and with such authenticity, like Hadhrat Muhammad ﷺ.

There were many classic Arabic works available on the life of Rasulullah ﷺ. The great scholars of Deoband then translated many of them and compiled various others in Urdu and Persian. One of the classic Urdu works that has been drawn from the many voluminous Arabic works is the masterpiece of Hadhrat Moulana Muhammad Idrees Kaandhlawi رحمه الله, Seeratul Mustafaa. For a long time, there was a call and need to have this work translated into English, and through the mercy of Allah Ta'ala, this has materialised after many years of hard work.

Looking at the need to present this classical work to the young mind, the Jamiatul Ulama (KZN) Ta'limi Board has abridged this wonderful book. We hope that this service is accepted in the court of Allah Ta'ala, and we make dua that the entire ummah draws maximum benefit from this beautiful work. *Aameen.*

(Hadhrat Moulana) Abdullah Amejee (Saahib)
Senior Ustaaz, Darul Uloom Azaadville
Head of Publication Department,
Madrasah Arabia Islamia, Azaadville,
South Africa
18 Zul Qa'dah 1434
24 September 2013

Foreword

by Hadhrat Maulana Ashraf 'Ali Thaanwi رحمة الله عليه

اَلْحَمْدُ لِلَّهِ الْعَلِيِّ الْحَكِيْمِ وَالصَّلٰوةُ عَلٰى نَبِيِّهِ ذِى الْخُلُقِ الْعَظِيْمِ

This humble servant Ashraf 'Ali hereby says that I have heard a few selected portions of the book, as mentioned below - recited before me by the honourable author himself Maulana Hafiz Muhammad Idrees Kaandhelwi Saahib.

The portions of the book recited to me are: firstly, the preface of the book, secondly, the topic dealing with the origination of divine revelation (Wahi) in which the author discusses pious dreams being an element of prophethood and its wisdom and underlying mysteries, thirdly, the lecture of Hadhrat Ja'far رضى الله عنه, in the royal court of Najaashi (Negus), fourthly, the part dealing with the As-haabe-Suffah and fifthly, the section discussing the unblemished nature of the Ambiyaa عليهم السلام even before prophet-hood. Masha Allah, the author certainly discharged all the vital aspects and necessary dues involved in the compilation of Seerah. May Allah Ta'ala reward him abundantly.

This humble servant offered the author some advice at some points of the compilation, which he enthusiastically accepted. This is a stark indication of his sincerity. *Allahumma Zid Fazid. Aameen.* If I had the time and ability to listen to the book from cover to cover, I would have, but my weakness and limited time has prevented me from this. Nonetheless, I anticipate that the rest of the book will prove to be a manifestation of the verse:

وَلَلْاٰخِرَةُ خَيْرٌ لَكَ مِنَ الْاُوْلٰى ۞

"Certainly the latter would be better for you than the former".

(In other words, I have sampled a few pages of the book and I anticipate the rest of the book to be more superior to the few pages I have sampled.)

I conclude this note with a word of exclusive advice, a word of general advice and finally with a dua.

My general advice is directed to the readers of the book at large. A person who has basic knowledge of Urdu should not deprive himself of either teaching or studying this book. The most beneficial advantage of this would be that the reader would somewhat familiarise himself with his master, Rasulullah ﷺ and this familiarity will naturally increase the love for Rasulullah ﷺ and this love, as promised, guarantees the company of Rasulullah ﷺ in Jannah. Who can have doubts about this being an immense fortune?

My dua is that may Allah Ta'ala bestow the author with spiritual and physical, worldly and eternal blessings and May He render this book meritoriously accepted and beneficial. *Aameen.*

Ashraf 'Ali
Thaanabowan
9th Shawwaal 1358

Preface

by Hadhrat Moulana Idrees Kaandhlawi رَحْمَهُ اللَّهُ

اَلْحَمْدُ لِلَّهِ رَبِّ الْعَلَمِيْنَ وَالْعَاقِبَةُ لِلْمُتَّقِيْنَ وَالصَّلٰوةُ وَالسَّلَامُ عَلٰى سَيِّدِنَا وَمَوْلَانَا مُحَمَّدٍ خَاتَمِ الْاَنْبِيَاءِ وَالْمُرْسَلِيْنَ وَعَلٰى اٰلِهِ وَاَصْحَابِهِ وَاَزْوَاجِهِ وَذُرِّيَّاتِهِ اَجْمَعِيْنَ -اَمَّا بَعْدُ-

For every Muslim it is more important to know about the Seerah of Nabi Muhammad ﷺ than to know about himself. In order to be able to protect and preserve our Imaan and to be able to act on the injunctions of Islam, we need to be aware of the Sunnah of Rasulullah ﷺ and the teachings he left behind for the Ummat. Allah Ta'ala forbid, if the existence of Rasulullah ﷺ is dismissed, the very survival of a believer's Imaan is in danger. This is why Allah Ta'ala says:

اَلنَّبِيُّ اَوْلٰى بِالْمُؤْمِنِيْنَ مِنْ اَنْفُسِهِمْ

"The Nabi is closer to the believers than what they are to their own lives." [Surah Ahzaab verse 6]

As for the disbelievers, the study of the Seerat of Rasulullah ﷺ will be a form of invitation towards Imaan and towards the truth. A number of nations compiled biographies and historical accounts of their prophets and other leaders but their compilations are unfortunately incomplete. Those who could not even preserve the scripture they regard as a heavenly book, those who are not even aware of when, how, upon whom and why certain verses were revealed, those who do not even have the slightest knowledge of the whereabouts of their leaders graves, how can such nations ever present a comprehensive biography and life history of their leaders? Let alone their life history, their disciples are unable to trace with any authenticity the teachings and scriptures of their religion.

Alhamdulillah, only the Ummah of Rasulullah ﷺ can lay claim to this honour. This is the only Ummah which is able to present the words and actions of their Nabi ﷺ with an uninterrupted chain of narrators. This is the only Ummah so familiarly attached to their Nabi ﷺ. From the time of Rasulullah ﷺ right up to this present day, there has never been a single moment when this Ummah was detached from its Nabi ﷺ.

The entire collection of Hadith makes up the Seerah of Rasulullah ﷺ. However, in the terminology of our earlier predecessors, Seerat referred to a combination of military expeditions and swift attacks during the lifetime of Rasulullah ﷺ.

Now I wish to conclude my preface and proceed with my actual objective of this book. I also make dua: "O Allah! Accept the services of this humble servant and render this compilation a source of perpetual reward and provision for the hereafter." *Aameen.*

اگرچہ یہ ہدیہ نہ میرا قابل منظور ہے

پر جو ہو مقبول کیا رحمت سے تیری دور ہے

"Although my gift may be unacceptable,

There is nothing beyond Your mercy."

رَبَّنَا تَقَبَّلْ مِنَّا اِنَّكَ اَنْتَ السَّمِيْعُ الْعَلِيْمُ وَتُبْ عَلَيْنَا اِنَّكَ اَنْتَ التَّوَّابُ الرَّحِيْمُ ۔ اٰمِيْنَ يَا رَبَّ الْعٰلَمِيْنَ

"O Allah! Accept from us. You are all-hearing, all-knowing. And forgive us, You are all-forgiving, merciful." *Aameen*

O Allah! Shower your mercy upon him who says *Aameen* upon this dua whether he says it audibly or inaudibly. Also forgive the person who raises his hands to make dua of forgiveness for this humble servant and recites Surah Faatihah and at least a few verses or whatever possible and conveys the reward to me.

سُبْحٰنَ رَبِّكَ رَبِّ الْعِزَّةِ عَمَّا يَصِفُوْنَ وَسَلٰمٌ عَلَى الْمُرْسَلِيْنَ وَالْحَمْدُ لِلّٰهِ رَبِّ الْعٰلَمِيْنَ وَالصَّلٰوةُ وَالسَّلَامُ عَلٰى سَيِّدِنَا وَ مَوْلَانَا مُحَمَّدٍ خَاتَمِ الْاَنْبِيَاءِ وَالْمُرْسَلِيْنَ وَعَلٰى اٰلِهٖ وَاَصْحَابِهٖ وَ اَزْوَاجِهٖ وَ ذُرِّيَّاتِهٖ اَجْمَعِيْنَ ۔

Chapter 1

Untainted Family Lineage

Allah Ta'ala says:

$$\text{لَقَدْ جَاۤءَكُمْ رَسُوْلٌ مِّنْ اَنْفُسِكُمْ}$$

"Verily a messenger has come to you from the best amongst yourselves...."

Hadhrat Anas ؓ reports that Rasulullah ﷺ recited the verse "Laqad Jaa akum ...." (with a Fat-hah on the word Anfas). In other words, verily a prophet of Allah has come to you from amongst your most superior, noble and virtuous families. After the recitation of this verse, Rasulullah ﷺ said: "In terms of family lineage, I am the most noble and superior of you. From the time of Aadam عليه السلام right up to me, there was no adultery. All of us (our ancestors) were born in wedlock."

When the Roman emperor asked Abu Sufyaan about the family lineage of Rasulullah ﷺ in the following words: "What is his family like amongst you?" Abu Sufyaan replied: "He is amongst us a man of prominent lineage."

When the Roman emperor heard the response of Abu Sufyaan, he remarked:

$$\text{"وَكَذَلِكَ الرُّسُلُ تُبْعَثُ فِيْ اَحْسَابِ قَوْمِهَا"}$$

"Similarly, all prophets are sent forth from the most distinguished families of their nations."

The lineage of our holy Prophet Muhammad ﷺ is the most noble and dignified lineage of all the diverse family lineages of the world. This golden lineage is recorded as follows:

Muhammad bin 'Abdullah bin 'Abdul Muttalib bin Haashim bin 'Abdu Manaaf bin Qusay bin Kilaab bin Murrah bin K'ab bin Luwayy bin Ghaalib bin Fihr bin Maalik bin Nadr bin Kinaanah bin Khuzaimah bin Mudrikah bin Ilyaas bin Mudar bin Nizaar bin Ma'ad bin 'Adnaan.

Maternal Lineage

The family lineage mentioned above was Rasulullah's ﷺ paternal lineage. His maternal lineage is as follows:

Muhammad bin Aaminah bint Wahab bin 'Abdu Manaaf bin Zuhrah bin Kilaab bin Murrah.

His paternal and maternal lineages meet up at Kilaab bin Murrah. Hereunder is a brief profile of a few of Rasulullah's ﷺ forefathers.

'Adnaan: He is from the progeny of Qaydar bin Ismaa'eel.

Ma'ad: Ma'ad was an extraordinarily strong and gallant warrior. He spent his entire life fighting against the Bani Israa'eel and he established his triumph in every one of these battles. Abu Nazar was his title.

Ma'ad bin 'Adnaan was a twelve year old lad during the reign of the famous king Bukhtenasr. Allah Ta'ala informed the prophet of that era Armiyaa bin Halqiyaa عليه السلام through divine revelation to convey the following message to Bukhtenasr: "We (i.e. Allah Ta'ala) pledge to grant you (i.e. Bukhtenasr) dominance over the Arabs. And you O Prophet! Take away this young boy, Ma'ad bin 'Adnaan with you on your horse (Buraaq) so that he does not suffer any harm. I will extract from Ma'ad's loins a noble prophet with whom I will seal the succession of prophets."

Accordingly, Hadhrat Armiyaa عليه السلام mounted his Buraaq, seated the young Ma'ad bin 'Adnaan with him and dropped him off in Syria. Here he lived with the Bani Israa-eel and grew up with them. This is one of the reasons the lineage of Ma'ad bin 'Adnaan is so well known amongst the 'Ulama of the Ahl-e-Kitaab (Jews and Christians).

Nizaar: When Nizaar was born, his forehead was glittering with the Nur (radiance) of Muhammad ﷺ. His father was overjoyed and in celebration of this joy, invited people over for a feast and remarked: "All this is Nazr (very little) in lieu of the rights of this child." This is how he got the name Nizaar.

Nizaar was the most strikingly handsome and exceptionally brilliant man of his times.

Some are of the opinion that Nizaar means skinny and weak. Since he was a man of slender build, he was referred to as Nizaar.

He is buried in Zaatul-Jaysh, an area close to Madinah Munawwarah.

Mudar: His actual name was 'Amr. Abu Ilyaas was his appellation whilst Mudar was his title. The name Mudar is derived from Madir, which literally means sour. He was incredibly fond of sour foods and sour milk.

He was a remarkably talented and wise man. Some of his words of wisdom are as follows:

$$\text{من يزرع شرا يحصد ندامة وخير الخير اعجله فاحملوا انفسكم على}$$
$$\text{مكروهها واصرفوها عن هواها فليس بين الصلاح والفساد الا الصبر}$$

"He who sows evil will reap sorrow. The best form of goodness is that which is done without delay. So influence your hearts to embrace whatever they loath to carry out and divert the hearts from succumbing to their base desires. There is no distinguishing feature between evil and good except patience."

He was a man with a remarkably melodious voice. The technique of Haadi (a chorus of chants sung to prompt the camels to move at a more rapid pace) was actually formulated by him.

'Abdullah bin Khaalid narrates that Rasulullah ﷺ said: "Do not speak ill of Mudar as he was a Muslim."

Ibn 'Abbaas رضي الله عنه said: "Adnaan, his father, his sons S'ad, Rabi'ah, Mudar, Qays, Tameem, Asad and Rudayyah all died on Millat-e-Ibraaheemi (the creed of Ibraaheem)."

Ilyaas: He was the namesake of Hadhrat Ilyaas عليه السلام. The Sunnah (tradition) of herding the Hadi (sacrificial) animals towards Baitullaah (in Makkah) was instituted by Ilyaas bin Mudar. It has been said that Ilyaas bin Mudar would quite often hear from his own back the Talbiyah of Haj being recited by Rasulullah ﷺ. It has also been narrated that Rasulullah ﷺ said: "Do not speak ill of Ilyaas as he was a Muslim."

Mudrikah: Most Ulama are of the opinion that Mudrikah's name was 'Amr. Mudrikah is derived from Idraak, literally meaning achievement. Since he achieved virtually every form of stature in his life, he was awarded the title of Mudrikah, the achiever.

Khuzaymah: Ibn 'Abbaas رضي الله عنه says that Khuzaymah died on Millat-e-Ibraaheemi (the creed of Ibraaheem عليه السلام).

Kinaanah: He was regarded in high esteem amongst all Arabs. Due to his noble graciousness and vast knowledge, people would travel far and wide just to pay him a special visit.

Nadr: Nadr is derived from Nadaarah, which means luminous and verdant. Owing to his exceptional handsomeness he was entitled Nadr. His actual name was Qays.

Maalik: His first name was Maalik whilst his title was Abul-Haarith. He was one of the most prominent chieftains of the Quraysh.

Fihr: Fihr was his first name whilst Quraysh was his title. According to some, his name was Quraysh whilst his title was Fihr. His descendants are referred to as Qurayshi whilst other Arab descendants not hailing from Fihr are referred to as Kinaani. Some 'Ulama are of the opinion that the term Quraysh is used to refer to the progeny of Nadr bin Kinaanah.

Hafiz 'Iraaqi writes:

اما قريش فالاصح فهر   جماعها والاكثرون النضر

As for Quraysh, the most authentic (opinion) is that they are (the descendants) of Fihr but most are of the (opinion) that they (are the descendants) of Nadr.

Reason for the name of Quraysh

Quraysh is actually the name of a marine animal, which, owing to its great strength, dominates all other marine animals. It promptly devours all other sea creatures but none dares to overwhelm it. Similarly, the Quraysh, owing to their unrivalled valour and incredible courage, always maintained their dominance over the other tribes. None dared to overwhelm them. This is why they were referred to as Quraysh.

K'ab: The person to initiate the weekly congregation on Fridays was K'ab bin Luway. K'ab bin Luway would assemble all the people every Friday and deliver a sermon. He would firstly praise Allah Ta'ala and explain that Allah Ta'ala created the skies, the earth, the moon, the sun and all other forms of creation. He would then go on to give them some advice. He would encourage them to maintain favourable family ties. He would also mention: "A prophet is to appear amongst my descendants. If you happen to encounter that time, make sure you follow him." At times he would recite the following stanza:

يَالَيْتَنِي شَاهِدٌ فَحْوَاءَ دَعْوَتِهِ   اِذَا قُرَيْشٌ تَبَغَّى الْحَقَّ خُذْلَانًا

"If only I could be present when he (Rasulullah ﷺ) proclaims his message, when the Quraysh will irrationally shun the truth and forsake him rather deplorably."

'Abdu Manaaf: Imaam Shaafi'ee رحمه الله says that 'Abdu Manaaf's name was Mughirah. He was exceptionally handsome and striking. This is why he was known as Qamar Al-Bathaa (the moon of the valley of Makkah). The following statement was found inscribed on a stone:

انا المغيرة بن قصي آمر بتقوى الله وصلة الرحم

"I, Mughirah bin Qusayy, enjoin Allah-consciousness and maintenance of favourable family ties."

Haashim: Imaam Maalik رحمه الله and Imaam Shaafi'ee رحمه الله say that Haashim's actual name was 'Amr. During a severe drought in Makkah, Haashim fed its inhabitants with roti crushed into gravy, hence the name Haashim. (Haashim means the crusher).

As a poet says:

عمرو العلا هشم الثريد لقومه   ورجال مكة مسنتون عجاف

"The exalted 'Amr crushed bread into Thareed (meat dish) and fed it to his people and to all others when the people of Makkah were left pathetically feeble by the drought."

This did not occur only once, but he fed them in this manner on a number of occasions. He was exceedingly generous. His food table was enormously wide. His table was open to every newcomer or traveller. He would provide the poor travellers with camels to complete their journeys. He was exceptionally handsome. The noor of prophethood would glimmer on his forehead. The Ulama of the Bani Israa'eel would fall into sajdah and kiss his hands whenever they caught sight of him.

A number of Arab tribes and the Ulama of the Banu Israa'eel would offer their daughters' hands in marriage to Haashim. In fact, on one occasion, Heraclius, the Byzantine emperor wrote to Haashim thus: "I have learnt of your unrivalled generosity. I wish to grant you my daughter's hand in marriage. She is a princess unparalleled in beauty. In order to perform the nikah with the princess, kindly come over to us." However, Haashim refused to accept the proposal. In actual fact, the emperor's key objective was to transmit the noor of prophethood that was glimmering on Haashims forehead into the royal family. It is said that Haashim passed away at the age of twenty-five.

Haashim was the first to initiate the custom of sending off two trade caravans a year; a caravan to Syria in summer and a caravan to Yemen in winter. According to this unvarying custom, a caravan would set out in every season of the year. Over desolate swathes of land, through scorching deserts and dangerous journeys by land and sea, these caravans would travel in winter towards Yemen and beyond going right up to as far as Ethiopia. Negus, the emperor of Ethiopia was exceedingly hospitable towards Haashim and would present a number of gifts to him. In summer, the caravans would travel to Syria (including Jordan and Lebanon), Gaza and Ankara (which was then the capital of Rome). Heraclius, the Byzantine emperor would also approach Haashim with utmost respect and would often present gifts to him.

A poet encapsulates:

$$سَفَرَيْنِ سَنَّهَا لَهُ وَلِقَوْمِهِ \qquad سَفَرَ الشِّتَآءِ وَرِحْلَةَ الْأَصْيَافِ$$

"Haashim initiated two journeys for himself and for his people, A journey in winter whilst another journey in summer."

Haashim secured assurances of extensive protection from the Yemeni as well as the Roman governments for his trade caravans. Since the trade routes of Arabia were not really safe from robbers, Haashim put in place a pact with all various tribes of the peninsula assuring them that we (the Makkans) would freely transport your basic necessities to you whilst you in turn should pledge a safe passage to all our caravans passing through your tribal lands. As a result of Haashim's brilliant strategy, all the trade routes leading to and from Makkah were rendered safe.

Allah Ta'ala also draws the attention of the Quraysh to this bounty in the following words:

$$لِإِيلَٰفِ قُرَيْشٍ ۝ إِۦلَٰفِهِمْ رِحْلَةَ الشِّتَآءِ وَالصَّيْفِ ۝ فَلْيَعْبُدُوا۟ رَبَّ هَٰذَا الْبَيْتِ ۝ الَّذِىٓ أَطْعَمَهُم مِّن جُوعٍ وَءَامَنَهُم مِّنْ خَوْفٍۭ ۝$$

"(With the grace of Allah) Due to the habituated custom of the Quraysh, their habitual custom of setting forth in winter and summer, (as a form of gratitude), they should worship Allah, the Lord of this house, He who has fed them against hunger and shielded them from fear." [Al-Quraysh verses 1-4]

During the days of Haj, Haashim would feed all the pilgrims with meat, roti, saweeq and dates. He would also provide water for them. He would make similar provisions for them at Mina, Muzdalifah and 'Arafaat.

Umayyah bin 'Abdu Shams was incredibly perturbed by Haashim's generosity and he became upset over Haashim's influence over the Arabs. Umayyah also attempted to feed the pilgrims just as Haashim was feeding them. However, in spite of his privileged affluence, he was unable to compete with Haashim.

This is the catalyst that sparked off a succession of the relentless hostilities between the Banu Haashim and the Banu Umayyah clans.

On one occasion, Haashim accompanied a trade caravan that halted at Madinah (probably en route to Syria). His gaze fell on a woman in the market place of Madinah. Apart from her exceptional beauty, her exquisite facial features portrayed a woman of noble reputation and keen intelligence. Haashim made some enquiries to establish whether she was married or single. He learnt that she was married to Asihah bin Jallah from whom she mothered two sons; 'Amr and Ma'bad. Asihah later divorced her.

Haashim sent her a proposal of marriage, which, due to his nobility of lineage and gracious character, she enthusiastically accepted and this Nikah was performed. The lady's name was Salma binte 'Amr who was from the Banu Najjaar tribe. After the Nikah, Haashim gave a ceremonial feast from which all his co-travellers partook and a few people from the Khazraj tribe were also invited.

Haashim stayed on in Madinah for a few days after the Nikah. Salma fell pregnant subsequent to which 'Abdul Muttalib was born. He was born with a single strand of white hair. This is why he was referred to as Shaybah (which means to turn white in old age). In the meantime, Haashim departed for Gaza with the trade caravan. He passed away in Gaza and he is also buried there.

'Abdul Muttalib: His name was Shaybatul-Hamd. He was incredibly handsome. A poet describes his beauty thus:

يضي ظلام الليل كالقمر البدري   على شيبة الحمد الذى كان وجهه

"Like the luminance of the fourteenth moon, Shaybatul-Hamd's face brightens the darkness of the night."

'Abdul Muttalib literally means 'the slave of 'Muttalib'. On the death of Haashim, 'Abdul Muttalib's mother lived with her people, the Banu Khazraj, for some time in Madinah Munawwarah. As he grew older, his uncle Muttalib from Makkah came to Madinah to fetch him. As they entered Makkah, 'Abdul Muttalib was seated on the camel behind his uncle. Shaybah's (i.e. 'Abdul Muttalib's) clothes were dirty and his features showed his orphaned status. When asked who this boy was, out of fear of embarrassment, Muttalib replied: "He is my slave." He did not want to declare that this was his nephew because people would question as to why his nephew was in such filthy attire. This is how he stuck with the name 'Abdul Muttalib (the slave of Muttalib). When he reached Makkah itself, Muttalib dressed him up in fine clothing and then revealed that this boy was his nephew.

Amongst the Quraysh, 'Abdul Muttalib was the most handsome, the most strong and robust, the most tolerant and composed, the most charitable and noble and the most shunning of evil and immorality. He was admittedly the greatest leader of the Quraysh.

'Abdul Muttalib's generosity significantly outshone that of his father Haashim. 'Abdul Muttalib's hospitality went beyond humankind to embrace even the beasts and birds. This is why the Arabs fondly remembered him as Fayyad (extremely generous) and Mut'imu Tayris-Sama (the sustainer of the birds of the sky). He made alcohol forbidden upon himself. He paid particular attention to feeding the destitute in the holy month of Ramadhaan. He initiated the tradition of seclusion and isolation in the cave of Hira.

'Abdul Muttalib's Dream and the Well of Zam Zam

The birthplace of the Jurhum tribe was actually Yemen. Due to divine intervention, a severe drought struck Yemen and this forced the Banu Jurhum to leave Yemen in search of more promising livelihood. During the course of their travels, they coincidentally met Hadhrat Ismaa'eel عَلَيْهِ السَّلَام and his honourable mother Hadhrat Haajrah رَضِيَ اللَّهُ عَنْهَا in the vicinity of the Zam Zam well. Banu Jurhum grew fond of this area and decided to settle down here. After some time, Hadhrat Ismaa'eel عَلَيْهِ السَّلَام married a lady from the same tribe. Once he was privileged with the title of prophethood, he was commissioned to the 'Amaliqah, Jurhum and the people of Yemen. He passed away at the age of one hundred and thirty and was buried in the Hateem area close to the grave of his honourable mother.

After his demise and in accordance with his parting advice, his son Qaydar assumed the role of trustee of the K'abah. In this manner, the Banu Ismaa'eel remained as trustees of the K'abah for quite some time. With the passage of time, hostilities and aggression erupted between the Banu Ismaa'eel and the Banu Jurhum. In due course the latter prevailed and subsequently established their rule over Makkah. Before long, the Jurhum rulers unleashed an aggressive bout of tyranny and cruelty over the people of Makkah. This ruthless brutality drove the Banu Ismaa'eel out of Makkah and forced them to settle on the outskirts. When their brutal tyranny, ghastly immorality and their disrespect of the Baitullah went beyond tolerable boundaries, all the Arab tribes joined hands to challenge their transgressions. As a consequence, the Banu Jurhum were compelled to flee from Makkah. However, as they were departing from Makkah, they buried a number of relics of the K'abah in the well of Zam Zam, filled sand into it and brought it level to the ground in such a manner that no sign of the well could be detected. After the evacuation of the Banu Jurhum, the Banu Ismaa'eel returned to Makkah and settled down but not a soul paid any attention to the well of Zam Zam. With the passage of time, not a single trace of the well was left and it fell into total oblivion.

When the rule of Makkah fell onto the shoulders of 'Abdul Muttalib and the divine will of Allah Ta'ala decreed that the well which had been totally forgotten should now be disclosed, by means of pious dreams 'Abdul Muttalib was directed to dig up the area of the well. Distinguishing markings and distinctive clues pointing out the whereabouts of the well were also revealed to him in the dream. 'Abdul Muttalib himself says: "I was once asleep in the Hateem area when a person came up to me in a dream and instructed: 'Dig up Barrah.' As I enquired, 'What is Barrah?' he departed. On the second day I was sleeping on the same spot when the same man again directed me in my dream: 'Go and dig up Al-Madnunah.' When I asked him: 'What is Al-Madnunah?' he went away. On the third day I was sleeping at the same spot when he again appeared in my dream and commanded: 'Go and dig up Tayyibah.' As I enquired what Tayyibah is, he once again headed off. On the fourth day, he ordered me: 'Go and dig up Zam Zam.' Again I asked: 'What is Zam Zam?' Upon this he replied: 'It is a well whose water neither runs dry nor decreases in volume and it provides countless number of pilgrims with drinking water.' He then went on to point out a few distinctive clues precisely indicating where I should dig."

The recurring nature of the dream coupled with a detailed location of the area convinced 'Abdul Muttalib that this is a true dream. 'Abdul Muttalib informed the

Quraysh of his dream and informed them of his decision to dig up a certain point of the Haram. The Quraysh opposed him but he could not be bothered with their resistance. Hoisting his pick and shovel, he set out with his son Haaris and commenced digging at the designated spot. 'Abdul Muttalib would go on burrowing whilst Haaris would scoop up and dispose of the sand. On the third day, he came across a deep hole. Out of extreme delight, he burst out chanting "Allahu Akbar, Allahu Akbar!" He then happily remarked:

هذا طوى اسمٰعيل

"This is evidently the well of Ismaa'eel."

'Abdul Muttalib thereafter constructed a few ponds close to the well of Zam Zam. He would fill these with Zam Zam water and readily provide it to the pilgrims. However, during the hours of darkness, some distressingly jealous people would maliciously cause damage to these ponds. 'Abdul Muttalib would then repair the damage early the next morning. Upset with such recurrent nasty acts, 'Abdul Muttalib implored Allah Ta'ala in dua. He was divinely instructed in a dream to recite the following dua:

اللّٰهُمَّ انى لا احلها لمغتسل ولكن هى لشارب حل

"O Allah! I do not render the water of Zam Zam Halaal for bathing but it is permitted only for drinking purposes."

The very next morning, 'Abdul Muttalib publicly announced this verdict. Thereafter, whoever attempted to damage any of the ponds, would indeed fall prey to some ailment or the other. When such woeful incidents of misfortune multiplied, the jealous people stopped damaging the ponds.

'Abdul Muttalib's Vow

Whilst in the process of excavating through the earth to get to the well of Zam Zam, besides his only son Haaris, 'Abdul Muttalib had no other assistant to lend a hand. This is why he took an oath to the effect that if Allah Ta'ala blesses him with ten sons, who would grow up to be his helping hands, he would slaughter one of them in the name of Allah.

When Allah Ta'ala fulfilled this cherished aspiration by granting him ten sons, he was fast asleep one night in front of the K'abah when he saw a vision of a person instructing him:

يا عبدالمطلب اوف بنذرك لرب هذا البيت

"O 'Abdul Muttalib! Fulfil your vow that you had pledged for the Lord of this sacred house."

On awakening from this dream, 'Abdul Muttalib summoned all his sons and revealed his vow and subsequent dream to them. With one voice they all submitted:

اوف بنذرك وافعل ما شئت

"Fulfil your vow and do as you please."

'Abdul Muttalib drew lots for all his sons and 'Abdullah, his most beloved son's name came up in the draw. He grasped 'Abdullah's hand and proceeded with a knife towards the sacrificial quarters. When 'Abdullah's sisters witnessed this distressing sight, they were moved to weeping in anguish. One of them pleaded with the father to draw another lot with ten camels against 'Abdullah's name. If the lot is drawn in favour of the ten camels, slaughter the camels but we implore you to leave 'Abdullah alone. At that time, ten camels was the blood money paid to a murdered victim's family. When he drew lots a second time, 'Abdullah's name came up again. 'Abdul Muttalib added on ten camels and drew lots again. Once more, 'Abdullah's name came up. 'Abdul Muttalib continued adding ten camels each time he drew lots but on every occasion, 'Abdullah's name came up. When he eventually reached a hundred camels, he was spared when finally the camels' name came up. At that instant, 'Abdul Muttalib and the bystanders cried out in delight: "Allahu Akbar." 'Abdullah's sisters carried him away from there and 'Abdul Muttalib slaughtered his hundred camels between mounts Safa and Marwah.

Ibn 'Abbaas ؓ says that initially, ten camels made up the blood money paid to a murdered victim's family. Amongst the Quraysh and other Arabs, 'Abdul Muttalib initiated the tradition of paying one hundred camels instead of the customary ten camels as blood money. Rasulullah ﷺ also maintained this Sunnah in Islam. Following this incident, 'Abdullah was described with the title of Zabeeh (the sacrificed or slaughtered one). This is the reason Rasulullah ﷺ was referred to as Ibnuz Zabeehain (the son of two Zabeeh's).

Hadhrat Mu'aawiyah ؓ says that he was once in the blessed company of Rasulullah ﷺ when a Bedouin addressed Rasulullah ﷺ as "O son of the two Zabeehs!" Rasulullah ﷺ merely smiled at him.

After narrating this incident, one of the attendees asked whom the two Zabeehs were. In response, Hadhrat Mu'aawiyah ؓ went on to recount this incident of 'Abdullah and said: "One was 'Abdullah whilst the other was Ismaa'eel عليه السلام."

'Allaamah Zarqaani رحمه الله says that whenever the Quraysh were afflicted by severe drought, they would take 'Abdul Muttalib to Mount Thabir. With his blessed presence they would then beg Allah Ta'ala for rain. Time and again the Quraysh solved their problems with the Barakah (sanctified presence or blessings) of 'Abdul Muttalib.

His position and conditions were immensely different from the conditions of the other Arabs at large. He would strongly prevent his children from any form of injustice and immorality. He would encourage them to adopt good character and shun evil behaviour.

'Abdul Muttalib would insist on fulfilling all vows. He forbade marriage between the Mahaarim (like marrying one's sister, aunt, etc.). He would restrain people from intoxicants, adultery, burying the daughters alive, and from making Tawaaf naked around the Baitullah. He would encourage amputating the hand of the thief. These are issues strongly endorsed by the Qur-aan and Hadith as well.

On closer examination of the aforementioned incidents and conditions it clearly appears that the closer the term of Nubuwwat (prophethood) approached, the more evident became the improvement in good character, etiquette, blessings, spiritual light and miraculous feats. This was remarkably evident in the life of 'Abdul Muttalib where on numerous occasions he saw truthful dreams and true dreams make up the very inception of prophethood. Whenever he was confronted with any serious issue, 'Abdul Muttalib would be appropriately guided by true dreams and divine insight.

Hadhrat Waasilah bin Asq'a رضى الله عنه reports that Rasulullah صلى الله عليه وسلم said: "Allah Ta'ala preferred Banu Kinaanah from the children of Ismaa'eel and from Banu Kinaanah He chose the Quraysh and from the Quraysh He favoured Banu Haashim and from the Banu Haashim, He preferred me."

Jibraa'eel عليه السلام traversed the earth in search of uncontaminated souls but since it was an era of spiritual ignorance, he did not search for outward actions but he focused on character and capability. In this aspect, Jibraa'eel عليه السلام did not find anyone better than the Arabs in general and Banu Haashim in particular.

At that time, in certain spheres, the Arabs enjoyed such supremacy over the other nations that none dared to challenge. For instance:

1. **Family Lineage:** The Arabs were so particular about family lineage that let alone humans they would even keep in memory a record of the lineage of their horses. They would even retain such (seemingly mundane) information as to who was born out of a free woman and who was mothered by a slave woman, who drank the milk of a noble woman and who was suckled by a despicable woman. This is evident from Hadhrat Salamah bin Akw'a's رضى الله عنه fiery statement he made on the battlefield when he declared: "I am the son of Akw'a and today's battle will attest who was nourished by a free woman and who was nursed by a slave woman." A poet of pre-Islamic times says:

لو كنت من مازن لم تستبح ابلى   بنو اللقيطة من ذهل بن شيبانا

"If I was of the Maazin tribe, the children of a foster woman attributed to Zuhal bin Shaybaan would not have outsmarted my camel."

As a form of ridicule, the poet refers to them as the children of an orphan. In other words, they are not the children of a noble woman but the children of an orphan who was abandoned on the roadside.

2. **Valour and heroism**: The influence of their valour was such that whilst the Romans or Persians reduced the rest of the world to subjugation or bondage, the Arabs in spite of their modest material possessions were not intimidated into imperial subjugation. Their spirit of determination was such that the most pitiable destitute would not be left awestruck whilst conversing with the greatest of emperors.

3. **Generosity and selflessness**: They were so big-hearted that they would not hesitate to slaughter a healthy camel in honour of an unexpected guest. They were eagerly prepared to remain hungry but it was just about impossible for the guest to go hungry.

4. **Memory and intellect**: The exceptional memory and outstanding intellectual talents of the Arabs was celebrated in every corner of the globe. They could commit to memory a hundred stanzas of a poem merely by listening to it once.

5. **Personal honour and prejudiced self-esteem**: They entertained such savage levels of chauvinism and patriotism that they were prepared to sacrifice their lives and wealth on the slightest hint of a provocative insult either against themselves or the tribe. In fact, most hostilities and unsympathetic behaviour amongst them were triggered by this sense of self-esteem and personal honour.

6. **Eloquence of Language and Expression**: No other language can rival the Arabic language in eloquence and expression. In fact, no other language can justifiably claim to possess books especially compiled on 'Ilm Al-Balaaghah (the science of eloquence and expression) and even if some may be found, they are taken from the Arabic books. Allah Ta'ala had entrusted these outstanding morals, exceptional abilities and excellent skills within their very nature and disposition but due to their ignorance and foolishness they were more inclined to focus these Allah-given talents in the wrong direction. However, when these same skills and talents were adorned with divine knowledge and heavenly direction, the same people who were in practice once worse than wild beasts turned out to become far superior than the celestial angels. The same folks who were blatantly steeped in vicious hostilities and ferocious conflicts, when they adopted to surrender their lives in the path of Allah Ta'ala, the celestial angels also turned up in white, yellow or black turbans fighting side by side with them and assisting them against their mutual enemy.

Nonetheless, although the Arabs were immorally corrupt in behaviour and deed, they were nonetheless relatively decent as far as their morals, disposition and talents were concerned.

It is relatively easier to rectify one's actions but to amend his character and innate disposition is almost impossible. For this reason Allah Ta'ala selected such a family for His prophethood so that the Prophet who hails from this family would also be a man of upright morals, untarnished nature and immaculate disposition. It is absolutely crucial for a Prophet to be a man of flawless character as this will enable him to rectify others.

'Abdullah: Hafiz 'Asqalaani رحمه الله says that this was Rasulullah's ﷺ honourable father's name and nobody disputes this fact.

This is the name most adored by Allah Ta'ala as a Hadith states that two names are most dear to Allah Ta'ala; 'Abdullah and 'Abdur-Rahmaan. This is so because the word "Allah" is the Ismul-A'azam (the supreme name of "Allah"). It would not be farfetched to believe that when 'Abdullah was born, his father 'Abdul Muttalib was divinely inspired by Allah Ta'ala to name this blessed son with a name most beloved to Allah Ta'ala.

Hadhrat 'Abdullah's Marriage to Hadhrat Aaminah

When 'Abdul Muttalib finally fulfilled the payment of the ransom in redemption of Hadhrat 'Abdullah's life, his next concern was to get him married. He sent a marriage proposal on behalf of 'Abdullah for the hand of Aaminah, the daughter of Wahab bin 'Abdu Manaaf of the eminently noble Banu Zuhrah tribe. She was then under the guardianship of her uncle, Wuhaib bin 'Abdu Manaaf. 'Abdul Muttalib also sent a marriage proposal himself for the hand of Haalah the daughter of Wuhaib bin 'Abdu Manaaf, Aaminah's uncle. Both proposals were accepted and both father and son were married in the same session. Hadhrat Hamzah رضي الله عنه, the son of 'Abdul Muttalib, was born from her (Haalah). Hadhrat Hamzah رضي الله عنه was Rasulullah's ﷺ paternal uncle as well as his milk-brother.

Ibn 'Abbaas رضي الله عنه says: "As 'Abdul Muttalib set out with his son 'Abdullah for the imminent marriage ceremony, they came across a Jewish woman by the name of Faatimah bintu Murr. She was well-versed with the Tawraat and Injeel. When her gaze fell on the light of Nubuwwat radiating from 'Abdullah's face, she imploringly beckoned him to come up to her and pleaded: "I will compensate you with a hundred camels (for being illicitly intimate with me)."

Hadhrat 'Abdullah responded with the following couplet:

اما الحرام فالممات دُونه   والحل فاستبينه

فكيف بالامر الذى تبغينه   يحمى الكريم عرضه ودينه

"Death is far easier than perpetrating a Haraam act. And such an action, which I cannot even envisage ever occurring, cannot be permitted.

So how is it possible to perpetrate the immoral deed you are longing for? An honourable man safeguards his honour and Deen."

As father and son were returning home, they came across the same woman once again. She enquired: "Where did you go after you left me?" 'Abdullah replied: "In the intervening period, I got married to Aaminah, the daughter of Wahab bin 'Abdu Manaaf. After the Nikah, I stayed with her for three days." The woman finally revealed: "By Allah! I am not a woman of loose morals. When my gaze fell on the light of prophethood emanating from your face, I was unable to curb my wistful longing to transmit that Noor (glow) from your body into mine."

Hadhrat 'Abdullah once set out on a trade journey with a caravan bound for Syria. Due to ill health, on the return journey, he was forced to break his journey in Madinah Munawwarah. The moment the caravan arrived in Makkah, 'Abdul Muttalib enquired as to the whereabouts of 'Abdullah. The travellers informed him that due to ill health, 'Abdullah decided to stop over at his maternal ancestor's family, the Banu Najjaar in Madinah Munawwarah. Without delay, 'Abdul Muttalib despatched his elder son Haaris, to Madinah Munawwarah. On reaching Madinah, he discovered that 'Abdullah had already departed from this world. He was ill for almost a month and he was buried in Naabighah's house in Madinah Munawwarah.

Haaris returned to Makkah informing 'Abdul Muttalib and other relatives of this unexpected tragedy. This cast all of them into a state of utter dejection and indescribable sorrow.

Qays Ibn Makhramah narrates that Rasulullah ﷺ was still in his mother's womb when his father 'Abdullah passed away. At the time of his death, 'Abdullah was – according to conflicting reports – either thirty, twenty five, twenty eight or eighteen years old. Hafiz 'Alaaie and Hafiz 'Asqalaani say that the view in favour of eighteen is most authentic.

On his demise, 'Abdullah's estate consisted of five camels, a few goats and a slave by the name of Barakah with the title of Umme Ayman.

Incident of the People of the Elephants

Fifty or fifty five days before the birth of Rasulullah ﷺ the incident involving the people of the elephants occurred as is prominently recorded in the books of history and Seerat. The holy Qur-aan also devotes a whole Surah to this particular incident. A comprehensive account of this incident is recorded in books of Tafseer. In short, Abrahah was the governor of Yemen appointed by Najaashi (Negus) the emperor of Abyssinia. When he noticed all the Arabs travelling to Makkah Mukarramah to perform Tawaaf of the Baitullah, he also decided to erect an imposing and magnificent structure in the name of Christianity so that the Arabs may renounce the simple K'abah and make Tawaaf of his fictitious K'abah instead. He therefore erected a beautiful church in the capital city of San'aa.

When the Arabs heard of this, a member of the Kinaanah tribe defaced the building by passing stool within its precincts and fled. Some are of the opinion that a few Arab youngsters lit a fire in the vicinity of the church. A gust of wind hoisted a smouldering ember, lobbed it onto the wooden structure of the church setting it ablaze and reducing it to ashes. This incited Abrahah into a fit of hysterical rage and he vowed that he would not rest until he had reduced the Kʿabah to ruins. With this wicked intention, he set out to attack Makkah. En route to Makkah, the tribes who put up resistance were subdued with the might of the sword. Together with his terrifying army of men, he was also accompanied by a herd of elephants. The livestock of the Makkans were grazing on the outskirts of Makkah. Abrahah's army seized all the grazing animals, which also comprised of two hundred camels belonging to Rasulullah's ﷺ grandfather ʿAbdul Muttalib. At that time, ʿAbdul Muttalib was the appointed leader of the Quraysh and a trustee of the Kʿabah. When he obtained intelligence of Abrahah's wicked intention, he gathered the Quraysh asking them to remain calm. "Do not worry," he advised, "Evacuate Makkah, nobody will be able to demolish the Kʿabah. This is the sacred house of Allah Taʿala and He will protect it."

Accompanied by a few leaders of Quraysh, ʿAbdul Muttalib set out to meet Abrahah. Before he set out, ʿAbdul Muttalib conveyed a message of his imminent arrival to Abrahah. Abrahah welcomed ʿAbdul Muttalib politely and graciously. Allah Taʿala had blessed ʿAbdul Muttalib with unparalleled handsomeness, remarkable eminence, imposing awe, refined dignity and arresting majesty that left all who came into contact with him utterly spellbound. Abrahah was also left awestruck with the imposing personality of ʿAbdul Muttalib leaving him no choice but to welcome his guest with absolute respect and reverence. He found it inappropriate to seat anyone on or in line with his throne. So instead, he descended from the throne out of respect for ʿAbdul Muttalib. During the course of their conversation, ʿAbdul Muttalib requested Abrahah to release all his camels detained by Abrahah's army. Astounded by this request, Abrahah exclaimed: "It is quite startling to hear you requesting for your camels but I see that you have not mentioned a word about the Kʿabah, which is a focal point of the Deen of your forefathers." ʿAbdul Muttalib calmly responded: "I am the owner of the camels whilst the owner of the house (Kʿabah) is someone else who will take care of it." In other words, I am the owner of the camels. This is why I have asked for their release whilst the custodian of the Kʿabah is Allah Taʿala and He will defend it. Following a few moments of silence, Abrahah ordered the release of all the camels. Taking delivery of his camels, ʿAbdul Muttalib returned to his people and asked them to evacuate Makkah. He then pledged all two hundred camels as an offering to the Kʿabah. Next, accompanied by a few people who would imploringly weep before Allah Taʿala, he presented himself before the door of the Kʿabah. These were his humble words of poetic dua:

اللهُمَّ اِنَّ الْمرءَ يَمْنَعُ رَحْلَهُ فَامْنَعْ رِحَالَكَ

"O Allah! A man takes care of his house, You take care of Your house.

وَانْـصُرْ عَلٰى اٰلِ الصليبِ وَعَابِدِيهِ اليومَ اٰلَكَ

And assist Your people against the people of the cross and its worshippers.

لَا يَغْلِبَنَّ صليبُهم وَمِحَالُهم اَبَدًا مِحَالَكَ

Their cross and their schemes will never dominate Your schemes.

جَرُّوا جَميعَ بلادِهم وَالفيلَ كَيْ يَسْبُوا عِيَالَكَ

They dragged along all their forces and their elephants to capture Your dependants.

مَدوا حِمَاكَ بِكَيْدِ هِمْ جَهْلًا وَمَا رَقَبُوا جَلَالَكَ

Out of ignorance they have turned up to ruin Your house with their evil plots, But they failed to consider Your unrivalled greatness."

On completing his earnest dua, ʿAbdul Muttalib, together with his companions, climbed the mountain leaving Makkah vacant for Abrahah and his army. As he pressed ahead to demolish the Kʿabah, miraculously and suddenly, huge flocks of small birds appeared. Each one of them had pebbles in its beak and claws. Without forewarning, with the divine power of Allah Taʿala, these pebbles swiftly rained down upon this army like volleys of lethal bullets. A pebble would strike the head and fatally emerge from the bottom. Whoever was wretched enough to be struck by these pebbles would be no more. This is how Abrahah's army was completely wiped out. Abrahah's whole body erupted with pox-like wounds, which left his body horribly decaying with pus and blood. One after the other, his limbs were severed and they fell to the ground. At long last, his chest split open and his heart popped out leaving him dead. When all of them perished, Allah Taʿala sent a flood that washed all of them into the sea.

فَقُطِعَ دَابِرُ ٱلْقَوْمِ ٱلَّذِينَ ظَلَمُوا ۚ وَٱلْحَمْدُ لِلَّهِ رَبِّ ٱلْعَٰلَمِينَ ﴿٤٥﴾

The roots of the oppressors have been cut off and all praise be to Allah Taʿala The Rabb of the worlds

Chapter 2

The Auspicious Birth

The greatest of humans, the leader of the children of Aadam ﷺ, Muhammad Mustafaa Ahmad Mujtabaa ﷺ made his blessed appearance into this world fifty or fifty five days after the incident of the elephants at dawn on Monday the 8th of Rabi'ul-Awwal corresponding to April 570 A.D. in Makkah Mukarramah in Abu Taalib's house.

Regarding the date of the blessed birth, the opinion favouring the 12th of Rabi'ul-Awwal is the most famous (amongst the common people). However, according to most Muhaddetheen and historians, the most preferred view is that Rasulullah ﷺ was born on the 8th of Rabi'ul-Awwal.

The mother of 'Usmaan bin Abul-Aas ﷺ, Faatimah bintu 'Abdullah says: "During the blessed birth of Rasulullah ﷺ, I was with his mother Aaminah. I clearly noticed the whole house radiating with Noor (brilliance) and I also saw the stars stooping so low down that I thought they would come crashing down onto me."

'Irbaad bin Saariyah ﷺ relates that during the blessed birth, Rasulullah's ﷺ mother observed a Noor (radiance) that illuminated the palaces of Syria.

According to another report, the palaces of Busra (not Basra) were illuminated.

It is reported on the authority of K'ab Ahbaar ﷺ that the old scriptures portray the destiny of Rasulullah ﷺ thus:

محمد رسول الله مولده بمكة ومهاجره بيثرب وملكه بالشام

"Muhammad, the Prophet of Allah; his birthplace will be Makkah and his migration will be towards Yasrib (Madinah) and his rule will be over Shaam."

Hadhrat 'Aa'ishah ﷺ relates: "For purposes of business, a Jew was residing in Makkah. On the night Rasulullah ﷺ was born, he asked the Quraysh if a baby boy was born that night. The Quraysh dismissed him by indicating their ignorance but he was adamant and insisted: 'At least make some enquiries because the Prophet of this Ummah was born tonight. This child has a symbol (seal) of prophethood between his shoulder blades. He would not be able to drink any milk for two days because a jinni has placed a finger over his mouth.' Without further delay the people got to their feet to investigate this matter. They discovered that a boy was born to 'Abdullah bin 'Abdul-Muttalib. The Jew begged to be taken along with them. When he caught sight of the symbol (seal) of prophethood between the shoulder blades, he fell down unconscious. As he regained consciousness he asserted: 'Prophethood has vanished from the Bani Israa'eel. O people of Quraysh! By Allah! This infant will launch such an attack upon you that news of this attack will rapidly spread from east to west.'"

The Collapse of Chosroes' Palace and the Sinking of Lake Sawah

On the same night an earth-tremor struck the palace of Chosroes causing all fourteen towers of the palace to crumble. Furthermore, the fire that was perpetually blazing for over a thousand years in the Persian fire-temple abruptly extinguished itself. Lake Sawah also unexpectedly dried up. The morning found Chosroes awfully distressed. His royal dignity prevented him from revealing his utter despair. He eventually convened court by assembling his ministers and other pillars of state. During the course of this assembly, he was informed that the "holy fire" has mysteriously extinguished. This fuelled his anguish even further. What further intensified his agony was when one of the Zoroastrian priests stood up before him in court and said: "I saw a dream last night in which powerfully built camels are dragging some Arabian horses. I then witnessed them crossing over the Tigris River and fanning out to each and every country in the world."

"So what is the interpretation of this dream, then?" asked the emperor. The priest replied: "Perhaps a momentous incident is about to occur from the direction of Arabia." In order to investigate further and to put his mind to rest, the emperor dispatched a royal edict to N'umaan bin Munzir instructing him to send him an eminent scholar who would be able to answer all his questions adequately.

N'umaan bin Munzir promptly despatched a celebrated scholar by the name of 'Abdul-Maseeh Gassaani to the emperor. When 'Abdul-Maseeh Gassaani appeared in court, the emperor asked: "Do you have any knowledge of whatever I wish to ask of you?" 'Abdul-Maseeh respectfully replied: "You may disclose to me whatever is distressing you. If I have any knowledge I will gladly assist you otherwise I will direct you to someone more enlightened than I am." The emperor then brought him up to date by describing in detail what was bothering him. 'Abdul-Maseeh advised him: "Perhaps my uncle, my mother's brother, Satih, who presently resides in Shaam would be able to assist you. Perhaps he has some information on this matter."

"You go ahead to your uncle and investigate this matter fully," commanded the emperor.

'Abdul-Maseeh set out for Shaam but reached his uncle Satih whilst he was in the agony of death. He was still in his senses though. 'Abdul-Maseeh greeted him with Salaam and recited a few couplets to him. When Satih heard him reciting these couplets, he turned towards him and said: "Abdul-Maseeh comes dashing to Satih when he is about to breathe his last. Have you been sent by the Sassanidae emperor because of the tremor that struck his palace, because the fire of the Zoroastrians mysteriously went out and because the priest saw a dream wherein powerfully built camels are dragging Arabian horses over the Tigris River and then fanning out across all cities? Is this why you have come? O 'Abdul-Maseeh! Bear in mind that when the word of Allah is recited in abundance, when the personality carrying an 'Asa (staff) becomes apparent, when the valley of Samawah is gushing forth, the lake of Sawah dries up and the Persian fire is extinguished, then Syria will not remain Syria for Satih any more. A few men and women from the Sassanidae dynasty will rule for a few years. The events that were ordained to happen, regard them as already coming to pass." Saying this, Satih breathed his last.

'Abdul-Maseeh returned to the emperor and fully informed him of what transpired. Upon hearing this, the emperor exclaimed: "The elapse of fourteen kingdoms takes a period of time but how long does it take for the passage of time? Time glides by rather rapidly."

Ten out of the fourteen kingdoms ceased to exist in just four years and the remaining four were reduced to oblivion by the time Hadhrat 'Usmaan ﷺ ascended the office of Caliphate.

Hadhrat Abbaas ﷺ narrates that Rasulullah ﷺ was born circumcised and furthermore, his navel was neatly cut. When his grandfather 'Abdul-Muttalib caught sight of this, he was amazed and remarked: "Verily, this son is bound to become a man of lofty status." This is exactly what transpired.

Ishaaq bin 'Abdullah ﷺ narrates from Hadhrat Aaminah that when Rasulullah ﷺ was born, he was exceptionally clean and dirt-free. He did not have the normal effects of after-birth or any form of dirt on his blessed body.

'Aqeeqah and Naming

On the seventh day after Rasulullah's ﷺ birth, 'Abdul Muttalib performed the 'Aqeeqah and invited all the Quraysh to this function. He then proposed to keep the child's name Muhammad. The Quraysh, startled by such an innovative name enquired: "O Abul Haaris! (This was the title of 'Abdul Muttalib) Why do you propose to keep a name that was certainly not kept by your forefathers or any of your family members?" 'Abdul Muttalib replied: "I propose to name him Muhammad (the praised one) because I want Allah Ta'ala in the sky and His creation on the earth to praise him."

Before the birth of Rasulullah ﷺ, 'Abdul Muttalib actually saw a dream that inspired him to keep the newborn child's name Muhammad. He dreamt that an iron chain is being extracted from his back. One end of the chain is towards the sky and the other end is towards the earth. One end is towards the west and the other towards the east. A little while later, the chain transforms itself into a huge tree. Every leaf of the tree was glittering with brightness seventy times more intense than the brilliance of the sun. People from the east as well as the west are clinging onto its branches. Some of the Quraysh are also clinging onto this tree whilst a few others from the Quraysh are determined to chop it down. Whenever this group decides to approach the tree with this intention, a handsome young man comes and pushes them aside.

In interpretation of his dream, 'Abdul Muttalib was informed that amongst his descendants, a boy will be born. People from the east to the west will follow him devotedly. The beings of the sky as well as the earth will sing his praises. This is why 'Abdul-Muttalib kept his name Muhammad.

Whilst 'Abdul Muttalib was reflecting over the name Muhammad, Rasulullah's ﷺ mother, on the other hand, saw a pious dream in which she was informed that she is carrying the most saintly creation and the most supreme leader of the nations. She was directed to keep his name Muhammad or according to another narration, she was instructed to name him Ahmad.

Allah Ta'ala also mentions the same two names in the Holy Qur-aan in the following verses:

مُحَمَّدٌ رَّسُوْلُ اللهِ

"Muhammad is the Prophet of Allah Ta'ala."

وَ اِذْ قَالَ عِيْسَى ابْنُ مَرْيَمَ يَبَنِىْٓ اِسْرَآءِيْلَ اِنِّىْ رَسُوْلُ اللهِ اِلَيْكُمْ مُّصَدِّقًا لِّمَا بَيْنَ يَدَىَّ مِنَ التَّوْرٰىةِ وَ مُبَشِّرًۢا بِرَسُوْلٍ يَّأْتِىْ مِنْۢ بَعْدِى اسْمُهٗٓ اَحْمَدُ ۚ

"And when 'Isa Ibn Maryam said: "O People of Israa'eel! I am a messenger of Allah unto you, confirming the Tourah (that appeared) before me and (a messenger) of glad tidings of a prophet to come after me, whose name shall be Ahmad."

[Surah Saff verse 6]

Muhammad: The origin of the name Muhammad is from the root letters of "Hamd". The word actually refers to a person of praiseworthy attributes whose practical virtues, indisputable achievements and outstanding character is repeatedly glorified.

اَللّٰهُمَّ صَلِّ عَلٰى مُحَمَّدٍ وَعَلٰى اٰلِهٖ وَصَحْبِهٖ وَبَارِكْ وَسَلِّمْ

"O Allah! Shower Your blessings upon Muhammad and his family and companions accompanied by blessings and peace."

According to some people, Muhammad means, 'that being in whom faultless character and commendable attributes are found on a perfectly flawless level'.

Abu Taalib would often recite the following stanza:

وَشَقَّ لَهُ مِنْ اِسْمِهِ لِيُجِلَّهُ   فَذُو الْعَرْشِ مَحْمُوْدٌ وَهٰذَا مُحَمَّدٌ

"Allah has extracted his (Muhammad's) name from His own so that he may be exalted, So the one on the throne is Mahmood whilst this is Muhammad."

Ahmad: This means the most praiseworthy person. And indisputably, he is the most praiseworthy in the entire creation. Nobody is more praiseworthy and nobody will ever be.

It can also mean one who praises and glorifies Allah Ta'ala the most.

Title (Kuniyyat)

His most well known title was Abul-Qaasim, designated after his eldest son Qaasim.

His second title was Abu Ibraaheem. Hadhrat Anas ؓ relates that when Ibraaheem ؓ was born to Maariyah Qibtiyyah ؓ, Hadhrat Jibraa'eel ؑ appeared before Rasulullah ﷺ addressing him thus: "O Abu Ibraaheem! O Abu Ibraaheem!"

Upbringing and Suckling

For about three or four days after he was born, Rasulullah ﷺ was breastfed by his mother. Thereafter his uncle Abu Lahab's slave woman Suwaybah ؓ suckled him.

When Suwaybah ؓ gave glad tidings of Rasulullah's ﷺ birth to his uncle Abu Lahab, out of sheer joy, he set her free. Prior to Rasulullah ﷺ, Suwaybah ؓ also suckled his uncle Hadhrat Hamzah ؓ. In this manner, apart from being his uncle (father's brother), Hadhrat Hamzah ؓ is also Rasulullah's ﷺ milk brother. After him Suwaybah ؓ also breastfed Hadhrat Abu Salmah ؓ.

Umme Habibah ؓ relates: "I once asked Rasulullah ﷺ: 'I heard that you wish to send a marriage proposal to Abu Salmah's daughter, Durrah.' In utter surprise, he said: 'Umme Salmah's daughter, Durrah, who is in my guardianship, even if she was not my Rabibah (foster daughter), then too she wouldn't be Halaal for me because she is my milk niece. Her father, Abu Salmah رضي الله عنه and I were breastfed by the same woman, Suwaybah رضي الله عنها.'"

Ibn 'Abbaas رضي الله عنه narrates that Rasulullah ﷺ was requested to marry Hadhrat Hamzah's daughter. However, he declined saying: "She is my milk niece."

Rasulullah ﷺ was exceptionally respectful towards Suwaybah رضي الله عنها. After his marriage to Hadhrat Khadijah رضي الله عنها, Suwaybah رضي الله عنها would frequently visit Rasulullah ﷺ. Even after his Hijrah to Madinah Munawwarah, Rasulullah ﷺ would send gifts to her in Makkah. Upon the conquest of Makkah, Rasulullah ﷺ made enquiries as to the whereabouts of Suwaybah رضي الله عنها and her son Masrooh. When informed that both of them had passed on, he made further enquiries to locate any of her living relatives so that he may bestow them with his kindness. However, he was informed that none of her relatives or kinsfolk were alive.

After his death, someone saw Abu Lahab in a dream in an awfully dreadful condition. He asked him how he was faring. Abu Lahab replied: "After I had left you, I haven't been comfortable in the least. However, because I freed Suwaybah رضي الله عنها, I am provided with a fingertip of water." In other words, in hell, he is provided with water equivalent to the finger he used in indicating to her that she is free.

After Suwaybah رضي الله عنها, Rasulullah ﷺ was breastfed by Halimah S'adiyyah رضي الله عنها. It was customary of the noble Arabs of those days to send their suckling infants out to the rural villages to grow up healthy and strong in the uncontaminated air of the countryside. The aim was also to expose the child to the eloquence and purity of the Arabic language and to pick up authentic Arab culture and unique Arab traditions.

Hadhrat 'Umar رضي الله عنه says:

تمعددوا و تمعزروا واخشو شنوا

"Adopt the appearance of M'adan bin 'Adnaan. (In other words, do not adopt the clothing and appearance of the non-Arabs.) Exercise patience upon all adversities, and wear coarse clothing. (In other words, adopt simplicity and do not fall into luxurious comforts.)"

Hadhrat Abu Bakr رضي الله عنه once remarked to Rasulullah ﷺ that he is a man of eloquence and purity in language. Rasulullah ﷺ admitted: "I am after all firstly from the Quraysh tribe. Moreover, I was suckled amongst the Banu S'ad tribe."

According to this established custom of the Arabs, the women of Banu S'ad would make an annual journey to Makkah in search of suckling infants. Halimah رضي الله عنها recalls: "A few women from the Banu S'ad and I set out for Makkah in search of suckling infants. Accompanying me on this journey was my husband and my infant son who was still breastfeeding. As our conveyance, we had an extremely thin donkey and a camel that wouldn't provide a single drop of milk. We were unable to fall asleep all night due to acute hunger. To add to our distress, the child, also suffering from pangs of hunger, cried in anguish all night long. I didn't even have sufficient breast milk to satiate the child.

Every single one of us women was offered to take Rasulullah ﷺ with her but the moment she discovered that the infant is an orphan she would bluntly refuse. After all, what remuneration can one expect from a child who does not have a father? But who knew that this child is not a Yateem (orphan) but he is a Durre-Yateem (a rare pearl). Who knew that the keys to the treasures of Chosroes and Caesar would be awarded to this child? Who knew that although the child has no apparent guardian and mentor who will award a meaningful remuneration but Allah Ta'ala in whose hands lies the incalculable treasures of the earth and skies is the guardian of this child. He would bestow upon those who nurture and nurse this child far more than the remuneration they had ever imagined possible."

All the women obtained at least one infant to return home with. Only Halimah رضى الله عنها was left empty-handed. As the hour of departure drew closer, Halimah رضى الله عنها found it somewhat punishing to return home empty-handed. All of a sudden, an impulsive but passionate urge to go and pick this poor orphan up divinely developed within her anxious heart. She leaped to her feet saying to her husband:

والله لاذهبن الى ذلك اليتيم فلآخذنه قال لا عليك عسى الله ان يجعل لنا فيه بركة

"By Allah! I will go to this orphan and I will by all odds take him with me."

Her husband responded: "This wouldn't be a problem. Who knows, perhaps Allah Ta'ala may bless us with Barakah because of him."

Barakah actually refers to goodness provided by Allah Ta'ala. In other words, Barakah refers to divine goodness that appears directly from Allah Ta'ala without any apparent exterior cause.

It appears in a Hadith-e-Qudsi that Allah Ta'ala says:

أنا عند ظن عبدى بى

"I will deal with my servant in the manner he expects Me to deal with him."

In fervent anticipation of this Barakah, Halimah رضى الله عنها went to fetch Rasulullah ﷺ. In conformity to this expectation, Allah Ta'ala threw open the doors of Barakah for Halimah رضى الله عنها and her family. The other women of Banu S'ad pinned their hopes on the creation whilst Halimah رضى الله عنها pinned her hopes on Allah

Ta'ala alone. Halimah رَضِيَ اللَّهُ عَنْهَا recounts: "I just grasped this blessed child to my dried-out bosom when they started filling up with milk. I produced so much of milk that both he and his milk-brother were able to drink to their fill. As we chanced to milk the scraggy camel, we saw its udders full of milk. My husband and I both satiated ourselves with its milk. We passed the night in splendid comfort."

The next morning, her husband commented:

تعلمى والله يا حليمة لقد اخذت نسمة مباركة

"Remember, O Halimah! By Allah! You have taken an exceptionally blessed child."

To this she replied:

والله انى لا رجو ذلك

"By Allah! With all true faith, I anticipate nothing but Barakah from Allah Ta'ala."

Now it was time to depart. All the travellers of the caravan mounted their conveyances and set out. Halimah رَضِيَ اللَّهُ عَنْهَا also mounted her camel with this blessed infant grasped to her bosom. Her thin camel, which previously would be repeatedly whipped to spur it forward, was now darting ahead in speed without a moments pause. It was, at that moment in time, the conveyance of the blessed Nabi of Allah Ta'ala. The other women of the caravan remarked: "Halimah! Is this the same camel you came with? By Allah! It now has a wholly different behaviour." In these circumstances we arrived in Banu S'ad.

At that time, no other region was affected by drought as severely as Banu S'ad. However, my goats would return home in the evening with udders swollen with milk whilst the other goats would return hungry without a drop of milk in their udders. On witnessing this, the people urged their shepherds to graze their goats where Halimah's goats grazed. They complied with this request but all the same, their goats returned empty whilst Halimahs goats returned at the end of the day with their udders bursting with milk. Halimah رَضِيَ اللَّهُ عَنْهَا says: "Allah Ta'ala continued exhibiting His Khair and Barakat (divine blessings and heavenly favours) in this manner whilst we continued witnessing this Khair and Barakat before our eyes. It continued like this until I weaned him at the end of two years."

At the end of two years, Halimah رَضِيَ اللَّهُ عَنْهَا returned to Makkah to hand over this trust back to his mother, Aaminah. However, due to the profuse divine blessings she had observed due to the presence of Rasulullah ﷺ in her home, Halimah رَضِيَ اللَّهُ عَنْهَا requested Hadhrat Aaminah to allow this orphan to stay on a few more days with her. On the one hand, an outbreak of plague in Makkah in those days and on the other hand, Halimah's رَضِيَ اللَّهُ عَنْهَا persistent entreaties made the mother give in and she permitted the child to be taken away for a few more days. Halimah رَضِيَ اللَّهُ عَنْهَا then returned home with this blessed infant. After a few months, he also started accompanying his milk-brothers to the grasslands to graze the family goats.

The Splitting of the Chest

Once Rasulullah ﷺ was out grazing goats with his milk-brothers when one of his milk-brothers came dashing home. Shocked into terror, he told his parents: "Two white-clothed men laid our Qurayshi brother onto the ground and slit open his chest. Now they are busy stitching him up." On hearing this, Halimah رضي الله عنها and her husband were left perplexed. In a state of total shock, both of them darted across to the grazing field where they saw the young boy standing on one side and his face looking pale. Halimah رضي الله عنها says, "I clutched him to my bosom to comfort him and his foster-father also held him onto his chest and asked him what happened. He then gave an account of what transpired." Halimah رضي الله عنها then returned home with him.

The splitting open of his chest occurred four times in Rasulullah's ﷺ life:

The first time was when he was merely a boy of four in the care of Halimah S'adiyyah رضي الله عنها. He was on the grazing-field when two angels, Jibraa'eel عليه السلام and Mikaa'eel عليه السلام, appeared as men in white garments bearing a golden tray laden with ice. They cut open his chest and removed his heart. They then split open his heart and fished out a few pieces of congealed blood and said: "This is shaytaan's portion." They then washed his heart with ice water in the tray and returned it to its original location after which they stitched him up.

This event of the splitting of the chest left Halimah رضي الله عنها exceptionally alarmed. She was anxious over Rasulullah's ﷺ well being. For fear of him coming to any harm, she returned to Makkah and described to his mother what transpired. Upon hearing what happened to the child, Hadhrat Aaminah was in no way left panic-stricken. She then recalled the divine Barakaat (blessings), Noor and good she experienced during pregnancy right up to birth. She then affirmed: "This son of mine is destined to be a great person. Shaytaan will be unable to approach him. Calm down. There's nothing to worry about. Nothing will harm him."

Halimah رضي الله عنها then returned home and Rasulullah ﷺ started living with his mother once again. When Rasulullah ﷺ was six, his mother decided to journey to Madinah. She took him along with her. Umme Ayman رضي الله عنها also accompanied them on this trip. She stayed at her ancestral home for a month and on her return to Makkah, she passed away at a place called Abwaa and she was buried there as well.

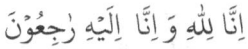

In the Guardianship of 'Abdul Muttalib

Umme Ayman ﷺ returned to Makkah with Rasulullah ﷺ and consigned him to the care of 'Abdul Muttalib. 'Abdul Muttalib always kept Rasulullah ﷺ with him. Whenever 'Abdul Muttalib appeared in Masjidul-Haraam, a special mat would be placed in the shadow of the Baitullah for his exclusive use. Not a soul would dare to even place a foot on this mat. Even 'Abdul Muttalib's own children would sit on the fringes of this mat but Rasulullah ﷺ would seat himself comfortably right on the centre of the mat. His uncles would try to steer him away from this seat but 'Abdul Muttalib, with unreserved affection would say: "Leave this son of mine alone. By Allah! This child is destined to an altogether unprecedented rank of eminence." He would then call him to sit nearby. Whenever 'Abdul Muttalib laid eyes upon Rasulullah ﷺ, he was unable to contain his utter joy.

The father of Kindir bin Sa'eed says: "During the era of ignorance, before the advent of Islam, I once came to Makkah to perform Hajj. I saw a person busy making Tawaaf of the K'abah whilst uttering the following couplet:

يا ربّ رُدَّه وَاصْطَنِعْ عِنْدِى يَدًا   رُدَّ اِلَى رَاكِبى مُحَمَّدًا

"O Allah! Return Muhammad, my conveyance to me, O Lord! Return him to me and do me a great favour."

I asked the people who this is and they replied that this is 'Abdul-Muttalib. He had just sent his grandson in search of some lost camels. Whenever he sends his grandson on an errand, the child returns successful. On this latest errand, the young boy was taking longer than usual. This is why 'Abdul Muttalib, frantically restless was repeatedly reciting the above poem. A little while later, Rasulullah ﷺ returned with the lost camels. The moment 'Abdul-Muttalib caught sight of him, he embraced him saying: "Son! I was dreadfully worried over your well-being. Now I will never allow you to part from me."

Death of 'Abdul Muttalib

Rasulullah ﷺ lived in the loving guardianship of 'Abdul Muttalib for a period of two years. When he turned eight, 'Abdul Muttalib also bid this world farewell. Depending on the differences of opinion, he passed away at the age of either eighty-two, eighty-five, ninety-five, one hundred and ten or one hundred and twenty. He was buried in Hajun.

Since Abu Taalib was 'Abdullah's blood brother, 'Abdul Muttalib consigned Rasulullah ﷺ to the charge of Abu Taalib and he made a bequest urging him to bring him up with great affection and care and with the greatest of love.

Umme Ayman ﷺ says: "When 'Abdul Muttalib's funeral bier was being carried along, I saw Rasulullah ﷺ trudging along behind his bier bitterly weeping in lamentation over his loss."

Once Rasulullah ﷺ was asked whether he could recall the death of 'Abdul Muttalib. Rasulullah ﷺ replied: "I was eight at that time."

In the Guardianship of Abu Taalib

Following the death of 'Abdul-Muttalib, Rasulullah ﷺ was taken into the custody of his uncle Abu Taalib. Rasulullah ﷺ was more beloved to him than his own children. He cared for him more affectionately than he cared for his own sons. Right up to his death, Abu Taalib reared him with such love and affection that as a matter of fact he wholly fulfilled the right of guardianship. Alas! In spite of this devoted guardianship and loving care of Rasulullah ﷺ, he was deprived of the wealth of Islam.

Following a severe drought in Makkah on one occasion, the people pleaded with Abu Taalib to make dua for rain. Accompanied by a substantial number of people, Abu Taalib together with Rasulullah ﷺ set out for the Masjidul-Haraam. Abu Taalib then positioned Rasulullah's ﷺ back against the K'abah. He then pointed his index finger to the sky. There was not a smidgen of cloud in the sky but the moment he pointed to the sky, clouds suddenly appeared all over the place. Within a few moments it started pouring so much so that the rivers and streams started gushing with water. It was in this context that Abu Taalib commented:

وَأَبْيَضُ يُسْتَسْقَى الْغَمَامُ بِوَجْهِهِ   ثِمَالُ الْيَتَامَى عِصْمَةٌ لِلْاَرَامِلِ

"He (Rasulullah ﷺ) is a person whose illuminated face is exploited to draw rain from Allah Ta'ala, he is a sanctuary for the orphans and a refuge for the widows."

The First Journey to Syria and his encounter with the Monk Bahira

When Rasulullah ﷺ turned twelve, his uncle Abu Taalib decided to travel to Syria with a trade caravan of the Quraysh. Owing to the difficult and long journey, Abu Taalib did not want to take him along but at the actual moment of departure, noticing signs of heartbreaking gloom and sorrow on his face, he finally relented and took him along.

En route to Syria, they halted at a city called Busra where a Christian monk by the name of Jarjis, popularly known as Bahirah the monk, lived. He was well acquainted with the signs of the final Prophet as mentioned in the divine books. The moment this trade caravan halted before Bahirah's monastery and his gaze fell on Rasulullah ﷺ, he at once recognised him as the Prophet referred to in the previous books. Bahirah then grasped Rasulullah's ﷺ hand in his own.

Abu Musa Ash'ari رضي الله عنه narrates that once Abu Taalib travelled with some high-ranking elders of Quraysh to Syria. A Christian priest was living in the vicinity of the area where they had halted over for the night. They passed this priest on numerous occasions in the past but he never cast a glance in their direction. This time though, when the trade caravan broke their journey, the monk unexpectedly emerged from his quarters, came to the caravan and started to scrutinise each one of the travellers until he came to Rasulullah ﷺ. The moment he laid eyes on Rasulullah ﷺ, he grasped him by the hand and exclaimed:

هذا سيّد العالمين هذا رسول رب العالمين يبعثه الله رحمة للعلمين

"This is the leader of the worlds. This is the messenger of the worlds. Allah Ta'ala will commission him as the embodiment of mercy for the people of the world."

The elders of the Quraysh, quite dazed at this, asked: "How do you know this? What prompts you to make such a claim?" The monk replied: "When you emerged from the valley of the mountain, every single boulder and tree stooped down in prostration. And trees and boulders don't bow down to anybody but a Prophet. Furthermore, I recognise him from his seal of prophethood that is similar to an apple and appears just below his shoulder blade."

Saying this, the monk departed. Because of Rasulullah ﷺ, he prepared a meal for the whole caravan of travellers. When all of them turned up to eat, Rasulullah ﷺ was conspicuously absent. When he enquired, the monk established that Rasulullah ﷺ was out herding the camels. He sent for him. When Rasulullah ﷺ appeared, a cloud was sheltering him from the fierce rays of the sun. As he approached his people, he noticed that they had already taken whatever available shade there was under a tree. Since there was no shade available, Rasulullah ﷺ sat down on one side. The moment he sat down, the tree stooped in his direction to offer him some shade. The monk remarked: "Look at this tree, how it is bending towards him." The monk then got on his feet committing the travellers by force of oath not to take the young boy with them to Rome. If they catch sight of him, the monk explained, they would identify him from his attributes and features and they would surely put him to death. Whilst pleading with them, the monk suddenly noticed a group of seven Romans coming his way diligently searching for something. The priest asked them what they were searching for. They replied: "We are hunting for that messenger (whose glad tidings have been cited in the Towrah and Injeel and whom we have learnt will be travelling some time this month). We have despatched men in all directions and launched an extensive search for him." The priest responded: "Okay, tell me, if the Almighty has already decreed something, is anyone able to prevent it happening?" They replied in the negative. The seven Romans thereafter pledged before Bahirah that they would refrain from hounding him. Furthermore, they eventually resolved to settle down with Bahirah because the very reason they set out for unexpectedly underwent a rapid transformation. They reckoned it to be unbecoming to return home. Hence, the decision to settle down with Bahirah.

Swearing an oath to the travellers, the monk then enquired who his guardian was. They pointed towards Abu Taalib. The monk pleaded with Abu Taalib to send him back to Makkah. Abu Taalib sent him back to Makkah with Abu Bakr and Bilal. The monk also provided some bread and olive oil as provisions for the return journey.

According to the narration of Baihaqi, Bahirah rose to inspect Rasulullah's ﷺ blessed back where he noticed the seal of prophethood between his shoulder blades. He discovered it to be exactly like how he had expected it to be.

Participation in Hilful-Fudool

For many years the Arabs were struggling with a succession of relentless battles but for how long could they allow this to continue? Following the truce agreed upon after Harbul-Fujjaar, some people decided that just as bloodshed and carnage in the past was brought to an end by a pact devised by Fadl bin Fudaalah, Fadl bin Wada'ah and Fudail bin Haaris thereby lending their names to this pact popularly known as Hilful-Fudool, in the same way, today there is an urgent need once again to revive this pact.

In some of his poems, Zubair bin 'Abdul-Muttalib revisits this pact:

اِنَّ الْفُضُوْل تَحَالَفُوْا وَتَعَاقَدُوْا   اَلَّا يُقِيْمَ بِبَطْنِ مَكَة ظَالِم

"Indeed, the three Fadls (Fadl bin Fudaalah, Fadl bin Wada'ah and Fudail bin Haaris) all made a solemn pledge that no oppressor would be permitted to live within the valley of Makkah.

اَمْر عَلَيْهِ تَعَاهَدُوْا وَتَوَاثَقُوْا   فالجار والمعترّ فِيْهِمْ سالِم

All of them also pledged that be it a neighbour or a visitor, everyone would be safe within its environs."

When Harbul-Fujjaar formally drew to a close, an unsteady revival of Hilful-Fudool was launched in the sacred month of Zul-Q'adah. The first person to initiate a revitalisation of this pact was Zubair bin 'Abdul-Muttalib. A conference was convened between the Banu Haashim and Banu Taym in 'Abdullah bin Jad'aan's house. 'Abdullah also prepared a sumptuous meal for all the delegates of this conference. Amongst other things, the members pledged to assist the oppressed at all costs. Whether the oppressed was a local inhabitant or a foreign visitor, they undertook to assist him to the best of their ability.

Rasulullah ﷺ says: "During the launch of this pledge, I was also present at 'Abdullah bin Jad'aan's house. Even if I were offered red camels in exchange of this pledge, I would never accept. Now, in Islam, if I were invited to a pledge of this nature, I would definitely accept this invitation."

'Abdullah bin Jad'aan was a cousin of Hadhrat 'Aa'ishah ﺭﺿﻲﷲﻋﻨﻬﺎ, (her father's brother's son). Once Hadhrat 'Aa'ishah ﺭﺿﻲﷲﻋﻨﻬﺎ asked: "O Prophet of Allah! 'Abdullah bin Jad'aan was an extraordinarily hospitable man. He was incredibly fond of feeding the people. Will this benefit him in any way on the day of Qiyaamah?" Rasulullah ﷺ replied: "No! This is because he fell short of saying the following dua:

$$رَبِّ اغْفِرْ لِيْ خَطِيْئَتِيْ يَوْمَ الدِّيْنِ$$

"O my sustainer! Pardon my sins on the day of reckoning."

In other words, he did not seek forgiveness for his sins nor beg for Allah Ta'ala's pardon at any time in his life.

Rasulullah ﷺ said: "Whilst walking during the hot summers, I would sometimes take shelter in the shade provided by the trough (or cooking pot) of 'Abdullah bin Jad'aan."

In other words, the trough (or cooking pot) of 'Abdullah bin Jad'aan was so gigantic that a person could stand in its shade. It was as though this trough or pot was a specimen of "basins as large as reservoirs".

Occupation of Trade and the Title of Al-Ameen

The people (of Makkah) maintained that Rasulullah ﷺ grew up as the most dignified, the most polite, the most supportive to his neighbours, the most forbearing, the most truthful and honest and the most remote from fighting, arguing, evil and immorality. This is why, as a young man, his people honoured him with the title of Al-Ameen (the truthful).

'Abdullah bin Abi Hamsaa ﺭﺿﻲﷲﻋﻨﻪ says: "Before prophethood, I once engaged in a trade transaction with Rasulullah ﷺ. I actually owed him some money. I promised him that I would return with it shortly but as fate would have it, I completely forgot about my promise. Only three days later I recalled my promise to return with the money. The moment I remembered this promise, I rushed out to the previous meeting place and found him waiting there patiently. All he said was,

'You put me into difficulty. I have been waiting here for you for the last three days.'"

'Abdullah bin Saaib رضي الله عنه says: "In the era of ignorance (pre-Islamic era), I was Rasulullah's ﷺ business partner. When I came to Madinah, he asked: "Do you recognise me?" "Surely!" I replied, "Why not? You were my business partner and what a pleasant partner you were. You would never dillydally nor would you squabble over anything."

Qays bin Saaib Makhzumi رضي الله عنه says: "I was Rasulullah's ﷺ business partner in the times of ignorance. He was the most favourable of partners. He would neither quarrel nor raise a dispute."

Grazing Goats

Just as Rasulullah ﷺ grazed goats in his childhood with his foster brothers whilst in the custody of Hadhrat Halimah رضي الله عنها, similarly, he grazed goats as he grew older. Jaabir bin 'Abdullah رضي الله عنه narrates: "We were with Rasulullah ﷺ in a place called Zahraan. When we started plucking some fruit off a peelu tree, Rasulullah ﷺ advised us to pick the black ones, as they were more succulent and tastier. We then asked him if he had ever grazed goats in his life (because how would he have known this.) Rasulullah ﷺ replied: "There is not a single messenger who did not graze goats."

Hadhrat Abu Hurayrah رضي الله عنه reports that Rasulullah ﷺ said: "There was not a single prophet who did not graze goats." The Sahaabah رضي الله عنهم asked in amazement: "Even you? O Prophet of Allah!" Rasulullah ﷺ replied: "Yes, I used to also graze the goats of the people of Makkah for a few Qaraarit (plural of Qeeraat, a coin weighing approximately 0.2 grams of silver)."

Second Journey to Syria and the Encounter with Nastoora, the Monk

Hadhrat Khadijah رضي الله عنها was an exceedingly wealthy woman of one of the most noble clans of the Arabs. Due to her noble lineage and her chastity, she was titled as Taahirah (pure) during the times of ignorance as well as the era of Islam.

When the Quraysh despatched their trade caravans, Hadhrat Khadijah رضي الله عنها would also despatch her trade goods with some reliable people as a form of Mudaarabah (business partnership). Her goods were equal to all the goods of the Quraysh put together. When Rasulullah ﷺ turned twenty-five and his trustworthiness became the talk of the town and when not a single person of Makkah failed to refer to him with the title of Al-Ameen, Hadhrat Khadijah رضي الله عنها sent him a message requesting him to take her goods to Syria with an offer to double his share of the profits in relation to her other normal business partners. Due to the financial constraints of his uncle Abu Taalib, Rasulullah ﷺ gladly accepted the offer and in the company of Hadhrat Khadijah's slave, Maysarah, he set off for Syria.

When Rasulullah ﷺ reached Busra, he took a seat under the shade of a tree. A monk by the name of Nastoora lived in the vicinity of this tree. On seeing Rasulullah ﷺ beneath this tree, he approached him and said: "From 'Isa bin Maryam عليه السلام right up to this present moment, besides you no other prophet has sat beneath this tree." He then remarked to Maysarah: "He (Rasulullah ﷺ) has this redness in his eyes." Maysarah responded by revealing: "Yes, this redness has never left his eyes."

The monk exclaimed:

هو هو وهو نبى وهو آخر الانبياء

"Yes, surely this is the Prophet. This is the final Messenger."

Rasulullah ﷺ thereafter continued engaging in his trading activities. During this time, a person once started arguing with Rasulullah ﷺ. The man demanded that Rasulullah ﷺ swear an oath on the idols of Laat and 'Uzza. Rasulullah ﷺ very calmly replied: "I have never taken an oath on Laat and 'Uzza. In fact, even if I perchance come across these idols, I try to avoid them altogether." The man replied: "Indisputably, you are right." In other words, you are truthful and trustworthy. The man then commented: "By Allah! This is a man whose description and attributes our 'Ulama find inscribed in their religious manuscripts."

Maysarah says: "In the severe heat of the afternoon, I would notice two angels offering shade to Rasulullah ﷺ."

As he was returning from Syria whilst the two angels were shading him from the fierce midday sun, Hadhrat Khadijah رضى الله عنها witnessed this extraordinary scene as she was sitting in one of the upper floors of her house. She summoned the women around her to come and view this incredible spectacle as well. This took all of them by surprise. Soon after, Maysarah gave her a detailed account of the strange phenomena and particulars of the journey. He then made over her goods and money to her. Due to the barakah (blessings) of Rasulullah ﷺ this time round, Hadhrat Khadijah رضى الله عنها realised such a huge profit from this trade caravan that she had never before made from a single trade caravan. Hadhrat Khadijah رضى الله عنها awarded Rasulullah ﷺ much more than the initial profit she had originally promised him.

Marriage to Hadhrat Khadijah ﴿رضى الله عنها﴾

Hadhrat Khadijah ﴿رضى الله عنها﴾, after listening to Maysarah's account of his travels including Nastoora the monk's statement and the spectacle of the angels providing shade etc., went to Waraqah bin Nawfal and conveyed the details of these miraculous events to him. Waraqah remarked: "Khadijah! If these incidents are true, then most certainly Muhammad is the prophet of this Ummah. I am well aware that this Ummah is patiently waiting to be graced by a prophet whose advent is imminent."

On hearing about these miraculous events, Hadhrat Khadijah ﴿رضى الله عنها﴾ developed a longing to be wedded to Rasulullah ﷺ. As a result, two months and twenty-five days after his arrival from the Syrian trade journey, she sent a proposal to Rasulullah ﷺ. Acting on the advice of his uncle, Rasulullah ﷺ accepted this proposal. On the predetermined date of the Nikah, together with his uncles Abu Taalib and Hamzah and a few other chieftains of the family, Rasulullah ﷺ set out for Hadhrat Khadijah's ﴿رضى الله عنها﴾ residence. Hadhrat Khadijah's ﴿رضى الله عنها﴾ father had already passed away before the battle of Fujjaar. Her uncle 'Amar bin Asad was present at her Nikah.

Abu Taalib recited the Khutbah of Nikah, the closing words of which were:

اما بعد فان محمدا ممن لا يوازن به فتى من قريش الا رجح به شرفا ونبلا وفضلا و عقلا وان كان فى المال قل فانه ظل زائل وعارية مسترجعة وله فى خديجة بنت خويلد رغبة ولها فيه مثل ذلك

"Muhammad is a young man who, if weighed against any other youngster from the Quraysh, Muhammad will outweigh the other in nobility, eminence, intellect and graciousness. He may be lacking in wealth but wealth is after all a passing shadow and a trust to be ultimately surrendered. He is interested in getting married to Khadijah bint Khuwailid and she also cherishes the same interest."

At the time of this blessed Nikah, Rasulullah ﷺ was twenty-five years old whilst Hadhrat Khadijah ﴿رضى الله عنها﴾ was forty. The Mahr (dowry) was fixed at twenty camels. According to Seerat Ibn Hishaam and Hafiz Abu Bishr Dawlami, the stipulated Mahr (dowry) was twelve and half awqiyah of silver. Each awqiyah is equivalent to forty Dirhams. Hence, the total dowry was five hundred Dirhams.

This was Rasulullah's ﷺ first Nikah whilst it was Hadhrat Khadijah's ﴿رضى الله عنها﴾ third. We will, Insha Allah Ta'ala, discuss this in more detail in the chapter dealing with the Azwaaj-e-Mutahharaat (the blessed wives of Rasulullah ﷺ).

The Renovation of the K'abah and Rasulullah's ﷺ Arbitration

From the very inception of this universe, the K'abah was reconstructed five times. Initially it was constructed by Hadhrat Aadam عليه السلام. 'Abdullah bin 'Amr bin 'Aas رضي الله عنه reports that Rasulullah ﷺ said: "Allah Ta'ala delegated Hadhrat Jibraa'eel عليه السلام to command Hadhrat Aadam عليه السلام to erect the K'abah. When he completed the building, he was instructed to walk around the house (Tawaaf). He was also informed: "You are the first man and this is the first house erected for the devotion of Allah Ta'ala."

When the flood of Nuh عليه السلام struck, no sign of the K'abah was left behind. Ibraaheem عليه السلام was then commanded to reconstruct the K'abah. There was no trace of even the foundation left behind. Hadhrat Jibraa'eel عليه السلام came and retraced the markings of the original foundation. Subsequently, Hadhrat Ibraaheem عليه السلام, with the wholehearted assistance of Hadhrat Ismaa'eel عليه السلام, began reconstructing the holy K'abah.

The third occasion the K'abah underwent reconstruction was just before prophethood when Rasulullah ﷺ was thirty-five and the Quraysh decided to reconstruct the K'abah. The original structure erected by Hadhrat Ibraaheem عليه السلام was roofless whilst the walls were not actually very high. The walls were just above the average height of a man, approximately nine hands in height. Over the passage of time, the structure fell into disrepair. Due to it lying on low ground, rainwater would often find its way into the structure itself. This is why the Quraysh decided to demolish the original structure and rebuild it afresh. When all the Qurayshi leaders unanimously agreed to demolish the K'abah and rebuild it, Abu Wahab bin 'Amr Makhzoomi, Rasulullah's ﷺ father's mother's brother, addressed the Quraysh thus: "Bear in mind that whatever we propose to spend in the reconstruction of the K'abah should be from Halaal sources. The income derived from adultery, theft and usury should not be applied to this sacred mission. Only exclusively Halaal wealth should be utilised in its construction. Allah Ta'ala is pure and He only approves of pure. In the erection of this structure, employ your purely Halaal wealth." With the reasoning that not a single person be deprived of this noble assignment of reconstructing the K'abah, the reconstruction was divided over the various clans in such a manner that the responsibility of each phase or element of the K'abah was consigned to a different clan. Each and every tribe or clan was assigned a particular task or portion in the reconstruction process.

The portion towards the door was assigned to Banu 'Abdu Manaaf and Banu Zuhrah. The area between the Hajr-e-Aswad and Rukn-e-Yamani was allocated to Banu Makhzoom and other Qurayhsi clans. The rear of the structure was allocated to Banu Jamh and Banu Sahm whilst the Hateem section was given over to Banu 'Abdud-Daar bin Qusayy and Banu S'ad. During the course of restoration, the

Quraysh got word of a merchant ship that was recently wrecked in the port of Jeddah. On hearing this, Waleed bin Mughirah immediately set off for Jeddah and managed to obtain the timber of this ruined vessel for the roof of the K'abah. Amongst the crewmembers of this vessel was a Roman mason (or carpenter) by the name of Baqum. Waleed bin Mughirah also took him along to assist in the reconstruction.

After these initial stages of groundwork, when it came to the actual moment of demolition of the original structure, not a soul had the courage to initiate the tearing down of the first brick. In the end, Waleed bin Mughirah, wielding a shovel, proclaimed before Allah Ta'ala:

"O Allah! Our intentions are nothing but good." In other words, Allah Ta'ala forbid, we harbour absolutely no evil intention in razing the K'abah. Saying this, he commenced demolishing the K'abah in the region of Hajr-e-Aswad and Rukn Yamani. The people of Makkah decided to hold back until the forthcoming night to ascertain if Waleed is struck by any divine punishment. If any form of divine reprisal assails him, we will restore the house of Allah Ta'ala to what it was otherwise we will all assist Waleed in demolishing the present structure. The next morning found Waleed hail and hearty wielding a shovel into the Haram area. People interpreted his safety as an indication of Allah Ta'ala's pleasure thereby boosting their courage even further. All of them then earnestly embarked on this task of demolishing the K'abah. They continued digging right down until the original foundation laid by Hadhrat Ibraaheem عَلَيْهِ السَّلَام became visible. When a Qurayshi delivered a blow to the Ibraaheemi foundation, a terrible explosion rocked the city of Makkah. At once, they discontinued digging further and started their construction on the same original foundation. As per the preceding division, each tribe amassed their respective stones and started to rebuild their allotted portion of the K'abah. Now when the building reached completion and the crucial moment of placing the Hajr-e-Aswad (black stone) surfaced, intensely violent disputes broke out between all interested parties. Swords were unsheathed and the people became fervently determined to go to war and kill one another to acquire this noble credit of raising the stone to its place. After a few days of severe tension and no lasting solution in sight, Abu Umayyah bin Mughirah Makhzoomi, one of the eldest members of the Quraysh, submitted the opinion that the decision to raise the stone should be conferred upon the first person that enters the doors of the Haram the next morning. All parties expressed their approval to this proposal. The next morning, when they reached the Haram, they saw none other than Muhammad Rasulullah صَلَّى اللهُ عَلَيْهِ وَسَلَّم as the first entrant of the Haram that morning. The moment they caught sight of him, with one voice they spontaneously proclaimed:

هذا محمد الامين رضينا هذا محمد الامين

"This is Muhammad, the trustworthy. We are extremely pleased with him as arbiter. This is after all Muhammad, the trustworthy."

Rasulullah ﷺ asked for a sheet and placing the black stone onto it, he directed: "The chief of each tribe should grasp the ends of the sheet so that none of the tribes are deprived of this grand opportunity." All of them wholeheartedly approved of this proposal and each leader grasped a side of the sheet and hoisted it to the vicinity the black stone was to be placed. Rasulullah ﷺ then went forward and with his blessed hands raised the stone and placed it in its proper place.

The fourth time the K'abah was reconstructed was during the Caliphate of Hadhrat 'Abdullah bin Zubair رضي الله عنه. The entire structure was raised to the ground and reconstructed anew.

The Ka'bah was reconstructed a fifth time by that Hajjaaj bin Yusuf whose oppression and transgression was unmatched in history. For further details, research the books of history.

His Divine Aversion to Pagan Customs

It is reported from Hadhrat Ali رضي الله عنه that Rasulullah ﷺ was once asked if he ever worshiped an idol. He replied in the negative. He was then asked if he ever consumed wine. Rasulullah ﷺ again replied in the negative and remarked: "I always considered such deeds to be Kufr even though I possessed no knowledge of Imaan and the Qur-aan at that stage."

Hadhrat 'Urwah bin Zubair رضي الله عنه relates that the neighbour of Hadhrat Khadijah رضي الله عنها narrates that she heard Rasulullah ﷺ declaring to Hadhrat Khadijah رضي الله عنها: "By Allah! I will never ever worship Laat. By Allah! I will never ever worship 'Uzza."

Zaid bin Haarisah رضي الله عنه narrates: "During the era of ignorance, the disbelievers would respectfully stroke the stone idols of Isaaf and Naa'ilah whenever they performed Tawaaf of the K'abah. Once I accompanied Rasulullah ﷺ in performing the Tawaaf of the Baitullah. As we passed these idols, I devotedly lay a hand on them. Rasulullah ﷺ forbade me from doing this. I thought to myself, what harm can there be in touching stone. So I stroked them again. A bit more sternly, he prohibited me again reminding me of the previous prohibition. By Allah! From that day on, I have never touched a single stone idol right up to the time when Allah Ta'ala bestowed his prophethood upon Rasulullah ﷺ and revealed His divine speech upon him."

It is reported from Hadhrat Ali رضي الله عنه that he heard Rasulullah ﷺ saying: "The notion of participating in any of these pagan rituals or customs had never crossed my mind except on two occasions when Allah Ta'ala safeguarded me from their evils. One night, I told my companion who usually grazed goats with us to keep an eye on the animals as I wished to go to Makkah to amuse myself with a bit of story-telling. As I entered Makkah, I was confronted with the sound of music. Upon enquiry I learnt that so and so is getting married. I also joined the ceremony but the moment I sat down, I was overcome with sleep. Moreover, Allah Ta'ala sealed my ears against the music and I dozed off utterly unaware of my surroundings. By Allah! Only the intensity of the sun beating down on my face the next morning jolted me awake. I returned to my companion only to be asked what I saw. I replied that I saw absolutely nothing. I then related my incident of falling off to sleep."

The next night, Rasulullah ﷺ again decided to join in the festivities but he fell asleep yet again. Rasulullah ﷺ says: "By Allah! After this occasion I never thought of indulging in any form of such Jaahiliyyah customs until Allah Ta'ala bestowed upon me His divine gift of prophethood." Bukhaari and Muslim narrate on the authority of Hadhrat Jaabir ؓ that during the reconstruction of the K'abah, Rasulullah ﷺ also joined the people in hauling boulders to the site. His uncle Hadhrat 'Abbaas ؓ advised him: "Son! Undo your lower garment and throw it over your shoulder so that you may be safe from the constant chafing caused by the boulders." On the advice of his uncle, he was about to undo his lower garment when he suddenly fell unconscious.

According to Abu Tufail, a mysterious voice cautioned Rasulullah ﷺ thus: "O Muhammad! Safeguard your private part." This was the first time Rasulullah ﷺ heard this mysterious voice.

According to the narration of Ibn 'Abbaas ؓ, Abu Taalib asked Rasulullah ﷺ what transpired. He replied: "A white-clothed person appeared before me and cautioned me to conceal my private parts."

On one occasion, the Quraysh placed some food before Rasulullah ﷺ. Zaid bin 'Amr bin Nufail was also present in this gathering. Rasulullah ﷺ refused to partake of this meal. Subsequently, Zaid also declined to eat this food saying: "I refuse to consume an animal slaughtered on the name of anyone other than Allah Ta'ala. I will not partake of food dedicated to a deity. I will only consume food upon which the name of Allah Ta'ala is taken exclusively." Zaid bin 'Amr bin Nufail would often reproach the Quraysh thus: "Allah Ta'ala created the goat and Allah Ta'ala Himself produced the grass for it to graze on. Then why do you slaughter the goat upon the name of someone other than Allah Ta'ala?"

Zaid bin 'Amr bin Nufail was the cousin (father's brother's son) of Hadhrat 'Umar ؓ. He was the father of Sa'eed bin Zaid, one of the 'Asharah Mubasharah (the ten companions conferred with glad tidings of Jannah). He was utterly revolted by idolatry and was in perpetual pursuit of the true religion. He passed away five years prior to prophethood whilst the K'abah was undergoing reconstruction.

Now I wish to return to the original topic. Bukhaari and Muslim narrate that Hadhrat 'Aa'ishah رَضِىَ اللّٰهُ عَنْهَا said:

اول ما بدئ به رسول الله صلى الله عليه وسلم من الوحى الرؤيا الصالحة فى النوم فكان لا يرى رؤيا الا جاءت مثل فلق الصبح

"Divine revelation upon Rasulullah ﷺ originated with pious dreams. Whatever he witnessed in his dreams, it would come to pass as true as the crack of dawn."

Ibn Abu Jamarah says: "The dreams of Rasulullah ﷺ are compared to dawn because the sun of prophethood had not as yet risen. Just as the crack of dawn signifies the imminent advent of the sun, similarly, pious dreams were an introduction to the imminent advent of the sun of prophethood." It was as though the 'dawn' of pious dreams is proclaiming: "Soon, the sun of prophethood will rise." Just as the radiance of the morning continues spreading in a flash, similarly, the light of these true dreams continued to flourish until such time that the luminance of prophethood extended to light up the mountains of Makkah. People like Abu Bakr رَضِىَ اللّٰهُ عَنْهُ who possessed the spiritual vision of the heart appeared before this sun and benefited from its brilliance whilst people like Abu Jahal who were enveloped in spiritual darkness, closed their eyes to this radiance and like bats they were unable to endure the radiance of this brilliant sun of prophethood.

گر نہ بیند بروز شپرہ چشم   چشمۂ آفتاب راچہ گناہ

چہرۂ آفتاب خود فاش است   بے نصیبی نصیب خفاش است

"If the bat is unable to see during the day, what is the fault of daylight? The face of the sun is naturally radiant, ill-fated is the bat."

As for the remainder of the people between the ranks of Abu Bakr رَضِىَ اللّٰهُ عَنْهُ and Abu Jahal, each and every person benefited from this sun of prophethood according to the level of his spiritual vision and luminance of his heart.

Ummul-Mumineen Hadhrat 'Aa'ishah رَضِىَ اللّٰهُ عَنْهَا further relates:

ثم حبب اليه الخلا وكان يخلو بغار حراء

"Thereafter, solitude was made dear to him. He would often go into seclusion in the cave of Hira."

When Allah Ta'ala intends to shower His special mercy upon a person, He cultivates the yearning for solitude and seclusion within this person's heart. Allah Ta'ala discloses in the story of the people of the Kahf (cave):

$$وَإِذِ اعْتَزَلْتُمُوهُمْ وَمَا يَعْبُدُونَ إِلَّا اللهَ فَأْوُوا إِلَى الْكَهْفِ يَنْشُرْ لَكُمْ رَبُّكُمْ مِنْ رَحْمَتِهِ وَيُهَيِّئْ لَكُمْ مِنْ أَمْرِكُمْ مِرْفَقًا$$

"And when you withdraw from them and from whatever else they worhisp besides Allah, then seek refuge in the cave so that your Lord may broaden for you His mercy and He may make your affairs easy for you." [Surah Kahf verse 16]

This does not necessarily entail that solitude begets prophethood because prophethood is not something that can be earned. Allah Ta'ala appoints as messenger whomsoever He wishes.

Chapter 3

The Sunrise of Prophethood on Mount Faran

When Rasulullah ﷺ reached forty, as per his earlier routine he was in the cave of Hira, when suddenly an angel appeared in the cave. He entered, greeted him with Salaam and said: "Read!" Rasulullah ﷺ replied: "I am unable to read." Rasulullah ﷺ recounts: "Upon this the angel embraced me so forcefully that there was no limit to my suffering. He then released me saying, 'Read!' Yet again, I responded:

ما انا بقارئ

"I am unable to read."

Continuing further, Rasulullah ﷺ relates: "The angel likewise forcefully embraced me a second and then a third time, released me and bade me to recite the following verses:

اِقْرَأْ بِاسْمِ رَبِّكَ الَّذِيْ خَلَقَ ۞ خَلَقَ الْاِنْسَانَ مِنْ عَلَقٍ ۞ اِقْرَأْ وَ رَبُّكَ الْاَكْرَمُ ۞ الَّذِيْ عَلَّمَ بِالْقَلَمِ ۞ عَلَّمَ الْاِنْسَانَ مَا لَمْ يَعْلَمْ ۞

"Read (with the aid) of the name of your Rabb Who has created (the entire universe). He has created (above all) man from a clot of blood. Read! And your Rabb is the most gracious Who has taught (knowledge) by the use of the pen. He has taught man that which he did not know." [Surah 'Alaq verse 1]

Thereafter, Rasulullah ﷺ returned home trembling in anxiety. The moment he entered, he requested Hadhrat Khadijah ﷺ to wrap him up. When his anxiety and agitation subsided, he related the whole incident to Hadhrat Khadijah ﷺ saying: "I was terrified of losing my life." In other words, since the spiritual illumination of divine revelation and the spiritual radiance of the angel were abruptly thrust upon the human nature of Rasulullah ﷺ and due to the magnitude of the divine revelation, Rasulullah ﷺ assumed that if the intensity of this Wahi persists in this manner, his human nature would very unlikely be able to withstand the burden of Wahi. It could also mean that saddled by the burden of prophethood, he thought he would perish. The following verse refers to this very burden:

اِنَّا سَنُلْقِیْ عَلَیْکَ قَوْلًا ثَقِیْلًا ۝

"We will reveal upon you a very burdensome word." [Surah Muzzammil: 5]

If Rasulullah ﷺ were receiving divine revelation whilst mounted upon a camel, the camel would be constrained to sit down. Hadhrat Zaid bin Thaabit رضي الله عنه narrates: "On one occasion, Rasulullah's ﷺ thigh was on my thigh when he started receiving divine revelation. His thigh suddenly became so unbearably heavy that I was afraid of my thigh being reduced to pulp."

Thereafter Jibraa'eel عليه السلام appeared before him giving him glad tidings of Allah Ta'ala choosing him as His messenger until Rasulullah ﷺ felt at ease. He then bade him to recite. Rasulullah ﷺ asked: "How must I recite?" Jibraa'eel عليه السلام replied: "Read in the name of your Rabb Who created...."up to the verse "that which he knew not." Rasulullah ﷺ accepted the message of Allah and returned. Every tree and stone he passed en route to his home greeted him with "As-Salaamu'alayka Yaa Rasulallah!" This is how he returned home in high spirits and with firm conviction that Allah Ta'ala has conferred upon him a rank of incalculable magnitude; prophethood."

Nonetheless, he returned home and furnished Hadhrat Khadijah رضي الله عنها with a detailed account of what transpired. He also expressed his fear of losing his life. Hadhrat Khadijah رضي الله عنها consoled him saying: "Congratulations to you! This is a source of glad tidings. Do not panic! By Allah! He will never disgrace you. You maintain favourable family ties. Your efforts at maintaining good family ties are notable. You always speak the truth. You bear the burdens of others. You shoulder the debts of others. You attend to the affairs of the poor. You are trustworthy; you return whatever has been entrusted to your care. You always fulfil the rights of the guests. You are always willing to assist in good works."

Hadhrat Khadijah رضي الله عنها also added: "You have never even been close to an evil woman."

In short, a person with such outstanding character, a man of such superior values, a human being with such purity, a man who is an embodiment of virtue and perfection can never be subject to any form of humiliation. He cannot be put to shame, neither in this world nor the hereafter. Whosoever Allah Ta'ala blesses with such exceptional character and virtue, Allah Ta'ala will shield him from all calamities and misfortune as well.

Khadijah ﷺ consoled him saying: "By Allah in whose absolute control lies Khadijah's life! I firmly expect you to be the messenger of this Ummah."

According to other narrations, Rasulullah ﷺ gave Khadijah ﷺ a detailed account of what transpired. She responded: "By Allah! Take heart and accept glad tidings. Allah Ta'ala will never do anything to you but good. So accept whatever status Allah Ta'ala has conferred upon you because it is distinctly authentic. And congratulations to you as I also maintain that you are truly the messenger of Allah."

Hadhrat Khadijah ﷺ then went alone to her cousin Waraqah bin Nawfal. He was a celebrated scholar of the old and the new testaments. He was busy translating the New Testament from Syriac into Arabic. During the pre-Islamic era of ignorance, he steered clear of idolatry and embraced Christianity. By this time he was very old and blind. On hearing the entire episode from Hadhrat Khadijah ﷺ, Waraqah remarked:

لئن كنت صدّقتِنى انه لياتيه ناموس عيسى

"If you are truthful in whatever you say, verily this is the same Angel who used to come to 'Isa عليه السلام."

Subsequent to this, Hadhrat Khadijah ﷺ took Rasulullah ﷺ along with her to Waraqah bin Nawfal. She addressed him saying: "O cousin! Why don't you hear it from your nephew (in his own words)?"

Waraqah then addressed Rasulullah ﷺ saying: "O nephew! Tell me, what did you observe? What happened?" Rasulullah ﷺ then narrated the entire incident.

فلما سمعَ كلامه ايقن بالحق واعترف به

"The moment he heard the details, he became absolutely convinced of the truth and he ardently accepted and wholeheartedly submitted to the truth."

On listening to these details, Waraqah submitted: "Indeed, this is the same angel that used to appear before Musa عليه السلام. If only I was strong enough during your prophethood when your people will banish you from your birthplace or at least I wish I am alive (to see those times)." Stunned by what he just said, Rasulullah ﷺ asked: "Will they really drive me out?" Waraqah replied: "This is not confined to you alone. All the Prophets who came with the divine message faced hostility from their own people. If I am fortunate enough to come across that era, I will assist you in all earnestness." However, not long thereafter, Waraqah passed away.

ہجر سے بڑھ کر مصیبت کچھ نہیں
اس سے بہتر ہے کہ مر جاؤں کہیں

Urdu Couplet: "There is no calamity more severe than separation from the beloved, it is better to die than suffer such anguish."

Nonetheless, whenever Rasulullah ﷺ would think about this, Jibraa'eel عليه السلام would appear before him and console him saying:

یا محمد انك رسول الله حقا

"O Muhammad! You are indeed the true Prophet of Allah."

On hearing such comforting words, Rasulullah ﷺ would feel somewhat relieved.

On one occasion, Hadhrat Khadijah رضى الله عنها requested Rasulullah ﷺ thus: "When the angel approaches you again, please inform me, if possible." When Jibraa'eel عليه السلام appeared yet again, Rasulullah ﷺ apprised her of his arrival. Hadhrat Khadijah رضى الله عنها then requested Rasulullah ﷺ to come onto her lap. As he placed his head on her lap, she removed her scarf exposing her head. "Can you still spot Jibraa'eel عليه السلام now?" she asked. When Rasulullah ﷺ replied in the negative, she remarked: "Glad tidings unto you. By Allah Ta'ala! This is an angel, not shaytaan."

Date of Prophethood

All the Muhadditheen and historians are unanimous over the fact that Rasulullah ﷺ was bestowed the mantle of prophethood on a Monday. However, there seems to be some disagreement on the actual month of his ordainment. Hafiz Ibn 'Abdul-Barr رحمه الله says that he was commissioned with the assignment of prophethood on the eighth of Rabi'ul-Awwal. According to this, Rasulullah ﷺ was exactly forty years old when he was ordained as a prophet.

Salaah - The Primary Obligation after Tauheed and Risaalat

Following Tauheed and Risaalat, the very first lesson imparted to Rasulullah ﷺ dealt with Wudu and Salaah. At the outset, Jibraa'eel عليه السلام stamped his heel on the ground that caused a spring to gush forth. Jibraa'eel عليه السلام performed wudhu with this water whilst Rasulullah ﷺ continued observing his actions. Then Rasulullah ﷺ also performed wudhu accordingly. Thereafter Jibraa'eel عليه السلام performed two Rakaats of Salaah with Rasulullah ﷺ keeping abreast by following him throughout. Following this lesson of Salaah and Wudhu, Rasulullah ﷺ returned home and imparted this ritual to Hadhrat Khadijah رضى الله عنها.

Usaamah bin Zaid رضى الله عنه narrates from his father Zaid bin Haarisah رضى الله عنه that Rasulullah ﷺ said: "During the initial stages of my prophethood and divine revelation, Jibraa'eel عليه السلام appeared before me and tutored me about Salaah and Wudhu."

وَأَقِمِ الصَّلٰوةَ طَرَفِ النَّهَارِ

"And establish Salaah in both parts of the day (i.e. morning and evening).

[Surah Hud verse 114]

Surah Muzzammil was revealed in which Qiyaamul-Layl (Tahajjud) was established.

In the early stages of Islam, Allah Ta'ala had prescribed two rakaats of Salaah for the morning and two rakaats for the evening. Later on five Salaahs were made compulsory on the night of Mi'raaj.

Chapter 4

The Earliest Pioneers

The very first person to embrace Islam was the beloved wife of Rasulullah ﷺ, Hadhrat Khadijatul-Kubraa رضي الله عنها and she was the first person to join him for Salaah (with Jamaat) on a Monday evening. Hence, she is regarded as the earliest member of Ahl-e-Qiblah (people who face the Qiblah as a reference to the Muslims).

Thereafter Waraqah bin Nawfal was honoured with embracing Islam followed by Hadhrat Ali رضي الله عنه who for some time was under the guardianship of Rasulullah ﷺ. He was ten when he embraced Islam. On the Tuesday following Rasulullah's ﷺ ordainment to prophethood, he joined Rasulullah ﷺ in Salaah as well.

When Hadhrat Ali رضي الله عنه observed Rasulullah ﷺ and Hadhrat Khadijah رضي الله عنها performing Salaah on the day following his ordainment, he asked: "What is this?" Rasulullah ﷺ replied: "This is the Deen of Allah Ta'ala. Each and every one of the Prophets imparted the same Deen to the peoples of this world. I am also inviting you towards Allah. Worship Him alone and renounce (the idols of) Laat and 'Uzza." Hadhrat Ali رضي الله عنه remarked: "This is something absolutely new to me. I haven't heard of anything quite like this. I am unable to make a decision without mentioning this to my father Abu Taalib." Since Rasulullah ﷺ was a bit reluctant to disclose his secret to anyone else, he said: "'Ali! If you do not wish to embrace Islam, don't mention it to anyone else." Hadhrat Ali رضي الله عنه remained silent. Not even a night passed when Islam was infused into his heart. The next morning he presented himself to Rasulullah ﷺ saying: "What are you inviting us to?" Rasulullah ﷺ replied: "Bear testimony that Allah is all alone and He has no partner. Renounce Laat and 'Uzza and express your hatred for idolatry." Hadhrat Ali رضي الله عنه then embraced Islam and for quite a while – possibly a whole year as mentioned in some narrations – he concealed his conversion to Islam from his father Abu Taalib.

Following this, Rasulullah's ﷺ freed slave Hadhrat Zaid bin Haarisah ؓ embraced Islam and performed Salaah with him.

Islam of Abu Bakr Siddeeq ؓ

When all his household members embraced Islam, Rasulullah ﷺ invited his intimate friends and close associates to embrace this great blessing of Islam. The first person he extended this invitation to was his devoted friend, his childhood acquaintance and his intimate confidant, Hadhrat Abu Bakr ؓ. Without even giving it a second thought, Hadhrat Abu Bakr ؓ enthusiastically accepted Rasulullah's ﷺ invitation the moment it was extended to him.

چشم احمد برابوبکرے زدہ

وزیکے تصدیق صدیق آمدہ

"Rasulullah ﷺ presented the truth and Abu Bakr submitted to it. A single Tasdeeq (belief) transformed him into a Siddeeq (passionate believer)."

In a Hadith, Rasulullah ﷺ said: "Whoever I presented Islam to, there was always some degree of hesitation except in the case of Abu Bakr. Without hesitation, he promptly embraced Islam."

When Imaam Abu Hanifah رحمه الله was asked who was the first person to embrace Islam, he replied: "Amongst the free men it was Hadhrat Abu Bakr ؓ. Amongst the women it was Hadhrat Khadijah ؓ. The first slave to embrace Islam was Hadhrat Zaid bin Haarisah ؓ whilst Hadhrat Ali ؓ was the first child to come into the fold of Islam."

Hadhrat Abu Bakr ؓ, on the other hand, started the propagation of Islam the moment he embraced Islam. Whenever he came into contact with his close friends or they came into contact with him, he would extend the invitation of Islam to them. As a result of his persistent efforts in communicating this message, the following personalities entered the fold of Islam: 'Usmaan bin 'Affaan, Zubair bin 'Awwaam, 'Abdur-Rahmaan bin 'Awf, Talhah bin 'Ubaidullah and S'ad bin Abi Waqqaas. These dignitaries of the Quraysh and the noble members of their respective families embraced Islam on the invitation of Abu Bakr ؓ. He brought all of them to Rasulullah ﷺ and they all embraced Islam at his blessed hands and joined him for Salaah.

After this, the following persons were honoured with Islam: Abu 'Ubaidah Aamir bin Jarraah, Arqam bin Abil-Arqam, the three sons of Maz'oon bin Habib; 'Usmaan bin Maz'oon, Qudaamah bin Maz'oon and 'Abdullah bin Maz'oon,

'Ubaidah bin Haaris, Sa'eed bin Zaid bin 'Amr bin Nufail and his wife Faatimah bint Khattaab – in other words, the sister of 'Umar bin Khattaab – Asma bint Abi Bakr, Khabbaab bin Arat, 'Umair bin Abi Waqqaas (brother of S'ad bin Abi Waqqaas), 'Abdullah bin Mas'ood, Mas'ood bin Qari, Salit bin 'Amr, 'Ayyaash bin Abi Rabi'ah and his wife Asma bint Salaamah, Khunais bin Huzaafah, 'Aamir bin Rabi'ah, 'Abdullah bin Jahsh and his brother Abu Ahmad bin Jahsh, Ja'far bin Abi Taalib and his wife Asma bint 'Umais, Haatib bin Haaris, his wife Faatimah bint Mujallal and his brother Khattaab bin Haaris with his wife Fakihah bint Yasar, M'amar bin Haaris, Saaib bin 'Usmaan bin Maz'oon, Mutallib bin Azhar with his wife Ramlah bint Abi 'Awf, Na'im bin 'Abdullah Al-Nahhaam, 'Aamir bin Fuhairah the emancipated slave of Abu Bakr Siddeeq, Khaalid bin Sa'eed bin Aas and his wife Umaniyyah bint Khalaf, Haatib bin 'Amr, Huzaifah bin 'Utbah, Waaqid bin 'Abdullah, the four sons of Bukair bin 'Abdyaalil; Khaalid, Aamir, 'Aqil and Iyaas, 'Ammaar bin Yaasir and Suhaib bin Sinaan the freed slave of 'Abdullah bin Jad'aan ﷺ.

Whenever the hour of Salaah approached, Rasulullah ﷺ would secretly perform his Salaah in a secluded valley or mountain pass. On one occasion, Rasulullah ﷺ was performing his Salaah with Hadhrat Ali ﷺ on an isolated mountain pass when all of a sudden Abu Taalib appeared in the distance coming their way. Up until that time, Hadhrat Ali ﷺ had not exposed his conversion to his parents, uncles and other relatives. Abu Taalib addressed Rasulullah ﷺ saying: "Nephew! What religion is this? What kind of devotion is this?" Rasulullah ﷺ replied: "Uncle! This is the Deen of Allah Ta'ala, His angels and all His prophets, especially the Deen of our great grandfather, Hadhrat Ibraaheem ﷺ. Allah Ta'ala has selected me as His messenger to all His servants. You are most eligible for my advice. I invite you towards goodness and divine guidance. You ought to accept this divine guidance and true religion first and prove your support and assistance towards me."

Abu Taalib replied: "Nephew! Personally I am unable to renounce my ancestral religion but I assure you that in my presence nobody will hurt you." He then turned to Hadhrat Ali ﷺ asking: "Son! What is this religion you have submitted to?" Hadhrat Ali ﷺ replied: "Father! I have faith in Allah and His Rasool ﷺ and I believe in whatever he conveys to us from Allah. I join him in Salaah and I am his devoted adherent." Abu Taalib remarked: "Very well then! He has unquestionably invited you to good. Don't ever abandon him."

The Islam of Ja'far bin Abi Taalib ﷺ

One day Hadhrat Ali ﷺ was engaged in Salaah standing on the right of Rasulullah ﷺ. Unexpectedly Abu Taalib happened to pass by. Hadhrat Ja'far was also with him. Abu Taalib addressed Ja'far advising: "Son! Like Ali, you should also lend your support to your cousin. Stand on his left and join them in Salaah." Ja'far ﷺ was also one of the foremost Sahaabah ﷺ to embrace Islam. He was either the twenty-first or the twenty-fifth person to embrace Islam.

Islam of 'Afeef Kindi ﷺ

'Afeef Kindi was a close friend of Hadhrat 'Abbaas ﷺ. He was a perfume merchant by trade. By virtue of his commercial activities, he would often travel to Yemen. 'Afeef Kindi ﷺ says: "I was once in Mina with Hadhrat 'Abbaas ﷺ when a man appeared, performed wudhu methodically and stood up for Salaah. Thereafter a woman appeared, performed wudhu in the same manner and stood up for Salaah. A little while later, an eleven-year-old boy came. He too performed wudhu and stood for Salaah in line with this man. I asked 'Abbaas: 'What religion is this?' He replied: 'This is the Deen of my nephew Muhammad who professes to be the apostle of Allah Ta'ala. This youngster is Ali bin Abi Taalib who is also my nephew whilst this woman is Muhammad bin 'Abdullah's wife.'" 'Afeef later embraced Islam. He would often lament: "If only I was the fourth person to embrace Islam."

Islam of Talhah ﷺ

Hadhrat Talhah ﷺ narrates: "I once went on a business trip to Busraa. One day I was in the market place of Busraa when I heard a monk shouting out: 'Ascertain if there is anyone from the Haram of Makkah (amongst these traders).' I responded: 'I am from the Haram of Makkah.' The monk asked: 'Has Ahmad ﷺ made an appearance as yet?' I posed: 'Come again! Who?' The monk replied: 'The son of 'Abdullah bin 'Abdul Muttalib. This is the month of his impending appearance. He is expected to appear in the Haram of Makkah and migrate to a rocky land abundant in date palms. He is the final messenger. Be vigilant. Do not get left behind.' This statement had a profound effect upon my heart. I immediately returned to Makkah enquiring if anything new had transpired recently. They replied: 'Yes, Muhammad, the trustworthy, has claimed prophethood and the son of Abu Quhaafah (i.e. Abu Bakr ﷺ) has committed himself with him.' Without delay, I set out for Abu Bakr ﷺ. He took me to Rasulullah ﷺ, before whom I embraced Islam and I also gave him a detailed account of what transpired between the monk and myself at Busraa."

Islam of S'ad bin Abi Waqqaas ﷺ

S'ad bin Abi Waqqaas ﷺ says: "Three nights before embracing Islam I saw a dream; I was in an appallingly intense darkness. It was so dark that I could see absolutely nothing. Suddenly, a moon appeared and I started trailing behind it. To my amazement, I observed that Zaid bin Haarisah, Ali and Abu Bakr have already preceded me to its light. On awakening, I set out for Rasulullah ﷺ and enquired: 'What do you preach?' Rasulullah ﷺ replied: 'I invite you towards the oneness of Allah Ta'ala and I invite you to attest that I am the messenger of Allah.' I submitted: 'I bear witness that there is none worthy of worship besides Allah and that Muhammad ﷺ is Allah's messenger.'"

Islam of Khaalid bin Sa'eed bin Aas ﷺ

He is among the earliest to embrace Islam. He was either the fourth or fifth person to embrace Islam.

Before embracing Islam, he had rather a strange dream. He says: "I dreamt that I am standing at the edge of a broad and deep abyss blazing with gigantic flames. My father, Sa'eed was about to shove me into the raging blaze when all of a sudden Rasulullah ﷺ appeared before us. He clutched me by the waist and hauled me away. I got up saying: 'By Allah! This dream is true.'"

I then proceeded to Abu Bakr ﷺ and related the dream to him. Abu Bakr ﷺ said: "Allah wants good for you. This is the messenger of Allah. Follow him and embrace Islam. Insha Allah, once you adhere to Rasulullah ﷺ and embrace Islam, your Islam will safeguard you from falling into the pit of fire but it appears as though your father is falling into the pit of fire." I then went to Rasulullah ﷺ and enquired: "O Muhammad! (ﷺ), to what are you inviting us?" Rasulullah ﷺ replied:

ادعوك الى الله وحده لا شريك له وان محمداً عبده و رسوله تخلع ما كنت عليه من عبادة حجر لا يضر ولا ينفع ولا يدرى من عبده ممن لم يعبده

"I am inviting you towards Allah Who is the One, He has no partner and verily Muhammad is His slave and messenger. And I invite you to relinquish your worship of stones (idols) that neither control benefit nor harm nor do they even comprehend who worships them or who desists from worshipping them."

Khaalid relates: "I then submitted before Rasulullah ﷺ: 'I testify that Allah is all alone and you (O Muhammad) are His true messenger.' In this manner I embraced Islam. When my father got wind of me embracing Islam, he beat me up so severely that I sustained a deep gash to the head. He broke a stick on my head and shrieked: 'You are taking after Muhammad (ﷺ) who is opposed to the whole nation. He condemns our deities and depicts our forefathers as stupid and ignorant.' I responded: 'By Allah! Muhammad ﷺ is true in his proclamations.' This statement enraged my father even further. He hurled stern abuse at me and bellowed: 'You contemptible idiot! Get out of here. Do not ever come close to me. By Allah! I will cut off your food.' I calmly replied: 'If you deprive me of food, Allah Ta'ala will provide me His sustenance.' Upon this, my father drove me out of the house and warned his children to sever relationship with me and to refrain from speaking to me. He cautioned them that if any of them were to speak to me, he would face the same fate."

Khaalid ؓ subsequently left his father's house and headed for the welcoming door of Rasulullah ﷺ. Rasulullah ﷺ held Khaalid ؓ in high esteem and always welcomed him warmly. A man does not bring dishonour to himself by leaving the door of anyone but he would definitely not find honour and respect wherever he goes if he has to leave the door of Allah Ta'ala and His Rasool ﷺ. Allah Ta'ala declares: "And to Allah alone is honour, and to His Rasool ﷺ and to the believers but the hypocrites are not aware." This verse clearly reveals that honour lies in Imaan whilst disbelief (kufr) is downright humiliation and shame. There is no likelihood whatsoever of honour in kufr.

Hadhrat Khaalid ؓ says: "My father once fell seriously ill. He vowed: 'If Allah restores my health from this illness, I will not allow the deity Muhammad urges us to worship to be worshipped here in Makkah.' I made dua to Allah Ta'ala: 'O Allah! Do not allow my father to get up from this illness.' He eventually died from this illness."

Islam of 'Usmaan bin 'Affaan ؓ

Hadhrat 'Usmaan ؓ says: "I once entered my house when I saw my aunt (mother's sister), Su'daa sitting amongst the house folks. My aunt frequently engaged in soothsaying. The moment she laid eyes on me, she said:

اَبْشِرْ وَحُيِّيْتَ ثَلَاثًا وِتْرًا ثُمَّ ثَلَاثًا وَثَلَاثًا اُخْرٰى

"Congratulations and glad tidings to you O 'Usmaan. Thrice, thrice again and thrice once more.

Chapter 4

لَقِيْتَ خَيْرًا وَوُقِيْتَ شَرًّا   ثُمَّ بِأُخْرَى لِكَيْ تُتِمَّ عَشْرًا

Then again once more to complete ten. You are fortunate to acquire good and you are privileged to be protected from evil.

وَأَنْتَ بِكْرٌ وَلَقِيْتَ بِكْرًا   نَكَحْتَ وَاللهِ حَصَانًا زَهْرًا

By Allah! You have wedded an incredibly chaste and beautiful woman. You are an unmarried man and you have married a virgin."

I was quite shocked at hearing these stanzas. I exclaimed: "Aunty! What are you saying." Upon this, she recited the following couplets:

لَكَ الْجَمَالُ وَلَكَ الشَّأْنُ   عُثْمَانُ يَا عُثْمَانُ يَا عُثْمَانُ

"Usmaan! O 'Usmaan! O 'Usmaan! You are a man of exceptional beauty coupled with great honour.

أَرْسَلَهُ بِحَقِّهِ الدَّيَّانُ   هَذَا نَبِيٌّ مَعَهُ الْبُرْهَانُ

This is a Prophet who possesses irrefutable proof. The Lord of reward (Allah Ta'ala) sent him with the truth.

فَاتَّبِعْهُ لَا تَغْيَابِكَ الْأَوْثَانُ   وَجَاءَهُ التَّنْزِيْلُ وَالْفُرْقَانُ

And the divine word, which differentiates between good and evil, descends upon him. So adhere to him and do not allow the idols to mislead you."

I responded: "Aunty! You mention such things the names of which have been unheard of in this city. I don't understand." Upon this S'udaa elaborated:

محمد بن عبدالله رسول من عند الله جاء بتنزيل الله يدعو الى الله قوله صلاح ودينه فلاح وامره نجاح ما ينفع الصياح لو وقع الرماح وسلت الصفاح و مدت الرماح

"Muhammad bin 'Abdullah, the Rasool of Allah ﷺ. He has appeared with the divine word of Allah beckoning everyone to come towards Allah. His proclamations are a source of guidance. His religion is a fountainhead of success.

His condition is one of victory. Screeching against him will be of no avail despite the numerous swords and abundant spears."

Saying this, she departed but her words left a profound impression upon my heart. I fell into a state of contemplation and anxiety. Since I had an excellent friendly relationship with Abu Bakr, I proceeded to him and sat down with him. Seeing my pensive mood, he asked: "What seems to distress you?" I related the entire incident about my aunt and her poetical predictions to Abu Bakr رضي الله عنه. Abu Bakr رضي الله عنه responded: "'Usmaan! You are, Maashaa Allah, intelligent and decisive. You are an expert in differentiating between the truth and falsehood. People like you are not bewildered between the truth and falsehood. What are these idols that our people are bowing down to? Are these idols not blind and deaf? They can neither hear nor see. Neither can they cause harm nor are they able to confer benefit." Hadhrat 'Usmaan رضي الله عنه replied: "By Allah! They are precisely as you profess." Upon this Abu Bakr رضي الله عنه commented: "By Allah! Your aunt spoke the truth. Muhammad bin 'Abdullah is the messenger of Allah. Allah Ta'ala commissioned him with His message to the people. If you deem it appropriate, you may attend one of his discourses and listen to what he says."

Hadhrat 'Usmaan رضي الله عنه says: "Whilst we were still in conversation, suddenly, as a stroke of fortune, Rasulullah ﷺ happened to pass by. Hadhrat Ali رضي الله عنه was with him. Rasulullah ﷺ had a cloth in one hand. On seeing Rasulullah ﷺ, Abu Bakr رضي الله عنه stood up and whispered something into his ear. Rasulullah ﷺ approached us and seated himself before us. He then addressed 'Usmaan رضي الله عنه saying: "O 'Usmaan! Allah invites you to Jannah. So accept His invitation. I am the messenger of Allah Ta'ala sent to you and the entire creation."

فوالله ما تمالكت حين سمعت قوله ان اسلمت واشهدت ان لا اله الا الله وحده لا شريك له وان محمدا عبده و رسوله

Hadhrat 'Usmaan رضي الله عنه relates: "By Allah! The moment I heard this, I was unable to restrain myself. Without any delay, I embraced Islam declaring: 'I bear witness that there is none worthy of worship but Allah, He is alone and has no partner and I bear witness that Muhammad is His slave and messenger.'"

Hadhrat 'Usmaan رضي الله عنه relates: "Not even a few days had passed when Rasulullah's ﷺ daughter Hadhrat Ruqayyaa رضي الله عنها came into my Nikah. Everyone viewed this union with a complimentary eye. To mark this auspicious occasion, my aunt Su'daa composed the following stanzas:

هَدَى اللهُ عُثْمَانَ الصيفِيَّ بِقَوْلِهِ فَأَرْشَدَهُ وَاللهُ يَهْدِي إِلَى الْحَقِّ

"Allah has guided 'Usmaan, His chosen servant. Only Allah has guided him and He is the only being Who leads the way.

فَتَابَعَ بِالرَّأْيِ الشَّدِيدِ مُحَمَّدًا وَكَانَ ابْنَ أَرْوَى لاَ يَصُدُّ عَنِ الْحَقِّ

Owing to his sound discretion, 'Usmaan has pursued Muhammad. After all, he is the son of Arwa. (Arwa literally means contemplative and understanding. In other words, 'Usmaan acted with sound thinking. Arwa the daughter of Kuraiz was actually Hadhrat 'Usmaan's ﷺ mother.) And he ('Usmaan ﷺ) is a man who does not desist from the truth.

وَأَنْكَحَهُ الْمَبْعُوثُ إِحْدَى بَنَاتِهِ فَكَانَ كَبَدْرٍ مَازَجَ الشَّمْسَ فِي الْأُفُقِ

And the commissioned personality (Rasulullah ﷺ) handed over one of his daughters to him in marriage. As though this union is like the sun and the full moon coming together on the horizon.

فِدًى لَكَ يَا ابْنَ الْهَاشِمِينَ مُهْجَتِي فَأَنْتَ أَمِينُ اللهِ أُرْسِلْتَ لِلْخَلْقِ

May my life be sacrificed for you O Son of the Hashimites! (Ref to Rasulullah ﷺ.) You are the trusted personage whom Allah Ta'ala has sent to His creation."

Subsequent to the day Hadhrat 'Usmaan ﷺ embraced Islam, Hadhrat Abu Bakr ﷺ brought the following luminaries to Rasulullah ﷺ: 'Usmaan bin Maz'oon, Abu 'Ubaidah bin Jarraah, Abu Salimah bin 'Abdul-Asad, Arqam bin Arqam ﷺ. All of them embraced Islam at the same time in one sitting.

Yazeed bin Rumaan narrates: "'Usmaan bin Maz'oon, 'Ubaidah bin Haaris, Abu 'Ubaidah Jarraah, 'Abdur-Rahmaan bin 'Awf and Abu Salimah bin 'Abdul Asad all got together and appeared before Rasulullah ﷺ. Rasulullah ﷺ presented them with Islam and enlightened them about the injunctions of Islam. All of them embraced Islam with one voice. These personages embraced Islam before they had taken refuge in Daar-e-Arqam."

Islam of 'Ammaar ﷺ and Suhaib ﷺ

'Ammaar bin Yaasir ﷺ says: "I met Suhaib bin Sinaan at the door of Daar-e-Arqam whilst Rasulullah ﷺ was inside. I asked Suhaib what his intention was. He surprised me by asking me the same question. 'What is your purpose for turning up here?' he enquired. I replied: 'I intend to go to him (Rasulullah

ﷺ) and listen to what he has to say.' Both of us then entered Daar-e-Arqam where Rasulullah ﷺ presented before us the teachings of Islam. Both of us, without further ado, embraced Islam."

Islam of 'Amr bin 'Abasah ؓ

'Amr bin 'Abasah ؓ says: "From the very outset, I had a horrid revulsion towards idolatry. I always considered these idols to be mere chunks of stone that possess absolutely no control over benefit or harm. I once came across a scholar from the Ahl-e-Kitaab (people of the scriptures – Jews or Christians) and asked him about the best and most virtuous religion. The scholar replied: 'A man is bound to appear in Makkah, who would invite people away from idolatry towards the unity of Allah. He will bring forth the best and most virtuous religion. If you happen to meet him, make sure you adhere to his teachings.'"

'Amr bin 'Abasah ؓ says: "From that day onwards, the city of Makkah was constantly in my thoughts. I would attempt to glean some information about Makkah from every traveller to the holy city until one day I got wind of Rasulullah's ﷺ appearance."

The moment I received news of Rasulullah's ﷺ appearance, I set out for Makkah. I met with Rasulullah ﷺ covertly and asked him: "Who are you?" "I am the messenger of Allah." He replied. I asked: "Did Allah Ta'ala commission you to this earth as a messenger?" He replied in the affirmative. I then asked him what message Allah Ta'ala has communicated through him to us. Rasulullah ﷺ replied: "The message from Allah Ta'ala is that He (Allah) be accepted as one, no partner be assigned to him, idols should be destroyed and favourable family ties maintained." I then enquired: "In this regard, who is with you?" He replied: "A free man and a slave." In other words, Abu Bakr ؓ and Bilal ؓ. I finally submitted: "I am also your ardent follower. I also wish to remain with you." Rasulullah ﷺ advised: "At this point in time, I suggest you return home. When you learn of my dominance, you may return."

'Amr bin 'Abasah ؓ says: "I embraced Islam and returned home but I continued keeping track of Rasulullah ﷺ and his sustained progress. When Rasulullah ﷺ ultimately migrated to Madinah Munawwarah, I presented myself before him and asked: "O Prophet of Allah! Do you remember me?" Rasulullah ﷺ replied: "Of course, you are the person who approached me whilst I was in Makkah (during the earlier times of Islam)." I responded: "Yes, I am the same person. O Prophet of Allah! Teach me something....."

Islam of Abu Zarr ؓ

Ibn 'Abbaas ؓ narrates that when Abu Zarr Ghifaari ؓ learnt of Rasulullah's ﷺ prophethood, he requested his brother, Unais, to proceed to Makkah saying: "Travel to Makkah and gather some information about this man who claims that he is the messenger of Allah Ta'ala and that divine revelation descends upon him from the heavens. Also listen to his discourse."

In accordance with Abu Zarr's proposal, Unais came to Makkah, met with Rasulullah ﷺ and returned home. When asked by Abu Zarr, what information he returned with, Unais replied: "When I landed in Makkah, I found some people referring to him as a fraud or a sorcerer whilst others referred to him as a soothsayer or poet. By Allah! He is definitely not a poet or soothsayer." Unais himself was a celebrated poet. This is why he remarked: "I have heard the speech of soothsayers but the discourses of this man does not bear any resemblance to the speech of soothsayers. I also appraised his discourses on poetical scales but I realised that it is not even poetry. By Allah! This man is truthful and honest." He also declared:

رأيته يأمر بالخير وينهي عن الشرو رأيته يأمر بمكارم الاخلاق
وسمعت كلاما ما هو بالشعر

"I have only witnessed him enjoining good and restraining evil. I have observed him bidding good character. And I have heard his discourse, which is definitely not poetry."

On hearing this report, Abu Zarr ؓ submitted: "I am not completely convinced." Perhaps Abu Zarr ؓ aspired to listen to additional details about Rasulullah ﷺ. Such sketchy and condensed information was probably not sufficient for him. This is why he took some provisions and a water bag and set out for Makkah by himself. Through the directions of Hadhrat Ali ؓ he reached Rasulullah ﷺ and after listening to Rasulullah ﷺ firsthand, he embraced Islam. He immediately thereafter proceeded to the Haram and publicly proclaimed his conversion to Islam. The infidels thrashed him so severely that he fell to the ground. The intervention of 'Abbaas barely saved him from further beating.

Rasulullah ﷺ advised him to return home and apprise his people about this message of Islam. Rasulullah ﷺ counselled him to return only when he hears of the Muslims' dominance. Subsequently, he returned home where both brothers invited their mother to embrace Islam. She very enthusiastically embraced Islam. He later invited his people, the Ghifaar tribe, towards Islam. Half of them accepted Islam there and then.

Assembly of the Muslims in Daar-e-Arqam

As people steadily embraced Islam, a small group of Muslims subsequently evolved. Thus it was proposed that all of them congregate in the house of Arqam. Hadhrat Arqam رضي الله عنه was one of the earliest Muslims. He was either the seventh or the tenth person to embrace Islam. His house was on Mount Safa. Right up to the Islam of Hadhrat 'Umar رضي الله عنه, Rasulullah صلى الله عليه وسلم and the Sahaabah رضي الله عنهم would congregate at Arqam's رضي الله عنه house. After Hadhrat 'Umar رضي الله عنه embraced Islam, the Muslims would assemble wherever they preferred.

Open Proclamation of Islam

Over a period of three years, Rasulullah صلى الله عليه وسلم continued inviting people to Islam secretly and people steadily embraced Islam. After this period of three years, Rasulullah صلى الله عليه وسلم was instructed to proclaim this invitation openly. The following verses were revealed:

فَاصْدَعْ بِمَا تُؤْمَرُ وَأَعْرِضْ عَنِ الْمُشْرِكِينَ ﴿٩٤﴾

"Therefore proclaim (Islam) openly that which you have been instructed and turn away from the disbelievers." [Surah Hijr verse 94]

وَأَنْذِرْ عَشِيرَتَكَ الْأَقْرَبِينَ ﴿٢١٤﴾ وَاخْفِضْ جَنَاحَكَ لِمَنِ اتَّبَعَكَ مِنَ الْمُؤْمِنِينَ ﴿٢١٥﴾

"And warn your close relatives and treat with affection those believers who have followed you." [Surah Shu'araa verses 214-215]

وَقُلْ إِنِّي أَنَا النَّذِيرُ الْمُبِينُ ﴿٨٩﴾

"And say (O Muhammad!) I am indeed an open warner." [Surah Hijr verse 89]

In response to such verses, Rasulullah صلى الله عليه وسلم ascended Mount Safa and summoned each of the tribes by name. When they had all assembled around him, he asked them: "If I caution you about an invading army on the other side of this mountain that is about to attack you, would you believe me?" In one voice they all responded: "Surely, why not! We have only known you to be honest and truthful." Rasulullah صلى الله عليه وسلم said: "I am warning you about a severe punishment that may befall you (if you do not accept my message from Allah Ta'ala)." Abu Lahab retorted: "Woe unto you. May you perish. Did you assemble us here for this reason only?" Upon this the Surah 'Tabbat Yadaa Abi Lahab' (May the hands of Abu Lahab perish.) This entire Surah was revealed on account of this incident.

Invitation to Islam and Ta'aam (meals)

Hadhrat Ali ؓ narrates: "When the verse: 'And warn your close relatives' was revealed, Rasulullah ﷺ instructed me to bring a Saa' (app.3.2 kg) of grain, a shoulder of a goat and a bowl of milk. He then requested me to summon all the children of Muttalib. I executed his instructions as directed. Approximately forty people assembled in response to his invitation. Amongst them were his uncles; Abu Taalib, Hamzah, 'Abbaas and Abu Lahab. Rasulullah ﷺ took the meat and shred it with his blessed teeth. Placing the meat into a bowl, he bade the others: 'Take the name of Allah Ta'ala and start eating.' Each and every one of them ate to their fill from this one small dish of food. In fact, there was a little left over as well. All of them were well satiated with this food whereas it was evidently sufficient for one person only. Rasulullah ﷺ then instructed me to produce the bowl of milk and offer it to all of them. All of them were quenched with just this one bowl whereas a bowl of milk is not really much. Let alone forty people, a bowl of milk is barely enough for just one person. When they finished eating, Rasulullah ﷺ was about to say something when Abu Lahab blurted out: 'People, get up! Muhammad has cast a spell over your food today. We have never witnessed such sorcery before this day!' The moment he uttered this disparaging remark, people dispersed and Rasulullah ﷺ did not get a chance to speak to them. The following day, Rasulullah ﷺ again instructed Hadhrat Ali ؓ to prepare the same meal. When they finished eating, Rasulullah ﷺ said: 'What I have presented to you, nobody else has presented anything better than that to his people. I have brought you news about this world as well as the next.'"

Although Abu Lahab was Rasulullah's ﷺ uncle, just as Abu Bakr ؓ remained in the forefront of personal sacrifice, passionate conviction and unstinting love, Abu Lahab ventured to remain in the forefront of downright disbelief, persistent harassment, disdainful mockery and concentrated hostility. May Allah's wrath descend on him. On account of this enmity he harboured against Rasulullah ﷺ, he forced his sons 'Utbah and 'Utaibah who were married to Rasulullah's ﷺ daughters Ruqayyah ؓ and Umme Kulsoom ؓ before prophethood to break up the marriage. Abu Lahab's objective was to intensify the sorrow of Rasulullah ﷺ as far as he possibly could. However, this divorce proved to be a source of Allah Ta'ala's mercy. One after the other, both these daughters were eventually married to Hadhrat 'Usmaan ؓ thereby meriting the title of Zun-Noorain (a man of two radiances). Amongst the one hundred and twenty four thousand Ambiyaa ؑ and the Sahaabah ؓ, only Hadhrat 'Usmaan ؓ had the honour of getting married to two daughters of a Rasool one after the other, thereby earning himself the title of Zun-Noorain. As long as Rasulullah ﷺ continued inviting the people individually to Islam, the Quraysh left him alone without impeding his endeavours but the moment he publicly proclaimed the message of Islam and started to speak ill of the idolaters and hampering the ideals of disbelief and polytheism, the Quraysh poised themselves for a spell of hostility and fierce opposition. However, Abu Taalib staunchly upheld his support for Rasulullah ﷺ. On one occasion, a delegation of the Quraysh appeared before Abu Taalib and said: "Your nephew speaks ill of our idols, degrades our religion and depicts us as fools and our forefathers as misguided. Either you prevent him or you desist from intervening between him and us. We will sort it out amongst ourselves." Abu Taalib very diplomatically and affectionately sidestepped the whole issue and somehow defused the situation whilst Rasulullah ﷺ continued with his invitation towards monotheism and his degrading of disbelief and polytheism. The fire of hatred and enmity of Abu Lahab and his friends flared up even more. They despatched another delegation to Abu Taalib saying: "We do acknowledge your nobility and graciousness amongst us but we will never tolerate the vilification of our idols and branding of our ancestors as fools. Either you stop your nephew or we will launch a full-scale battle in which one of us will perish." Saying this, they returned.

The unrelenting hostilities of the tribe and the bitterness of his family members had a profound effect on Abu Taalib. When Rasulullah ﷺ came to him, Abu Taalib said: "Dear nephew! People of your tribe came to me and this is what they had to say." Abu Taalib then went on to recount what transpired between him and the Qurayshi delegation. Abu Taalib said: "So I urge you to take pity on me and take pity on yourself as well. Please do not weigh me down with an unbearable burden."

Judging from this conversation, Rasulullah ﷺ was led to believe that perhaps Abu Taalib wanted to withdraw his assistance and support from him. So with tearful eyes and a dejected heart, Rasulullah ﷺ said: "Uncle! By Allah, if these people place the sun in my right hand and the moon in my left and beg me to relinquish this work, I will never relinquish it until Allah either grants this Deen dominance or until I perish."

Saying this, Rasulullah ﷺ burst into tears and stood up to leave. Abu Taalib called for him and said: "My beloved nephew! You do what you want. I will never surrender you to your enemies."

When the Quraysh noticed the determined assistance and support of Abu Taalib for Rasulullah ﷺ, they conferred for a third time and coming to Abu Taalib they said: "'Amaarah bin Wahid is an incredibly handsome and exceptionally intelligent young man of the Quraysh. Take him instead and surrender to us your nephew who is responsible for causing such severe friction amongst the people. We wish to kill him and release the people from this nuisance."

Abu Taalib replied: "Wow! How can this ever be possible? How can I surrender to the execution of the child that I have brought up myself whilst I foster your child in his place? By Allah! This can never happen!"

Mut'im bin 'Adi remarked: "Abu Taalib! Your people have presented you with a reasonably fair ruling and a wonderful method of ridding themselves of this calamity but you failed disappointingly in accepting this decision."

Abu Taalib retorted: "By Allah! My people have not been fair to me. You can do whatever you want!"

When the Quraysh lost all hope upon Abu Taalib, they declared their open hostility towards him (and the Muslims). They started inflicting a range of torturous punishments against the weak and vulnerable Muslims they came across amongst the other tribes. Abu Taalib invited the Banu Haashim and Banu Muttalib to support and assist Rasulullah ﷺ. Upon these summons, all the members of the Banu Haashim and Banu Muttalib clans gave their assurance of all-out support and protection. From amongst the Banu Haashim, only Abu Lahab joined the enemy against Rasulullah ﷺ.

Rabi'ah bin 'Ibaad ؓ says: "I saw Rasulullah ﷺ in the markets of 'Ukkaaz and Banul-Majaaz inviting people towards Islam declaring: "People! Say *Laa Ilaaha Illallahu*, you will be successful."

Following his footsteps I saw a squint-eyed man calling out to the people: "This man has turned into a heathen and he is a liar. (Do not believe in what he says.)"

When I enquired who this man was, I was informed that it is Rasulullah's ﷺ uncle Abu Lahab. This version of the Hadith says that Rasulullah ﷺ was calling the people thus:

يَا أَيُّهَا النَّاسُ اِنَّ اللّٰهَ يَأْمُرُكُمْ أَنْ تَعْبُدُوْهُ وَلَا تُشْرِكُوْا بِهِ شَيْئًا

"O People! Allah commands you to worship Him and to abstain from ascribing any partner unto him."

Whilst Rasulullah ﷺ was engaged in inviting the people towards Islam, Abu Lahab, walking behind Rasulullah ﷺ, would shout:

يايها الناس ان هذا يا مركم ان تتركوا دين آبآءكم

"O People! This man is commanding you to renounce the religion of your forefathers."

The most select of the entire creation was inviting the people towards Islam and Darus-Salaam (Jannah) whilst Abu Lahab was calling the people towards a fire of Lahab (blazing fire).

Qurayshi conference for hampering the spread of Islam

When the Quraysh witnessed Islam progressing day by day, they assembled before Waleed bin Mughirah who was one of their higher-ranking elders and said: "The Haj season is almost upon us and your eminence is celebrated throughout the lands. Pilgrims from far-flung lands will soon ask you about this man (Rasulullah ﷺ). So we need to formulate a consistent opinion about him. All of us should be unanimous in our opinion about him. There should not be any conflict of view lest we falsify or contradict one another and this will obviously not be good for us. O Abu 'Abdush-Shams! (This was Waleed's title.) Why do you not devise a cohesive verdict, which all of us will adhere to? Waleed said: "You put your thoughts forward, I will listen and then I will formulate my opinion." Some people suggested: "This man (Rasulullah ﷺ) is, Allah Ta'ala forbid, a soothsayer." Waleed commented: "You are wrong. By Allah! This man can never be a soothsayer. I have had an opportunity to meet a number of soothsayers. This man neither has a single hint of a soothsayer around him nor does his speech correspond with the humming noises of the soothsayers." Some suggested that Rasulullah ﷺ is mad. Waleed replied: "No, he is not mad. I am fully aware of the reality of insanity and mental illnesses. I don't perceive an iota of insanity in this man." People said that he is a poet. Waleed remarked: "I am a poet myself. I am thoroughly acquainted with the poetic rhythms and styles of poetry. For instance, I am intimately familiar with the poetic meters of Rajz, Hajz, Maqbud, Mabsut, etc. His speech has no parallel to poetical compositions." The people then suggested that Rasulullah ﷺ is a sorcerer. Waleed commented: "He is not a sorcerer. He does not blow or engage in incantations or fasten knots like the sorcerers do." The people finally surrendered saying: "O Abu 'Abdish-Shams! Then what can we assert?" Waleed replied: "By Allah! In Muhammad's (ﷺ) speech is an extraordinary sweetness and alluring attraction. His speech is embellished with a peculiar magnificence. The roots of his speech are incredibly fresh and its branches are fruit bearing. (In other words, Islam is like a wonderful tree. Its roots are firm and solid in the ground and its branches, laden with fruit, are growing up to the sky.)"

Waleed continued: "I know that whatever description you have opted for, each and every one of them is baseless and fictitious. I think that the description of 'sorcerer' would be most appropriate. I suppose we should just let it be known to the masses that this man is a sorcerer and his speech is also bewitching. His speech triggers a rift between husband and wife, between blood brothers and between members of the same clan. This is after all the peculiarity of sorcery."

Saying this, the meeting came to a close. With the approach of the Haj season, as people started streaming into Makkah, the Quraysh posted people onto every road leading into Makkah dispensing the following words of caution to every foreign pilgrim: "Beware of this man (Rasulullah ﷺ) as he is a sorcerer."

This malicious strategy of the Quraysh failed to harm Islam in the least. In fact, the pilgrims coming into Makkah from far and wide were, by now, well acquainted with Rasulullah ﷺ.

In reference to the same Waleed bin Mughirah (mentioned in the aforementioned incident) Allah Ta'ala revealed the following verse of Surah Muddhatthir:

ذَرْنِىْ وَ مَنْ خَلَقْتُ وَحِيْدًا ۞ وَّجَعَلْتُ لَهٗ مَالًا مَّمْدُوْدًا ۞ وَّبَنِيْنَ شُهُوْدًا ۞ وَّمَهَّدْتُّ لَهٗ تَمْهِيْدًا ۞ ثُمَّ يَطْمَعُ اَنْ اَزِيْدَ ۞ كَلَّا ۖ اِنَّهٗ كَانَ لِاٰيٰتِنَا عَنِيْدًا ۞ سَاُرْهِقُهٗ صَعُوْدًا ۞ اِنَّهٗ فَكَّرَ وَقَدَّرَ ۞ فَقُتِلَ كَيْفَ قَدَّرَ ۞ ثُمَّ قُتِلَ كَيْفَ قَدَّرَ ۞ ثُمَّ نَظَرَ ۞ ثُمَّ عَبَسَ وَبَسَرَ ۞ ثُمَّ اَدْبَرَ وَاسْتَكْبَرَ ۞ فَقَالَ اِنْ هٰذَآ اِلَّا سِحْرٌ يُّؤْثَرُ ۞ اِنْ هٰذَآ اِلَّا قَوْلُ الْبَشَرِ ۞ سَاُصْلِيْهِ سَقَرَ ۞

"And leave me and he whom I had created alone. (I will deal with him on my own. You don't bother yourself with him.) And I granted him abundant wealth and sons who are in attendance and I made life comfortable and smooth for him (by bestowing upon him worldly honour). Then (in spite of all this) he desires that I bestow him with more. Never! He has been hostile to our signs (verses or proofs). I will compel him to climb (a slippery) mountain (of hell and then hurl him down). Verily, he deliberated and plotted. So let him be cursed: how he plotted. And again let him be cursed: how he plotted. Then he glanced about. Then he scowled and assumed a furious countenance. Then he turned away and displayed arrogance and said: 'This (Qur-aan) is nothing but sorcery that is being transmitted (through the generations). This is nothing but the word of a human being.' I will cast him into the fire of Hell……." [Surah Muddatthir verses 11-26]

According to a narration, Rasulullah ﷺ had recited before him the following verse that is the synopsis of good character:

اِنَّ اللّٰهَ يَأْمُرُ بِالْعَدْلِ وَالْاِحْسَانِ وَاِيْتَآئِ ذِى الْقُرْبٰى وَيَنْهٰى عَنِ الْفَحْشَآءِ وَالْمُنْكَرِ وَالْبَغْىِ ۚ يَعِظُكُمْ لَعَلَّكُمْ تَذَكَّرُوْنَ ۞

"Verily Allah decrees justice, beneficence, and giving to the relatives and He prohibits evil, abominable deeds and oppression. He advises you that you may take heed." [Surah Nahl verse 90]

Islam of Hamzah رَضِىَ اللَّهُ عَنْهُ

Whilst walking near Mt. Safa one day, Rasulullah ﷺ suddenly came upon Abu Jahal who also happened to be passing that way. The moment his eyes fell on Rasulullah ﷺ, he let off a string of curses and words of condemnation against Rasulullah ﷺ. However, Rasulullah ﷺ didn't utter a word against Abu Jahal's deplorable choice of words and calmly departed from the scene. After all 'Silence is the best response to a fool'. 'Abdullah bin Jud'aan's slave girl witnessed this awful spectacle. In the meantime, Hadhrat Hamzah رَضِىَ اللَّهُ عَنْهُ, who was just returning from one of his hunting trips, happened to come that way clutching his bow and quiver of arrows. The moment she laid eyes on him, 'Abdullah bin Jud'aan's slave girl exclaimed: "Abu 'Ammaarah! If only you were around when Abu Jahal was busy uttering obscenities and foul language against your nephew."

On hearing this, Hadhrat Hamzah رَضِىَ اللَّهُ عَنْهُ became enraged. From there, he set out in search of Abu Jahal. It was the custom of Hadhrat Hamzah رَضِىَ اللَّهُ عَنْهُ that he would first visit the Haram whenever he returned from hunting. In compliance with his routine, he came to the Haram first where he saw Abu Jahal sitting with a few other members of the Quraysh tribe. The moment he reached him, Hadhrat Hamzah رَضِىَ اللَّهُ عَنْهُ struck him so severely with the bow on his head that he suffered a serious head injury. He then yelled at him: "You have the audacity to verbally abuse Muhammad (ﷺ). In fact, I am also an adherent of his religion." Some of the onlookers wanted to come to Abu Jahal's aid but he himself prevented them saying: "Yes, I am guilty; today I verbally abused his nephew. Leave Hamzah alone." Some of those in attendance addressed Hadhrat Hamzah رَضِىَ اللَّهُ عَنْهُ saying: "Hamzah! What, have you also turned Saabi (irreligious)?" Hadhrat Hamzah رَضِىَ اللَّهُ عَنْهُ replied: "Muhammad's ﷺ truthfulness and credibility has been laid bare before me. I hereby testify that Muhammad is the messenger of Allah and I believe that whatever he says is absolutely true. I will never ever forsake this belief. Do whatever you can!" Saying this, Hadhrat Hamzah رَضِىَ اللَّهُ عَنْهُ returned home.

When he reached home, shaytaan embarked on a campaign of waswasah (devilish insinuation) against him. Shaytaan insinuated: "Hamzah! You are one of the chieftains of the Quraysh. How dare you tag along behind a Saabi? Why did you renounce the religion of your forefathers? You should rather perish instead of doing this." This devilish insinuation threw Hadhrat Hamzah رَضِىَ اللَّهُ عَنْهُ in a bit of uncertainty and doubt. Hadhrat Hamzah رَضِىَ اللَّهُ عَنْهُ relates: "This is when I turned to Allah Ta'ala in dua. I pleaded to Allah in the following words:

اللّٰهُمَّ ان كان رشدا فاجعل تصديقه فى قلبى والافاجعل لى مما وقعت فيه مخرجا

> "O Allah! If this is guidance, insert its conviction into the depths of my heart otherwise devise a way out for me from this situation."

According to another narration, he passed the night in this state of anxious restlessness. He was unable to doze off even for a moment. When he realised that he was unable to rid himself of this agitation, he proceeded to the Haram and with utmost humility he made the following dua:

"O Allah! Open my heart to enthusiastically accept the truth and liberate me from these doubts and misgivings." Hadhrat Hamzah ﷺ relates: "I barely lowered my hands from the dua when all my futile reservations disappeared and my heart was swiftly infused with conviction and true faith. Immediately the next morning, I set out towards the blessed company of Rasulullah ﷺ and gave him an account of what had transpired. Rasulullah ﷺ made dua for my staunch dedication and steadfastness upon Islam."

According to the narration of Mustadrak Haakim, when Hadhrat Hamzah ﷺ appeared before Rasulullah ﷺ, he submitted:

اشهد انك لصادق شهادة المصدق والعارف

> "I hereby testify that you are undeniably truthful. I offer this testimony as a dedicated and perceptive believer."

He went on further: "O nephew! Proclaim your religion publicly now. By Allah! Even if I am offered the whole world and whatever is contained therein, I would certainly not renounce this religion in favour of my ancestral creed." Saying this, he composed the following stanzas:

حمدت الله حين هدى فوادى   الى الاسلام والدين الحنيف

> "I praise Allah Who has steered my heart towards Islam and towards the Ibraaheemi creed.

لدين جاء من رب عزيز   خبير بالعباد بهم لطيف

> The religion that came to us from the venerable Lord, who is sensitive and affectionate towards His servants.

اذا تليت رسائله علينا   تحدر دمع ذى اللب الحصيف

> When His messages are recited before us, the tears of the intellectually gifted flow freely.

رسائل جاء احمد من هداها   باياب مبينة الحروف

> The messages brought by Ahmad for the guidance of the people, messages that are unambiguous and clear-cut.

| فلا تغشوه بالقول العنيف | واحمد مصطفى فينا مطاع |

And Ahmad, the chosen one amongst us is to be obeyed. So do not conceal it with coarse language.

| ولما نقض فيهم بالسيوف | فلا والله نسلمه لقوم |

By Allah! As long as our swords do not make the final judgement amongst us, we will never surrender him to anyone."

Hadhrat Hamzah's ﷺ embracing of Islam was a clear sign to the Quraysh that from now on it wouldn't be as easy to harass and persecute Rasulullah ﷺ.

Chapter 5

The Spread of Islam and the Quraysh of Makkah

When the Quraysh realised that Hadhrat Hamzah ﷺ embraced Islam and the numbers of the Muslims were progressively increasing, Abu Jahal, 'Utbah, Shaybah, Waleed bin Mughirah, Umayyah bin Khalaf, Aswad bin Muttalib and other chieftains of the Quraysh convened a meeting to deliberate over this issue. Based upon the decision reached by this consultative meeting, the members appointed 'Utbah bin Rabi'ah as their spokesman to Rasulullah ﷺ. He was a man unrivalled by any of his contemporaries in sorcery, soothsaying and poetry.

'Utbah came to Rasulullah ﷺ and said: "O Muhammad! There is no doubt about your distinguished lineage and superior status but alas, you are guilty of rupturing the unity of our nation. You condemn our idols and proclaim our forefathers as fools. This is why I wish to make a statement." Rasulullah ﷺ replied: "Go ahead, Abul-Waleed, I am listening."

'Utbah said: "O Nephew! Why do you have to concern yourself with these issues? If wealth is what you desire, we will amass so much of wealth for you that even the richest man will not be able to compete with you. If you wish to get married, we will get you married to whichever woman you fancy and to how many women you want. If leadership is what you crave for, we will elect you as our leader. If you aspire to take on the reins of government and kingship, we will designate you as our king. If an evil spirit possesses you, we will provide the treatment to remove it."

Rasulullah ﷺ replied: "O Abul-Waleed! Are you over with whatever you wanted to say?" When 'Utbah replied in the affirmative, Rasulullah ﷺ said: "Okay, now listen to what I have got to say. I don't crave for your riches and wealth and I have no inclination towards your leadership and power. I am the Rasool of Allah Ta'ala whom He has sent to you with His divine message. He has revealed a divine book unto me and has charged me to issue His glad tidings of reward and warnings of punishment. I have conveyed His message unto you and as a form of good counsel I have cautioned you. If you accept this message, it would be a source of success for you in both the worlds. However, if you fail to accept this message, I am willing to exercise patience until Allah Ta'ala passes judgment between us."

Saying this Rasulullah ﷺ recited the following verses:

حٰمٓ ۚ تَنْزِيْلٌ مِّنَ الرَّحْمٰنِ الرَّحِيْمِ ۚ كِتٰبٌ فُصِّلَتْ اٰيٰتُهٗ قُرْاٰنًا عَرَبِيًّا لِّقَوْمٍ يَّعْلَمُوْنَ ۙ بَشِيْرًا وَّ نَذِيْرًا ۚ فَاَعْرَضَ اَكْثَرُهُمْ فَهُمْ لَا يَسْمَعُوْنَ وَ قَالُوْا قُلُوْبُنَا فِيْۤ اَكِنَّةٍ مِّمَّا تَدْعُوْنَاۤ اِلَيْهِ وَ فِيْۤ اٰذَانِنَا وَقْرٌ وَّ مِنْۢ بَيْنِنَا وَ بَيْنِكَ حِجَابٌ فَاعْمَلْ اِنَّنَا عٰمِلُوْنَ قُلْ اِنَّمَاۤ اَنَا بَشَرٌ مِّثْلُكُمْ يُوْحٰۤى اِلَيَّ اَنَّمَاۤ اِلٰهُكُمْ اِلٰهٌ وَّاحِدٌ فَاسْتَقِيْمُوْۤا اِلَيْهِ وَ اسْتَغْفِرُوْهُ ؕ وَ وَيْلٌ لِّلْمُشْرِكِيْنَ ۙ الَّذِيْنَ لَا يُؤْتُوْنَ الزَّكٰوةَ وَ هُمْ بِالْاٰخِرَةِ هُمْ كٰفِرُوْنَ اِنَّ الَّذِيْنَ اٰمَنُوْا وَ عَمِلُوا الصّٰلِحٰتِ لَهُمْ اَجْرٌ غَيْرُ مَمْنُوْنٍ ۬ قُلْ اَئِنَّكُمْ لَتَكْفُرُوْنَ بِالَّذِيْ خَلَقَ الْاَرْضَ فِيْ يَوْمَيْنِ وَ تَجْعَلُوْنَ لَهٗۤ اَنْدَادًا ؕ ذٰلِكَ رَبُّ الْعٰلَمِيْنَ ۚ وَ جَعَلَ فِيْهَا رَوَاسِيَ مِنْ فَوْقِهَا وَ بٰرَكَ فِيْهَا وَ قَدَّرَ فِيْهَاۤ اَقْوَاتَهَا فِيْۤ اَرْبَعَةِ اَيَّامٍ ؕ سَوَآءً لِّلسَّآئِلِيْنَ ثُمَّ اسْتَوٰۤى اِلَى السَّمَآءِ وَ هِيَ دُخَانٌ فَقَالَ لَهَا وَ لِلْاَرْضِ ائْتِيَا طَوْعًا اَوْ كَرْهًا ؕ قَالَتَاۤ اَتَيْنَا طَآئِعِيْنَ فَقَضٰىهُنَّ سَبْعَ سَمٰوَاتٍ فِيْ يَوْمَيْنِ وَ اَوْحٰى فِيْ كُلِّ سَمَآءٍ اَمْرَهَا ؕ وَ زَيَّنَّا السَّمَآءَ الدُّنْيَا بِمَصَابِيْحَ ۖ وَ حِفْظًا ؕ ذٰلِكَ تَقْدِيْرُ الْعَزِيْزِ الْعَلِيْمِ فَاِنْ اَعْرَضُوْا فَقُلْ اَنْذَرْتُكُمْ صٰعِقَةً مِّثْلَ صٰعِقَةِ عَادٍ وَّ ثَمُوْدَ ؕ

"Haa Meem. This is a revelation from the Beneficent and Merciful. This is a book whose verses are clearly detailed, a Qur-aan in Arabic for people who are aware. It (the Qur-aan) is an issuer of glad tidings and an admonisher. (Rightfully they should have embraced this Qur-aan) but most of them turn away so they hear not. And they say: 'Our hearts are sealed against what you are inviting us to and in our ears are plugs and between us and between you is a screen (because of which we are unable to understand what you say). So, you do (your work) whilst we continue doing our work. Say! (in response to them O Muhammad!) I am but a human being like you (but) divine revelation is revealed upon me that your deity is only one. So take a straight path towards Him and seek His forgiveness and woe to the disbelievers; those who do not pay Zakaat and they disbelieve in the hereafter. Truly, those who believe and do righteous deeds, for them will be a reward that will never cease. Say (O Muhammad!) Do you really disbelieve in the being Who had created the earth in two days and you ascribe partners unto Him? That is the Lord of all the worlds. And He placed therein (in the earth) mountains above it (the earth) and He blessed it (the earth) and He measured therein its sustenance in four *days equal (in duration) for those who enquire (about His creation). Thereafter, he focussed upon the sky when it was smoke and said to it (the sky) and the earth: 'Come both of you enthusiastically or reluctantly.' Both of them replied: 'We come enthusiastically.' So He completed seven skies in two days and He transmitted to every sky its affair. And we adorned the sky of the world with lamps (stars for adornment) and protection (against the Shayaateen by using the stars as projectiles against them). Such is the strategy of the all-powerful, the all-knowing. And if they turn away, then say (O Muhammad!) I have warned you of a thunderbolt like the thunderbolt that had befallen 'Aad and Thamud." [Surah Haa Meem Sajdah verses 1–13]*

Rasulullah ﷺ continued reciting this Surah whilst 'Utbah was sitting leaning with both his hands behind his back listening in bewildered amazement to the recitation. When Rasulullah ﷺ reached the final verse, 'and if they turn away', 'Utbah abruptly placed his hand over Rasulullah's ﷺ mouth and swearing an oath surrendered: "By Allah! For Allah's sake, take pity on us."

Actually, 'Utbah was terrified lest the punishment of 'Aad and Thamud suddenly befell him. Thereafter, Rasulullah ﷺ continued reciting right up to the verse of Sajdah after which he performed a Sajdah. Following his recitation, Rasulullah ﷺ addressed 'Utbah saying: "Abul-Waleed! You have heard whatever you have heard. The choice now rests with you."

'Utbah took his leave from Rasulullah ﷺ and returned to his associates but the 'Utbah who returned was not the same 'Utbah who went. This is why Abu Jahal blurted out: "'Utbah doesn't look like the same 'Utbah. It seems as though 'Utbah has transformed into a Saabi." 'Utbah replied: "I have lent my ears to his words. By Allah! I have never come across such words. His words are neither poetry nor sorcery nor soothsaying. It is something totally alien to me. O People! If you would care to heed my advice, leave Muhammad alone. By Allah! The words I have just heard are surely something to keep an eye on. If the Arabs assassinate him, you have nothing to be anxious about and alternatively, if he prevails over the Arabs, his honour will be your honour and his reign will be your reign because after all, he is a constituent of your own tribe."

To this the Quraysh chieftains responded: "Abul-Waleed! Muhammad has cast a spell of black magic over you." 'Utbah replied: "My opinion will remain unchanged. You do whatever you please!"

Revelation of Qul Yaa Ayyuhal-Kaafirun

The Quraysh pleaded with Rasulullah ﷺ to refrain from condemning their idols. They further requested that if this was not possible, they could come to some settlement where both parties could be accommodated. They proposed that

Rasulullah ﷺ should worship their idols for a year and they would worship his deity for the forthcoming year and so forth. When the Quraysh made this bizarre proposal, the following Surah was revealed:

$$\text{قُلْ يَاأَيُّهَا الْكَافِرُونَ ۞ لَا أَعْبُدُ مَا تَعْبُدُونَ ۞ وَلَا أَنْتُمْ عَابِدُونَ مَا أَعْبُدُ ۞ وَلَا أَنَا عَابِدٌ مَا عَبَدْتُّمْ ۞ وَلَا أَنْتُمْ عَابِدُونَ مَا أَعْبُدُ ۞ لَكُمْ دِينُكُمْ وَلِيَ دِينِ ۞}$$

"Say! O You disbelievers! I will not worship what you worship nor will you worship that which I worship. Neither would I be a devotee to what you worship nor would you be devoted to that which I worship. For you is your religion and for me is my religion." [Surah Kaafirun]

Apart from Surah Kaafirun, the following verse was also revealed:

$$\text{قُلْ أَفَغَيْرَ اللهِ تَأْمُرُونِّي أَعْبُدُ أَيُّهَا الْجَاهِلُونَ ۞ وَلَقَدْ أُوحِيَ إِلَيْكَ وَإِلَى الَّذِينَ مِنْ قَبْلِكَ لَئِنْ أَشْرَكْتَ لَيَحْبَطَنَّ عَمَلُكَ وَلَتَكُونَنَّ مِنَ الْخَاسِرِينَ ۞ بَلِ اللهَ فَاعْبُدْ وَكُنْ مِنَ الشَّاكِرِينَ ۞}$$

"Say! (to them): 'O you fools! Do you instruct me to worship anyone other than Allah? And indeed it has been revealed to you (O Muhammad!) and to those before you that 'if you assign partners (unto Allah), your actions will be in vain and you will certainly be amongst the losers. Nay! Allah Alone should you worship and be from amongst the grateful." [Surah Zumar verses 64-66]

Pointless and absurd questions of the Makkan disbelievers

Following this confrontation, the Quraysh suggested another proposition. They proposed to Rasulullah ﷺ: "Fine, if you don't consent to our previous proposal, we wish to advocate another strategy in which we anticipate your enthusiastic approval. You are quite conscious of the impoverishment of your people. This city of Makkah is also very restricted. We are surrounded by mountains on all sides with scarcely any greenery around us. So, request the Lord Who has commissioned you as a messenger to transfer the mountains of this city elsewhere so that the city becomes more spacious. Also request Him to bring forth rivers in this city akin to the cities of Syria and Iraq. Furthermore, resurrect our forefathers particularly Qusayy bin Kilaab so that we may enquire from him about the veracity or fallacy of your claims. If our forefathers, upon being resurrected, endorse what you claim and they believe in you, only then would we regard you as the messenger of Allah and only then would we believe in you." Rasulullah ﷺ replied: "I was not commissioned as a messenger for this purpose. I have conveyed to you the divine message I was sent with. If you accept the message, it would be for your own good fortune and if you fail to believe in it, I will exercise patience until such time that Allah Ta'ala's celestial judgement prevails over us."

"Okay", enjoined the Quraysh, "if you are unable to accomplish our demands, make dua for your own benefit that Allah Ta'ala sends an angel from the heavens to accompany you wherever you go. This angel will verify whatever you utter. Also request Allah to bless you with gardens, palaces and treasures of gold and silver, as this will enhance your noble status and piety. We observe that you also walk about in the market places in search of sustenance. (We find this rather strange from a divine messenger.)" Rasulullah ﷺ replied: "I will never dare pose such requests before Allah Ta'ala. I was not commissioned for this purpose. I was commissioned to this world as a Basheer (provider of glad tidings) and as a Nazeer (warner). If you believe in what I say, I guarantee you success in this world as well as the next. And if you fail to believe, I will exercise patience until Allah Ta'ala passes judgement between us."

The Quraysh replied: "Very well, beseech Allah Ta'ala to thrust His divine punishment upon us." Rasulullah ﷺ countered: "It is up to Allah Ta'ala to decide. It is His prerogative either to punish you or to grant you respite."

Upon this, 'Abdullah bin Umayyah sprang up saying: "O Muhammad! Your people have made a number of proposals but you have refused to consent to even a single one. O Muhammad! Even if you were to hoist a ladder and ascend to the sky and return with a written permit authorising your prophethood and even if four angels return with you proclaiming your prophethood, then too I will not believe you."

Burdened with torturous heartache, Rasulullah ﷺ headed home.

Since Rasulullah ﷺ was commissioned to this world as Rahmatan-lil 'Aalameen (a mercy unto the worlds), the diverse forms of divine punishment that had befallen the previous Ummahs were withdrawn from this Ummah due to the barakah (blessing) of Rasulullah ﷺ. It appears in one narration that the Quraysh requested Rasulullah ﷺ to transform the mountain of Safa into gold. On this occasion, Rasulullah ﷺ planned to make dua before Allah Ta'ala but Hadhrat Jibraa'eel عليه السلام appeared, saying: "O Rasulullah ﷺ! Inform them that they will get what they ask for but also warn them that if they fail to believe even after witnessing these definite signs, it will not be good for them. They will be destroyed immediately." The Quraysh retorted: "We are not in need of this."

Quraysh of Makkah consult Jewish scholars

When the Quraysh realised that their line of questioning was foolish and prejudiced, they, after mutual consultation, sent Nasr bin Haaris and 'Uqbah bin Abi Mu'eet to Madinah Munawwarah to make meticulous enquiries about Rasulullah ﷺ from the Jewish scholars stationed there. They were reasonably acquainted with the knowledge of the Ambiyaa and relatively more knowledgeable with the signs of prophethood. These two representatives went to Madinah and apprised the Jewish scholars of what was happening back in Makkah. The Jews proposed that they pose three questions to Muhammad (Rasulullah ﷺ). The first question they proposed was: who were the people who sought refuge in a cave and what is their story? In other words, ask Muhammad (Rasulullah ﷺ) about the story of the people of the cave. The second question they proposed was; who was the man who traversed the whole earth from east to west? In other words, ask him about the story of Zul-Qarnain. And the third question they suggested was: what is the ruh (soul)?

These Jewish scholars additionally advised that if Muhammad ﷺ provides answers to the first two questions and remains silent about the third, this is a sure sign of his prophethood otherwise he is a liar and fraud.

Filled with joy, Nasr and 'Uqbah returned to Makkah and notified the Quraysh that they returned with a decisive proposal. They appeared before Rasulullah ﷺ and posed these questions to him. On the assumption that he would get some response in the form of divine revelation the next day, Rasulullah ﷺ said: "I will provide an answer tomorrow." In keeping with his human nature, Rasulullah ﷺ forgot to say Insha Allah (if Allah Ta'ala wills). A few days later, a number of verses recounting the stories of the people of the cave and the story of Zul-Qarnain were revealed. In response to the third question, the following verse was revealed: "Say! (O Muhammad) The Rooh (soul) is from the affairs of my Lord." In other words, you will not be able to unravel the reality of the soul. All you need to know is that the soul is something that when it enters the body, it comes to life with the directive of Allah and when it departs, the body dies."

In keeping with his human nature when Rasulullah ﷺ forgot to say Insha Allah, the following verses were revealed:

$$\text{وَلَا تَقُوْلَنَّ لِشَاْئٍ اِنِّىْ فَاعِلٌ ذٰلِكَ غَدًا ۝ اِلَّا اَنْ يَّشَاۤءَ اللّٰهُ ۖ وَاذْكُرْ رَّبَّكَ اِذَا نَسِيْتَ}$$

"And never say about anything that I will do it tomorrow except by adding Insha Allah to it and when you forget remember your Lord (as this will make amends for this forgetfulness)." [Surah Kahf verse 23,24]

This is why Ibn 'Abbaas ؓ would say that even if a person recalls after a whole year, he should still say Insha Allah, as this would compensate for his slip-up or forgetfulness.

When one omits mentioning the will of Allah Ta'ala and relies on his own will by saying I will do this tomorrow, Allah Ta'ala despises it. This is why, if a person forgets to say Insha Allah presently, he may redress this act of forgetfulness by saying Insha Allah whenever he remembers. This will compensate for his forgetfulness.

Disbelievers persecute Rasulullah ﷺ

When the Quraysh noticed Islam being proclaimed publicly and idolatry being openly condemned, they could not tolerate this any further. They became sworn enemies to anyone engaged in inviting to one Lord. They geared their strains of hostility against the principles of Tauheed (monotheism). They resolved to hound Rasulullah ﷺ to such an extent that he gives in and abandons his mission to invite people towards Islam.

Muneeb Ghaamidi رضي الله عنه relates: "I observed Rasulullah ﷺ summoning the people to Islam pleading with them: 'O people! Say *'Laa Ilaaha Illallahu'*, you will be successful.' But alas, I also witnessed some ill-fated souls hurling abuse at him. Some people were spitting at him whilst others were busy flinging sand at him. In this manner they relentlessly abused him when a young girl carrying water appeared on the scene. She approached Rasulullah ﷺ and washed his blessed face and hands. When I enquired who she is, I was informed that she is Rasulullah's ﷺ daughter, Zainab رضي الله عنها."

A man of the Banu Kinaanah tribe narrates that he saw Rasulullah ﷺ in the market of Zul-Majaaz proclaiming: 'O people! Say *'Laa Ilaaha Illallahu'*, you will be successful' whilst Abu Jahal was busy hurling sand at Rasulullah ﷺ saying: 'O people! Do not be hoodwinked by this man's motives. He wants you to sever your connection with Laat and 'Uzza'. However, Rasulullah ﷺ calmly continued with his efforts without even a glance at Abu Jahal.

'Urwah bin Zubair رضي الله عنه says: "I once asked 'Abdullah bin 'Amr bin 'Aas رضي الله عنه to relate to me the disbeliever's unrelenting persecution of Rasulullah ﷺ. 'Abdullah bin 'Amr bin 'Aas رضي الله عنه replied: 'On one occasion, Rasulullah ﷺ was engaged in Salaah in the Hateem area when 'Uqbah bin Abi Mu'eet yanked a cloth over Rasulullah's ﷺ neck and tugged it so rigidly that he almost strangled him. Abu Bakr رضي الله عنه unexpectedly appeared on the scene and jostled 'Uqbah aside. He then recited the following verse:

$$\text{اَتَقْتُلُوْنَ رَجُلًا اَنْ يَّقُوْلَ رَبِّیَ اللّٰهُ وَ قَدْ جَآءَكُمْ بِالْبَيِّنٰتِ مِنْ رَّبِّكُمْ}$$

"Are you killing a man who says my only Lord is Allah and he has presented to you corroborating evidence from your Lord?"

When Fir'aun and Haamaan conspired to kill Hadhrat Musa عليه السلام, one of Fir'aun's people who had secretly embraced Imaan upon Musa عليه السلام exclaimed: "How can you kill someone who declares 'my Lord is Allah'?"

Allah Ta'ala recounts this incident in Surah Mu'min as follows:

وَ قَالَ رَجُلٌ مُّؤْمِنٌ ۙ مِّنْ اٰلِ فِرْعَوْنَ يَكْتُمُ اِيْمَانَهٗۤ اَتَقْتُلُوْنَ رَجُلًا اَنْ يَّقُوْلَ رَبِّیَ اللّٰهُ

"A believing man from the folk of Fir'aun who was concealing his Imaan said: 'Do you wish to kill a man simply because he says 'My Lord is Allah!'?"
[Surah Mu'min Verse 28]

During the course of his Khutbah (public address), Hadhrat Ali رَضِىَ اللّٰهُ عَنْهُ asked the people: "Tell me, who is the most brave and valiant person?" The people replied: "Unquestionably, it is you." Hadhrat Ali رَضِىَ اللّٰهُ عَنْهُ responded: "My condition is such that anyone who challenged me, I have settled my scores with him. (In other words, my valour is limited to taking revenge only when someone confronts me.) The most daring and courageous person was Abu Bakr رَضِىَ اللّٰهُ عَنْهُ. I recall one incident when the Quraysh were battering Rasulullah صَلَّى اللّٰهُ عَلَيْهِ وَسَلَّمَ around whilst taunting him repeatedly with the words:

انت جعلت الالهة الها واحدا

"So you are the one who has united all the gods into a single deity?"

Whilst they were kicking him around, none of us had the courage to intervene and fend off the enemy but by good fortune, Abu Bakr رَضِىَ اللّٰهُ عَنْهُ happened to pass by. He swiftly leaped into the mob and landed a punch here and delivered a blow there and just as that believing man addressed Fir'aun and Haamaan, Abu Bakr رَضِىَ اللّٰهُ عَنْهُ addressed the disbelievers: "Shame on you! Do you wish to kill a man (simply because) he says Allah is my Lord?"

Recounting this incident, Hadhrat Ali رَضِىَ اللّٰهُ عَنْهُ burst into tears. He then addressed his audience saying: "I entreat you in the name of Allah, was Abu Bakr more superior or was the believing man from the people of Fir'aun more superior?" When the audience didn't answer, Hadhrat Ali رَضِىَ اللّٰهُ عَنْهُ proclaimed: "By Allah! One moment of Abu Bakr's life was far superior than that of the entire life of that believing man. That man concealed his beliefs whilst Abu Bakr رَضِىَ اللّٰهُ عَنْهُ gallantly exposed his beliefs. Furthermore, that believing man was content with mere verbal advice whilst Abu Bakr رَضِىَ اللّٰهُ عَنْهُ employed his verbal as well as his physical abilities in the defence of Rasulullah صَلَّى اللّٰهُ عَلَيْهِ وَسَلَّمَ."

'Usmaan bin Affaan رَضِىَ اللّٰهُ عَنْهُ narrates: "I once saw Rasulullah صَلَّى اللّٰهُ عَلَيْهِ وَسَلَّمَ performing Tawaaf of the K'abah. 'Uqbah bin Abi Mu'eet, Abu Jahal and Umayyah bin Khalaf were sitting in the Hateem area. The moment Rasulullah صَلَّى اللّٰهُ عَلَيْهِ وَسَلَّمَ passed by, they uttered a few obscenities at Rasulullah صَلَّى اللّٰهُ عَلَيْهِ وَسَلَّمَ. The second time round, they again told him something repulsive. When they uttered these obscenities on the third round, Rasulullah's صَلَّى اللّٰهُ عَلَيْهِ وَسَلَّمَ countenance changed. He stopped and said: 'By Allah! You will never give up until the punishment of Allah Ta'ala does not swiftly befall you.'" Hadhrat 'Usmaan رَضِىَ اللّٰهُ عَنْهُ comments: "There wasn't a single one of them who was not trembling with fear. Saying this, Rasulullah ﷺ set out for home whilst we moved off behind him. This is when Rasulullah ﷺ prophesised:

ابشروا فان الله مظهر دينه و متم كلمته و ناصر دينه ان هؤلاء الذين ترون ممن يذبح بايديكم عاجلا فوالله لقد رأيتهم ذبحهم الله بايدينا، اخرجه الدارقطني

"Accept glad tidings from me. Allah will make His Deen prevail and He will complete His word and assist His Deen. These people whom you are staring at, Allah Ta'ala will rapidly slaughter them at your hands."

Hadhrat 'Usmaan ؓ says: "By Allah! I saw them all slaughtered at our hands."

'Abdullah bin Mas'ood ؓ narrates: "Rasulullah ﷺ was once performing Salaah in the Haram area. Abu Jahal and his friends were also present. Abu Jahal challenged his friends: "Is there anyone amongst you who has the courage to go and fetch the tripe of so and so camel and place it on Muhammad's back as he goes into Sajdah?" The most ill-fated of the lot i.e. 'Uqbah bin Abi Mu'eet roused himself to take up this challenge. He fetched a load of tripe and hurled it on Rasulullah's ﷺ back whilst he was in Sajdah. 'Abdullah bin Mas'ood ؓ narrates: "I was busy witnessing this whole scene but I could do absolutely nothing. The disbelievers on the other hand, glancing at one another, burst out in laughter and were actually falling upon each other in gleeful laughter. In the meantime, Hadhrat Faatimah ؓ who was about four or five years old at that time, scampered to the scene and swiftly removed the tripe from his back. Rasulullah ﷺ serenely raised himself from Sajdah and thrice invoked the curse of Allah Ta'ala upon these wicked people. This curse proved quite punishing upon the Quraysh because they firmly believed that duas are readily accepted in this blessed city. Thereafter Rasulullah ﷺ invoked the curses of Allah Ta'ala particularly upon Abu Jahal, 'Uqbah bin Rabi'ah, Shaybah bin Rabi'ah, Waleed bin 'Utbah, Umayyah bin Khalaf, 'Uqbah bin Abi Mu'eet and 'Amaarah bin Waleed. He cursed each person by name most of whom were put to death in the battle of Badr.

The verse "And purify your clothing" was revealed after the aforementioned incident.

Hadhrat 'Aa'ishah ؓ narrates that Rasulullah ﷺ said: "I used to live in the midst of two of the most evil neighbours; Abu Lahab and 'Uqbah bin Abi Mu'eet. These two would frequently hurl impurity at my door."

Islam of Dimaad bin Tha'labah ﷺ

From the very pre-Islamic days of ignorance, Dimaad bin Tha'labah Azdi ﷺ was a close acquaintance of Rasulullah ﷺ. He would use invocations and other techniques to treat people afflicted by sorcery and other such ailments. When he came into Makkah after Rasulullah ﷺ was bestowed with prophethood, he caught sight of a group of people trailing behind Rasulullah ﷺ. Some were calling him a sorcerer and fortune-teller whilst others proclaimed him a man suffering from insanity. Dimaad appeared before Rasulullah ﷺ and submitted: "I am skilfully competent in treating insanity. Give me your consent to treat you. Perhaps Allah Ta'ala will cure you at my hands." Rasulullah ﷺ replied by reciting the following Khutbah:

الحمد لله نحمده ونستعينه ونستغفره ونعوذ بالله من شرور انفسنا من يهده الله فلا مضل له ومن يضلله فلا هادى له وانى اشهد ان لا اله الا الله وحده لا شريك له واشهد ان محمدا عبده و رسوله

> "All praise is due to Allah! We pay tribute to Him and ask of His assistance and beg His forgiveness. We seek the refuge of Allah from the evils of our base desires. He whom Allah guides none can lead him astray and he whom Allah leads astray, none can guide him. I bear witness that there is none worthy of worship but Allah, He is alone and has no partner and I bear witness that Muhammad ﷺ is His slave and true messenger."

Dimaad relates: "I requested Rasulullah ﷺ to repeat his words once again. By Allah! I have come across an abundance of poetry and I have heard a great many mantras (chants) of the fortune-tellers but I have never come across such words. I swear by Allah! These words are submerged in the deepest end of the ocean of eloquence. I also declare that I bear testimony that there is none worthy of worship but Allah, He is alone and has no partner and I bear witness that Muhammad ﷺ is His slave and true messenger."

In this manner, Dimaad embraced Islam and on behalf of his people, he pledged allegiance at the hands of Rasulullah ﷺ.

Chapter 6

Arch-enemies

Following his proclamations of Tauheed (monotheism) and invitation towards Islam, by and large, most of the residents of Makkah turned out to be Rasulullah's ﷺ enemies but some of them had reached the limits of blatant hostility. Some of these people were:

- Abu Jahal bin Hishaam
- Abu Lahab bin 'Abdul-Muttalib
- Aswad bin 'Abdu-Yaghuth
- Haaris bin Qays
- Waleed bin Mughirah
- Umayyah bin Khalaf
- Ubayy bin Khalaf
- Abu Qays bin Faakihah
- 'Aas bin Waa'il
- Nadr bin Haaris
- Munabbah bin Hajaaj
- Zuhair bin Abi Umayyah
- Saa'ib bin Saifi
- Aswad bin 'Abdul-Asad
- 'Aas bin Sa'eed
- 'Aas bin Haashim

- 'Uqbah bin Abi Mu'eet
- Ibnul-Asda Hakam bin 'Aas
- 'Adi bin Hamra

Most of them were Rasulullah's ﷺ neighbours and men of high standing in society. They were relentlessly engaged in hostility against Rasulullah ﷺ. Night and day, they were obsessed with this single mission of antagonism. Abu Jahal, Abu Lahab and 'Uqbah bin Abi Mu'eet were the three most bitter enemies of the lot.

It is a conventional custom of Allah Ta'ala that when He creates something, He also creates its opposite. Allah Ta'ala states:

$$\text{وَمِنْ كُلِّ شَيْءٍ خَلَقْنَا زَوْجَيْنِ لَعَلَّكُمْ تَذَكَّرُونَ}$$

"And of everything We have created pairs so that you may comprehend the (perfection of the Creator)." [Surah Zaariyaat verse 49]

So just as every Pharaoh has a Musa, similarly, every Musa has a Pharaoh in opposition to him. After all, things are recognised by their opposites.

For this reason we have decided to present a brief outline of each of Rasulullah's ﷺ sworn enemies.

Abu Jahal bin Hishaam

He was the Pharaoh of the Ummah of Rasulullah ﷺ. He left no stone unturned in his wave of deep-seated hostility and fierce resistance against Rasulullah ﷺ. A few incidents depicting his hatred towards Rasulullah ﷺ were mentioned in the past and more are to follow. Readers will be able to clearly ascertain the intensity of his enmity towards Rasulullah ﷺ from the words he uttered even while breathing his last on his death-bed (the details of which will follow under the chapter dealing with the battle of Badr, Insha Allah). Abu Jahal's original name was Abul-Hakam (which literally means the father of wisdom) but Rasulullah ﷺ changed this to Abu Jahal (the father of ignorance).

Abu Jahal would often blow his own trumpet by asserting: "I am 'Aziz and Kareem (revered and noble)." Upon this, the following verses were revealed:

$$\text{اِنَّ شَجَرَتَ الزَّقُّوْمِ ۞ طَعَامُ الْاَثِيْمِ ۞ كَالْمُهْلِ ۚ يَغْلِىْ فِى الْبُطُوْنِ ۞ كَغَلْىِ الْحَمِيْمِ ۞ خُذُوْهُ فَاعْتِلُوْهُ اِلٰى سَوَآءِ الْجَحِيْمِ ۞ ثُمَّ صُبُّوْا فَوْقَ رَاْسِهٖ مِنْ عَذَابِ الْحَمِيْمِ ۞ ذُقْ ۖ اِنَّكَ اَنْتَ الْعَزِيْزُ الْكَرِيْمُ ۞}$$

"Verily, the tree of Zaqqum, will be the food of the sinner. Like boiling oil, it will boil in the bellies, like the boiling of scalding water. (It will be said) 'Seize him and drag him into the midst of the blazing fire. Then pour over his head the agony of boiling water. Taste this! You (are the one who claimed) you are revered and noble".
[Surah Dukhaan verse 43-49]

Abu Lahab

Abu Lahab was his title. His actual name was 'Abdul-Uzza bin 'Abdul Muttalib. He was Rasulullah's ﷺ blood uncle (Rasulullah's ﷺ father's brother). When Rasulullah ﷺ assembled the Quraysh to preach the message of Islam to them, Abu Lahab was the first person to falsify him saying:

$$\text{تبالك سائر اليوم الهذا جمعتنا}$$

"Woe unto you! Did you assemble us here for this?"

Upon this incident, Surah Lahab was revealed. Since Abu Lahab was extremely wealthy, whenever he was cautioned about the punishment of Allah Ta'ala, he would say: "If my nephew is true in his assertions, I will absolve myself by paying money and children in ransom. The verse "Neither his wealth nor his earnings will spare him from it" is a reference to this assertion. His wife, Umme Jameel bintu Harb, the sister of Abu Sufyaan bin Harb also harboured a streak of bitter hostility towards Rasulullah ﷺ. She would often strew Rasulullah's ﷺ path with sharp thorns at night.

When Umme Jameel learnt that a Surah of the Holy Qur-aan was revealed about her and her husband, she picked up a stone and dashed out to strike Rasulullah ﷺ. At that moment, Rasulullah ﷺ was seated with Abu Bakr Siddeeq in Masjidul-Haraam. When Umme Jameel got to the Masjid, Allah Ta'ala placed a veil over her eyes. Only Abu Bakr ؓ was visible. She failed to spot Rasulullah ﷺ. Umme Jameel asked Abu Bakr ؓ: "Where is your companion? I heard that he ridicules me and makes mocking remarks about me. By Allah! If I come across him now, I will smash him with this stone. By Allah! I am a celebrated poetess." Saying this, she sang the following stanzas:

$$\text{مذمما عصينا   وامره ابينا   ودينه قلينا}$$

"Muzammam we disobeyed and his instructions we rebuffed and his religion we despised."

Due to her seething rage and fanatical hatred she cherished against Rasulullah ﷺ, she referred to him as Muzammam instead of Muhammad. Muzammam is actually the antonym of Muhammad. Muhammad means commendable whilst Muzammam means lamentable.

Expressing her hatred with these few lines, she went away.

Whenever the Quraysh hurled scorn upon Rasulullah ﷺ and labelled him Muzammam, Rasulullah ﷺ would say: "O people! Don't you find it strange? Don't you notice how Allah Ta'ala has repelled their vulgarities away from me? They refer to me as Muzammam but I am actually Muhammad."

According to another narration when Hadhrat Abu Bakr ؓ spotted Umme Jameel rushing towards them, he cautioned Rasulullah ﷺ saying: "O Prophet of Allah! Here is Umme Jameel speeding towards us. I fear for your safety." Rasulullah ﷺ replied: "She will never be able to catch sight of me." Rasulullah ﷺ then recited a few Qur-aanic verses.

Musnad Bazzaar mentions that Umme Jameel came up to Abu Bakr ؓ and said: "This man says poetry." Abu Bakr ؓ replied: "By the Lord of this building! Whatever he says is not poetry." Umme Jameel fumed: "You are a man who indisputably believes in him."

Saying this, she walked away. Hadhrat Abu Bakr ؓ then said: "O Prophet of Allah! Perhaps Umme Jameel failed to spot you." Rasulullah ﷺ replied: "Right until she left, an angel continued shrouding me from her."

Barely seven days after the battle of Badr, a terminal cyst erupted on Abu Lahabs' body and this brought about an agonizing death. Out of fear of infection, his family members refused to even touch his corpse. In this manner, his corpse remained decomposing for a period of three days. Finally, out of fear of disgrace and dishonour, they employed a few Abyssinian labourers to remove his body. They dug a hole and with the aid of long wooden poles, they shoved his body and dumped him into the hole. They then swiftly covered him up with sand and stones. This was the humiliation of this world. What about the disgrace of the hereafter that is still to follow? May Allah Ta'ala protect us from this. Aameen.

Abu Lahab had three sons; 'Utbah, Mu'attab and 'Utaibah. The first two embraced Islam at the conquest of Makkah. As for 'Utaibah, who, at the command of his father, divorced his wife – Rasulullah's ﷺ daughter – and was rude to Rasulullah ﷺ, he perished after Rasulullah ﷺ cursed him. At the conquest of Makkah, Rasulullah ﷺ asked his uncle Hadhrat 'Abbaas ؓ: "I don't see your nephews, 'Utbah and Mu'attab around, where are they?" Hadhrat 'Abbaas ؓ replied: "It seems as though they have gone into hiding." Rasulullah

ﷺ asked him to search for them. After an exhausting search, he found them in the field of 'Arafaat. Hadhrat 'Abbaas ؓ brought both of them to Rasulullah ﷺ. Rasulullah ﷺ presented them with Islam and both of them enthusiastically embraced Islam and pledged their allegiance at his hands. Upon this Rasulullah ﷺ remarked: "I beseeched Allah Ta'ala for these two cousins. Allah Ta'ala handed over both of them to me."

Umayyah bin Khalaf Jumahi

Umayyah had the audacity to publicly abuse Rasulullah ﷺ. Whenever he passed Rasulullah ﷺ, he would mockingly wink his eyes. His dreadful conduct brought about the revelation of the following Surah:

$$\text{وَيْلٌ لِكُلِّ هُمَزَةٍ لُمَزَةٍ ۞ الَّذِيْ جَمَعَ مَالًا وَّ عَدَّدَهُ ۞ يَحْسَبُ اَنَّ مَالَهٗ اَخْلَدَهُ ۞ كَلَّا لَيُنْۢبَذَنَّ فِي الْحُطَمَةِ ۞ وَمَآ اَدْرٰىكَ مَا الْحُطَمَةُ ۞ نَارُ اللّٰهِ الْمُوْقَدَةُ ۞ الَّتِيْ تَطَّلِعُ عَلَى الْاَفْـِٕدَةِ ۞ اِنَّهَا عَلَيْهِمْ مُّؤْصَدَةٌ ۞ فِيْ عَمَدٍ مُّمَدَّدَةٍ}$$

"Woe unto every slanderer and backbiter! He, who accumulates wealth and repeatedly counts it (like some of the Hindus who tally their Rupees with relish). What! Is he under the impression that his wealth will bring him eternity? Never! Verily, he will be hurled into the crushing fire. And do you know what is the crushing fire? It is the kindled fire of Allah Ta'ala, which will leap over the hearts. Verily, the fire will be sealed over them in long pillars."
[Surah Humazah verses 1 - 9]

Umayyah bin Khalaf was slain in the battle of Badr at the hands of Hadhrat Khubaib ؓ or at the hands of Hadhrat Bilal ؓ.

Ubayy bin Khalaf

Ubayy bin Khalaf also rivalled his brother Umayyah bin Khalaf in his hostility towards Rasulullah ﷺ. Once, he picked up a decomposed bone and crushing it in his hand and hurling its dust into the wind, he demanded: "Will Allah be able to resurrect this?" Rasulullah ﷺ replied: "Yes, when you and your bones decompose like the bone in your hand, Allah will resurrect you and hurl you into the fire."

This was the background to the following verses:

$$\text{وَضَرَبَ لَنَا مَثَلًا وَنَسِيَ خَلْقَهُ ۖ قَالَ مَن يُحْيِي الْعِظَامَ وَهِيَ رَمِيمٌ ۝ قُلْ يُحْيِيهَا الَّذِي أَنشَأَهَا أَوَّلَ مَرَّةٍ ۖ وَهُوَ بِكُلِّ خَلْقٍ عَلِيمٌ ۝ الَّذِي جَعَلَ لَكُم مِّنَ الشَّجَرِ الْأَخْضَرِ نَارًا فَإِذَا أَنتُم مِّنْهُ تُوقِدُونَ ۝ أَوَلَيْسَ الَّذِي خَلَقَ السَّمَاوَاتِ وَالْأَرْضَ بِقَادِرٍ عَلَىٰ أَن يَخْلُقَ مِثْلَهُم ۚ بَلَىٰ وَهُوَ الْخَلَّاقُ الْعَلِيمُ ۝ إِنَّمَا أَمْرُهُ إِذَا أَرَادَ شَيْئًا أَن يَقُولَ لَهُ كُن فَيَكُونُ ۝ فَسُبْحَانَ الَّذِي بِيَدِهِ مَلَكُوتُ كُلِّ شَيْءٍ وَإِلَيْهِ تُرْجَعُونَ ۝}$$

"And he puts forth for us a parable and he forgets his own creation; he says: 'Who will resurrect these bones in this state of decomposition?' Say! (O Muhammad!), "He will resurrect them Who created them the first time round and He is all-knowing of the entire creation, He who produces fire for you from the green tree and then you kindle your fires with it. Is not He who created the skies and the earth able to create the like of them? Indeed! He is the all-knowing, supreme creator. Verily, His command, when He intends something, is merely to say to it: "Be" - and it is. So, glorified is He in whose dominion is all things and to Him shall you be returned."
[Surah Yaaseen verses 78 - 83]

Ubayy bin Khalaf was killed in the battle of Uhud at the hands of Rasulullah ﷺ.

'Uqbah bin Abi Mu'eet

'Uqbah was the bosom friend of Ubayy bin Khalaf. One day, 'Uqbah took a seat in the company of Rasulullah ﷺ attentively listening to the words of Rasulullah ﷺ. When Ubayy learnt of this, he hurried over to 'Uqbah and voiced his concerns: "I learnt that you sat in the company of Muhammad ﷺ attentively listening to his words. By Allah! Until you do not go and spit on his face, it is Haraam for me to talk to you and even look at your face." Accordingly, the wretched 'Uqbah rose and ejected his saliva right onto the blessed face of Rasulullah ﷺ. Upon this, the following verses were revealed:

$$\text{وَيَوْمَ يَعَضُّ الظَّالِمُ عَلَىٰ يَدَيْهِ يَقُولُ يَا لَيْتَنِي اتَّخَذْتُ مَعَ الرَّسُولِ سَبِيلًا ۝ يَا وَيْلَتَىٰ لَيْتَنِي لَمْ أَتَّخِذْ فُلَانًا خَلِيلًا ۝ لَقَدْ أَضَلَّنِي عَنِ الذِّكْرِ بَعْدَ إِذْ جَاءَنِي ۗ وَكَانَ الشَّيْطَانُ لِلْإِنسَانِ خَذُولًا ۝ وَقَالَ الرَّسُولُ يَا رَبِّ إِنَّ قَوْمِي اتَّخَذُوا هَٰذَا الْقُرْآنَ مَهْجُورًا ۝ وَكَذَٰلِكَ جَعَلْنَا لِكُلِّ نَبِيٍّ عَدُوًّا مِّنَ الْمُجْرِمِينَ ۗ وَكَفَىٰ بِرَبِّكَ هَادِيًا وَنَصِيرًا ۝}$$

"And the day when the evil-doer will bite his hands (in despair) saying: "Oh! If only I had taken the path of the messenger. Ah! Woe unto me! If only I did not assume so and so as an intimate friend. He indeed led me astray from the Zikr (reminder and advice i.e. the Qur-aan) after it had come to me." And shaytaan is a deserter to man (in the hour of need). And the messenger said: "O my Lord! My people have discarded (the teachings of) this Qur-aan. (O Nabi! Do not become despondent because) in this manner We have assigned to every Nabi an enemy from amongst the criminals. Your Lord is sufficient as a guide and helper."
[Surah Furqaan verses 27-31]

'Uqbah was captured as a prisoner in the battle of Badr and he was executed in a place called Safra.

Waleed bin Mughirah

Waleed bin Mughirah would say: "It is rather strange that Muhammad was preferred for the revelation of divine Wahi whilst Abu Mas'ood Thaqafi and I were excluded from this privilege whereas both of us are reputable leaders of this city. I am the leader of the Quraysh whilst he is the leader of the tribe of Thaqif."

Upon this, the following verses were revealed:

$$\text{وَقَالُوا لَوْلَا نُزِّلَ هَٰذَا الْقُرْآنُ عَلَىٰ رَجُلٍ مِّنَ الْقَرْيَتَيْنِ عَظِيمٍ ۝ أَهُمْ يَقْسِمُونَ رَحْمَتَ رَبِّكَ ۚ نَحْنُ قَسَمْنَا بَيْنَهُم مَّعِيشَتَهُمْ فِي الْحَيَاةِ الدُّنْيَا ۚ وَرَفَعْنَا بَعْضَهُمْ فَوْقَ بَعْضٍ دَرَجَاتٍ لِّيَتَّخِذَ بَعْضُهُم بَعْضًا سُخْرِيًّا ۗ وَرَحْمَتُ رَبِّكَ خَيْرٌ مِّمَّا يَجْمَعُونَ ۝}$$

'And they say, 'Why was this Qur-aan not revealed to some great man of the two cities?' Is it they who portion out the mercy of your Lord? It is We who portion out amongst them their livelihood in this worldly life and We raise some of them amongst others in rank so that some may employ the others (in their work). And the mercy of your Lord is far better than (the wealth) they are amassing.' (In other words, the fortunes of the hereafter are far superior to the blessings of this world. So, if the distribution of worldly livelihood is not based on their opinion, how can the fortune related to the hereafter (prophethood) ever be based on their opinions?)
[Surah Zukhruf verse 31-32]

Put differently, material wealth, affluence, worldly honour and reputation is certainly not the basis of prophethood. On one occasion, a few chieftains of the Quraysh including Waleed bin Mughirah, Umayyah bin Khalaf, Abu Jahal, 'Utbah bin Rabi'ah and Shaybah bin Rabi'ah approached Rasulullah ﷺ to make some enquiries about Islam. Whilst Rasulullah ﷺ was in the process of preaching to them, 'Abdullah ibn Ummi Maktum رضى الله عنه – the blind Muazzin of Rasulullah's ﷺ Masjid – also came to enquire about some issue. Rasulullah ﷺ thought to himself that Ibn Ummi Maktum رضى الله عنه is after all a Muslim. He can enquire later on at some other time. These people on the other hand, are the influential folks of society. If they embrace Islam, thousands of others will follow. This is why Rasulullah ﷺ did not pay much attention towards Ibn Ummi Maktum رضى الله عنه. In fact, owing to his ill-timed intrusion, a few traces of a frown appeared on Rasulullah's ﷺ blessed face. He should have waited for the first meeting to conclude before intruding the gathering. However, the mercy of Allah Ta'ala flared up and the following verses were revealed:

عَبَسَ وَتَوَلَّى ۞ اَنْ جَآءَهُ الْاَعْمٰى ۞ وَمَا يُدْرِيْكَ لَعَلَّهٗ يَزَّكّٰى ۞ اَوْ يَذَّكَّرُ فَتَنْفَعَهُ الذِّكْرٰى ۞ اَمَّا مَنِ اسْتَغْنٰى ۞ فَاَنْتَ لَهٗ تَصَدّٰى ۞ وَمَا عَلَيْكَ اَلَّا يَزَّكّٰى ۞ وَاَمَّا مَنْ جَآءَكَ يَسْعٰى ۞ وَهُوَ يَخْشٰى ۞ فَاَنْتَ عَنْهُ تَلَهّٰى ۞ كَلَّآ اِنَّهَا تَذْكِرَةٌ ۞

"He (Rasulullah ﷺ) frowned and turned away because there came to him the blind man. And how do you know? He may just purify himself (from all sins). Or perhaps he might receive admonition and this advice may benefit him. As for him who considers himself independent, to him you attended. There is (no blame) upon you if he does not become pure (from disbelief and kufr etc.). But as for he who came running to you whilst he was afraid (of Allah Ta'ala), you are neglectful of him (by diverting your attention to others). Nay, this (Qur-aan) is an admonition..... [Surah 'Abasa verses 1-11]

Subsequent to this incident, whenever 'Abdullah ibn Ummi Maktum رضى الله عنه appeared before Rasulullah ﷺ, he would reverently lay his sheet down for him saying: "Welcome to him in whose regards my Rabb reprimanded me."

Abu Qays bin Faakihah

He was also instrumental in ruthlessly persecuting Rasulullah ﷺ. He was one of the select assistants and sidekicks of Abu Jahal. Abu Qays was killed in the battle of Badr at the hands of Hadhrat Hamzah رضى الله عنه.

Nadr bin Haaris

He was also one of the chieftains of the Quraysh. He would often travel to Persia on business. On his travels, he would purchase stories and historical accounts of the non-Arab monarchs. He would then relate these narratives to the Quraysh. He would tell the Quraysh: "Muhammad relates the stories of 'Aad and Thamud to you but I will share with you the legends of Rustam, Asfandiyaar and the Persian monarchs." People took great delight in listening to these stories (like the novels of today). People would pay more attention to the accounts of his legendary fables than they paid to the Holy Qur-aan. He also purchased a singing slave girl whose musical talents he exploited by making people listen to her melodious voice. Whenever he learnt of anyone being inclined towards Islam, he would take this slave to him and bid her to entertain him with food, drink and music. He would then ask him: "Tell me, is this better than what Muhammad invites you to? Is this better than his directives on Salaah, Saum and Jihaad against the enemies of Allah?"

Upon this, the following verses were revealed:

وَ مِنَ النَّاسِ مَنْ يَّشْتَرِىْ لَهْوَ الْحَدِيْثِ لِيُضِلَّ عَنْ سَبِيْلِ اللّٰهِ بِغَيْرِ عِلْمٍ ۖ وَّ يَتَّخِذَهَا هُزُوًا ؕ اُولٰٓئِكَ لَهُمْ عَذَابٌ مُّهِيْنٌ ۝ وَ اِذَا تُتْلٰى عَلَيْهِ اٰيٰتُنَا وَلّٰى مُسْتَكْبِرًا كَاَنْ لَّمْ يَسْمَعْهَا كَاَنَّ فِىْٓ اُذُنَيْهِ وَقْرًا ۚ فَبَشِّرْهُ بِعَذَابٍ اَلِيْمٍ ۝

"And amongst people there is a person who purchases idle talk (music, singing etc.) to mislead people from the path of Allah without knowledge and he takes this (path of Allah or the Holy Qur-aan) as a form of mockery. For such people there is a humiliating punishment (in hell). And when our verses are recited to him, he turns away in arrogance as though he hasn't heard them, as if there is a mass (deafness) in his ears. So offer him glad tidings of an agonizing punishment."

[Surah Luqmaan verses 6-7]

Note: Entertaining people with food, drink and singing girls to deflect them from their religious convictions are an ancient ploy of the people of falsehood. The Christians in particular are exceedingly skilful in this and in emulation of them, the Aryans (modern reformist but fanatical Hindu sect) also adopted this approach. A person whom Allah Ta'ala has given a little bit of intellect will realise that this is not the approach of those who worship Allah Ta'ala but the approach of those who worship their desires. May Allah Ta'ala protect us all.

Nadr bin Haaris was captured in the battle of Badr and on the instruction of Rasulullah ﷺ, was slain by Hadhrat Ali ﷢.

'Aas bin Waa'il Sahmi

'Aas bin Waa'il Sahmi was the father of Hadhrat 'Amr bin 'Aas ﷢. He (the father) was also one of the people who vigorously engaged in poking fun at and ridiculing the blessed personality of Rasulullah ﷺ.

All Rasulullah's ﷺ sons passed away in infancy. In deriding Rasulullah ﷺ, 'Aas bin Waa'il commented:

$$\text{ان محمدا ابتر لا يعيش له ولد}$$

"Indeed Muhammad is an Abtar. None of his sons survive."

The word Abtar refers to an animal with a severed tail. A person who is not survived by male descendants or a person not remembered by anyone is like an animal with a severed tail. (it is as though the person's lineage is now severed and terminated.)

Upon this, the following verse was revealed:

$$\text{اِنَّ شَانِئَكَ هُوَ الْاَبْتَرُ}$$

"Verily your enemy is an Abtar (cut off from all good in the hereafter)."
[Surah Kauthar verse 3]

Rasulullah ﷺ is fondly remembered by millions of people (unlike his enemies).

A month after Hijrah, 'Aas was bitten by an animal on his leg. This caused such swelling that his leg turned as thick as a camel's neck. This casualty ultimately led to his death.

Nubaih and Munabbihah, the sons of Hajaaj

Nubaih and Munabbihah were also bitter enemies of Rasulullah ﷺ. Whenever they laid eyes on Rasulullah ﷺ, they sarcastically commented: "What, could Allah not find anyone else to appoint as His messenger?"

Both of them were killed in the battle of Badr.

Aswad bin Muttalib

Whenever Aswad bin Muttalib and his friends came across Rasulullah ﷺ and his Sahaabah ؓ, they would roll their eyes, wink at each other and mockingly say: "Are these the people who propose to rule the earth and seize the treasures of Caesar and Chosroe?" Making such sarcastic remarks, they would whistle and clap hands. Rasulullah ﷺ cursed him in the following words: "O Allah? Make him blind (so that he is unable to wink his eyes in mockery) and destroy his son." As a result, Aswad immediately turned blind whilst his son was killed in the battle of Badr. Whilst the Quraysh were frantically making preparations for the battle of Uhud, he was ill but, notwithstanding this, his efforts in inciting his people against Rasulullah ﷺ persisted. He died before the battle of Uhud.

Aswad bin 'Abdi-Yaghuth

Aswad bin 'Abdi-Yaghuth was Rasulullah's ﷺ mother's brother's son. His family lineage is as follows: Aswad bin 'Abdi-Yaghuth bin Wahab bin Munaaf bin Zuhrah. He was also one of the most bitter enemies of Rasulullah ﷺ. Whenever he saw the poor Muslims, he would sarcastically remark: "These are the future kings of the world who will become the heirs of Chosroes' kingdom." Whenever he laid eyes on Rasulullah ﷺ, he would sarcastically say things like: "What is the matter, has nothing descended from the heavens today?"

Haaris bin Qays Sahmi

He was also referred to as Haaris bin 'Aytalah. 'Aytalah was his mother's name whilst his father was Qays. He was also one of those who ardently engaged in deriding and mocking the companions of Rasulullah ﷺ. He would often remark: "Muhammad has deceived his companions by leading them to believe in life after death."

Allah Ta'ala portrays this in the verse:

$$وَمَا يُهْلِكُنَا إِلَّا الدَّهْرُ$$

"They say, by Allah! Nothing but time annihilates us." [Surah Jaathiyah verse 24]

When their mockery and scorn went beyond reasonable limits, Allah Ta'ala revealed the following verses to comfort Rasulullah ﷺ:

$$فَاصْدَعْ بِمَا تُؤْمَرُ وَأَعْرِضْ عَنِ الْمُشْرِكِينَ ۝ إِنَّا كَفَيْنَاكَ الْمُسْتَهْزِئِينَ ۝$$

"So proclaim what you have been commanded and (if the disbelievers refuse to comply) turn away from the disbelievers. Verily, We will suffice for you against the mockers." [Surah Hijr verse 94-95]

The most active in mocking Rasulullah ﷺ were the following five people: Aswad bin 'Abdi-Yaguth, Waleed bin Mughirah, Aswad bin 'Abdul-Muttalib, 'Aas bin Waa'il and Haaris bin Qays.

On one occasion Rasulullah ﷺ was busy making Tawaaf of the Baitullah when Jibraa'eel عليه السلام appeared before him. Whilst Rasulullah ﷺ was complaining to Jibraa'eel عليه السلام about the excessive mockery of these people, Waleed bin Mughirah happened to pass before Rasulullah ﷺ. Rasulullah

ﷺ pointed out that this is Waleed. Jibraa'eel علیہ السلام indicated towards Waleed's jugular vein. Rasulullah ﷺ asked: "What? What have you done?" Jibraa'eel علیہ السلام replied: "You are sufficed against Waleed." Thereafter, Aswad bin Muttalib happened to pass by. Rasulullah ﷺ commented: "This is Aswad bin Muttalib." Jibraa'eel علیہ السلام indicated towards his eyes. Rasulullah ﷺ asked: "What have you done?" Jibraa'eel علیہ السلام replied: "You are sufficed against Aswad bin Muttalib. Thereafter Aswad bin 'Abdi-Yaghuth came along. Jibraa'eel علیہ السلام indicated towards his head and as per the previous inquiry of Rasulullah ﷺ, Jibraa'eel علیہ السلام said: "You have been sufficed." Thereafter, Haaris happened to pass by. Jibraa'eel علیہ السلام pointed to his stomach and said: "You have been sufficed." Thereafter along came 'Aas bin Waa'il. Pointing towards the soles of his feet, Jibraa'eel علیہ السلام said: "You have been sufficed."

In due course, what happened to Waleed is that once he came across a man from the Khuzaa'ah tribe who was engaged in the manufacture of arrows. Accidentally, Waleed's foot fell onto one of his arrows thereby causing a minor injury to his foot. He barely pointed to his foot when the injury started spurting blood. This minor injury proved fatal for him. The story of Aswad bin Muttalib is that he sat beneath an acacia tree when he suddenly screamed out to his sons: "Help me! Help me! Someone is poking thorns into my eyes." His sons replied: "We don't see anyone around." He went on yelling like this until he turned blind. What transpired with Aswad bin 'Abdi-Yaguth is that Jibraa'eel علیہ السلام merely indicated towards his head when suddenly his whole head erupted in pustules and pimples. He ultimately died from this affliction. As for Haaris, he abruptly fell so ill that he started evacuating faecal matter from his mouth. This in due course led to his death. Finally 'Aas bin Waa'il was on his way to Taa'if on a donkey when he unexpectedly fell off the donkey onto a patch of thorny grass. He was pricked by an insignificant thorn but the injury caused by this rather tiny thorn was so severe that it proved fatal for him.

On the basis of the aforementioned incidents, readers are urged to contemplate whether force and pressure was employed in the spread of Islam or whether cruelty and transgression was used for the eradication and suppression of Islam.

Persecution of the Muslims

Just as Islam continued spreading far and wide and just as the Muslims continued growing in number, the rage and hatred of the disbelievers of Makkah intensified proportionately. The disbelievers really didn't have much influence and dominance over the Muslims who had backing and support (within their respective clans) but the pitiable Muslims who neither enjoyed any support nor sanctuary fell victim to the merciless persecution and brutality of the disbelievers of Makkah. Some

Muslims fell prey to their relentless beatings whilst others were confined to dark and narrow cages.

Hereunder we recount a few incidents highlighting the sheer brutality and ruthlessness of the Makkan disbelievers and the firm endurance and forbearance of the Sahaabah رضى الله عنهم.

Sayyidina Bilal bin Rabaah رضى الله عنه (The Imaam of the callers to Salaah and success)

He was an Abyssinian by lineage. He was the slave of Umayyah bin Khalaf. In the midst of the afternoon, when the heat was at its fiercest and the boulders of the desert turned blazing hot, he (Umayyah, the master) would direct his servants to lay Bilal down onto the baking stones of the desert and place a boulder onto his chest to restrict his movements. He would then bellow at him: "You will die like this. If you have any hope of salvation, renounce Muhammad and start praying to Laat and 'Uzza." Even in these trying times, nothing but the words, "Ahad Ahad (He is one, He is one)" would stem from his mouth.

He would occasionally drape him in cowhide or fit him out with a suit of armour and force him to sit in the scorching sun. Even in this state of horrible torture, the words, "Ahad, Ahad" would emanate from his tongue.

When Umayyah, his master, realised that Bilal's determination and firmness was not influenced in the least, he tied a rope around his neck and committed him to the charge of some young boys who continued dragging him around the city but despite these odds he persisted in uttering the words "Ahad, Ahad". Consistent with this wave of unrelenting torture, Hadhrat Bilal رضى الله عنه was being turned into a target of their ruthless tyranny when Hadhrat Abu Bakr رضى الله عنه happened to pass by. Witnessing this pitiful and intolerable scene before him, he addressed Umayyah, the master, saying:

"Don't you fear Allah? Until when will this unbearable torture continue?"
Umayyah replied: "You are responsible for turning him into this wreck. Now you are obliged to release him." Abu Bakr رضى الله عنه replied: "Very well. I have a slave who is extremely strong and he is passionately devoted to your faith. Take him in exchange of Bilal and surrender Bilal to my care." Umayyah consented to this offer. Hadhrat Abu Bakr رضى الله عنه then took Bilal رضى الله عنه along with him and subsequently set him free.

The brutal torture and dreadful injuries inflicted by the disbelievers upon the best of Muazzins Hadhrat Bilal رضى الله عنه left horrible scars on his back. These scars were clearly visible whenever his back happened to be exposed.

'Ammaar bin Yaasir رضي الله عنه

'Ammaar bin Yaasir رضي الله عنه was essentially a man of Qahtaani descent. His father Yaasir came to Makkah in search of one of his missing brothers. His two brothers, Haaris and Maalik also accompanied him on this journey. Haaris and Maalik returned to Yemen whilst Yaasir decided to stay over in Makkah Mukarramah. He then established an alliance with Abu Huzaifah Makhzumi. Abu Huzaifah got him married to his slave woman Sumayyah bintu Khayyat and from this union 'Ammaar was born. Yaasir and 'Ammaar lived with Abu Huzaifah right until the end of his life. When Allah Ta'ala subsequently exposed Islam, Yaasir رضي الله عنه, Sumayyah رضي الله عنها, 'Ammaar رضي الله عنه and his brother 'Abdullah bin Yaasir رضي الله عنه all embraced Islam. Hadhrat 'Ammaar رضي الله عنه also had another elder brother by the name of Huraith bin Yaasir who was murdered at the hands of Banud-Dail in the times of Jaahiliyyah (pre-Islamic era).

Since 'Ammaar bin Yaasir رضي الله عنه had no family or tribe in Makkah to support him, the Quraysh severely persecuted him and inflicted him with a multitude of tormenting afflictions. In the midst of the scorching noon heat, they would lay him onto the blazing sand and beat him up so severely that he would fall unconscious. At times they would hurl him into (a dam) of water and at times they would force him to lie down on a bed of blazing coals. On such occasions, whenever Rasulullah صلى الله عليه وسلم happened to pass by, he would pass his hands over 'Ammaar's head and say:

يانار كوني بردا و سلاما على عمار كما كنت على ابراهيم

"O Fire! Turn cool and safe upon 'Ammaar as you had transformed yourself for Ibraaheem."

Whenever Rasulullah صلى الله عليه وسلم witnessed 'Ammaar رضي الله عنه, his father Yaasir رضي الله عنه or his mother Sumayyah رضي الله عنها in hardship, he would advise them: "O family of Yaasir! Exercise patience." Sometimes, he would utter: "O Allah! Forgive the family of Yaasir." Sometimes he would remark: "Glad tidings upon you! Jannat is eagerly awaiting your arrival."

Hadhrat Ali رضي الله عنه narrates that he heard Rasulullah صلى الله عليه وسلم saying: "From head to toe, 'Ammaar is imbued with faith. (He is an embodiment of Imaan.)" Once Hadhrat 'Ammaar رضي الله عنه removed his shirt when a few bystanders happened to catch sight of black scars covering his back. When asked about these scars, he replied: "The Quraysh of Makkah would lay me down on the scorching stones (of the Makkan desert). These are the scars of those injuries."

The same brutality was meted out to his father Yaasir رضي الله عنه and his mother Sumayyah رضي الله عنها. Initially, just seven people openly proclaimed their belief in Islam. They were, Rasulullah صلى الله عليه وسلم, Abu Bakr رضي الله عنه, Bilal رضي الله عنه, Khabbaab

, Suhaib ﷺ, 'Ammaar ﷺ and Sumayyah ﷺ. Owing to their noble family connections, the disbelievers of Makkah were unable to wield absolute domination over Rasulullah ﷺ and Abu Bakr ﷺ. However, the remaining five; Bilal, Khabbaab, Suhaib, 'Ammaar and Sumayyah ﷺ were persistently subject to their relentless brutality. In the midst of the midday heat, they would dress them in metallic armour and force them to stand in the blistering heat. One day, Abu Jahal appeared before them. (In a fit of rage), he thrust a spear into Hadhrat Sumayyah's ﷺ private part. This wound proved fatal. She subsequently died a Shaheed.

The first martyr in Islam was Hadhrat Sumayyah ﷺ who was exceptionally old and weak. When Abu Jahal was put to death on the occasion of the battle of Badr, Rasulullah ﷺ addressed Hadhrat 'Ammaar ﷺ thus: "Allah has slain your mother's killer."

In the same difficult and brutal circumstances, Hadhrat Yaasir ﷺ passed away before Hadhrat Sumayyah ﷺ.

Suhaib bin Sinaan ﷺ

Suhaib was actually a native of the vicinity of Musil. His father and uncle were governors of Ubullah whilst it was a dominion of the Persian Empire under the rule of Chosroe. Once, this area came under fierce attack from the Romans. Suhaib was barely a young boy at that time. During the course of the Roman pillage and plunder, he was seized by the Romans and hauled away to Rome. This is where he grew up, hence the name "Suhaib Rumi" (Suhaib, the Roman). A person of the Banu Kalb tribe purchased him from the Romans and brought him over to Makkah. In Makkah, 'Abdullah bin Jad'aan purchased him and set him free. When Rasulullah ﷺ launched his public invitation towards Islam, Hadhrat 'Ammaar ﷺ and Hadhrat Suhaib ﷺ both appeared together in Daaru Arqam and embraced Islam. Just as they persecuted Hadhrat 'Ammaar, the disbelievers of Makkah also subjected Hadhrat Suhaib ﷺ to a stream of wide-ranging modes of torture. When he intended to emigrate from Makkah, the Quraysh of Makkah demanded that he may only depart if he leaves behind all his goods and wealth in Makkah otherwise he is prohibited from emigrating. Hadhrat Suhaib ﷺ consented to this ultimatum and giving a boot to the temporary vanities of this world, he emigrated. When he reached Madinah Munawwarah and related this incident to Rasulullah ﷺ, he commented: "Suhaib has unquestionably profited in his trade." In other words, by him trading in his dunya in exchange for his hereafter, he has netted a healthy profit. In regards to this, Allah Ta'ala revealed the following verse:

وَ مِنَ النَّاسِ مَنْ يَشْرِىْ نَفْسَهُ ابْتِغَآءَ مَرْضَاتِ اللّٰهِ ۗ وَاللّٰهُ رَءُوْفٌۢ بِالْعِبَادِ ۝

"And there are some people who sell themselves in pursuit of the pleasure of Allah. And Allah is exceptionally kind to the servants." [Surah Baqarah verse 207]

According to another narration, Rasulullah ﷺ repeatedly affirmed:

ربح صهيبٌ ربح صهيب

"Suhaib has earned a healthy profit. Suhaib has earned a healthy profit."

The disbelievers of Makkah would torment 'Ammaar, Suhaib, Abu Faaidah and 'Aamir bin Fuhayrah ؓ to such an unbearable level that they would often fall unconscious and at times they would be beaten senseless. This state of senselessness was so severe that quite often, they did not even realise what they were uttering.

In regards to such people, the following verse was revealed:

ثُمَّ اِنَّ رَبَّكَ لِلَّذِيْنَ هَاجَرُوْا مِنْۢ بَعْدِ مَا فُتِنُوْا ثُمَّ جَاهَدُوْا وَصَبَرُوْا ۙ اِنَّ رَبَّكَ مِنْۢ بَعْدِهَا لَغَفُوْرٌ رَّحِيْمٌ ۝

"Then, your Lord - for those who migrated after suffering misfortunes and then they migrated and exercised forbearance, verily your Lord, thereafter, is most Forgiving and Merciful." [Surah Nahl verse 110]

This verse was revealed in respect of the abovementioned people.

Khabbaab bin Aratt ؓ

Khabbab bin Aratt ؓ was amongst the first group of persons to embrace Islam. It is said that he was the sixth person to enter Islam. He was honoured with Islam even before entering Daaru Arqam. He was a slave of Umme Anmaar. When she learnt of his conversion to Islam she subjected him to an assortment of pain and suffering.

Once Hadhrat Khabbaab ؓ went to meet Hadhrat 'Umar ؓ. Assigning him a seat on his personal seating place, Hadhrat 'Umar ؓ remarked: "Nobody is more eligible to this seat than you except Bilal ؓ." Upon this, Hadhrat Khabbaab ؓ remarked: "O Ameerul-Mumineen! Even Bilal is not more eligible than I am because Bilal enjoyed some support from at least a few disbelievers during that period of suffering and anguish. At any rate, some of them supported and protected him whilst I enjoyed absolutely no support from any one of them. I recall one day when the Quraysh laid me flat over blazing coals. One of them placed his foot over my chest so that I was unable to move." Hadhrat Khabbaab رضي الله عنه then lifted his kurtah to expose ashen scars covering his back.

Khabbaab bin Aratt رضي الله عنه says: "In the pre-Islamic days of ignorance, I was a blacksmith by trade. I was well skilled in the forging of swords. On one occasion I produced a sword for 'Aas bin Waa'il. When the time came to pay for his sword, he declared: "I refuse to pay you a cent until you renounce Muhammad (صلى الله عليه وسلم)." I replied: "Even if you had to die and be resurrected, I will never renounce Muhammad Rasulullah صلى الله عليه وسلم." 'Aas sarcastically enquired: "Will I be resurrected after my death?" Khabbaab رضي الله عنه replied: "Yes, of course." To this, 'Aas scornfully replied: "When Allah puts me to death and resurrects me once again and I have the same wealth and children in my possession, I will settle my debt with you."

Upon this, Allah Ta'ala revealed the following verses of the Holy Qur-aan:

$$\text{اَفَرَءَيْتَ الَّذِيْ كَفَرَ بِاٰيٰتِنَا وَقَالَ لَاُوْتَيَنَّ مَالًا وَّ وَلَدًا ۞ اَطَّلَعَ الْغَيْبَ اَمِ اتَّخَذَ عِنْدَ الرَّحْمٰنِ عَهْدًا ۞ كَلَّا ؕ سَنَكْتُبُ مَا يَقُوْلُ وَنَمُدُّ لَهٗ مِنَ الْعَذَابِ مَدًّا ۞ وَّ نَرِثُهٗ مَا يَقُوْلُ وَيَاْتِيْنَا فَرْدًا ۞}$$

"Did you behold the one who denies our signs and says: 'I will certainly be bestowed with wealth and children (in the hereafter).' Is he conscious of the unseen or has he taken a covenant from Allah? Never! We will record what he says (as a form of evidence against him in the hereafter) and We will persist in prolonging his torment (in the hereafter). And We shall inherit all what he speaks of (wealth and children) and he will appear before us alone." [Surah Maryam verses 77-80]

Abu Fukayhah Juhani رضي الله عنه

Abu Fukayhah was actually his title. His name was Yasaar although he was better known by his title of Abu Fukayhah. He was the slave of Safwaan bin Umayyah. Umayyah bin Khalaf would sometimes get a rope tied to his feet and pitilessly drag him around. At times, he would shackle his feet with leg irons and force him to lie face down on the scorching sand with a huge boulder placed on his back. This was so agonizing that he often fell unconscious. Sometimes he would viciously throttle him.

One day Umayyah bin Khalaf had him pinned to the scorching ground and he was busy throttling him when Umayyah bin Khalaf's brother Ubayy bin Khalaf happened to pass by. Instead of this heartless man taking pity on him, he urged his brother to throttle him even more. He throttled him so ruthlessly that people thought he was no more. Fortunately Abu Bakr رضي الله عنه happened to pass that way. He purchased Abu Fukayhah رضي الله عنه and set him free.

Zanirah رضي الله عنها

Hadhrat Zanirah رضي الله عنها was amongst the first group of women to embrace Islam. She was the slave of Hadhrat 'Umar رضي الله عنه. (Before he embraced Islam), 'Umar would relentlessly beat her until he himself would be exhausted. Abu Jahal also harassed her a great deal. Whenever Abu Jahal and the other chieftains of Makkah caught sight of Zanirah رضي الله عنها, they would scornfully say: "If Islam was an admirable religion and if it was something grand, people like Zanirah would not have beaten us to it."

In reaction to this, Allah Ta'ala revealed the following verse:

$$\text{وَ قَالَ الَّذِيْنَ كَفَرُوْا لِلَّذِيْنَ اٰمَنُوْا لَوْ كَانَ خَيْرًا مَّا سَبَقُوْنَآ اِلَيْهِ}$$

"And the disbelievers said to the believers: 'If this was any good, they wouldn't have preceded us to it." [Surah Ahqaaf verse 11]

They failed to realise that if they possessed any good within them they themselves would have preceded others towards goodness and the true Deen and they would not be hesitant to embrace the true Deen. They failed to understand that the failure of the leaders and prosperous members of society to accept the advice of the Ambiyaa and the acceptance of the teachings of the Ambiyaa by these ascetics whose hearts are uncontaminated by the love of wealth and power, is undeniably not proof of the truth being false. In fact it is a glaring proof of the pride, arrogance and haughtiness of those who reject this Deen. That the poor and weak readily accept the truth is no dishonour to the truth but by them accepting the truth they raise themselves from the gutters of wretchedness and secure the lofty pinnacles of honour. On the other hand, by refuting the truth, the rich and influential leaders debase and demean themselves in the eyes of the men of insight. Yes, if the rich and influential are not reluctant in accepting the truth – like Abu Bakr, 'Usmaan Ghani and 'Abdur-Rahmaan bin 'Awf رضي الله عنهم - then this adds additional lustre to the gleam of their nobility and honour.

Due to these relentless ordeals, Hadhrat Zanirah رضي الله عنها lost her eyesight. The disbelievers of Makkah claimed that their idols, Laat and 'Uzza, rendered her blind. In response to this claim, Hadhrat Zanirah رضي الله عنها told these disbelievers: "Laat and 'Uzza are not even aware of who worships them. This tragedy (of my blindness) was destined by none other than Allah Ta'ala. If He wishes, He will restore my eyesight." Look at the marvel of Allah Ta'ala, the very next morning she awoke with her eyesight restored. Upon this, the disbelievers of Makkah remarked: "Muhammad (صلى الله عليه وسلم) has cast a spell of black magic over her." Eventually, Hadhrat Abu Bakr رضي الله عنه purchased her and set her free.

Similarly, Hadhrat Abu Bakr رضي الله عنه is said to have purchased a number of slaves – male and female – and subsequently set them free. Thus he rescued a number of victims of oppressive brutality. Some of these liberated slaves were Bilal, Abu Fukayhah, 'Aamir bin Fuhayrah, Zanirah, Nahdiyyah, Nahdiyyah's daughter, Labinah, Mutiyyah and Abu 'Ubais ﷺ.

Hadhrat Abu Bakr's ﷺ father Abu Quhaafah had not as yet embraced Islam. One day, he told Abu Bakr ﷺ: "I observe you purchasing only the weak and feeble slaves and then liberating them. If you purchase and free strong and robust slaves they will at least be of some use to you." Abu Bakr ﷺ replied: "The motive for setting them free is within my heart." Upon this, Allah Ta'ala revealed the following verses:

فَاَمَّا مَنْ اَعْطٰى وَ اتَّقٰى ۞ وَ صَدَّقَ بِالْحُسْنٰى ۞ فَسَنُيَسِّرُهٗ لِلْيُسْرٰى ۞ وَ اَمَّا مَنْ بَخِلَ وَ اسْتَغْنٰى ۞ وَ كَذَّبَ بِالْحُسْنٰى ۞ فَسَنُيَسِّرُهٗ لِلْعُسْرٰى ۞ وَ مَا يُغْنِىْ عَنْهُ مَالُهٗ اِذَا تَرَدّٰى ۞ اِنَّ عَلَيْنَا لَلْهُدٰى ۞ وَ اِنَّ لَنَا لَلْاٰخِرَةَ وَ الْاُوْلٰى ۞ فَاَنْذَرْتُكُمْ نَارًا تَلَظّٰى ۞ لَا يَصْلٰىهَآ اِلَّا الْاَشْقَى ۞ الَّذِىْ كَذَّبَ وَ تَوَلّٰى ۞ وَ سَيُجَنَّبُهَا الْاَتْقَى ۞ الَّذِىْ يُؤْتِىْ مَالَهٗ يَتَزَكّٰى ۞ وَ مَا لِاَحَدٍ عِنْدَهٗ مِنْ نِّعْمَةٍ تُجْزٰى ۞ اِلَّا ابْتِغَآءَ وَجْهِ رَبِّهِ الْاَعْلٰى ۞ وَ لَسَوْفَ يَرْضٰى

"As for him who gives (in charity) and maintains Allah-consciousness, and believes in the best (i.e. the religion of Islam), We will grant him the divine ability for the pathway of ease (i.e. virtuous deeds that may lead him towards Jannah). And as for him who is miserly and indifferent (and regards himself self-sufficient) and he disbelieves in the best (i.e. the religion of Islam), We will make easy for him the pathway of evil. And his wealth will not avail him when he goes down (in destruction). Verily, in our power alone lies guidance. And truly, to Us belongs the last (the hereafter) and the first (this world). So I am warning you of a blazing fire. None shall enter it except the most wretched who disbelieves and turns away. And the most Allah-conscious person would be far removed from it (the fire), the one who spends his wealth to purify it, and who has no favour to be returned to anyone except to seek the pleasure of his Lord, the most exalted. He will surely be pleased (when he enters paradise)." [Surah Layl verses 5-21]

It is unanimously agreed that the aforementioned verses were revealed with regards to Abu Bakr Siddeeq ﷺ wherein he is referred to as "Al-Atqaa", in other words, the most devout and the most Allah-fearing person. The verse in Surah Hujuraat reads:

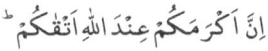

"Verily, the most noble of you (in the eyes of Allah Ta'ala) are those amongst you who are most Allah-conscious." [Surah Hujuraat verse 13]

This clearly indicates that in this Ummah, the most devout person in the sight of Allah Ta'ala after Rasulullah ﷺ is the personage of Abu Bakr Siddeeq ﷺ. After Rasulullah ﷺ, he is the most virtuous person. From the very inception of Islam he sacrificed his life and his wealth for Islam and regularly purchased and freed a great number of slaves. It is said that in the first thirteen years he spent a capital amount of nothing less than forty thousand Dirhams for the benefit of Islam and the Muslims. Whatever was left over was spent in Hijrat and for the purchase of the land for the construction of Masjid-e-Nabawi. When he had not a stitch of clothing left, he wrapped a blanket over himself and appearing before Rasulullah ﷺ declared: "I am extremely pleased with my Lord."

In a nutshell, the Quraysh left no stone unturned in their persecution of the Muslims. They suspended them from the tree-tops, sometimes they tied their feet and pitilessly dragged them about. They even placed heated iron bars on their backs and stomachs. The disbelievers did all sorts of vile things to them but not one of them wavered a notch from the true Deen. They died tolerating these agonising hardships but they did not digress from Islam. May Allah Ta'ala be pleased with them and may they be pleased with Him.

These were people who were either held in servitude by their masters or they were foreigners residing in Makkah. However, even those who enjoyed family honour and social esteem were not spared from the brutal victimisation of the disbelievers. Some of them are as follows:

1. When Hadhrat 'Usmaan Ghani ﷺ embraced Islam, his uncle Haakim bin Abul-'Aas tied him up with a rope and in an attempt to terrify him bellowed at him: "You have the audacity to renounce the creed of your forefathers and embrace a new religion!" To this Hadhrat 'Usmaan ﷺ replied: "By Allah! I will never ever forsake this Deen and I will certainly not abandon it." When his uncle Haakim realised how steadfast and committed he was to this Deen, he released him.

2. When Hadhrat Zubair bin 'Awwaam ﷺ embraced Islam, his uncle wrapped him in a sack and subjected him to incessant palls of smoke. He left no stone unturned in an attempt to compel him to return to Kufr but Hadhrat Zubair bin 'Awwaam ﷺ would utter: "Never! I will certainly not go back to Kufr."

3. When Hadhrat 'Umar's ﷺ brother-in-law, who was also his cousin, Sa'eed bin Zaid embraced Islam, Hadhrat 'Umar ﷺ tied him up with ropes.

4. When Khaalid bin Sa'eed bin 'Aas embraced Islam, his father subjected him to such a bashing that he suffered serious head injuries. His father also deprived him of all meals.

5. When Hadhrat Abu Bakr رضى الله عنه and Hadhrat Talhah رضى الله عنه accepted Islam, Nafal bin Khuwaylid – who was celebrated as 'the lion of the Quraysh' – got hold of both of them and tied them up with one rope. This is why Abu Bakr and Talhah were referred to as Qarnain. (In other words, two people yoked together with a single rope.)

6. When Waleed bin Waleed, 'Ayyaash bin Rabi'ah and Salamah bin Hishaam embraced Islam, the disbelievers of Makkah put them through such pitiless hardships that they did not even allow these people to migrate. At least this migration would have brought them some respite from their difficulties. Whilst in Madinah Munawwarah, in the Fajr Salaah, Rasulullah صلى الله عليه وسلم continued making dua for their safe release from the clutches of the Makkan disbelievers. He would plead with Allah: "O Allah! Liberate Waleed bin Waleed, 'Ayyaash bin Rabi'ah and Salamah bin Hishaam from the tyrannical clutches of the disbelievers."

7. When Hadhrat Abu Zarr Ghifaari رضى الله عنه embraced Islam and publicly proclaimed his conversion in the midst of the Masjidul-Haraam, the disbelievers gave him such a beating that he fell unconscious to the ground. Hadhrat 'Abbaas رضى الله عنه rescued him from their clutches.

The Miracle of the Splitting of the Moon

اِقْتَرَبَتِ السَّاعَةُ وَ انْشَقَّ الْقَمَرُ ۝

"The hour has dawned and the moon has split asunder." [Surah Qamar, verse 1]

Approximately five years prior to the migration to Madinah, the disbelievers of Makkah approached Rasulullah صلى الله عليه وسلم. Amongst them were Waleed bin Mughirah, 'Aas bin Waa'il, 'Aas bin Hishaam, Aswad bin 'Abdi Yaghuth, Aswad bin Muttalib, Zam'ah bin Aswad, Nadr bin Haaris, etc. They challenged Rasulullah صلى الله عليه وسلم to exhibit some sign that would corroborate the authenticity of his prophethood. According to some narrations, they demanded that he split the moon into two parts to demonstrate the legitimacy of his claim. They challenged him at night when the fourteenth moon was shining in all its glory. Rasulullah صلى الله عليه وسلم replied: "Fine, if I exhibit this miracle, would you embrace Islam?" "Surely," they replied, "We would certainly believe in you." Rasulullah صلى الله عليه وسلم then implored Allah Ta'ala and thereafter directed his blessed finger towards the moon. The moment he pointed towards the moon, it split into two; one part towards Mt. Abu Qubais and the other towards Mt. Qayqa'an. For quite a while, people were left dumbfounded staring at this incredible sight. Some of them were so astounded that they repeatedly wiped their eyes with their clothing and gaped at the moon only to discover that it really was in two parts. Rasulullah ﷺ continued prompting them: "Ish-hadoo! Bear witness: Bear witness!" The moon remained like this for a duration of time equivalent to the time between 'Asr and Maghrib. It subsequently reverted to its original condition. In disgust, the disbelievers of Makkah exclaimed: "Nay, Muhammad! You have cast a wizardly spell over all of us. Wait for some travellers coming into Makkah from the outer regions. Ask them about this miracle because it is not possible for Muhammad to cast his spell over everybody. If they testify to this miraculous sighting, then consider Muhammad to be genuine and if they say that they have not witnessed any sighting of this nature, then consider yourselves bewitched by his sorcery." Nonetheless, a number of travellers were asked about this. Travellers from every direction testified that they had seen the moon split into two.

In spite of their own sighting and the testimony of others, these obstinate individuals refused to accept Imaan saying: "This is enduring sorcery." In other words, very soon, the effects of it will wear away. Upon this, the following verses were revealed:

$$ \text{اِقْتَرَبَتِ السَّاعَةُ وَ انْشَقَّ الْقَمَرُ ۞ وَ اِنْ يَّرَوْا اٰيَةً يُّعْرِضُوْا وَ يَقُوْلُوْا سِحْرٌ مُّسْتَمِرٌّ ۞} $$

"The hour has dawned and the moon has split asunder. And if they witness any sign, they turn away and say: 'enduring sorcery'." [Surah Qamar, verse 1-2]

The Miracle of the Return of the Sun

From amongst the prominent miracles of Rasulullah ﷺ, one of them is the return of the sun, in other words, the re-emergence of the sun after sunset. Hadhrat Asma bint 'Umais رضى الله عنها relates: "Rasulullah ﷺ was in a place called Sahba near Khaybar. He was resting with his head on Ali's رضى الله عنه lap. Hadhrat Ali رضى الله عنه had not as yet performed his 'Asr Salaah when Wahi (divine revelation) started streaming forth. The descent of revelation continued until sunset. Rasulullah ﷺ enquired from Hadhrat Ali رضى الله عنه if he had performed his 'Asr Salaah. When he replied in the negative, Rasulullah ﷺ raised his hands in dua and beseeched Allah Ta'ala: "O Allah! Ali was in the submission of Your Rasool. I beg You to return the sun so that he may perform his 'Asr Salaah on time."

Hadhrat Asma رضى الله عنها continues: "After sunset, the sun re-emerged with its rays falling on the earth and the mountains."

The Miracle of the Halting of the Sun

This miracle (of the halting of the sun) occurred in Makkah Mukarramah. When Rasulullah ﷺ returned from Mi'raaj, he informed the Quraysh of some of the details of this journey. The Quraysh insisted he recount a few specific details about Baitul-Maqdis. They even asked him about one of their trade caravans which had journeyed to Syria, (that since he claims that he went to Syria) when was it expected to return to Makkah. Rasulullah ﷺ replied: "The caravan is expected to enter Makkah on Wednesday." As Wednesday was drawing to a close and the sun was about to set, the disbelievers caused a huge uproar. At that moment Rasulullah ﷺ made dua. Allah Ta'ala halted the sun at that point until the caravan entered the city of Makkah. In this manner, Allah Ta'ala further verified the credibility of Rasulullah ﷺ.

The First Migration to Abyssinia

When the disbelievers noticed that day-by-day more and more people are entering the fold of Islam and the sphere of Islam is growing progressively larger, they unanimously resolved to step up their persecution of the Muslims. In this manner, they started to systematically harass the Muslims in an all-out bid to force them to renounce Islam. Rasulullah ﷺ then advised the Sahaabah ﷺ thus:

تفرقوا فى الارض فان الله سيجمعكم قالوا الى اين نذهب قال الى هنا و اشار بيده الى ارض الحبشه

"Spread out onto the earth. Soon Allah Ta'ala would assemble all of you." They enquired: "Where should we go to?" Rasulullah ﷺ indicated with his hand towards the land of Habshah (Abyssinia).

Rasulullah ﷺ also informed them that a king, in whose territory nobody is oppressed by another, rules this land.

The Sahaabah ﷺ did not wish to flee because of their physical persecution or because of their external agony but because they were distressed by the spiritual turmoil of disbelief and polytheism and in order to protect themselves from the oppressive opposition to Deen and Imaan, thus they fled towards Allah Ta'ala. Their purpose of emigration was to take the name of Allah Ta'ala in peace and tranquillity.

In the month of Rajab in the fifth year of prophethood a small group of men and women made the first Hijrah towards Abyssinia. They were:

Men:

1. 'Usmaan bin Affaan ﷺ
2. Abu Huzaifah bin 'Utbah ﷺ
3. Abu Salamah bin 'Abdul Asad ﷺ
4. 'Aamir bin Rabi'ah ﷺ
5. Abu Sabrah bin Abu Rahm 'Aamiri ﷺ
6. 'Abdur-Rahmaan bin 'Awf ﷺ
7. Zubair bin 'Awwaam ﷺ
8. Mus'ab bin 'Umair ﷺ
9. 'Usmaan bin Maz'oon ﷺ
10. Suhail bin Bayda ﷺ
11. Haatib bin 'Amr ﷺ

Women:

1. Ruqayyah ﷺ, the daughter of Rasulullah ﷺ and the wife of 'Usmaan ﷺ.
2. Sahlah bint Suhail ﷺ, the wife of Abu Huzaifah ﷺ
3. Umme Salamah bint Abu Umayyah ﷺ, the wife of Abu Salamah ﷺ. She married Rasulullah ﷺ after the death of Abu Salamah ﷺ gaining the title of mother of the believers.
4. Layla bint Abi Hathamah ﷺ, the wife of 'Aamir bin Rabi'ah ﷺ
5. Umme Kulsoom bint Suhail bin 'Amr ﷺ, the wife of Abu Sabrah bin Abu Rahm ﷺ

These eleven men and five women secretly slipped out of Makkah. Some of them were mounted whilst the others were on foot. To their good fortune, when they landed at the port (of Jeddah), two merchant ships were on the point of setting sail to Abyssinia. For a fare of just five dirhams, they took all of them on board. When the disbelievers of Makkah got wind of their stealthy departure from Makkah, they despatched their people to hunt them down. By the time these trackers reached the port, the ships had already set sail. These emigrants boarded ship from the coast of Jeddah.

They settled in Abyssinia from Rajab right up to Shawwaal. In Shawwaal they got word of the people of Makkah embracing Islam. So they all set off for Makkah. As they drew close to Makkah, they learnt that the information they received was only a rumour. This threw all of them into an agonising dilemma. Some of them secretly slipped into Makkah whilst others entered the city under the protection of someone or the other.

The Second Migration to Abyssinia

The disbelievers started harassing the Muslims even more than ever. This is why Rasulullah ﷺ permitted a second migration towards Abyssinia.

When the Quraysh realised that the Sahaabah رضى الله عنهم were quite at ease in Abyssinia and they were peacefully adhering to the tenets of Islam, the Quraysh held an urgent meeting. At this meeting they resolved to appoint 'Amr bin Aas and 'Abdullah bin Abi Rabi'ah as their representatives to Negus, the emperor of Abyssinia. The assembly resolved to despatch these two emissaries with gifts and presents to Negus and his ministers to try and win them over.

Accordingly, 'Amr bin 'Aas and 'Abdullah bin Abi Rabi'ah landed in Abyssinia and to start with, they offered their gifts to Negus' consorts and confidants. They appealed to them saying: "A few foolish and immature fugitives of our city have renounced their ancestral religion and taken refuge in your city. In fact, they abandoned their ancestral religion not in favour of your religion of Christianity but they have opted for an entirely new religion, of which, neither of us are aware. The leaders of our clan have commissioned us to request the emperor to hand them over to us. We plead with you to intercede to the emperor on our behalf to hand them over to us without discussion and deliberation." Nonetheless, after presenting their gifts and pleading their case before the courtiers, the Makkan emissaries received overwhelming support. 'Amr bin 'Aas and 'Abdullah bin Abi Rabi'ah were not in favour of the emperor summoning the Sahaabah رضى الله عنهم and speaking to them. They did not want the emperor to give the Sahaabah رضى الله عنهم a fair hearing.

The readers can very well imagine why they were averse to the emperor interviewing and speaking to the Sahaabah رضى الله عنهم and why they wanted the emperor to hand them over without any form of investigation and discussion. The reason is quite obvious; they very well knew that the moment the truth left their tongues, it would entrench itself into the heart.

In short, these emissaries pleaded their case before the emperor whilst the courtiers conveyed their overwhelming support in favour of surrendering the Sahaabah رضى الله عنهم to these people, but what they dreaded is exactly what happened. The emperor was thrown into a rage. He made it clear to them that he is unable to hand them over without proper investigation and without speaking to them. He said: "How can I, without any form of formal investigation, surrender to their enemies those who have sought refuge in my kingdom?" He then sent one of his messengers to summon the Sahaabah رضى الله عنهم. When the messenger conveyed the royal summons, a Sahaabi alarmingly asked: "What would you say when you are in the emperor's court?" (In other words, the emperor is a Christian whilst we are Muslims. We clash on a number of fundamental beliefs.) Another Sahaabi confidently said: "In the imperial court, we will say whatever our Nabi ﷺ has taught us and we will do as he had coached us. We will not breach his instructions."

Nonetheless, when they landed at the imperial court, they made do with Salaam only instead of the customary prostration before the emperor. The royal courtiers were naturally quite enraged at the Muslims by this apparent disregard for royal etiquette. The courtiers at once challenged the Muslims and asked: "Why didn't you bow down before the majestic presence of the emperor?" According to another narration, the emperor himself asked why they failed to bow down before him. Hadhrat Ja'far رضى الله عنه replied: "We do not bow down before anyone other than Allah. Allah Ta'ala has sent a messenger to us and he instructed us not to prostrate to anyone but Allah." The other Muslims added: "We Muslims greet Rasulullah ﷺ also in this manner with Salaam only. Our Rasool ﷺ also informed us that the inhabitants of Jannah would greet each other in a similar manner with Salaam. As for prostrating before anyone, Allah Ta'ala forbid, how can we prostrate before you and equate you with Allah?"

Addressing the Muslims, Negus then enquired: "Apart from idol-worship and Christianity, what other faith did you adopt?" In response to the emperor's enquiry, Hadhrat Ja'far رضى الله عنه got to his feet to address the court on behalf of the Sahaabah رضى الله عنهم.

The Inspirational Sermon of Ja'far رضى الله عنه in the Court of Negus

"O emperor! All of us were ignorant. We would worship idols and devour carrion. We were immersed in a host of vices. We would cut off family relationships and ill-treat our neighbours. The powerful amongst us would oppress the weak. Whilst we were wallowing within such an abyss of spiritual decadence, Allah Ta'ala favoured us with one of His messengers whose noble lineage, truthfulness, honesty and chastity we are fully aware of. He ordered us to worship Allah Ta'ala and believe in Him alone. He instructed us to devote ourselves to the sole worship of Allah Ta'ala and to renounce the idols we and our forefathers used to revere. He charged us to speak the truth, be honest, maintain favourable family ties and good neighbourly relations and to abstain from bloodshed and other prohibitions. He also prevented us from immorality, falsehood, devouring the wealth of orphans and from falsely slandering a chaste woman. He commanded us to worship Allah Ta'ala Alone without ascribing any partners unto Him. He enjoined us to perform

Salaah, pay Zakaat and observe fasting. In short, we should not be hesitant with our lives and wealth in the path of Allah Ta'ala."

Enumerating a number of other Islamic injunctions, Hadhrat Ja'far رَضِىَاللهُعَنْهُ ultimately said: "So we believe in him and we have faith in him. And we have adhered to whatever he has conveyed to us from Allah Ta'ala. We worship Allah alone and we do not ascribe any partner unto Him. We do what is Halaal and we abstain from Haraam. Because of this, our people have started to harass us. They have subjected us to numerous forms of mistreatment in a bid to force us to renounce the worship of Allah Ta'ala and revert to our former days of shamelessness. When we were unable to bear their ruthless persecution any longer and the worship of Allah Ta'ala and adherence to His Deen became somewhat difficult, we decided to emigrate with the hope that you would not oppress us. We gave preference to your neighbourliness over everything else."

Negus asked: "Do you remember any part of the divine word your Messenger has brought from Allah Ta'ala?" When Hadhrat Ja'far replied in the affirmative, Negus requested him to recite a portion of it. Hadhrat Ja'far رَضِىَاللهُعَنْهُ commenced reciting the opening verses of Surah Maryam. The emperor and all his courtiers were unable to contain themselves. They started weeping profusely so much so that the emperor's beard was drenched in tears. (It appears that the emperor had a beard and this is also the way of all the Ambiyaa. Not a single Nabi ever shaved his beard. Keeping a beard is a distinctive Sunnah of all the Ambiyaa عَلَيْهِمُالسَّلَام.)

When Hadhrat Ja'far رَضِىَاللهُعَنْهُ terminated his recitation, the emperor exclaimed: "These words and the words imparted by 'Isa عَلَيْهِالسَّلَام are of the same spiritual order." He then bluntly addressed the Qurayshi delegation saying: "I will neither surrender these people to you nor is there a remote possibility of me doing so."

When 'Amr bin 'Aas and 'Abdullah bin Abi Rabi'ah emerged terribly unproductive from the imperial court, 'Amr bin 'Aas confidently declared: "Tomorrow I will once more present my case before the king and I will make such an effective claim that the emperor will annihilate them all." 'Abdullah bin Abi Rabi'ah pleaded: "Don't ever do something that would put their lives in danger. They are, after all, our own flesh and blood. These are our relatives even though we are poles apart as far as our religion is concerned." But 'Amr bin 'Aas was adamant. He did not bother with 'Abdullah's plea. On the following day, 'Amr bin 'Aas presented himself once again in the imperial court and said: "O Emperor! These people express somewhat offensive words in regards to 'Isa عَلَيْهِالسَّلَام." The emperor summoned the Sahaabah رَضِىَاللهُعَنْهُم yet again. The Sahaabah رَضِىَاللهُعَنْهُم were pretty distraught by this sudden turn of events. When one of the Sahaabah رَضِىَاللهُعَنْهُ asked what they would say about 'Isa عَلَيْهِالسَّلَام, all of them unanimously pledged that they will say precisely what Allah Ta'ala and His Rasool صَلَّىاللهُعَلَيْهِوَسَلَّم said. They would not waver on this subject.

When they reached the imperial court, the emperor addressed the Muslims saying: "What is your opinion about 'Isa عَلَيْهِالسَّلَام? Hadhrat Ja'far رَضِىَاللهُعَنْهُ replied:

"Our view is precisely the same as our Prophet's ﷺ view; Hadhrat 'Isa عَلَيْهِ السَّلَام was a servant and a Prophet of Allah. He was the Ruh (soul) and Kalimah (word) of Allah." Upon this account, emperor Negus picked up a particle from the ground and raising it said: "By Allah! Whatever the Muslims have professed, 'Isa عَلَيْهِ السَّلَام is nothing more than that, not even to the extent of this particle."

This proclamation really threw the courtiers into dismay. All of them wrinkled their brows in displeasure but Emperor Negus was not bothered in the least. He told them in no uncertain terms that you may frown in displeasure as much as you like but this is the reality. He then addressed the Muslims: "You may live here in absolute peace. I would not want to harass you even after procuring a mountain of gold (from your enemies)." He then bade his courtiers to return the gifts of the Quraysh saying: "I have no need for their offerings. By Allah! Allah has blessed me with power and empire without bribery of any sort. So I will definitely not accept any bribery and hand the Muslims over to you."

This signalled the end of the royal assembly. The Muslims emerged from the court delighted and in high spirits whilst the Qurayshi delegation left the court in shame and dejection.

Hadhrat 'Aa'ishah رَضِيَ اللهُ عَنْهَا narrated that Negus's father was the emperor of Abyssinia. He had no other son besides Negus whilst the emperor's brother i.e. Negus's uncle had twelve sons. Once, some of the citizens of Abyssinia were struck with a rather weird idea. They reasoned that since Negus is the only son of his father and the emperor's brother i.e. Negus's uncle has a number of children, we should assassinate the current emperor and install his brother on the throne. They felt that since he has a number of children, the reign of power would persist in the same family for a much longer period of time. Accordingly, they assassinated him and installed his brother as the next emperor. Negus fell into the custody of his uncle, the present emperor. Negus was exceptionally bright and intelligent. This is why nobody else enjoyed such status in the eyes of the emperor as he did, so much so that Negus was seen to be taking charge in virtually all the affairs of the kingdom. The citizens of Abyssinia were perturbed at his intelligence, which they imagined would drive him to seek revenge for the assassination of his father. This is why they tried to influence the emperor to kill him. The emperor retorted: "Yesterday you killed his father and today you wish to kill him. It is not possible for me to meet your demands. Yes, the most I can do is to expel him from here and separate him from us." The people agreed to this proposal. The emperor subsequently sold Negus off to a merchant for six hundred Dirhams. The trader took possession of him and set off. The same evening the emperor was fatally struck by lightning. Now the public was left in turmoil. Who should they appoint as their next emperor? None of the twelve sons seemed appropriate for this task. All twelve of them, from the eldest to the youngest, were foolish and immature. Some people voiced their opinion that if you really wish to be successful, bring Negus back and elect him as your next ruler. People scampered in all directions in search for the merchant who purchased him. They managed to retrieve him from the merchant and installed him as the new emperor. Once he assumed the role of emperor, the merchant returned demanding compensation. Negus returned his six hundred Dirhams to him."

Ummul-Mumineen Hadhrat 'Aa'ishah ﷺ says: "It was a reference to this incident when Negus addressed the Qurayshi emissaries saying: 'Allah has blessed me with power and empire without bribery of any sort'.

Subsequent to this royal proclamation, the Muhaajireen (emigrants) settled down in Abyssinia with ease and tranquillity. When Rasulullah ﷺ migrated to Madinah Munawwarah, most of them left Abyssinia and headed for Madinah. Twenty-four of them took part in the battle of Badr. The remaining Muhaajireen left Abyssinia for Madinah in the company of Hadhrat Ja'far ﷺ in the seventh year of Hijrah around the time of the conquest of Khaybar.

Three questions of Ja'far ﷺ to the Qurayshi delegates

Hadhrat Ja'far ﷺ said to emperor Negus: "I have a few questions for these people. I request you to ask them to respond to my questions.

1. Are we slaves who have absconded from their masters? If we are slaves, then indeed we deserve to be returned to our masters.

When Negus asked 'Amr bin Aas if these people were slaves, he replied: "No! They are not slaves but free and noble."

2. Hadhrat Ja'far ﷺ addressed the king: "Ask them if we have fled after murdering someone? If we killed someone unlawfully, you may promptly surrender us to the custody of the victim's guardians."

Negus addressed 'Amr bin 'Aas:

هل اهرقوا دما بغير حقه

"Did these people unlawfully shed anyone's blood before they fled here?"

'Amr bin 'Aas replied:

لا قطرة من دم

"No! Not a single drop of blood."

3. Hadhrat Ja'far ﷺ asked the emperor to ask them: "Have we fled after usurping someone's wealth? Suppose we are guilty of usurping someone's wealth, we are prepared to reimburse him."

Emperor Negus addressed 'Amr bin 'Aas saying: "If these people fled after illicitly seizing someone's wealth, I am accountable and answerable for it. I stand as guarantor for all penalties as well."

'Amr bin 'Aas replied: "They have not usurped a single Qiraat (cent)."

The emperor then accosted the Qurayshi emissaries saying: "Then what are your demands?"

'Amr bin 'Aas replied: "All of us were adherents of the same religion. Now these people have renounced their own religion and assumed a totally novel religion."

Addressing the Sahaabah رضى الله عنه, the emperor asked: "What was the religion you renounced and what is this new religion you have adopted?"

Hadhrat Ja'far رضى الله عنه replied:

اما الذى كنا عليه فدين الشيطان وامر الشيطان نكفر بالله ونعبد الحجارة واما الذى نحن عليه فدين الله عزوجل نخبرك ان الله بعث الينا رسولا كما بعث الى الذين من قبلنا فاتانا بالصدق والبر ونهانا عن عبادة الاوثان فصدقناه وامنا به واتبعناه فلما فعلنا ذلك عادانا قومنا وارادوا قتل النبى الصادق و ردنا فى عبادة الاوثان ففررنا اليك بديننا ودمائنا ولوا قرنا قومنا لاستقررنا فذلك خبرنا

"As for our previous religion, it was the creed of shaytaan and the mandate of shaytaan. It was a creed wherein we disbelieved in Allah Ta'ala and worshipped stones. As for the religion we have now adopted, it is the religion of Allah Ta'ala. Allah Ta'ala sent a Messenger to us as He had sent prophets and divine messengers to those before us. This Prophet appeared before us with truthfulness and virtue and he forbade us from idol-worship. So we placed our faith in him and believed in everything he said. We have become his true adherents. As a result of this, our people turned against us in hostile enmity. They wish to slay this truthful Prophet and they expect us to return to idol-worship. So we fled with our religion and lives towards you. Had our people allowed us to remain within our native land, we would have remained. This is our story."

When Hadhrat Ja'far ؓ and his companions ultimately decided to leave Abyssinia for Madinah, emperor Negus bore all their travel costs and supplied them with provisions for the journey as well. Furthermore, he presented them with a number of gifts and he sent a messenger along with them saying: "Kindly inform Rasulullah ﷺ about my conduct with you. Also notify him that I bear testimony that there is none worthy of worship save Allah and I also bear testimony that you are His Messenger. I also plead with you to seek forgiveness from Allah Ta'ala on my behalf."

Hadhrat Ja'far ؓ relates: "We left Abyssinia and headed towards Madinah. When we reached the presence of Rasulullah ﷺ, he hugged me and remarked: 'I wonder if the conquest of Khaybar has brought me more joy or the arrival of Ja'far has brought me more joy.'

Rasulullah ﷺ then took a seat. The messenger of Negus stood up and said: '(O Prophet of Allah Ta'ala!) Here Ja'far is right before you. Ask him how our emperor had treated him.' Hadhrat Ja'far replied: 'No doubt, Negus gave us a warm welcome. He treated us in such and such manner. In fact, when we decided to depart from Abyssinia, he provided us with conveyances and provisions for the journey. He offered us his constant assistance. He also testified that there is none worthy of worship save Allah and he testified that you are the Messenger of Allah. He also requests that you make dua of forgiveness in his favour.'"

Rasulullah ﷺ instantly got to his feet, performed wudhu and recited the following dua thrice:

اللّٰهم اغفر للنجاشى

"O Allah! Forgive Najaashi (Negus)."

The Muslims uttered Aameen upon this dua.

Hadhrat Ja'far ؓ relates: "I requested the emperor's messenger to describe whatever he has witnessed about Rasulullah ﷺ to his emperor on his return to Abyssinia."

Islam of 'Umar bin Khattaab ؓ - 6th year of Prophethood

The actual cause of Hadhrat 'Umar's ؓ conversion to Islam was the dua of Rasulullah ﷺ.

Initially Rasulullah ﷺ would make dua (secretly) as follows: "O Allah! Boost the honour of Islam with either Abu Jahal or 'Umar bin Khattaab, whoever is most dear to You."

Ibn 'Asaakir says that subsequently, Rasulullah ﷺ was enlightened by divine revelation that Abu Jahal would certainly not embrace Islam. So he made dua exclusively for Hadhrat 'Umar ؓ in the following words:

اللهم اید الاسلام بعمر بن الخطاب خاصةً

"O Allah! Strengthen Islam particularly with 'Umar bin Khattaab."

In short, the actual cause of 'Umar's ﷺ conversion to Islam was the magnetic dua of Rasulullah ﷺ. As for the external cause of his conversion, it is what he himself narrates.

Hadhrat 'Umar ﷺ relates: "In the beginning I was a bitter enemy of Rasulullah ﷺ and I harboured a vehement loathing towards Islam."

بد عمر رانام ایں جابت پرست
لیک مؤمن بود نامش در الست

"In this world, 'Umar's name was amongst the idolaters but in the realm of the souls, his name was inscribed amongst the Mumineen."

Hadhrat 'Umar ﷺ narrates: "Abu Jahal publicly proclaimed that he guaranteed to confer one hundred camels in prize money to whoever killed Muhammad. I went directly to Abu Jahal enquiring whether this guarantee was genuine or not. When he replied in the affirmative, I set out with my sword in quest of Muhammad's blood. As I was walking, I came across a calf, which some people were about to slaughter. I also stood by to watch. Suddenly, I heard a voice coming out from the calf's stomach exclaiming:

يَا آلَ ذَرِيْحٍ. اَمْرٌ نَجِيْحٌ. رَجُلٌ يَصِيْحُ بلسانٍ فصيح يدعو الى شهادة ان لا اله الا الله وان محمدا رسول الله

"O family of Zarih! This is a mighty successful affair. There is a man who proclaims in an eloquent tongue. He invites people to the testimony of Laa Ilaaha Illallahu wa Anna Muhammadar-Rasulullah."

The moment this voice fell onto my ears I guessed that this voice is being directed towards me. I am the addressee of this voice.

In spite of this, 'Umar did not detract from his disgusting ambition and he pressed on. He barely took a few steps when he met Nu'aim bin 'Abdullah Nahhaam. "Where are you off to at this time of the afternoon?" he asked. "'Umar replied: "I am on my way to eliminate Muhammad (ﷺ)." Nu'aim commented: "Once you assassinate Muhammad (ﷺ), how do you expect to protect yourself from the families of Bani Haashim and Bani Zuhrah?" 'Umar furiously retorted: "It seems you too have turned Saabi (apostate). You also renounced the religion of your ancestors!" Nu'aim defended himself saying: "Why are you accusing me? Don't you know that your sister Faatimah bint Khattaab and your brother-in-law Sa'eed bin Zaid also turned Saabi? Have you not heard that they also renounced your ancestral religion in favour of Islam?"

'Umar was thrown into a rage of fury at this 'distasteful' news and set out at once for his sister's place. Hadhrat Khabbaab رضي الله عنه who was engaged in teaching Umar's sister and brother-in-law, hid away the moment he heard the footsteps of Umar.

'Umar stormed into the house and enraged with his sister and brother-in-law, yelled: "It seems both of you have become apostates?" His brother-in-law replied: "Umar! Tell me, if your religion is not true whilst another religion is true, what should one do?" The moment this statement left his lips, Umar pounced onto him. His sister valiantly intervened to protect her husband but he struck her so brutally that her face was left full of blood. His sister remarked: "O Son of Khattaab! Do whatever you can. We have embraced Islam. O enemy of Allah! You are subjecting us to this misery merely because we believe in the Oneness of Allah? Bear in mind that we have embraced Islam in spite of your bitterness against this."

On hearing these daring words from his sister, 'Umar was left somewhat embarrassed. "Okay," he addressed his sister: "Show me the book you were reading just now." The instant Umar said this, Hadhrat Khabbaab رضي الله عنه, who was hiding in a corner of the house suddenly emerged.

His sister said:

انك رجس وانه لا يمسه الا المطهرون فقم فتوضأ

"You are unclean. Nobody but the pure are allowed to touch it (the Qur-aan). Go and perform wudhu before you touch it."

'Umar got to his feet and either performed wudhu or ghusal. He then took hold of the sacred writings and started reciting from Surah Taa-Haa until he reached the verse:

اِنَّنِىٓ اَنَا اللّٰهُ لَآ اِلٰهَ اِلَّآ اَنَا فَاعْبُدْنِىْ وَ اَقِمِ الصَّلٰوةَ لِذِكْرِىْ ﴿١٤﴾

"Certainly I am Allah! There is no other being worthy of worship but Me. So worship Me and establish Salaah for My remembrance." (Surah Maryam: Verse 14)

The moment he came across this verse, he could not help but declare: "What magnificent and gracious words!"

On hearing Umar say this, Hadhrat Khabbaab رضي الله عنه joyously remarked: "O Umar! Glad tidings unto you! I imagine the dua Rasulullah ﷺ made in your favour has been accepted." Umar رضي الله عنه said: "O Khabbaab! Take me to Rasulullah ﷺ."

Hadhrat Khabbaab رضي الله عنه took Umar along and headed off in the direction of Daarul Arqam where Rasulullah ﷺ and the Sahaabah رضي الله عنهم would frequently congregate. The door was closed. He knocked on the door and requested permission to enter. When the occupants gathered that Umar sought to enter, none of them dared to open the door. However, Hadhrat Hamzah رَضِىَ اللهُ عَنْهُ said: "Go on, open the door and allow him to enter. If Allah Ta'ala wishes to grace Umar with His good fortune, He will certainly guide him towards Islam. He will embrace Islam, adhere to the commandments of Allah Ta'ala and comply with the teachings of Rasulullah ﷺ. If he intends otherwise, you will be safe from his evil by the will of Allah. All praises to Allah, it is no great feat for us to put Umar to the sword." According to another narration, Hadhrat Hamzah رَضِىَ اللهُ عَنْهُ said: "If Umar comes to us with a good intention, we will also deal with him favourably but if he has set foot here with evil intentions, we will kill him with his very own sword."

Rasulullah ﷺ also permitted them to open the door. Hadhrat Umar رَضِىَ اللهُ عَنْهُ narrates: "Once the door was thrown open, two people grasped me by the arms and led me before Rasulullah ﷺ. Rasulullah ﷺ asked them to release me and clutching my kurtah (shirt), he drew me towards him saying: "O son of Khattaab! Accept Islam." Saying this, Rasulullah ﷺ made the following dua:

اللّٰهم اهده

"O Allah! Grace Umar with Your divine guidance."

According to another narration, Rasulullah ﷺ made the following dua:

اللّٰهم هذا عمر بن الخطاب اللّٰهمَّ اعز الدين بعمر بن الخطاب

"O Allah! This is Umar bin Khattaab before You. O Allah! Honour the Deen with Umar bin Khattaab."

He then addressed Umar رَضِىَ اللهُ عَنْهُ saying: "O Umar! Would you renounce (your evil) only when Allah Ta'ala drives His humiliating punishment upon you?"

Umar رَضِىَ اللهُ عَنْهُ replied: "O Prophet of Allah! I have presented myself before you to profess my faith in Allah and His Rasool ﷺ and in whatever has been divinely revealed by Him. I bear testimony that there is none worthy of worship but Allah and you are the messenger of Allah."

Gripped by a wave of ecstatic joy, Rasulullah ﷺ called out Takbeer at the top of his voice, by which all the occupants of the house realised that Umar رَضِىَ اللهُ عَنْهُ had embraced Islam.

Ibn 'Abbaas رَضِىَ اللهُ عَنْهُ narrates: "When Umar رَضِىَ اللهُ عَنْهُ entered the fold of Islam, Jibraa'eel عَلَيْهِ السَّلَام descended and said: "O Muhammad ﷺ! All the inhabitants of the heavens are overjoyed at the Islam of Umar."

'Umar ﷺ embraced Islam and this almost instantaneously heralded the honour, exposure and dominance of Islam. People started performing their Salaah openly in the Haram. The dissemination of and invitation towards Islam was carried out more freely and openly. This was the day that laid bare the distinction between truth and falsehood. This is why Rasulullah ﷺ named Umar ﷺ "Al-Faarooq" –the one who distinguishes between truth and falsehood.

Hadhrat Umar ﷺ relates: "When I embraced Islam, I thought to myself that I should inform someone who is proficient in publicising this so that one and all is aware of my Islam. Accordingly, I went up to Jameel bin Mu'ammar who was quite proficient in such a task. I submitted: "O Jameel! Are you aware that I embraced Islam? I have entered the religion of Muhammad ﷺ."

The instant this fell onto Jameel's ears, he, dragging his sheet behind him, scuttled to the Masjidul-Haraam where the chieftains of the Quraysh had assembled. On reaching them, he yelled out: "O People! Umar has turned Saabi (apostate)." I was closely following on his heels. I exclaimed: "No! He is mistaken. I have not turned into a Saabi but I have become a Muslim. I testify that there is none worthy of worship but Allah and that Muhammad ﷺ is His slave and messenger."

The moment people gathered what happened, they fell onto 'Umar striking and hitting him until the day retreated when coincidentally 'Aas bin Waa'il happened to pass by. When asked what happened, the people replied that Umar had become a Saabi. "So what," 'Aas retorted, "A person has the liberty to choose whatever religion he fancies. Why are you interfering in his affairs? Do you think Bani 'Adi will just abandon a member of their clan like this? Go on. Leave him alone, I have offered sanctuary to Umar." The moment 'Aas offered sanctuary to Umar, the crowd dispersed.

Boycott of Banu Haashim and the Penning of an Oppressive Decree

When the Qurayshi emissaries returned disappointed from Abyssinia and the disbelievers learnt of Emperor Negus' admiration for Hadhrat Ja'far ﷺ and his companions, whilst here in Makkah Hadhrat Hamzah ﷺ and Hadhrat 'Umar ﷺ embraced Islam, which further fractured the might of the disbelievers, the Muslims seemed to be growing day by day and when no other strategy appeared to be as effective, all the Qurayshi tribes unanimously agreed to endorse an accord that would summarily suspend all dealings with Muhammad ﷺ, the Banu Haashim and their allies. Amongst others, they resolved not to marry any member of the Banu Haashim tribe or to maintain any sort of cordial relationship with them until the Banu Haashim undertook to surrender Muhammad's ﷺ life to the Quraysh.

They drew up an accord outlining such details and pinned it onto the interior wall of the K'abah. Mansoor bin 'Ikramah, the writer of this oppressive and malicious accord, was instantaneously punished by Allah Ta'ala; his fingers became paralysed and he was unable to use his fingers to write again.

Constrained by these unfavourable circumstances, Abu Taalib, together with members of his family, sought refuge in the valley of Abu Taalib. The Banu Haashim and the Banu-Muttalib – believers and disbelievers – both gave him their full support. The believers offered their support for religious reasons whilst the disbelievers offered their support in honour of family relationship. From the Banu Haashim, only Abu Lahab opted to remain with the Quraysh.

For three long years, these people lived in such dreadful isolation and under the most appalling conditions. The wailing of infants out of acute hunger could be heard right outside the valley where the pitiless Quraysh would hear this anguished crying and cheer in happiness. However, the compassionate from amongst them found this behaviour rather distasteful and bluntly said: "Don't you see what divine retribution was meted out to Mansoor bin 'Ikramah?"

During this dreadful social sanctions imposed upon them, the Muslims lived on Kekar (acacia) leaves and somehow managed to survive. S'ad bin Abi Waqqaas رَضِىَ اللهُ عَنْهُ relates: "I was extremely hungry to the point of starvation. One night, I stepped onto something moist. I immediately picked it up and swallowed it. Up until now I have absolutely no idea what it was."

S'ad bin Abi Waqqaas رَضِىَ اللهُ عَنْهُ relates another such incident. He says: "One night I was on my way to relieve myself when I came across a shrivelled out camel skin. I picked it up, washed it with water and burnt it. I thereafter pounded it into a powder, which I then gulped down with water. I survived on this for full three days."

The restrictions imposed upon the Muslims were further escalated when Abu Lahab instructed the trade caravans not to supply goods to the companions of Muhammad صَلَّى اللهُ عَلَيْهِ وَسَلَّمَ at normal prices but at enormously inflated prices. In fact, Abu Lahab even agreed to bear the traders' losses if any. The Sahaabah رَضِىَ اللهُ عَنْهُمْ would come to purchase from the trade caravans but noticing the outrageous prices would return empty-handed. In short, on the one hand they were distressed by their destitution and tormented by the heavy-handedness of the enemy whilst on the other hand, they were challenged with the heartrending cries and hunger-pangs of the children.

Some people could not stand their family members suffering such anguish and would secretly send some food for them. One day Hakeem bin Hizaam, accompanied by his slave, was taking some provisions for his aunt (father's sister) Hadhrat Khadijah رَضِىَ اللهُ عَنْهَا when Abu Jahal spotted him. He bellowed in fury: "You are taking grains to Banu Haashim! I will never tolerate you taking any food for them. I will humiliate you in front of everyone." Coincidentally, Abul-Bakhtari happened to pass by. On ascertaining what happened, he addressed Abu Jahal saying: "The man is sending some food to his aunt. Why do you have to interfere?" This really added to his fury and he let stream a few abusive words. Abul-Bakhtari picked up a camel bone and whacked Abu Jahal so hard on the head that he sustained a terrible injury to his head. What hurt Abu Jahal more than the actual injury was that Hadhrat Hamzah رَضِىَ اللّٰهُ عَنْهُ was busy witnessing this whole scenario from the valley of Abu Taalib.

Due to these agonising and pathetic hardships the Muslims were facing, some of the disbelievers thought about violating this gruesome accord. The first person who reflected over this was Hishaam bin 'Amr. He dwelled on the fact that they are eating and drinking to their fill whilst their close relatives are longing for just a few grains and they are passing their days in starvation. So every night he would leave a camel-load of grain at the mouth of the valley of Abu Taalib.

One day, Hishaam bin 'Amr took this thought to Zuhair bin Umayyah. He was the grandson of 'Abdul-Muttalib and the son of 'Aatikah bint 'Abdul-Muttalib. In other words, he was Rasulullah's صَلَّى اللّٰهُ عَلَيْهِ وَسَلَّمَ cousin – his father's sister's son. Hishaam went up to Zuhair saying: "O Zuhair! Are you pleased to eat, drink, wear and marry however you want whilst your mother's brother pines for a few grains of food? By Allah! If Abu Jahal's uncle and maternal relations were to suffer such hardships, he would never have bothered about this accord." Zuhair replied: "Alas! I am alone in this. What can I achieve single-handed? If only I can get another sympathiser to assist me I will readily stand up against this immoral accord."

Hishaam bin 'Amr then went to Mut'im bin 'Adi and convinced him as well. Mut'im bin 'Adi in turn convinced another person to defy this accord.

From here, Hishaam went to Abul-Bakhtari and then to Zam'ah bin Al-Aswad to gather further support against this treaty.

When these five people resolved to challenge the treaty, they unanimously agreed to touch on the topic when all the other people gather. Zuhair undertook to steer the conversation towards this topic. The next morning, when the people had assembled in the Masjid, Zuhair rose saying: "O people of Makkah! It is a matter of grave concern and shame that we eat, drink, marry and attire ourselves whilst the Banu Haashim are dying with starvation. By Allah! I will not sit at ease until this oppressive accord is not shredded up." Abu Jahal retorted: "This divine accord of Allah can never be shredded."

Zam'ah bin Aswad commented: "By Allah! It will certainly be shred. Even when this accord was drawn up we were not happy about it." Abul-Bakhtari said: "Yes, Zam'ah is speaking the truth. We were not pleased with the accord." Mut'im added: "Certainly, both of them are true in what they say." Hishaam bin 'Urwah again endorsed what he said. Witnessing the tones of the gathering, Abu Jahal was left thunderstruck and exclaimed: "It seems like some decision was already taken the previous night."

In the meantime, Rasulullah صَلَّى اللّٰهُ عَلَيْهِ وَسَلَّمَ informed his uncle that apart from the names of Allah Ta'ala, ants had eaten up the written accord. Apart from the sentence *Bismika Allahumma* which generally headed every document, the rest of the words had been devoured by ants.

Abu Taalib, whilst narrating this to the Quraysh said: "This is what my nephew says and up to this day, my nephew has never uttered a lie. Whatever he has claimed thus far has never proven to be fictitious. Come, let us make a decision; if Muhammad's claim is true you will refrain from this cruelty and if his claim proves false, I am prepared to surrender Muhammad to you. You may then slay him or set him free." The people said: "Surely, Abu Taalib! You have been reasonably fair."

The written accord was then sent for. When they caught sight of it, they were shocked to discover that apart from the names of Allah Ta'ala, ants had eaten up the rest of the document. All of them lowered their heads in shame and embarrassment.

In this manner, this oppressive accord was finally put to rest. In the tenth year of prohethood, Abu Taalib and all his companions emerged from this desolate valley. Abu Taalib then went to the Haram Shareef and clinging onto the curtain of the K'abah, he and his companions made the following dua: "O Allah! Those who oppressed us, those who severed our family ties and those who put us through such dishonour, O Allah! We beg of You to retaliate on our behalf."

Abu Taalib also composed a poem in this regard. One couplet reads:

الم يأتكم ان الصحيفة مزقت   وان كل مالم يرضه الله يفسد

"Do you not know that the accord was ripped up and whatever displeases Allah Ta'ala is ruined in this manner?"

Hafiz Ibn Katheer says: "When Rasulullah and the Banu Haashim were besieged in the valley of Abu Taalib, Abu Taalib composed his celebrated poem called Qasidah Laamiyyah".

This brought an end to three years of protracted misery and in the tenth year of prohethood, three years before Hijrah, the Muslims were liberated from the valley of Abu Taalib.

Migration of Abu Bakr

During this period, when the Banu Haashim were restrained in the valley of Abu Taalib, Abu Bakr set out with the intention to migrate to Abyssinia (to join the other Abyssinian migrants). When he reached a place called Barkul-Ghamaad, he happened to meet the chieftain of the Qaarah tribe, Ibnud-Daghinah.

"Where are you off to, O Abu Bakr?" asked Ibnud-Daghinah. Abu Bakr replied: "My people have driven me out. I wish to travel in the land of Allah Ta'ala and worship my Lord." Ibnud-Daghinah said: "Abu Bakr! A man of your status does not leave nor is he driven out. You offer provisions to the needy, you maintain favourable family ties, you bear the burdens (debts, penalties etc.) of others, you are exceptionally hospitable and you support the truth. I will take you under my protection. Go on, return home." Ibnud-Daghinah headed towards Makkah and performed Tawaaf in the presence of the chieftains of Quraysh. He then addressed them saying: "A man like Abu Bakr does not just leave nor is he ever banished. You are driving out a man who offers provisions to the needy, who maintains favourable family ties, who bears the burdens of others, who is incredibly hospitable and who supports the truth. I have offered him my personal protection."

The Quraysh accepted this protection offered by Ibnud-Daghinah but added: "Ask Abu Bakr to worship his Lord within the confines of his home. He may perform his Salaah and recite the Qur-aan within his home but he may not publicise whatever he is doing. He may not recite the Qur-aan in an audible tone as this distresses us a great deal. Furthermore, we fear our children and womenfolk may become attracted to Islam."

Ibnud-Daghinah informed Hadhrat Abu Bakr رَضِيَ اللهُ عَنْهُ of their demands and returned home. So Abu Bakr رَضِيَ اللهُ عَنْهُ limited his devotions to his home only. A few days later, Abu Bakr رَضِيَ اللهُ عَنْهُ erected a Masjid (a place exclusively devoted to 'Ibaadah) within the courtyard of his house for the performance of Salaah and the recitation of the Qur-aan.

In spite of him confining his rituals to this area alone, the women and children of the Quraysh would gather around him in rapt concentration. Struck by wonder, they would unceasingly stand and stare at Abu Bakr رَضِيَ اللهُ عَنْهُ. The focus of attention of every single one of them was concentrated upon Abu Bakr رَضِيَ اللهُ عَنْهُ. Due to his intense fear of Allah Ta'ala, Abu Bakr رَضِيَ اللهُ عَنْهُ was a man who wept a lot. Despite being a man (who could control his emotions), Abu Bakr رَضِيَ اللهُ عَنْهُ was helpless in restraining the tears of his eyes whilst reciting the Holy Qur-aan. Notwithstanding his best efforts, he was unable to control his weeping. (This is why the audience were unable to control their hearts. Notwithstanding their best efforts, they were unable to control their hearts whenever Abu Bakr رَضِيَ اللهُ عَنْهُ engaged in tilaawat of the Holy Qur-aan.)

When the chieftains of the Quraysh got wind of this, they were hurled into a state of absolute anxiety and they immediately summoned Ibnud-Daghinah. As he appeared before them, they complained: "We assured Abu Bakr of our non-interference upon your surety provided he worships his Lord in the privacy of his home. We were given the assurance that he will neither worship openly nor will he recite the Qur-aan audibly. Contrary to our stipulated conditions, Abu Bakr has started performing Salaah and reciting the Qur-aan openly. We fear our women and children becoming 'morally corrupt'. We urge you to request Abu Bakr to commit himself to these pre-arranged conditions or alternatively you may withdraw your personal protection from him. We have no intention of violating your personal protection."

To this Hadhrat Abu Bakr ؓ replied: "I am returning your personal protection back to you. I am content with the protection and sanctuary offered by Allah Ta'ala."

Note: The benevolent features of Abu Bakr ؓ as mentioned by Ibnud-Daghinah are precisely the same features of Rasulullah ﷺ as mentioned by Hadhrat Khadijah ؓ (as referred to under the chapter of the commencement of prophethood). This clearly indicates the virtue and excellence of Abu Bakr Siddeeq ؓ and the close correlation between the status of nubuwwat (prophethood) and the status of Siddeeqiyyat.

The Year of Anguish and Bereavement - The death of Khadijatul-Kubra ؓ and Abu Taalib

Merely a few days after emerging from Shi'b Abi Taalib, in the month of Ramadhaan or Shawwaal in the tenth year of prophethood, Abu Taalib passed away and just three or five days after this, Hadhrat Khadijatul-Kubra ؓ also departed from this world.

When Abu Taalib was about to breathe his last, Rasulullah ﷺ drew close to him. Abu Jahal and 'Abdullah bin Umayyah were also present at his bedside. Rasulullah ﷺ pleaded with him: "O uncle! Say *Laa Ilaaha Illallahu* once only so that I may have some basis to intercede on your behalf before Allah Ta'ala." Alarmed by this probability, Abu Jahal and 'Abdullah bin Umayyah exclaimed: "O Abu Taalib! Do you wish to renounce the creed of 'Abdul Muttalib?"

Abu Taalib refused to utter *Laa Ilaaha Illallahu* and the very last words to leave his tongue were "'*Alaa Millati 'Abdil Muttalib*. In other words, I am committed to the creed of 'Abdul Muttalib."

Abu Taalib died saying this but Rasulullah ﷺ pledged, "I will continue to make dua of forgiveness for Him as long as Allah Ta'ala does not prohibit me." Upon this the following verse was revealed:

$$\text{مَا كَانَ لِلنَّبِيِّ وَالَّذِيْنَ اٰمَنُوْۤا اَنْ يَّسْتَغْفِرُوْا لِلْمُشْرِكِيْنَ وَلَوْ كَانُوْۤا اُولِيْ قُرْبٰى مِنْۢ بَعْدِ مَا تَبَيَّنَ لَهُمْ اَنَّهُمْ اَصْحٰبُ الْجَحِيْمِ}$$

"It is not permissible for the Prophet and the believers to seek forgiveness for the disbelievers even if they are relatives when it is evident to them that they are inmates of hell. (In other words, they died in disbelief.)" [Surah Taubah verse 113]

The following verse was also revealed in this regard:

$$\text{اِنَّكَ لَا تَهْدِيْ مَنْ اَحْبَبْتَ وَلٰكِنَّ اللّٰهَ يَهْدِيْ مَنْ يَّشَآءُ}$$

"You are unable to guide whom you wish but Allah guides whomsoever he chooses to." [Surah Qasas verse 56]

Hadhrat 'Abbaas ﷺ relates: "I asked Rasulullah ﷺ, 'Of what benefit were you to your uncle? After all, he was your benefactor and he provided you his unstinting support.' Rasulullah ﷺ replied: 'He is up to his ankles in the fire. Had I failed to intercede on his behalf, he would have been in the midst of the fire of Jahannam.'"

Note: 'Allaamah Suhayli says: "Abu Taalib was fully immersed in supporting and assisting Rasulullah ﷺ. Only his feet (so to say) were ensnared in the creed of 'Abdul Muttalib. This is why only his feet were enveloped by the divine chastisement (as mentioned above)."

$$\text{رَبَّنَا اَفْرِغْ عَلَيْنَا صَبْرًا وَّثَبِّتْ اَقْدَامَنَا وَانْصُرْنَا عَلَى الْقَوْمِ الْكٰفِرِيْنَ}$$

"O our Lord! Dispense upon us patience and secure our feet and assist us against the disbelieving nation."

Hadhrat Ali ﷺ narrates: "When Abu Taalib died, I notified Rasulullah ﷺ: 'O Prophet of Allah! Your deviated uncle has died.' Rasulullah ﷺ responded: 'Go and bury him.' I submitted: 'He died a Mushrik.' Rasulullah ﷺ said: 'All the same, go and bury him.'"

According to another narration, when Hadhrat Ali ﷺ reappeared before Rasulullah ﷺ on his return from burying Abu Taalib, Rasulullah ﷺ instructed him to take a bath. This is why the jurists and 'Ulama maintain that it is preferable to take a bath after administering the Ghusl and burial of a disbeliever.

Journey to Taaif for the Propagation of Islam

Following the departure of Abu Taalib from this world, Rasulullah ﷺ was left with no apparent benefactor and supporter and after the demise of Hadhrat Khadijah ﷺ, he was left with no sympathiser and comforter. This is why, at the end of Shawwaal in the tenth year of prophethood, strained by the heavy-handedness of the Quraysh of Makkah, Rasulullah ﷺ decided to journey to Taaif. Perhaps, he reflected, these inhabitants would embrace the divine guidance of Allah Ta'ala and turn out to be the supporters and benefactors of this Deen. Accompanied by Zaid Bin Haarisah ﷺ, Rasulullah ﷺ set out for Taaif.

Rasulullah ﷺ presented Islam to 'Abdiyaalil, Mas'ood and Habib – three brothers who were the chieftains of that area. Instead of lending an ear to the words of truth, they responded in an awfully ruthless manner. One of them remarked: "Did Allah Ta'ala commission you as a prophet to rip apart the curtains of the K'abah?" Another mockingly commented: "Could Allah Ta'ala not choose someone else for His prophethood?" The third brother bellowed: "By Allah! I absolutely refuse to speak to you! If you have truly been commissioned as a divine messenger, it is terribly dangerous to defy you. (This foolish man failed to understand that ridiculing and poking fun at a prophet is even more dangerous than that.) If you are not the Prophet of Allah, then you neither merit my attention nor are you worth our consideration."

He then incited the immoral vagrants and other uncouth youngsters to hurl stones at him and poke fun at him. These heartless inhabitants lobbed so many stones upon his blessed body that they gravely wounded him. Whenever Rasulullah ﷺ was overwhelmed by his injuries and forced to sit down, these unfortunate souls would seize him by the arm and force him to stand up again for another spell of stone throwing and mockery.

Zaid bin Haarisah ؓ, who also went along on this journey, selflessly tried to protect Rasulullah ﷺ by bodily shielding him from the barrage of stones. This left him with serious head injuries whilst Rasulullah ﷺ suffered serious injuries to his (body and) legs so much so that blood streamed down his legs (into his shoes).

On his return from Taaif, Rasulullah ﷺ decided to take a breath under a tree in the garden of 'Utbah bin Rabi'ah and Shaybah bin Rabi'ah. As he sat down, he humbly expressed his helplessness before Allah Ta'ala by offering the following dua:

اللّٰهُمَّ اِلَيْكَ اَشْكُوْ ضُعْفَ قوتى وقلة حيلتى وهوانى على الناس يا ارحم الراحمين انت رب المستضعفين الى من تكلنى الى عدو بعيد يتجهمنى ام الى صديق قريب ملكته امرى ان لم تكن غضبانا على فلا ابالى غير ان عافيتك اوسع لى اعوذ بنور وجهك الذى اشرقت له الظلمات وصلح عليه امر الدنيا والاخرة من ان تنزل بى غضبك او يحلَّ بى سخطك ولك العتبى حتى ترضى ولا حول ولا قوة الا بك

"O Allah! Only to You do I complain of my infirmity, my inadequate strategies and of my humiliation before the people. O most merciful of the merciful! You are the Lord of the weak and helpless. To whom do You consign me? Would You condemn me to an impolite and ill-tempered enemy who will enrage me or would You consign me to a close friend to whom You would entrust my affairs? If You are not angry with me, I am not concerned in the least but Your protection and safety is more accommodating and pleasant to me. I seek refuge with the Noor (radiance) of Your

being that has brightened the darkness and the radiance upon which the affairs of this world and the hereafter depend, with the medium of this radiance I seek Your refuge, O Allah, from Your wrath descending upon me or from Your fury being unleashed over me. And only to You (do I wish to express my lamentations) until You are content. There is no power (to repel evil) nor might (to do good) but only that which You have decreed."

The status of prophethood would have sufficed for the acceptance of duas because every prophet is a Mustajaabud-D'awaat (one whose duas are promptly accepted by Allah Ta'ala). However, at this moment, apart from the attribute of prophethood, a pitiable condition of adversity, victimisation, alienation and Musaafarat (a state of travelling) further complemented this condition of acceptance of duas. Allah Ta'ala says:

اَمَّنْ يُّجِيْبُ الْمُضْطَرَّ اِذَا دَعَاهُ وَ يَكْشِفُ السُّوْٓءَ

"Who is the one who would respond to (the duas) of the person afflicted by adversity when he calls unto Him, and He removes evil."

Furthermore, in regards to a traveller and an oppressed person, both of them are clearly and independently mentioned in the Hadith that their duas are indisputably accepted.

بترس از آہ مظلوماں کہ ہنگام دعا کردن
اجابت از در حق بہر استقبال می آید

"Beware the sigh of the oppressed for the gates of acceptance readily welcomes his dua in the Divine Court of Allah Ta'ala."

You can very well imagine the duas of a personage of such noble character who besides being a divine messenger is also a victim of adversity, oppression, alienated and travelling on a journey. Such a dua barely left his lips when the doors of acceptance were flung open.

The same 'Utbah and Shaybah, whose hearts were harder than stone, turned soft when they caught sight of Rasulullah's ﷺ sad and pitiable condition. The blood of their kinship and the veins of their patriotism surged forth (in their concern for his welfare). They charged their slave 'Addaas to fill a tray with grapes and take it to the man sitting in the garden. They instructed him to request the man to partake of it. 'Addaas brought the tray to Rasulullah ﷺ and placed it before him. Rasulullah ﷺ recited *Bismillah* and commenced eating. 'Addaas commented: "By Allah! Nobody in that city has ever expressed such words." Rasulullah ﷺ asked: "Where are you from and what religion do you follow?" 'Addaas replied: "I am a resident of the city of Nenwaa and I am a

Christian by faith." Rasulullah ﷺ enquired: "Is this the same Nenwaa where the devout servant of Allah, Yunus bin Matta lived?" Taken aback, 'Addaas responded: "What knowledge do you have about Yunus bin Matta?" Rasulullah ﷺ replied: "He was my brother, a Messenger and I am also a Messenger." 'Addaas kissed Rasulullah ﷺ on his forehead, hands and legs and submitted: "I bear testimony that you are the slave and messenger of Allah." When 'Addaas returned to 'Utbah and Shaybah, they reproached him for kissing Rasulullah ﷺ on his hands and feet. They also warned him: "Make sure this man does not deviate you from your religion. Your religion is far better than his religion."

Hakeem bin Hizaam رحمة الله narrates: "When 'Utbah and Shaybah were all primed to take part in the battle of Badr with the Quraysh of Makkah, 'Addaas grasped their feet and beseeched: "By Allah! This man is the Messenger of Allah. These people are being drawn to their annihilation."

'Addaas was busy weeping when 'Aas bin Shaybah happened to pass by. He asked 'Addaas why he was weeping so profusely. 'Addaas replied: "I am shedding tears over my two masters who are on their way to do battle with the Messenger of Allah." 'Aas bin Shaybah enquired: "Is he really the Messenger of Allah?" 'Addaas replied: "Certainly, by Allah! He has been commissioned as a messenger of Allah to the entire world."

Hadhrat 'Aa'ishah رضي الله عنها narrates: "I once asked Rasulullah ﷺ if he ever encountered a day more gruelling than the day of Uhud. Rasulullah ﷺ replied: "Well, the rigorous ordeals I suffered at the hands of your people, were trials I had somehow endured, but the most punishing day to me was the day I presented myself before the sons of 'Abdiyaalil (at Taaif). I returned from them dreadfully disillusioned and dejected. I recovered somewhat as I reached a place called Qarn Al-Tha'aalib when all of a sudden I raised my head and caught sight of a cloud sheltering me. Jibraa'eel عليه السلام who was also within the cloud called out to me: "Allah is well-aware of the response of your people. Allah has presently despatched to you Malakul-Jibaal (the angel of the mountains). You may bid him to do as you instruct." Presently, the angel in charge of the mountains greeted me with Salaam and said: "O Muhammad! Allah has sent me to you. I am Malakul-Jibaal (the angel in charge of the mountains). The mountains are in my control. You may instruct me to do as you prefer. If you instruct me, I will combine these two mountains (on either side of Makkah and Taaif) and crush everyone within them." Rasulullah ﷺ responded: "No, I cherish hope that Allah Ta'ala will create from their very own descendants, people who will worship Him alone without ascribing any partners unto Him."

Note: In spite of their ruthless brutalities, this personification of mercy unto mankind, this embodiment of affection did not make dua for their annihilation because even though these people may not embrace Islam, their descendants may comprise of obedient, sincere and devoted servants of Allah Ta'ala.

Chapter 6

Return from Taaif and Attendance of the Jinn

On his return from Taaif, Rasulullah ﷺ spent a few days in a place called Nakhlah. As Rasulullah ﷺ was performing Salaah one night, seven Jinnaat of Naseebayn happened to pass by. They stood listening to his recitation of the Qur-aan for a little while and departed. Rasulullah ﷺ was totally unaware of their appearance until the following verses were revealed:

وَإِذْ صَرَفْنَآ إِلَيْكَ نَفَرًا مِّنَ الْجِنِّ يَسْتَمِعُونَ الْقُرْاٰنَ ۖ فَلَمَّا حَضَرُوهُ قَالُوْٓا اَنْصِتُوْا ۚ فَلَمَّا قُضِيَ وَلَّوْا اِلٰى قَوْمِهِمْ مُّنْذِرِيْنَ ۝ قَالُوْا يٰقَوْمَنَآ اِنَّا سَمِعْنَا كِتٰبًا اُنْزِلَ مِنْۢ بَعْدِ مُوْسٰى مُصَدِّقًا لِّمَا بَيْنَ يَدَيْهِ يَهْدِيْٓ اِلَى الْحَقِّ وَاِلٰى طَرِيْقٍ مُّسْتَقِيْمٍ ۝ يٰقَوْمَنَآ اَجِيْبُوْا دَاعِيَ اللّٰهِ وَاٰمِنُوْا بِهٖ يَغْفِرْ لَكُمْ مِّنْ ذُنُوْبِكُمْ وَيُجِرْكُمْ مِّنْ عَذَابٍ اَلِيْمٍ ۝ وَمَنْ لَّا يُجِبْ دَاعِيَ اللّٰهِ فَلَيْسَ بِمُعْجِزٍ فِى الْاَرْضِ وَلَيْسَ لَهٗ مِنْ دُوْنِهٖٓ اَوْلِيَآءُ ۚ اُولٰٓئِكَ فِيْ ضَلٰلٍ مُّبِيْنٍ ۝

"And remember the time when We directed towards you a group of Jinn listening attentively to the (recitation of) the Qur-aan. When they turned up before him, they said (to one another): 'Remain silent (and listen to his words).' And when it was concluded (by the termination of the Salaah), they returned to their people warning (them). They said: 'O Our People! We have heard (the recitation) of a book revealed after Musa that endorses the previous books and it guides towards the truth and towards the right path. O our People! Respond to the caller of Allah and believe in him; Allah will forgive your sins and deliver you from a grievous punishment. And he who does not respond to the caller of Allah, he is unable to flee in the earth and he will have no supporter besides Him (Allah). Such people are in clear misguidance.'" [Surah Ahqaaf verses 29-32]

As they approached Makkah, Hadhrat Zaid bin Haarisah ؓ asked: "How will you enter Makkah when the inhabitants of Makkah had forcefully ousted you from the city?" Rasulullah ﷺ replied: "O Zaid! Allah Ta'ala will surely bring about some solution from this predicament. Allah Ta'ala Himself is the supporter and guardian of His Deen. Certainly He will grant His messenger dominance over everyone else."

When Rasulullah ﷺ reached the cave of Hira, he dispatched a message to Akhnas bin Shareeq asking whether he could enter Makkah under his (Akhnas') protection. Akhnas responded: "Since I am an ally of the Quraysh, I am unable to afford you this protection." Thereafter Rasulullah ﷺ sent the same message to Suhail bin 'Amr. He replied: "The Banu 'Aamir are unable to offer protection in defiance of Banu K'ab." Finally Rasulullah ﷺ sent a message to Mut'im bin

'Adi appealing to him whether he could enter Makkah under his protection. Mut'im accepted this appeal. He then drew his sons and people of his clan together and instructed them to assemble fully armed at the door of the Haram. He declared to them: "I have offered Muhammad my protection." Saying this, he himself mounted his camel and headed for the Haram. As he reached the door of the Haram, he proclaimed: "O people of the Quraysh! I have offered Muhammad my protection. None of you should interfere with him."

Rasulullah ﷺ then entered the Haram. After kissing the Hajr-e-Aswad (the black stone) he performed Tawaaf of the K'abah followed by two Rakaats of Salaah. He then returned home. Mut'im and his sons had actually taken Rasulullah ﷺ into their personal protection.

It was due to this demonstration of his goodwill, Rasulullah ﷺ, in regards to the captives of Badr, said:

لو كان المطعم بن عدى حيا ثم كلمنى فى هولاء النتنى لتركتهم له

"If Mut'im bin 'Adi was alive today and he spoke to me about these (spiritually) filthy people, I would have released all of them in consideration of him."

Islam of Tufail bin 'Amr Dawsi

During this period, Tufail bin 'Amr Dawsi turned up in Makkah. Rasulullah ﷺ was actively engaged in Tableegh (inviting towards Allah Ta'ala) during this period. Apart from being a man of noble lineage, Tufail was a celebrated poet and a man of remarkable wisdom. He was also renowned for his great hospitality. He enjoyed friendly alliances with the Quraysh.

When he came to Makkah, some of the Quraysh informed him: "There is a man who has turned up amongst us who has caused a lot of friction within the nation. His speech is like sorcery and black magic as it causes hostile division between father and son, between brother and brother and between husband and wife. You should also be vigilant of him lest you or your people fall prey to his menace. As far as possible, refrain from listening to anything he has to say."

The Quraysh terrified him to such an extent that he inserted wads of cotton into his ears lest the speech of this man accidentally falls onto his ears. He relates: "This action led the people to dub me Zul-Qutnatain (the man with two wads of cotton wool). Coincidentally, I was one day passing the Masjidul Haraam where I came across Rasulullah ﷺ performing Salaah before the K'abah. I edged closer to him. Although I personally had no intention to listen to his words, Allah Ta'ala wanted to make me listen to some of His words. I involuntarily managed to listen to these words, which I found extraordinarily pleasant and delightful. I thought to myself, 'I am an intelligent man and a celebrated poet. The charismatic grace or the repulsive lewdness of any speech is not strange to my ears. I will definitely lend my ears to this speech. If his words are pleasant, I will accept them and if his words are revolting or inappropriate, I will reject them."

He further relates: "Subsequently, when Rasulullah ﷺ returned from the Haram, I tagged along behind him. When he reached his house, I submitted: 'Your people have left me so terrified of listening to your words that I have inserted cotton wool into my ears lest I fall prey to your words. However, the divine will of Allah Ta'ala has disallowed this decision of abstaining from your words. Your words fell onto my ears and I found them to be exceptionally graceful. Why don't you present your religion to me?'

Rasulullah ﷺ then presented Islam to me and recited a portion of the Holy Qur-aan before me."

According to another narration Rasulullah ﷺ recited Surah Ikhlaas and Mu'awwazatain before him.

He relates: "By Allah! I have never come across any words similar to the words of the Holy Qur-aan and I have not encountered any religion more moderate and reasonable than the religion of Islam. I immediately embraced Islam. I then appealed: 'O Rasool of Allah! I am the chief of my people. After my return, I aspire to invite my people towards Islam. Make dua unto Allah Ta'ala to grant me some symbol that would assist me in my ambitions.' Rasulullah ﷺ then made dua:

اللّٰهُمَّ اجعل له اية

"O Allah! Grant him some symbol."

He relates: "Subsequently, as I neared my hometown, a Nur (radiance) like the radiance of a lantern suddenly formed between my eyes. I pleaded with Allah Ta'ala to transfer this Nur onto some other part of my body instead of positioning it right on my face lest my people regard this as a type of Muthlah (mutilation) as a form of divine reprisal against me for denouncing my ancestral religion. This Nur was instantly transferred to my whip, which miraculously turned into something like a lantern.

In the morning, I presented Islam first to my father and then to my wife. Both of them cleaned their clothing, took a bath and embraced Islam. I pacified my wife by saying: 'If you are concerned about any harm afflicting the children due to us abandoning the idols, I accept full responsibility.'

I then presented Islam to the Daws tribe but they were a bit hesitant to accept Islam. I returned to Makkah and once again presented myself to Rasulullah ﷺ exclaiming: 'O Prophet of Allah! The tribe of Daws declined to embrace Islam. Why don't you invoke the curse of Allah against them?' Rasulullah ﷺ raised his hands in supplication:

اللّٰهُمَّ اهد دوسًا وائت بهم

'O Allah! Guide the tribe of Daws and (following their conversion to Islam) bring them here.'

He then advised Tufail: 'Go and invite them towards Islam with affection and compassion.'"

He says: "As per his advice, I persisted in inviting the people towards Islam. Up to the seventh year of Hijrah, between seventy to eighty households embraced Islam. In the year 7 A.H., I brought all of them with me to Madinah Munawwarah in the presence of Rasulullah ﷺ. Following the conquest of Makkah, I requested Rasulullah ﷺ to permit me to set ablaze the idol of 'Amr bin Hameemah called Zul-Kaffain."

Once Tufail gained his approval, he set out for his village and set fire to this idol. As he was in the process of setting it alight, he disdainfully continued reciting the following stanzas:

$$\text{يَا ذَا الْكَفَّيْنِ لَسْتُ مِنْ عُبَّادِكَا مِيْلَادُنَا اَكْبَرُ مِنْ مِيْلَادِكَا}$$

$$\text{اِنِّيْ حَشَوْتُ النَّارَ فِيْ فُؤَادِكَا}$$

"O Zul-Kaffain! I am not one of your devotees. My birth is far superior to your birth. Indeed, I have thrust blazing fire within your heart."

Half the tribe had already embraced Islam. Subsequent to the torching of this idol, the other half repented from their polytheism and embraced Islam.

According to another narration, after accepting Islam, Tufail returned to his hometown on an incredibly dark rainy night. As a result, he was unable to see the road ahead. This is when Allah Ta'ala created this Nur (light). The people were left in utter bewilderment. They surrounded him from all sides attempting to clutch his whip. This brilliance then radiated from their fingertips. Whenever a dark night fell, this whip would turn radiant with Nur. This is why Hadhrat Tufail was prominently known as Zun-Nur (a man of radiance).

Chapter 7

Mi'raaj

After his return from Taaif, Allah Ta'ala took Rasulullah ﷺ for Mi'raaj from Masjidul-Haraam to Masjidul-Aqsa and from there to the seven heavens all in one night with the same physical body and soul in a state of absolute consciousness and wakefulness. This journey is referred to as Mi'raaj or Israa, the details of which will be described in the chapter dealing with divine miracles, Insha Allah. The scholars of Seerah have differed over the exact month in which the Mi'raaj took place. The most accepted view is that it occurred on the twenty-seventh night of Rajab. And Allah Ta'ala knows best.

Wisdom behind Mi'raaj

Ten years of prophethood had gone by. All avenues of trials and tribulations were covered. Not a facet of humiliation was left untouched in the path of Allah Ta'ala. Clearly what better outcome can there be of trials and tribulations suffered in the path of Allah Ta'ala than honour, reverence and Mi'raaj (ascension)?

So when Rasulullah ﷺ experienced the extreme levels of distress after his emergence from the valley of Abu Taalib and after his return from Taaif, Allah Ta'ala bestowed him with the privilege of Mi'raaj and ascension and Allah Ta'ala elevated him to such a lofty level that even the most revered of the closest angels were left behind. Allah Ta'ala made him journey to the extremity of the universe. He was taken right up to the divine throne after which there is no further rank.

This is why some Aarifeen (sufis) say that this journey to the divine throne was an indication of Khatm-e-Nubuwwat (the termination of prophethood). The entire creation and universe terminates at the divine throne. The existence of any creation beyond the throne is not established from the Qur-aan and Hadith. Similarly, the merits of prophethood terminate upon the existence of Rasulullah ﷺ.

Mi'raaj in Detail

Allah Ta'ala says:

$$\text{سُبْحٰنَ الَّذِيْۤ اَسْرٰى بِعَبْدِهٖ لَيْلًا مِّنَ الْمَسْجِدِ الْحَرَامِ اِلَى الْمَسْجِدِ الْاَقْصَا الَّذِيْ بٰرَكْنَا حَوْلَهٗ لِنُرِيَهٗ مِنْ اٰيٰتِنَا ؕ اِنَّهٗ هُوَ السَّمِيْعُ الْبَصِيْرُ ۝}$$

"Glory be to the Being who had taken His (special) servant in (a little part of) the night from Masjidul-Haraam to Masjidul-Aqsa the environs of which We had blessed. (The actual aim of this was) to show him from Our signs (some of which are mentioned in Surah Najm like journeying to Sidratul-Muntahaa, witnessing Jannah and Jahannam and other divine phenomena). Verily, He (Allah Ta'ala) is all-hearing, all-seeing." [Surah Israa verse 1]

One night Rasulullah ﷺ was lying down in Umme Haani's house. He just dozed off when the roof of the house suddenly split open. Through this gap, Jibraa'eel عليه السلام accompanied by other angels descended upon Rasulullah ﷺ. They woke him up and took him to Masjidul-Haraam. As he reached there, he went into the Hateem area and fell asleep. Jibraa'eel عليه السلام and Mikaa'eel عليه السلام woke him up again and took him to the well of Zam Zam. There they laid him down and split his chest open. They extracted his blessed heart and rinsed it with the water of Zam Zam. A tray containing Imaan and wisdom was then brought to him. Implanting this Imaan and wisdom into his blessed heart, they restored the heart to its original position and resealed his chest. They then inscribed the seal of prophethood between his shoulder blades. (This was a physical symbol of Rasulullah ﷺ being the seal of all divine messengers.)

The Buraaq was then brought before him. Buraaq is actually the name of a celestial animal that is smaller than a mule but bigger than a donkey. It was white in colour and it was so fast that one step would fall as far as the eye could see. When Rasulullah ﷺ mounted this animal, it fell into a state of energetic friskiness. Jibraa'eel عليه السلام reproached: "O Buraaq! Why this friskiness? To this day, not a single servant of Allah more honourable than Muhammad (ﷺ) has mounted you." Buraaq almost kneeled over in shame. It then set off with Rasulullah ﷺ. Jibraa'eel عليه السلام and Mikaa'eel عليه السلام also accompanied Rasulullah ﷺ on this animal.

According to certain narrations, Jibraa'eel Ameen عليه السلام assisted Rasulullah ﷺ in mounting Buraaq after which he himself took a seat behind Rasulullah ﷺ.

Shaddaad bin Aws رضي الله عنه narrates that Rasulullah ﷺ related: "En route we came across a land with numerous date-palms. Jibraa'eel عليه السلام asked me to descend and perform Nafl Salaah. I dismounted and performed Salaah. Jibraa'eel عَلَيْهِ السَّلَام then enquired: 'Do you have any idea where you performed Salaah?' I replied: 'I have absolutely no idea.' Jibraa'eel عَلَيْهِ السَّلَام said: 'You performed Salaah in Yasrib (Madinah Tayyibah) where you are going to migrate.' We then set off once again when we passed another area. Jibraa'eel عَلَيْهِ السَّلَام asked me to alight and perform Salaah here as well. I dismounted and performed Salaah. Jibraa'eel عَلَيْهِ السَّلَام informed me: 'You performed Salaah in the valley of Saynaa near the tree of Musa عَلَيْهِ السَّلَام where Allah Ta'ala spoke to Musa عَلَيْهِ السَّلَام.' We then passed another area where I was again instructed to perform Salaah. I dismounted once again and performed Salaah. Jibraa'eel عَلَيْهِ السَّلَام informed me that I had just performed Salaah in Madyan (the native land of Shu'aib عَلَيْهِ السَّلَام). We set off once again until we came to another area where Jibraa'eel عَلَيْهِ السَّلَام asked me to dismount and perform Salaah. I alighted from the animal and performed Salaah. Jibraa'eel عَلَيْهِ السَّلَام informed me that this place is called Baitul-Lahm (Bethlehem) where 'Isa عَلَيْهِ السَّلَام was born."

The Marvels of this Celestial journey

Whilst Rasulullah ﷺ was on this celestial voyage, he came across an old woman who called out to him. Jibraa'eel عَلَيْهِ السَّلَام advised Rasulullah ﷺ to proceed ahead without taking any heed of her in the least. As he proceeded, he came across an old man who also called out to him. Hadhrat Jibraa'eel عَلَيْهِ السَّلَام again advised Rasulullah ﷺ to move on. As he proceeded further, Rasulullah ﷺ came across a group of people who greeted him thus:

السلام عليك يا اول، السلام عليك يا اخر، السلام عليك يا حاشر

"Assalaamu 'Alayka Yaa Awwal, Assalaamu 'Alayka Yaa Aakhir, Assalaamu 'Alayka Yaa Haashir."

Jibraa'eel عَلَيْهِ السَّلَام asked Rasulullah ﷺ to respond to their Salaam. He then explained to him, "The old woman you caught sight of at the roadside is actually the dunya (the world). The remaining age of this world is now limited to the remaining life span of this old woman. The old man you noticed was actually shaytaan. Both of them aspire to incline you towards them. The group that greeted you with Salaam comprised of Hadhrat Ibraaheem عَلَيْهِ السَّلَام, Hadhrat Musa عَلَيْهِ السَّلَام and Hadhrat 'Isa عَلَيْهِ السَّلَام."

Rasulullah ﷺ said: "On the night of my ascension (to the heavens) I passed Musa عَلَيْهِ السَّلَام who was standing engaged in Salaah in his grave."

According to the narration of Ibn 'Abbaas ﷺ, Rasulullah ﷺ said: "On the night of Mi'raaj, I caught sight of Musa ﷺ, Dajjaal and the superintendent of Jahannam whose name is Maalik."

En route, Rasulullah ﷺ also came across a group of people with copper fingernails. They were busy scraping the skin of their faces and chests with these copper fingernails. When asked about these people, Jibraa'eel ﷺ replied: "These are the people who consume the flesh of others." In other words, they backbite and vilify others.

Rasulullah ﷺ also witnessed a person swimming in a river. He was busy consuming morsels of stones. When Rasulullah ﷺ asked about this man, Jibraa'eel ﷺ replied: "This man is a consumer of interest."

Rasulullah ﷺ also came across a group of people who, during the course of just one day, could sow their land and harvest the crop. The field would then revert to its original condition. When Rasulullah ﷺ asked about this, Jibraa'eel ﷺ replied: "These are people who wage Jihaad in the path of Allah. Their good deeds are multiplied seven hundred fold. Whatever they spend, Allah Ta'ala recompenses them with a far better substitute."

Rasulullah ﷺ then passed a group of people whose heads were being crushed by boulders. Each time the heads were crushed, they would revert to their normal condition. This cycle continued ceaselessly. When Rasulullah ﷺ enquired about these people, Jibraa'eel ﷺ replied: "These are people who are indifferent towards their Fard Salaah."

He then came across a group of people whose anterior and posterior private parts were wrapped in rags and they were grazing like camels and oxen. Rasulullah ﷺ asked who they were. Jibraa'eel ﷺ replied: "These are people who do not pay Zakaat on their wealth."

Rasulullah ﷺ then came across a group of people in front of whom were two cauldrons. One contained cooked flesh and the other cauldron contained raw and decomposing flesh. These people were consuming the decomposing flesh without partaking of any of the wholesome cooked flesh. Rasulullah ﷺ asked: "Who are these people?" Jibraa'eel ﷺ replied: "These people are made up of men of your Ummah who, in spite of having Halaal and decent women available to them, spend the entire night with adulteresses and women of loose morals, and this group is made up of women who leave their Halaal and decent husbands to pass the night with adulterers and unchaste men."

Rasulullah ﷺ then came across a pole positioned on a main road. It slashed or hacked up clothing or anything else that happened to come close to it. When Rasulullah ﷺ asked Jibraa'eel ﷺ about this, he replied: "This is the image of people who lie in wait at the roadsides and plunder the property of passers-by."

Then Rasulullah ﷺ happened to pass a man who had amassed a huge pile of sticks. Although he was unable to bear this huge burden, he was nonetheless fetching more and more sticks and adding to the burden. When Rasulullah ﷺ asked what this signified, Jibraa'eel عليه السلام replied: "This is a man of your Ummah who is burdened by numerous rights and responsibilities which he is unable to execute but notwithstanding this, he continues saddling himself with even more obligations."

He then came across a group of people whose tongues and lips were being sheared by iron scissors. As soon as their lips and tongues were sheared off, they reverted intact to their original condition. This cycle continued relentlessly without any sign of termination. When Rasulullah ﷺ asked about this, Jibraa'eel عليه السلام said: "These are the preachers of your Ummah (who befit the verse 'they preach what they do not do')," in other words, they preach to others but fail to practise themselves.

Thereafter Rasulullah ﷺ passed an area with appealing fragrances and cool breezes. Jibraa'eel عليه السلام informed him that this was the fragrance of Jannah (paradise). They then passed an area reeking of repulsive odours. Jibraa'eel عليه السلام said that this was the stench of Jahannam (hell).

Baitul-Muqaddas

Rasulullah ﷺ arrived at Baitul-Muqaddas in this splendour and dismounted from the Buraaq. Rasulullah ﷺ tied the animal to the iron loop on which all the previous Ambiyaa عليهم السلام tethered their animals.

Thereafter Rasulullah ﷺ entered Masjidul-Aqsa and offered two Rakaat (of Tahiyyatul-Masjid).

On this auspicious occasion of Rasulullah's ﷺ advent, the other Ambiyaa عليهم السلام were already awaiting his arrival in the Masjid. Hadhrat Ibraaheem عليه السلام and Hadhrat Musa عليه السلام were also amongst the luminaries awaiting Rasulullah ﷺ.

Barely a few moments passed when a number of people happened to assemble in Masjidul-Aqsa. A Muazzin called out the Azaan followed by the Iqaamah. Now the entire congregation was waiting to see who would lead them in prayer? Jibraa'eel عليه السلام held Rasulullah ﷺ by the hand and led him forward. Rasulullah ﷺ says: "I led all of them in Salaah. When I completed the Salaah, Jibraa'eel عليه السلام asked me if I knew whom I led in Salaah. When I replied in the negative, he said: 'All the prophets who were commissioned before you, every single one of them offered Salaah behind you.'"

According to another narration, even the angels descended from the skies upon this momentous advent of Rasulullah ﷺ. Rasulullah ﷺ then led all the Ambiyaa عليهم السلام and the angels in Salaah.

Upon the termination of the Salaah, the angels asked Jibraa'eel عليه السلام: "Who is this companion with you?" Jibraa'eel عليه السلام replied: "This is Muhammad ﷺ, the seal of all divine messengers." The angels asked: "Is he already commissioned as a messenger?" When Jibraa'eel عليه السلام replied in the affirmative, the angels commented: "May Allah keep him alive and well. He is a wonderful brother and vicegerent." In other words, he is our brother and the vicegerent of Allah Ta'ala.

Thereafter Rasulullah ﷺ met with the souls of the Ambiyaa عليهم السلام. Each one of them praised and glorified Allah Ta'ala in his distinctive manner.

Glorification of Ibraaheem عليه السلام:

Ibraaheem عليه السلام praised Allah Ta'ala in the following words:

الحمد لله الذى اتخذنى خليلا واعطانى ملكا عظيما وجعلنى امة قانتا يؤتم بى وانقذنى من النار وجعلها علىّ بردا و سلاما

"All praises are due to Allah Who had adopted me as His Khalil (bosom friend) and granted me great authority, and Who has rendered me an obedient leader who is adhered to and has saved me from the fire by making it cool and safe for me."

Glorification of Musa عليه السلام:

الحمد لله الذى كلمنى تكليما وجعل هلاك ال فرعون ونجاة بنى اسرائيل على يدى وجعل من امتى قوما يهدون بالحق وبه يعدلون

"All praises are due to Allah Who had spoken to me directly without an intermediary, Who had destroyed Fir'awn and rescued the Bani Israa'eel at my hands and Who had made such people from my Ummah who guide towards the truth and with the truth do they mete out justice."

Glorification of Dawood ﷺ:

الحمد لله الذى جعل لى ملكا عظيما وعلمنى الزبور والان لى الحديد وسخر لى الجبال يسبحن والطير واعطانى الحكمة وفصل الخطاب

"All praises are due to Allah Who had granted me great authority, taught me the Psalms, made iron easily flexible for me, made the mountains and birds subservient to me in that they chant His praises, and had granted me wisdom and a sound faculty of judgement."

Glorification of Sulaymaan ﷺ:

الحمد لله الذى سخر لى الرياح وسخرلى الشياطين يعملون ما شئت من محاريب و تماثيل وجفان كالجواب وقدور راسيات وعلمنى منطق الطير واتانى من كل شىء فضلا وسخر لى جنود الشياطين والانس والطير و فضلنى على كثير من عباده المؤمنين وأتانى ملكا عظيما لا ينبغى لاحد من بعدى وجعل ملكى ملكا طيبا ليس فيه حساب

"All praises are due to Allah Who had rendered the winds subservient to me, He made the shayaateen submissive to my commandments; they did work as I wished by making high rooms, images, basins as large as reservoirs and cauldrons fixed (in their places), who has taught me the language of the birds, who has blessed me with every grace, who has rendered the armies of the Shayaateen, humankind and birds all submissive to me, who had favoured me over a number of His faithful servants, who had granted me a grand supremacy, which is inappropriate for anyone after me and who has made this supremacy an admirable one for which there is no reckoning."

Glorification of 'Isa ﷺ:

الحمد لله الذى جعلنى كلمة وجعل مثلى مثل ادم خلقه من تراب ثم قال له كن فيكون وعلمنى الكتاب والحكمة والتوراة والانجيل

$$\text{اخلق من الطين كهيئة الطير فانفخ فيه فيكون طيرا باذن الله}$$
$$\text{وجعلنى ابرئ الاكمه والابرص واحى الموتى باذن الله و رفعنى}$$
$$\text{وظهرنى و اعاذنى و امى من الشيطان الرجيم فلم يكن للشيطان}$$
$$\text{علينا سبيل}$$

"All praises are due to Allah Who had made me (His) word, who had created me like Aadam ﷺ (without a father), He created him from sand and commanded the mould: 'be' and it came into existence, who taught me the book, wisdom, the Taurah and Injeel, who bestowed me with the ability to form the figures of birds in which I breathe and they turn into birds by the will of Allah, who had also bestowed on me the miracle to heal the one born blind and the lepers and the miracle to bring the dead to life with the command of Allah, who had elevated me and protected my mother and I from the accursed shaytaan so that he (shaytaan) has no hold over us."

Glorification of Rasulullah ﷺ:

$$\text{الحمد لله الذى ارسلنى رحمة للعالمين وكافة للناس بشيرا ونذيرا}$$
$$\text{وانزل على الفرقان فيه بيان لكل شىء وجعل امتى خير امة اخرجت}$$
$$\text{للناس وجعل امتى هم الاولون والاخرون وشرح لى صدرى و وضع}$$
$$\text{عنى وزرى و رفع لى ذكرى وجعلنى فاتحا و خاتما}$$

"All praises are due to Allah who has sent me as a source of mercy unto the world and to all the people as a warner and a heralder (of glad tidings), who has revealed upon me the Furqaan in which there is an explanation of everything, who has made my Ummah the best of nations, my Ummah is the first (as far as its status) and the last (in terms of its emergence in this world), who has opened my chest and purged me of my burdens, who has elevated my status and who has made me an opener (by creating me spiritually before everyone else) and a seal (by creating my physical form and making me the seal of all the prophets)."

When Rasulullah ﷺ completed his address on the glorification of Allah Ta'ala, Ibraaheem ﷺ rose and addressed the other Ambiyaa ﷺ saying:

بهذا افضلكم محمد صلى الله عليه وسلم

"Due to these virtues and merits, Muhammad has surpassed you."

When Rasulullah ﷺ emerged from the Masjid, three cups were presented before him. One contained water, the other milk and the third contained wine. Rasulullah ﷺ chose the cup of milk. Upon this Jibraa'eel عليه السلام commented: "You have chosen Deenul-Fitrah (the natural Deen). Had you chosen wine, your Ummah would have gone astray and had you chosen the cup with the water, your Ummah would have drowned."

According to some narrations, a cup of honey was also presented to him. He partook a bit of this as well.

Ascension to the Heavens

Subsequent to this, Rasulullah ﷺ, in the company of Jibraa'eel عليه السلام and other honourable angels embarked on their ascension to the heavens. According to some narrations, Rasulullah ﷺ ascended the skies mounted upon the Buraaq animal similar to the preceding leg of the journey. However, according to some narrations, after his emergence from Masjidul-Aqsa, Rasulullah ﷺ ascended the skies with the aid of a ladder studded with gems and emeralds with the entourage of angels on either side of him.

Abu Sa'eed Khudri رضي الله عنه said that he heard Rasulullah ﷺ saying: "When I concluded my rituals at Masjidul-Aqsa, a ladder was brought before me. I have never set eyes on a ladder more beautiful than this ladder. This is the same ladder that enables the souls of people to climb to the heavens and it is the same ladder that a dying person casts his gaze upon when he is about to breathe his last. My travelling companion Jibraa'eel hoisted me upon this ladder (and I continued ascending) until I reached one of the doors of heaven, which is referred to as 'the door of the Hafazah."

Meeting the Ambiyaa عليهم السلام

In this majestic manner, Rasulullah ﷺ reached the first heaven. Jibraa'eel عليه السلام requested to be let in. The overseer of the first heaven enquired: "Who is with you?"

"Muhammad Rasulullah ﷺ is with me," he replied.

"Was he invited over here?" he asked.

When Jibraa'eel عليه السلام replied in the affirmative, the angels warmly welcomed him and opened the door for him. Rasulullah ﷺ entered the porch of the first heaven where he came across a rather elderly man. Jibraa'eel

ﷺ revealed: "This is your father Aadam ؑ. Go ahead! Make Salaam to him." Rasulullah ﷺ made Salaam to him. He affectionately responded to the Salaam and added: "Marhabaa! Welcome to a pious son and a pious Prophet." He then went on to make dua for Rasulullah ﷺ.

Whilst meeting him, Rasulullah's ﷺ glance fell on some figures on Hadhrat Aadam's ؑ right and some on his left. When Aadam ؑ glanced to the figures on his right, he would smile in delight and when he cast his gaze to the figures on his left, he would weep in sorrow. Jibraa'eel ؑ revealed: "The figures on his right represent his pious children, those destined for Jannah. When he casts his eyes towards them he is pleased. The figures on his left represent his evil children, those who are doomed to Jahannam. He weeps in anguish when he casts his eyes upon them."

Then Rasulullah ﷺ ascended the second heaven. In the same manner, Jibraa'eel ؑ requested to be let in. When the overseer asked who was with him, Jibraa'eel ؑ replied: "Muhammad Rasulullah ﷺ is with me."

"Was he invited?" he asked.

When Jibraa'eel ؑ replied in the affirmative, the overseer commented: "Welcome! Welcome to such a majestic guest." Here on this level, Rasulullah ﷺ saw Hadhrat Yahya ؑ and Hadhrat 'Isa ؑ.

Jibraa'eel ؑ ushered him into their company saying: "Here, this is Yahya ؑ and 'Isa ؑ. Go on, make Salaam to them." Rasulullah ﷺ went up to them and offered his Salaam to both of them. They replied to his Salaam and remarked: "Welcome to a pious brother and a pious Prophet."

Thereafter Rasulullah ﷺ ascended the third heaven and here again Jibraa'eel ؑ asked to be let in as mentioned previously. Here Rasulullah ﷺ met Yusuf ؑ and as per the previous occasions, Rasulullah ﷺ made Salaam etc. with him. Rasulullah ﷺ, (whilst relating this event) commented: "Yusuf ؑ was bestowed with immense handsomeness."

Thereafter Rasulullah ﷺ visited the fourth heaven where he met Hadhrat Idrees ؑ. He then proceeded to the fifth heaven where he met Hadhrat Haroon ؑ. From there, he ascended to the sixth heaven where he met Hadhrat Musa ؑ, then to the seventh heaven where he met Hadhrat Ibraaheem ؑ. He spotted him resting his back against the Baitul-Ma'mur. The Baitul-Ma'mur is the Qiblah of the angels and falls directly in line with the Ka'bah. If, hypothetically speaking, the Baitul-Ma'mur had to come crashing down; it would fall directly onto the Ka'bah. Seventy thousand angels make Tawaaf of this Baitul-Ma'mur every single day never to get another chance again.

Jibraa'eel ؑ informed Rasulullah ﷺ that this is his father and he should make Salaam with him. Rasulullah ﷺ went ahead and made Salaam with him. Ibraaheem عَلَيْهِ ٱلسَّلَام replied to the Salaam and remarked: "Welcome to a pious son and to a pious Prophet."

Sidratul-Muntaha:

Following this meeting with Ibraaheem عَلَيْهِ ٱلسَّلَام, Rasulullah ﷺ was raised to the Sidratul-Muntaha. This is a lotus tree towering above the seventh heaven. Whatever rises from the earth stops at Sidratul-Muntaha (the lotus-tree of the outer extremity), and from this point onwards, it is raised further into the heavens. On the other hand, whatever descends from the Malaul-A'laa first descends upon Sidratul-Muntaha and from there it descends further to the other heavens and beyond, thus the name Sidratul-Muntaha.

At this very location, Rasulullah ﷺ beheld Jibraa'eel عَلَيْهِ ٱلسَّلَام in his original form. He also witnessed some strange and amazing celestial radiances of Allah Ta'ala. He also saw innumerable angels and golden moths hovering about the Sidratul-Muntaha.

Observation of Jannah and Jahannam:

Jannah is in close proximity to Sidratul-Muntaha. The Holy Qur-aan depicts:

عند سدرة المنتهى عندها جنة الماوى

"At Sidratul-Muntaha, near it is the abode of Jannah."

This is why Abu Sa'eed Khudri's رَضِيَ ٱللَّهُ عَنْهُ narration mentions that after his performance of Salaah in Baitul-M'amur, Rasulullah ﷺ was elevated to Sidratul-Muntaha. From Sidratul-Muntaha, Rasulullah ﷺ was raised to Jannah. After his visit to Jannah, Jahannam was presented before him. In other words, the horrors of Jahannam were laid bare to him.

Rasulullah ﷺ says: "I reached Sidratul-Muntaha where I beheld astounding colours and incredible embellishments. I have no idea what they were. I was then admitted into Jannah where the domes were constructed from (mammoth-sized) pearls and the soil was of musk."

Sareeful-Aqlaam - The Site of the Scratching of the Pens:

Thereafter Rasulullah ﷺ ascended even further where he was able to perceive the sounds made by the pens (recording predestination). The sound produced by the scratching of these pens of predestination is referred to as Sareeful-Aqlaam. This is the location where the pens of fate are engaged in recording everything that is to transpire in the future. The angels were busy transcribing the divine edicts and religious commandments from the Lawh-e-Mahfooz (the preserved tablet).

Divine Proximity - (Celestial vision, divine conversation and the conferral of sacred edicts)

From Sareeful-Aqlaam, Rasulullah ﷺ traversed through a number of concealed realms until he finally arrived in the sacred presence of Allah Ta'ala. It is said that a Rafraf (a green silken seat) was provided for his conveyance. Rasulullah ﷺ mounted this seat and was thus conveyed to the closest of the celestial realms before the majesty of Allah Ta'ala.

When Rasulullah ﷺ reached this area of 'close proximity', he fell into Sajdah. Here he caught sight of the magnificence of the radiance of Allah Ta'ala from beyond the divine screen and without any intermediary he was honoured to converse directly with Allah Ta'ala.

Rasulullah ﷺ said: "I caught sight of the greatest of (divine radiances). Thereafter Allah Ta'ala communicated whatever He wished to communicate to me."

Rasulullah ﷺ was blessed with setting eyes on Allah Ta'ala and communicating with Him directly without any intermediary between them.

Allah Ta'ala conversed with Rasulullah ﷺ and endowed him with three gifts on this great occasion; the first gift was made up of the five daily Salaah; the second gift was the closing verses of Surah Baqarah, which includes the mercy, affection, ease and forgiveness of Allah Ta'ala upon this Ummah and it focuses upon victory and assistance to the Muslims against the disbelievers. Although these verses are in the form of duas, the verses are more of an educative and enlightening nature. It is as though Allah Ta'ala is enlightening this Ummah in these closing verses that they should make a point of imploring Allah Ta'ala and He will respond to their duas.

وَلَوْ لَمْ تُرِدْ نَيْلَ مَا نَرْجُو وَ نَطْلُبُهُ   مِنْ فَيْضِ جُودِكَ مَا عَلَّمْتَنَا الطَّلَبَا

If You had no intention to bestow upon us from Your oceans of grace, You wouldn't have enlightened us on the method of begging from You.

In other words, You wouldn't have even informed us of what to beg of You.

The third gift awarded to Rasulullah ﷺ on this night was that Allah Ta'ala would pardon the major sins of any Ummati who does not ascribe partners unto Him. In other words, Allah Ta'ala will not condemn a perpetrator of major sins to eternal hellfire, as He would do to the disbelievers. Some of them will be pardoned through the intercession of the Ambiyaa عَلَيْهِمُ السَّلَامُ. Others will be forgiven due to the intercession of the noble angels whilst others will be forgiven solely by the mercy and grace of Almighty Allah. Any person whose heart embraces even an iota of faith (Imaan) will, in due course, be released from Jahannam.

According to a lengthy Hadith of Abu Hurayrah ؓ, during the course of his conversation with Allah Ta'ala, Rasulullah ﷺ was addressed by Allah Ta'ala thus:

فقال له ربه قد اتخذتك خليلا وحبيبا وارسلتك الى الناس كافة بشيرا ونذيرا و شرحت لك صدرك و وضعت عنك وزرك و رفعت لك ذكرك فلا اذكر الا اذكرت معى وجعلت امتك خير امة اخرجت للناس وجعلت امتك وسطا وجعلت امتك هم الاولين والاخرين وجعلت من امتك اقواما قلوبهم اناجى لهم وجعلتك اول النبيين خلقا واخرهم بعثا واعطيتك سبعا من المثانى لم يعطها نبيا قبلك واعطيتك خواتيم سورة البقرة من كنز تحت العرش لم يعطها نبيا قبلك واعطيتك الكوثر واعطيتك ثمانية اسهم الاسلام والهجرة والجهاد والصلاة والصدقة وصوم رمضان والامر بالمعروف والنهى عن المنكر وجعلتك فاتحا و خاتما الى اخر الحديث اخرجه ابن جرير فى تفسير سورة الاسراء عن ابى هريرة رضى الله عنه بطوله

كذا فى الخصائص الكبرى

"I have adopted you as my Khalil (bosom friend) and Habib (beloved). I have sent you to all the peoples of the world as a Basheer (presenter of glad tidings) and as a Nazeer (warner). I have opened your breast for you, I have relieved you of your burden and I have elevated your mention. My oneness is not mentioned but with you as My slave. I have made your Ummah the best of Ummahs that was ever raised from the people. I have declared your Ummah as the most just and moderate Ummah. I have rendered your Ummah as the first (in terms of its virtue) and last (in terms of its appearance in this world). I have made from your Ummah a group of people whose hearts contain the Injeel. (In other words, the divine words of the Qur-aan will be etched onto their hearts.) I have made you the first Prophet in terms of the creation of your Nur and the last Prophet in terms of your commission. I have *awarded you the Sab'ul-Mathaani (Surah Fatihah), which I had not given to any messenger prior to you. I have bestowed upon you the closing verses of Surah Baqarah from the treasures beneath the divine throne, which I had not bestowed to any messenger prior to you. I have granted you the Kauthar (the pond), and I have bestowed your Ummah with eight distinctive merits; Islam, Hijrah, Salaah, Sadaqah (charity), Saum of Ramadhaan, Amr bil M'aroof (enjoining good) and Nahy 'anil-Munkar (forbidding evil). I made you a Faatih (opener or forerunner to the Ambiyaa) and Khaatam (seal of all the Prophets)……"*

In short, Allah Ta'ala bestowed Rasulullah ﷺ with many bounties and blessed him with many glad tidings and awarded him with distinctive injunctions and directives. One of the most significant directives issued to Rasulullah ﷺ was the obligation to observe fifty daily Salaahs. Accepting all these directives and injunctions with delight, Rasulullah ﷺ turned back to return to this earth. On his return journey, he met Hadhrat Ibraaheem عليه السلام. He made no comment about these injunctions of Salaah, etc.,.

"Thereafter I passed Musa عليه السلام who asked me what I was commanded with. I replied: 'During the day and night, fifty Salaahs have been prescribed for us.' Musa عليه السلام remarked: 'I have a great deal of experience with the Bani Israa'eel. Your Ummah is far weaker; they will be unable to cope with this commandment. So return to your Lord and request him to reduce this obligation.'" Rasulullah ﷺ returned to Allah and requested Him to reduce the number of Salaahs. Allah Ta'ala reduced it by five. When Rasulullah ﷺ passed Musa عليه السلام again, he posed the same question. Once more he requested Rasulullah ﷺ to beg for a reduction in this obligation. This going back and forth ensued a number of times until just five daily Salaah remained. Even then, Musa عليه السلام pleaded with Rasulullah ﷺ to return to Allah and get yet another reduction. Rasulullah ﷺ replied: "I have requested a reduction a number of times already. Now I am embarrassed to approach Him for a further reduction." Saying this Rasulullah ﷺ continued ahead. A voice from the unseen then called out: "These are five but equivalent to fifty." That is, these are just five Salaah but the reward of these five Salaah is equal to fifty Salaah. "And My verdict will not be altered. This obligation of just five Salaah was predetermined within My knowledge."

In the same order, Rasulullah ﷺ returned from the heavens and landed first at Baitul-Muqaddas. From here he mounted the Buraaq and reached Makkah before the break of dawn. The same morning, he recounted this incident to the Quraysh. They, as expected, were left flabbergasted in disbelief. Some of them held their hands over their heads in exasperation whilst others scornfully started clapping their hands. They scoffed at him and exclaimed: "How can he possibly go to Baitul-Muqaddas and return in just one night!" In order to test him, those who had been to Baitul-Muqaddas started throwing questions at him about the distinguishing features of Baitul-Muqaddas. The instant they started interrogating him, Allah Ta'ala brought Baitul-Muqaddas right before his very eyes and he continued responding to their questions. Now when all their questions pertaining to Baitul-Muqaddas were exhausted, they asked: "Okay, tell us some incident about the road leading to Baitul-Muqaddas." Rasulullah ﷺ replied: "On my way I came across a trade caravan at a certain place that was returning to Makkah from Syria. They lost one camel and later retrieved it. Insha Allah, this trade caravan should reach Makkah within three days. Leading the way would be a khaki-coloured camel laden with two sacks of goods."

Accordingly, on the third day, this caravan entered Makkah in precisely the same manner as foretold by Rasulullah ﷺ and they also narrated the incident of the lost camel. On seeing and hearing this, Waleed bin Mughirah dismissed the whole incident by declaring: "This is nothing but sorcery." The people also concurred with him saying: "Yes, Waleed is speaking the truth."

Stalling the Sun

Rasulullah ﷺ informed the Quraysh that the trade caravan that was returning from Syria would be in Makkah by Wednesday evening before sunset. However, by Wednesday evening the caravan failed to make an appearance and the sun was about to set. Rasulullah ﷺ made dua unto Allah Ta'ala. Allah Ta'ala delayed the setting of the sun for a little while until the caravan entered Makkah the same evening before sunset, in accordance with Rasulullah's ﷺ prophesy.

According to the scholars of Seerat, this miracle is referred to as the miracle of Habsush-Shams (the stalling of the sun). Shaikh Taqiyyud-Deen Subki رحمه الله says:

$$\text{وَشَمْسُ الضُّحَى طَاعَتْكَ عِنْدَ مَغِيبِهَا} \qquad \text{فَمَا غَرَبَتْ بَلْ وَافَقَتْكَ بِوَقْفِهِ}$$

"The setting sun complied with you, it did not set but it submitted to you by you stalling it."

In this manner Allah Ta'ala confirmed the truthfulness of Rasulullah ﷺ. The Quraysh witnessed his honesty with their very own eyes. They heard the truth with their very own ears but they remained committed to their obstinacy and refutation of the truth. They were bent on rebelling against the truth. Some of them went to Abu Bakr رضي الله عنه and said: "Your friend, Muhammad (Rasulullah ﷺ) says that he went to Baitul-Maqdis last night and returned before dawn. Do you believe him?" Abu Bakr رضي الله عنه asked: "Did Muhammad ﷺ say that?" When they replied in the affirmative, Abu Bakr رضي الله عنه declared: "Then it has to be the truth. I wholeheartedly believe in whatever he says. In fact, day and night I believe in the heavenly news he conveys to us which is even beyond that." From that moment on, he was conferred with the title of Siddeeq.

On the second heaven, Rasulullah ﷺ met Hadhrat 'Isa عليه السلام and Hadhrat Yahya عليه السلام.

It appears in the Hadith:

انا اقرب الناس بعيسى بن مريم ليس بينى و بينه نبى

"From all the Ambiyaa, I am closest to 'Isa bin Maryam; there is no prophet between him and me."

Furthermore, towards the latter times, Hadhrat 'Isa عليه السلام will descend from the skies to kill Dajjaal. Within Ummat-e-Muhammadiyyah he will implement the Shari'ah of Muhammad Rasulullah ﷺ as a revivalist. On the day of Qiyaamah, Hadhrat 'Isa عليه السلام will appear before Rasulullah ﷺ with the entire creation, from beginning to end, and he will request Rasulullah ﷺ to initiate the process of intercession before Allah Ta'ala. For this reason, Rasulullah ﷺ was made to meet Hadhrat 'Isa عليه السلام. Hadhrat Yahya عليه السلام accompanying Hadhrat 'Isa عليه السلام on this occasion was merely due to their close family relationship. They were maternal cousins. (Their mothers were sisters.) This meeting denoted the relentless harassment of the Jews. The Jews would leave no stone unturned in frustrating him and they would devise a range of plans to assassinate him. However, just as Allah Ta'ala protected Hadhrat 'Isa عليه السلام from their wicked schemes, similarly Allah Ta'ala would protect Rasulullah ﷺ also from their evils.

On the third heaven he met Hadhrat Yusuf عليه السلام. This meeting implied that like Yusuf عليه السلام, Rasulullah ﷺ will also suffer at the hands of his brothers but he will ultimately prevail over them and forgive them their wrongs. On the day of the conquest of Makkah, Rasulullah ﷺ addressed the Quraysh in the same manner as Yusuf عليه السلام addressed his brothers when he said:

لاَ تَثْرِيْبَ عَلَيْكُمُ الْيَوْمَ يَغْفِرُ اللهُ لَكُمْ وَهُوَ اَرْحَمُ الرَّاحِمِيْنَ اذهبوا فانتم الطلقاء اى العتقاء

"Today there is no blame upon you. May Allah forgive you. He is the most affectionate of all the merciful. Go on! You are free."

Furthermore, when the Ummah of Rasulullah ﷺ will enter Jannah, they will all be as handsome as Hadhrat Yusuf عليه السلام.

Rasulullah's ﷺ meeting with Hadhrat Idrees عَلَيْهِ السَّلَامُ signified that Rasulullah ﷺ will despatch letters of invitation to Islam to the rulers of the world because Hadhrat Idrees عَلَيْهِ السَّلَامُ was the pioneer of letter writing. Also, in regards to Hadhrat Idrees عَلَيْهِ السَّلَامُ, Allah Ta'ala declares: "And We raised him up to an elevated rank." Meeting him was an indication that Allah Ta'ala will bestow Rasulullah ﷺ also with an elevated rank and majestic position. As a consequence, even the emperor of Rome was left awestruck when he received the letter of Rasulullah ﷺ. As mentioned in Sahih Bukhaari, when Abu Sufyaan left the emperor's court, in amazement he remarked:

امر امر ابن ابى كبشة حتى يخاف ملك بنى الاصفر

"The affair of the son of Abu Kabshah has developed into something so enormous that even the king of the children of Asfar is alarmed by him."

His meeting with Hadhrat Haroon عَلَيْهِ السَّلَامُ was an indication that just as Saamiri and the calf-worshippers utterly defied Hadhrat Haroon عَلَيْهِ السَّلَامُ and they were subsequently executed due to this apostasy, in the same way, on the day of Badr, seventy Qurayshi leaders were slain and another seventy taken as prisoners. Also, some members of the 'Uraynah tribe were executed due to their apostasy.

Rasulullah's ﷺ meeting with Hadhrat Musa عَلَيْهِ السَّلَامُ implied that just as Hadhrat Musa عَلَيْهِ السَّلَامُ waged Jihaad against the Jabaarin in Syria and Allah Ta'ala granted him victory over them, similarly, Rasulullah ﷺ will enter the regions of Syria to wage Jihaad. Rasulullah ﷺ went towards Syria for the expedition to Tabuk. There the leader of Dawmatul-Jundul begged Rasulullah ﷺ for a truce on a promise of paying Jizyah (security tax levied on non-Muslims living under Muslim rule). Rasulullah ﷺ consented to the truce.

And just as Syria was conquered after Hadhrat Musa عَلَيْهِ السَّلَامُ at the hands of his successor Hadhrat Yush'a عَلَيْهِ السَّلَامُ, similarly, after the demise of Rasulullah ﷺ, Syria fell into Muslims hands during the Caliphate of Hadhrat 'Umar رَضِيَ اللَّهُ عَنْهُ.

On the seventh heaven, Rasulullah ﷺ met Hadhrat Ibraaheem عَلَيْهِ السَّلَامُ. He saw him sitting with his back leaning on the Baitul-M'amur. The Baitul-M'amur is actually a Masjid on the seventh heaven directly parallel to the K'abah. Seventy thousand angels make Tawaaf of this structure every day (and they do not ever get a second chance to do so). Since Ibraaheem عَلَيْهِ السَّلَامُ is the builder of the K'abah, he was honoured with this distinction. This final meeting indicated to Hajatul-Wadaa (the farewell Haj). It implied that Rasulullah ﷺ would perform Haj before his demise from this world. According to the interpreters of dreams, a vision of Hadhrat Ibraaheem عَلَيْهِ السَّلَامُ in one's dream is a glad tiding of an imminent Hajj.

Ibn Muneer says: "Up to this point, seven Mi'raajs (ascensions) took place. The eighth ascension was up to Sidratul-Muntaha. This ascension was symbolic of the forthcoming conquest of Makkah that occurred in the eighth year of Hijrah. The ninth ascension took place from Sidratul-Muntaha to Sareeful-Aqlaam (the site of the scratching of the pens). This ascension was a sign of the expedition of Tabuk that occurred in the ninth year of Hijrah. The tenth ascension was the ascension on the silken seat towards the location of the utmost divine proximity to Allah Ta'ala where Rasulullah ﷺ heard the words of Allah Ta'ala. Since Rasulullah ﷺ acquired Baqaa (spiritual immortality) in this tenth ascension, this was an indication that in the tenth year of Hijrah Rasulullah ﷺ would leave this world for the Liqaa (reunion) with Allah Ta'ala. He would depart from this world to meet his Rafeeq-e-A'laa (the greatest of companions)."

During his journey to the heavens, Rasulullah ﷺ found the divine angels engaged in various positions of worship. Some of them with their hands clasped together in the Qiyaam position. Some of them were in perpetual Ruk'u without raising their heads up. Some of them were in eternal Sajdah whilst others were in perpetual Qu'ood position. Allah Ta'ala drew all these positions into one Rakaat for this Ummah so that the 'Ibaadah of this Ummah is a consolidation of all the various positions of Ibaadat of the angels. Furthermore, the Holy Qur-aan reveals that everything sings the praise and glory of Allah Ta'ala. Allah Ta'ala says:

$$\text{وَ اِنْ مِنْ شَيْءٍ اِلَّا يُسَبِّحُ بِحَمْدِهٖ وَلٰكِنْ لَّا تَفْقَهُوْنَ تَسْبِيْحَهُمْ}$$

"And there is nothing but it glorifies Him (Allah Ta'ala) with His praise but you do not understand their glorification (Tasbeeh). [Surah Israa verse 44]

Every single thing in this universe is engaged in the Tasbeeh (glorification) of Allah Ta'ala. Not a moment passes without them being engaged in his Tasbeeh. Obviously, this Tasbeeh of the universe would not be all of the same nature. They differ in their methods of Tasbeeh. The Tasbeeh of the trees and plants is in the state of Qiyaam (standing posture). The Tasbeeh of the animals is in the state of Ruk'u and the Tasbeeh of the insects is in perpetual Sujood. Their heads are always bowed to the earth in submission. The Tasbeeh of stones and other inanimate objects is the position of Qu'ood. In our Salaah, Allah Ta'ala has assembled all the various types of Tasbeeh and Tahmeed.

Furthermore, man is created from the four basic elements. This is why his Ibaadat also constitutes four basic postures of Qiyaam, Qu'ood, Ruk'u and Sujood. Since there are five sources that initiate the ghaflat (negligence) of Allah Ta'ala – i.e. the five senses – the five Salaah have been prescribed for every single day of the year.

Chapter 8

Invitation to Islam during the days of Haj

When Rasulullah ﷺ realised that the Quraysh are stubbornly clinging onto their aggression, he would himself go to the camping-grounds of the pilgrims who would congregate at Makkah during the days of Haj and there he would invite them towards Islam. He would advise them to support the true religion. He would bid the people towards Tauheed, truth and sincerity. However, his uncle Abu Lahab, whose actual name was 'Abdul-'Uzza bin 'Abdul-Muttalib would cast aside all his other duties and trailing behind Rasulullah ﷺ, he would proclaim: "People! This man wants you to abandon Laat and 'Uzza. He is tempting you towards Bid'ah (innovation) and misguidance. Don't ever adhere to what he says."

Nonetheless, Rasulullah ﷺ presented Islam to a number of tribes inviting them to support and aid Islam. Some of them responded encouragingly whilst others reacted harshly and unsympathetically. Some of them pledged their support on condition they are appointed vicegerents upon his victory. Rasulullah ﷺ replied: "That is not in my control. Allah Ta'ala appoints whomsoever He wishes." They retorted: "This is quite strange; we should fight side by side with you sacrificing our lives in support of this cause, sticking out our necks, making our chests a target of the arrows of the Arabs and when you are triumphant somebody else is appointed your deputy!"

During this time, Rasulullah ﷺ also visited the tribe of Banu Zuhal bin Shaybaan. Abu Bakr رضي الله عنه and Ali رضي الله عنه also accompanied him on this venture. Mafrooq bin 'Amr and Haani bin Qabisah were chieftains of this tribe. Abu Bakr رضي الله عنه addressed Mafrooq saying: "Haven't you heard about the prophet-hood of Rasulullah ﷺ? Here, this is the Prophet of Allah Ta'ala with me." Mafrooq replied: "Well, I have heard about him." Addressing Rasulullah ﷺ, he asked: "O Qurayshi brother! What are you inviting people to?" Stepping ahead, Rasulullah ﷺ answered: "Believe in Allah alone without ascribing any partners unto Him and accept me as His Prophet and lend your support to His religion. The Quraysh declined to accept the commandment of Allah. They have falsified His Prophet and in their intoxication of falsehood they have become independent of the truth. And Allah Ta'ala is the most independent." In other words, this independent being of Allah Ta'ala is absolutely not in need of you embracing Deen. He really does not require your support and aid. Yes, if you are concerned about your personal success, embrace the truth, accept the divine guidance and repent from falsehood and deviation.

"Then what do you invite to?" asked Mafrooq. Rasulullah ﷺ recited the following verses in response:

$$\text{قُلْ تَعَالَوْا أَتْلُ مَا حَرَّمَ رَبُّكُمْ عَلَيْكُمْ أَلَّا تُشْرِكُوا بِهِ شَيْئًا وَبِالْوَالِدَيْنِ إِحْسَانًا وَلَا تَقْتُلُوا أَوْلَادَكُم مِّنْ إِمْلَاقٍ نَّحْنُ نَرْزُقُكُمْ وَإِيَّاهُمْ وَلَا تَقْرَبُوا الْفَوَاحِشَ مَا ظَهَرَ مِنْهَا وَمَا بَطَنَ وَلَا تَقْتُلُوا النَّفْسَ الَّتِي حَرَّمَ اللّهُ إِلَّا بِالْحَقِّ ذَلِكُمْ وَصَّاكُم بِهِ لَعَلَّكُمْ تَعْقِلُونَ}$$

"Say (O Muhammad!) Come! I will recite what your Lord has made forbidden over you; that you do not ascribe any partner unto Him, favourable relationship with the parents, and that you do not kill your children out (of fear) of poverty – We sustain you as well as them – and do not come close to evils – whether they are exposed or veiled – and do not kill the being whom Allah has forbidden but for a just cause. This is what He has commanded you to do so that you may understand." [Al-An'aam verse 151]

After listening to the recitation of these verses, Mafrooq replied: "By Allah! This is indisputably not the word of an earthly being."

He further requested: "O Qurayshi brother! What do you summon people to?" Rasulullah ﷺ responded by reciting the following verses:

$$\text{إِنَّ اللّهَ يَأْمُرُ بِالْعَدْلِ وَالْإِحْسَانِ وَإِيتَاءِ ذِي الْقُرْبَى وَيَنْهَى عَنِ الْفَحْشَاءِ وَالْمُنكَرِ وَالْبَغْيِ يَعِظُكُمْ لَعَلَّكُمْ تَذَكَّرُونَ}$$

"Verily Allah ordains justice, Ihsaan (performance of good) and giving to the relatives and He prohibits evils, repulsive deeds and injustice. He advises you so that you may take heed." [Surah Nahl verse 90]

With good grace, Mafrooq responded: "By Allah! You have invited towards excellent character and outstanding actions but the problem is that I am a bit reluctant to conclude an accord with you without consulting my people. I feel it inappropriate to take such steps in their absence. I am uncertain about whether they will sanction this accord or not. Furthermore, we fall within the royal administrative control of Chosroe. We had assured him that we would not appoint any leader without consulting with him first. I am convinced that if we were to enter into any accord with you, Chosroe would certainly treat this as an insult to his authority."

Delightfully approving of his frankness and truthfulness, Rasulullah ﷺ said: "Allah Himself is the protector and assistant of His Deen. Those who support the Deen of Allah, soon Allah Ta'ala will make them the heirs of the riches and lands of Chosroe."

Thereafter Rasulullah ﷺ, grasping Abu Bakr's رضي الله عنه hand, rose from this meeting and proceeded to meet the tribes of Aws and Khazraj of Madinah. (Details of this meeting are coming up soon, Insha Allah.) These tribes enthusiastically embraced Islam and pledged their unstinting support for the cause of Islam.

Islam of Iyaas bin Mu'aaz رضي الله عنه

In the same year, Abul-Haysar Anas bin Raaf'i came to Makkah with a few of his friends in search of an ally amongst the Quraysh against the Khazraj tribe. Amongst these youth was a man by the name of Iyaas bin Mu'aaz. When Rasulullah ﷺ heard of their arrival, he went up to them and said: "I will present before you something better than what you have come for." Abul-Haysar and his friends enquired: "What is that?" Rasulullah ﷺ replied: "I am the messenger of Allah. Allah Ta'ala has commissioned me to summon His servants towards Him and to worship Him without ascribing any partner unto Him. Allah Ta'ala has also revealed a book upon me." Rasulullah ﷺ then recited a few verses of the Holy Qur-aan and presented them with Islam.

Iyaas bin Mu'aaz said: "People! This far outweighs what you have come for."

Flinging a few pebbles on Iyaas's face, Abul-Haysar retorted: "We have not come here for this." This silenced Iyaas. Thereafter Rasulullah ﷺ rose from the meeting and this group returned to Madinah Munawwarah.

A few days later, Iyaas passed away. As he was breathing his last, words like *Laa ilaaha illallahu, Allahu Akbar, Subhaanallah* and *Alhamdulillah* were spilling over from his tongue. All those who were in attendance heard these words and this left no doubt in their minds that he passed away as a Muslim.

The Inception of Islam in Madinah Munawwarah – 11th Year of Prophethood

Most of the citizens of Madinah were made up of the Aws and Khazraj tribes who were idol worshippers. Living amongst them were Jews as well, who were regarded as people of the book. Since the Jews were in the minority in Madinah, whenever they had a conflict with the Aws or Khazraj, the Jews would say: "Very soon the final messenger is going to be commissioned to this earth. We will follow him. And joining our forces with him, we will destroy you like the people of 'Aad and Iram."

During the days of Haj a few pilgrims of the Khazraj tribe arrived in Makkah. This was the eleventh year of prophethood. Rasulullah ﷺ appeared before them inviting them towards Islam. He also recited to them a few verses of the Holy Qur-aan. The moment these people laid eyes on him they recognised him and addressing one another they exclaimed: "By Allah! This is the very same Prophet whom the Jews longingly talk about. Take heed! Let not the Jews beat you to this good fortune and virtue."

In this very meeting, this group embraced Islam before rising from their seats. They then said: "O Prophet of Allah! We have embraced Islam and we believe in you. The Jews and us are always at odds with one another. If you permit, may we return and invite them to this religion of Islam as well? If they embrace Islam and both of us live in harmony, nobody will be more dear to us than you." (Rasulullah ﷺ permitted them to invite them to Islam.)

These six fortunate men of the Khazraj tribe were:

1. As'ad bin Zuraarah رضي الله عنه
2. 'Awf bin Haaris رضي الله عنه
3. Raaf'i bin Maalik رضي الله عنه
4. Qutbah bin 'Aamir رضي الله عنه
5. Uqbah bin 'Aamir رضي الله عنه
6. Jaabir bin 'Abdullah bin Rabaab رضي الله عنه

These six personalities took leave from Rasulullah ﷺ and returned to Madinah. Whomsoever they met they couldn't help but mention Rasulullah ﷺ. As a result, in Madinah, not a house nor meeting was devoid of the mention of Rasulullah ﷺ.

The First Pledge of the Ansaar – 12th year prophethood

In the following year, which was the twelfth year of prophethood, twelve people came to Makkah to meet Rasulullah ﷺ. Five of them were from the abovementioned six people whilst another seven joined them. These seven people are:

1. Mu'aaz bin Haaris رضي الله عنه (brother of 'Awf bin Haaris رضي الله عنه)
2. Zakwaan bin 'Abduqays رضي الله عنه
3. 'Ubaadah bin Saamit رضي الله عنه

4. Yazeed bin S'alabah رضى الله عنه

5. 'Abbaas bin 'Ubaadah bin Nadlah رضى الله عنه

6. Abul-Haysam Maalik bin Tayhaan رضى الله عنه

7. 'Uwaym bin Saa'idah رضى الله عنه

On this occasion, Jaabir bin 'Abdullah bin Rabaab رضى الله عنه was not present (although he was present on the first occasion as mentioned above).

These twelve personalities presented themselves before Rasulullah ﷺ and at night in Mina they pledged their allegiance at the hands of Rasulullah ﷺ just near a place called 'Aqabah, hence the name of this allegiance, Bay'atul-'Aqabah.

They pledged their allegiance not to ascribe partners unto Allah, to abstain from theft, fornication, infanticide, false accusation and slander. This was the foremost allegiance of the Ansaar, which is referred to as Bay'atul-'Aqabah Al-Ulaa (the first allegiance at 'Aqabah).

As this group was returning to Madinah Munawwarah after pledging their allegiance, Rasulullah ﷺ despatched 'Abdullah bin Ummu Maktoom رضى الله عنه and Mus'ab bin 'Umair رضى الله عنه with them to teach the people of Madinah the Holy Qur-aan and the regulations of Islam. When they reached Madinah, they were accommodated in the house of As'ad bin Zuraarah رضى الله عنه.

Mus'ab bin 'Umair رضى الله عنه would invite the people towards Islam and lead them in Salaah. He was their Imaam. One day, as he was delivering a sermon about the magnificence of Islam in front of a huge crowd of people, Usaid bin Hudhair, bearing a sword in hand, appeared before him and demanded: "What have you come here for? Why are you misleading our women and children? It would be better if you left this place!"

Mus'ab bin 'Umair رضى الله عنه replied: "Is it possible for you to sit down for a little while and listen to what I have to say? If it pleases you, well and good otherwise you may choose to withdraw." Usaid replied: "Very well, this seems quite fair." He then took a seat. Mus'ab bin 'Umair رضى الله عنه portrayed the magnificence of Islam and recited verses of the Holy Qur-aan before him. On hearing this, Usaid remarked:

ما احسن هذا الكلام واجمله

"How beautiful and splendid are these words."

He then enquired about the process of entering into the fold of Islam. Mus'ab bin 'Umair رضى الله عنه replied: "Firstly, you should cleanse your body and clothing. Take a bath. Recite the Kalimah Shahaadah and perform Salaah."

Usaid right away stood up, cleaned his clothing, took a bath, recited the Kalimah Shahaadah and offered two Rakaat of Salaah. He then said: "There is another man – meaning S'ad bin Mu'aaz, the chief of the Aws tribe – who, if he embraces Islam, not a single member of the Aws tribe will remain unconverted. Let me go and I will send him to you now."

As S'ad bin Mu'aaz saw Usaid bin Hudhair رضي الله عنه approaching, he said: "The Usaid returning does not seem like the same Usaid who left from here earlier on." As he drew closer, S'ad asked Usaid: "What happened?" Usaid replied: "I did not find anything objectionable in his (Mus'ab's) words."

S'ad bin Mu'aaz was thrown into a fit of rage and wielding his sword, he set out for As'ad bin Zuraarah's home (the host of Mus'ab رضي الله عنه).

As he reached him, S'ad fumed: "If it was not because of your family relationship with me, if you were not my cousin I would have sorted you out with this sword. Have you brought this man (Mus'ab) here to deceive the people?"

Mus'ab replied: "S'ad, is it possible for you to sit and listen to me for a few moments? If you like what you hear you may accept it otherwise you are free to do as you please." "Okay," replied S'ad, "what you say is rather fair." Saying this, he sat down. Mus'ab presented the magnificence of Islam before him and recited a few verses of the Holy Qur-aan to him. He barely heard the verses of the Qur-aan when his colour changed. He pleaded: "How do I enter this religion?"

Mus'ab رضي الله عنه replied: "Firstly, you should cleanse your clothing and take a bath. Recite the Kalimah Shahaadah and perform two Rakaat of Salaah."

Without more ado, S'ad got up, took a bath, recited the Kalimah Shahaadah and performed two Rakaat of Salaah.

The moment he was done here, he headed off towards his people. As his people saw him coming from a distance, they realised that his colour has changed. There was something different about him. As he reached their gathering, S'ad addressed them saying: "What do you think of me?" In one voice they all agreed: "You are our leader. As far as your discretion and good counsel is concerned, you are the best amongst us." S'ad said: "By Allah! I will never speak to you until and unless each one of you believes in Allah and His Rasool ﷺ."

Even before nightfall, not a single man or woman of the Banu 'Abdul-Ashal tribe was left without embracing Islam.

From the entire tribe of Banu 'Abdul-Ashal, only one man by the name of 'Amr bin Thaabit who was known as Usayrim was left to embrace Islam. He embraced Islam on the day of Uhud. He accepted Islam and immediately set out for the battlefield where he was martyred. On this occasion, Rasulullah ﷺ issued glad tidings of his entry into Jannah. Hadhrat Abu Hurayrah رضي الله عنه would ask as a riddle: "Show me a person who is a Jannati without even performing a single Salaah."

When the people failed to answer, he would say: "He is Usayrim from the tribe of Banu Abdul-Ashal."

Islam of Rifa'ah ﷺ

Rifa'ah bin Raaf'i Zuraqi ﷺ narrates: "Even before those six Ansaaris could come to Makkah, my cousin (my mother's sister's son) Mu'aaz bin 'Afraa and I came to Makkah. We met with Rasulullah ﷺ and he presented the beauty of Islam to us. He asked me: "O Rifa'ah! Tell me, who created the earth, skies and mountains?" We replied: "Allah created them." He then asked: "Who is more worthy of being worshipped; the Creator or the created?" We replied: "The Creator." Rasulullah ﷺ then advised: "So you are entitled to be worshipped by these idols whilst you worship Allah because you created these idols whilst you were created by Allah. I am inviting you to the worship of just one Allah. Believe in the oneness of Allah and do not ascribe any partners unto him and regard me as the messenger and Prophet of Allah. Maintain favourable relationship with your kith and kin and refrain from oppression and transgression."

To this I replied: "You have certainly invited us towards outstanding character and magnificent characteristics"

I then rose from there and headed off towards the Haram where I loudly proclaimed: "I bear witness that there is none worthy of worship besides Allah and that Muhammad ﷺ is His messenger."

The Institution of Jumu'ah at Madinah

In the same year As'ad bin Zuraarah ﷺ established Jumu'ah at Madinah Munawwarah. When he observed that the Jews and Christians have a special day of the week in which they congregate; the Jews on Saturday and the Christians on Sunday, he reflected that the Muslims should also observe a day of the week in which they congregate to remember Allah, to express their Shukr (appreciation) before him, to offer Salaah and to worship Him. As'ad bin Zuraarah proposed the day of Friday as this special day for the Muslims and on this day he led everyone in Salaah.

In short, the Sahaabah ﷺ, on the basis of their own Ijtihaad (inference), firstly established the performance of Jumu'ah and secondly they proposed that the name of that auspicious day be referred to as the day of Jumu'ah. Previously, during the times of ignorance, the day was referred to as the day of 'Arubah. The divine revelation of Allah approved of both these inferences, as evident from the following verse:

يَا أَيُّهَا الَّذِيْنَ اٰمَنُوْا اِذَا نُوْدِيَ لِلصَّلٰوةِ مِنْ يَّوْمِ الْجُمُعَةِ فَاسْعَوْا اِلٰى ذِكْرِ اللهِ

"When the call for prayer is proclaimed on the day of Friday, hasten towards the Zikr of Allah..." [Surah Jumu'ah]

Besides establishing the compulsion of Jumu'ah, this verse also proves that Allah Ta'ala approved the name Jumu'ah. The divine revelation of Allah Ta'ala refrained from using the name Yawm-e-'Arubah (day of 'Arubah) for Friday as was prevalent in the pre-Islamic days of ignorance and employed exactly the same name proposed by the Ansaar. Judging from this perspective, Allah Ta'ala has endorsed and approved of the Ijtihaad (inference) of the Ansaar.

Merely a few days later, Rasulullah's ﷺ letter addressed to Mus'ab bin 'Umair ؓ reached the people of Madinah wherein he instructed them to congregate and perform two Rakaat of Salaah after midday.

'Abdur-Rahmaan bin K'ab bin Maalik ؓ says: "Whenever my father K'ab bin Maalik ؓ heard the Azaan of Jumu'ah being called he would fondly bring to mind As'ad bin Zuraarah and make dua of forgiveness for him. When I once enquired about this, he replied: 'In Madinah, he was the first person to lead us in Jumu'ah Salaah.'"

Second Pledge of the Ansaar – 13th year of prophet-hood

The following year, which was the thirteenth year of prophet-hood, Mus'ab bin 'Umair ؓ, in the company of a group of Muslims, set out for Makkah with the intention of performing Haj. Accompanying these Muslim pilgrims were a number of disbelievers from the Aws and Khazraj tribes who had not as yet embraced Islam. Most of the group, which numbered more than four hundred, comprised of these people. According to the most popular view, the Muslims numbered seventy-five; seventy-three men and two women, who pledged their allegiance at the hands of Rasulullah ﷺ in the same valley where the very first group had pledged their allegiance. This second pledge is referred to Bay'atul 'Aqabah Saaniyah (the second pledge of allegiance).

'Allaamah Jawzi ؒ says that the people who pledged their allegiance on this occasion numbered a few more than seventy five.

Hadhrat Jaabir ؓ narrates: "For ten long years Rasulullah ﷺ would go to meet the people in their houses, in the market places and in their social functions. He would invite them towards Islam pleading with them: 'Who will grant assistance to me? Who will support me? Who will assist me in conveying the message of my Lord? For him I guarantee Jannah.' But alas, he would return in vain without any support or assistance.

This continued until such time that Allah Ta'ala sent us from Yasrib to Rasulullah ﷺ. We placed our trust in him and offered him assistance. Everyone of us who appeared before him returned as a Muslim. When Islam penetrated almost every home in Madinah, we convened a meeting in which we deliberated over the plight of Rasulullah ﷺ. We thought, for how long more are we going to forsake Rasulullah ﷺ in this bleak condition? For how long more will we observe him anxiously walking about on the mountains of Makkah?

Nonetheless, from Madinah, seventy of us came to Makkah for Haj that year……." (up to the end of the Hadith).

When this caravan reached Makkah, they secretly sent a message to Rasulullah ﷺ informing him that they wished to meet him. Rasulullah ﷺ promised to meet them during the days of Tashreeq (Haj) in the same valley in Mina where the other fortunate pilgrims of Madinah had pledged their allegiance the preceding year.

At the appointed hour, in the company of his uncle Hadhrat 'Abbaas رضي الله عنه, Rasulullah ﷺ met them in the valley of Mina. Although Hadhrat 'Abbaas رضي الله عنه had not as yet embraced Islam, he was nonetheless a devoted supporter of Rasulullah ﷺ. The moment he took a seat, Hadhrat 'Abbaas رضي الله عنه addressed the Ansaar saying: "Muhammad (ﷺ) is an exceptionally esteemed and well-regarded man in his community. (Although people were antagonistic towards Rasulullah's ﷺ Deen but the honour and admiration they cherished for him was not accorded to anyone else.) We are his staunch supporters and loyal protectors. He wishes to come over to you. If you are capable of providing your loyal support and absolute protection to him and you sincerely believe you would remain committed to this unto death, well and good otherwise give me an honest answer now."

The Ansaar replied: "Okay, we understand what your concerns are."

Addressing Rasulullah ﷺ, they then said: "O Prophet of Allah! Whatever you want from us, we are eager to comply. Whatever the demands are of you and Allah, we are enthusiastic and you may even take a pledge from us."

Rasulullah ﷺ replied: "I am inviting you towards Allah." He then presented them with Islam and recited a few portions of the Holy Qur-aan. He then proclaimed: "For Allah, I urge you to worship Him Alone and refrain from ascribing any partner unto Him. For my friends, I request you to grant us refuge, offer us your protection just as you would protect your own wives and children, and that you will obey me in times of bliss and despair, in comfort and adversity, in prosperity and in poverty. In every condition you will take heed and abide by my instructions."

"What will we get in return," asked the Ansaar "if we comply?"

Rasulullah ﷺ replied: "Jannah!" (In other words, the eternal bounties of the hereafter.)

The Ansaar replied: "We accept all your conditions. Come, stretch out your blessed hand, we wish to pledge our allegiance."

Abul-Haysam bin Tayhaan رضي الله عنه anxiously asked: "O Prophet of Allah! I am a bit concerned about something. We enjoy some relationships with the Jews. Since we have established a relationship with you, the Jews are bound to sever these relationships. Let it not be such that when Allah Ta'ala makes you victorious and provides you with assistance, you return to Makkah leaving us (floundering) here in Madinah." Rasulullah ﷺ smiled and said: "Never! Your life is my life. You are mine and I am yours. Your adversaries are my adversaries and your allies are my allies."

Upon this, all of them enthusiastically stretched their hands in a pledge of allegiance.

Hadhrat 'Abbaas رضي الله عنه replied: "The first person to pledge allegiance at the blessed hands of Rasulullah ﷺ was As'ad bin Zuraarah (who was the most fortunate). Thereafter Baraa bin M'arur رضي الله عنه and then Usaid bin Hudhair رضي الله عنه."

(In order to lend more support and underpin this pledge), 'Abbaas bin 'Ubaadah, addressing the Khazraj, said: "O people of Khazraj! Do you realise what you are pledging? Bear in mind that you are pledging to wage war with the Arabs and the non-Arabs. If you have even an inkling that in future, when faced with devastating catastrophes, you would apprehensively abandon this, you might as well give up now. By Allah! Giving up then out of fearfulness will be a source of indignity in this world as well as the next. If, however, you are prepared to suffer the adversities of the future, if you are willing to sacrifice your wealth and lives and you are eager to remain staunch upon this pledge, then, by Allah, this will be a source of your success and fortune in this world as well as the next."

In one voice they all agreed: "Yes, we are pledging our allegiance upon this. We are not reluctant to sacrifice our wealth and lives for Rasulullah ﷺ. Even when faced with danger, by Allah, we will never violate this pledge."

Assigning Nuqabaa (Leaders)

When all of them had given their pledge, Rasulullah ﷺ said: "Musa عليه السلام had chosen twelve Nuqabaa (leaders) from the Jews. In a similar vein, as per the counsel of Jibraa'eel عليه السلام, I also choose twelve leaders from amongst you."

He then addressed these leaders saying: "You twelve are representatives of your people just as the Hawaariyyeen were the representatives of 'Isa عليه السلام."

Names of the Nuqabaa

The twelve whom Rasulullah ﷺ had elected as the Nuqabaa (leaders) over the Ansaar are as follows:

1. As'ad bin Zuraarah رضي الله عنه

2. 'Abdullah bin Rawaahah رضي الله عنه

3. S'ad bin Rab'i رضي الله عنه

4. Raaf'i bin Maalik رضي الله عنه

5. Abu Jaabir 'Abdullah bin 'Amr ﺭﺿﻲ ﺍﻟﻠﻪ ﻋﻨﻪ

6. Baraa bin Ma'rur ﺭﺿﻲ ﺍﻟﻠﻪ ﻋﻨﻪ

7. S'ad bin 'Ubaadah ﺭﺿﻲ ﺍﻟﻠﻪ ﻋﻨﻪ

8. Munzir bin 'Amr ﺭﺿﻲ ﺍﻟﻠﻪ ﻋﻨﻪ

9. 'Ubaadah bin Saamit ﺭﺿﻲ ﺍﻟﻠﻪ ﻋﻨﻪ

10. Usaid bin Hudhair ﺭﺿﻲ ﺍﻟﻠﻪ ﻋﻨﻪ

11. S'ad bin Khaysamah ﺭﺿﻲ ﺍﻟﻠﻪ ﻋﻨﻪ

12. Rifa'ah bin 'Abdul-Munzir ﺭﺿﻲ ﺍﻟﻠﻪ ﻋﻨﻪ

Zuhri says that Rasulullah ﷺ addressed the Ansaar saying: "I want to appoint twelve leaders from amongst you. None of you should be offended if he is not chosen as a Naqeeb because I am obliged to do as I am instructed." Jibraa'eel ﻋﻠﻴﻪ ﺍﻟﺴﻼﻡ who was seated next to Rasulullah ﷺ would gesture to the proposed Naqeeb and Rasulullah ﷺ would in turn go on appointing them.

The next morning when news of this pledge started spreading in Makkah, the Quraysh came to the Ansaar to verify this news. Since there were some disbelievers and idolaters in this caravan as well and they were unaware of this pledge, they utterly rejected this as a rumour saying that if this had some substance of truth in it, they would have known something.

After some time, this caravan, comprising of Muslims and non-Muslims alike, left for Madinah. Only once they had departed, the Quraysh learnt that the information they received about this pledge was authentic. They swiftly despatched some people to give chase but the caravan had already covered some distance and they were unable to catch up. They only managed to seize S'ad bin 'Ubaadah ﺭﺿﻲ ﺍﻟﻠﻪ ﻋﻨﻪ who was left behind the caravan. They collared him and subjected him to a severe beating. Jubair bin Mut'im ﺭﺿﻲ ﺍﻟﻠﻪ ﻋﻨﻪ managed to release him from their clutches.

Bay'at – the pledge, what is it?

Bay'at is an Arabic word derived from Bay'a, which means to sell. In technical terms, it refers to enthusiastically selling one's life and wealth at the hands of Allah in exchange of Jannah.

So when this pledge was underway, 'Abdullah bin Rawaahah enquired: "O Prophet of Allah! You are at liberty to take whatever assurances you want from us but tell me, what will we attain in exchange of this?" Rasulullah ﷺ replied: "Jannah."

'Abdullah bin Rawaahah ﺭﺿﻲ ﺍﻟﻠﻪ ﻋﻨﻪ remarked:

ربح البيع لا نقيل ولا نستقيل

"This is a rather profitable transaction. We will neither dissolve this transaction nor will we solicit its termination."

Upon this, Allah Ta'ala revealed the following verses:

اِنَّ اللهَ اشْتَرٰى مِنَ الْمُؤْمِنِيْنَ اَنْفُسَهُمْ وَ اَمْوَالَهُمْ بِاَنَّ لَهُمُ الْجَنَّةَ ۚ يُقَاتِلُوْنَ فِىْ سَبِيْلِ اللهِ فَيَقْتُلُوْنَ وَ يُقْتَلُوْنَ ۖ وَعْدًا عَلَيْهِ حَقًّا فِى التَّوْرٰىةِ وَ الْاِنْجِيْلِ وَ الْقُرْاٰنِ ۚ وَمَنْ اَوْفٰى بِعَهْدِهٖ مِنَ اللهِ فَاسْتَبْشِرُوْا بِبَيْعِكُمُ الَّذِىْ بَايَعْتُمْ بِهٖ ۚ وَ ذٰلِكَ هُوَ الْفَوْزُ الْعَظِيْمُ ۞

"Verily Allah has purchased from the believers their lives and wealth in exchange for Jannah. They wage battle in the path of Allah in which they sometimes kill and sometimes get killed. This is the true promise of Allah in the Taurah, Injeel and the Qur-aan. And who is more conforming to his promises than Allah? So rejoice in this transaction you have concluded. That is the supreme success." [Taubah verse 111]

In Jannah, a unique market will be erected. Those who have sold their wealth and lives to Allah and they have surrendered their lives and properties to Him will be at liberty to choose whatever they desire from this market because they have already made advance payment (with their lives and wealth).

How well an Arab poet describes this when he says:

حى على السُّوْقِ الذى فيه يلتقى   المحبون ذاكَ السُّوْقُ للقوم مَعْلَمُ
فما شئت خُذْ مِنْهُ بِلَا ثَمَنٍ لَهُ   فَقَدْ اَسْلَفَ التُّجَّارُ فيه وَاَسْلَمُوْا

"Hasten to the market wherein the devotees would meet, that market would be reserved for some people. (They will be told) 'Take whatever you desire from therein.' Verily the traders had made exceedingly profitable transactions in future trading."

Important Note

Whilst taking the oath of allegiance, Rasulullah ﷺ would clasp the hands of men only. He did not shake the hands of women. He would accept a verbal pledge from them and inform them that their pledge of allegiance is complete and they may return.

Open proclamation of Islam in Madinah

This caravan of the Ansaar left Makkah and eventually reached Madinah where they openly proclaimed their conversion to Islam. Most of the tribes of Madinah had already embraced Islam although there were a few obstinate elders who were fiercely clinging onto their ancient ways of idolatry. One of them was 'Amr bin Jamooh, the leader of the Banu Salmah tribe and whose son Mu'aaz bin 'Amr bin Jamooh had just returned from Makkah after pledging his allegiance at the blessed hands of Rasulullah ﷺ. 'Amr bin Jamooh had crafted a wooden idol for himself to which he accorded great respect and he held in high esteem. One night, his own son, Mu'aaz bin 'Amr, Mu'aaz bin Jabal and a few youngsters of the Banu Salmah tribe whisked away this idol and dumped it upside-down into a large gutter. In the morning, 'Amr bin Jamooh discovered that his own handcrafted god has disappeared. He started muttering: "Alas! I wonder who took my god away." He promptly went around the area in search of this idol and found it lying upside down in a huge cesspit. He retrieved it from the pit, washed it thoroughly and applied some perfume to it. On the second night, these youngsters once again hauled the idol away and dumped it into another large pit. The next morning, 'Amr bin Jamooh went out in search for it again. He recovered it from the pit, bathed it and applied fragrance to it.

When this happened ceaselessly over a period of few days, 'Amr bin Jamooh placed a sword over the idol's neck saying: "By Allah! I wonder who is doing this to you. If you have any good in you, here, take this sword and protect yourself."

That night, these youngsters removed the sword from its neck. They got hold of a dead dog and tied it to this idol. They then suspended both of them over a well. The next morning, 'Amr bin Jamooh learnt that his idol has disappeared once again. He went out in search of it and found his idol attached to a dead dog hanging over a well. The moment he laid eyes on this spectacle, his eyes opened and addressing the idol, he called out: "By Allah! If you were truly a god, you would not have been subject to such utter humiliation!"

Chapter 9

Migration to Madinah Munawwarah

Just as the inception of prohethood was launched with pious dreams, similarly, the origins of Hijrah (migration) were initiated in the form of pious dreams. At the beginning, Rasulullah ﷺ was shown dreams about the location of his migration but not the name of the place. He was merely shown that his place of migration was a place abounding in date palms. This is why he was under the impression that the place was perhaps Yamaamah or Hajar. Whilst he was reflecting over this, divine revelation singled out Madinah Munawwarah as the place of migration. On the basis of this divine directive, Rasulullah ﷺ commanded his Sahaabah رضي الله عنهم to emigrate to Madinah Munawwarah.

According to another Hadith, Allah Ta'ala revealed to Rasulullah ﷺ that whichever city you are drawn to from Madinah, Bahrain or Qinasriyyeen, that city will be regarded as your Daarul-Hijrah (place of migration).

Note: Just as a number of various homes are offered to an honoured guest to choose whichever one he wishes, similarly, as a mark of honour, Rasulullah ﷺ was offered a number of locations for Hijrah. Madinah was ultimately chosen as his place of Hijrah.

After the termination of Bay'atul-Aqabah, Rasulullah ﷺ commanded the Sahaabah رضي الله عنهم to emigrate to Madinah Munawwarah. The moment they were made aware of this divine commandment, frantic but secretive preparation began. The first person to brace himself for this Hijrah was Rasulullah's ﷺ milk-brother Abu Salmah 'Abdul-Asad Makhzumi رضي الله عنه with his wife and son. However, Hijrah was not a stroll in the park. Whoever intended to emigrate would meet fierce resistance from the Quraysh. They would leave no stone unturned in preventing them from Hijrah because, after all, who would they employ as their targets of tyranny?

Nonetheless, Abu Salmah, with his wife and child, got ready to depart for Madinah. His carriage was put over his camel and his wife and child were already mounted on the camel. He was about departing when people heard about his migration. His wife Umme Salmah's ﷺ family, rushed up to him and said: "You can do whatever you want with your life but you are not at liberty to take our daughter away." Saying this, they grasped her hand and hauled her away. From the other side, Abu Salmah's ﷺ relatives came up to him saying: "This child belongs to our family and nobody has the right to take him away." They then snatched the child from her lap and made off with him. The father, mother and child all were pitilessly drawn apart in this manner. Abu Salmah ﷺ ultimately set out all alone for Madinah Munawwarah.

Umme Salmah ﷺ relates: "(Following this incident) I would go to Abtah every morning and cry my heart out. A whole year passed like this before one of my paternal cousins took pity upon me and rebuked my people of Banul-Mughirah saying: "Don't you have any pity for this miserable woman?" Upon this, Banul-Mughirah relented and allowed me to migrate to Madinah. The people of Banul-Asad also returned my son to me. I took the child on my lap, mounted the camel and set out for Madinah all alone.

When I landed at Tan'eem (just on the outskirts of Makkah), I was met by 'Usmaan bin Talhah ﷺ who asked me where I was off to. I replied: "I am on my way to Madinah to meet my husband." He asked: "Is there anybody accompanying you?" I replied:

$$\text{لا والله الا الله وبُنَيَّ هذا}$$

"No, nobody but Allah and this infant son of mine."

On hearing this, 'Usmaan ﷺ was on the verge of weeping. He took hold of the reins of the camel and started walking ahead of us. Whenever we halted, he would make the camel sit and move away. When I would dismount, he would take the camel a distance away, tie it to a tree and lie down under its shade. When we had to continue on our journey, he would bring the camel and move aside saying: "Go on, mount the camel." When I was mounted, he would take its reins and walk ahead. Whenever we broke our journey, he would maintain this attitude of modesty until we reached Madinah. As we caught sight of the buildings of Quba from a distance, he said: "Your husband resides in this village. Enter this village with the Barakah (blessings) of Allah Ta'ala." Delivering me to my husband, he returned to Makkah. By Allah! I haven't come across another man more noble and gracious than 'Usmaan bin Talhah ﷺ."

Thereafter 'Aamir bin Rabi'ah ﷺ migrated with his wife Layla bint Khaysamah ﷺ. Then Abu Ahmad bin Jahsh ﷺ with his brother 'Abdullah bin Jahsh رضي الله عنه with both their families set out for Madinah after locking their homes.

'Utbah and Abu Jahal were both sullenly viewing this spectacle where one by one, people were departing from Makkah. The houses of Makkah were all falling eerily vacant. Almost on the verge of tears, 'Utbah took a deep breath and wailed:

$$\text{كُلُّ دَارٍ وَإِنْ طَالَتْ سَلَامَتُهَا} \quad \text{يَوْمًا سَتُدْرِكُهَا النَّكْبَاءُ وَالْحُوْبُ}$$

"Every house, no matter how long it remains safe and homely, one day it is bound to turn into a house of bereavement and sorrow."

He then exclaimed: "This is all because of our nephew. He is responsible for causing such a turbulent division within our society."

Thereafter the following personalities migrated: 'Ukkaashah bin Mihsan, 'Uqbah bin Wahab, Shuj'a bin Wahab, Arbad bin Jamirah, Munqiz bin Nabatah, Sa'eed bin Ruqaish, Muhriz bin Nadlah, Yazeed bin Ruqaish, Qays bin Jaabir, 'Amr bin Mihsan, Safwaan bin 'Amr, Saqeef bin 'Amr, Rabi'ah bin Aktham, Zubair bin 'Ubaid, Tamaam bin 'Ubaidah, Sanjarah bin 'Ubaidah and Muhammad bin Jahsh رضي الله عنهم. Amongst the ladies who migrated in this wave were: Zainab bint Jahsh, Umme Habibah bint Jahsh, Juzamah bint Jundul, Umme Qays bint Mihsan, Umme Habib bint Sumaamah, Aaminah bint Ruqaysh, Sanjarah bint Tameem, Hamnah bint Jahsh رضي الله عنهن.

They were followed by Hadhrat 'Umar رضي الله عنه and 'Ayaash bin Abi Rabi'ah رضي الله عنه in the company of twenty other mounted emigrants.

Hishaam bin 'Aas رضي الله عنه was also supposed to migrate with Hadhrat 'Umar رضي الله عنه but his people intensely protested against his departure and prevented him from departing.

When Hadhrat 'Umar رضي الله عنه and 'Ayaash bin Abi Rabi'ah رضي الله عنه landed in Madinah, Abu Jahal bin Hishaam and his brother Haaris bin Hishaam (Abu Jahal's brother who later embraced Islam) travelled to Madinah. They located 'Ayaash and said to him: "Your mother has vowed that as long as she does not lay eyes on you she will neither comb her hair nor will she take shade from the sunshine." This touching vow hurled him onto the brink of tears and he promptly agreed to return to Makkah with them. They barely set out when Abu Jahal tied his hands behind his back. He brought him to Makkah and locked him up for a long period of time. During this incarceration, he subjected him to all forms of physical anguish.

During Fajr Salaah, Rasulullah ﷺ would recite the Qunoot and make special dua for him as well. He would beseech Allah Ta'ala saying:

$$\text{اللّٰهُمَّ انج الوليد بن الوليد وسلمة بن هشام و عياش بن ابى ربيعه}$$

"O Allah! Deliver Waleed bin Waleed, Salmah bin Hishaam and 'Ayaash bin Abi Rabi'ah (from the persecution of the disbelievers)."

Subsequently, Allah Ta'ala released him from this agony and he fled to Madinah.

The following people joined Hadhrat 'Umar رضي الله عنه in the Hijrah: Zaid bin Khattaab (Hadhrat 'Umar's elder brother), 'Amr and 'Abdullah (the sons of Suraaqah), Khunais bin Huzaafa Sahmi, Sa'eed bin 'Amr bin Nufail, Waaqid bin 'Abdullah Tameemi, Khawla bin Khawla, Maalik bin Abi Khawla and the four sons of Bukair; Iyaas, 'Aamir, 'Aaqil and Khaalid رضي الله عنهم.

After this group, a procession of others followed. Some of them were: Talhah bin 'Ubaidullah, Suhaib bin Sinaan, Hamzah bin 'Abdul-Muttalib, Zaid bin Haarisah, Abu Marthad Kanaaz bin Hasan, Anasah, Abu Kabshah, Abu 'Ubaidah bin Haaris and his two brothers Tufail bin Haaris and Husain bin Haaris, Mistah bin Athaathah, Suwait bin S'ad, Tulaib bin 'Umair, Khabbaab bin Aratt, 'Abdur-Rahmaan bin 'Awf, Zubair bin 'Awwaam, Abu Sabrah bin Abi Riham, Mus'ab bin 'Umair, Abu Huzaifah bin 'Utbah, Saalim the emancipated slave of Abu Huzaifah, 'Utbah bin Ghazwaan and 'Usmaan bin Affaan رضي الله عنهم. In short, gradually, one by one, group by group, all the Sahaabah رضي الله عنهم emigrated to Madinah Munawwarah.

In Makkah it was only Rasulullah ﷺ, Hadhrat Abu Bakr رضي الله عنه and Hadhrat Ali رضي الله عنه who remained. Yes, a few helpless and vulnerable Muslims trapped within the brutal clutches of the disbelievers still remained behind in Makkah.

Assembly of Quraysh in Daarun-Nadwah and their Resolution to Assassinate Rasulullah ﷺ

When the Quraysh realised that gradually all the Sahaabah رضي الله عنهم had migrated to Madinah and Rasulullah's ﷺ departure was also imminent, a number of chieftains convened in Daarun-Nadwah to deliberate over this 'predicament'. Amongst the chieftains gathered were: 'Utbah bin Rabi'ah, Shaybah bin Rabi'ah, Abu Sufyaan bin Harb, Ta'imah bin 'Adi, Jubair bin Mut'im, Haaris bin 'Aamir, Abul-Bakhtari bin Hishaam, Zam'ah bin Aswad, Hakeem bin Hizaam, Abu Jahal bin Hishaam, Nabihah and Munabbihah sons of Hajaaj and Umayyah bin Khalaf.

Iblees the accursed appeared in this gathering in the form of an old man. As he turned up at the door people asked him whom he was. He replied: "I am a Shaikh from Najd. I wish to listen to your discussion and if possible, I would assist you by voicing my personal opinion and counsel."

The people allowed him entry and the discussion began. One of them suggested that Rasulullah ﷺ should be imprisoned within a fully enclosed closet. To this the 'Najdi Shaikh' responded: "No, this is not the ideal solution because if his companions learn of his imprisonment, they would overwhelm you and release him." Someone else proposed to banish him from Makkah altogether. To this the 'Najdi Shaikh' countered: "No! This opinion is definitely not acceptable. Are you not aware of the sweetness, allure and captivating nature of his speech? If you drive him out of here, perhaps the inhabitants of another city would listen to his sweet words and believe in him. Then all of them may just get together and launch an attack against us."

Abu Jahal said: "I am of the opinion that neither should we incarcerate him nor should we banish him. Rather we should select a young man from each and every tribe and all of them should jointly assassinate Muhammad. In this manner, Muhammad's ﷺ blood will be fanned out over all the tribes and his tribe, Banu Abdu Manaaf, would not be able to hit back against any particular tribe. They will be forced to settle the matter by accepting blood money."

The 'Najdi Shaikh' responded quite excitedly to this proposal. With fervent enthusiasm he said: "By Allah! This seems like the most excellent plan." Other members of the meeting also sanctioned this proposal.

It was also agreed in this meeting that this baneful plan be carried out that very night.

This assembly barely dispersed when Hadhrat Jibraa'eel عليه السلام appeared before Rasulullah ﷺ with divine revelation enlightening him about their evil plot in the following verses:

وَاِذْ يَمْكُرُ بِكَ الَّذِيْنَ كَفَرُوْا لِيُثْبِتُوْكَ اَوْ يَقْتُلُوْكَ اَوْ يُخْرِجُوْكَ ۚ وَيَمْكُرُوْنَ وَيَمْكُرُ اللّٰهُ ۖ وَاللّٰهُ خَيْرُ الْمٰكِرِيْنَ ۞

"And remember when the disbelievers were conspiring against you either to incarcerate, kill or banish you. They were plotting and Allah was plotting but Allah Ta'ala is the best of plotters." [Surah Anfaal verse 30]

He was then fully apprised of the sinister plot of the disbelievers and he was divinely commanded to emigrate to Madinah Munawarrah. Rasulullah ﷺ was also advised to recite the following dua:

وَقُلْ رَّبِّ اَدْخِلْنِيْ مُدْخَلَ صِدْقٍ وَّاَخْرِجْنِيْ مُخْرَجَ صِدْقٍ وَّاجْعَلْ لِّيْ مِنْ لَّدُنْكَ سُلْطٰنًا نَّصِيْرًا ۞

"And say: 'My Lord! Let my entry (into Madinah) be good and (similarly) let my exit (from Makkah) be good. And grant me from Your side a dominion and assistance. [Surah Israa verse 80]

Hadhrat Ali رضي الله عنه narrates that Rasulullah ﷺ asked Jibraa'eel عليه السلام who would accompany him in the emigration. Jibraa'eel عليه السلام replied: "Abu Bakr رضي الله عنه will emigrate with you."

Hadhrat 'Aa'ishah رضي الله عنها narrates: "Right at high noon, Rasulullah ﷺ appeared at Abu Bakr's رضي الله عنه house and informed him that his emigration to Madinah had been divinely sanctioned by Allah Ta'ala. Overcome with excitement, Abu Bakr رضي الله عنه asked: "May my parents be sacrificed for you, O Prophet of Allah!

Will this unworthy man get the honour of travelling with you?" Rasulullah ﷺ replied: "Yes, surely."

On hearing this elating news, Abu Bakr ؓ burst into tears. Hadhrat 'Aa'ishah ؓ says: "Before this, I never knew that anyone could cry out of downright elation and joy. Long before this, Abu Bakr ؓ, in anticipation of this impending journey, set aside two camels, which he was feeding with acacia leaves for the last four months. He offered one of these camels to Rasulullah ﷺ saying: "O Prophet of Allah! may my parents be sacrificed for you! Please select one of these camels, it is a gift for you." Rasulullah ﷺ replied: "No, I would not accept it without paying for it." Abu Bakr replied: "Okay, if you want to pay for it, well and good. You may pay for it."

In other words, my personal desire is of no concern. My desires and inclinations are all subject to your directives.

That night as darkness spread across the land, the Quraysh, as per their predetermined resolution, besieged Rasulullah's ﷺ house planning to attack him later that night. Rasulullah ﷺ directed Hadhrat Ali ؓ to don his green sheet and lie down on his (Rasulullah's ﷺ) bed. He also advised him saying: "Do not panic. Nothing will happen to you."

Although the Quraysh were his nasty enemies, they still regarded him as trustworthy and honest. They would customarily entrust their valuables to his care. Rasulullah ﷺ handed over these entrusted items to Hadhrat Ali ؓ advising him to return them to their rightful owners.

Abu Jahal, the accursed, was standing outside and with riotous laughter he was mockingly telling his cohorts: "Muhammad is under the impression that if you follow him you will become the rulers of the Arabs and non-Arabs alike and you will get eternal paradise after your death. And if you fail to follow him, you will be killed at the hands of his companions and thereafter you will burn in the fire of Hell.

Whilst he was scornfully saying this, Rasulullah ﷺ emerged from the door. Taking a handful of sand, he said: "Yes, this is what I assure you would happen. You are also one of those who are destined to die at the hands of my companions and to burn in the fire of Hell." Over this handful of sand, Rasulullah ﷺ then recited the opening verses of Surah Yaaseen until the verse "Fa Aghshaynaahum Fa Hum Laa Yubsiroon (and We have swathed them so they cannot see)" and hurled this sand over their heads. Allah Ta'ala placed a veil over their eyes. He passed right before their very eyes without them realising it.

Rasulullah ﷺ then proceeded to Hadhrat Abu Bakr's ؓ house. Together they left home and headed off to the road leading to Mount Saur. They ascended the mountain and took cover in one of its caves. During this time, a man passed Rasulullah's ﷺ house and saw a number of the Quraysh milling about. When he enquired what they were waiting for, they replied: "We are waiting for Muhammad to emerge. The moment he sets foot out of his house, we will kill him." The man countered: "May Allah Ta'ala make your efforts go in vain. Muhammad (ﷺ) has hurled sand over your heads and passed by."

The next morning, when they saw Hadhrat Ali رضي الله عنه rising from Rasulullah's ﷺ bed, they exclaimed: "By Allah! That man was right." With untold misery dripping from their voices, they asked: "Where is Muhammad?" Hadhrat Ali رضي الله عنه replied: "I have no idea."

Note: The disbelievers of Makkah laid siege to his house but they did not break into the house itself because the Arabs considered it unethical to enter the female sections of anyone's home.

Thereafter Rasulullah ﷺ continued his journey. As he was leaving the environs of Makkah, he ascended a hillock and addressed Makkah lamentably saying:

$$\text{والله انك لخير ارض الله واحب ارض الله الىّ ولولا اني اخرجت منك ما خرجت}$$

"By Allah! You are the best of lands. You are the most dear to Allah. If I was not expelled from you, I would never have left you."

Ibn 'Abbaas رضي الله عنه narrates that Rasulullah ﷺ addressed the land of Makkah saying:

$$\text{ما اطيبك من بلد واحب الي ولولا ان قومي اخرجوني ما سكنت غيرك}$$

"What a pure land you are. You are very much dear to me. If my people did not expel me from you, I would not take up residence but in you."

Hadhrat Abu Bakr's رضي الله عنه elder daughter Hadhrat Asma رضي الله عنها, prepared their provisions for the road. Driven by haste, instead of using a cord, she ripped her girdle apart and used it as a cord to tie the provisions. From that day hence, she was referred to as Zaatun-Nitaaqayn (a woman with a double girdle). She used one portion of it to tie the provisions and the other to tie the mouth of the water-skin.

'Abdullah, the son of Abu Bakr رضي الله عنه, who was a still a young man, would spend the day in Makkah and in the evenings he would come to his father in the cave and give a report on the activities of the Quraysh. 'Aamir bin Fuhayrah, who was the emancipated slave of Hadhrat Abu Bakr رضي الله عنه would graze goats all day long and at Isha time he would come to the cave and feed Rasulullah ﷺ and Abu Bakr رضي الله عنه with goat's milk.

'Abdullah bin Uraiqeet was hired as a guide to take the pair of them via the relatively unknown route to Madinah. Although the guide, 'Abdullah bin Uraiqeet was a disbeliever, Rasulullah ﷺ and Hadhrat Abu Bakr ؓ still trusted him and counted upon (his navigational skills). They entrusted the camels to the guide requesting him to meet them on the third day at Mount Saur from where they would set out for Madinah.

Cave of Saur

In short, both of them left home the same night and set out for the cave of Saur.

When Rasulullah ﷺ proceeded towards the cave, his cave-companion, his devoted disciple, his dedicated companion, his sincere devotee, and his incomparable friend Hadhrat Abu Bakr ؓ was struck with an unusual sense of restlessness. Sometimes he would walk behind Rasulullah ﷺ and sometimes in front of him. At times he would walk on his right and sometimes to his left. In due course, Rasulullah ﷺ asked: "What is the matter Abu Bakr? Sometimes you walk ahead of me and sometimes behind me?" Abu Bakr ؓ replied: "O Rasulullah ﷺ! When I envisage someone hunting for you from the back, I promptly move behind you. When I dread someone waiting in ambush for you, I reposition myself to get ahead of you." Rasulullah ﷺ asked: "Abu Bakr! Your purpose for acting in this manner is to sacrifice your life for mine?" Hadhrat Abu Bakr ؓ replied: "Yes, O Prophet of Allah! I swear by the Being who has commissioned you with the truth, I wish to sacrifice my life in favour of yours." As they reached the cave, Abu Bakr ؓ said: "O Prophet of Allah! Just hold on a moment. I will enter the cave and clean it for you."

Abu Bakr ؓ entered the cave first and after a little while Rasulullah ﷺ followed him through. Soon thereafter, with the grace of Almighty Allah, a spider spun its web over the mouth of the cave.

The Quraysh surrounded Rasulullah's ﷺ house all night long. The next morning, they were startled to notice Ali ؓ awakening from Rasulullah's ﷺ bed. When they enquired from Hadhrat Ali ؓ about his whereabouts, he replied: "I have no idea." They promptly scurried about in all directions hunting for him until they reached the cave. When their glances fell onto the web screening the mouth of the cave, they said:

لو دخل هنا لم يكن نسيج العنكبوت على بابه

"This web would not have been here if he had entered the cave."

Whilst Rasulullah ﷺ sought refuge in the cave of Saur, with the will of Allah, a tree miraculously sprouted up before him. A pair of wild doves then laid their eggs in the nests that were on the tree. Whilst the disbelievers were hunting for Rasulullah ﷺ, they came across the cave but when they caught sight of the nests covering the tree, they retreated. Rasulullah ﷺ says: "Allah Ta'ala defended us from their (evils)."

Abu Bakr ؓ recounts: "When Rasulullah ﷺ and I were in the cave whilst the Quraysh were frenziedly searching for us and they somehow managed to get to the mouth of the cave, I anxiously submitted: 'O Prophet of Allah! If one of them has to lower his gaze, he is certainly bound to spot us.' Rasulullah ﷺ replied:

ماظنك يا ابا بكر باثنين الله ثالثهما

'What is your opinion, O Abu Bakr, of those two people amongst whom the third is Allah.'

(In other words), we are not alone. Allah is with us and He will shield us from their evil."

When Rasulullah ﷺ noticed Abu Bakr ؓ looking miserably sad, he said:

لَا تَحْزَنْ إِنَّ اللّٰهَ مَعَنَا

"Do not grieve. Certainly Allah is with us."

He also made special dua for Abu Bakr's ؓ pacification after which, a unique form of tranquillity and serenity descended over Abu Bakr ؓ. In this regard Allah Ta'ala states in the Holy Qur-aan:

إِذْ هُمَا فِى الْغَارِ إِذْ يَقُولُ لِصَاحِبِهٖ لَا تَحْزَنْ إِنَّ اللّٰهَ مَعَنَا ۖ فَأَنْزَلَ اللّٰهُ سَكِيْنَتَهٗ عَلَيْهِ وَأَيَّدَهٗ بِجُنُوْدٍ لَّمْ تَرَوْهَا وَجَعَلَ كَلِمَةَ الَّذِيْنَ كَفَرُوا السُّفْلٰى ۗ وَكَلِمَةُ اللّٰهِ هِىَ الْعُلْيَا ۗ وَاللّٰهُ عَزِيْزٌ حَكِيْمٌ

"When both of them were in the cave, when he (Rasulullah ﷺ) told his companion: 'Do not grieve. Certainly Allah is with us.' So Allah transmitted His special tranquillity over him and strengthened him with forces (angels) that you were unable to see and He rendered the word of the disbelievers the lowermost, and the word of Allah is always uppermost. And Allah is all-mighty, all-wise."

[Surah Taubah verse 40]

For three long days, Rasulullah ﷺ remained hidden in the cave. 'Abdullah, the son of Abu Bakr ؓ would spend the day in Makkah gathering information about the disbelievers and in the evenings, he would give them a detailed report of the happenings in Makkah and quickly depart as early as possible. 'Aamir bin

Fuhayrah رضي الله عنه (the emancipated slave of Abu Bakr رضي الله عنه) would come daily to the cave after 'Isha when it was somewhat dark. He would come with a few she-goats so that Rasulullah ﷺ and Abu Bakr رضي الله عنه could drink whatever milk they required. This is how they passed three nights in the cave.

On the fourth morning, 'Abdullah bin Uraiqeet (who was appointed as their guide to Madinah), as per his pledge, turned up at the cave with two she-camels. Casting aside the normal route to Madinah, he took them on the more unfamiliar coastal route to Madinah Munawwarah.

Rasulullah ﷺ mounted one camel whilst Abu Bakr رضي الله عنه mounted the other. In order to serve them, Abu Bakr رضي الله عنه also took his emancipated slave, 'Aamir bin Fuhayrah, along with him and seated him behind him on the same camel. 'Abdullah bin Uraiqeet mounted his own camel and since he was the guide, he would ride slightly ahead of them.

When Abu Bakr رضي الله عنه embraced Islam, he had a princely sum of forty thousand Dirhams in his possession. He spent most of this amount in the path of Allah. He would regularly purchase slaves and set them free. He had just five thousand from the original forty at the time of Hijrah. He took this money along as well. Even this was exhausted in purchasing the land for Masjide-Nabawi and in other religious projects. Hadhrat 'Aa'ishah رضي الله عنها says: "When Abu Bakr رضي الله عنه passed away, he did not leave behind a single Deenar nor Dirham."

Nonetheless, 'Abdullah bin Uraiqeet took Rasulullah ﷺ and Hadhrat Abu Bakr رضي الله عنه towards the lower regions of Makkah along the coastal route. From here they made their way to the lower regions of 'Asfaan travelling a stage at a time until they ultimately reached Quba (on the outskirts of Madinah).

Note: Rasulullah ﷺ left home and went straight to Abu Bakr's رضي الله عنه house. Taking Hadhrat Abu Bakr with him, both of them went into hiding in the cave of Saur. In the meantime, the disbelievers laid siege to his home but when they failed to locate him, a comprehensive search was launched. They frantically dispatched trackers to all areas and some of them eventually landed at the mouth of the cave but to no avail. Allah Ta'ala availed the services of a spider that could not have been provided by a hundred coats of mail. He remained concealed within this cave for three long days whilst the disbelievers kept up their exhaustive search for this period as well. When they ultimately became despondent of finding him, they sat down in frustration. In spite of their substantial offers of a reward of one hundred camels for the person who locates Rasulullah ﷺ and Abu Bakr رضي الله عنه, all their efforts went in vain. Exasperated by these turn of unexpected events, the intensity of their search subsequently subsided. This is when Rasulullah ﷺ and Abu Bakr رضي الله عنه slipped out of the cave and taking the coastal route, set out for Madinah Munawwarah.

Abu Bakr رضي الله عنه was well recognised amongst the people whilst Rasulullah ﷺ was not as well recognised. So whenever they encountered anyone en route who asked Abu Bakr who this man accompanying him was, he would reply: "This is the man showing me the way." In his mind, he would mean that this is the man showing me the proper road to goodness and to the hereafter.

Date of Departure

About three months after the pledge of 'Aqabah, on Thursday, the first of Rab'i-ul-Awwal, Rasulullah ﷺ set out from Makkah Mukarramah. He halted over in the cave for three days. On Monday he left the cave and set out for Madinah Munawwarah. He arrived in Madinah on a Monday.

Asma bint Abi Bakr says: "After the departure of Rasulullah ﷺ, some people came to my father's house enquiring about the whereabouts of Abu Bakr ؓ. Amongst them was Abu Jahal. When he asked me about the whereabouts of my father, I responded: 'By Allah! I have no idea whatsoever.' Abu Jahal delivered such an awful slap to my face that my ear-ring fell off."

Story of Umm-e-Ma'bad

As he slipped out of the cave en route to Madinah Munawwarah, Rasulullah ﷺ passed the tent of Umm-e-Ma'bad. She was a remarkably noble and incredibly hospitable woman. She would often sit on the porch of her tent. People of Rasulullah's ﷺ caravan approached her to purchase some dates and meat but she had nothing to offer them. Rasulullah's ﷺ glance fell onto a young goat in the corner of the tent. When he enquired about it, Umm-e-Ma'bad replied: "This goat is dreadfully frail and weak. This is why it is unable to graze with the rest of the herd out in the fields." Rasulullah ﷺ asked: "Does she have any milk?" She replied: "How can she ever have milk in this condition?" Rasulullah ﷺ asked: "Do I have your permission to milk her?" She replied: "May my parents be sacrificed for you. If there is any milk in them, you are more than welcome to help yourself." Reciting *Bismillah*, Rasulullah ﷺ placed his blessed hand over its udders, which miraculously started filling up with milk. Rasulullah ﷺ then set about milking the goat. A huge container, from which about eight to ten people could satiate themselves, filled up with its milk. Rasulullah ﷺ offered the milk to Umm-e-Ma'bad first. She drank to her fill. He then offered the container to his companions and then he drank right at the end. He once again milked the goat until the container was brimming with milk yet again. He then handed the container over to her and after accepting her in Bay'at (pledge of allegiance), he set out on his journey once more. In the evening, when Abu Ma'bad returned home after grazing the goats, he noticed a huge container of milk lying there. Taken aback by this startling spectacle, he asked: "Where did this milk come from, Umm-e-Ma'bad? This goat had not a drop of milk." She replied:

"Today an exceptionally blessed man happened to pass this way. By Allah! This is due to his Barakah (blessings)." She then went on to recount what transpired. Abu Ma'bad remarked: "Enlighten me a bit more about this man." Umm-e-Ma'bad recounted Rasulullah's ﷺ countenance, his divine nobility, his awe-inspiring nature and his indefinable dignity.

Abu Ma'bad remarked: "Okay, now I know who you are talking about. This is the same man from the Quraysh tribe. I will certainly present myself before him as well."

Incident of Suraaqah bin Maalik

The Quraysh publicly proclaimed a reward of one hundred camels each for the person who kills or captures either Muhammad (ﷺ) or Abu Bakr (رضي الله عنه).

Suraaqah bin Maalik bin J'usham narrates: "I was sitting in my usual place when a man came up to me saying that he caught sight of a few people sneaking off onto the coastal route. He also added that he believes that these people were Muhammad and his companions."

Suraaqah continues: "I was positive that these people were really Muhammad and his friends but out of fear of this man receiving the promised prize of one hundred camels instead of myself, I somehow skirted the whole issue and convinced him that it was someone else and not Muhammad."

Suraaqah continues: "A little while later, I got up from my place and asked my slave girl to take the horse to a certain hillock and wait for me there. I clutched my spear and crept out of the back of the house. I reached the horse and with lightning speed I mounted the horse and shoved him into a full gallop."

As Suraaqah reached Rasulullah ﷺ, Abu Bakr رضي الله عنه noticed someone riding fast in their direction. Abu Bakr رضي الله عنه anxiously submitted: "O Rasulullah ﷺ! Now we will really be captured. This man is coming in search of us." Rasulullah ﷺ responded:

لَا تَحْزَنْ إِنَّ اللهَ مَعَنَا

"Don't worry! Certainly Allah is with us."

He then cursed Suraaqah. He barely uttered the curse when Suraaqah's horse slumped into the rocky ground right up to its knees. Suraaqah submitted: "I am certain that this happened because of your curse. I beseech both of you to make dua for me. By Allah! I swear that I will turn back whoever is hunting for you."

Rasulullah ﷺ prayed for him and Suraaqah's horse was forthwith released by the ground. Suraaqah says: "From this I promptly gathered that Allah Ta'ala was bound to grant Rasulullah ﷺ dominance. I went on to inform him about the Quraysh's sinister plot to assassinate him and I also apprised him of the reward of one hundred camels offered by them. I then offered him whatever food provisions I had on me but he declined to accept it. However, he requested me not to disclose his condition to anyone.

As an added precautionary measure, I asked him to write out a note of security and pardon in my favour. With Rasulullah's ﷺ directive, 'Aamir bin Fuhayrah wrote out a note of clemency on a piece of leather. Issuing the note to me, they set forth. Clutching the note of clemency, I also headed off towards Makkah. Whenever I came across anyone searching for Rasulullah ﷺ, I would turn him back saying: "There is no need for you to go this way. I have already searched this area."

In the same regard, Suraaqah poetically addresses Abu Jahal as follows:

ابا حكم والله لو كنت شاهدا   لامر جوادي حين ساخت قوائمه

"By Allah! Abu Hakam (Abu Jahal), if you were present when my horse's legs sank into the ground,

علمت ولم تشكك بان محمدا   نبي ببرهان فمن ذا يقاومه

You would have been convinced without a shadow of doubt that Muhammad is a messenger who has come with indisputable proofs. So, who will be able to oppose him?"

Note: This miracle of Rasulullah ﷺ was similar to the miracle of Hadhrat Musa عليه السلام. Just as Qaarun was sunk into the earth with the curse of Musa عليه السلام, similarly, Suraaqah's horse sank into the ground with the dua of Rasulullah ﷺ.

Nonetheless, without further incident and fear, they proceeded with the rest of the journey.

As they drew closer to Madinah Munawwarah, Rasulullah ﷺ met Hadhrat Zubair رضي الله عنه who was returning with a trade caravan from Syria. Hadhrat Zuabir رضي الله عنه presented Rasulullah ﷺ and Hadhrat Abu Bakr رضي الله عنه with white clothing.

According to Ibn Abi Shaybah's narration, Hadhrat Talhah رضي الله عنه also offered some clothing to these two personalities.

Incident of Buraidah Aslami

As they pushed ahead, Buraidah Aslami, like Suraaqah, was also hunting for Rasulullah ﷺ with seventy other searchers. He also fancied the coveted one hundred-camel-reward offered by the Quraysh. As he drew closer, Rasulullah ﷺ asked him: "Who are you?" "I am Buraidah," he replied.

Turning towards Abu Bakr رَضِىَ اللهُ عَنْهُ, Rasulullah صَلَّى اللهُ عَلَيْهِ وَسَلَّمَ, taking a favourable omen, remarked: "O Abu Bakr! Our concerns have cooled down and they have been resolved." (His name was Buraidah. It is a diminutive of Bard, which means coolness. So when he mentioned that his name is Buraidah, Rasulullah صَلَّى اللهُ عَلَيْهِ وَسَلَّمَ took this as a good omen that now their anxieties will be cooled down.)

He then asked: "From which tribe do you hail?"

"From Aslam," he replied.

Turning towards Abu Bakr رَضِىَ اللهُ عَنْهُ, Rasulullah صَلَّى اللهُ عَلَيْهِ وَسَلَّمَ, as a good omen, said: "We will remain safe."

"From which clan of the Aslam tribe do you come?" asked Rasulullah صَلَّى اللهُ عَلَيْهِ وَسَلَّمَ.

He replied: "From the Banu Sahm."

To this Rasulullah صَلَّى اللهُ عَلَيْهِ وَسَلَّمَ responded: "Your Sahm (share of Islam) has materialised." In other words, you will get a share of Islam.

Buraidah then asked: "Who are you?"

Rasulullah صَلَّى اللهُ عَلَيْهِ وَسَلَّمَ replied:

انا محمد بن عبدالله ورسول الله

"I am Muhammad, the son of 'Abdullah and the Prophet of Allah."

To this Buraidah said:

اَشْهَدُ اَنْ لَا اِلٰهَ اِلَّا اللهُ وَاَنَّ مُحَمَّدًا عَبْدُهُ وَ رَسُوْلُهُ

"I bear witness that there is none worthy of worship besides Allah and certainly Muhammad is His servant and messenger."

Buraidah, together with the seventy others accompanying him all embraced Islam.

Buraidah then voiced his advice to Rasulullah صَلَّى اللهُ عَلَيْهِ وَسَلَّمَ saying: "You should hoist a flag abreast of you as you are entering Madinah." Rasulullah صَلَّى اللهُ عَلَيْهِ وَسَلَّمَ removed his 'Imaamah (turban) and lashing it onto a spear, he offered it to Buraidah رَضِىَ اللهُ عَنْهُ. When Rasulullah صَلَّى اللهُ عَلَيْهِ وَسَلَّمَ ultimately entered Madinah Munawwarah, Buraidah was walking ahead of him bearing this flag.

The delightful news of Rasulullah's صَلَّى اللهُ عَلَيْهِ وَسَلَّمَ departure and his imminent arrival in Madinah Munawwarah had already reached the inhabitants of Madinah. Driven by an ardent yearning to lay eyes on him, every single individual of Madinah would come and await his arrival at a place called Harrah (on the outskirts of Madinah). This was their daily ritual. One day, as they were leaving without catching sight of him, a Jew who was atop one of the hillocks of Madinah, ecstatically and inadvertently shouted out:

يَا بَنِيْ قِيْلَه هٰذَا جَدُّكُمْ

"O children of Qilah! Here comes your source of good fortune and blessings."

The moment the Ansaar heard this delightful news, they were overcome with ecstatic joy and in unreserved exhilaration, they hastened to welcome him. The entire locality of Bani 'Amr bin Awf reverberated with the cries of Takbeer.

Approximately three miles (South of) Madinah is a locality called Quba. Here, a few families of the Ansaar resided. These inhabitants were predominantly made up of the family of 'Amr bin 'Awf and the chieftain of this family was Kulsoom bin Hadam. When Rasulullah ﷺ landed at Quba, he put up at the house of Kulsoom bin Hadam whilst Hadhrat Abu Bakr ؓ stayed at the house of Khabib bin Isaaf. The Ansaar would come to him in droves from all around the vicinity and with fervent conviction they would present themselves to offer their enthusiastic and passionate Salaam.

After the departure of Rasulullah ﷺ from Makkah, Hadhrat Ali ؓ stayed over in Makkah for another three days. Once he surrendered the property of the people entrusted to him by Rasulullah ﷺ just before he set out for Hijrah, Hadhrat Ali ؓ also left Makkah. He joined Rasulullah ﷺ in Quba and he also put up with Rasulullah ﷺ at the house of Kulsoom bin Hadam.

Foundation of Masjidut Taqwa

Subsequent to his arrival in Quba, the first task Rasulullah ﷺ undertook to do was the laying of the foundation of a Masjid. He brought a stone with his own blessed hands and placed it in the direction of the Qiblah. Abu Bakr ؓ and then 'Umar ؓ also placed a stone each in the same direction. After them, the other Sahaabah ؓ fetched a stone each and then the actual construction of the Masjid started in earnest. With the Sahaabah ؓ, Rasulullah ﷺ would also lug heavy boulders. At times, to clutch it more firmly, he would hold it close to his blessed stomach. The Sahaabah ؓ would urge him to leave it but Rasulullah ﷺ would not yield to their appeals.

In regards to this very Masjid, the following verse was revealed:

لَمَسْجِدٌ أُسِّسَ عَلَى التَّقْوٰى مِنْ أَوَّلِ يَوْمٍ أَحَقُّ أَنْ تَقُوْمَ فِيْهِ ۚ فِيْهِ رِجَالٌ يُحِبُّوْنَ أَنْ يَتَطَهَّرُوْا وَاللّٰهُ يُحِبُّ الْمُطَّهِّرِيْنَ ۝

"Surely the Masjid that was erected upon Taqwa (Allah-consciousness) from the first day is more befitting that you stand (for Salaah) within it. In it are men who

love (physical and spiritual) cleanliness. And Allah loves those who purify themselves." [Surah Taubah verse 108]

When this verse was revealed, Rasulullah ﷺ asked 'Amr bin 'Awf: "On what type of Tahaarat (purity) did you attract the praise of Allah?"

The people of Bani 'Amr replied: "O Rasulullah ﷺ! After using clods of earth, we make Istinjaa (cleansing of the private parts) with water as well. Perhaps this type of twofold Tahaarat (purity) appeals to Allah Ta'ala, hence, our commendation in the Qur-aan."

Rasulullah ﷺ remarked: "Yes, this is the practice which has attracted divine recognition. You should stick firmly to this custom and remain attached to it."

'Abdullah bin 'Umar رضي الله عنه relates: "Rasulullah ﷺ would visit Masjid-e-Quba every Saturday. Sometimes he would go on foot and at times he would go mounted on a conveyance. He would offer two Rakaat Salaah in the Masjid."

Sahal bin Hunaif رضي الله عنه narrates: "Rasulullah ﷺ said: 'He who performs Wudhu at home and performs two Rakaat Salaah in Masjid-e-Quba will acquire the Sawaab of an Umrah'."

Date of Hijrah

The day Rasulullah ﷺ made his regal presence in Quba during the journey of Hijrah, was a Monday and the date was the twelfth of Rabi-ul-Awwal thirteen years after prophethood.

According to the scholars of Seerah, Rasulullah ﷺ left Makkah on Thursday the twenty-seventh of Safar. Following his sojourn of three days in the cave of Saur, he left for Madinah Munawwarah on Monday, the first of Rabi-ul-Awwal. Travelling on the coastal route, Rasulullah ﷺ made his august appearance in Quba on Monday afternoon the eighth of Rabi-ul-Awwal.

The Inception of the Islamic Calendar

In accordance with the directive of Rasulullah ﷺ, this day signals the start of the Islamic calendar. When Rasulullah ﷺ appeared in Madinah Munawwarah, he instructed (the Muslims) to use the month of Rabi'ul-Awwal of that year as the launch of the Islamic calendar. The more favoured view is that the inception of the Islamic calendar was launched during the Caliphate of Hadhrat 'Umar رضي الله عنه. Once Hadhrat Abu Musa Ash'ari رضي الله عنه wrote to Hadhrat 'Umar رضي الله عنه saying that although his imperial correspondence reaches him, his letters are all undated. Subsequently, in the seventeenth year of Hijrah, Hadhrat 'Umar رضي الله عنه summoned the Sahaabah رضي الله عنهم to discuss the issue regarding the inception of the

Islamic calendar. Some of them proposed that the day Rasulullah ﷺ was blessed with Prophethood should be the day of the inception of the Islamic calendar. Others suggested the Hijrah whilst some felt that the date of Rasulullah's ﷺ demise should be the inception of this calendar. Finally Hadhrat 'Umar رضي الله عنه proposed: "The inception of the Islamic calendar should be the Hijrah because this migration was the differentiating factor between truth and falsehood. It was the Hijrah that heralded the honour and dominance of Islam." Everyone unanimously sanctioned this proposal.

Some of the Sahaabah رضي الله عنهم suggested that the year commence with the month of Ramadhaan. To this Hadhrat 'Umar رضي الله عنه replied: "No, Muharram seems the most appropriate month to start the calendar because people generally return from Haj in the month of Muharram." Subsequently, they all agreed to this proposal.

Imaam Sarakhsi رحمه الله writes: "When 'Umar رضي الله عنه assembled the Sahaabah رضي الله عنهم to discuss the issue of determining the Islamic calendar, some of the Sahaabah رضي الله عنهم suggested that the inception of the calendar be determined from the day of Rasulullah's ﷺ blessed birth. However, Hadhrat 'Umar رضي الله عنه was somewhat averse to this view as this bore a resemblance to the practice of the Christians. The Christian calendar commences from the holy birth of Hadhrat 'Isa عليه السلام. Some people proposed that the Islamic calendar commence from the demise of Rasulullah ﷺ. Hadhrat 'Umar رضي الله عنه declined to adopt this proposal as well. The demise of Rasulullah ﷺ was a tragic calamity and a misfortune to befall this Ummah. This is why Hadhrat 'Umar رضي الله عنه was disinclined to this proposal. After much debate and deliberation, the attendees agreed that the Islamic calendar commence from the Hijrah. Farooq A'zam (Hadhrat 'Umar رضي الله عنه) was inclined to this view because Hijrah was the differentiating factor between truth (Haq) and falsehood (Baatil). This was when the Sha'aair (prominent Ibaadaat) like Jumu'ah and 'Eidain were openly observed.

Following a short stay of a few days in Quba, Rasulullah ﷺ mounted his camel and departed for Madinah on a Friday. En route lies the locality of Banu Saalim. Since the time of Jumu'ah had set in, Rasulullah ﷺ performed Jumu'ah here. This was the first Khutbah and Jumu'ah in Islam.

Khutbatut-Taqwa (First Khutbah and Jumu'ah)

This is such a Khutbah (sermon) whose every single letter was saturated in eloquence, whose every letter was a source of spiritual remedy for spiritual ailments, whose words were a source of life for spiritually numb hearts and whose every word is more sweeter and delectable than exquisite wine. The celebrated Khutbah is as follows:

(اَلْحَمْدُ لِلّٰهِ) احمده واستعينه واستغفره واستهديه واومن به ولا اكفر. واعادى من يكفره واشهد ان لا اله الا الله وحده لا شريك له وان محمدا عبده و رسوله ارسله بالهدى والنور والموعظة على فترة من الرسل وقلة من العلم وضلالة من الناس وانقطاع من الزمان و دنو من الساعة و قرب من الاجل. من يطع الله و رسوله فقد رشد ومن يعصهما فقد غوى و فرط وضل ضلا بعيدا واوصيكم بتقوى الله فانه خير ما اوصى به المسلمُ المسلمَ ان يحضه على الاخرة وان يامره بتقوى الله فاحذروا ما حذركم الله من نفسه ولا افضل من ذلك نصيحةً ولا افضل من ذلك ذكرى وان تقوى الله لمن عمل به على وجل ومخافة من ربه عون صدق على ما تبغون من امر الاخرة ومن يصلح الذى بينه و بين الله من امره فى السر والعلانية لا ينوى بذلك الا وجه الله يكن له ذكرا فى عاجل امره وذخراً فيما بعد الموت حين يفتقر المرء الى ما قدم وما كان من سوى ذلك يود لو ان بينه و بينه امدا بعيدا. ويحذركم الله نفسه والله رؤوف بالعباد والذى صدق قوله انجز وعده لا خلف لذلك فانه يقول عزوجل ما يبدل القول لدى وما انا بظلامٍ للعبيد فاتقوا الله فى عاجل امركم واجله فى السر والعلانية فانه من يتق الله يكفر عنهُ سيّأته ويعظم له اجراً ومن يتق الله فقد فاز فوزاً عظيما وان تقوى الله يُوَقِّ مقته ويوق عقوبته و يوق سخطه وان تقوى الله يبيض الوجوه ويرضى الرب ويرفع الدرجة خذوا بحظكم. ولا تفرطوا فى جنب الله قد

Chapter 9

علمكم الله كتابه ونهج لكم سبيله ليعلم الذين صدقوا و يعلم الكاذبين فاحسنوا كما احسن الله اليكم و عادوا اعداءه. هواجتباكم وسَمَّاكُمُ المسلمين ليهلك من هلك عن بينةٍ ويحى من حى عن بينة ولا قوة الا بالله فاكثروا ذكر الله واعملوا لما بعد اليوم فانه من يصلح ما بينه وبين الله يكفه الله ما بينه و بين الناس ذلك بان الله يقضى على الناس ولا يقضون عليه و يملك من الناس ولا يملكون منه. والله اكبر ولا قوة الا بالله العظيم

"All praise is due to Allah. I glorify Him, I beseech His assistance, I beg His forgiveness and I plead for His divine guidance. I believe in Him and I renounce disbelief in Him. In fact I oppose those who disbelieve in Allah. I bear witness that there is none worthy of worship besides Allah, He has no partner and I testify that Muhammad ﷺ is His slave and messenger. He was commissioned by Allah (to this earth) with guidance, spiritual radiance and good counsel at a time when the succession of Prophets had terminated and at a time when there was a dearth of knowledge and when people were spiritually deviated and close to the day of judgement.

He who obeys Allah and His Rasool is rightly guided whilst he who disobeys them has gone astray, transgressed and he is awfully deviated.

I advise you to adhere firmly to Taqwa (Allah-consciousness) because the best advice one Muslim can impart to another Muslim is that he persuades him to harbour concern for the hereafter and that he enjoins him to adhere to Taqwa. So beware of that which Allah Himself has warned you about. There is no better advice than Taqwa. Certainly the Taqwa of Allah Ta'ala and fear for Him is an ideal benefactor for the hereafter.

He who rectifies his external as well as his internal affairs with Allah Ta'ala and his intention is nothing but the pleasure of Allah Ta'ala, this spiritual and physical rectification will be a source of esteem for him in this world and a source of immense treasure for him upon his death when a person is in dire need of his good deeds. As for him who adopts anything contrary to this Taqwa, he would, on that day, wish there be a considerable distance between him and his evil deeds. And Allah cautions you about Himself (His punishment etc.) and (this caution is because) Allah is most kind to His servants.

The word of Allah is true. He executes His promises. There is no reneging on His promises because Allah Ta'ala declares: 'The word that emanates from Me cannot be altered'.

So fear Allah in your external and internal affairs and in the issues related to this world and the hereafter. 'He who adopts Taqwa, Allah will wipe out his sins and grant him an enormous reward. And he who adopts Taqwa has attained enormous success. Taqwa is something that thwarts the wrath, punishment and anger of Allah. The Taqwa of Allah will spiritually illuminate the faces on the day of judgement and it will be a source of acquiring the pleasure of Allah and a source of elevated ranks in the hereafter. Take your share (of this Taqwa) whatever you can manage and do not be lacking in the affairs of Allah. Allah has revealed a book for your guidance and He has clarified His path to differentiate between the truthful and the liars. So, just as Allah has favoured you, you should also be favourable (in complying with His instructions). Harbour enmity towards His enemies and implement Jihaad in His path.

Allah has chosen you and He has named you as Muslims (His obedient servants). The objective of Allah is: that he who is to be destroyed will be destroyed even after clear evidence and he who is to live (as a believer) will live (with insight) after clear evidence.

There is no might and power besides Allah. Remember Allah abundantly and practice for the time after this day (hereafter). He who rectifies his affairs with Allah, Allah will suffice for him against the people and nobody will be able to harm him because the decree of Allah is executed upon the people and the will of the people is not implemented upon Allah. He is the exclusive master and owner of the people whilst the people do not own anything of Allah. He controls the people and they have no control whatsoever over Him.

Allah is the greatest. And there is no power and might save in the control of Allah, the most magnificent."

Note: This was the first Khutbah delivered by Rasulullah ﷺ after the Hijrah. In spite of spending thirteen long years in the tyrannical grip of the disbelievers, he uttered neither a scathing word nor a complaint against his enemies. Besides Taqwa, Allah-consciousness and preparation for the hereafter, he mentioned nothing else. No doubt Rasulullah ﷺ perfectly fitted the verse 'certainly you are upon magnificent character'.

Upon the completion of Jumu'ah, Rasulullah ﷺ mounted his camel and set out in the direction of Madinah. He seated Abu Bakr رضي الله عنه directly behind him on the camel. A vast number of Ansaar, armed with their weaponry, were walking to his right, to his left and behind him.

Every single resident of Madinah cherished a hope of entertaining Rasulullah ﷺ in his home. From every corner, fervently excited and impassioned pleas of invitation were extended to Rasulullah ﷺ. Each resident implored him to come to his house. Rasulullah ﷺ would make dua for them and reply: "This camel is commanded by Allah. Wherever she sits down with the decree of Allah, I will put up there."

Rasulullah ﷺ left the reins absolutely loose. He would not even nudge the animal in any direction.

There was such an enthusiastic atmosphere in the air that to catch a glimpse of this prophetic magnificence, the ladies clambered upon the roofs of their houses singing:

طَلَعَ الْبَدْرُ عَلَيْنَا مِنْ ثَنِيَّاتِ الْوَدَاعِ

"The full moon has glowed upon us from the valley of Wad'aa.

وَجَبَ الشُّكْرُ عَلَيْنَا مَا دَعَا لِلَّهِ دَاعٍ

Gratitude towards Allah is essential upon us as long as there remains a caller to Allah.

اَيُّهَا الْمَبْعُوثُ فِيْنَا جِئْتَ بِالْاَمْرِ الْمُطَاعِ

O you who has been sent unto us! You have come to us with something that has to be adhered to."

The younger girls of Banu Najjaar were chanting:

نحن جوارٍ من بنى النجار يا حبذا محمد من جار

"We are the lasses of Banu Najjaar, Oh! What a pleasure having Muhammad ﷺ as a neighbour."

Unable to control their delight, every single tongue was exclaiming:

جاء نبى الله. جاء رسول الله

"Here comes the Nabi of Allah. Here comes the Rasool of Allah."

Baraa bin 'Aazib رضي الله عنه says: "I have not witnessed the people of Madinah as ecstatic as they were on the day Rasulullah ﷺ appeared in Madinah."

Anas رضي الله عنه says: "When Rasulullah ﷺ landed in Madinah, the Abyssinians, as an expression of their delight, put on a demonstration of skilful archery. When Rasulullah ﷺ appeared in Madinah, every single particle glowed with radiance and the day he passed away, everything was looking gloomy.

We barely dusted our hands after burying him when we found that our hearts had already undergone (some spiritual) transformation."

Nonetheless, this blessed camel with its majestic mount forged ahead with these enthusiasts thronging around him from the right and left. These were the chosen souls whom Allah Ta'ala had selected for the fervent love and sincere devotion of His beloved Rasool ﷺ. Their love for him was so intense that not an iota of space was left for anyone else. By Allah! What I am saying is unquestionably true. This is not merely metaphorical language and an occasion for figurative expressions. The Sahaabah رضي الله عنهم were indeed like this. Whilst Rasulullah ﷺ was riding his camel, each one of them lowered his gaze in longing as though they 'spread their eyes as a carpet' before him.

Overwhelmed with unbridled joy and overcome with uncontainable emotions of love, some of the Sahaabah رضي الله عنهم would attempt to seize the reins of the camel but Rasulullah ﷺ would gently advise them:

دَعُوْهَا فَاِنَّهَا مَأْمُوْرَةٌ

"Leave her alone as she is divinely commanded."

In due course, the camel ended up in the locality of Banu Najjaar (Rasulullah's ﷺ maternal relatives) where, without any prompting, she halted right at the spot where the door of Masjidun-Nabawi would be. However, Rasulullah ﷺ did not alight. The camel then got up and proceeded to sit down at Abu Ayyub Ansaari's رضي الله عنه door. A little while later, she arose and proceeded to sit at the first location where she lowered her head onto the ground.

At this moment, Rasulullah ﷺ alighted from his camel and Abu Ayyub رضي الله عنه carried his goods into the house.

Rasulullah ﷺ also felt predisposed to residing in the locality of Banu Najjaar. Najjaar was Rasulullah's ﷺ grandfather, 'Abdul-Muttalib's mother's brother. Rasulullah ﷺ aimed to enhance their status and reverence as well. However, Allah Ta'ala also fulfilled Rasulullah's ﷺ heartfelt desire in a rather miraculous manner. Rasulullah ﷺ was made to let the reins of the camel hang loose so that it appeared that he had no say in the direction the camel took. Furthermore, Rasulullah ﷺ did not target any specific house to settle in. This was done to ensure that his enthusiasts' hearts remain free from any form of personal rivalry and contention and so that they appreciate the fact that Rasulullah ﷺ himself had no part in this decision. The camel was divinely commanded by Allah Ta'ala. It would halt wherever it was directed to. Rasulullah ﷺ was merely waiting for Allah Ta'ala's signal.

So in this manner, Allah Ta'ala fulfilled the aspiration of Rasulullah ﷺ and in regards to the Sahaabah رضي الله عنهم, Allah Ta'ala rendered this descent a miraculous feat that ensured that their hearts remain free of rivalry, jealousy and malice. All of them realised that choosing Abu Ayyub Ansaari's ؓ home was not of his own accord but this was pre-ordained by Allah Ta'ala.

$$\text{ذٰلِكَ فَضْلُ اللّٰهِ يُؤْتِيْهِ مَنْ يَّشَآءُ وَاللّٰهُ ذُوالْفَضْلِ الْعَظِيْمِ}$$

"That is the Fadl (grace) of Allah that He bestows upon whosoever He wishes. And Allah is magnificent, great."

Furthermore, when Tubb'a, the emperor of Yemen, happened to pass by the land of Madinah, four hundred 'Ulama of the Tawrat were also with him. They requested the king to allow them to settle down in this area. When he enquired the reason, they replied: "We find in the manuscripts of the Prophets that towards the end of time, a Prophet by the name of Muhammad will appear. This region is reported to be his Daarul-Hijrah (place of migration)." The emperor allowed them to settle down there. He constructed a separate house for each one of them. He got them all married and liberally provided them with ample wealth. He put up a home especially for Rasulullah ﷺ with the belief that when the final Messenger migrates to this area, he may reside therein. He even composed a letter to Rasulullah ﷺ in which he expressed his faith in him and his ardent desire to behold him.

The focus of the letter is summed up in the following poetic words:

$$\text{شهدت على احمد انه رسول من الله بارى النسم}$$

"I bear testimony upon Ahmad that he is the messenger of Allah, the Creator of life.

$$\text{فلو مد عمرى الى عمره لكنت وزيرا له وابن عم}$$

If my era has to connect with his era I would certainly become his supporter and devotee.

$$\text{وجاهدت بالسيف اعدآءه وفرجت عن صدره كل غم}$$

I would challenge his enemies with the sword and I would eliminate all woe from his heart."

Tubb'a, the emperor then sealed the letter with a royal seal. Entrusting the letter to one of the 'Ulama, he said: "If you happen to come across the era of this final messenger, hand this epistle over to him otherwise hand it over to your children and enjoin them with the same advice I am imparting to you."

Hadhrat Abu Ayyub ؓ is a descendant of this very Aalim and his house was the very same house which Emperor Tubb'a constructed for the final messenger to reside in whenever he happened to migrate this way. The Ansaar were descendants of these four hundred 'Ulama.

Nonetheless, the camel went and halted at the door of the house, which Tubb'a had constructed with Rasulullah ﷺ in mind.

It is said that on the arrival of Rasulullah ﷺ in Madinah Munawwarah, Abu Ayyub Ansaari ؓ presented the royal poetic epistle of emperor Tubb'a to Rasulullah ﷺ. And Allah Ta'ala knows best.

Abu Ayyub Ansaari ؓ insisted that Rasulullah ﷺ reside on the upper floor whilst he and his family would reside on the lower floor. However, Rasulullah ﷺ felt that since he would be getting a stream of visitors all the time, it would be inconvenient for Abu Ayyub and his family to reside on the lower floor. This is why Rasulullah ﷺ did not agree to reside on the upper floor. He preferred the lower floor.

Hadhrat Abu Ayyub ؓ says: "This is how we came to live on the upper floor. One day a water container fell and broke. Flushed with agitation, we swiftly spread our blanket over it to absorb the water before it seeped down to the lower floor. Umme Ayyub and myself promptly mopped up the area with our blanket. This was the only blanket we possessed.

"Daily we would prepare meals for Rasulullah ﷺ and send it down to him. He would send the leftover back to us. As a form of acquiring his Tabarruk (blessings), Umme Ayyub and I would search for the spot he ate from and we would also eat from there as well. One day we added a bit of garlic and onions to the food. When he sent it back to us, we were quite perturbed to find no impressions of his fingers on any part of the food. Overcome with agitation, I went to Rasulullah ﷺ and submitted: "O Rasulullah! You sent the food back to us without partaking any morsel of it. We found no impression of your fingers in it. Umme Ayyub and I deliberately eat from the spot that your blessed fingers left impressions on."

Rasulullah ﷺ replied: "I perceived the odour of garlic and onions in the food. You may go ahead and eat it. Since I communicate with the angels, I abstain from such food-stuffs."

Abu Ayyub ؓ says: "From that day on, we did not add onions and garlic to his food."

The Appearance of the Rabbis before Rasulullah ﷺ

When Rasulullah ﷺ landed at Madinah Munawwarah, the 'Ulama of the Jews (Rabbis) appeared before him and posed a variety of questions to him. On the basis of the glad tidings of the previous Ambiyaa عليهم السلام, they were well aware of the imminent emergence of the final Messenger. They were well enlightened that the final Messenger about whom Musa عليه السلام issued glad tidings was on the verge of emerging from the land of Bathaa. The 'Ulama of the Jews (Rabbis) were all eagerly anticipating his arrival.

As mentioned earlier under the chapter dealing with Hijrah, when Rasulullah ﷺ first presented Islam to the Ansaar, they conferred amongst themselves agreeing that this was the very same Prophet about whom the Jews often referred to. They said: "It must not be such that the Jews beat us to this good fortune and virtue."

It seems that the Jews were well aware that the appearance of the final Messenger - in regards to whom Musa عَلَيْهِ السَّلَام had prophesied, was imminent. This is why the Jews made a point of coming to visit Rasulullah ﷺ. Those who were divinely fortunate recognised him as the true Prophet the moment their eyes fell on Rasulullah ﷺ. Without a hint of hesitancy they embraced Islam whilst those whose fate had decreed deprivation remained deprived of this immeasurable gift of Imaan.

Ibn 'Aaiz narrates on the authority of 'Urwah bin Zubair رَضِيَ اللهُ عَنْهُ that from amongst the Rabbis, the first person to appear before Rasulullah ﷺ was Yaasir bin Akhtab, the brother of Huyayy bin Akhtab. When he heard the blessed words of Rasulullah ﷺ and returned to his people, he addressed them:

اطیعونی فان هذا النبی الذی کنا ننتظر

"Take heed of my advice and comply with me. This is the Nabi we were eagerly awaiting."

However, his brother Huyayy bin Akhtab refused to listen to him. Huyay was considered the chief of his people. His people always adhered to what he required them to do. Shaytaan subdued him and prevented him from acknowledging the truth. The people complied with him and declined to obey his brother Yaasir.

When Rasulullah ﷺ arrived in Madinah Munawwarah, the Rabbis of Madinah assembled in Baitul-Midraas (the Madrasah of the Jews) and following mutual consultation, they resolved to put a few questions to this man (a reference to Rasulullah ﷺ).

A Rabbi appeared before Rasulullah ﷺ whilst he was reciting the verses of Surah Yusuf. The Rabbi enquired: "Muhammad! Who imparted the knowledge of this Surah to you?" "Allah imparted its knowledge to me," replied Rasulullah ﷺ. The Rabbi, overwhelmed with astonishment, hastened back to the Jews and said: "Muhammad is reciting from a book that seems similar to the Tauraat revealed upon Musa عَلَيْهِ السَّلَام."

Taking a group of Jews along with him, this Rabbi appeared once again before Rasulullah ﷺ. The moment they set eyes upon his physical appearance and attributes, they realised that this was the very Nabi the Tauraat referred to. They even scrutinised the seal of prophethood that appeared between his shoulder blades. As Rasulullah ﷺ continued reciting Surah Yusuf, the amazement of the Jews also intensified in proportion. All of them embraced Islam.

Abu Hurayah ؓ narrates: "Once Rasulullah ﷺ addressed Ibn Surya (a Rabbi), saying: 'I appeal to you in the name of Allah to speak the truth. Tell me, what is the punishment for a married adulterer in the Tauraat? What is the ruling on stoning to death?' Ibn Surya replied:

اللّٰهم نعم اما والله يا ابا القاسم انهم ليعرفون انك نبى مرسل ولكنهم يحسدونك

'O Allah! Yes! By Allah, this ruling is explicitly mentioned in the Taurah. O Abul-Qaasim, the Jews are well-aware that you are a divinely commissioned Prophet but they are unreservedly jealous of you.'

Jaabir bin Samurah ؓ narrated: "A Maqani Rabbi appeared before some Sahaabah ؓ and said: 'Where is your companion who claims he is a Prophet? I wish to pose a few questions to him that would enable me to determine whether he really is a true Prophet or not.' In the meantime, Rasulullah ﷺ turned up before him. This Rabbi said: 'Recite a bit what had been revealed to you.' Rasulullah ﷺ recited a few verses of the Qur-aan before him. The instant these verses fell onto his ears, he submitted: 'By Allah! These words are similar to the words conveyed by Musa ؑ'."

There are many similar incidents regarding the Rabbis and Jews who embraced Islam at the hands of Rasulullah ﷺ, eg. Zaid bin Sa'nah ؓ etc.

Islam of 'Abdullah bin Salaam ؓ

'Abdullah bin Salaam ؓ was an eminent Aalim of the Tawrat. He was a descendant of Hadhrat Yusuf ؑ. His original name was Husain. After he embraced Islam, Rasulullah ﷺ changed his name to 'Abdullah bin Salaam. 'Abdullah bin Salaam ؓ narrates his conversion to Islam thus:

فلما رأيت وجهه عرفت ان وجهه ليس بوجه كذاب

"The moment I received news of Rasulullah's ﷺ arrival in Madinah, I set out to meet him. The instant my gaze fell onto his face, I realised that this can never be the face of a fraud."

The first words I heard from his tongue were:

Chapter 9

ايها الناس اطعموا الطعام وافشوا السلام وصلوا الارحام وصلوا بالليل والناس نيام تدخلوا الجنة بسلام

"O People! Feed people, observe widespread Salaam, maintain favourable family ties and perform Salaah at night whilst people are asleep, you will enter Jannah with ease."

'Abdullah bin Salaam ؓ narrates: "I was aware of Rasulullah's ﷺ name, attributes and physical appearance long before this. When I heard of Rasulullah's ﷺ imminent arrival in Madinah I was perched on a date palm and from there I ecstatically called out the chant of Allahu Akbar. My father's sister, Khaalidah bint Haaris commented: 'If you had heard of the arrival of Musa عليه السلام, you wouldn't have been as ecstatic as you are now.' I replied: 'By Allah! This is also the brother of Musa. He is commissioned with the same Deen that Musa عليه السلام was commissioned with.' My Aunt said: 'Nephew! Is this the same Nabi about whom we have been informed that he will be commissioned before the advent of Qiyaamah (resurrection)?' 'Yes,' I replied, 'this is the same Nabi'.

I then left home and presenting myself before Rasulullah ﷺ, I embraced Islam. Thereafter I returned home and bade my family members to embrace Islam as well. They too embraced Islam."

'Abdullah bin Salaam ؓ continues: "I then requested Rasulullah ﷺ to conceal me in a room and ask the Jews about me because the Jews are a rather slanderous nation. When the Jews appeared before Rasulullah ﷺ, he hid 'Abdullah bin Salaam ؓ in a room and said to them: "O assembly of Jews! Fear Allah! I swear in the name of that being besides Whom there is none worthy of worship, you are well aware that I am the true Messenger of Allah and I have been commissioned with the truth. So embrace Islam." The Jews, however, said: "We know nothing of this sort." Three times Rasulullah ﷺ appealed to them to accept Islam and each time their response was the same.

He then asked them: "What type of person is 'Abdullah bin Salaam amongst you?" They replied: "He is our leader and the son of our leader. He is the best amongst us and the son of the best." Rasulullah ﷺ then asked: "If 'Abdullah bin Salaam expresses his faith in me, would you then believe that I am a true Prophet?" They replied: "Under no circumstances would 'Abdullah bin Salaam embrace Islam." Rasulullah ﷺ asked: "If, hypothetically speaking, he does embrace Islam?" They shrieked: "Certainly not! He can never ever embrace Islam."

Rasulullah ﷺ said: "O 'Abdullah bin Salaam! Show yourself to these people." As he emerged from this room, he revealed:

اَشْهَدُ اَنْ لَّا اِلٰهَ اِلَّا اللّٰهُ وَاَشْهَدُ اَنَّ مُحَمَّدًا رَّسُوْلُ اللّٰهِ

"I bear witness that there is none worthy of worship besides Allah and Muhammad is the Messenger of Allah."

He then addressed the Jews saying: "O assembly of Jews! Fear Allah! I swear in the name of that being besides Whom there is none worthy of worship, you are well aware that he is the true Messenger of Allah and he has been commissioned with the truth."

They barely heard this when they screeched: "You ('Abdullah bin Salaam) are a liar and a fraud. You are the worst amongst us and the son of the worst."

In this regard Allah Ta'ala revealed the following verses:

قُلْ أَرَءَيْتُمْ إِنْ كَانَ مِنْ عِنْدِ اللّٰهِ وَ كَفَرْتُمْ بِهٖ وَ شَهِدَ شَاهِدٌ مِّنْ بَنِىۡ اِسْرَآءِيْلَ عَلٰى مِثْلِهٖ فَاٰمَنَ وَ اسْتَكْبَرْتُمْ ۚ اِنَّ اللّٰهَ لَا يَهْدِى الْقَوْمَ الظّٰلِمِيْنَ ۞

"Say: 'Tell me! If this (Qur-aan) is from Allah and you deny it whilst a witness from the Bani Israa'eel ('Abdullah bin Salaam رضي الله عنه) testifies (that this Qur-aan is from Allah) and he believes whilst you are too arrogant (to believe). Verily, Allah does not guide the transgressing people." [Surah Ahqaaf verse 10]

Islam of Maymun bin Yaameen رضي الله عنه

Maymun bin Yaameen was also one of the Jewish leaders. He embraced Islam the moment he set eyes upon Rasulullah ﷺ. His conversion to Islam is similar to that of 'Abdullah bin Salaam رضي الله عنه.

Maymun bin Yaameen appeared before Rasulullah ﷺ and said: "O Rasulullah! Summon the Jews and appoint me as a mediator. They will ultimately confer with me."

Rasulullah ﷺ bade him to sit in a concealed room and sent someone to call the Jews. When they appeared before him, Rasulullah ﷺ requested them to appoint an arbitrator between him and the Jews. They replied: "We are pleased to appoint Maymun bin Yaameen as our arbitrator. We will gladly accept whatever decision he makes."

Rasulullah ﷺ then called out for Maymun رضي الله عنه saying: "Maymun! Come out." As he emerged, he declared: "I testify that he is the messenger of Allah."

However, the Jews utterly refused to endorse this testimony.

Chapter 9

Islam of Salmaan bin Islam ﷺ

Salmaan was his name. Abu 'Abdullah was his Kuniyyat (title). He is popularly called Salmaan Al-Khayr (goodness), as though Salmaan was an embodiment of goodness. He hailed from the town of Huyay in the vicinity of Hormuz in Persia. He was a descendant of the Persian emperors. When anyone asked him: "Whose son are you?" He would reply: "I am Salmaan, the son of Islam."

In other words, Islam is the source of my spiritual presence. Islam is my mentor and guide. What a wonderful father and what a majestic son.

Hadhrat Salmaan ﷺ reached a very old age. It is said that he was around during the era of Hadhrat Maseeh 'Isa bin Maryam ﷺ. Some say that although he was not around at that time, he was around during the time of one of his Hawaari (disciples) or executors. All are unanimous that his age exceeded two hundred and fifty.

Ibn 'Abbaas ﷺ says: "Salmaan Faarsi ﷺ related to me his story of embracing Islam in the following manner:

'I was a resident of a town called Huyay in Persia. My father was the chieftain of this town. I was extraordinarily dear to him. He would protect me just as virgin girls are protected. He would not allow me to step out of the house. We were Zoroastrians (fire-worshippers) by faith. My father appointed me as an overseer and guard over one of the fire-temples to ensure that the fire never goes out. On one occasion, since my father was busy with some construction work, he was forced to send me to inspect a farm or a piece of land. He stressed upon me not to be late. I set out from home. En-route I came across a church from which I heard some sounds. On closer inspection from the inside, I noticed a group of Christians occupied in prayer. Their manner of prayer was tremendously appealing to me. I thought to myself: 'This religion far surpasses our religion'. I enquired from them: 'Where is the origin of this religion?' They replied: 'In Palestine'.

The sun had already set by then. Nervously impatient, my father sent someone to search for me. When I finally reached home, my father enquired: 'Son! What happened? Where were you?' I recounted the whole incident to him. My father commented: 'There is nothing good in this religion (Christianity). The religion of your forefathers (Zoroastrianism) is far better.'

I replied: 'Never! The religion of the Christians is far better than our religion.' My father shackled me in leg-irons and restricted me from leaving the house. This was just like how Fir'aun told Musa ﷺ: 'If you take anyone other than myself as your lord, I will render you amongst the incarcerated.'

I forwarded a secret message to the Christians asking them to inform me when the next caravan was departing for Syria (Palestine). Soon they sent me a message that a trade caravan made up of Christians was about to return to Syria. The moment I got the opportunity, I hurled my shackles aside, fled from home and joined them.

As I reached Palestine, I made enquiries about the most distinguished priest amongst the Christians. People directed me to a certain priest. I went to him and related my whole story to him. I said to him: 'I wish to stay in your company to learn about your religion. I am incredibly fond of your religion and it really appeals to me. If you permit, I would like to stay in your service and study this religion. I would also like to perform my prayers with you.'

He responded favourably.

A few days later, I realised that this priest was not a morally upright person. He was dreadfully greedy. He would instruct others to give alms. When they brought their charities to him, he would not distribute it amongst the poor but he would keep it for himself. In this manner, he had accumulated seven earthen-vessels of gold coins. When he died and in good faith, people assembled to prepare for his burial and shrouding etc., I disclosed his actual condition to them and showed them the seven vessels of gold coins.

On ascertaining his true condition the people exclaimed: 'By Allah! We will never bury such a person. Eventually, his body was left suspended from a cross where people furiously continued to pelt it with stones. Another priest was appointed as his successor.'

Hadhrat Salmaan رضى الله عنه continues: '(Prior to Islam) I have not come across a person more abstinent from the dunya (worldly pursuits), more devoted to the hereafter and more engrossed in his prayers than this priest. The level of adoration I cherished for this man I had never cherished for anyone else. I remained in this man's company for many years. As his last moments in this world approached, I submitted: 'Offer me some parting advice; who should I stay with after your departure?' He replied: 'In Musil there is a great Aalim. Go to him.'

I went to him and after his death, on his parting advice, I set off for another Aalim in Nasibayn. I stayed in his company for some time. After his death, also according to his counsel, I went to an Aalim in the city of 'Umuriyyah where I stayed in his company for a considerable time as well. On his deathbed, I submitted: 'I have lived in the company of so and so 'Ulama. Tell me, where should I head now?' This Aalim said: 'To the best of my knowledge there is not a single Aalim on the straight path I can refer you to. However, the era for the appearance of a Prophet is pretty close. This Prophet will tread the path of the creed of Ibraaheem عليه السلام. He will make an appearance in the land of Arabia. He will subsequently migrate to a land of date palms. If it is possible to gain access to him, make sure you get there. His distinctive feature would be that he would not consume charity but he would accept gifts. The seal of prophethood would be embedded between his shoulder blades. Once your glance falls onto him you will surely recognise him.'

During this time, I had accumulated a few goats and cows for myself. Coincidentally I met up with a caravan heading towards Arabia. I begged them: 'Take me along with you. I will pay you all these goats and cows I have in my possession.' They accepted my offering and took me along with them.

As we reached the valley of Qura, they turned out to be treacherous to me. They sold me as a slave to a Jew. When I joined him (to his house) I came across a number of date palms. I imagined that perhaps this was the land I was seeking. However, I was not at ease about this land when another Jew from Banu Qurayzah approached this master and purchased me from him. He then brought me along with him to Madinah. The moment I set foot in Madinah, I realised, by Allah, this is the very land that was previously described to me."

It appears in Sahih Bukhaari that Hadhrat Salmaan ﷺ says: "In this manner I was purchased and sold more than ten times." (Although people nonchalantly purchased him for a few Dirhams, nobody realised his true worth.)

"I continued living with this Jewish master attending to his date palms in Banu Qurayzah. In the meantime, Allah commissioned Rasulullah ﷺ at Makkah but since I was in bondage and engaged in the service of my master, I was completely in the dark about this. Rasulullah ﷺ migrated and landed in Quba at Banu 'Amr bin 'Awf. One day, as I was busy right on the top of a date palm whilst my master was seated beneath it, another Jew – my master's father's brother's son i.e. his cousin, appeared before him and said: 'May Allah destroy the Qilah (the Ansaar)! They are gathering around a Makkan man in Quba and they claim that he is a Prophet and Messenger of Allah.'"

Salmaan ﷺ says:

فوالله ان هو الا اخذتنى العُروآءُ حتى ظننت انى ساسقط على صاحبى

"By Allah! This barely landed on my ears when I was seized by a spell of shivering. I almost lost control of myself and thought I would collapse onto my master."

The advent of the Basheer (bringer of glad tidings) and Nazeer (warner) left Salmaan ﷺ enraptured with delight and ravished by ecstasy so much so that if it wasn't for the divine spirit of "Had we not fortified her (Musa's ﷺ mother's) heart, she would have disclosed it (that this is her son)", he would have plummeted headlong from the date palm.

Looking up at him, both the Jews were left astounded.

Nonetheless, he brought his heart under control and warily descended from the palm. He continues: "I then asked the arriving Jew: 'Tell me! What were you just talking about? Enlighten me about this news as well.'

On hearing me soliciting this information, my master, raging with fury, struck a severe blow to my face and warned: 'What does this concern you?'

"As I wrapped up my work in the evening, I gathered up whatever wealth I possessed and presented myself before Rasulullah ﷺ. He was residing in Quba at that time. I submitted: 'I heard that you and your companions do not have anything. All of you are in need. I wish to present some charity to you and your friends.' Rasulullah ﷺ declined to accept the charity for himself saying: 'I do not consume of charity.' He then permitted the Sahaabah ﷺ to accept it."

Salmaan ﷺ says: "I told myself that by Allah! This is one of the three signs. I then returned home where I busied myself in accumulating a bit more wealth. When Rasulullah ﷺ appeared in Madinah, I presented myself to him a second time and submitted: 'My heartfelt desire is to present something to you. Since you do not accept charity, I have appeared before you with a gift.' Rasulullah ﷺ accepted the gift from me. He himself ate from it and fed his companions as well. I said to myself that this is the second sign.

"I then returned home and after a few days I presented myself before him yet again. In the company of a Janaazah, Rasulullah ﷺ had just come into Baqi cemetery. A group of the Sahaabah ﷺ were also with him. Whilst he was sitting amongst them, I ventured up to him and offered Salaam. From there I rose and went and sat behind him to get a view of the seal of prohethood. Rasulullah ﷺ guessed my intention and removed his upper sheet from his blessed back. I identified the seal the moment my gaze fell onto it. I stood up, tenderly kissed the seal and burst out crying. Rasulullah ﷺ said: 'Come in front of me.' I went before him and just as I am narrating this incident before you O Ibn 'Abbaas, I recounted my entire story to Rasulullah ﷺ and his Sahaabah ﷺ and in that very noble assembly I embraced Islam. Rasulullah ﷺ was overjoyed.

After this I occupied myself in the service of my master. This is why I was unable to take part in the battles of Badr and Uhud. Once, Rasulullah ﷺ advised me: 'Salmaan! Make a deal of Kitaabat with your master.'

When I spoke to my master, he said: 'Surely, on condition you pay me forty Awqiyah of gold. Furthermore, you should plant three hundred date palms. After you have paid the forty Awqiyahs of gold and the date palms start bearing fruit, you are free.' On the advice of Rasulullah ﷺ, Salmaan ﷺ accepted this arrangement. Rasulullah ﷺ then encouraged the people to assist me in providing the saplings. The people wholeheartedly responded by providing these saplings. Someone provided thirty saplings, another person twenty whilst a third person provided fifteen and someone brought along ten. When we had accumulated all three hundred palm-saplings, Rasulullah ﷺ said: 'O Salmaan! Dig holes for them.' Once the holes were dug, Rasulullah ﷺ planted them all with his own blessed hands and he made dua for Barakah as well.

Barely a year passed by when all of them started flowering and bearing fruit. Not a single sapling died. Each and every one of them flourished with fruit. In this manner, I managed fulfilling my obligation as far as the palms were concerned. Only the liability of the gold remained.

One day a man appeared before Rasulullah ﷺ with gold equivalent to a miniature egg. Rasulullah ﷺ asked: 'Where is that poor Mukaatab slave? Go and call him.' When I turned up before him, he made over the gold to me saying: 'Take this. Allah will pay out your debts.' I said: 'This gold is very little, O

Prophet of Allah. How will I manage paying my debts off?' Rasulullah ﷺ replied: 'Go, Allah will pay your debts with this very amount.'

When I weighed it, I found it to be precisely forty Awqiyah of gold. In this manner, I managed fulfilling my entire obligation and I, at long last, became a free man. I then joined Rasulullah ﷺ in the battle of Khandaq. Even after this, I stayed close to Rasulullah ﷺ in every subsequent battle."

Erection of Masjid-e-Nabawi

The first spot the camel chose to sit on was a dates-drying area belonging to orphans. Upon inquiry, Rasulullah ﷺ learnt that the plot of land belongs to two orphans; Sahal and Suhail. Rasulullah ﷺ summoned both of them to purchase this plot of land to erect a Masjid. Rasulullah ﷺ also spoke to their uncle, in whose care these orphans were, about purchasing the land. Both of them expressed a desire to donate the land to Rasulullah ﷺ without any compensation whatsoever saying that they hoped to reap the compensation from Allah Ta'ala alone. However, Rasulullah ﷺ declined to accept it without any remuneration. He paid them for the land.

Rasulullah ﷺ instructed Abu Bakr ؓ to pay for the plot of land. Abu Bakr ؓ paid ten Dinaars (gold coins) as a price for the land.

Thereafter Rasulullah ﷺ instructed the Sahaabah ؓ to chop down the date palms and level the graves of some disbelievers that were on the land. He then instructed them to produce unbaked bricks and he himself joined the Muhaajireen and Ansaar in the production of these bricks.

With the Sahaabah ؓ, Rasulullah ﷺ would lug these bricks and chant:

هذا الحمال لا حمال خيبر هذا ابر ربنا واطهر

"These loads are not the burdens of Khaybar, O our Lord, these loads are far better and virtuous."

Intermittently he would recite:

اللّهم ان الاجر اجر الاخره فارحم الانصار والمهاجره

"O Allah! The actual reward is the reward of the hereafter. So shower Your mercy upon the Muhaajireen and the Ansaar (who are focused upon the reward of the hereafter only.)"

According to another narration, the words are:

اللّٰهم لاخير الاخير الاخره فانصر الانصار والمهاجره

"O Allah! There is no goodness except in the goodness of the hereafter. So assist the Muhaajireen and the Ansaar (who are aiming for the goodness of the hereafter only)."

The Sahaabah رضى الله عنهم, in the meantime were chanting:

لئن قعدنا والنبى يعمل لذاك من العمل المضلل

"If we sit down whilst the Prophet toils, this action of ours (this sitting) would be extremely detestable."

Hadhrat Ali رضى الله عنه was chanting the following couplet:

لايستوى من يعمر المساجدا   يدأب فيها قائما و قاعدا

ومن يرى عن التراب حائدا

"He who indefatigably perseveres whilst standing and sitting in the erection of the Masjid can never be on par with that person who protects his clothing from dust."

Amongst those carrying stones was Hadhrat 'Usmaan bin Maz'oon رضى الله عنه. He was by nature an exceedingly neat and clean person. He was absolutely pre-disposed to cleanliness and tidiness. Whenever he would lug the stones, he would carry them away from his clothing. The moment a speck of dust would get onto his clothing, he would promptly dust it off.

Hadhrat Ali رضى الله عنه would humorously chant the words "he who protects his clothing from dust" to Hadhrat 'Usmaan bin Maz'oon رضى الله عنه.

It would not be surprising to learn that perhaps in this humorous indulgence, Hadhrat Ali رضى الله عنه wished to highlight the point that in such circumstances, dust and dirt is far superior than being fussy about cleanliness, as it appears in the Hadith, that a Haaji is he who has dishevelled hair and is dirty.

Talq bin Ali رضى الله عنه narrates: "Rasulullah ﷺ instructed me to mix the mortar. Taking a shovel in hand, I got up to mix the mortar." He says: "I asked, O Rasulullah ﷺ! Should I not carry the bricks as well?" Rasulullah ﷺ replied: "No, you should rather stick to mixing mortar, as you are more skilled in this field."

This Masjid was unique in its simplicity. The walls were constructed of unbaked brick. The pillars were hewn from the trunks of date palms. The roof was fabricated from the leaves and branches of date palms. Whenever it rained, water would seep through into the Masjid. Later on, the roof was plastered with mortar. It was a hundred cubits long and approximately a hundred cubits wide. The foundations were about three cubits deep. The height was slightly higher than the height of an average man. The Qiblah wall was facing Baitul-Muqaddas (in Jerusalem). Three doors were erected in the Masjid structure. One door was placed on the side where the Qiblah is today. The second door was positioned on the western wall and is today referred to as Baabur-Rahmah. The third door was the door frequently used by Rasulullah ﷺ and is today referred to as Baabu Jibraa'eel.

After about sixteen or seventeen months, when the Qiblah direction was moved from Baitul-Muqaddas to the K'abah for the performance of Salaah, the door at the back (previously the front) of the Masjid was sealed off and another door was erected directly opposite it.

Masjid-e-Nabawi underwent contruction twice (during the time of Rasulullah ﷺ). The first when it was erected when Rasulullah ﷺ migrated and put up at Abu Ayyub Ansaari's house. The second time it was renovated in the year seven Hijri after the battle of Khaybar when the Masjid fell into disrepair.

In the initial construction, the length and the breadth of the Masjid was under a hundred cubits whilst it was extended to just over a hundred cubits in the subsequent construction.

When Rasulullah ﷺ planned to extend the Masjid, he approached the Ansaari owner of the adjoining plot of land and said: "Sell us this land in exchange of a palace in Jannah." However, the Ansaari, due to his poverty and excessive dependants, was unable to offer the land for free. This is why Hadhrat 'Usmaan ؓ purchased this plot in exchange of ten thousand Dirhams from this Ansaari. Appearing before Rasulullah ﷺ, he submitted: "O Rasulullah ﷺ! The plot of land you wished to purchase from the Ansaari in exchange of a palace in Jannah, please purchase it from me (in exchange of that palace)." Rasulullah ﷺ purchased this plot from Hadhrat 'Usmaan ؓ in exchange of a palace in Jannah and incorporated this plot of land into the Masjid. Rasulullah ﷺ placed the first brick with his own blessed hand and, as per his instructions, the next brick was placed by Abu Bakr ؓ, then by 'Umar ؓ, followed by 'Usmaan ؓ and then by Ali ؓ.

Hadhrat Abu Hurayrah ؓ, who embraced Islam in the seventh year of Hijrah, also joined them in this reconstruction of the Masjid. Abu Hurayrah ؓ himself narrates: "Rasulullah ﷺ himself was lugging the stones with the Sahaabah ؓ in the reconstruction of the Masjid. He was supporting the stones onto his chest. I thought that he was holding them close to his chest because of their substantial weight. I submitted: 'O Rasulullah! Hand them over to me. I will carry them.' Rasulullah ﷺ replied: 'Take another lot of stones, Abu Hurayrah. There is no life but the life of the hereafter.'"

Erection of Rooms for the Wives

Once he completed the construction of the Masjid, Rasulullah ﷺ laid foundations for the houses of his pure wives. Initially he built two rooms; one for Hadhrat Sawdah bint Zama'ah رضى الله عنها and the other for Hadhrat 'Aa'ishah رضى الله عنها. The additional rooms were built later on as the need arose.

Adjacent to the Masjid were the houses of Haarisah bin Nu'maan Ansaari رضى الله عنه. Whenever the need arose, Hadhrat Haarisah رضى الله عنه would offer a house to Rasulullah ﷺ. In this manner, he offered all his houses, one after the other to Rasulullah ﷺ. Most of the rooms were built from branches of date palms whilst some of them were built from unbaked brick. The doorways were covered with rough Hessian or thick cloth. These structures were not even rooms. They were examples of their asceticism and contentment. These rooms were epitomes of the transitory nature of the dunya. Although lanterns were rarely lit at night within these homes, there was really no need for any other source of illumination. What is the need for a lantern or candle in a home wherein resides the Basheer and Nazeer and the Siraaj-e-Muneer (illuminating lantern)? How aptly a poet describes it when he says:

يا بديع الدل والغنج لك سلطان على المهج

"O you with unique and exquisite features! Your kingship extends over the hearts.

ان بيتا انت ساكنه غير محتاج الى السرج

Certainly the home wherein you reside does not require a lantern.

وجهك الما مول حجتنا يوم يأتى الناس بالحجج

Your blessed countenance will suffice for us as proof, the day when people will present their proofs."

Hasan Basri رحمه الله says: "When I grew up a bit, whilst standing, my outstretched hand could touch the roof of these rooms."

These rooms were situated on the eastern side of the Masjid. There were no rooms on the western side.

After the Demise of the Pure Wives

Following the demise of the wives of Rasulullah ﷺ, on the royal decree of Waleed bin 'Abdul Malik, these rooms were demolished and the area included into the Masjid. When this royal directive reached Madinah, the entire population of Madinah cried out in anguish.

Abu Umaamah Sahl bin Hunaif would often lament: "If only the original structure of the rooms were left intact, people would have witnessed for themselves how the Messenger who was divinely awarded the keys to the treasures of the world passed his life in such simple rooms and huts."

During this time, Rasulullah ﷺ sent Zaid bin Haarisah رضي الله عنه and Abu Raafi' رضي الله عنه to Makkah to fetch Hadhrat Faatimah رضي الله عنها, Hadhrat Umme Kulsoom رضي الله عنها and Ummul-Mumineen Hadhrat Sawdah رضي الله عنها. In their company, Hadhrat Abu Bakr رضي الله عنه sent his son 'Abdullah to fetch Hadhrat 'Aa'ishah, Hadhrat Asma, Hadhrat Umme Rumaan and 'Abdur-Rahmaan bin Abi Bakr رضي الله عنهم.

By the time Hadhrat Zaid bin Haarisah رضي الله عنه returned to Madinah, Rasulullah ﷺ had already relocated from Abu Ayyub Ansaari's رضي الله عنه house to these rooms.

Expansion of the Masjid by the Khulafaa

During his Caliphate, Hadhrat Abu Bakr رضي الله عنه did not extend any portion of the Masjid. He merely replaced with exactly the same date trunks some of the pillars that had decomposed with age.

In the seventeenth year of Hijrah, Hadhrat 'Umar رضي الله عنه extended the Masjid towards the Qiblah and the western side. Since the rooms of the Azwaaj-e-Mutahharaat were situated towards the eastern side, he did not extend the Masjid in this direction.

Although Hadhrat 'Umar رضي الله عنه extended the Masjid, he did not bring about any substantial change in the actual façade and appearance of the structure. As was in the case of Rasulullah ﷺ, Hadhrat 'Umar رضي الله عنه also built the Masjid with unbaked bricks. He hewed its pillars from the trunks of date palms and erected the roof from branches and leaves. He upheld the former simplicity of the original structure.

During his reign of Caliphate, Hadhrat 'Usmaan رضي الله عنه extended the Masjid and instead of simple unbaked bricks, he reconstructed the Masjid using decorative stones and lime as mortar. He remodelled the pillars from stone and replaced the roof using a kind of hardwood timber.

When Hadhrat 'Usmaan رضي الله عنه resolved to revamp the Masjid in this manner, the Sahaabah رضي الله عنهم were a bit offended to see the simplicity of Masjid-e-Nabawi subject to such elaborate transformation. When Hadhrat 'Usmaan رضي الله عنه noticed the Sahaabah's رضي الله عنهم relentless refusal and their aversion for this, he addressed them in one of his sermons saying:

$$\text{انكم اكثرتم وانى سمعت النبى صلى الله عليه وسلم، من بنى لله}$$
$$\text{مسجدا يبتغى به وجه الله له مثله فى الجنة}$$

"You people have expressed numerous comments (about this proposed elaborate structure). I heard Rasulullah ﷺ saying: 'He who builds a Masjid for the pleasure of Allah, Allah will surely build a palace similar to it in Jannah'."

Construction commenced in Rabi'ul-Awwal 29 A.H. and reached completion in Muharram 30 A.H. According to this, the construction took at least ten months.

Imaam Maalik رحمه الله narrates: "When Hadhrat 'Usmaan رضي الله عنه initiated the renovation of the Masjid, K'ab Ahbar would make dua thus: 'O Allah! May this construction never reach completion.' When people enquired the reason for him making dua like this, he replied: 'The moment the renovation draws to a close, the Fitnahs (divine tribulations) will start to descend from the sky.'"

Site of Janaazah Salaah

Abu Sa'eed Khudri رضي الله عنه narrates: "When Rasulullah ﷺ migrated to Madinah and if any of us was close to breathing his last, we would promptly notify him. Rasulullah ﷺ would then come and make dua of Istighfaar (forgiveness) for him. He would stay with the deceased right up to after his burial. Quite often, Rasulullah ﷺ would get incredibly late. This is why we decided to notify him after the actual death. This routine continued for a few days. We would inform Rasulullah ﷺ of the death. He would come, perform the Salaah and make dua of forgiveness etc. for the deceased. Sometimes he would participate in the burial whilst at times he would return immediately after the Salaah.

Afterwards, in view of Rasulullah's ﷺ ease, we decided to take the Mayyit (deceased) directly to his house. Rasulullah ﷺ would perform the Janaazah Salaah in the vicinity of his house. This is why that area came to be known as Mawda'ul-Janaa'iz (place of Janaazah)."

Chapter 10

Brotherhood between the Muhaajireen and Ansaar

When the Muhaajireen migrated from Makkah leaving behind their children, kinsfolk, homes and property and arrived in Madinah, Rasulullah ﷺ established bonds of brotherhood between the Muhaajireen and Ansaar so that their perplexing agitation brought about by their traumatic departure may be replaced by the love and affection of the Ansaar. At times of need, they may assist one another and console one another at times of bereavement. The weak may acquire some strength from the brotherhood of the strong and powerful and the weak may underpin his support for the strong. The fortunate may benefit from the unfortunate whilst the unfortunate may benefit from the fortunate. The scattered pearls of the Muhaajireen and Ansaar may be threaded into a single strand of brotherhood and develop into a single entity without any form of disunity and disharmony. All of them may hold firmly onto the rope of Allah Ta'ala. This Ummah should be entirely safe from the dissension and disunity that brought about the destruction of the Banu Israa'eel. Due to their unassailable unity, Allah Ta'ala's hand would remain over their heads. If, per chance, some arrogance of the pre-Islamic days still remained within the hearts, this brotherhood would totally eradicate it and instead of the heart harbouring pride, arrogance and conceit, the hearts may cherish humility, meekness, brotherhood and beneficence. The servant and the master, the superior and inferior, the king and the subjects were all brought to stand on a single platform. All the ludicrous distinctive features of the world were eliminated and Allah-consciousness and piety was restored as the sole benchmark of nobility and eminence. Allah Ta'ala declares:

$$\text{اِنَّ اَكْرَمَكُمْ عِنْدَ اللّٰهِ اَتْقٰىكُمْ ۚ اِنَّ اللّٰهَ عَلِيْمٌ خَبِيْرٌ}$$

"Certainly, the most noble amongst you in the eyes of Allah are those who are the most Allah-conscious." [Surah Hujuraat verse 13]

It was with these benefits in mind that Rasulullah ﷺ, even before Hijrah, established bonds of brotherhood amongst the Muhaajireen whilst in Makkah. After his migration to Madinah, he again instituted this union of brotherhood, this time between the Muhaajireen and Ansaar. This association of brotherhood was launched on two separate occasions; first amongst the Muhaajireen whereby one Muhaajir was allied with another Muhaajir. This took place in Makkah. The second phase of brotherhood took place in Madinah between the Muhaajireen and Ansaar.

Ibn 'Abbaas ؓ narrates that Rasulullah ﷺ established a bond of brotherhood between Zubair ؓ and 'Abdullah bin Mas'ood ؓ whereas both of them were from the Muhaajireen.

Ibn 'Umar ؓ narrates: "Rasulullah ﷺ established a bond of brotherhood between Abu Bakr ؓ and 'Umar ؓ, between so and so and so and so"…..and he went on to mention a few others. Ali ؓ enquired: "Who is my brother, O Rasulullah ﷺ?" Rasulullah ﷺ replied: "I am your brother."

The bond of brotherhood established in Makkah before Hijrah was instituted amongst the Muhaajireen as follows:

Brotherhood between:

1. Abu Bakr ؓ & 'Umar ؓ
2. Hamzah ؓ & Zaid bin Haarisah ؓ
3. 'Usmaan Ghani ؓ & 'Abdur Rahmaan bin 'Awf ؓ
4. Zubair bin 'Awwaam ؓ & 'Abdullah bin Mas'ood ؓ
5. 'Ubaidah bin Haaris ؓ & Bilal bin Rabah ؓ
6. Mus'ab bin 'Umair ؓ & S'ad bin Abi Waqqaas ؓ
7. Abu 'Ubaidah ؓ & Saalim, slave of Huzaifah ؓ
8. Sa'eed bin Zaid ؓ & Talhah bin 'Ubaidullah ؓ
9. Sayyidina Rasulullah ﷺ & Ali ؓ

Second Occasion of Brotherhood

The second occasion of brotherhood was launched five months after Hijrah in Hadhrat Anas's ؓ house between forty-five Muhaajireen and forty-five Ansaar. Each Muhaajir was paired off with an Ansaari.

Some of them are listed below:

Muhaajireen & Ansaar

1. Abu Bakr Siddeeq ﷺ & Khaarijah bin Zaid ﷺ
2. 'Umar bin Khattaab ﷺ & 'Atbaan bin Maalik ﷺ
3. Abu 'Ubaidah bin Jarraah ﷺ & S'ad bin Mu'aaz ﷺ
4. 'Abdur-Rahmaan bin 'Awf ﷺ & S'ad bin Rab'i ﷺ
5. Zubair bin 'Awwaam ﷺ & Salaamah bin Salaamah bin Wuqaish ﷺ
6. 'Usmaan bin Affaan ﷺ & Aws bin Saabit ﷺ
7. Talhah bin 'Ubaidullah ﷺ & K'ab bin Maalik ﷺ
8. Sa'eed bin Zaid bin 'Amr bin Nufail ﷺ & Ubayy bin K'ab ﷺ
9. Mus'ab bin 'Umair ﷺ & Abu Ayyub Khaalid bin Zaid Ansaari ﷺ
10. Abu Huzaifah bin 'Utbah ﷺ & 'Abbaad bin Bishr ﷺ
11. 'Ammaar bin Yaasir ﷺ & Huzaifah bin Yamaan ﷺ
12. Abu Zar Ghifaari ﷺ & Munzir bin 'Amr ﷺ
13. Salmaan Faarsi ﷺ & Abud-Dardaa 'Uwaymir bin S'alabah ﷺ
14. Bilal ﷺ & Abu Ruwayhah 'Abdullah bin 'Abdur-Rahmaan ﷺ
15. Haatib bin Abi Balta'ah ﷺ & 'Uwaim bin Saa'idah ﷺ
16. Abu Marsad ﷺ & 'Ubaadah bin Saamit ﷺ
17. 'Abdullah bin Jahash ﷺ & 'Aasim bin Thaabit ﷺ
18. 'Utbah bin Ghazwaan ﷺ & Abu Dujaanah ﷺ
19. Abu Salamah bin 'Abdul-Asad ﷺ & S'ad bin Khaysamah ﷺ
20. 'Usmaan bin Maz'oon ﷺ & Abul-Haysam bin Tayhaan ﷺ
21. 'Ubaidah bin Haaris ﷺ & 'Umair bin Hammaam ﷺ
22. Tufail bin Haaris ﷺ & 'Ubaidah's brother - Sufyaan Nasr Khazraji ﷺ
23. Safwaan bin Baydaa ﷺ & Raaf'i bin Mu'allaa ﷺ
24. Miqdaad ﷺ & 'Abdullah bin Rawaahah ﷺ
25. Zush-Shimaalain ﷺ & Yazeed bin Haaris ﷺ
26. Arqam ﷺ & Talhah bin Zaid ﷺ

27. Zaid bin Khattaab رضي الله عنه & M'an bin 'Adi رضي الله عنه

28. 'Amr bin Suraaqah رضي الله عنه & S'ad bin Zaid رضي الله عنه

29. 'Aaqil bin Bukair رضي الله عنه & Mubashir bin 'Abdul-Munzir رضي الله عنه

30. Khunais bin Huzaafah رضي الله عنه & Munzir bin Muhammad رضي الله عنه

31. Surrah bin Abi Ruhm رضي الله عنه & 'Ubaadh bin Khashkhash رضي الله عنه

32. Mistah bin Usaasah رضي الله عنه & Zaid bin Muzayyan رضي الله عنه

33. 'Ukkaashah bin Mihsan رضي الله عنه & Mujazzir bin Dammaar رضي الله عنه

34. 'Aamir bin Fuhayrah رضي الله عنه & Haaris bin Simmah رضي الله عنه

35. Muhajj'a رضي الله عنه, slave of 'Umar رضي الله عنه & Suraaqah bin 'Amr bin 'Atiyyah رضي الله عنه

The right of brotherhood fulfilled by the Ansaar and the overriding degree of the sincere sacrifices demonstrated by them is absolutely unique and without comparison. Their generosity with the Muhaajireen as far as their wealth, lands and assets is concerned is somewhat understandable in that they gave away their physical wealth like date orchards etc. to the Muhaajireen but even beyond that, they even offered their wives to the Muhaajireen. An Ansaari who had two wives would offer his Muhaajir brother one of his two wives saying: "Select whichever one you wish. I will divorce her and you may marry her (after the 'Iddah period)."

Hadhrat Anas رضي الله عنه narrates: "None of the Ansaar would ever regard anyone more eligible to his wealth than his Muhaajir brother."

When the Muhaajireen witnessed the unparalleled empathy and unrivalled sacrifices of the Ansaar, they asked: "O Rasulullah صلى الله عليه وسلم! We have not come across anyone more compassionate, sincerely dedicated and more enthusiastically devoted – whether in times of comfort or hardship – than these people amongst whom we have put our roots. We fear that they will acquire all the reward whilst we will be deprived." Rasulullah صلى الله عليه وسلم replied: "No, as long as you continue making dua for them."

In other words, your good turn of making dua for them is not in any way inferior to their kindness of providing tangible wealth to you. In fact, making dua is more superior to that. Let alone a few coins, if the riches of the entire world were to be placed on one pan of the scale and just a single sincere dua is placed on the other pan, Insha Allah, the pan of dua would far outweigh the pan of riches. Whenever a beggar appeared before Hadhrat 'Aa'ishah رضي الله عنها, showering duas upon her, as is the norm of beggars, she would first recompense him by responding with dua and then she would give him some charity. Someone asked her: "O Ummul-Mumineen! Why is it that you give a beggar charity and make dua for him in the words he made dua for you?" She replied: "If I refrain from praying for him and simply give him alms only, his favour over me would be more superior to my kindness over him because dua is far superior to alms-giving. This is why I offset my dua against his dua so that my charity remains pure, it will not be in exchange of anything." So he who can give a few coins and earn himself sincere dua in the process should not allow this opportunity to pass by.

Nonetheless, this union of brotherhood was so strong that it was considered as enduring as a family relationship. When an Ansaari would leave this world, his Muhaajir brother would inherit from him. Allah Ta'ala says:

اِنَّ الَّذِيْنَ اٰمَنُوْا وَهَاجَرُوْا وَجٰهَدُوْا بِاَمْوَالِهِمْ وَاَنْفُسِهِمْ فِىْ سَبِيْلِ اللّٰهِ وَالَّذِيْنَ اٰوَوْا وَّنَصَرُوْۤا اُولٰٓئِكَ بَعْضُهُمْ اَوْلِيَآءُ بَعْضٍ ۭ

"Certainly those who believed and migrated and executed Jihaad in the path of Allah with their wealth and lives, and those who provided refuge and help – these are all allies (heirs) unto one another." [Surah Anfaal verse 72]

However, this injunction favouring inheritance was subsequently rescinded and all believers were declared to be brothers unto one another. The following verse was revealed:

اِنَّمَا الْمُؤْمِنُوْنَ اِخْوَةٌ

"Certainly the believers are brothers (unto one another)." [Surah Hujuraat verse:10]

Now the bond of brotherhood was left only for mutual assistance, protection and sympathy and inheritance was allotted specifically to family members only.

Inception of the Azaan

The Salaah's of 'Asr and Fajr were made mandatory right at the beginning of prophethood. Subsequently, the remaining Salaahs were enjoined on the night of Mi'raaj. All the Salaahs with the exception of Maghrib consisted of just two Rakaats. After Hijrah the two Rakaats were left intact when travelling, whilst a further two Rakaats were added in Zuhr, 'Asr and Isha for those not travelling.

The prevailing practice was that people would assemble in the Masjid whenever the time for Salaah would set in. Rasulullah ﷺ felt that there should be some signal that would allow the people from the community to easily assemble in the Masjid at once.

Someone suggested striking a Naaqus (bell) whilst someone else suggested blowing a Buq (horn) to summon the faithful to Salaah. However, Rasulullah ﷺ rejected the use of such devices as this would resemble the practice of the Jews and Christians. The Christians used the Naaqus whilst the Jews used a

Buq. In short, Rasulullah ﷺ detested this degree of resemblance with the Christians and Jews.

Someone proposed lighting a fire at an elevated spot. When people would notice the flames, they would come to Salaah. Rasulullah ﷺ replied that this is the custom of the Fire Worshippers. He abhorred resemblence with them as well.

The assembly dispersed without reaching any concrete resolution. This concern and unease of Rasulullah ﷺ had a profound effect on 'Abdullah bin Zaid bin 'Abdi Rabbihi ؓ.

During the course of these discussions, 'Abdullah bin Zaid saw a dream. He says: "I saw a man dressed in green apparel clutching a bell in his hand walking past me. I asked him: 'Will you sell this bell to me?' 'What will you do with it?' he asked. I replied: 'I will summon the people to Salaah by chiming the bell.' The man with the green apparel remarked: 'Should I not enlighten you on something far more superior than this?' 'Why not?' I replied, 'Surely.'

The man said: 'Say the following words (to summon the people to prayer):

اَللّٰهُ اَكْبَرُ اَللّٰهُ اَكْبَرُ   اَللّٰهُ اَكْبَرُ اَللّٰهُ اَكْبَرُ

'Allahu Akbar Allahu Akbar.

اَشْهَدُ اَنْ لَّا اِلٰهَ اِلَّا اللّٰهُ   اَشْهَدُ اَنْ لَّا اِلٰهَ اِلَّا اللّٰهُ

Ash-hadu Al-Laailaaha Illallah,   Ash-hadu Al-Laailaaha Illallah.

اَشْهَدُ اَنَّ مُحَمَّدًا رَسُوْلُ اللّٰهِ   اَشْهَدُ اَنَّ مُحَمَّدًا رَسُوْلُ اللّٰهِ

Ash-hadu Anna Muhammadar-Rasulullah,

حَىَّ عَلَى الصَّلٰوةِ   حَىَّ عَلَى الصَّلٰوةِ

Hayya 'Alas-Salaah,   Hayya 'Alas-Salaah.

حَىَّ عَلَى الْفَلاَحِ   حَىَّ عَلَى الْفَلاَحِ

Hayya 'Alal-Falaah   Hayya 'Alal-Falaah.

اَللّٰهُ اَكْبَرُ اَللّٰهُ اَكْبَرُ   لَا اِلٰهَ اِلَّا اللّٰهُ

'Allahu Akbar Allahu Akbar.

Laa Ilaaha Illallah.'

Shifting onto one side, the man then taught me the words of the Iqaamah saying: 'Recite the same words when you stand for Salaah. After the words Hayya 'Alal-Falaah, add on the words 'Qad Qaamatis-Salaah' twice.'"

'Abdullah bin Zaid رضي الله عنه further relates: "The next morning, I presented myself before Rasulullah صلى الله عليه وسلم and related the dream to him. On hearing the dream, Rasulullah صلى الله عليه وسلم pronounced:

ان هذه الرؤيا حق ان شاء الله تعالى

"Surely this dream is true, Insha Allah."

Rasulullah صلى الله عليه وسلم then directed 'Abdullah bin Zaid رضي الله عنه to teach Bilal رضي الله عنه the words of the Azaan so that he, Bilal رضي الله عنه, may call out the Azaan. Rasulullah صلى الله عليه وسلم told 'Abdullah bin Zaid رضي الله عنه: "Let Bilal call out the Azaan as his voice is louder than yours."

Hadhrat Bilal رضي الله عنه then called out the Azaan. When the words of the Azaan reached the ears of Hadhrat 'Umar رضي الله عنه, he hastened to Rasulullah صلى الله عليه وسلم heaving his sheet behind him. As he appeared before Rasulullah صلى الله عليه وسلم, 'Umar رضي الله عنه submitted:

والذى بعثك بالحق لقد رايت مثل الذى أرى

"O Rasulullah صلى الله عليه وسلم! By the Being Who has ordained you with Haqq (truth), I have also seen (in the dream) what he ('Abdullah bin Zaid) had been shown."

Upon hearing this, Rasulullah صلى الله عليه وسلم exclaimed: "So Allah be praised!"

Treaty with the Jews

The majority of the population of Madinah was made up of the Aws and Khazraj tribes. However over an extended period of time, a significant number of Jews also settled in Madinah. They had a number of Madrasahs and educational institutes in Khaybar and Madinah. They also had a few fortresses in Khaybar. They were referred to as Ahl-e-Kitaab (people of the scripture). Compared to the disbelievers, they enjoyed educational superiority and distinction in the land of Hijaaz. On the basis of their celestial scriptures, they were conscious of the conditions and attributes of the final Messenger. Allah Ta'ala declares: "They recognise him just as they recognise their (own) sons." However, they were not people of sound disposition. Jealousy, pride, obstinacy and defiance were their second nature. Allah Ta'ala states: "And they (the Jews) refuted it (the Aayaat) wrongfully and arrogantly even though their hearts were convinced (of the truth)."

Even whilst Rasulullah ﷺ was in Makkah, the Jews would persistently incite the Makkan Quraysh against Rasulullah ﷺ. The Jews would often persuade the Quraysh to ask Rasulullah ﷺ about certain topics like Ashaab-e-Kahf, Ruh (soul), Zul-Qarnain, etc. When Rasulullah ﷺ migrated to Madinah, this jealousy and defiance flared even further. In due course, they came to grips with the fact that the days of their educational and academic superiority had drawn to a close and the deviants from amongst them trailed their predecessors in flouting the truth. They elected to adhere to the ways of the 'people of Saturday (Ashaab-e-Sabt)' and the conduct of those who 'assassinated the Prophets'.

The pious and those of sound disposition from amongst the Rabbis and the learned divulged the prophecies of the final messenger to their people and these selected few embraced Islam. However, most of them preferred the route of defiance. Jealousy and rebelliousness proved to be their downfall in this path of righteousness.

In view of their jealousy and defiance and in order to contain their civil strife, rebellion and depravity, Rasulullah ﷺ decided to draw up a written treaty with them. The idea behind this treaty was to at least ensure that their opposition and defiance does not intensify any further and so that the Muslims may be safe from their strife and depravity. The Holy Qur-aan is replete with the evils and rabble-rousing of the Jews. So in order to contain this problem and mischief from swelling any further, Rasulullah ﷺ formed a treaty with the local Jews of Madinah.

Five months after his migration to Madinah, Rasulullah ﷺ established a written treaty with the Jews of Madinah in which he promised to allow them to retain their Deen, wealth and assets subject to certain conditions. These will be discussed shortly. A summary of this treaty follows:

$$\text{بِسْمِ اللهِ الرَّحْمٰنِ الرَّحِيْمِ}$$

Treaty from Muhammad, the unlettered Prophet between the Muslims of the Quraysh and Muslims of Madinah and between the Jews who wish to ally themselves with the Muslims, that every affiliate of the treaty will, whilst retaining his own faith, be bound by the following conditions:

1. Qisaas and the ancient system of blood money will be retained with justice and integrity.

2. With fairness, each member will be obliged to pay the ransom of its own tribe. In other words, if a prisoner (of war) is to be released by the payment of ransom, the obligation of payment rests upon the tribe from which the prisoner hails.

3. All members will remain committed against tyranny, transgression, hostility and civil strife. There will be no exceptions to this rule even if the offender is the son (of one of the leaders).
4. No Muslim will be permitted to execute another Muslim in retaliation of the murder of a disbeliever. Furthermore, no disbeliever will be assisted against a Muslim.
5. A lowest ranking Muslim will enjoy the same right of offering sanctuary and refuge as that of the highest-ranking Muslim.
6. The safety of Jews living under the Muslims will be the responsibility of the Muslims. They will not be harassed or tyrannised and their enemies will not be assisted against them.
7. A disbeliever will neither have the right against Muslims to offer asylum to the lives and wealth of the Quraysh nor will he have the right to interfere between the Muslims and the Quraysh.
8. In times of war, the Jews will be obliged to support the Muslims with their wealth and lives. They will not be permitted to assist the enemy against the Muslims.
9. If an enemy of Rasulullah ﷺ attacks Madinah, the Jews will be duty-bound to assist Rasulullah ﷺ.
10. From the tribes who are affiliated to this treaty, none of them will have the right to withdraw from the obligations of this treaty without the permission of Rasulullah ﷺ.
11. Assistance or asylum to a trouble monger will not be permitted. (He who assists or offers asylum to a Bid'ati attracts the wrath and curse of Allah. None of his good actions will be accepted right until Qiyaamah.)
12. If the Muslims enter into a peace treaty with anyone, the Jews will also be obliged to observe the conditions of this treaty.
13. He who murders a Muslim and there is evidence to support this, will be executed in Qisaas except if the guardian agrees to accept blood money etc.
14. In cases of dispute or mutual disagreement, matters will be referred to Allah and His Rasool ﷺ.

The tribes with which Rasulullah ﷺ concluded this treaty included three major tribes of the Jews who lived in and around Madinah. These three tribes were Banu Qaynuqaa, Banu Nazeer and Banu Qurayzah. Since these three tribes declined to comply with Rasulullah ﷺ, he entered into this treaty with them to stop the spreading of their evil and mischief. However, all three tribes, one after the other, violated the terms of the treaty and took extensive part in their hostility and conspiracy against the Muslims. They were thus punished for their misdeeds as mentioned in the chapter dealing with military expeditions.

This treaty was endorsed before the injunction of jizyah (tax levied on non-Muslims living under Muslim rule). Islam was still vulnerable and weak at that moment in time. Initially, the ruling was that if the Jews join the Muslims in any military expedition, they are to be given a percentage of the booty. This is why one of the conditions of this treaty was that the Jews will be obliged to share the burden of the expenditure incurred in these campaigns.

Miscellaneous Incidents of the First Year of Hijrah

1. After Rasulullah's ﷺ arrival in Madinah, Kulsoom bin Hadam, in whose house Rasulullah ﷺ lodged during his stay in Quba, passed away.

2. Even before Rasulullah ﷺ could complete the construction of the Masjid, As'ad bin Zuraarah, the head of Banu Najjaar tribe passed away. Banu Najjaar appeared before Rasulullah ﷺ and requested: "O Rasulullah ﷺ! Appoint someone as his successor." Rasulullah ﷺ replied: "You are my maternal kinsfolk. I am from amongst you and I am your head."

3. Rasulullah's ﷺ acceptance of the post of head over the Banu Najjaar tribe is enumerated as one of the merits of this tribe. This tribe considered this a source of their pride.

4. In the same year, two chieftains of the disbelievers died; Waleed bin Mughirah and 'Aas bin Waa'il, the father of the conqueror of Egypt 'Amr bin 'Aas ﷜.

5. In the same year, eight months after arriving in Madinah, Rasulullah ﷺ consummated his marriage with Hadhrat 'Aa'ishah ﷞ with whom he had performed Nikah before Hijrah after the demise of Hadhrat Khadijah ﷞.

6. At the time of her Nikah, Hadhrat 'Aa'ishah ﷞ was six years old and she was nine when she went to live with Rasulullah ﷺ. Some Ulama that Rasulullah ﷺ consummated his marriage with her eighteen months after Hijrah in the second year.

7. When the Muslims arrived in Madinah, the water of all the wells of Madinah was salty. Only one well called 'the well of Roomah' gave sweet water. This well belonged to a Jew who would not provide its water except at a price. The poor Muslims were left in a fix. Hadhrat 'Usmaan ﷜ purchased this well and sold it to Rasulullah ﷺ in exchange for a fountain in Jannah. He

donated it to the Muslim Ummah at large. Whoever wanted could avail himself of its water.

Islam of Sarumah bin Abi Anas ﷺ

Sarumah bin Abi Anas Najjaari ﷺ was enthusiastic about Tauheed right from the beginning. He abhorred disbelief. In fact, once he even aimed to embrace Christianity but abandoned this idea (perhaps after witnessing the sceptical ideologies of the Christians).

He was a great Aabid and Zaahid (devoted and abstinent). He lived a frugal life of an ascetic. He never wore fine cloth. He was always dressed in rough course clothing.

He built a special room exclusively for his devotions. Women in their menses and people in the state of Janaabat (impurity) were not allowed entry into this room. He would often declare: "I am worshipping the Lord of Ibraaheem."

He was a celebrated poet of his era. His poetry was replete with words of wisdom, advice and good counsel.

When Rasulullah ﷺ arrived in Madinah after his migration, Sarumah was by then a rather aged man. He appeared before Rasulullah ﷺ, embraced Islam and recited the following lines of poetry:

ثوى فى قريش بضع عـشرة حجة يذكر لو يلقى صديقا مواتيا

"He (Rasulullah ﷺ) resided for over ten years amongst the Quraysh offering them advice and good counsel whilst expecting some friend and supporter to assist him.

ويعرض فى اهل المواسم نفسه فلم يرمن يؤوى ولم يرداعيا

And he would present himself to the pilgrims during the season (of Haj) but he failed to find anyone willing to offer him sanctuary or anyone to assist him in inviting.

فلما اتانا اظهر الله دينه فاصبح مـسرورا بطيبة راضيا

When he appeared before us, Allah awarded His Deen dominance and he was overjoyed and content with Madinah.

والقى صديقا اطمأنت به النوى وكان له عونا من الله باديا

Coming here he found a friend and he felt consoled from the grief brought about by separation from his birthplace. And his friend turned out to be a sincere companion and supporter from Allah's side.

يقص لنا ما قال نوح لقومه وما قال موسى اذا جاب المناديا

He (Rasulullah ﷺ) relates to us about that which Nuh عليه السلام and Musa عليه السلام enlightened their people.

فاصبح لا يخشى من الناس واحدا قريبا ولا يخشى من الناس نائيا

And coming here to Madinah, he has taken a sigh of relief; he does not fear anything close nor distant.

بذلنا له الاموال من جل مالنا وانفسنا عند الوغى والتآسيا

We have surrendered all our wealth to him whilst at times of war we sacrifice our lives for him.

ونعلم ان الله لا شيء غيره ونعلم ان الله افضل هاديا

And we harbour firm conviction that there is nothing of substance save Allah and we firmly believe that He is the best guide.

نعادي الذي عادى من الناس كلهم جميعا وان كان الحبيب مصافيا

We regard his enemy as our enemy even though he may be intently dear to us."

Change of Qiblah direction – 2nd Year of Hijrah

As long as Rasulullah ﷺ lived in Makkah he continued performing Salaah whilst facing Baitul-Muqaddas but in such a manner that he would face the K'abah as well. When he migrated to Madinah Munawwarah, he was unable to maintain this practise of facing both Qiblahs simultaneously. This is why, on the divine directive of Allah Ta'ala, he performed his Salaah whilst facing Baitul-Muqaddas for about sixteen to seventeen months.

Even before Allah revealed the divine commandment of transforming the direction of the Qiblah, He kindled the eagerness within Rasulullah's ﷺ heart to face the K'abah whilst performing Salaah. Quite frequently, Rasulullah ﷺ would raise his gaze to the skies in anticipation of the divine commandment directing him to turn towards the K'abah for Salaah.

Subsequently, on the fifteenth of Sh'abaan 2 A.H., the following verse was revealed:

فَوَلِّ وَجْهَكَ شَطْرَ الْمَسْجِدِ الْحَرَامِ

"And turn your face towards the direction of Masjidul-Haraam."

Chapter 10

Suffah and As-haabus Suffah

Following the change of the Qiblah direction when the direction of Qiblah from Masjid-e-Nabawi was changed to Baitullah, the walls of the former Qiblah and the area immediately adjacent to it was left intact for the accommodation of the poor and destitute who had no home or place to live. This place was popularly known as Suffah.

A Suffah is actually a ledge or a covered veranda. The weak Muslims and grateful destitute were not only patient over their poverty but they were more content and grateful than the affluent and powerful rulers. When these poverty-stricken souls would come to listen to the words of Allah and His Rasool ﷺ, they would stay behind at this spot. People would refer to this group as As-haabus Suffah. It was as though this was the Khaanqah of Rasulullah ﷺ, the abstinent Prophet, who enthusiastically preferred poverty to the dominion of the world.

The As-haabus Suffah were a group of people made up of ascetics and Mutawakkileen whose principal objective day and night was their spiritual purity and the acquisition of the knowledge of the Qur-aan and the wisdom of Rasulullah ﷺ. They were neither interested in trade nor was farming of any concern to them.

These people had dedicated their sight to behold Rasulullah ﷺ and their ears to listen to his sacred words and they had surrendered their physical bodies to the companionship of Rasulullah ﷺ.

Hadhrat Abu Hurayrah ﷺ narrates: "I have observed seventy As-haabus Suffah who did not even possess a single sheet to cover themselves. They merely owned a sheet or a blanket to cover the lower portion of their bodies, which they would fasten to their necks. Even these blankets were so short that they would barely reach half their calves or their ankles and they would clasp it close to their bodies lest their Satar become exposed."

Waasilah bin Asq'a ﷺ relates: "I was also one of the members of As-haabus Suffah. None of us even had a complete set of clothing. Due to excessive perspiration, our bodies were encrusted with grime and dust." (This grime was more cherished by them than extreme cleanliness. These were the dishevelled and grubby personalities who, if they had to take an oath upon Allah Ta'ala, He would ensure that their oaths are fulfilled.)

Mujaahid says that Abu Hurayrah ﷺ relates: "I swear by that Being besides whom there is no other deity that quite often, overwhelmed with hunger, I would lay my chest and stomach onto the ground (so that the moisture and coolness of the ground may alleviate the heat of my hunger to some extent). Occasionally I would fasten a stone to my stomach merely to keep my back straight.

One day I seated myself at one of the main thoroughfares when Abu Bakr رَضِيَ اللَّهُ عَنْهُ happened to pass by. I asked him to explain a certain verse of the Qur-aan to me but my actual aim was that he might catch sight of my pitiful condition and take me along for a meal. However, Abu Bakr رَضِيَ اللَّهُ عَنْهُ went away (without a notion of my objective).

A little later Hadhrat 'Umar رَضِيَ اللَّهُ عَنْهُ happened to pass by. In a like manner, on the pretext of explaining a Qur-aanic verse to me I intercepted him. However he too went on his way.

A little while later Abul-Qaasim صَلَّى اللَّهُ عَلَيْهِ وَسَلَّمَ (whom Allah Ta'ala commissioned as a Qaasim – distributor – of blessings) happened to pass by the same way.

The moment his gaze fell on me, he realised my intentions. Smiling at me, he said: 'O Abu Hirr!'

'I am at your service', I replied, 'O Rasulullah صَلَّى اللَّهُ عَلَيْهِ وَسَلَّمَ!'

'Come along with me'" he said.

I went along with him to his house. As he entered his home, he found a bowl of milk there. When he enquired about it, his family replied: 'So and so sent it as a gift to you.' Looking towards me, he bade me to call the As-haabus Suffah."

Abu Hurayrah رَضِيَ اللَّهُ عَنْهُ relates: "The As-haabus Suffah were the guests of Islam. They neither had a place to live nor were they in possession of any wealth. Whenever any charity came to Rasulullah صَلَّى اللَّهُ عَلَيْهِ وَسَلَّمَ, he would send it over to them without partaking of any part of it (because Sadaqah was Haraam for him). Whenever he received a gift, he would partake of it and include the As-haabus Suffah in it as well. Now when he asked me to call the As-haabus Suffah, I found it a bit tough. I reflected to myself, how would this one bowl of milk suffice for all the As-haabus Suffah? I am most eligible to drink this milk. At least I would be able to regain some of my strength. Furthermore, after the arrival of the As-haabus Suffah, I myself would be instructed to distribute the milk to them. I do not think there would be any leftover for me, I thought. Nevertheless, there was no getting away from compliance with Allah and His Rasool صَلَّى اللَّهُ عَلَيْهِ وَسَلَّمَ.

I called the As-haabus Suffah and as per Rasulullah's صَلَّى اللَّهُ عَلَيْهِ وَسَلَّمَ instructions, I summoned them one by one. When all of them drank to their fill, Rasulullah صَلَّى اللَّهُ عَلَيْهِ وَسَلَّمَ smiled at me and said: 'Only you and I are left now.'

I submitted: 'That is correct, O Rasulullah صَلَّى اللَّهُ عَلَيْهِ وَسَلَّمَ!' Rasulullah صَلَّى اللَّهُ عَلَيْهِ وَسَلَّمَ bade me to start drinking. As I was drinking, he repeatedly bade me to drink saying: 'Drink more! Drink more!' until such time that I was utterly satiated and cried out: 'By that Being Who has sent you with the truth! I do not have room for any more.' Taking the bowl from my hand, Rasulullah صَلَّى اللَّهُ عَلَيْهِ وَسَلَّمَ recited some praise of Allah, said *Bismillah* and drank up whatever remained within the bowl."

'Abdur-Rahmaan bin Abi Bakr رَضِيَ اللَّهُ عَنْهُ relates: "The As-haabus Suffah were extremely destitute. Rasulullah صَلَّى اللَّهُ عَلَيْهِ وَسَلَّمَ would distribute them amongst the Sahaabah رَضِيَ اللَّهُ عَنْهُمْ saying: "He who has food for two should take a third person with him and he who has food for three should take a fourth person with him," and so forth.

Muhammad bin Seereen رَحْمَةُاللّٰه says: "Towards the evening, Rasulullah صَلَّى اللّٰهُ عَلَيْهِ وَسَلَّم would distribute the As-haabus Suffah amongst his Sahaabah رَضِىَ اللّٰهُ عَنْهُم. Some of them would take two whilst others would take three of them home with them. S'ad bin 'Ubaadah رَضِىَ اللّٰهُ عَنْه would sometimes take up to eighty people home with him for meals."

Abu Hurayrah رَضِىَ اللّٰهُ عَنْه relates: "I was also from amongst the As-haabus-Suffah. Every evening we would present ourselves before Rasulullah صَلَّى اللّٰهُ عَلَيْهِ وَسَلَّم. He would distribute us in ones or twos amongst the more affluent Sahaabah رَضِىَ اللّٰهُ عَنْهُم. He would then take those who were left. After meals, we would all sleep in the Masjid.

A string was tied between two pillars of the Masjid. The Ansaar who had date orchards would hang up a few clusters of dates for the exclusive consumption of the As-haabus Suffah. They would strike the dates with a stick and eat as they fell to the ground. Mu'aaz bin Jabal رَضِىَ اللّٰهُ عَنْه was in charge of this."

'Awf bin Maalik Ashj'ai رَضِىَ اللّٰهُ عَنْه narrates: "Rasulullah صَلَّى اللّٰهُ عَلَيْهِ وَسَلَّم once emerged (from his house into the Masjid) bearing a staff when his gaze fell onto a spoilt cluster of dates suspended in the Masjid. He commented: "If the donor wished, he could have brought a better bunch of dates."

According to another Hadith, Rasulullah صَلَّى اللّٰهُ عَلَيْهِ وَسَلَّم instructed every date palm owner to bring a bunch of dates and hang it up in the Masjid for the destitute.

Jaabir bin 'Abdullah رَضِىَ اللّٰهُ عَنْه narrates that Rasulullah صَلَّى اللّٰهُ عَلَيْهِ وَسَلَّم said:

فى كل عشرة اقناء قنو يوضع فى المسجد للمساكين

"From every ten clusters of dates, one cluster should be placed in the Masjid for the destitute."

'Abdullah bin Shaqeeq رَحْمَةُاللّٰه says: "I lived for a whole year in the company of Abu Hurayrah رَضِىَ اللّٰهُ عَنْه. One day he commented: 'If only you had witnessed our past days when for days on end we did not even have that much food by which we could at least straighten our backs. We would be forced to tie stones to our stomachs merely to straighten our backs.'"

Fudaalah bin 'Ubaid رَضِىَ اللّٰهُ عَنْه narrates: "Quite often, overwhelmed with acute hunger, the As-haabus Suffah would fall down unconscious whilst performing Salaah. If a villager or Bedouin stranger had to lay eyes on them, he would reckon them to have lost their senses or regard them as lunatics. Rasulullah صَلَّى اللّٰهُ عَلَيْهِ وَسَلَّم would come to them and console them thus:

لو تعلمون مالك عندالله لاحببتم ان تزدادوا فقرا و حاجة

"If only you knew what awaits you by Allah, you would yearn for an increase in this poverty and need."

Attributes of As-haabus Suffah

'Ayaad bin Ghanam رَضِيَ اللَّهُ عَنْهُ relates that he heard Rasulullah ﷺ saying: "The best and high ranking people of my Ummah – as I was enlightened by the Malaul-A'alaa (close angels) – are those people who overtly smile whilst contemplating over the infinite mercy of Allah Ta'ala but their hearts are sobbing in trepidation of the severity of His divine chastisement. Morning and evening they remember Allah in His uncontaminated houses (i.e. the Masaajid). With their tongues brimming with hope mingled with fear, they call unto Allah Ta'ala and their hearts are replete with a passionate longing to meet Him. Their burden unto others is extremely light whilst their own burdens unto themselves are enormously heavy. They walk on the ground with humility and tranquillity and not with arrogance and pride. They walk like ants. In other words, humility and neediness is exuded from their gaits.

They recite the Holy Qur-aan. They are dressed in old frayed clothing. They are always in the divine care and protection of Allah Ta'ala. Their souls are in this world whilst their hearts are attached to the hereafter. They have no concern but of the hereafter. They are perpetually engaged in preparation for the grave and the hereafter."

Thereafter Rasulullah ﷺ recited the following verse of the Holy Qur-aan:

$$ذٰلِكَ لِمَنْ خَافَ مَقَامِيْ وَخَافَ وَعِيْدِ$$

"This (promise) is for that person who fears standing before Me and he fears My warning."

Names of As-haabus Suffah

The actual number of As-haabus Suffah continued fluctuating from time to time. Aarif Seharwardi رَحْمَةُ اللَّهِ writes in 'Awaarif that the roll of the As-haabus Suffah once reached four hundred.

Some of these illustrious souls are listed below:

1. Abu 'Ubaidah 'Aamir bin Jarrah رَضِيَ اللَّهُ عَنْهُ
2. 'Ammaar bin Yaasir رَضِيَ اللَّهُ عَنْهُ
3. 'Abdullah bin Mas'ood رَضِيَ اللَّهُ عَنْهُ
4. Miqdaad bin 'Amr رَضِيَ اللَّهُ عَنْهُ

5. Khabbaab bin Aratt ؓ
6. Bilal bin Rabah ؓ
7. Suhaib bin Sinaan ؓ
8. Zaid bin Khattaab ؓ, brother of 'Umar ؓ
9. Abu Marthad Kanaaz bin Husain 'Adawi ؓ
10. Abu Kabshah ؓ, emancipated slave of Rasulullah ﷺ
11. Safwaan bin Baydaa ؓ
12. Abu 'Abas bin Jabr ؓ
13. Saalim ؓ, the emancipated slave of Huzaifah ؓ
14. Mistah bin Asaasah ؓ
15. 'Ukaashah bin Mihsan ؓ
16. Mas'ood bin Rab'i ؓ
17. 'Umair bin 'Awf ؓ
18. 'Uwaim bin Saa'idah ؓ
19. Abu Lubaabah ؓ
20. Saalim bin 'Umair ؓ
21. Abu Bishr K'ab bin 'Amr ؓ
22. Khubaib bin Siyaaf ؓ
23. 'Abdullah bin Unais ؓ
24. Jundub bin Junaadah Abu Zarr Ghifaari ؓ
25. 'Utbah bin Mas'ood Huzali ؓ
26. 'Abdullah bin 'Umar ؓ
27. Salmaan Faarsi ؓ
28. Huzaifah bin Yamaan ؓ
29. Abud-Dardaa 'Uwaymir bin 'Aamir ؓ
30. 'Abdullah bin Zaid Juhani ؓ
31. Hajaaj bin 'Amr Aslami ؓ

32. Abu Hurayrah Dawsi ﷺ

33. Sawbaan ﷺ, emancipated slave of Rasulullah ﷺ

34. Mu'aaz bin Haaris ﷺ

35. Saaib bin Khallaad ﷺ

36. Saabit Wadi'ah ﷺ

Fasting of Ramadhaan

In the same year, (2nd year) during the latter ten days of Sha'baan, fasting during the month of Ramadhaan was made obligatory. In this regard, the following verse was revealed:

$$شَهْرُ رَمَضَانَ الَّذِيَ اُنْزِلَ فِيْهِ الْقُرْاٰنُ هُدًى لِّلنَّاسِ وَبَيِّنٰتٍ مِّنَ الْهُدٰى وَالْفُرْقَانِ ۚ فَمَنْ شَهِدَ مِنْكُمُ الشَّهْرَ فَلْيَصُمْهُ$$

"The month of Ramadhaan, in which the Qur-aan was revealed – a source of guidance for the people and clear proofs for guidance and criterion (to distinguish between good and evil). And whosoever witnesses the month, he should observe the fast." [Surah Baqarah verse 185]

Ummul-Mumineen Hadhrat 'Aa'ishah ﷺ and Hadhrat 'Abdullah bin 'Amr ﷺ narrates: "When Rasulullah ﷺ arrived in Madinah, he instructed us to observe the fast of 'Aashurah (10th of Muharram). When the fast of Ramadhaan was prescribed, he said: "As far as the fast of 'Aashurah is concerned, one is at liberty to observe it or to abstain from it."

Salamah bin Akw'a ﷺ relates: "On the day of 'Aashurah, Rasulullah ﷺ instructed a man to publicly announce: 'He who has not eaten as yet should fast whilst he who has already eaten should also abstain from food and drink like the fasting ones.'"

Sadaqatul-Fitr and Eid Salaah

Just two days before the termination of the month of Ramadhaan, the divine commandment obligating Sadaqatul-Fitr and Salaatul-Eid was revealed. In this regard the following verse was revealed:

$$\text{قَدْ اَفْلَحَ مَنْ تَزَكّٰى ۙ وَ ذَكَرَ اسْمَ رَبِّهٖ فَصَلّٰى ؕ}$$

"Successful is he who has spiritually cleansed himself and he has mentioned the name of his Lord then performed the Salaah (of Eid). [Surah A'laa]

'Umar bin 'Abdul-Aziz رحمه الله interpret the verse thus: "Successful is he who has disbursed his Sadaqatul-Fitr and performed the Salaatul-Eid."

Salaatul-Adhaa and Qurbaani

In the same year, Qurbaani and the Salaah of Eidul-Adhaa was made obligatory. The following verse was revealed in this regard:

$$\text{فَصَلِّ لِرَبِّكَ وَ انْحَرْ ؕ}$$

"So perform Salaah (of Eid) for your Lord and slaughter (perform Qurbaani)."
[Surah Al kausar verse 2]

Hasan Basri رحمه الله says: "This verse makes reference to Salaatul-Adhaa (Eidul-Adhaa Salaah) and to Qurbaani."

Durood Shareef

Abu Zarr رضي الله عنه narrates: "Conveying Salaah and Salaam (salutations) upon Rasulullah صلى الله عليه وسلم was also prescribed in this year, the second year of Hijrah."

According to some scholars, this commandment was enjoined on the night of Mi'raaj.

Zakaat on wealth

The 'Ulama have differed as to exactly when the annual Zakaat was enjoined. Most are of the opinion that it was prescribed after the Hijrah. Some say it was in the first year whilst others maintain that it was in the second year of Hijrah after the compulsion of the Saum of Ramadhaan. And Allah Ta'ala knows best.

Chapter 11

Ghazawaat and Saraaya (Military Expeditions)

This chapter deals with the unique sacrifices of the Sahaabah ﷺ in the path of Allah Ta'ala and the execution of the rebellious villains in the various military campaigns.

Only when the divine commandment of Jihaad was issued, did Rasulullah ﷺ launch an offensive attack against the disbelievers and he despatched an army to the various regions.

The battle in which Rasulullah ﷺ himself participated is referred to as a Ghazwah in the technical terminology of the scholars whilst the expedition in which he did not participate is referred to as Sariyyah.

Sariyyah of Hadhrat Hamzah ﷺ

The very first squad of thirty Muhaajireen was despatched by Rasulullah ﷺ seven months after the Hijrah either in the month of Ramadhaan or in the month of Rabi'ul-Awwal of the second year, towards Siful-Bahr under the leadership of Hadhrat Hamzah ﷺ. This contingent was sent out to check on a trade caravan of three hundred travellers returning from Syria under the commandership of Abu Jahl. This was the first Sariyyah after Hijrah. This contingent was made up exclusively of the Muhaajireen without any of the Ansaar. When Hadhrat Hamzah ﷺ landed at Siful-Bahr and both parties drew their battle lines poised for attack, Majdi bin 'Amr Juhani mediated between the two rivals. Abu Jahl returned to Makkah with his caravan and Hadhrat Hamzah ﷺ to Madinah.

Sariyyah of 'Ubaidah bin Haaris ﺭﺿﻲ ﺍﻟﻠﻪ ﻋﻨﻪ

Eight months after Hijrah, in the month of Shawwaal in the first year A.H., Rasulullah ﷺ despatched a contingent of sixty or eighty Muhaajireen under the commandership of 'Ubaidah bin Haaris ﺭﺿﻲ ﺍﻟﻠﻪ ﻋﻨﻪ towards Rabigh. This contingent consisted of no Ansaar.

When they reached Rabigh, they had a confrontation with two hundred Qurayshi mounted cavalry. However, no actual battle took place. Only S'ad bin Abi Waqqaas ﺭﺿﻲ ﺍﻟﻠﻪ ﻋﻨﻪ launched a single arrow against the enemy. This was recorded as the first arrow to be let loose in the history of Islam.

The Qurayshi cavalry – according to conflicting narrations - was under the commandership of Abu Sufyaan bin Harb, 'Ikramah bin Abi Jahal or Mikraz bin Hafs.

Miqdaad bin 'Amr and 'Utbah bin Ghazwaan, who had earlier embraced Islam but as they were in the malicious clutches of the Quraysh, were unable to migrate, also joined the Quraysh in this expedition with the intention of breaking away from the Quraysh and joining the Muslims the moment an opportunity presented itself. Accordingly, when the two hostile parties confronted one another, these two slipped away from the ranks of the kuffaar and joined the Muslims.

Sariyyah of S'ad bin Abi Waqqaas ﺭﺿﻲ ﺍﻟﻠﻪ ﻋﻨﻪ

In the first year of Hijrah, in the month of Zul-Q'adah, Rasulullah ﷺ despatched an infantry unit comprising of twenty Muhaajireen under the command of S'ad bin Abi Waqqaas ﺭﺿﻲ ﺍﻟﻠﻪ ﻋﻨﻪ to Kharrar.

This infantry unit would hide during the day and travel at night. When they landed at the valley of Kharrar, they learnt that the Qurayshi caravan (that they were pursuing) had already left. This group then returned to Madinah.

Expedition of Abwa

This was the very first military campaign in which Rasulullah ﷺ actively participated whilst the battle of Tabuk was his last.

In the beginning of the month of Safar, in the second year of Hijrah, taking sixty Muhaajireen with him without any Ansaar, Rasulullah ﷺ set out for Abwa to launch an offensive against a Qurayshi caravan and upon the Banu Damrah tribe. He appointed S'ad bin 'Ubaadah ﺭﺿﻲ ﺍﻟﻠﻪ ﻋﻨﻪ as his vicegerent in Madinah. The battle flag in this expedition was held by Hadhrat Hamzah ﺭﺿﻲ ﺍﻟﻠﻪ ﻋﻨﻪ.

When Rasulullah ﷺ landed at Abwa, the Qurayshi caravan had already departed. Concluding a truce with the chief of the Banu Damrah tribe,

Makhshi bin 'Amr, Rasulullah ﷺ returned to Madinah. Some of the conditions of this truce were that the Banu Damrah would neither wage war against the Muslims nor would they support the Muslims' enemy in any way. They would not betray the Muslims and in times of need, they are required to extend a helping hand to the Muslims.

This expedition is also referred to as the battle or expedition of Wuddaan. Abwa and Wuddaan are names of places barely six miles apart form one another.

In this expedition, within fifteen days, Rasulullah ﷺ returned to Madinah Munawwarah without actually engaging in any physical combat.

The Battle of Bawaat

Through divine revelation Rasulullah ﷺ was informed of a trade caravan of the Quraysh heading towards Makkah. Rasulullah ﷺ set out for Bawaat with at least two hundred Mujaahideen in the month of Rabi'ul-Awwal or Rabi'us-Saani 2 A.H. The purpose of this expedition was to launch an attack against this trade caravan. Rasulullah ﷺ appointed 'Usmaan bin Maz'oon ؓ, who was amongst the first group of people to embrace Islam and also amongst the emigrants to Abyssinia, as his governor in Madinah Munawwarah.

This trade caravan of the Quraysh comprised of two thousand five hundred camels and one hundred tribesmen of the Quraysh under the leadership of Umayyah bin Khalaf.

When Rasulullah ﷺ reached Bawaat, he discovered that the trade caravan had somehow slipped away undetected. So without engaging in any hostilities, Rasulullah ﷺ returned to Madinah Munawwarah.

Expedition of 'Ushayrah

During Jumaadal-Ula, 2 A.H., Rasulullah ﷺ, in the company of two hundred Muhaajireen, set out for 'Ushayrah to attack the Qurayshi caravan. 'Ushayrah is close to Yambu'u. He appointed Abu Salamah bin 'Abdul-Asad ؓ as his vicegerent in Madinah.

Thirty camels were available for this expedition and the Sahaabah ؓ took turns riding them.

A number of days before Rasulullah ﷺ turned up at 'Ushayrah, the trade caravan that he was pursuing had already slipped away. Rasulullah ﷺ then stayed on for the rest of the month of Jumaadal-Ula and a few days of Jumaadas-Saaniyah. He then concluded a peace treaty with Bani Mudlij tribe and without actually engaging in any form of combat, Rasulullah ﷺ returned to Madinah Munawwarah.

This is what the peace treaty looked like:

بِسْمِ اللهِ الرَّحْمٰنِ الرَّحِيْمِ ، هذا كتاب من محمد رسول الله لبنى ضمرة بانهم آمنون على اموالهم وانفسهم وان لهم النصر على من رماهم ان لا يحاربوا فى دين الله ما بل بحر صوفة وان النبى اذ دعاهم لنصره اجابوه عليهم بذلك ذمة الله وذمة رسوله ولهم النصر على من برواتقى

"Bismillahir-Rahmaanir-Raheem. This is an accord from Muhammad Rasulullah in favour of Banu Damrah tribe. Their lives and property are protected and safe. They will be assisted against whosoever attacks them provided Banu Damrah themselves do not interfere with the Deen of Allah. This treaty will remain in force until Lake Sufah dries up. (In other words, this treaty will remain perpetually intact.) When the Rasool ﷺ beckons them to assist, they will be required to offer their (unstinting) support. This is the pledge of Allah and His Rasool ﷺ over them. The pious and Allah-conscious from amongst them will be aided and supported."

First Battle of Badr - Also referred to as the battle of Safwaan or the minor battle of Badr

Barely ten days had passed after Rasulullah's ﷺ return to Madinah from the battle of 'Ushayrah when Kurz bin Jaabir Fahri launched a late night attack on the pastures of Madinah and made off with a number of camels and goats.

The instance Rasulullah ﷺ received news about this offensive, he immediately set out in pursuit of him towards Safwaan. This was a location close to Badr. However, Kurz had already sneaked off even before Rasulullah ﷺ landed at Safwaan. This is why he decided to return to Madinah.

Safwaan is a region close to Badr. Since Rasulullah ﷺ trailed him all the way to Badr, this expedition is referred to as the first battle of Badr and it is also referred to as the battle of Safwaan. Before setting out for this expedition, Rasulullah ﷺ appointed Zaid bin Haarisah ؓ as his deputy in Madinah Munawwarah.

Kurz bin Jaabir ؓ was one of the chieftains of the Quraysh tribe. He later embraced Islam. Rasulullah ﷺ appointed him the Ameer of the unit that was despatched to give chase to the 'Uraniyyeen. He was martyred in the conquest of Makkah.

Sariyyah of 'Abdullah bin Jahsh ﷺ

On his return from the expedition of Safwaan, Rasulullah ﷺ despatched 'Abdullah bin Jahsh ﷺ towards a place called Nakhlah in the month of Rajab 2 A.H. Eleven Muhaajireen, who are listed hereunder, were also despatched with him:

1. Abu Huzaifah bin 'Utbah ﷺ
2. 'Ukkaashah bin Mihsan ﷺ
3. 'Utbah bin Ghazwaan ﷺ
4. S'ad bin Abi Waqqaas ﷺ
5. 'Aamir bin Rabi'ah ﷺ
6. Waaqid bin 'Abdullah ﷺ
7. Khaalid bin Bukair ﷺ
8. Suhail bin Baydaa ﷺ
9. 'Aamir bin Iyaas ﷺ
10. Miqdaad bin 'Amr ﷺ
11. Safwaan bin Baydaa ﷺ

S'ad bin Abi Waqqaas ﷺ narrates: "Rasulullah ﷺ planned to send us out on a Sariyyah and revealed: 'I will appoint such a man as an Ameer (leader) over you who is the most tolerant over hunger and thirst.' He then appointed 'Abdullah bin Jahsh ﷺ as an Ameer over us."

Jundub Bajali ﷺ relates: "As Rasulullah ﷺ was sending off 'Abdullah bin Jahsh ﷺ, he wrote out a letter and handing it over to him instructed: 'Do not open this letter until you are two days into your journey. Once you are two days into your expedition, read this letter and act accordingly but do not compel any of your companions to do so.'

Accordingly, two days into the journey, 'Abdullah bin Jahsh ﷺ opened the letter of Rasulullah ﷺ and found the following instructions written therein: 'Continue on your journey until you land at a place called Nakhlah between Makkah and Taaif and wait there for the Quraysh. Also continue to provide us intelligence on their movements.'

On reading the contents of this letter, 'Abdullah bin Jahsh ﷺ declared: 'Sam'an wa Taa'atan – I submit and adhere to the instructions of Rasulullah ﷺ.' He then notified his companions about the contents of the letter, adding: 'I am not compelling any of you to adhere to these instructions. Whomsoever cherishes martyrdom may join me.' Every single one of them enthusiastically agreed to accompany him on this mission and they subsequently set out for Nakhlah.

En route, S'ad and 'Utbah's camel went astray (somewhere in the desert) and whilst searching for the lost camel, both of them got left behind and they lost their way. The remaining members of this unit proceeded to Nakhlah and stayed there (for a few days)."

The first spoils of war in Islam

A Qurayshi trade caravan was returning from Syria to Makkah on the last day of Rajab. Engagement in hostilities and combat was forbidden in this month. However, mistakenly thinking that it was already the first of Sh'abaan, the Sahaabah رضى الله عنهم launched an attack on this trade caravan.

Waaqid bin 'Abdullah رضى الله عنه shot an arrow at the leader of this caravan 'Amr bin Al-Hadrami that proved instantaneously fatal. The moment the travellers of the caravan learnt what happened to their leader, they anxiously fled in confusion and despair. The Muslims then seized their goods and property. Also, 'Usmaan bin 'Abdullah and Hakam bin Kaysaan were captured as prisoners of war.

Up until that time, no divine instruction existed in regards to the distribution of the war booty. Purely on the basis of his inference, 'Abdullah bin Jahsh رضى الله عنه divided the booty into five parts. Of that, he distributed four parts amongst the Mujaahideen and the remaining one fifth he kept aside for Rasulullah ﷺ. When they returned to Madinah and apprised Rasulullah ﷺ of these events, he remarked: "I did not instruct you to fight during the Haraam (sacred) month. Be that as it may, keep the prisoners and the booty safely aside until a divine commandment is revealed in this regard."

Upon this reprimand, 'Abdullah bin Jahsh رضى الله عنه and his companions were exceptionally grieved and dreadfully agitated, whilst on the other hand, the disbelievers and the Jews set out alleging: "Muhammad and his companions have made fighting in the sacred months permissible." On this occasion, the following verse was revealed:

$$\text{يَسْـَٔلُونَكَ عَنِ الشَّهْرِ الْحَرَامِ قِتَالٍ فِيهِ ۖ قُلْ قِتَالٌ فِيهِ كَبِيرٌ ۚ وَصَدٌّ عَنْ سَبِيلِ اللَّهِ وَكُفْرٌ بِهِ وَالْمَسْجِدِ الْحَرَامِ ۚ وَإِخْرَاجُ أَهْلِهِ مِنْهُ أَكْبَرُ عِنْدَ اللَّهِ ۚ وَالْفِتْنَةُ أَكْبَرُ مِنَ الْقَتْلِ ۗ وَلَا يَزَالُونَ يُقَاتِلُونَكُمْ حَتَّىٰ يَرُدُّوكُمْ عَنْ دِينِكُمْ إِنِ اسْتَطَاعُوا}$$

"They ask you (O Muhammad!) about fighting in the sacred month. Say (to them), undoubtedly fighting in this month is a great (sin) but forestalling people from the

path of Allah, disbelief in Allah, preventing people from Masjidul-Haraam and expelling the people of the Haram from the Haram, all these are far greater sins in the sight of Allah. The fitnah (trial and misery of polytheism and disbelief) is far worse than this fighting. These disbelievers will continue fighting you until they turn you away from your religion if they have the ability."
[Surah Baqarah verse 217]

In short, fighting in this sacred month either due to confusion or misunderstanding, is no great deal. Yes, the fitnah of disbelief and polytheism and calculatedly preventing the Muslims from entering Masjidul-Haraam is a colossal fitnah, beyond which there is no greater transgression.

Subsequent to the revelation of this verse, Rasulullah ﷺ accepted his one fifth of the booty whilst the remaining four fifths were distributed amongst the Mujaahideen.

On hearing the details of this verse, 'Abdullah bin Jahsh رضي الله عنه and his companions were cast into a sense of utter delight. Yearning for a reward, they felt rather buoyant to ask Rasulullah ﷺ if they can expect any reward for this. They enquired: "O Rasulullah ﷺ! Can we hope for any reward from this expedition?" Upon this, the following verse was revealed:

إِنَّ الَّذِينَ آمَنُوا وَالَّذِينَ هَاجَرُوا وَجَاهَدُوا فِي سَبِيلِ اللَّهِ أُولَٰئِكَ يَرْجُونَ رَحْمَتَ اللَّهِ ۚ وَاللَّهُ غَفُورٌ رَحِيمٌ

"Verily those who believed, and those who migrated and executed Jihaad in the path of Allah, such people (may) entertain hope of the mercy of Allah, (and why not when) Allah is all-forgiving, merciful." [Surah Baqarah verse 218]

This was the very first war-booty in Islam and 'Amr bin Hadrami was the first disbeliever to be slain at the hands of the Muslims.

The Quraysh remitted a sum of money for the release of the two captives, 'Usmaan bin 'Abdullah and Hakam bin Kaysaan, held by the Muslims. When presented with this demand, Rasulullah ﷺ said: "As long as my companions, S'ad and 'Utbah, do not return, I will not release your captives. I dread that you may kill them. If you kill my companions, I will also retaliate by executing your people."

A few days later, S'ad and 'Utbah returned safely. Rasulullah ﷺ then accepted the ransom and released 'Usmaan and Hakam. The instant he was released, 'Usmaan returned to Makkah where he died a disbeliever whilst Hakam bin Kaysaan embraced Islam and stayed over at Madinah. He was martyred in the expedition of Bir Ma'unah.

As an insight to the aforementioned incident, 'Abdullah bin Jahsh رضي الله عنه composed the following verses of poetry:

$$\text{تَعُدُّونَ قَتْلًا فِى الْحَرَامِ عَظِيمَةً} \quad \text{وَأَعْظَمُ مِنْهُ لَوْ يَرَى الرُّشْدَ رَاشِدُ}$$

$$\text{صدودُكم عمَّا يقول مُحَمَّدُ} \quad \text{وكُفْرٌ بهِ واللهُ راءٍ وشاهدُ}$$

"You view fighting within the sacred months as a great sin but worse than that, if only an intelligent person would grasp, is your hindrance from what Muhammad ﷺ is saying and your disbelief in him. Allah is an observer and witness.

$$\text{وَإِخراجكم من مسجدِ اللهِ أَهلَهُ} \quad \text{كَيْلَا يُرَى فِى الْبَيْتِ لِلَّهِ سَاجِدُ}$$

Your expulsion of the people of Allah Ta'ala from His Masjid so that not a single person prostrating may be seen, is even worse than fighting in the sacred months.

$$\text{فانا وان عيَّر تُمُونَا بقتلهِ} \quad \text{وَأَرْجَفَ بالاسلامِ باغٍ وحاسدُ}$$

$$\text{سَقَيْنَا مِن ابنِ الحضرمى رماحنَا} \quad \text{بنَخْلَةَ لمَّا أوقدَ الحربَ واقدُ}$$

$$\text{دماً وابنُ عبداللهِ عثمانُ بيننا} \quad \text{ينازعُهُ غُلٌّ مِن القَيدِ عانِدُ}$$

Over our action of fighting in this month, you may attempt to humiliate us as much as you please and the jealous may spread as many rumours as they like, it would not matter to us in the least. We quenched our spears with the blood of 'Amr bin Hadrami at Nakhlah when Waaqid bin 'Abdullah stoked the flames of war. 'Usmaan bin 'Abdullah was a captive amongst us with chains and shackles burdening him down to the ground."

Chapter 12

Battle of Badr – 2 A.H.

This battle was the most decisive battle in the annals of Islam because this battle was the forerunner to the honour and splendour of Islam and it marked the beginning of the fall and humiliation of disbelief.

Through the divine mercy of Allah Ta'ala, without any form of external and material resources, the Deen of Islam was fortified from the unseen whilst a powerful blow was dealt to the skull of disbelief and polytheism. Perhaps no other battle can be equated with the battle of Badr. This is why Allah Ta'ala refers to that day as the day of Furqaan – the differentiating factor between truth and falsehood. In fact it was also the month of Furqaan. It was the month of Ramadhaan in which, by revealing the Qur-aan, Allah Ta'ala exposed the distinction between truth and falsehood, between guidance and deviation.

Preamble to the Battle of Badr

During the early stages of the month of Ramadhaan, Rasulullah ﷺ learnt that Abu Sufyaan was returning to Makkah with a trade caravan fully laden with commercial merchandise and other goods.

Rasulullah ﷺ gathered the Sahaabah رضى الله عنهم and addressed them: "This is a fully laden trade caravan of the Quraysh. Proceed towards this caravan. It would not surprise me if Allah Ta'ala decides to award this caravan to you as 'the spoils of war'."

Since they entertained not a hint of engaging in hostilities, they had set out without any military preparations. Abu Sufyaan, who was also anxious of such an interception, continued soliciting every traveller on his journey for some news about Rasulullah ﷺ as he got closer to Hijaaz. On one of his enquiries, a traveller enlightened him about Rasulullah ﷺ instructing his companions to pursue his trade caravan. Without further ado, Abu Sufyaan paid Damdam Ghifaari a sum of money and sent him off to the Quraysh of Makkah with the message: "As quick as you can, protect your caravan and salvage your capital because Muhammad and his companions have already departed to intercept this caravan."

This is the very same caravan against which Rasulullah ﷺ set out with two hundred Muhaajireen in the expedition of 'Ushayrah. Now the caravan was returning from Syria. Since Rasulullah ﷺ merely intended to intercept the caravan, in haste very few people were able to accompany him on this journey. Since this journey was not undertaken with the intention of fighting and Jihaad, those who failed to participate were neither rebuked nor criticised.

Departure

On the twelfth of Ramadhaan, Rasulullah ﷺ set out from Madinah Munawwarah. Three hundred and thirteen Mujaahideen accompanied him on this lofty expedition. They were so ill equipped for this expedition that the entire group had just two horses and seventy camels. One horse belonged to Hadhrat Zubair bin 'Awwaam رضي الله عنه and the other to Hadhrat Miqdaad رضي الله عنه. Each camel was allocated to a group of two or three people. Hadhrat 'Abdullah bin Mas'ood رضي الله عنه narrates: "In the expedition of Badr, just one camel was allocated to a group of three people, which they would take turns in riding. Abu Lubaabah رضي الله عنه and Ali رضي الله عنه were partnered with Rasulullah ﷺ. When it was Rasulullah's ﷺ turn to walk, Abu Lubaabah رضي الله عنه and Ali رضي الله عنه would plead: "O Rasulullah ﷺ! You continue riding, we will walk on your behalf." To this Rasulullah ﷺ would reply: "You are neither stronger than I am nor am I more independent of the divine reward of walking than you are."

When they reached Bir Abi 'Inabah (approximately a mile out of Madinah), Rasulullah ﷺ assembled all of them for a visual inspection. Youngsters, who were eager to participate in this expedition, were sent back home from this point. When he reached a place called Rawhaa, he appointed Abu Lubaabah bin 'Abdul-Munzir as his deputy in Madinah and sent him on his way.

There were three battle flags in this army. One was held by Hadhrat Ali رضي الله عنه, the second one was held by Mus'ab bin 'Umair رضي الله عنه and the third by an Ansaari Sahaabi رضي الله عنه.

As they drew closer to a place called Safraa, Rasulullah ﷺ despatched Basbas bin 'Amr Juhani رضي الله عنه and 'Adi bin Abi Zaghbaa Juhani رضي الله عنه as forward scouts to spy on Abu Sufyaan's trade caravan.

In the meantime, Damdam Ghifaari landed in Makkah with Abu Sufyaan's message warning the people of Makkah that their caravan was under imminent threat of attack. "Hurry", he urged the people of Makkah, "run and save your property."

The moment this news reached the people of Makkah, the entire city was thrown into a state of riotous uproar because not a single man, woman and child remained in Makkah who did not inject capital into this trade caravan. Threatened by the loss of their capital, the citizens of Makkah were gripped by a state of frantic enthusiasm. A thousand fully equipped men were rapidly deployed and they subsequently set out to engage this threat. Abu Jahal was the commander of this force.

Fully laden with appliances of fun and amusement and accompanied by singing women, drums, tambourines and other musical instruments, the Quraysh puffed up with arrogance, emerged from Makkah with all their splendour and glory, as Allah Ta'ala depicts:

وَلَا تَكُوْنُوْا كَالَّذِيْنَ خَرَجُوْا مِنْ دِيَارِهِمْ بَطَرًا وَّ رِئَآءَ النَّاسِ

"Do not resemble those who emerged from their homes conceitedly and flaunting (their splendour) before people." [Surah Anfaal verse 47]

Almost all the chieftains of the Quraysh participated in this campaign. Only Abu Lahab, for some reason, was unable to join the expedition. He sent Abu Jahal's brother, 'Aas bin Hishaam in his place instead.

'Aas bin Hishaam was in debt to Abu Lahab to the sum of four thousand dirhams. Due to his poverty-stricken circumstances, he was unable to repay this debt. Under pressure of this debt, he agreed to go to battle on behalf of Abu Lahab.

Similarly, Umayyah bin Khalaf declined to participate in Badr but with the insistence and intimidation of Abu Jahal, he ultimately relented and joined them.

The background to his initial refusal to join the expedition is that S'ad bin Mu'aaz Ansaari رضي الله عنه was a close friend to Umayyah bin Khalaf during the pre-Islamic days of ignorance. When Umayyah would travel to Syria on business, he would stay over in Madinah at S'ad bin Mu'aaz's رضي الله عنه house and when S'ad bin Mu'aaz رضي الله عنه would come to Makkah, he would put up at Umayyah's house.

On one occasion, after the Hijrah of Rasulullah صلى الله عليه وسلم, S'ad bin Mu'aaz رضي الله عنه decided to perform Umrah. He came to Makkah and as was his previous routine, he stayed over with Umayyah. As he settled down, S'ad bin Mu'aaz رضي الله عنه requested Umayyah to take him to the Haram for Tawaaf at a time when the Haram was empty, in other words, when the Haram was relatively quiet and uncrowded. Umayyah took S'ad رضي الله عنه to the Haram towards the early afternoon. As he was busy in Tawaaf, Abu Jahal appeared before them demanding: "O Abu Safwaan! (This was the title of Umayyah) Who is this person with you?" "This is S'ad رضي الله عنه," replied Umayyah. Abu Jahal snapped: "I see that this person is performing his Tawaaf with such ease and comfort. Why do you provide assistance and refuge to such irreligious people?" Addressing S'ad bin Mu'aaz ﷺ, Abu Jahal warned: "O S'ad ﷺ! I swear by Allah, that if Abu Safwaan (Umayyah) was not with you, you would not have returned safely from here." To this, S'ad ﷺ stridently retorted: "If you prevent me from performing Tawaaf, by Allah, I will ensure that your access through Madinah to Syria is curtailed."

Umayyah said to S'ad ﷺ: "Do not raise your voice before Abul-Hakam (Abu Jahal). He is the chief of this valley."

Furiously, S'ad ﷺ shot back: "O Umayyah! Let it be. I heard Rasulullah ﷺ predicting that you would be slain at the hands of his companions." Umayyah anxiously asked: "Will I be killed in Makkah?" S'ad ﷺ replied: "I have no idea of the exact location you will be put to death."

On hearing this, Umayyah was thrown into overwhelming panic and foreboding. He scuttled to his wife Umme Safwaan and narrated the incident to her. According to another narration, Umayyah said: "By Allah! Muhammad never speaks a lie." He was so terrified of this forewarning that he almost wet his pants.

He was gripped with such fear that he resolved never to leave the boundaries of Makkah. So when Abu Jahal bade the people to participate in the expedition of Badr, he was awfully reluctant to go. He was terrified of losing his life in this battle.

However, Abu Jahal insisted that he join the campaign. When Abu Jahal noticed his reluctance, he pleaded with him: "You are one of the leaders. If you are unwilling to join in this campaign, the masses will also follow suit and they too would be reluctant to join us."

Anyway, Abu Jahal persisted and continued pressurising Umayyah. He ultimately persuaded him by pledging to him: "O Abu Safwaan! I will purchase a graceful and fast horse especially for you. (The moment you feel threatened you can mount it and return home.)" This finally swung his reluctance to strained agreement. He then went home and requested his wife to make his preparations for this journey. His wife pleaded with him: "O Abu Safwaan! Do you not recall the forewarning of your Yathrabi (Madani) brother?" He replied: "Yes, I intend to travel just a bit out of Makkah and return home."

Anyway, Umayyah set out with this intention and wherever the caravan halted, he would keep his camel close at hand but destiny did not allow him a chance to escape. He somehow landed in Badr and was slain at the hands of the Sahaabah ﷺ.

In short, Umayyah was convinced of his impending doom but under pressure from Abu Jahal, he grudgingly agreed to join them. Abu Jahal destroyed himself and destroyed others as well. "They made their people dwell in the abode of destruction; Hell, in which they will burn and what a dreadful abode it is."

Chapter 12

Mashwarah with the Sahaabah ﷺ and their Staunchly Devoted Discourses

As Rasulullah ﷺ left Rawhaa and reached Safraa, Basbas ﷺ and 'Adi ﷺ turned up with news that the Quraysh were on their way. Rasulullah ﷺ assembled all the Muhaajireen and Ansaar for a consultation. Rasulullah ﷺ alerted them about the departure of the well-equipped army of the Quraysh. The moment Abu Bakr ﷺ heard this, he swiftly got to his feet and gracefully expressed his devoted allegiance to Rasulullah ﷺ. He enthusiastically subscribed to the hints of Rasulullah ﷺ with all his heart and soul and pushed himself to comply with the wishes of Rasulullah ﷺ. Thereafter, Umar ﷺ stood up and he too brilliantly expressed his enthusiasm to sacrifice his life for this cause.

Selfless sermon of Miqdaad bin Aswad ﷺ

Thereafter, Miqdaad bin Aswad ﷺ got to his feet and submitted:

امض لما امرك الله (تعالى) فنحن معك والله لا نقول كما قالت بنو اسرائيل لموسى اذهب انت و ربك فقاتلا انا ههنا قاعدون ولكن اذهب انت و ربك فقاتلا انا معكما مقاتلون

"O Rasulullah ﷺ! Go ahead and accomplish what you have been divinely instructed to do. We are with you all the way. By Allah! We will never be like the Jews who told Musa عليه السلام: 'You and your Lord go to engage the enemy whilst we take a seat here.' (We on the contrary pledge to you): 'You and your lord go and engage the enemy and we will fight side by side with you.'"

The narrator of this Hadith, Hadhrat 'Abdullah bin Mas'ood ﷺ relates: "(Upon this pledge) I noticed Rasulullah's ﷺ blessed countenance glowing in delight."

Rasulullah ﷺ made a special dua for the welfare of Hadhrat Miqdaad ﷺ.

Abu Ayyub Ansaari ﷺ narrates: "We were in Madinah when Rasulullah ﷺ notified us about the trade caravan of Abu Sufyaan and company, saying: 'If you advance towards this caravan, it would not be surprising if Allah Ta'ala awards you with the spoils of war.' To this we commented: 'Very well,' and we set out. One or two days into our journey, Rasulullah ﷺ informed us about the departure of the Quraysh from Makkah. He also petitioned us to prepare ourselves for imminent battle. Some of us were a bit hesitant (because they did not leave home with the intention of engaging in hostilities). At that moment, Hadhrat Miqdaad رضي الله عنه got to his feet and conveyed his selfless commitment to Rasulullah ﷺ. If only all of us could express the same spirit of selflessness like Miqdaad رضي الله عنه."

On this occasion the Sahaabah رضي الله عنهم vowed:

لا نقول كما قالت بنو اسرائيل ولكن انطلقا انت وربك فقاتلا انا معكما مقاتلون

"We will not say what the Jews said but go, you and your Lord and we will fight alongside you."

In spite of these adequate assurances, Rasulullah ﷺ once again, for a third time, asked the Sahaabah رضي الله عنهم:

اشيروا عَلَىَّ ايها الناس

"O people! What is your opinion? Give me your Mashwarah."

The leader of the Ansaar S'ad bin Mu'aaz رضي الله عنه promptly understood what Rasulullah ﷺ, the most eloquent of the Arabs and non-Arabs, was trying to say. He instantly submitted: "O Rasulullah ﷺ! Perhaps your speech is directed to the Ansaar?" Rasulullah ﷺ replied in the affirmative.

The Valiant Speech of S'ad bin Mu'aaz رضي الله عنه

Upon this, Hadhrat S'ad bin Mu'aaz رضي الله عنه passionately declared:

يا رسول الله قد امنا بك وصدقناك وشهدنا ان ما جئت به هو الحق واعطيناك على ذالك عهودا ومواثيق على السمع والطاعة ولعلك يا رسول الله خرجت لامر فاحدث الله غيره فامض لما شئت وصل حبال من شئت واقطع حبال من شئت وسالم من شئت و عاد من شئت وخذ من اموالنا ما شئت واعطنا ما شئت وما أخذت منا كان

Chapter 12

احب الينا مما تركت وما امرت به من امرنا فامرنا تبع لامرك لئن سرت حتى تاتى برك الغماد لنسيرن معك فوالذى بعثك بالحق لو استعرضت بنا هذا البحر لخضناه وما تخلف منا رجل واحد وما نكره ان نلقى عدونا انا لصبر عندالحرب صدق عنداللقاء ولعل الله يريك منا ما تقربه عينك فسربنا على بركة الله

"O Rasulullah ﷺ! We affirmed our faith in you, we believe in you, we bear testimony to the fact that whatever you came with is the truth and upon this we had wholeheartedly pledged our absolute submission. O Rasulullah ﷺ! Perhaps you emerged from Madinah with a specific purpose but Allah has brought about something else. So proceed as you deem fit. You may maintain ties with whom you wish and you may sever ties with whomsoever you wish. You may enter into a peace agreement with whom you wish and you may engage in hostilities with whom you wish. We are with you all the way. You may take from our wealth whatever you please and you may bestow upon us whatever you please. Whatever you take from our wealth would be dearer to us than what you would leave behind, and whatever you charge us to do we will unquestionably abide by it. If you bid us to set off for Barkul-Ghamaad with you, we will eagerly accompany you. I swear by the Being Who has deputed you with the truth, if you direct us to leap into the ocean we would eagerly hurl ourselves into it and not one of us would be left behind. We do not detest confronting the enemy. Yes, during the heat of battle we are tolerant and we are committed to meet the enemy head-on. We hope Allah Ta'ala will exhibit something of ours that would bring about the coolness of your eyes. So, in the name of Allah, take us along with you."

Listening to these selfless words of sacrifice of these Sahaabah ؓ brought great joy to Rasulullah ﷺ. He proclaimed: "Come on. Let us depart in the name of Allah and many glad tidings for you. Allah Ta'ala had promised me that He would grant me victory over one of the two parties; either the party of Abu Jahal or the party of Abu Sufyaan."

He revealed further: "I was also shown the location of where the disbelievers will fall in defeat. I was shown that this is where so and so will fall slain and this is where so and so will perish."

Allah Ta'ala says:

وَإِذْ يَعِدُكُمُ اللّٰهُ إِحْدَى الطَّآئِفَتَيْنِ أَنَّهَا لَكُمْ وَتَوَدُّوْنَ أَنَّ غَيْرَ ذَاتِ الشَّوْكَةِ تَكُوْنُ لَكُمْ وَيُرِيْدُ اللّٰهُ أَنْ يُّحِقَّ الْحَقَّ بِكَلِمٰتِهٖ وَيَقْطَعَ دَابِرَ الْكٰفِرِيْنَ ۞

"And remember when Allah promised you one of the two parties (of the enemies i.e. either the caravan or the enemy) that it would be yours and you wished that the unarmed party (the caravan) be yours but Allah willed to justify the truth by His words and to cut off the roots of the disbelievers." [Surah Anfaal verse 7]

Dream of Aatikah bint 'Abdul Muttalib

Whilst Rasulullah ﷺ was busy informing the Sahaabah رضي الله عنه about the revelation regarding the locations of the disbelievers dropping in defeat, there in Makkah, even before Damdam Ghifaari could reach Makkah (forewarning the disbelievers about the impending doom), Rasulullah's ﷺ aunty (father's sister) Aatikah bint 'Abdul-Muttalib saw a dream.

She dreamt that a person mounted on a camel appeared, made his camel sit in the valley of Bathaa and yelled:

انفروا يا آل غدر لمصارعكم فى ثلاث

"O people of deception! Head off towards the locations in which you are doomed to fall in defeat within three days."

A number of people then gathered around this man. Holding onto his camel, this man then proceeded to the Masjidul-Haraam where he delivered the same proclamation. He then ascended the mountain of Abu Qubais from where he hurled a gigantic boulder. As the boulder landed at the foot of the mountain it shattered into smithereens and not a single house in Makkah was spared but a smidgen of this rock filtered through it.

Aatikah narrated this dream to her brother 'Abbaas adding: "Brother! By Allah, I have seen such a dream that I dread a horrendous calamity is to befall your people. Listen, I beg of you not to narrate this dream to anyone else."

When 'Abbaas left home, he narrated this dream to his friend Waleed bin 'Utbah and stressed upon him not to relate this dream to anyone else but Waleed related this dream word for word to his father 'Utbah. In this manner, news of this dream spread to the whole city of Makkah.

A few days later, when 'Abbaas entered the Masjidul-Haraam, he caught sight of Abu Jahal sitting in the company of a group of people. The moment Abu Jahal noticed 'Abbaas entering the Masjid, he sneered: "Abul-Fadl ('Abbaas)! All along your men were claiming prophethood. Now even your womenfolk are laying claim to it!"

"What do you mean?" asked 'Abbaas. Upon this Abu Jahal referred to the dream of Aatikah. Whilst these people were engaged in this conversation, Damdam Ghifaari reached Makkah with Abu Sufyaan's message of the impending catastrophe. This messenger entered Makkah with torn clothing, with the nose of his camel severed and bellowing at the top of his voice: "O people of Quraysh! Salvage your caravan and with due haste, assist the caravan of Abu Sufyaan."

The moment the Quraysh heard this message they rallied their equipment and men and headed out of Makkah. They reached Badr where they witnessed a true interpretation of this dream.

Dream of Juhaim bin Salat

In all their ceremonial glory, the Quraysh headed out of Makkah serenading to the accompaniment of drums and musical instruments. When they reached a place called Juhfah, Juhaim bin Salat saw a dream. He saw a person riding a horse and this person also had a camel with him. This rider drew closer and pronounced: "'Utbah bin Rab'iah is slain, Shaybah bin Rabi'ah is slain, Abul-Hakam (Abu Jahal) is slain, Umayyah bin Khalaf is slain, so and so and so and so are also slain." This man then struck a spear into the camel and set it loose within the army. Not a single tent in the army remained but blotches of blood spattered onto it.

When Abu Jahal heard of this dream, he was fuming with rage. He sarcastically exclaimed: "This is the second prophet born in the Banu Muttalib. Tomorrow when we confront the enemy then only will it be known which of us has been slain."

When Basbas رضي الله عنه and 'Adi رضي الله عنه, the two Sahaabah رضي الله عنهم whom Rasulullah صلى الله عليه وسلم sent to spy on Abu Sufyaan's caravan, reached Badr, they seated their camels at the foot of a hillock close to a water spring. In the interim, they spied two women in the vicinity chatting with one another. When one of them demanded payment of a debt from the other, the debtor replied: "Tomorrow or the day after that, when the trade caravan returns from Syria, I will toil and labour and pay you whatever is due to you."

Mujaddaa bin 'Amr Juhani, who was also near this water spring, was busy listening to this intriguing exchange between these two women. When the indebted woman pledged to repay her creditor what was due to her after doing some manual labour for the trade caravan that was expected to arrive the next or the following day, Mujadda commented: "It appears that she is speaking the truth." Saying this, he promptly withdrew himself from the area and sneaked away.

The instant Basbas رضي الله عنه and 'Adi رضي الله عنه gathered this intelligence, they mounted their camels and rapidly made tracks back to Rasulullah صلى الله عليه وسلم. They appeared before him and apprised him of this incident.

After the departure of Basbas رضي الله عنه and 'Adi رضي الله عنه, Abu Sufyaan, who was attempting to get some intelligence about the whereabouts and movements of

Rasulullah ﷺ also happened to come to this spring. He asked Mujjada bin 'Amr: "Did you notice anyone coming or going in this area?" He replied: "Not really. I only saw two men mounted on camels passing this way. They halted at the foot of that hillock, rested and watered their camels and after filling their water skins they moved off. Abu Sufyaan immediately went to the spot where he noticed some animal droppings. He picked up one of the droppings and split it open. Upon closer scrutiny, he noticed a seed embedded within it and he exclaimed: "By Allah! This is a Yasrib (Madinah) date-seed."

At once, he returned from this area and slightly altering the direction of the caravan, he proceeded towards the coastal road via which he safely reached Makkah undetected by the Muslims.

As he reached Makkah, he despatched a message to the Quraysh advising them: "You primarily set out with the express purpose of safeguarding your property, wealth and the lives of the travellers. Allah has saved your property and lives. So why do you not return to Makkah?"

To this Abu Jahal responded: "Until and unless we do not proceed to Badr to eat, drink and celebrate for three days, we will never return to Makkah."

Akhnas bin Shariq, the chieftain of the Banu Zuhrah tribe counselled his people: "O people of Banu Zuhrah! You originally set out to protect your merchandise. So Allah Ta'ala has safeguarded your goods from ruin. Now there is no need to fight. There is no need for us to hurl ourselves into pointless jeopardy as this man (Abu Jahal) is beckoning us to do. So you might as well return home."

On the counsel of their leader Akhnas bin Shariq, the entire Banu Zuhrah tribe returned home. Not one of them participated in the battle of Badr. A number of others also cautioned their people against fighting the enemy. They argued that since the caravan had returned safe and sound, there was absolutely no need to go into battle. However, Abu Jahal was adamant. He failed to listen to reason and he determinedly set out for Badr.

By the time Rasulullah ﷺ and the Sahaabah رضي الله عنهم landed at Badr, the disbelievers had already seized control of the water springs. They also promptly took control of the better areas of Badr. On the contrary, the Muslims neither had any water nor were any suitable areas available to them. Their area was made up of rough terrain where it was a dreadful challenge to walk. Their feet would sink into the ground.

Allah Ta'ala sent down rain. The soft yielding sand turned to hard ground and the Muslims dug up a few small ponds for Ghusal and Wudhu purposes. In Surah Anfaal, Allah Ta'ala describes this boon in the following manner:

وَيُنَزِّلُ عَلَيْكُمْ مِنَ السَّمَاءِ مَاءً لِيُطَهِّرَكُمْ بِهِ وَيُذْهِبَ عَنْكُمْ رِجْزَ الشَّيْطٰنِ وَلِيَرْبِطَ عَلٰى قُلُوْبِكُمْ وَيُثَبِّتَ بِهِ الْاَقْدَامَ ۞

"And He caused water to descend upon you from the sky so that He may purify you with it and remove from you the filth (evil insinuations) of shaytaan and to strengthen your hearts with it and make your feet firm thereby."
[Surah Anfaal verse 11]

Although this water rained down to meet the needs of the Muslims, out of His sheer mercy, Rasulullah ﷺ, who was a personification of compassion, keenly allowed his enemies also to drink from the water.

The same evening, Rasulullah ﷺ despatched Hadhrat Ali رضي الله عنه, Zubair bin 'Awwaam رضي الله عنه, S'ad bin Abi Waqqaas رضي الله عنه and a few other Sahaabah رضي الله عنهم to gather some intelligence about the Quraysh.

Coincidentally they chanced upon two slaves whom they apprehended and returned to base camp with. Rasulullah ﷺ was engaged in Salaah whilst they started interrogating them. The slaves whined: "We are merely water bearers of the Quraysh. We simply came out to fetch some water for them."

However, their statement failed to convince the Muslims and they started beating them in the hope that, under pressure of further aggression, they will reveal the whereabouts or conditions of Abu Sufyaan. They changed their statements forthwith and whimpered: "Yes, yes! We are members of Abu Sufyaan's caravan." The moment they said this, they left them alone.

When Rasulullah ﷺ completed his Salaah, he remarked: "When they were speaking the truth, you beat them and when they were telling lies, you left them alone. By Allah! These slaves belong to the Quraysh (and not to Abu Sufyaan's people)."

Rasulullah ﷺ then went about questioning the slaves personally. He asked: "Where are the Quraysh?" "By Allah", they replied: "they are at the foot of Muqanqas mountain." "What is the total number of people?" asked Rasulullah ﷺ.

They replied: "They are quite a few in number."

"How many in number are they?" he asked. The slaves replied that they had no idea what their numbers were. Rasulullah ﷺ asked: "Okay, tell me, how many camels do they slaughter daily?" They replied: "One day nine and one day ten." To this Rasulullah ﷺ pointed out: "They are between nine hundred to a thousand."

After this, Rasulullah ﷺ asked them which of the Quraysh chieftains were in attendance. They replied: "Utbah bin Rabi'ah, Shaybah bin Rabi'ah, Abul-Bakhtari bin Hishaam, Hakeem bin Hizaam, Nawfal bin Khuwaylid, Haaris bin 'Aamir, T'amiyyah bin 'Adi, Nadr bin Haaris, Zam'ah bin Aswad, Abu Jahal bin Hishaam, Umayyah bin Khalaf, Nubayh bin Hajaaj, Munabbih bin Hajaaj, Suhail bin 'Amr and 'Amr bin 'Abdud."

When Rasulullah ﷺ heard of this 'impressive lineup' of the chieftains, he turned to his companions and commented: "Today Makkah has consigned all her treasured souls to you."

In short, this was how Rasulullah ﷺ went about gaining information from these slaves.

Preparation for War

The next morning Rasulullah ﷺ made preparation for the actual battle. As per the advice of S'ad bin Mu'aaz رضي الله عنه, a simple thatched hut was erected at the peak of the hillock for Rasulullah ﷺ.

S'ad bin Mu'aaz رضي الله عنه submitted: "O Rasulullah ﷺ! May we erect a thatched structure for you, in which you will be able to sit? We will have your mounts ready for you whilst we go and engage the enemy. If Allah Ta'ala honours us and bestows us with victory over the enemy, this is precisely what we aspire for. On the contrary, Allah forbid, something else happens, you will still be able to mount your conveyances and take off to join our other compatriots who have stayed behind (in Madinah). O Rasulullah ﷺ! We are not dearer to you than they are. If those people had only known that you are going to engage the enemy in battle, they would never have remained behind. Perhaps Allah Ta'ala would shield you through them, and they would have engaged in Jihaad with absolute devotion and goodwill." Rasulullah ﷺ commended S'ad bin Mu'aaz رضي الله عنه on his devoted enthusiasm and made dua for him. Thereafter a simple thatched hut was erected for Rasulullah ﷺ in which he took shelter. This structure was erected right on the summit of a hillock that afforded a bird's-eye-view of the entire battle ground.

Hadhrat Anas رضي الله عنه narrates from Hadhrat 'Umar رضي الله عنه that on the eve of the impending battle of Badr, Rasulullah ﷺ took us with him to the battlefield so that we may see for ourselves the locations of those who would be slain in battle. As we reached the battleground, he continued pointing out to us with his blessed hand: "This is the spot so and so would collapse and this is the spot so and so would fall, in the morning Insha Allah." Gesturing with his hand, he proceeded to reveal the exact location of where each person would be slain.

Hadhrat Anas رضي الله عنه says: "I swear by the Being Who has sent Rasulullah ﷺ with the truth, not one of them had fallen beyond a hair's breadth than the location that was pointed out by Rasulullah ﷺ."

Thereafter, Rasulullah ﷺ, in the company of his most dear companion of the cave, the Siddeeq of the Muhaajireen, Hadhrat Abu Bakr رضي الله عنه, entered his hut and offered two Rakaat of Salaah. Meanwhile, the Siddeeq of the Ansaar, S'ad bin Mu'aaz رضي الله عنه stood guard at the door, wielding a sword.

Hadhrat Ali ﷺ narrates: "On the night preceding the battle of Badr, there was not a single one of us who did not fall off to sleep except Rasulullah ﷺ. He passed the entire night in Salaah and earnest dua right until the morning."

At the onset of Fajr, Rasulullah ﷺ announced: "As-Salaah! O people! The time for Salaah has arrived." The instant the people heard this announcement, they rapidly gathered for Salaah. Rasulullah ﷺ led them in Salaah whilst standing at the base of a tree. After Salaah, Rasulullah ﷺ spurred the Sahaabah ﷺ to engage the enemy with fearless valour and daring zeal.

Thereafter Rasulullah ﷺ straightened the files of the Mujaahideen for battle whilst the ranks of the disbelievers had already been imposingly arrayed for conflict. It was a Friday the seventeenth of the holy month of Ramadhaan. On one side of the battlefield was the assembly of Haq whilst the other end of the battlefield was blustering with the forces of Baatil (falsehood). Both parties advanced towards the arena of Furqaan.

When Rasulullah ﷺ laid eyes on the well-equipped Qurayshi army pressing ahead with all their swaggering glory, he submitted before Allah Ta'ala:

اللهم هذه قريش قد اقبلت بخيلائها وفخرها تحادك وتكذب رسولك اللهم فنصرك الذى وعدتنى اللهم احنهم الغداة

"O Allah! Here are the Quraysh marching ahead in all their arrogance and pomp. They have come to challenge You and falsify Your Messenger. O Allah! I beg of You Your victory and assistance over them as promised by You. O Allah! Annihilate them (these forces of Baatil)."

Thereafter, Rasulullah ﷺ arranged the ranks of the Muslims in proper fighting formation. He held a small spear in his hand, which he used to straighten the ranks of the fighters. As he was forming the rows, he caught sight of one Sahaabi, Sawaad bin Ghaziyyah ﷺ sticking out of the line a bit. In a measure of compassion, Rasulullah ﷺ nudged Sawaad on his stomach with this spear. Amiably poking him in the stomach, Rasulullah ﷺ said: "O Sawaad! Get in line."

To this Sawaad submitted:

يا رسول الله او جعتنى وقد بعثك الله بالحق والعدل فاقدنى

"O Rasulullah ﷺ! You hurt me whereas Allah Ta'ala sent you with truth and justice. So allow me to take revenge against you."

Rasulullah ﷺ gladly raised his upper garment and exposing his stomach, said to him: "Go on, take your revenge."

Sawaad رضي الله عنه embraced his blessed stomach and pressed his lips to it. Addressing Rasulullah ﷺ, he then said: "O Rasulullah ﷺ! Perhaps this is our final meeting." This certainly brought unbridled delight to Rasulullah ﷺ and he made dua for him.

Once Rasulullah ﷺ formed the lines of battle similar to that of the ranks of the Malaaikah (angels), he went into his hut. Only Abu Bakr رضي الله عنه went along with him into his hut whilst S'ad bin Mu'aaz رضي الله عنه stood sentry at the door wielding a sword in his hand.

As the Quraysh settled down, before engaging in actual combat, they decided to send 'Umair bin Wahab Jumahi to ascertain the numbers of the Muslims. After casting a fleeting glimpse at the Muslims, mounted on his horse, 'Umair returned and reported: "The Muslims merely number about three hundred but give me a chance and I will check if they have any backup forces lying in ambush for us."

Once again he mounted his horse and rode far and wide checking for backup forces. He returned to the Quraysh and said: "I've checked but I could not find any backup force. However, O People of the Quraysh! I see these Madani camels carrying red death (murder) on their backs. These people have no sanctuary or support besides their own swords. By Allah! I foresee that as long as these people do not kill their opponents, they themselves will not be killed. So even if from our own ranks, an equal number of people are killed, what joy would the future hold (with over three hundred of our people dead)? Deliberate over what I am saying and let us decide on how to proceed further."

To this, Hakeem bin Hizaam commented: "What you say is absolutely correct." Hakeem then went to 'Utbah and said: "Abul-Waleed! You are one of the leaders of the Quraysh. Would you not be pleased to hear your name being remembered with goodness?"

'Utbah asked: "What is the problem?" Hakeem said: "Take your people and return (to Makkah) and take the responsibility of the blood money of 'Amr bin Hadrami onto your own shoulders."

To this 'Utbah promised: "I take full responsibility for the blood money of 'Amr bin Hadrami but discuss the dilemma with Abu Jahal as well."

Saying this, he got to his feet and delivered the following speech:

Battleground speech of 'Utbah

"O people of Quraysh! I swear by Allah, you will get absolutely no benefit from fighting with Muhammad (ﷺ) and his companions. These are all your blood relatives. If you are adamant on engaging them in battle, then you will counter members of your immediate family; your fathers, brothers, maternal and paternal cousins. I exhort you to leave Muhammad and the Arabs to their own devices. If the Arabs finish him off, then you have achieved your goal and if Allah confers victory and dominance to him, then too this is an opportunity of honour for you because, after all, he is a member of your own clan. His supremacy is your supremacy. Do not shun my advice and do not pronounce me a fool."

Hakeem bin Hizaam relates: "I then proceeded to Abu Jahal, who, at that moment, was busy donning his armour. I said: 'Utbah sent me with this message.' I then conveyed 'Utbah's message to him.

The moment he heard the message, he exploded with rage and huffed: '(This is not the only reason 'Utbah is shirking from war). 'Utbah is also reluctant to engage the Muslims because his son Abu Huzaifah is with the Muslims. No harm should come to him. I swear by Allah! We will never retreat until Allah makes a decisive decision between Muhammad and us.'

Abu Jahal then summoned 'Amr bin Hadrami's brother, Aamir bin Hadrami, and said to him: 'Your ally, 'Utbah, wishes to take everyone back with him without engaging the enemy whereas the blood of your brother is right before your eyes!' On hearing this, Aamir wailed in sorrow: 'O 'Amr! O 'Amr! How dreadful!' His distressing wails of sorrow stirred their flagging spirits and once again, they were incited to take on the Muslims."

Inception of the war

Abu Jahal's reproach at his people had such a profound impression that even 'Utbah ardently donned his armour and geared himself for battle.

In fact, from the disbelievers, 'Utbah, his brother Shaybah bin Rabi'ah and his son Waleed were the first combatants to swagger out of the ranks of the disbelievers and emerging onto the battlefield they mockingly growled for their challengers to approach the field.

From the files of the Muslims, three contenders stepped forward; 'Awf bin Haaris, Mu'awwiz bin Haaris and 'Abdullah bin Rawaahah.

"Who are you?" bellowed 'Utbah.

They countered:

رهط من الانصار

"We are a group of the Ansaar."

To this 'Utbah replied: "We have no need to engage you. We wish to fight with our own people." Saying this, he shrieked:

يا محمد اَخرِج اِلينا اكفاء نا مِنْ قَوْمِنَا

"O Muhammad! Why don't you send us evenly-matched contenders from our own tribe!"

Rasulullah ﷺ then bade the Ansaar to withdraw to their ranks and petitioned Hadhrat Ali ؓ, Hadhrat Hamzah ؓ and Hadhrat 'Ubaidah bin

Haaris ﷺ. He called each of them by name and exhorted them to stride out and fight.

As per Rasulullah's ﷺ directive, the three of them emerged from their ranks. Since their faces were concealed by protective masks, 'Utbah asked them to identify themselves. "I am 'Ubaidah," said Hadhrat 'Ubaidah bin Haaris ﷺ. Hadhrat Hamzah ﷺ rejoined: "I am Hamzah." Hadhrat Ali ﷺ replied: "I am 'Ali."

'Utbah reacted by exclaiming:

نعم اكفاءٌ كِرامٌ

"Yes! Now these are equally-matched noble combatants."

Rasulullah ﷺ said:

قوموا يا بنى هاشم بحقكم الذى بعث الله به نبيكم اذ جاؤا بباطلهم ليطفؤا نور الله

"Rise O children of Haashim, with the truth with which Allah Ta'ala has sent your Prophet. Stand against this falsehood with which they have appeared in order to extinguish the light of Allah."

Slaying of 'Utbah, Shaybah and Waleed

Now the contestants confronted one another. 'Ubaidah ﷺ clashed with 'Utbah. Hamzah ﷺ challenged Shaybah and Ali ﷺ was pitted against Waleed.

Hadhrat Ali ﷺ and Hadhrat Hamzah ﷺ laid their foes to rest with a single stroke of the sword. Meanwhile 'Ubaidah ﷺ who was clanging swords with 'Utbah was seriously injured. Both combatants suffered injuries but continued fighting. Eventually, 'Utbah dealt such a severe blow with his sword that 'Ubaidah ﷺ sustained a serious injury to his leg. In the interim, Hadhrat Hamzah ﷺ and Hadhrat Ali ﷺ, dismissing their rivals, swiftly went to the aid of 'Ubaidah ﷺ. They then promptly despatched 'Utbah to his death. Thereafter, they carried 'Ubaidah ﷺ and brought him to Rasulullah ﷺ. He was bleeding profusely from his shin area. 'Ubaidah ﷺ expectantly asked: "O Rasulullah ﷺ! Am I a martyr?" When Rasulullah ﷺ replied in the affirmative, 'Ubaidah ﷺ said: "If only Abu Taalib was alive he would have utterly been convinced that indisputably, we are more deserving of his poem than he ever was:

وَنُسْلِمُ حَتَّى نُصْرَعَ حَوْلَه ۞ وَنَذْهَلَ عَنْ اَبْنَائِنَا وَالْحَلَائِلِ

"We will surrender Muhammad to the enemy only when all of us around him are slain and when we are absolutely oblivious of even our own wives and children."

'Ubaidah رضي الله عنه then recited the following stanzas:

فَاِنْ يَقْطَعُوْا رِجْلِي فَاِنِّيْ مُسْلِمٌ ۞ اَرْجٰى بِهٖ عَيْشًا مِنَ اللهِ عَالِيَا

"If they (disbelievers) severed my leg, this is not a problem. In compensation of this injury, I anticipate a far more superior life from Allah Ta'ala. (In other words, although the severance of my leg foretells the end to my transitory life in this world, I hope that in compensation I would get a far better life of eternal bliss.)

وَاَلْبَسَنِيَ الرَّحْمٰنُ مِنْ فَضْلِ مَنِّهٖ ۞ لِبَاسًا مِنَ الْاِسْلَامِ غَطَّى الْمَسَاوِيَا

And why not? Why should not I anticipate this? After all, Allah Ta'ala, out of His infinite compassion has adorned me with the religion of Islam that has concealed all my defects."

Note: Initially, 'Utbah and Shaybah were awfully reluctant to go into battle. Firstly, because of Aatikah's ominous dream and this was closely followed by the foreboding dream of Juham bin Salat, these people were agonizingly terrified. Secondly, on their departure from Makkah, 'Addaas رضي الله عنه (the slave of 'Utbah and Shaybah who had renounced Christianity and embraced Islam at the hands of Rasulullah صلى الله عليه وسلم on his return from Taaif) grasped his master's feet and pleaded:

بابى وامى انتما والله انه رسول الله وما تساقان الا الى مصار عكما

"May my parents be sacrificed for both of you! Please! He is the Rasool of Allah صلى الله عليه وسلم. You are not being driven except to your deaths."

Saying this, he burst out crying.

When 'Aas, the son of Shaybah noticed 'Addaas weeping, he asked what made him so upset. 'Addaas replied: "I am weeping for both my masters who are about to go into battle with the Prophet of Allah." 'Aas enquired: "Really? Is he really the Prophet of Allah?" Trembling in fear, 'Addaas replied:

اى والله انه رسول الله الى الناس كافة

"Off course! He is unquestionably the Prophet of Allah to all peoples of the world."

These solemn pleadings of 'Addaas رضي الله عنه and his startling revelation of their impending doom had a profound effect on both 'Utbah and Shaybah. This is why both 'Utbah and Shaybah didn't want to take part in this battle. Only because of Abu Jahal's taunts did they march along. Time and time again, Abu Jahal would scornfully taunt 'Utbah and Shaybah with insulting comments of cowardice and unmanliness. So, in order to put an end to such vulgar criticism and to inhibit allegations of cowardice and effeminacy thrown at them, these two strode out into battle.

Abu Usaid رضي الله عنه narrates: "On the day of the battle of Badr, Rasulullah صلى الله عليه وسلم said: 'Reserve your arrows for the moment the disbelieving mob rushes upon you. Release your arrows only when they are close to you.'"

Rasulullah's صلى الله عليه وسلم Dua for Victory

Following the deaths of 'Utbah and Shaybah, the rage of the battle kicked off in earnest. Rasulullah صلى الله عليه وسلم emerged from his hut and strategically laid out the ranks of the Sahaabah رضي الله عنهم and then, in the company of Abu Bakr رضي الله عنه, he returned to his hut. Wielding a sword, Hadhrat S'ad bin Mu'aaz رضي الله عنه stood sentry at the door.

When Rasulullah صلى الله عليه وسلم laid eyes on his companions' negligible numbers and their minimal equipment confronted by the vast and well-equipped legion of the disbelievers, he got to his feet and performed two Rakaats of Salaah. He then absorbed himself in dua. He implored Allah Ta'ala thus:

اللهم انى انشدك عهدك ووعدك اللهم ان شئت لم تعبد

"O Allah! I plead with you to honour Your word (of victory over the enemy). O Allah! If You wish, You may not be worshipped (after this day)."

Rasulullah صلى الله عليه وسلم was overcome with an extraordinary condition of humility and submissiveness. Sometimes he would humbly bow down in Sajdah before Allah Ta'ala and at times he would piteously spread his hands out in supplication and beg Allah Ta'ala for His assistance and victory. He was so immersed in this state of humility that his upper garment repeatedly fell off his shoulders.

Hadhrat Ali رضي الله عنه narrates: "On the day of Badr, I engaged the enemy for a little while and then I hurried to check on Rasulullah صلى الله عليه وسلم. I found him prostrating before Allah Ta'ala piteously begging Allah Ta'ala repeatedly with the words 'Yaa Hayyu Yaa Qayyum!' I returned and busied myself with fighting. I went to check on him a second and then a third time but still found him prostrate. However, when I went to check on him the fourth time, by then Allah Ta'ala had favoured him with victory."

Chapter 12

Ibn 'Abbaas ﷜ says: "Hadhrat 'Umar ﷜ related to me that on the day of Badr, when Rasulullah ﷺ noticed the thousand-strong force of the disbelievers of Makkah on one hand, confronted by his three hundred odd ill-equipped companions on the other hand, he went into his hut, faced the Qiblah and spread his hands out in supplication:

اَللّٰهُمَّ اَنْجِزْ لِى مَا وعدتنى اَللّٰهُمَّ ان تهلك هذه العصابة من اهل الاسلام لا تعبد فى الارض

"O Allah! Fulfil Your promise You had made to me. O Allah! If this small group of Muslims is eliminated, You will never again be worshipped on the earth."

In other words, Rasulullah ﷺ was the seal of all the Prophets and his Ummah is the final Ummah. So if, Allah forbid, Rasulullah ﷺ and his Ummah is wholly eliminated, not a single person will remain on this earth to worship Allah Ta'ala. Furthermore, we learn from this that his dua of victory and divine assistance was not only to safeguard the lives of the Muslims but also to consistently maintain the Ibaadat of Allah Ta'ala on the earth. It should not be such that the earth is entirely devoid of the Ibaadat of Allah Ta'ala.

For an incredibly long period of time, Rasulullah ﷺ continued making this dua about Allah Ta'ala not being worshipped if this group of Muslims was destroyed. He was so engrossed with this dua that his sheet fell of his blessed shoulders. Abu Bakr ﷜ picked the sheet up and replaced it on his blessed shoulders. Coming up from his rear, Abu Bakr ﷜ clasped Rasulullah's ﷺ hand and implored:

حَسْبُكَ فَقَدْ اَلْحَحْتَ عَلٰى رَبِّكَ

"O Rasulullah ﷺ! This is enough for you. You have persistently implored your Lord."

Rasulullah's ﷺ gaze was concentrated upon the grandeur, greatness and absolute independence of Allah Ta'ala, as Allah Ta'ala declares:

اِنَّ اللهَ لَغَنِيٌّ عَنِ الْعٰلَمِيْنَ

"Verily, Allah is independent of the worlds."

Allah Ta'ala says in another verse:

وَاللهُ هُوَ الْغَنِيُّ الْحَمِيْدُ ۝ اِنْ يَّشَاْ يُذْهِبْكُمْ وَيَأْتِ بِخَلْقٍ جَدِيْدٍ ۝

"And Allah is independent (free of all needs) and worthy of all praise. If He willed, He could eliminate you and bring forth a new creation."

This is why the tears of humility gushed forth from his blessed eyes. However, judging from the fretful persistence and intense anguish of Rasulullah ﷺ, Abu Bakr ؓ was firmly convinced that Rasulullah's ﷺ dua would be accepted, as Allah Ta'ala says:

$$\text{اَمَّنْ يُّجِيْبُ الْمُضْطَرَّ اِذَا دَعَاهُ وَ يَكْشِفُ السُّوْٓءَ وَ يَجْعَلُكُمْ خُلَفَآءَ الْاَرْضِ}$$

"Is He not better (than your false gods) who responds to the distressed one when he calls unto Him and He removes evil and He makes you the inheritors of the earth (generation after generation)?" [Surah Naml verse 62]

In short, Abu Bakr ؓ was overwhelmed by a condition of hope whilst Rasulullah ﷺ was overcome by a condition of fear.

Upon this, Allah Ta'ala revealed the following verse:

$$\text{اِذْ تَسْتَغِيْثُوْنَ رَبَّكُمْ فَاسْتَجَابَ لَكُمْ اَنِّيْ مُمِدُّكُمْ بِاَلْفٍ مِّنَ الْمَلٰٓئِكَةِ مُرْدِفِيْنَ ۞ وَ مَا جَعَلَهُ اللّٰهُ اِلَّا بُشْرٰى وَ لِتَطْمَئِنَّ بِهٖ قُلُوْبُكُمْ ۚ وَ مَا النَّصْرُ اِلَّا مِنْ عِنْدِ اللّٰهِ ۗ اِنَّ اللّٰهَ عَزِيْزٌ حَكِيْمٌ ۞}$$

"Remember the time when you sought the aid of your Lord and He responded to you (saying): 'I will assist you with a thousand angels one behind the other in succession. Allah made this (divine assistance) only as glad tidings and so that your hearts are comforted therewith. There is no assistance (of victory) except from Allah. Verily Allah is the All-mighty, the All-wise." [Surah Anfaal verses 9-10]

At the revelation of this verse, Rasulullah ﷺ emerged from his shelter with the following verse on his tongue:

$$\text{سَيُهْزَمُ الْجَمْعُ وَ يُوَلُّوْنَ الدُّبُرَ ۞}$$

"Their multitudes will be routed and they will turn their backs and flee."
[Surah Qamar verse 45]

Whilst Rasulullah ﷺ was beseeching Allah Ta'ala in dua, he dozed off. When he awakened, he addressed Abu Bakr ؓ saying:

ابشر يا ابابكر اتاك نصر الله هذا جبريل اخذ بعنان فرسه يقوده على ثنا ياه الغبار

"O Abu Bakr! Glad tidings to you. Allah's aid has come. Here is Jibraa'eel عَلَيْهِ السَّلَام clutching the reins of his horse and driving it along. It has dust on its teeth."

Descent of the angels to assist the Muslims

Allah Ta'ala sent down a thousand angels, then three thousand and finally five thousand angels to lend a hand to the Muslims.

Note: Since Iblees (shaytaan) and his cohorts were all set and primed to assist the disbelievers in this battle, Allah Ta'ala sent down a group of angels under the command of Jibraa'eel عَلَيْهِ السَّلَام, Mikaa'eel عَلَيْهِ السَّلَام and Israafeel عَلَيْهِ السَّلَام to assist the Muslims. Since shaytaan appeared in the disguise of Suraaqah bin Maalik and his cohorts appeared in the form of the menfolk of the Banu Mudlij, the angels also appeared in the form of normal men as mentioned.

The angels who descended from the skies came to assist. They were such creations who ostensibly were human, but in reality were divine angels.

Abu Usaid Sa'idi رَضِيَ اللهُ عَنْهُ (who was also a Badri Sahaabi) relates: "On the day of the battle of Badr, the angels descended from the skies wearing yellow turbans. The tail ends of their turbans were suspended between their shoulders. Zubair رَضِيَ اللهُ عَنْهُ was himself wearing a yellow turban on the day of this battle."

According to some narrations, the colour of the turbans of the angels was black and according to other narrations, they had white turbans on their heads.

Rab'i bin Anas رَضِيَ اللهُ عَنْهُ narrates: "On the day of Badr, those slain by humans could easily be distinguished from those killed by the angels. Those slain by the angels had dark fire-scars on their necks and fingertips."

A Muslim would run behind a scuttling disbeliever when suddenly he heard the crack of a whip accompanied by a voice: 'Hayzum! Go on! Charge!' The moment he located the disbeliever, he found him lying flat on the ground. His face, especially his nose, was bruised green with the lash of a whip.

When this Ansaari reported this incident to Rasulullah صَلَّى اللهُ عَلَيْهِ وَسَلَّمَ, he commented: "You have spoken the truth. This is divine aid from the third heaven."

On the day of Badr, Rasulullah صَلَّى اللهُ عَلَيْهِ وَسَلَّمَ remarked:

هذا جبرئيل آخذٌ براس فرسه عليه اداة الحرب

"Here, this is Jibraa'eel عَلَيْهِ السَّلَام clutching the reins of his horse, adorned with the weapons of war."

Suhail bin Hunaif رَضِيَ اللهُ عَنْهُ narrates: "On the day of Badr, we observed that when any of us would merely gesture towards the Mushrik and even before our swords made contact with him, his head would be chopped off and fall to the ground."

Sahl bin S'ad رَضِيَ اللهُ عَنْهُ narrates: "Describing the battle of Badr, Abu Usaid رَضِيَ اللهُ عَنْهُ addressed me saying: 'O nephew! If you and I were on the battlefield of Badr, I would have pointed out to you the valley from which the angels appeared to offer us divine assistance. There is not an iota of doubt in this.'"

The attendance of the angels mounted on horses is also established from authentic Ahaadith. According to some narrations, they were mounted on piebald (spotted) horses.

Rasulullah ﷺ emerged from his shelter and after motivating them to engage the enemy, declared: "I swear by the Being in whose absolute control lies Muhammad's life, today whosoever puts up a bold front and engages the enemy with forbearance and sincerity and he is subsequently martyred, Allah Ta'ala will certainly admit him into Jannah."

Whilst Rasulullah ﷺ was making this declaration, 'Umair bin Hamaam رضي الله عنه had a few dates in his hand, which he was busy eating. The moment he heard these enthralling words, he bounded up in delight and exclaimed:

بخ بخ فما بيني وبين ان ادخل الجنة الا ان يقتلني هؤلاء

"Bakh! Bakh! (Hooray! Bravo!) The only intervention between me and my admittance into Jannah is my martyrdom at these people's hands."

Saying this, he flung those dates aside and wielding a sword he hurled himself into the thick of battle and fought valiantly until he was martyred. May Allah Ta'ala shower His boundless mercy upon him. Aameen.

Also on this occasion, 'Awf bin Haaris رضي الله عنه asked Rasulullah ﷺ:

يا رسول الله ما يضحك الرب من عبده

"O Rasulullah! Which action of the servant makes the Lord laugh (pleases Him)?"

Rasulullah ﷺ replied: "To confront the enemy without armour and to colour his hands with the blood of the enemy." The moment 'Awf رضي الله عنه heard these words, he threw off his armour and clutching his sword, he went to fight the enemy until he was martyred. May Allah Ta'ala shower him with His infinite mercy. Aameen.

Abu Jahal's dua and his Incitement of War

Subsequent to the slaying of 'Utbah, Shaybah and Waleed, Abu Jahal encouraged his troops to fight valiantly and in a frantic bid to spur them on, he addressed them saying:

"O people! Do not be flustered over the deaths of 'Utbah, Shaybah and Waleed. They fell victim to the sword because of their imprudent haste. I swear by Laat and 'Uzza! We will never return until we truss them up in ropes."

He then beseeched Allah Ta'ala with the following dua:

"O Allah! He who is guilty amongst us of severing family ties and of perpetrating strange actions, O Allah, destroy him, and amongst us, he who is most dear and beloved to You, O Allah, grant him victory."

Upon this Allah Ta'ala revealed the following Qur-aanic verse:

$$ اِنْ تَسْتَفْتِحُوْا فَقَدْ جَآءَكُمُ الْفَتْحُ ۚ وَاِنْ تَنْتَهُوْا فَهُوَ خَيْرٌ لَّكُمْ ۚ وَاِنْ تَعُوْدُوْا نَعُدْ ۚ وَلَنْ تُغْنِىَ عَنْكُمْ فِئَتُكُمْ شَيْئًا وَّلَوْ كَثُرَتْ ۙ وَاَنَّ اللّٰهَ مَعَ الْمُؤْمِنِيْنَ ۞ $$

"(O disbelievers!) You were seeking victory. So, here victory has come unto you. And if you desist (from evil) it will be better for you. And if you return (to fight) so shall We return and your forces will be of no avail to you however numerous they may be. Verily Allah is with the believers." [Surah Anfaal verse 19]

As Abu Jahal made his dua, Rasulullah ﷺ also raised his hands in supplication before Allah Ta'ala and implored: "O Allah! If (Allah forbid) this group of people is annihilated, you will never be worshipped again on the face of this earth."

Here on this side Abu Jahal was engaged in dua whilst on the other end Rasulullah ﷺ was also engaged in imploring Allah Ta'ala. After this, both parties started fighting in earnest. Rasulullah ﷺ emerged from his shelter and exhorting the Sahaabah رضي الله عنهم to fight, he promised: "Whoever is slain in the path of Allah, Allah will admit him into Jannah."

On the direction of Jibraa'eel عليه السلام, Rasulullah ﷺ then picked up a fistful of sand and hurled it towards the faces of the Mushrikeen. He then bade the Muslims to launch an attack against them. Not a single Mushrik remained but a particle of this sand penetrated his eyes, nose and mouth.

Only Allah Ta'ala knows what impact this sand had on the disbelievers. The instant Rasulullah ﷺ hurled this fistful of sand at them they took flight. In this regard, Allah Ta'ala revealed:

$$ وَمَا رَمَيْتَ اِذْ رَمَيْتَ وَلٰكِنَّ اللّٰهَ رَمٰى $$

"And you did not throw (the sand) when you threw it but Allah threw it."
[Surah Anfaal verse 17]

In other words, although Rasulullah ﷺ himself tossed a fistful of sand particles that got into the eyes and noses of the thousand-strong army, this was no achievement on his part as such but this was a divine deed, a manifestation of the omnipotence of Allah Ta'ala.

As the fighting intensified, Rasulullah ﷺ uttered thrice: "Shaa-hatil-Wujooh (may the faces (of the enemy) become disfigured)." He then picked up a handful of pebbles and hurled them towards the Quraysh and charged the Sahaabah رضي الله عنهم to attack.

Barely a moment passed when the metaphorical dust of humiliation settled on the faces of the enemies of Allah Ta'ala, then they started rubbing their eyes whilst the Muslims opportunely unleashed a quick attack against the confused enemy. Allah Ta'ala cast a peculiar attribute within this handful of sand that left each and every one of them humbled and bewildered. In downright perplexity, they had no idea where to turn.

Rasulullah ﷺ barely hurled the fistful of sand when the entire army of disbelievers was left bewildered and thrown into turmoil. 'Eminent' heroes and 'noble warriors' were either getting captured or slain at the hands of the Muslims. During this time Rasulullah ﷺ was in his shelter with Hadhrat S'ad bin Mu'aaz رضي الله عنه clutching a sword and standing sentry at the door, protecting Rasulullah ﷺ.

Whilst the Muslims were engaged in apprehending the disbelievers, Rasulullah ﷺ noticed signs of disgust on the face of Hadhrat S'ad bin Mu'aaz رضي الله عنه as though this revulsion was a tangible thing placed on his face. Rasulullah ﷺ asked: "O S'ad! Perhaps you resent the Quraysh being captured?" S'ad رضي الله عنه submitted:

اجل والله يا رسول الله كانت اول وقعة اوقعها الله تعالى باهل الشرك

فكان الاثخان فى القتل احب الى من استبقاء الرجال

"Yes, O Rasulullah ﷺ! By Allah! This is the first encounter in which Allah Ta'ala has inflicted (such loss) against the disbelievers. Personally, I feel it is far superior to put these disbelievers to the swords than allowing them to live."

Where will those whose hearts are brimming with the Tauheed (oneness) of Allah Ta'ala, ever be able to accommodate those who ascribe partners unto Allah Ta'ala?

Furthermore, divine disposition also demands that the sin of Shirk (polytheism) be unpardonable, as Allah Ta'ala declares:

اِنَّ اللهَ لَا يَغْفِرُ اَنْ يُشْرَكَ بِهٖ وَ يَغْفِرُ مَا دُوْنَ ذٰلِكَ لِمَنْ يَّشَآءُ ۚ وَمَنْ يُّشْرِكْ بِاللهِ فَقَدِ افْتَرٰٓى اِثْمًا عَظِيْمًا ۝

"Verily Allah does not forgive polytheism and He forgives everything else apart from that for whomsoever He wishes. And he who ascribes partners unto Allah, he is guilty of a grave sin indeed." [Surah Nisaa verse 48]

Ibn 'Abbaas رضي الله عنه narrates: "Rasulullah ﷺ had notified us beforehand, 'Some people like the Banu Haashim and other tribes simply turned up on the battlefield under pressure from the Quraysh. They have not come on their own free will. So they should not be harmed in any way. We have no need to kill them or to fight with them.' Rasulullah ﷺ also advised: 'If any of you come across Abul-Bakhtari bin Hishaam and 'Abbaas bin 'Abdul Muttalib during the course of this campaign, do not kill any of them.'"

This is why the Sahaabah ﷺ, instead of killing the enemy, were predominantly predisposed to capturing them alive.

So when Mujazzar bin Ziyaan Ansaari ﷺ caught sight of Abul-Bakhtari on the battlefield, he said: "Rasulullah ﷺ forbade us to put you to the sword."

Abul-Bakhtari was accompanied by one of his Makkan friends by the name of Junaadah bin Malihah. Abul-Bakhtari, when enlightened about this prohibition, appealed: "My friend too should be spared." Mujazzar ﷺ retorted: "Never! By Allah! We will never spare the life of your friend. Rasulullah's ﷺ amnesty extends to you only. To this Abul-Bakhtari replied: "By Allah! It is ludicrous for me to abandon my friend in this hour of need. Tomorrow the womenfolk of Makkah would taunt me for deserting my friend merely to save my own life!"

Reciting the following stanza, he audaciously stepped out to fight:

لَنْ يُسْلِمَ اِبن حُرّةٍ زَمِيْلَهُ   حتى يموتَ او يرى سَبِيْلَه

"A noble man will never forsake his companion in need until he dies or he detects a way out."

No sooner had Abul-Bakhtari stepped foot into the combat area than Mujazzar ﷺ finished him off with his sword. He then proceeded to Rasulullah ﷺ and submitted:

والذى بعثك بالحق لقد جهدت ان يستاسر فاتيك به فابى الا ان يقاتلنى فقاتلته فقتلته

"O Rasulullah ﷺ! I swear by the Being Who has sent you with the truth! I certainly tried to capture Abul-Bakhtari alive and bring him before you but he refused and elected to fight. So I killed him."

Slaying of Umayyah bin Khalaf and his Son

Umayyah bin Khalaf was one of the most bitter enemies of Rasulullah ﷺ. He had already heard the warning of his assassination from the mouth of S'ad bin Mu'aaz ﷺ in Makkah long before there was even a notion of the battle of Badr. This is why he was dreadfully reluctant to take part in this campaign.

Abu Jahal incited the people to participate in this campaign saying: "Save your trade caravan." (The caravan of Abu Sufyaan.) However, Umayyah tried his utmost to steer clear of this campaign. Abu Jahal continued persuading him saying: "Abu Safwaan! You are the chief of this valley. If you attempt to avoid this campaign, the masses are bound to follow suit and they too would try to find a way out." Abu Jahal persisted until Umayyah was forced to grudgingly agree. However, he added: "I will purchase a very fine, daring and fast camel. I will join you, but the moment I get a chance I will return." He then went home to his wife Umme Safwaan and asked her to make his travel arrangements. She asked: "Do you not recall the menacing words of your Yasribi brother (where he forewarned you about being assassinated at the hands of the companions of Muhammad)?" Umayyah replied: "Yes, I remember very well but I do not really intend to actively participate in this campaign. I will just tag along with them for a few leagues and I will return soon."

However, he somehow accompanied them through every stage of the journey until he reached the battlefield of Badr.

Umayyah was the same villain who subjected Hadhrat Bilal رضي الله عنه to an array of brutal punishments. He would make Bilal رضي الله عنه lie on the scorching boulders of Makkah. When Ummayah appeared on the battlefield of Badr and Hadhrat Bilal's رضي الله عنه gaze fell on him, he yelled out a shriek of challenge to the Ansaar.

'Abdur-Rahmaan bin 'Awf رضي الله عنه, who was a friend of Umayyah bin Khalaf in times of pre-Islamic ignorance, did not want Ummayah killed. He preferred that he rather be captured as a prisoner. (Perhaps, he reflected, Allah Ta'ala would guide Umayyah somewhere along the line and save him from eternal hellfire.)

Hadhrat 'Abdur-Rahmaan bin 'Awf رضي الله عنه, who was clutching a few coats of armour that he had seized from the kuffaar, flung them aside and clasped the hands of Umayyah and his son. When Bilal رضي الله عنه got a glimpse of this, he shouted: "Seize the head of the kaafir Umayyah! I am not safe if Umayyah is saved."

The instant the Ansaar heard this rallying cry they darted over. Hadhrat 'Abdur-Rahmaan bin 'Awf رضي الله عنه thrust Umayyah's son in front of him and the Ansaar summarily finished him off. They then raced to Umayyah who was being shielded by Hadhrat 'Abdur-Rahmaan bin 'Awf رضي الله عنه. When he saw them tearing towards Umayyah, he quickly lied down over him as a human shield but the Ansaar breached this human shield and driving their swords from his legs, they killed him. In the clash, Hadhrat 'Abdur-Rahmaan bin 'Awf رضي الله عنه sustained a serious injury to his foot, the scar of which remained for a long time.

Hadhrat 'Abdur-Rahmaan bin 'Awf رضي الله عنه used to remark: "May Allah Ta'ala shower His mercy on Bilal رضي الله عنه. On this occasion I lost my coats of armour (that I had seized from the enemy) and my captive too."

Slaying of Abu Jahal – Pharaoh of this Ummah

Hadhrat 'Abdur-Rahmaan bin 'Awf ﷺ narrates: "I was standing poised to attack on the battle lines of Badr when suddenly I caught sight of two youngsters to my left and right. I was a bit concerned (perhaps the enemy, spotting me between two youngsters, would try to rush me). I was reflecting over this when one of them came up to me and murmured: 'Uncle! Would you point out Abu Jahal to me?'

"What would you want to do with Abu Jahal?" I asked in amazement.

This young man replied: "I have made a vow unto Allah Ta'ala that when I lay eyes on Abu Jahal I will surely kill him or I will be killed in the process. I heard that he is guilty of verbally abusing Rasulullah ﷺ. By Allah in Whose absolute control lies my life! The moment I lay eyes on Abu Jahal, I will ensure that my shadow does not break away from his shadow until one of us is killed.'

The moment I heard his zealous words, my expectation of being flanked by two men instead of two youngsters, rapidly dwindled away.

When I pointed out Abu Jahal to this young man, he dashed over to him and like a swooping raptor, he pounced on him and finished him off."

These two youngsters were Mu'aaz and Mu'awwiz, the sons of 'Afraa.

Mu'aaz bin 'Amr bin Jamooh ﷺ relates: "I was maintaining a vigilant lookout for Abu Jahal. The moment I was presented with an opportunity, I pounced on him with my sword and dealt him such a powerful blow that left his leg severed."

The narrator continues: "In defence of his father, Abu Jahal's son 'Ikramah (who embraced Islam at the conquest of Makkah), struck Mu'aaz bin 'Amr bin Jamooh with such force that left his arm hanging by its tendons. However, this handicap did not deter Mu'aaz and he continued fighting valiantly right until the evening. When fighting with this dangling hand became excruciatingly painful, he placed the hand beneath his foot and ripped off the hand completely. He lived until the Caliphate of Hadhrat 'Usmaan Ghani ﷺ."

After finishing off with Abu Jahal, Mu'awwiz bin 'Afraa, however, continued fighting until he drank from the nectar of martyrdom. We belong to Allah and to Him shall we return.

Searching for Abu Jahal's Body after the Victory

Although Abu Jahal suffered extensive injuries, he still had some life left in him. Hadhrat Anas ﷺ relates: "On the day of Badr, Rasulullah ﷺ bade the Sahaabah ﷺ: 'Is there anyone who would provide some information about Abu Jahal?' 'Abdullah bin Mas'ood ﷺ went in search of him amongst the corpses. When he located him, he realised that he still had a bit of life in him."

Ibn Mas'ood ﷺ planted his foot on Abu Jahal's neck and remarked:

اخزاك الله يا عدو الله

"O enemy of Allah! Allah has humiliated and disgraced you."

Saying this, he severed his head from his body. He then carried the head and deposited it before Rasulullah ﷺ saying:

هذا راس عدو الله ابى جهل

"This is the head of Abu Jahal, the enemy of Allah."

Rasulullah ﷺ asked, "Really? By Allah, besides Whom there is no other deity! Is this really the head of Abu Jahal?"

He replied: "By Allah besides whom there is no other deity! This is really the head of Abu Jahal."

Rasulullah ﷺ expressed his profound gratitude before Allah Ta'ala thrice and remarked:

الحمد لله الذى اعز الاسلام واهله

"All praise is due to Allah Who has honoured Islam and its people."

Rasulullah ﷺ even prostrated in gratitude before Allah Ta'ala.

According to another narration, Rasulullah ﷺ performed two Rakaat Salaah as an expression of his gratitude before Allah Ta'ala.

'Abdullah bin Mas'ood ؓ relates: "I climbed onto Abu Jahal's chest and sat astride him. Abu Jahal opened his eyes and said: "O sheep herder! You have parked yourself astride a very honourable place."

I replied:

الحمد لله الذى مكننى من ذلك

"All praise is due to Allah Who has awarded me the ability to do so."

He then asked me: "Who triumphed and who lost?" I replied: "Allah and His Rasool ﷺ have prevailed."

"What is your intention now?" he asked. I replied: "I wish to behead you." He said: "Very well. Here, this is my sword. It is incredibly sharp. It would assist you in fulfilling your objective rather swiftly. But listen, be sure to sever my head closer to my shoulders as this would instil more awe within my onlookers. Furthermore, when you return to Muhammad, give him this message that I cherish more animosity and disgust for him today than I did yesterday."

Ibn Mas'ood ؓ further relates: "I then lopped his head off and brought it to Rasulullah ﷺ saying: "O Rasulullah! This is the head of the enemy of

Allah, Abu Jahal." I then relayed his message to Rasulullah ﷺ. Rasulullah ﷺ glorified Allah and pronounced: "This man was the Pharaoh to me and my Ummah. His evil by far overshadowed the evil of the Pharaoh of Musa عليه السلام. At least the Pharaoh of Musa عليه السلام attempted to recite the Kalimah at his death but the Pharaoh of this Ummah snapped out words of arrogance and disbelief even at the instant of his death." Rasulullah ﷺ then awarded Abu Jahal's sword to 'Abdullah bin Mas'ood رضي الله عنه.

In other words, just as Rasulullah ﷺ surpassed all the Ambiyaa عليهم السلام in virtue and perfection, similarly, his Ummah's Pharaoh eclipsed all the other Pharaohs in disbelief and immorality. Even at the time of death his eyes failed to open and the throes of death did not nudge him in the least from his disbelief and arrogance. In fact, his kufr (disbelief) and conceit mushroomed even further at the time of his death. (May Allah Ta'ala protect us from this. Aameen.)

Note: Ibn 'Abbaas رضي الله عنه narrates that the night in which Rasulullah ﷺ decided to visit the Jinn, he addressed them saying:

ليقم معي من لم يكن في قلبه مثقال ذرة من كبر فقام ابن مسعود فحمله رسول الله صلى الله عليه وسلم مع نفسه

"The person who does not harbour an iota of pride should stand and accompany me." Ibn Mas'ood رضي الله عنه stood up. Rasulullah ﷺ took him along with him.

Perhaps it would not be farfetched to believe that 'Abdullah bin Mas'ood رضي الله عنه was given the honour to kill Abu Jahal for 'Abdullah رضي الله عنه was a unique servant of Allah Ta'ala, whose heart was absolutely devoid of even an iota of pride. On the contrary, Abu Jahal was en epitome of pride and arrogance who did not even have a trace of humility within his heart.

This is why Allah Ta'ala decreed the killing of Abu Jahal at the hands of a fortunate man who harboured not a grain of pride. May Allah Ta'ala be pleased with 'Abdullah bin Mas'ood رضي الله عنه and may He please him too and may Allah Ta'ala recompense him abundantly on behalf of Islam with a reward that pleases him. Aameen.

Note: Abu Jahal's actual title was Abul-Hakam (father of wisdom). Rasulullah ﷺ changed his title to Abu Jahal. In other words, Rasulullah ﷺ awarded him a title of 'father of downright ignorance'. As long as this father remained alive, every variety of ignorance was brought forth.

Whilst waging an intense battle against the enemy, 'Ukkaashah bin Mihsan's رضي الله عنه sword broke. Rasulullah ﷺ replaced it with a stick. The instant he got hold of the stick, it miraculously transformed itself into a sharp sword. He continued fighting valiantly with this sword until Allah Ta'ala awarded them victory. The name of this sword was 'Awn (assistance) and it accompanied him in every subsequent battle.

In the battle of Badr, 'Ubaidah bin Sa'eed bin 'Aas - one of the disbelievers – was entirely covered in body armour. Nothing but his eyes could be seen. Undeterred by this, Hadhrat Zubair ﷺ aimed for this tiny chink in his armour. He hurled a spear with such force and accuracy that it went all the way through his head. He died instantaneously. Hadhrat Zubair ﷺ relates: "Only when I placed my foot on his head and pulled with all my strength was the spear released but its edges were slightly bent."

As a memento, Rasulullah ﷺ asked Hadhrat Zubair ﷺ to give the spear to him. After Rasulullah's ﷺ demise, the spear went to Hadhrat Abu Bakr ﷺ then to Hadhrat 'Umar ﷺ then to Hadhrat 'Usmaan ﷺ then to Hadhrat Ali ﷺ and finally it came into the possession of Hadhrat 'Abdullah bin Zubair ﷺ (the son of the original owner).

In the battle of Badr, Hadhrat Zubair ﷺ sustained a number of wounds to his body. One of the wounds to his shoulder was so deep that after it healed, his young son 'Urwah ﷺ in his childhood days would insert his fingers within the folds of the healed skin and amuse himself.

Once 'Abdul-Malik bin Marwaan asked 'Urwah bin Zubair ﷺ: "Do you recognise the sword of Zubair (your father)?" He replied: "Yes, surely." "How would you recognise the sword?" asked 'Abdul-Malik. 'Urwah replied: "In the battle of Badr, the sword developed serrations on its edges (due to the intensity of the battle)."

To this 'Abdul-Malik replied: "Yes, you are right." To endorse this further, he recited the following poem:

$$بهن فلول من قراع الكتائب$$

"They (the swords) sport serrations notched into them after confronting titanic battalions."

The Prisoners of Badr

Alhamdulillah, after a sweeping defeat of the disbelievers, the battle came to an end. Seventy of the Quraysh were killed and seventy were taken as prisoners. Rasulullah ﷺ directed that the bodies of the disbelievers be dumped into the well of Badr. However, the corpse of Umayyah bin Khalaf was so badly bloated that when they tried to remove his armour, his body started disintegrating. This is why his remains were put into the ground there and then.

As 'Utbah bin Rabi'ah's corpse was being cast into the well, Rasulullah ﷺ noticed 'Utbah's son Abu Huzaifah ﷺ, visibly distraught. Rasulullah

ﷺ asked him: "O Abu Huzaifah! Looking at your father in this pitiful condition perhaps causes your heart grave concern?" He replied: "O Rasulullah ﷺ! By Allah, I am not distressed by this but the only thing that really concerns me is that my father was an intelligent, graceful and forbearing man. That is why I had expected his intellect and perception to guide him towards Islam. However, when I realised that he died with kufr (disbelief), I was awfully disappointed."

Rasulullah ﷺ then made dua in favour of Abu Huzaifah رضي الله عنه.

Disposing of the Corpses in the well of Badr

Anas bin Maalik رضي الله عنه narrates from Abu Talhah رضي الله عنه that on the day of Badr, Rasulullah ﷺ instructed that twenty-four bodies of the slain Qurayshi chieftains be disposed off in a dreadfully dirty, filthy and polluted well. All those who were cast into the well were the leaders of the kuffaar. The remaining corpses were dumped elsewhere.

Whenever Rasulullah ﷺ would secure victory over any nation, it was his noble habit to spend an additional three days at that location. As was his noble tradition, on the third day, Rasulullah ﷺ ordered his mount to be saddled and he set out. The Sahaabah رضي الله عنهم followed guessing that Rasulullah ﷺ was perhaps going for some important work. They followed until Rasulullah ﷺ reached the edge of that well and he called out each occupant by name. He called out: "O 'Utbah! O Shaybah! O Umayyah! O Abu Jahal! You did not find submission to Allah and His Rasool very appealing. Verily, whatever our Lord has promised us; we found it to be true. Did you also find the promise of your Lord to be true?"

Rasulullah ﷺ then addressed them saying:

"O dwellers of the pit! You were a dreadfully wretched tribe for your Prophet. You falsified me whilst others believed in me. You banished me whilst others offered sanctuary to me. You waged war against me whilst others assisted me. You declared a trustworthy person as dishonest. You pronounced a truthful person to be a liar. May Allah severely punish you."

Hadhrat 'Umar رضي الله عنه exclaimed: "O Rasulullah ﷺ! You are speaking to lifeless corpses?" Rasulullah ﷺ replied: "Yes! I swear by Him in whose absolute control lays my soul! You are not more perceptive of my words than they are. The only difference is that they are unable to respond."

In his description of this event, Hadhrat Hassaan bin Thaabit رضي الله عنه mentions in one of his lengthy poems:

يناديهم رسول الله لما   قذفنا هم كباكب فى القليب

"When we pitched them into the well, Rasulullah ﷺ addressed them thus:

الم تجدوا كلامى كان حقا   وامر الله ياخذ بالقلوب

'Did you not find my words to be true? And Allah is the absolute controller of the hearts.'

فما نطقوا ولو نطقوا لقالوا   صدقت وكنت ذا رأى مصيب

But none of them uttered a word. Were they able to speak, they would have responded: 'You have spoken the truth and you have turned out to be a judicious man.'"

Despatching a Messenger to Madinah with News of Victory

Thereafter, to share the glad tidings of victory with the others, Rasulullah ﷺ despatched his messengers to Madinah Munawwarah. He sent 'Abdullah bin Rawaahah رضي الله عنه towards the upper regions and Zaid bin Haarisah رضي الله عنه towards the lower regions of Madinah.

Usaamah bin Zaid رضي الله عنه narrates: "The good news of victory reached us whilst we were engaged in burying Hadhrat Ruqayyah رضي الله عنها, the daughter of Rasulullah ﷺ and the wife of Hadhrat 'Usmaan رضي الله عنه. Rasulullah ﷺ left Hadhrat 'Usmaan رضي الله عنه to care for her in Madinah. This is why Hadhrat 'Usmaan رضي الله عنه was unable to participate in the battle of Badr. However, since his absence from the battle was on the instruction of Rasulullah ﷺ, he was considered to have, in principle, attended the battle. I saw Zaid bin Haarisah رضي الله عنه standing on the Musallaa with the people encircling him from all sides. Sharing the glad tidings of victory with the people, I heard him cheerfully saying: "A number of the chieftains have been slain including 'Utbah bin Rabi'ah, Shaybah bin Rabi'ah, Abu Jahal bin Hishaam, Zam'ah bin Aswad, Abul-Bakhtari bin Hishaam, Umayyah bin Khalaf, Nabihah bin Hajaaj and Munabbihah bin Hajaaj."

I excitedly enquired: "Father! Is this really true?" He replied: "Yes, by Allah! This is true."

After despatching Zaid bin Haarisah رضي الله عنه and 'Abdullah bin Rawaahah رضي الله عنه to Madinah, Rasulullah ﷺ, in due course, set out for Madinah Munawwarah. The pack of prisoners also tagged along with Rasulullah ﷺ. The spoils of war was consigned to the custody of 'Abdullah bin K'ab Ansaari رضي الله عنه.

When Rasulullah ﷺ reached a place called Rawhaa, he was met by a few Muslims who congratulated him and the Sahaabah رضي الله عنهم on this triumphant campaign. Upon this Salamah bin Salaamah ﷺ remarked: "Why do you congratulate us? We confronted a few old hags resembling trussed-up camels. We slaughtered them and dumped them." (In other words, we did not accomplish any great feat for which we deserve congratulations.)

On hearing this, Rasulullah ﷺ smiled and said: "These were, after all, the chieftains and leaders of Makkah."

Distribution of the booty

Following the conquest, Rasulullah ﷺ stayed over in Badr for a further three days. Before setting out for Madinah, he consigned the war booty in the care of Abdullah bin K'ab Ansaari ﷺ. When he reached a place called Safraa, he went about dividing the booty. Rasulullah ﷺ barely started partitioning the booty when the participants of Badr started squabbling about its distribution. The younger Sahaabah ﷺ argued that since they had killed the enemy, they deserved the booty more than anyone else. On the contrary, the elder Sahaabah ﷺ, who did not take much part in the actual fighting, maintained that they should also be included in the booty. They said: "We won this battle because of our backup and support. If, Allah forbid, you youngsters suffered defeat, you would have fallen back onto our strength." Yet again, another group who was guarding Rasulullah ﷺ reckoned that they were the most eligible for this wealth.

Upon this, the following verse was revealed:

$$\text{يَسْـَٔلُوْنَكَ عَنِ الْاَنْفَالِ ۖ قُلِ الْاَنْفَالُ لِلّٰهِ وَ الرَّسُوْلِ}$$

"They ask you (O Muhammad!) about the spoils of war. Inform them that the spoils are for Allah and the Rasool." [Surah Anfaal verse 1]

In other words, the spoils of war belong to Allah and His Rasool ﷺ is His representative. He may dispense it as he deems appropriate. Once Rasulullah ﷺ reached Safraa, he distributed this booty equally amongst the Sahaabah ﷺ.

Furthermore, an additional eight people who, with the consent of Rasulullah ﷺ, did not physically participate in this campaign were also allotted a share from the booty. They are:

1. 'Usmaan bin Affaan ﷺ. Rasulullah ﷺ left him in Madinah to attend to his ill wife Hadhrat Ruqayyah, the daughter of Rasulullah ﷺ.

2. Talhah bin 'Ubaidullah ﷺ.

3. Sa'eed bin Zaid ﷺ. Both these Sahaabis were despatched from Madinah to gather information about Abu Sufyaan's trade caravan.

4. Abu Lubaabah رضي الله عنه. Rasulullah ﷺ left him in Madinah to attend to the day-to-day administrative affairs.

5. 'Aasim bin 'Adi رضي الله عنه. Rasulullah ﷺ left him (as his representative) in Aaliyah (upper regions of Madinah Munawwarah).

6. Haaris bin Haatib رضي الله عنه. For some reason Rasulullah ﷺ sent him back to 'Amr bin 'Awf.

7. Haaris bin Al-Sammah رضي الله عنه. He was sent back because he was injured.

8. Khuwaat bin Jubair رضي الله عنه. He was sent back due to an injury to his calf.

Although these Sahaabah رضي الله عنهم did not actively participate in the battle of Badr, Rasulullah ﷺ allotted them a standard share of the war booty and included them from amongst the Sahaabah رضي الله عنهم of Badr.

Nadr bin Haaris was executed by Hadhrat Ali رضي الله عنه whilst 'Uqbah bin Abi Mu'it was slain by 'Aasim bin Saabit رضي الله عنه. With the remaining prisoners in tow, Rasulullah ﷺ then set out to Madinah Munawwarah.

Note: Nadr bin Haaris and 'Uqbah bin Abi Mu'eet were bitter enemies of Rasulullah ﷺ. They were blasphemous and foulmouthed. Either in speech or action, they left no stone unturned in belittling, ridiculing and mocking Rasulullah ﷺ. This is why these two wretched souls were particularly singled out from the other prisoners and condemned to death. This was the same 'Uqbah bin Abi Mu'eet who dumped a bucketful of camel intestines upon the blessed back of Rasulullah ﷺ whilst he was in Sajdah. He also throttled Rasulullah ﷺ. This ill-fated person also spat on the blessed face of Rasulullah ﷺ. In short, a relentless torrent of abuse and ridicule against Rasulullah ﷺ was what sustained him.

Hostile opposition and antagonistic confrontation against a Prophet of Allah Ta'ala is a major sin and an obvious source of depravity. However, verbal abuse against the reputation of a Prophet and mockery and contempt of his honour is a far more serious crime than hostile opposition because this in effect, is tantamount to denigrating the status of prophethood.

Halting at various points along the way, Rasulullah ﷺ eventually reached Madinah Munawwarah with his war captives.

Distribution of the War Captives amongst the Muslims

As Rasulullah ﷺ reached Madinah Munawwarah, he distributed the captives amongst the Muslims accompanied by the admonishment:

$$\text{استوصوابا لاسارى خيرا}$$

"Treat the captives favourably and kindly."

As a result of this prophetic caution, the Sahaabah ﷺ who had captives in their care would first feed their captives and then feed themselves if there was anything left over, otherwise they would suffice simply on dates.

Mus'ab bin 'Umair's ﷺ blood brother Abu Aziz bin 'Umair was also one of the prisoners of war. Abu Aziz recalls: "The family members of the Ansaari household were such gracious people that whatever little bread they baked morning and evening, they would feed it to me whilst they simply lived on dates. I was certainly embarrassed by this and I would always insist that they eat the bread but they would not yield to my appeals. They would say: 'Rasulullah ﷺ enjoined us to treat the captives well.'"

Consultation over the Captives of Badr

A few days after reaching Madinah Munawwarah, Rasulullah ﷺ held a meeting with the Sahaabah ﷺ about the captives of Badr. Hadhrat Anas ﷺ narrates: "Rasulullah ﷺ sought the opinion of the Sahaabah ﷺ over the prisoners of Badr. At the outset, he addressed the Sahaabah ﷺ saying:

$$\text{إِنَّ اللهَ أَمْكَنَكُمْ مِنْهُمْ}$$

"Surely Allah has awarded you control over them."

Hadhrat 'Umar ﷺ proposed: "O Rasulullah! I think that each one of them should be put to the sword."

However, the embodiment of mercy and the epitome of compassion, Rasulullah ﷺ declined this proposal and once more he said:

$$\text{يَا أَيُّهَا النَّاسُ إِنَّ اللهَ قَدْ أَمْكَنَكُمْ وَإِنَّمَا هُمْ إِخْوَانِكُم بالامس}$$

"O People! Allah has awarded you control over these people. Yesterday they were your brothers."

Once again Hadhrat 'Umar ﷺ made the same proposal only to be countered by the same prophetic statement: "Allah has awarded you control over these people. Yesterday they were your brothers."

Hadhrat Abu Bakr ﷺ submitted: "O Rasulullah! My suggestion is that these prisoners be released on payment of a ransom." Ibn 'Abbaas ﷺ relates that Hadhrat 'Umar ﷺ proposed: "O Rasulullah! Each of us should slay his close relative. Instruct Ali to kill his brother 'Aqeel and allow me to strike the neck of so and so relative as these are the leaders of kufr."

Hadhrat Abu Bakr رضي الله عنه submitted: "O Rasulullah! These people are, after all, members of your own family. I suggest that you release them on payment of ransom. It would not be strange to imagine that perhaps Allah Ta'ala would guide the same people towards Islam and then they would assist us against the disbelievers." Rasulullah صلى الله عليه وسلم eagerly accepted this proposal.

'Abdullah bin Mas'ood رضي الله عنه narrates: "On receiving the proposals put forward by Abu Bakr رضي الله عنه and 'Umar رضي الله عنه, Rasulullah صلى الله عليه وسلم remarked: "O 'Umar! Your nature is similar to that of Hadhrat Nuh عليه السلام and Hadhrat Musa عليه السلام who made dua against their people. And you O Abu Bakr! Your nature is akin to that of Hadhrat Ibraaheem عليه السلام and Hadhrat 'Isa عليه السلام who implored Allah to pardon their people. Hadhrat Nuh عليه السلام made the following dua:

$$\text{وَ قَالَ نُوحٌ رَّبِّ لَا تَذَرْ عَلَى الْأَرْضِ مِنَ الْكَافِرِينَ دَيَّارًا ۝ إِنَّكَ إِنْ تَذَرْهُمْ يُضِلُّوا عِبَادَكَ وَ لَا يَلِدُوا إِلَّا فَاجِرًا كَفَّارًا ۝}$$

"My Lord! Leave not a single person from the disbelievers dwelling on the earth. If You leave them, they will lead Your servants astray and they will not give birth but to immoral disbelievers." [Surah Nuh verses 26-27]

and Musa عليه السلام made the following dua:

$$\text{رَبَّنَا اطْمِسْ عَلَى أَمْوَالِهِمْ وَاشْدُدْ عَلَى قُلُوبِهِمْ فَلَا يُؤْمِنُوا حَتَّى يَرَوُا الْعَذَابَ الْأَلِيمَ ۝}$$

"Our Lord! Destroy their wealth and seal their hearts so that they will not believe until they see the painful torment." [Surah Yunus verse 88]

Ibraaheem عليه السلام made the following dua:

$$\text{فَمَنْ تَبِعَنِي فَإِنَّهُ مِنِّي ۖ وَمَنْ عَصَانِي فَإِنَّكَ غَفُورٌ رَحِيمٌ ۝}$$

"So whomsoever follows me, he is of me and whomsoever disobeys me, You are most forgiving, most merciful." [Surah Ibraaheem verse 36]

and 'Isa عليه السلام made the following dua:

$$\text{إِنْ تُعَذِّبْهُمْ فَإِنَّهُمْ عِبَادُكَ ۖ وَإِنْ تَغْفِرْ لَهُمْ فَإِنَّكَ أَنْتَ الْعَزِيزُ الْحَكِيمُ ۝}$$

"If You punish them, they are Your servants and if You pardon them, You are All-mighty, All-wise (You can pardon any offender You wish and Your pardon is not devoid of wisdom)." [Surah Maa'idah verse 118]

Rasulullah's ﷺ nature of 'embodiment of mercy to mankind' came to the fore, thus agreeing with Abu Bakr ؓ. He then instructed them to release the captives on payment of ransom."

Whilst Rasulullah ﷺ was engaged in consulting with the Sahaabah ؓ, divine revelation charged Rasulullah ﷺ to give the Sahaabah ؓ the option of execution or ransom. Hadhrat Ali ؓ narrates: "Jibraa'eel ؑ appeared before Rasulullah ﷺ and said: 'O Rasulullah! Give your companions an option; either they execute their captives or they release them on payment of ransom. However, the proviso for accepting a ransom is that the same number of Sahaabah ؓ will be killed the forthcoming year.' The Sahaabah ؓ assented to the second option of accepting a ransom from the disbelievers thus exposing themselves to martyrdom in the forthcoming year."

Jibraa'eel ؑ appeared before Rasulullah ﷺ and submitted: "O Rasulullah! Your Lord has given you liberty with the captives of Badr." When Rasulullah ﷺ sought the counsel of the Sahaabah ؓ, they submitted: "O Rasulullah! Today we are willing to set them free in lieu of a ransom so that we may attain a degree of strength against them and in the forthcoming year, Allah Ta'ala may confer martyrdom upon whomsoever He wishes." The Sahaabah ؓ added:

"Perhaps in the forthcoming year, seventy of us will be admitted into Jannah."

Divine Admonishment upon the Acceptance of Ransom

Nonetheless, Rasulullah ﷺ endorsed Hadhrat Abu Bakr's ؓ opinion and instructed the Sahaabah ؓ to accept a ransom and liberate the captives. A number of senior Sahaabah ؓ also suggested the ransom route on the thought that these same captives would perhaps embrace Islam, thus boosting the cause of Islam, and the ransom that they would collect now could be utilised for further Jihaad expeditions and other Deeni activities. Amongst those who proposed taking a ransom, the odds are that there were some Sahaabah ؓ whose primary objective was the accumulation of worldly wealth. This was spurred by their love for this material world. Although this wealth was from Halaal sources – as part of the war booty – such love attracted severe divine admonishment. The following verse was revealed:

مَا كَانَ لِنَبِيٍّ اَنْ يَّكُوْنَ لَهٗۤ اَسْرٰى حَتّٰى يُثْخِنَ فِى الْاَرْضِ ؕ تُرِيْدُوْنَ عَرَضَ الدُّنْيَا ۖ وَاللّٰهُ يُرِيْدُ الْاٰخِرَةَ ؕ وَاللّٰهُ عَزِيْزٌ حَكِيْمٌ ۝ لَوْلَا كِتٰبٌ مِّنَ اللّٰهِ سَبَقَ لَمَسَّكُمْ فِيْمَاۤ اَخَذْتُمْ عَذَابٌ عَظِيْمٌ ۝

"It is not (appropriate) for a Prophet that he has captives (and sets them free with ransom) until he causes a massacre in the earth (by killing the enemy). You desire

the goods of the world (the ransom) but Allah desires the hereafter. And Allah is all prevailing, all wise. Were it not for a previous ordainment from Allah, you would have been inflicted with a grave pusnihment due to what you had taken."
[Surah Anfaal verse 67-68]

This reproachful censure is specifically directed to those whose focus was centred on monetary gain and worldly benefit and thus proposed that ransom be taken in lieu of the captives' liberation. This is evident from the verse "you desire the goods of the world". As for those who proposed the taking of ransom for the benefit of Deen and the hereafter, they are not, in reality, included in this admonishment. Rasulullah ﷺ applauded the opinion of ransom simply on the grounds of maintaining favourable family ties and on the grounds of compassion. Furthermore, he wished to give the others an opportunity to get some financial gain. This was motivated by his spirit of selfless generosity, which in itself is commendable. Yes, what is deplorable is to have one's personal financial gain in mind. So this verse slams those whose primary objective was the acquisition of worldly gain.

When Rasulullah ﷺ and Abu Bakr رضى الله عنه learnt of this divine admonishment, they burst out crying. Hadhrat 'Umar رضى الله عنه narrates: "When I enquired as to what makes him weep so much, Rasulullah ﷺ replied:

ابكى للذى عرض على اصحابك من اخذهم الفداء لقد عرض على عذابهم ادنى من هذه الشجرة

'I am weeping because of the divine punishment that was presented before me for those of your companions who consented to accept ransom. Their divine punishment was presented before me even closer than this tree in front of us.'

Note: The punishment was not meted out but merely shown to him. The objective was simply to caution them.

Rasulullah ﷺ then declared: "Had the punishment struck, none of us except 'Umar would have been saved." Another Hadith says, "except S'ad bin Mu'aaz."

Since S'ad bin Mu'aaz رضى الله عنه also proposed that the captives be killed, he was also absolved with Hadhrat 'Umar رضى الله عنه. Although 'Abdullah bin Rawaahah رضى الله عنه was also opposed to taking ransom, he proposed that all the captives be thrown into a fire but Shari'ah disapproves of this as well. This is why his name was not mentioned here.

The reason for this is that the primary aim of this campaign was to establish the truth and obliterate falsehood as Allah Ta'ala says:

$$وَيُرِيدُ اللّٰهُ اَنْ يُّحِقَّ الْحَقَّ بِكَلِمٰتِهٖ وَيَقْطَعَ دَابِرَ الْكٰفِرِيْنَ ۞ لِيُحِقَّ الْحَقَّ وَيُبْطِلَ الْبَاطِلَ وَلَوْ كَرِهَ الْمُجْرِمُوْنَ ۞$$

"And Allah wishes to establish the truth with His words and to sever the roots of the disbelievers. And that He may render the truth triumphant and frustrate falsehood even though the sinners detest it." [Surah Anfaal verses 7-8]

The Muslims, particularly in this battle, were divinely commanded to kill the disbelievers.

This is further confirmed in this verse:

$$فَاضْرِبُوْا فَوْقَ الْاَعْنَاقِ وَاضْرِبُوْا مِنْهُمْ كُلَّ بَنَانٍ ۞$$

"And strike them (the disbelievers) on the necks and smite all the fingertips." [Surah Anfaal verse 12]

Another verse ordains:

$$فَاِذَا لَقِيْتُمُ الَّذِيْنَ كَفَرُوْا فَضَرْبَ الرِّقَابِ ۚ حَتّٰى اِذَآ اَثْخَنْتُمُوْهُمْ فَشُدُّوا الْوَثَاقَ ۙ فَاِمَّا مَنًّا بَعْدُ وَاِمَّا فِدَآءً حَتّٰى تَضَعَ الْحَرْبُ اَوْزَارَهَا ۚ$$

"So when you meet the disbelievers (in Jihaad) smite their necks until when you have shed their blood, then bind them securely (by taking them as prisoners). Thereafter, there is a favour (by setting them free) or there is a ransom until the war divests its burdens (arms)...." [Surah Muhammad verse 4]

Ransom Amount

As per the financial abilities of the captives, the ransom per captive was fixed at anything from one thousand to four thousand dirhams. As for the poor captives who were unable to afford anything, they were set free without the payment of any tangible ransom whatsoever.

The literate amongst these indigent captives were charged to tutor ten children each in reading and writing. Once they taught ten children each, they would be set free. This was their ransom. Hadhrat Zaid bin Saabit رَضِىَ اللّٰهُ عَنْهُ learnt to read and write in this very manner.

Amongst the captives of Badr was Abu 'Uzzah 'Amr bin 'Abdullah bin 'Usmaan. He too could not afford to pay any ransom. He appeared before Rasulullah صَلَّى اللّٰهُ عَلَيْهِ وَسَلَّم pleading: "O Rasulullah! You are well aware that I am a destitute with a number of dependants. I beg you to be compassionate towards me." Rasulullah صَلَّى اللّٰهُ عَلَيْهِ وَسَلَّم showered him with his compassion and set him free without demanding any ransom from him. However, Rasulullah ﷺ released him on condition that he would not assist anyone against Rasulullah ﷺ and the Muslims. Abu 'Uzzah consented to this condition. He even went as far as saying a few laudatory couplets in honour of Rasulullah ﷺ. However, he did not embrace Islam and was killed in the state of kufr in the battle of Uhud. Similarly, Muttalib bin Hantab and Sayfi bin Abi Rifa'ah were released without ransom.

Back in Makkah

When news of Quraysh's humiliating defeat reached Makkah, the whole city was thrown into a state of mystified panic. The first person to reach Makkah was Haysamaan Khuzaa'i. When the residents asked him about the news of the war, he lamented: "'Utbah bin Rabi'ah has been killed, Shaybah bin Rabi'ah has been killed, Abul-Hakam bin Hishaam (Abu Jahal) has been killed, Umayyah bin Khalaf has been killed, Zam'ah bin Aswad has been killed, Nabihah bin Hajaaj has been killed, Munabbihah bin Hajaaj has been killed, so and so has been killed." He then went on to enumerate a few more chieftains who were killed in the battle.

Safwaan bin Umayyah, who was seated in the Hateem area listening to this dismal report, remarked: "I cannot understand. Is this man perhaps gone mad! Why do you people not put his sanity to the test and ask him where is Safwaan bin Umayyah?" When asked, Haysamaan replied: "Here is Safwaan bin Umayyah sitting here in the Hateem. With my own eyes, I saw his father and brother being put to the sword."

Ibn 'Abbaas ؓ narrates: "Abu Raaf'i related to me that at this moment in time, Islam had already filtered into the home of 'Abbaas but we (his children) would conceal our Islam.

When the Quraysh set off for the battle of Badr, daily we would wait in anticipation of some news. When Haysamaan Khuzaa'i brought news of the Quraysh's defeat in Badr, we were thrown into a state of unbridled ecstasy at Rasulullah's ﷺ victory." 'Abbaas ؓ says: "At that moment, my wife, Ummu Fadl, and I, were sitting beneath the Zam Zam canopy when Abu Lahab happened to pass by."

When the people noticed Abu Sufyaan bin Haaris approaching them, they addressed Abu Lahab saying: "Here is Abu Sufyaan returning from Badr."

Abu Lahab invited Abu Sufyaan to sit next to him and to enlighten him about the battle of Badr. Abu Sufyaan replied:

والله ما هو الا ان لقينا القوم فمنحنا هم اكتافنا يضعون السلاح منا حيث شاؤا وياسروننا كيف شاؤا وايم الله مع ذلك ما لمت الناس

Chapter 12

لقينا رجالا بيضا بيض على خيل بلق بين السماء والارض والله ما تليق شيئا ولا يقوم لها شيء

"By Allah! I know nothing except that we fought a people before whom we submitted our shoulders. They were thrusting their weapons against us as they wished and they rounded us up as captives as they wished. By Allah! I do not blame our people (for surrendering before them) because we caught sight of white-robed men mounted on piebald horses suspended between the sky and the earth. By Allah! They would not leave anything and nothing remains intact before them."

Abu Raaf'i says:

قلت والله تلك الملائكة

"On hearing this strange occurrence, I commented: "By Allah! Incontestably, these were angels."

The moment Abu Lahab heard me make this comment, he flew into a towering rage and landed a nasty smack to my face. He lifted me up and pitilessly hurled me onto the ground. With the purpose of inflicting more pain on me, he came and plopped himself right onto my chest. I was a weak bodied person.

Umme Fadl got up and clutching a wooden column in her hand, went up to him and dealt him an injurious blow to his head. She then added: "His master (Abbaas رضي الله عنه) is not around. Is this why you regard him as so weak?"

Barely a week later, Abu Lahab was struck with plague-like eruptions on his entire body and he died. The stench given off by his corpse was so disgusting that nobody could approach it.

After three days, his sons, driven by a fear of public disgrace, got a hole dug and with the aid of long poles, roughly shoved him into it.

It is related that whenever Hadhrat 'Aa'ishah رضي الله عنها would pass the spot where Abu Lahab disgracefully died, she would cover her face with a cloth.

When Rasulullah ﷺ happened to pass the dwellings of Samood, he covered his face with a cloth and bade his mount to move faster. He implied that one should do so when passing through areas struck by divine punishment. Hadhrat 'Aa'ishah رضي الله عنها was actually observing a Sunnah of Rasulullah ﷺ.

When the Quraysh confirmed the death of their kinsfolk, they fell into a state of mourning. For a whole month, they bewailed the loss of their loved ones but before long, an announcement was made advising the people not to engage in any form of mourning because if Muhammad and his companions happen to hear of their mourning, they will be thrilled with delight. Further, it was announced that nobody should pay ransom in lieu of his or her captives lest Muhammad (ﷺ) attempts to inflate the amount payable.

However, in spite of these announcements and warnings, Muttalib bin Abi Widaaʻah sneaked away from the Quraysh and one night, with a sum of four thousand dirhams, he set out for Madinah. On reaching there, he paid the ransom, secured the release of his father Abu Widaaʻah and returned with him to Makkah. Following his example, a procession of others followed suit and remitting their ransoms; they released their captives one after the other.

Amongst these captives was also Suhail bin ʻAmr. He was exceptionally shrewd and eloquent in speech. In the gatherings of (the disbelievers) he would often lavish words of scorn and disrespect against the blessed person of Rasulullah ﷺ. Since Suhail was being held by the Muslims, Hadhrat ʻUmar رضى الله عنه inquired: "O Rasulullah! Allow me to draw out two of his lower teeth so that he never wags his tongue against you in the future." Rasulullah ﷺ replied: "No, leave him alone. It would not surprise me if Allah shows you some source of bliss through Suhail."

Subsequently, the peace accord signed at Hudabiyyah, which Allah Taʻala transformed into an 'obvious victory', came about through his laborious efforts. He embraced Islam at the conquest of Makkah.

According to Ibn Hishaam's narration, Rasulullah ﷺ responded to Hadhrat ʻUmar's رضى الله عنه request by saying: "I do not wish to disfigure him lest Allah Taʻala disfigures me, even though I may be a Prophet."

Amongst the captives was also Abu Sufyaan's son ʻAmr. When Abu Sufyaan was asked to pay ransom for the release of his son, he replied: "How is it possible that I pay ransom for one family member while another is slain? One of my sons, Hanzalah, is already murdered. How am I expected to pay ransom for the release of my other son ʻAmr? They may keep him captive as long as they wish."

During this period, Sʻad bin Nʻumaan Ansaari came to Makkah from Madinah to perform Umrah. Abu Sufyaan detained him in place of his son. On the request of the Ansaar, Rasulullah ﷺ surrendered ʻAmr bin Abu Sufyaan to his father Abu Sufyaan and secured the release of Sʻad bin Nʻumaan.

Abul ʻAas bin Rabiʼ رضى الله عنه

Amongst the captives was also the son-in-law of Rasulullah ﷺ, Abul ʼAas bin Rabiʼ. Rasulullah's ﷺ daughter Hadhrat Zainab رضى الله عنها was married to him.

Hadhrat Khadijah رضى الله عنها was the aunt (mother's sister) of Abul ʼAas bin Rabiʼ. Hadhrat Khadijah رضى الله عنها regarded him as her own son. With the approval of Rasulullah ﷺ, Hadhrat Khadijah رضى الله عنها got Zainab رضى الله عنها married to Abul ʼAas even before prophethood. Abul ʼAas was a rich, honest and distinguished trader. After prophethood, all the daughters of Rasulullah ﷺ embraced Islam but Abul 'Aas remained committed to shirk (polytheism).

The Quraysh repeatedly badgered: "Why do you not divorce Muhammad's daughter, Zainab, just as Abu Lahab's sons divorced his daughters? We will get you married to a woman of your choice." However, Abul 'Aas bluntly refused to do so and declared: "In comparison to a noble woman as Zainab, I will never fancy any other woman."

When the Quraysh left for the campaign of Badr, Abul 'Aas also joined them. Amongst others, he was also captured as a prisoner of war. When the inhabitants of Makkah remitted their ransoms in lieu of the release of their respective captives, Hadhrat Zainab ؓ sent a necklace that was given to her as a wedding gift by her mother Hadhrat Khadijah ؓ, to release her husband Abul 'Aas. The moment his glance fell onto the necklace, Rasulullah's ﷺ eyes welled up with tears (in memory of Hadhrat Khadijah ؓ). Rasulullah ﷺ advised the Sahaabah ؓ: "If you consider it appropriate, return the necklace and release the captive as well."

They instantly lowered their heads in submission to this request. They returned the necklace and set the captive free as well. However, Rasulullah ﷺ obtained an assurance from Abul-'Aas that he will send Zainab to Madinah the moment he gets back to Makkah.

When he arrived in Makkah, Abul 'Aas permitted her to leave for Madinah and he sent his brother Kinaanah bin Rab'i with her.

Towards the middle of the afternoon, Kinaanah seated Hadhrat Zaynab ؓ on a camel and clutching his bow and arrows, he set out.

Rasulullah's ﷺ daughter flagrantly heading out of Makkah in this manner was enormously upsetting to the Quraysh. Subsequently, Abu Sufyaan and a few other chieftains turned up at the valley of Tuwaa and barring the camel from going any further, they said: "We have no reason to prevent Muhammad's daughter, but for her to set out so brazenly is demeaning to us. Why do you not return to Makkah now and leave in the darkness of night?" Kinaanah consented to this proposal and returned to Makkah.

Before Abu Sufyaan, another person by the name of Habbaar bin Aswad (who later embraced Islam) blocked the passage of the camel. He threatened her so terrifyingly that she suffered a miscarriage. At his intimidating attitude, Kinaanah got his bow and arrow out and warned them: "Any of you dare to come close to the camel, I will leave his body looking like a sieve."

Nonetheless, Kinaanah reached Makkah and after about two days he slipped out of Makkah one night and proceeded towards Madinah.

Whilst he was leaving Makkah, in Madinah Rasulullah ﷺ instructed Zaid bin Haarisah ؓ and another Ansaari to proceed to a place called Batn-

Yaajuj and advised, "When Zainab ﵂ reaches this place, bring her along with you."

When these people reached Batn-Yaajuj, they met Kinaanah bin Rab'i coming from the opposite direction. Kinaanah returned to Makkah whilst Zaid bin Haarisah ﵁ and his companion took Zainab ﵂ to Madinah. They reached Madinah about a month after the battle of Badr.

Hadhrat Zainab ﵂ started living with Rasulullah ﷺ whilst Abul 'Aas continued living in Makkah. Before the conquest of Makkah, Abul 'Aas left on a business trip to Syria. Since the people of Makkah were confident of his honesty and reliability, they also invested capital into this trade expedition.

On his return from Syria, a unit of the Muslim army waylaid the caravan. They seized all their merchandise from the caravan. However, Abul 'Aas managed to sneak away and turned up in Madinah at the door of Zainab ﵂.

When Rasulullah ﷺ emerged for the Fajr Salaah, Hadhrat Zainab ﵂ called out from the women's hut: "O people! I have offered sanctuary to Abul 'Aas bin Rabi'."

Once he completed the Salaah, Rasulullah ﷺ turned to the people and said:

ايها الناس هل سمعتم ما سمعت قالوا نعم قال اما والذى نفسى بيده ما علمت بشىء من ذلك حتى سمعت ما سمعتم انه يجير على المسلمين ادناهم

"O people! Did you hear what I heard?" "Yes," they replied. "I swear by the Being in whose absolute control lies Muhammad's life! I had absolutely no idea about this until I heard what you heard. Bear in mind that the lowest-ranking Muslim may offer sanctuary to anyone he (or she) pleases."

Saying this, he went up to his daughter and cautioned: "My dearest daughter! You may honour him but do not allow him to be intimate with you because you are not Halaal for him." In other words, you are a Muslim whilst he is a disbeliever.

He then addressed the military unit saying: "You are aware of this man's (Abul 'Aas') relationship with me. If you feel that it is appropriate, you may return his goods to him otherwise it is a gift from Allah and you are most eligible to receive it."

The moment they heard this request, they returned all his possessions. Someone returned a bucket, another a rope whilst a third person brought a piece of leather and so forth. In short, they surrendered every last bit of his goods back to him.

Abul 'Aas acquired all his confiscated goods and returned to Makkah where he returned all the merchandise to their respective owners. Once he handed over their goods, he addressed them saying:

يا معشر قريش هل بقى لاحد منكم عندى مال ياخذه قالوا لا
فجزاك الله خيرا فقد وجدناك وفيا كريما قال فانا اشهد ان لا اله الا
الله وان محمدا عبده و رسوله والله ما منعنى من الاسلام عنده الا
تخوفا ان آكل اموالكم فلما اداها الله اليكم و فرغت عنها اسلمت

"O Quraysh! Is there anything outstanding in favour of anyone of you who has not collected what is due to him?" "No," they replied. "May Allah reward you favourably. We have found you to be an honest and noble man of integrity." He then revealed: "I bear witness that there is none worthy of worship but Allah and Muhammad is His slave and messenger." He added further: "By Allah! I did not reveal my Islam until now lest people imagine I embraced Islam simply to usurp your wealth. However, since Allah has now returned your wealth to you and I am absolved of any liability over this, I have embraced Islam."

Thereafter Abul 'Aas ؓ left Makkah and when he returned to Madinah, Rasulullah ﷺ reinstated Hadhrat Zainab ؓ into his Nikah.

Abbaas bin Abdul Muttalib ؓ

Amongst these captives was Rasulullah's ﷺ uncle (father's brother) Hadhrat 'Abbaas ؓ. He was captured by K'ab bin 'Amr Abul-Yusr ؓ. Hadhrat 'Abbaas ؓ was burly and powerful whilst Abul-Yusr ؓ was scrawny, weak and short in stature. Rasulullah ﷺ asked him: "O Abul-Yusr! How did you manage capturing 'Abbaas?" He replied: "O Rasulullah! Another man whom I have neither seen before nor since, assisted me in capturing him." He then went on to describe the man's features. Rasulullah ﷺ remarked: "Beyond doubt, you were assisted by a noble angel."

The shackles binding 'Abbaas were a bit tight. When Rasulullah ﷺ heard the mournful cries of 'Abbaas, he was deeply moved and overwhelmed with grief. When the Ansaar heard of this, they promptly removed his shackles and even went to the extent of recommending: "O Rasulullah! If you consent to it, we wish to absolve our nephew 'Abbaas from payment of the ransom." Rasulullah ﷺ replied: "By Allah! Do not even yield for a single dirham."

Nonetheless, when Hadhrat 'Abbaas ؓ was demanded to pay the ransom, he pleaded poverty. To this Rasulullah ﷺ responded: "Okay, so where is the treasure that you and your wife Umme Fadl buried?"

Jolted beyond surprise, Hadhrat 'Abbaas ؓ declared: "I bear testimony that you are indisputably the Prophet of Allah. Apart from Umme Fadl and I, nobody else knows about it."

Ibn 'Abbaas ؓ narrates that Rasulullah ﷺ fixed one hundred Awqiyah of silver as ransom for 'Abbaas and eighty for 'Aqeel bin Abi Taalib." (From all the captives, Hadhrat 'Abbaas's ransom was the highest.)

Hadhrat 'Abbaas ؓ pleaded: "Did you set my ransom at the highest due to our close family relationship?" (In other words, our kinship demands that you offer me some concession in the ransom but instead of a concession, you fixed my ransom at the highest.)

Upon this, the following verse was revealed:

يَاَيُّهَا النَّبِيُّ قُلْ لِّمَنْ فِىْٓ اَيْدِيْكُمْ مِّنَ الْاَسْرٰۤى اِنْ يَّعْلَمِ اللّٰهُ فِىْ قُلُوْبِكُمْ خَيْرًا يُّؤْتِكُمْ خَيْرًا مِّمَّآ اُخِذَ مِنْكُمْ وَ يَغْفِرْ لَكُمْ ۚ وَاللّٰهُ غَفُوْرٌ رَّحِيْمٌ ۞

"O Nabi! Inform the captives who are in your possession (that they should not bemoan the payment of this ransom), if Allah is aware of any goodness within your hearts (by you sincerely embracing Islam) then He would award you something far superior than what was taken from you and He will forgive you. And Allah is most-forgiving, merciful." [Surah Anfaal verse 70]

Hadhrat 'Abbaas ؓ would later comment: "If only the ransom demanded from me was multiplied manifold."

He further relates: "Whatever Allah Ta'ala has taken from me, He has rewarded me with something far more superior. He had taken a hundred Awqiyah of silver from me and rewarded me with a hundred slaves and each and every one of them is a trader. Allah Ta'ala has fulfilled His promise in this very world and His second promise was about Maghfirat (forgiveness). I am optimistic of this promise as well."

This humble servant adds: Insha Allah, the second promise will also be fulfilled, for Allah Ta'ala does not breach His promise. I mentioned 'Insha Allah' here, more out of blessing and not as a condition.

Amongst the prisoners of Badr was Nawfal bin Haaris. When Rasulullah ﷺ asked him to pay ransom, he beseeched: "I have absolutely nothing to pay in ransom."

Rasulullah ﷺ responded by saying: "Where are those spears you left in Jeddah?" Nawfal replied: "By Allah! After Allah nobody but I know of their existence. I testify that verily you are the Prophet of Allah."

Nawfal surrendered these spears to Rasulullah ﷺ as payment of his ransom. They numbered a thousand spears in all. Rasulullah ﷺ established a bond of brotherhood between Hadhrat 'Abbaas رضي الله عنه and Hadhrat Nawfal رضي الله عنه. Both of them were friends during the days of pre-Islamic ignorance. They were business associates as well.

'Umair bin Wahab Jumahi was one of the most bitter enemies of Islam. During the Makkan period, Rasulullah ﷺ and his Sahaabah رضي الله عنهم were subjected to severe torture and persecution at his hands. His son Wahab bin 'Umair was also one of the captives of Badr.

'Umair bin Wahab and Safwaan bin Umayyah were one day seated in the Hateem area when Safwaan broached the subject of the captives of Badr saying: "Nowadays there is no joy left in our lives." 'Umair responded: "Yes. That is right, by Allah! Since the slaying of the chieftains of Quraysh, life really holds no bliss for us. If it was not for the concern of my debts and children, I would have promptly went up to Muhammad and finished him off."

This brought profound delight to Safwaan who promised: "The burden of your debts, family and children is all on my shoulders." Safwaan then burnished his sword and tempering it with a deadly toxin, he handed it over to 'Umair.

Taking the sword, 'Umair set out for Madinah. He proceeded straight to the door of the Masjid and halted his camel there.

The moment Hadhrat 'Umar رضي الله عنه laid eyes on him, he figured out that this man has turned up with some wicked plan. Hadhrat 'Umar رضي الله عنه at once, grasped his sword-belt and yanked him along into the presence of Rasulullah ﷺ.

Rasulullah ﷺ asked Hadhrat 'Umar رضي الله عنه to release him and addressed 'Umair: "What brings you here?" "I have come," he replied, "to secure the release of one of our captives." Rasulullah ﷺ insisted: "No, speak the truth. What really brings you here? Speak the truth, what discussion did you and Safwaan hold in the Hateem?"

Agitated by this, 'Umair nervously asked: "What did I propose in that discussion?" Rasulullah ﷺ replied: "You assumed the responsibility of assassinating me on condition that Safwaan would bear the burdens of your family and debts."

'Umair responded:

اشهد انك رسول الله ان هذا الحديث كان بيني وبين صفوان فى الحجر لم يطلع عليه احد غيرى وغيره فاخبرك الله به فامنت بالله ورسوله

> "I testify that you are certainly the Rasool of Allah. This discussion was solely between Safwaan and myself in the Hateem. Nobody save the two of us was aware of what transpired. Only Allah could have informed you. So I believe in Allah and His Rasool."

According to the narration of Ibn Ishaaq, 'Umair said:

والله انى لا علم ما آتاك به الا الله فالحمد لله الذى هدانى للاسلام وساقنى هذا المساق ثم تشهد

"By Allah! I am convinced that nobody but Allah could have informed you of this incident. So all praise is due to Allah Who has guided me towards Islam and Who has driven me to this end." He then recited the Kalimah.

Rasulullah ﷺ addressed the Sahaabah رضي الله عنه: "Teach your brother the knowledge of Deen and teach him the Qur-aan and release his prisoner."

The captive was immediately released into the care of 'Umair رضي الله عنه. 'Umair رضي الله عنه then addressed Rasulullah ﷺ saying: "O Rasulullah! I was awfully persistent in trying to smother the Deen of Allah Ta'ala and I subjected the Muslims to an assortment of agonising afflictions. Now allow me to return to Makkah and call the people to Allah and His Rasool and to invite them towards Islam. Perhaps Allah Ta'ala would guide them to the right path. Allow me to torment His enemies as I was previously tormenting His friends." Rasulullah ﷺ conceded to his request.

Whilst 'Umair was leaving from Madinah, in Makkah, Safwaan was gleefully informing everyone he met: "Do not worry, in a few days I will give you such delightful news that would make you forget about the sorrow of Badr."

He also continued making enquiries from other travellers about 'Umair. When he heard about 'Umair embracing Islam, he flew into a rage and pledged: "By Allah! I will neither speak to 'Umair nor will I benefit him in any way."

'Umair رضي الله عنه landed in Makkah and set about inviting people to Islam. Due to his determined efforts, many people turned to Islam. As for the enemies of Islam, he put them through a great deal of aggravation.

Salaatul-Eid

After his return from Badr, Rasulullah ﷺ performed Eid Salaah on the first day of Shawwaal. This was the first Eidul-Fitr ever performed.

Chapter 13

Virtues of the Badriyeen

Hadhrat Ali ﷺ narrates that in the incident of Haatib bin Abi Balta'ah (the details of which will be mentioned later on, Insha Allah), Rasulullah ﷺ addressed Hadhrat 'Umar ﷺ saying:

لعل الله اطلع الى اهل بدر فقال اعملوا ماشئتم فقد وجبت لكم الجنة

"Verily Allah Ta'ala focused His (compassionate) attention towards the participants of Badr and said: "Do whatever you wish, for Jannah has become inevitable for you."

Hadhrat Jaabir ﷺ relates that Rasulullah ﷺ said:

لن يدخل النار احد شهد بدرا

"A participant of Badr will never enter the fire of Jahannam."

Rifa'ah Raaf'i ﷺ narrates that once Jibraa'eel ﷺ appeared before Rasulullah ﷺ and asked: "What do you think of the Badri Sahaabah ﷺ?" Rasulullah ﷺ replied: "They are the best of people." To this Jibraa'eel ﷺ remarked: "Yes, similarly, the angels who participated in the battle of Badr are also regarded as the best of angels."

Number of Badri Sahaabah ﷺ

The total number of the Badri Sahaabah ﷺ were three hundred and thirteen.

There were eight people who, for some reason or the other, were unable to participate in the battle of Badr but they are counted as Badri Sahaabah ﷺ and Rasulullah ﷺ also awarded them a share of the spoils.

Register of the Badri Angels

The descent of the angels during the battle of Badr and their subsequent assistance to and combat with the ranks of Muslims has already been established from the texts of the Qur-aan and Ahaadith. However, on the basis of the narrations of Ahaadith, only three names of the participating angels could be ascertained with certainty. They are as follows:

1. The most noble angel and loyal emissary of Allah Ta'ala to the Ambiyaa عَلَيْهِمُالسَّلَامْ, Sayyidina Jibraa'eel عَلَيْهِالسَّلَامْ.

2. Sayyidina Mikaa'eel عَلَيْهِالسَّلَامْ.

3. Sayyidina Israafeel عَلَيْهِالسَّلَامْ.

Since the Ahaadith make mention of the heavenly descent of the angels in the order of Jibraa'eel عَلَيْهِالسَّلَامْ followed by Mikaa'eel عَلَيْهِالسَّلَامْ and then by Israafeel عَلَيْهِالسَّلَامْ, the same sequence of descent was observed in the above list as well.

Register of the Martyrs of Badr

Allah Ta'ala says:

وَلَا تَحْسَبَنَّ الَّذِيْنَ قُتِلُوْا فِيْ سَبِيْلِ اللهِ أَمْوَاتًا ۚ بَلْ أَحْيَاءٌ عِنْدَ رَبِّهِمْ يُرْزَقُوْنَ ۞ فَرِحِيْنَ بِمَآ اٰتٰهُمُ اللهُ مِنْ فَضْلِهٖ ۙ وَيَسْتَبْشِرُوْنَ بِالَّذِيْنَ لَمْ يَلْحَقُوْا بِهِمْ مِنْ خَلْفِهِمْ ۙ اَلَّا خَوْفٌ عَلَيْهِمْ وَلَا هُمْ يَحْزَنُوْنَ ۞

"And do not regard those who have been killed in the path of Allah as dead. Nay, they are alive by their Lord, they are provided with sustenance. They rejoice in what Allah has bestowed upon them from His bounty and they take delight for the sake of those who have not yet joined them but are left behind (not martyred) that no fear shall befall them, nor will they grieve." [Surah Aal-'Imraan verses 169-170]

مکن گریہ بر گور مقتول دوست
برو خرمی کن کہ مقبول اوست

"There is no need to shed tears over the grave of a beloved, Take solace from the fact that he is the accepted servant of the 'true beloved (Allah Ta'ala).'"

(1) 'Ubaidah bin Haaris bin Muttalib ؓ.

He was severely wounded on his leg at Badr. He lost the leg and succumbed to his injuries by the time he reached Safraa. Rasulullah ﷺ buried him there.

It is said that on one occasion, Rasulullah ﷺ and his Sahaabah ؓ broke their journey in Safraa. Some of the Sahaabah ؓ exclaimed: "O Rasulullah! We perceive the fragrance of musk from around here." Rasulullah ﷺ said: "What is surprising about that? Abu Mu'aawiyah's grave is here." (Abu Mu'aawiyah was the title of Hadhrat 'Ubaidah bin Haaris ؓ.)

(2) 'Umair bin Abi Waqqaas ؓ

He was the younger brother of S'ad bin Abi Waqqaas ؓ. S'ad bin Abi Waqqaas ؓ narrates: "When the combatants of Badr assembled to depart, I caught sight of my brother 'Umair ؓ ducking about in the crowd. I asked him: 'Brother! What is happening with you?' He replied: 'I fear that Rasulullah ﷺ will spot me and send me back home due to my young age. I yearn to go into battle. Perhaps Allah Ta'ala would honour me with martyrdom.' When Rasulullah ﷺ inspected the ranks of the Sahaabah ؓ, he caught sight of 'Umair and declared that he be sent back due to his age. Upon this, 'Umair ؓ burst out crying. However, when Rasulullah ﷺ noticed his zealous enthusiasm to participate in the campaign, he allowed him to stay on. Subsequently, he took part in the battle and was martyred. 'Umair ؓ was only sixteen at that time."

(3) Zush-Shimaalain bin 'Abdi 'Amr Muhaajiri ؓ

(4) Aaqil bin Bukair ؓ

He was from amongst the earliest Muslims. He embraced Islam in Daaru Arqam. Initially his name was Ghaafil (which means negligent). Rasulullah ﷺ later changed his name to Aaqil (which means intelligent and alert). Prior to him embracing Islam, he was Ghaafil - negligent and ignorant of the hereafter but he turned out to be Aaqil - intelligent and alert after he embraced Islam. This is why Rasulullah ﷺ preferred this name for him. And Allah Ta'ala knows best. He was martyred in the battle of Badr. He was thirty-four at that time.

(5) Mihj'a bin Saalih, the emancipated slave of 'Umar bin Khattaab ؓ

Sa'eed bin Musayyab narrates: "During the battle, the following words were on Mihj'a's tongue: "انا مهجع والى ربى ارجع" 'I am Mihj'a and unto my Lord do I intend to return.'"

(6) Safwaan bin Baydaa Muhaajiri ؓ

Him being a Badri Sahaabi is undisputed but whether he was martyred at Badr is something the scholars have failed to agree upon. Some are of the opinion that he was martyred in the battle of Badr at the hands of Tu'aimah bin 'Adi.

(7) S'ad bin Khaysamah ؓ

He was a Sahaabi and the son of a Sahaabi. Both father and son were martyrs. The son, S'ad was martyred in Badr whilst the father, Khaysamah was martyred in the battle of Uhud.

Hadhrat S'ad ؓ also participated in the pledge of 'Aqabah. Rasulullah ﷺ appointed him as the head of the Banu 'Amr tribe.

When Rasulullah ﷺ enjoined the Sahaabah ؓ to step forth against the trade caravan of Abu Sufyaan, Khaysamah implored his son S'ad saying: "Son! One of us will have to stay behind at home to take care of the women and children. I request you to give me preference and allow me to go in the company of Rasulullah ﷺ whilst you stay here at home." S'ad ؓ bluntly refused and said:

لو كان غير الجنة آثر تك به انى ارجو الشهادة فى وجهى هذا

"If it was in any other affair besides Jannah, I would have undeniably given you this honour and given you preference over myself but I entertain high aspirations of martyrdom in this campaign."

Thereafter, lots were drawn between father and son. Thus the lot was drawn in favour of the son. The son turned out to be more fortunate than the father and with unbridled enthusiasm he set out with Rasulullah ﷺ towards Badr. During the battle of Badr he was martyred at the hands of either 'Amr bin 'Abd Wadd or Tu'aimah bin 'Adi. May Allah Ta'ala be pleased with S'ad.

(8) Mubasshir bin 'Abdi Munzir Ansaari ؓ

(9) Yazeed bin Haaris Ansaari ؓ

(10) 'Umair bin Hamaam Ansaari ؓ

It is reported from Hadhrat Anas ؓ that on the day of Badr, Rasulullah ﷺ said: "O People! Rise for the Jannah whose breadth is as extensive as the expanse of the earth and sky." To this 'Umair ؓ remarked: "Bakh! Bakh! (Wow! Wow!)" Rasulullah ﷺ asked: "'Umair! What drove you to utter Bakh!

Bakh!" 'Umair رضى الله عنه replied: "O Rasulullah! Nothing but the earnest desire to be counted amongst the inhabitants of Jannah had driven me to utter this." Rasulullah صلى الله عليه وسلم declared: "Undoubtedly, you are of the inhabitants of Jannah." He then took out a few dates and began eating them when suddenly he cast them aside and said: "If I am to occupy myself in consuming these dates, life would then be too long." Casting these dates aside, he leaped into the thick of battle and continued fighting until he was martyred.

According to Ibn Ishaaq's narration, 'Umair رضى الله عنه clutched a sword in his hand whilst the following words of poetry were streaming forth from his tongue:

ركضا الى الله بغير زاد   الا التقى وعمل المعاد

"Hasten to Allah without any provision but the provision of Taqwa (Allah-consciousness) and deeds for the hereafter.

والصبر فى الله على الجهاد

And ensure you take with you in the path of Allah the provision of patience and fortitude.

وكل زاد عرضة النفاد   غير التقى والبر والرشاد

Every provision will come to an end except the provision of Taqwa, righteousness and virtue."

(11) Raaf'i bin Mu'allaa Ansaari رضى الله عنه

(12) Haarisah bin Suraaqah Ansaari رضى الله عنه

Haarisah bin Suraaqah bin Haaris Ansaari رضى الله عنه was a Sahaabi and the son of a Sahaabi. He was a martyr and the son of a martyr. The son, Hadhrat Haarisah رضى الله عنه was martyred in the battle of Badr whilst his father, Hadhrat Suraaqah رضى الله عنه was martyred in the battle of Hunain.

Hadhrat Anas رضى الله عنه reports that Haarisah was martyred in Badr whilst he was a very young man. When Rasulullah صلى الله عليه وسلم returned from the battle of Badr, his mother Rubayy'i bint Nadr رضى الله عنها appeared before Rasulullah صلى الله عليه وسلم and submitted: "O Rasulullah! You are well aware how profound my love for my son Haarisah was. So if he is in Jannah I will exercise patience and hope for reward from Allah. However, if it is something else, you will see what I will do. (I will mourn him a great deal and weep profusely in sorrow and pain.)" Rasulullah صلى الله عليه وسلم remarked: "He is favoured with not one but many Jannahs. And most certainly, he is dwelling in Jannatul-Firdaus (the highest rank of Jannah)."

(13) 'Awf bin Haaris Ansaari رضى الله عنه

(14) Mu'awwiz bin Haaris Ansaari رضى الله عنه

Both of them are brothers. Their mother was 'Afraa رضى الله عنها. The incident relating to the martyrdom of 'Awf bin Haaris رضى الله عنه has already been mentioned previously.

'Abdullah bin Mas'ood رضى الله عنه narrates that the companions of Rasulullah ﷺ who were martyred in the battle of Badr were blessed with the spectacle of the noor (light) of Allah Ta'ala. He enquired from them: "O My servants! What do you wish for?" The Sahaabah رضى الله عنهم replied: "O Almighty! Are there any bounties greater than the bounties of Jannah that You had blessed us with?" Allah Ta'ala again asked: "Tell Me, what do you wish for?" The fourth time when Allah Ta'ala repeated the question, the Sahaabah رضى الله عنهم submitted: "O Allah! We yearn for our souls to be returned to our physical bodies so that we may be slain in Your path once again."

Prisoners of Badr

As established previously on the basis of authentic Ahaadith, in the battle of Badr, seventy disbelievers were killed and seventy were captured as prisoners.

(1) 'Abbaas bin 'Abdul-Muttalib
He was the respected uncle (father's brother) of Rasulullah ﷺ. He was merely two years elder than Rasulullah ﷺ. He openly declared his Islam just before the conquest of Makkah.

(2) Aqil bin Abu Taalib
He was Rasulullah's ﷺ cousin (father's brother's son). He embraced Islam around the time of the treaty of Hudaybiyyah.

Hadhrat Aqil رضى الله عنه was ten years elder than Hadhrat Ja'far رضى الله عنه. Similarly, Hadhrat Ja'far رضى الله عنه was also ten years elder than Hadhrat Ali رضى الله عنه. Abu Taalib's eldest son, Taalib (after whom he acquired his title) was also ten years elder than Hadhrat Aqil رضى الله عنه. However, the eldest son, Taalib was deprived of the bounty of Islam. Three of these four brothers were blessed with Islam; Aqil, Ja'far and Ali رضى الله عنهم.

(3) Nawfal bin Haaris رضى الله عنه
The story of his embracing Islam has been cited previously. It is said that he embraced Islam in the year the battle of Khandaq (trench) took place. In other words, he embraced Islam in 5 A.H.

Chapter 14

Other Expeditions

Assassination of 'Asma, the Jewess – 26th Ramadhaan 2 A.H.

'Asma was a Jewess who maliciously recited poetry in denigration of the honour of Rasulullah ﷺ. She would persistently search for a variety of ways to cause harm to Rasulullah ﷺ. She would endeavour to instil feelings of revulsion in the hearts of people against Rasulullah ﷺ and Islam. Rasulullah ﷺ had not even returned from Badr when she recited some derogatory poetry once again. The moment 'Umair bin 'Adi ؓ heard these offensive lines, he was overwhelmed with rage and vowed: "By the grace of Allah, if Rasulullah ﷺ returns safe and sound from the battle of Badr, I will kill her."

When Rasulullah ﷺ returned triumphant and safe from the battle of Badr, 'Umair ؓ set out at night wielding a sword. When he reached her house, he searched for her with his hand, as he was blind. There were some children around her whom he drove away. He then positioned his sword on her chest and plunged it with such force that it penetrated all the way through and emerged from her back.

As he fulfilled this vow, he returned and performed his Fajr Salaah with Rasulullah ﷺ and informed him about the incident. He then submitted: "O Rasulullah! Will I be taken to task for what I did?" Rasulullah ﷺ replied: "This is something over which not even two goats would butt one another." In other words, this is something over which there is virtually no difference of opinion. Let alone humans, even animals would have no reservations about this.

This despicable woman would dispose of her soiled sanitary pads right within the sacred confines of the Masjid.

In short, Rasulullah ﷺ was exceptionally delighted at 'Umair's ؓ accomplishment and addressing the Sahaabah ؓ, he said:

اذا احببتم ان تنظروا الى رجل نصر الله ورسوله بالغيب فانظروا الى عمير بن عدى

"If you wish to lay your eyes on a man who assisted Allah and His Rasool secretly, then cast your gaze upon 'Umair bin 'Adi."

Hadhrat 'Umar ؓ remarked: "Just look at this blind man who stealthily set out in the obedience of Allah." Upon this Rasulullah ﷺ commented: "Do not call him blind. This man is sighted." In other words, he may be physically blind but he possesses profound insight of the heart.

This woman was slain on the twenty-fifth of Ramadhaan.

Hadhrat Jaabir ؓ narrates that 'Umair ؓ fell ill. Rasulullah ﷺ enjoined:

انطلقوا بنا الى البصير الذى فى بنى واقف، نعوده

"Come, let us go and visit the sighted man who is in Banu Waaqif."

Hafiz 'Iraaqi رحمه الله sums up in poetic words:

فَبَعْثُهُ عُمَيرا الخَطْمِيّا لِقَتْلِ عصما هَجّتِ النبيّا

"Umair ؓ was despatched to assassinate 'Asma who vilified Rasulullah ﷺ."

Battle of Qarqaratul-Kudr

On his return from the battle of Badr, at the beginning of the month of Shawwaal, when Rasulullah ﷺ heard of the build up of the Sulaim and Ghitfaan forces, he set out with two hundred men. When Rasulullah ﷺ landed at the springs of Kudr, he was informed that the enemies of Islam had already dispersed when they got news of Rasulullah ﷺ. After staying over for three days, Rasulullah ﷺ returned without engaging the enemy in combat.

According to some narrations, Rasulullah ﷺ despatched a small contingent in pursuit of the enemy and they returned with a booty of five hundred camels.

For the rest of Shawwaal and Zul-Q'adah, Rasulullah ﷺ stayed in Madinah and during this period, the captives of Badr were set free after paying their ransom.

Assassination of Abu 'Afak, the Jew

Within the same month of Shawwaal, Rasulullah ﷺ charged Saalim bin 'Umair ؓ with the killing of Abu 'Afak.

By religion Abu 'Afak was a Jew. He was an extremely old man. He was one hundred and twenty years old. He would often recite poetry in defamation of Rasulullah ﷺ and he would incite hostility and aggression against Rasulullah ﷺ. However, when his audacious impudence went beyond the extremes, Rasulullah ﷺ enquired from the Sahaabah ؓ: "Who (will stand in preservation of my honour) against this evil man?"

Upon this, Saalim bin 'Umair ؓ remarked: "O Rasulullah ﷺ! I have already sworn an oath that either I would kill Abu 'Afak or I would die (in the process)." Clutching his sword, he set out for Abu 'Afak. It was a hot summer's night and Abu 'Afak was fast asleep, dead to the world. As Saalim ؓ appeared before his sleeping form, he placed his sword on his liver and drove it in with such force that the sword went all the way through the bed. This brazen enemy of Allah uttered a shriek and people dashed to his assistance but he was over and done with.

Campaign of Qaynuqaa - Saturday 15th of Shawwaal 2 A.H.

The Banu Qaynuqaa were the kinsfolk of 'Abdullah bin Salaam ؓ. (They were Jews). They were incredibly daring and an extremely courageous people. On Saturday, the fifteenth or sixteenth of Shawwaal, Rasulullah ﷺ went into their market place, assembled them in one area and addressed them saying:

يا معشر يهود احذروا من الله مثل ما نزل بقريش من النقمة
واسلموا فانكم قد عرفتم انى نبى مرسل تجدون ذلك فى كتابكم
وعهد الله اليكم

"O Jewish people! Fear from Allah a doom similar to the punishment that had befallen the Quraysh. Embrace Islam because you very well know that I am a true Messenger of Allah. You will find this written in your book (the Tourah) and Allah has taken a covenant from you about this."

The moment the Jews heard this, their fury knew no bounds and they indignantly replied: "Do not be deceived by your victory over an inexperienced and ignorant enemy (the Quraysh). By Allah! If you had to fight us, you will realise that we are men in the true sense of the word." Upon this, Allah Ta'ala revealed the following verse:

$$\text{قَدْ كَانَ لَكُمْ اٰيَةٌ فِىْ فِئَتَيْنِ الْتَقَتَا ۖ فِئَةٌ تُقَاتِلُ فِىْ سَبِيْلِ اللّٰهِ وَاُخْرٰى كَافِرَةٌ يَّرَوْنَهُمْ مِّثْلَيْهِمْ رَاْىَ الْعَيْنِ ۚ وَاللّٰهُ يُؤَيِّدُ بِنَصْرِهٖ مَنْ يَّشَآءُ ۗ اِنَّ فِىْ ذٰلِكَ لَعِبْرَةً لِّاُولِى الْاَبْصَارِ ﴿١٣﴾}$$

"Verily there is a sign for you (O Jews!) in those two groups who met in combat; one group was fighting in the path of Allah whilst the other was made up of the disbelievers. They (the Muslims) saw them (the disbelievers) with their own eyes twice their number. And Allah supports with His assistance whom He wills. Surely in this is a lesson for those who have insight." [Surah Aal-'Imraan verse 13]

When Rasulullah ﷺ migrated to Madinah Munawwarah, he formed a pact with the Jewish tribes of Banu Qaynuqaa, Banu Qurayzah and Banu Nazeer. The peace accord with these Jewish tribes commissioned all parties to refrain from waging war against the Muslims and to refrain from assisting their enemies. However, the Banu Qaynuqaa were the first to break this accord. They responded to Rasulullah's ﷺ sermon with unreserved rudeness and braced themselves for war against the Muslims.

This tribe was living on the outskirts of Madinah. Appointing Abu Lubaabah bin 'Abul-Munzir Ansaari as his representative in Madinah, Rasulullah ﷺ set out for the Banu Qaynuqaa. When they learnt of the Muslim army approaching, they took refuge in one of their forts and sealed the doorway. From the fifteenth of Shawwaal up to the first of Zul-Q'adah, Rasulullah ﷺ laid siege to the fort. Constrained by the circumstances, they were eventually forced to surrender. Rasulullah ﷺ then ordered their hands to be tied to their backs.

Owing to the lamenting pleas of the chief of the hypocrites, 'Abdullah bin Ubayy bin Salool, Rasulullah ﷺ spared their lives but after first confiscating their property, Rasulullah ﷺ condemned them to a life of banishment.

Rasulullah ﷺ then returned with their property to Madinah where he distributed four fifths of the booty amongst the combatants and the remaining one fifth he kept for himself. After Badr, this was the first khums (one fifth) that Rasulullah ﷺ took with his own blessed hands.

'Ubaadah bin Saamit ؓ says: "I had entered into a treaty of alliance with the Banu Qaynuqaa but when I observed their wicked behaviour and treacherous nature, I broke off with them and publicly declared my detachment and revulsion against them."

'Ubaadah bin Saamit ؓ submitted before Rasulullah ﷺ:

$$\text{يا رسول الله اتبرأ الى الله والى رسوله وأتولى الله و رسوله والمؤمنين وابرأ من حلف الكفار و ولايتهم}$$

"O Rasulullah! I have declared my detachment from your enemy and proclaim my association with Allah, His Rasool and the believers. I affirm my disengagement from the alliance of the kuffaar and their friendship."

Campaign of Saweeq – 5th Zul-Hijjah 2 A.H.

After the Battle of Badr, when the routed army of the Mushrikeen returned to Makkah utterly defeated, Abu Sufyaan bin Harb swore an oath that he will never take a clean bath until he launched an attack on Madinah.

Subsequently, in order to discharge this oath, at the beginning of Zul-Hijjah, he set out with two hundred mounted men towards the direction of Madinah. When they reached a place called 'Uraid, just three miles before Madinah, they crept into a date orchard where two people were busy cultivating the land. One was an Ansaari whilst the other was a labourer. He killed both of them and set fire to a few trees on the notion that he was now absolved of his oath. He then promptly fled from the area.

When Rasulullah ﷺ learnt of this, he set out in pursuit of Abu Sufyaan with two hundred Muhaajireen and Ansaar on Sunday the fifth of Zul-Hijjah. However, they failed to apprehend anyone because Abu Sufyaan and his people had long since departed. Whilst fleeing, in order to lighten their burden, they dumped their bags of Saweeq (crushed wheat flavoured with ghee). The pursuing Muslims army managed to salvage these bags, hence the name of this campaign, the campaign of Saweeq.

Eidul-Adhaa

On the ninth of Zul-Hijjah, Rasulullah ﷺ returned from the campaign of Saweeq and on the tenth of Zul-Hijjah, he performed two Rakaats of Eid Salaah. He then sacrificed two sheep and instructed the Muslims to perform Qurbaani as well. This was the first Eidul-Adhaa of the Muslims.

Nikah of Hadhrat Faatimah ﷺ

In the same year Rasulullah ﷺ got his youngest daughter, Hadhrat Faatimah ﷺ, married to Hadhrat Ali ﷺ.

First Hadhrat Abu Bakr ﷺ and then Hadhrat 'Umar ﷺ expressed a desire to achieve this auspicious eminence but Rasulullah ﷺ remained silent on both occasions. According to another narration, Rasulullah ﷺ replied: "I am awaiting the divine commandment of Allah Ta'ala in this regard." Thereafter, Hadhrat Abu Bakr ﷺ and Hadhrat 'Umar ﷺ both advised Hadhrat Ali ﷺ to submit a proposal for the hand of Hadhrat Faatimah ﷺ.

On the basis of this sincere and whole-hearted advice, Hadhrat Ali ﷺ appeared before Rasulullah ﷺ and put forward this request. As per divine revelation, Rasulullah ﷺ accepted the proposal of Hadhrat Ali ﷺ.

Hadhrat Ali ﷺ narrates: "When I aimed to present my marriage proposal, I reflected: 'By Allah! I have nothing whereas expenses are certain to arise on the occasion of marriage.' However, Rasulullah's ﷺ benevolence, good character and compassion boosted my courage to put this proposal before him.

Rasulullah ﷺ asked me: "Do you possess anything that you may pay as Mehr?" When I replied in the negative, Rasulullah ﷺ enquired: "Where is the body armour you received in the battle of Badr?" I replied: "I still have it with me." Rasulullah ﷺ said: "Very well. You may offer that to Faatimah as her Mehr."

Hadhrat Ali ﷺ sold the body armour to Hadhrat 'Usmaan ﷺ for 480 Dirhams. When Hadhrat Ali ﷺ placed these Dirhams before Rasulullah ﷺ, he advised: "Arrange for some scent and clothing from this money."

The following negligible goods made up the Jahez (dowry) which Rasulullah ﷺ gave to his daughter Hadhrat Faatimah ﷺ: a quilt, a leather mattress filled with the bark of a tree instead of cotton padding, two hand-mills, a water-skin and two earthenware pots.

As the time for the consummation of the marriage approached, Rasulullah ﷺ requested Hadhrat Ali ﷺ to arrange a house. Hadhrat Ali ﷺ arranged for a house on rent and consummated his marriage therein. Hadhrat Faatimah ﷺ requested him to ask Haarisah bin N'umaan ﷺ for his house but Hadhrat Ali ﷺ felt ashamed to make such a request. When Haarisah bin Nu'maan ﷺ somehow learnt of this request, he went to Rasulullah ﷺ and pleaded: "O Rasulullah! I swear by Allah that whatever you take from me will be more cherished than what you do not take from me." Rasulullah ﷺ replied: "You have spoken the truth. May Allah bless you." Haarisah ﷺ then shifted to another house and offered this house to Hadhrat Ali ﷺ and Hadhrat Faatimah ﷺ.

Campaign of Ghitfaan 3 A.H. - Also referred to as the campaign of Anmaar and the campaign of Zu Amar

On his return from the campaign of Saweeq, Rasulullah ﷺ spent the rest of Zul-Hijjah in Madinah. During this period, Rasulullah ﷺ learnt that the Banu S'alabah and Banu Mahaarib (both subdivisions of the Ghitfaan tribe) were assembling in Najd with the express intention of plundering the surrounding areas of Madinah. They were under the command of D'asoor Ghitfaani.

Intending to launch an attack on the Ghitfaan tribe, Rasulullah ﷺ set out from Madinah in the company of four hundred and fifty Sahaabah ؓ in the month of Muharram 3 A.H. after appointing Hadhrat 'Usmaan ؓ as his representative in Madinah.

The moment the Ghitfaan tribe got wind of Rasulullah's ﷺ approach, they took flight and dispersed into the mountains. The Sahaabah ؓ managed to apprehend just one member of the Banu S'alabah tribe. He was brought before Rasulullah ﷺ who invited him towards Islam and he accepted. Rasulullah ﷺ spent the whole month of Safar there but not a single soul dared to attack him. Without engaging the enemy in battle, Rasulullah ﷺ then returned to Madinah in Rabi'ul-Awwal.

During the course of this journey, a heavy downpour left Rasulullah ﷺ and the Sahaabah ؓ drenched. Rasulullah ﷺ hung his clothes on a nearby tree to dry and he lay down to rest under the same tree. The Bedouins of the area continued keeping Rasulullah ﷺ in sight. They challenged their commander D'asoor, a gallant young man, by saying: "Muhammad (ﷺ) is lying down all alone under that tree and his companions are all scattered about. Why do you not go and finish him off?"

Grasping an exceptionally sharp sword, D'asoor strode up to Rasulullah ﷺ and wielding the naked sword before him, D'asoor arrogantly demanded: "O Muhammad! Tell me! Who will save you from my sword today?" Rasulullah ﷺ calmly responded: "Allah will." Rasulullah ﷺ barely uttered this statement when Jibraa'eel ؑ dealt D'asoor a severe punch to his chest causing his sword to fly out of his hand.

Rasulullah ﷺ retrieved the sword and asked: "Now tell me, who will save you from my sword?" D'asoor replied: "Nobody."

D'asoor embraced Islam and recited the Kalimah of Shahaadah. (I bear witness that there is none worthy of worship besides Allah and that Muhammad is the messenger of Allah.) D'asoor also pledged not to assemble forces of combat against Rasulullah ﷺ.

Rasulullah ﷺ handed his sword back to him. As D'asoor left the company of Rasulullah ﷺ, he took a few steps and returned pronouncing: "By Allah! You are far better than I am."

When D'asoor returned to his people, they chided him saying: "What is the problem? What happened about the mission you set out for?" He recounted the extraordinary incident to them. He also mentioned: "Out of the blue, I was struck by an unseen fist with such incredible force that I was thrown flat on my back. Falling in this manner convinced me to believe that only an angel could have delivered a punch like that. That is why I embraced Islam and I proclaimed the prophethood of Rasulullah ﷺ." From then on, D'asoor embarked on a mission to invite his people towards Islam.

In reference to this incident, the following verse was revealed:

$$\text{يَاأَيُّهَا الَّذِينَ آمَنُوا اذْكُرُوا نِعْمَتَ اللّٰهِ عَلَيْكُمْ إِذْ هَمَّ قَوْمٌ أَنْ يَبْسُطُوا إِلَيْكُمْ أَيْدِيَهُمْ فَكَفَّ أَيْدِيَهُمْ عَنْكُمْ}$$

"O you who believe! Remember the favour of Allah over you when some people planned to stretch their hands against you but Allah held back their hands from you." [Surah Maa'idah verse 11]

Campaign of Buhraan

On his return from the campaign of Ghitfaan, Rasulullah ﷺ spent the rest of Rabi'ul-Awwal in Madinah. During the month of Rabi'us-Saani, he got word that the Banu Sulaim are amassing against Islam in a place called Buhraan, which was regarded as the mine of Najd. On hearing about this, Rasulullah ﷺ set out in the company of three hundred Sahaabah ؓ towards Buhraan and he appointed 'Abdullah ibn Ummi Maktoom ؓ as his representative in Madinah.

The moment the Banu Sulaim heard of Rasulullah's ﷺ imminent arrival, they promptly dispersed. Without engaging in actual combat, Rasulullah ﷺ returned to Madinah.

Assassination of K'ab bin Ashraf

When news of the Muslims' victory in Badr filtered through to Madinah, K'ab bin Ashraf the Jew was overwhelmed by profound anguish and lamented: "If the news that the noble chieftains of Makkah have been killed turns out to be true then the interior of the earth is far superior than its exterior." In other words, it is better to die than to face the humiliation of such a defeat.

When he verified the credibility of this news, he instantly set out for Makkah to offer solace to the families of the victims of Badr. In praise of the victims of Badr, he composed poetic eulogies, which he would frequently recite before the Makkans. Whilst reciting, he himself would weep and bring his listeners to tears as well. During his visit in Makkah, he would deliver fiery speeches inciting the Quraysh to take up arms once more against Rasulullah ﷺ. One day, he gathered all the Quraysh leaders in the Haram and clinging onto the curtains of the K'abah, all of them swore an oath to wage battle against the Muslims. After a few more days in Makkah, he returned to Madinah where he composed flirtatious love-poems against the Muslim women.

K'ab bin Maalik رضي الله عنه narrates: "K'ab bin Ashraf was a poet of great repute. He would compose mocking couplets to dishonour Rasulullah ﷺ. He was relentless in his attempts to incite the disbelievers of Makkah to launch an attack against Rasulullah ﷺ. He was perpetually involved in inflicting much anguish against the Muslims.

Rasulullah ﷺ continued advising the Muslims to adopt patience and forbearance in the face of such distress but when this man persisted in his insidious mischief, Rasulullah ﷺ commanded that he be put to death."

According to another narration, K'ab bin Ashraf once called Rasulullah ﷺ on the pretext of inviting him to meals. Meanwhile, he positioned a few men in the house to assassinate Rasulullah ﷺ the moment he entered. Rasulullah ﷺ barely sat down when Jibraa'eel عليه السلام apprised him of these people's malicious intentions. Rasulullah ﷺ immediately moved out of there under the shade of Jibraa'eel's عليه السلام wings and on his return, he issued an edict authorising the assassination of K'ab bin Ashraf.

Rasulullah ﷺ said: "Which of you is willing to kill K'ab bin Ashraf? He has caused lots of harm (disobedience) to Allah and His Rasool." On hearing this appeal, Muhammad bin Maslamah رضي الله عنه stood up and said: "O Rasulullah! Do you want him put to death?" When Rasulullah ﷺ replied in the affirmative, Muhammad bin Maslamah رضي الله عنه asked: "O Rasulullah! Would you permit me to make certain (ambiguous) statements that would bring delight to K'ab bin Ashraf?" Rasulullah ﷺ replied: "Yes, you are permitted."

Subsequently, Muhammad bin Maslamah رضي الله عنه went to visit K'ab and during the course of their conversation, Muhammad bin Maslamah said: "This man (i.e. Rasulullah ﷺ) demands charity and Zakaat from us (to distribute it amongst the poor and destitute). Verily, this man has put us into distress. (Undoubtedly, this is gruelling on those who are insatiably greedy but for those who are genuinely sincere, for them the giving of charity and assisting the poor and destitute is exceptionally pleasing. In fact, not spending in the path of Allah is distressing to them.)"

"I turned up before you," continued Muhammad bin Maslamah رضي الله عنه "to request a loan from you." K'ab replied: "What's the hurry? Let's wait and see. By Allah! You will surely get fed up with him in due course." Muhammad bin Maslamah رضي الله عنه responded: "Now that we have become his adherents, we cannot just abandon him. We are now waiting for the outcome of events." (In his heart he meant the inevitable outcome of the triumph of Allah and His Rasool and the crushing defeat of the enemy, in which there was absolutely no doubt.)

Muhammad bin Maslamah رضي الله عنه continued: "At this moment, why do you not lend us some grain?" K'ab replied: "Agreed, but you will have to lodge some security against the loan." They (Muhammad bin Maslamah and his companions) asked: "What would you prefer us to lodge as security against the loan?" He replied: "Why don't you lodge your womenfolk as collateral?" They responded: "How can we pledge our womenfolk as collateral? Firstly, our Ghayrat (self respect) will not tolerate this and secondly, you are a handsome and graceful young man." K'ab said: "All right, then why don't you pawn your children against this loan?" They replied: "This will then be a lifelong source of indignity and shame for these children. People would, in time to come, mock them and taunt them by saying: 'You are the children who were pawned for a few bushels of grain.' However, we would be willing to pledge our weapons as security against this loan."

They further added: "You are well aware of how essential our weapons are to us. However, we are willing to pawn our arms against the loan. As for pawning our wives and children, this is definitely out of the question." K'ab agreed to this proposal and committed them to return the same night with the weapons and to take delivery of the grain.

As per the arrangements, these people returned the same night and called out to him. As K'ab prepared to descend from his fortress, his wife anxiously asked: "Where are you off to at this moment?" "There is absolutely nothing to worry about," replied K'ab. "It is just Muhammad bin Maslamah and my milk-brother Abu Naa'ilah." With a hunch of foreboding, his wife said: "I perceive the sound of blood dripping from this man's voice." K'ab replied: "When a noble man is summoned at night, he should respond even if he is summoned to hurl a spear."

In the interim, Muhammad bin Maslamah رضى الله عنه had outlined his strategy to his companions. He explained to them: "When K'ab appears, I will attempt to smell the fragrance of his hair. When you notice his hair firmly gripped by my hands, quickly finish him off."

When K'ab appeared before them, he was radiating a most pleasant fragrance. Head to toe, he was emitting a heady scent. Muhammad bin Maslamah exclaimed: "I have never come across such a pleasant fragrance before this." To this K'ab commented: "I have with me the most beautiful woman of Arabia and she is a most fragrant woman." Muhammad bin Maslamah رضى الله عنه asked: "May I have an opportunity to smell your fragrant head?" K'ab replied: "Sure! You may do so." Muhammad bin Maslamah رضى الله عنه stepped forth and sniffed him and made his companions also smell his fragrance. A little while later, Muhammad رضى الله عنه asked: "Will you permit me to inhale your fragrance once again?" "Surely!" replied K'ab, "by all means you may do so." Muhammad bin Maslamah رضى الله عنه stood up and as he was busy inhaling the scent of his head, he got hold of K'ab's hair and clutching firmly onto it, he indicated to his companions. They promptly stepped forward and beheaded him. In the blink of an eye, he was no more.

In the latter part of the night, they returned to Rasulullah ﷺ, who, the instant he laid eyes on them, remarked: "These faces have triumphed." To this they replied: "And your face as well, O Rasulullah!"

They then placed K'ab bin Ashraf's head before Rasulullah ﷺ. Rasulullah ﷺ said Alhamdulillah! and expressed his profound gratitude before Allah Ta'ala.

When the Jews heard of the assassination of K'ab bin Ashraf, they were left awestruck and were pitched into a state of utter panic. The next morning, a group of Jews appeared before Rasulullah ﷺ and complained about their leader being slain by the Muslims. Rasulullah ﷺ responded: "He was guilty of causing endless misery to the Muslims and he would frequently incite others to wage war against us." This reply left them expressly dumbfounded and they were unable to respond. Rasulullah ﷺ then initiated them into signing a formal agreement wherein they pledged not to engage in such subversive activities.

Islam of Huwayyisah bin Mas'ood ﷜

Following the assassination of K'ab bin Ashraf the Jew, Rasulullah ﷺ enjoined the Sahaabah ﷢ to eliminate such evil Jews wherever they find them. Consequently, Huwayyisah bin Mas'ood's younger brother Muhayyisah bin Mas'ood killed Ibn Sabinah, a merchant Jew who conducted business with Huwayyisah, Muhayyisah and some other inhabitants of Madinah.

Huwayyisah had not yet embraced Islam whilst Muhayyisah was a Muslim. Since Huwayyisah was the elder brother, he caught hold of his younger sibling Muhayyisah, and whilst whacking him bellowed: "O enemy of Allah! How could you have killed him? By Allah, you benefitted tremendously from his wealth and yet you kill him!"

To this Muhayyisah replied:

والله لقد امرنى بقتله من لو امرنى بقتلك لضربت عنقك

"By Allah! Such a personality has charged me to kill him that if he asked me to kill you, I would not hesitate in chopping your head off."

Taken aback, Huwayyisah asked:

الله لو امرك محمد بقتلى لقتلتنى

"What? If Muhammad asked you to kill me, would you kill me?"

Muhayyisah replied:

نعم والله لو امرنى بضرب عنقك لضربتها

"Of course! By Allah! If Muhammad instructs me to behead you I will not hesitate to do so."

In other words, in the face of Rasulullah's ﷺ instruction, you being my brother would not have crossed my mind in the least.

Downright shocked on hearing this, Huwayyisah spontaneously exclaimed: "By Allah, this is really the true religion that penetrates the hearts with such intense fervour and permeates every vein of the body with such intensity."

Thereafter Huwayyisah appeared before Rasulullah ﷺ and embraced Islam with a sincere heart.

Sariyyah of Zaid bin Haarisah رضي الله عنه - 3 A.H.

Following the victory of the Muslims at Badr, the Quraysh of Makkah were left so terrified and awestruck of the Muslims that out of fear of harassment, they stopped using their ancient trade routes altogether. Instead of using the well-established route that took them towards Syria, they started using the road that led towards Iraq, and they employed Furaat bin Hayyaan 'Ajali as their guide. Once, a well-laden trade caravan left Makkah towards the Iraq road. Abu Sufyaan bin Harb, Safwaan bin Umayyah, Huwaytib bin 'Abdul-'Uzza and 'Abdullah bin Abi Rabi'ah were also with this caravan. (During the conquest of Makkah, all four of them embraced Islam.)

When Rasulullah ﷺ heard of this caravan, he despatched a group of one hundred Sahaabah رضي الله عنهم under the command of Zaid bin Haarisah رضي الله عنه. They attacked the caravan and although they were successful in appropriating the goods, the noblemen and other members of the caravan managed to flee. Only Furaat bin Hayyaan was captured as a prisoner and brought back with them. However, he embraced Islam when he reached Madinah.

The abundance of the booty can be gauged from the khums (one fifth allocated to Rasulullah ﷺ and the Baitul-Maal) which amounted to twenty thousand dirhams. From this, we deduce that the total booty amounted to one hundred thousand dirhams.

Assassination of Abu Raaf'i - Jumaadath-Thaani 3 A.H.

Abu Raaf'i was a prominent Jew merchant. Abu Raaf'i was his title. His name was 'Abdullah bin Abil-Huqaiq. He was also known as Sallaam bin Abil-Huqaiq. He lived in a fortress in Khaybar.

He was a bitter enemy of Rasulullah ﷺ and he devised varied methods of harassing Rasulullah ﷺ. He was a staunch supporter and collaborator of K'ab bin Ashraf. This was the same vile man who incited the Quraysh of Makkah against the Muslims in the battle of Ahzaab. He provided great financial assistance to the Quraysh of Makkah. He was forever willing to spend his wealth in pursuit of his aggressive hostility against Rasulullah ﷺ and the Muslims.

The assassins of K'ab bin Ashraf were Muhammad bin Maslamah رضي الله عنه and his companions. Since all of them hailed from the Aws tribe, the people of the Khazraj reasoned that the people of the Aws tribe acquired the honour of eliminating a bitter enemy and a blasphemous rascal like K'ab bin Ashraf, so why should they not get rid of the other blasphemous and insolent instigator, Abu Raaf'i and thereby also acquire this privilege of honour in both the worlds?

Subsequently, they appeared before Rasulullah صلى الله عليه وسلم and requested permission to eliminate Abu Raaf'i from this world. Rasulullah صلى الله عليه وسلم sanctioned his assassination.

Rasulullah صلى الله عليه وسلم despatched the following Sahaabah رضي الله عنهم to kill Abu Raaf'i: 'Abdullah bin 'Atik, Mas'ood bin Sinaan, 'Abdullah bin Unais, Abu Qataadah Haaris bin Rib'i and Khuzaa'i bin Aswad and he appointed 'Abdullah bin 'Atik as their Ameer (leader). Before they set out, Rasulullah صلى الله عليه وسلم stressed upon them not to kill a woman or child.

Towards the middle of Jumaadal-Ukhraa, in 3 A.H., 'Abdullah bin 'Atik set out for Khaybar in the company of his companions.

This group of Sahaabah رضي الله عنهم landed in Khaybar after sunset when the people had returned home with their animals. As the fortress of Abu Raaf'i drew closer, 'Abdullah bin 'Atik رضي الله عنه told his companions: "Why don't all of you wait here. I will hatch a plan to penetrate the fortress." When he drew close to the door of the fortress, he covered himself up and sat down as though relieving himself. The doorkeeper, imagining him to be one of their people, called out: "O servant of Allah! If you are coming inside, you better come quickly because I am about to shut the door."

'Abdullah bin 'Atik رضي الله عنه continues: "Without further ado, I slipped in and hid in a corner. Abu Raaf'i lived on the upper floor.

Every night they would be entertained with story telling. When the session for that night ended, the occupants of the fortress returned to their respective homes and the doorkeeper locked all the doors and hung the ring of keys on a peg.

When I determined that all of them had fallen asleep, I crept out of my hiding place, got hold of the keys hanging on the peg and went along opening the doors leading to the upper floor. As I passed through each door, I would lock it from the inside so that even if people got wind of my presence, I will still be able to accomplish my mission.

As I reached the upper floor, it was extremely dark and Abu Raaf'i was fast asleep with his wife and children. I had no idea whatsoever where exactly he was sleeping. So I called out softly: "Abu Raaf'i! Abu Raaf'i!" He asked: "Who's there!" Full of apprehension, I lunged with my sword in the direction of the sound but to no avail. Abu Raaf'i let out a shriek of terror. A little while later, I altered my voice and in a sympathetic tone asked: "Abu Raaf'i, what sound is that? What is the problem?" In a terrified voice he replied: "Someone attacked me with a sword just now." He barely uttered this when I attacked him a second time that left him seriously wounded. I then placed the tip of the sword on his stomach and pressed it down with such force that it reached his spine. When I was convinced that this would finish him off, I turned around the way I had come, opening each door as I went along. As I was climbing down the stairs, I thought that I was close to the ground and misjudged the stairs. I fell down breaking my shinbone in the process. It was a moonlit night. I unwound my turban and wrapped it securely around my calf. As I reached my companions, I urged them to set off and convey the good news to Rasulullah ﷺ and added: 'I will wait here until I hear some announcement of his assassination.'

As dawn broke out with the roosters crowing, a caller mounted the rampart of the fortress and made a public announcement of his death. Only then did I set forth and join my friends. I appealed to them: 'Come on, faster. Allah Ta'ala has eliminated Abu Raaf'i.'

From there we proceeded straight to Rasulullah ﷺ and shared the glad tidings with him. I then went on to describe the full details of this mission. Rasulullah ﷺ asked me to stretch out my leg. When I extended my leg, he rubbed his blessed hand over it. After this, I felt as though nothing had ever afflicted my shin."

Chapter 15

The Battle of Uhud - Shawwaal 3 A.H.

Allah Ta'ala says:

$$\text{وَ إِذْ غَدَوْتَ مِنْ أَهْلِكَ تُبَوِّئُ الْمُؤْمِنِينَ مَقَاعِدَ لِلْقِتَالِ}$$

"And remember when you (O Muhammad!) left your family in the morning organising the believers for battle."

When the Quraysh returned woefully beaten back to Makkah, they discovered that the trade caravan which Abu Sufyaan managed to keep safe by slipping away onto the coastal route, its capital and profit was secure in Daarun-Nadwah. All of them suffered the anguish of the woeful defeat and humiliating thrashing of Badr but those who lost their fathers, brothers, nephews and other close relatives in Badr were particularly overwhelmed with a concentrated fervour. Their hearts were brimming with a raging passion for rapid revenge.

Eventually, Abu Sufyaan bin Harb, 'Abdullah bin Abi Rabi'ah, 'Ikramah bin Abi Jahal, Haaris bin Hishaam, Huwaytib bin 'Abdul-'Uzza, Safwaan bin Umayyah and other leading members of the Quraysh convened a special meeting in which they proposed that the capital amount of the trade caravan which is still held in trust be distributed to the respective shareholders and the entire profit be used in preparation for war against Muhammad (ﷺ). This, they advocated, would settle the score with the Muslims who killed our fathers, brothers, relatives and leaders in Badr. In one voice, all of the attendants of this meeting enthusiastically approved this proposal. Subsequently, the profits of this trade expedition, which amounted to about fifty thousand Dinaars (gold coins) were set aside for this purpose.

In this regard, Allah Ta'ala revealed the following verse:

$$\text{اِنَّ الَّذِيْنَ كَفَرُوْا يُنْفِقُوْنَ اَمْوَالَهُمْ لِيَصُدُّوْا عَنْ سَبِيْلِ اللّٰهِ ۚ فَسَيُنْفِقُوْنَهَا ثُمَّ تَكُوْنُ عَلَيْهِمْ حَسْرَةً ثُمَّ يُغْلَبُوْنَ ۚ}$$

"Verily the disbelievers who spend their wealth to prevent from the path of Allah, they will spend (more) of it and then it will be (a source) of despair against them. Then they will be vanquished." [Surah Anfaal verse 36]

Quraysh Taking the Womenfolk Along

The Quraysh made frantic preparations for this expedition. They also elected to take some women along to sing poems to rouse the courage of the warriors and to kindle the shame of the deserters. Furthermore, out of fear of the women being dishonoured, the warriors were prone to fight with more valour and they would not consider retreating as easily.

The Quraysh despatched messengers to the various tribes inviting them to display their bravery and valour. In this manner, they amassed a force of three thousand people including seven hundred well-armoured warriors. They had two hundred horses, three thousand camels and fifteen women with them. This imposing army set out from Makkah with great splendour and majestic grandeur under the command of Abu Sufyaan on the 5th of Shawwaal 3 A.H.

'Abbaas ؓ Notifies Rasulullah ﷺ of the Quraysh's Plan

Hadhrat 'Abbaas ؓ made a comprehensive note of these details and forwarded it to Rasulullah ﷺ with a high-speed messenger. He also stressed upon him to make sure he gets this message to Rasulullah ﷺ somehow or the other within three days.

Rasulullah ﷺ Consulting the Sahaabah ؓ

The moment Rasulullah ﷺ received this intelligence, he despatched Anas ؓ and Munis ؓ to acquire additional information about the Quraysh. They returned and informed Rasulullah ﷺ that the Qurayshi army was almost upon Madinah. Thereafter, Rasulullah ﷺ sent Habbaab bin Munzir ؓ to determine the number of people in the army. He returned and provided an accurate estimate to Rasulullah ﷺ.

All night long, S'ad bin Mu'aaz ﷺ, Usaid bin Hudhair ﷺ and S'ad bin 'Ubaadah ﷺ were on guard in Masjidun-Nabawi and sentinels were posted all around the town as well.

This occurred on Friday night. The next morning, Rasulullah ﷺ consulted the Sahaabah ﷺ and invited them to express their opinions. The senior Muhaajireen and Ansaar proposed that the Muslims engage the enemy whilst taking refuge within the boundaries of the city. However, the younger Sahaabah ﷺ, who were unable to participate in Badr and were ardently enthusiastic to drink from the cup of martyrdom, suggested that they attack the enemy outside Madinah.

After giving them all a hearing Rasulullah ﷺ said: "I saw a dream wherein I was dressed in a strong impregnable armour whilst a cow was being slaughtered nearby. I interpret this dream to mean that Madinah is this impregnable armour whilst the slaughter of the cow suggests that some of my Sahaabah ﷺ will soon die as martyrs. So, my suggestion is that we engage the enemy whilst taking refuge in Madinah."

Rasulullah ﷺ continues: "I also saw in a dream that as I shook my sword, its tip broke and fell off. I then shook the sword once again and it transformed itself into a better sword than what it was previously. The interpretation of this dream is that the Sahaabah ﷺ are like the sword, which would strike the enemy. Taking the Sahaabah ﷺ into battle is like shaking the sword. When I shook it the first time i.e. in the battle of Uhud, the tip of the sword broke off. In other words, some of the Sahaabah ﷺ will be killed as martyrs. Thereafter the sword was employed in another battle and it turned out to be far better and sharper and was used much more liberally on the enemy."

Since 'Abdullah bin Ubayy, the chief of the hypocrites, was a talented and experienced man in such affairs, he was also consulted. He said: "Past experience will attest to the fact that whenever an enemy attacked Madinah and the residents of Madinah confronted the enemy within the boundaries of the city, the Madanis triumphed. On the contrary, whenever they challenged the enemy on the outside, they were defeated. O Rasulullah! Do not step out of the boundaries of the city. By Allah! Whenever we stepped out of Madinah we were subject to a great deal of suffering at the hands of the enemy and when the enemy launched an attack upon us whilst we took up a defensive position within the boundaries of Madinah, the enemy suffered a dreadful thrashing at our hands. Why don't you blockade and fortify the entire city and if, per chance, the enemy somehow manages to breach this blockade, the men will confront them with swords whilst the women and children will rain down volleys of stones upon them. And if the enemy retreats disappointed without penetrating the city, then the objective is fulfilled."

Nonetheless, some of the senior Sahaabah ﷺ also joined the ranks of the younger Sahaabah ﷺ and insisted even further that the enemy be engaged out of the city of Madinah. They said: "O Rasulullah! We were eagerly expecting such a day and we begged Allah Ta'ala to show us this day soon. Now Allah Ta'ala has given us the chance and the journey is also a short one."

Hadhrat Hamzah رضى الله عنه, S'ad bin 'Ubaadah رضى الله عنه and Nu'maan bin Maalik رضى الله عنه said: "O Rasulullah ﷺ! If we defend ourselves whilst holed up within the boundaries of the Madinah, our enemy will disdainfully regard us as weak cowards in the path of Allah Ta'ala."

Hadhrat Hamzah رضى الله عنه said:

وَالَّذِىْ اَنْزَلَ عَلَيْكَ الْكِتَابَ لا اطعم اليوم طعاما حتى اجادلهم بسيفى خارج المدينة

"I swear by the Being Who has revealed the book upon you! I will not eat until I have engaged the enemy with my sword out of Madinah."

Nu'maan bin Maalik Ansaari رضى الله عنه said:

يا رسُول الله لا تحرمنا الجنة ، فوالذى بعثك بالحق لادخلن الجنة

"O Rasulullah! We beg of you not to deprive us of this opportunity to enter Jannah. I swear by the Being Who has sent you with the truth! I will surely enter Jannah."

Rasulullah ﷺ asked: "On what grounds?" Nu'maan رضى الله عنه replied:

لانى اشهد ان لا اله الا الله وانك رسول الله ولا افر ليوم الزحف

"Owing to the fact that I testify that there is none worthy of worship but Allah and that you are His messenger and also due to the fact that I am not prone to flee from the battlefield."

According to another narration, he said:

لانى احب الله ورسوله

"Owing to the fact that I love Allah and His Rasool."

To this Rasulullah ﷺ remarked: "You have spoken the truth."

When Rasulullah ﷺ noticed the enthusiasm of the devotees of Jannah, i.e. the younger Sahaabah رضى الله عنهم, to fight out of Madinah and when he detected a similar passion for martyrdom from some of the senior Muhaajireen and Ansaar like Hadhrat Hamzah رضى الله عنه and S'ad bin 'Ubaadah رضى الله عنه, then Rasulullah ﷺ also elected to do the same.

This happened on Friday. After the Jumu'ah Salaah, Rasulullah صَلَّى اللَّهُ عَلَيْهِ وَسَلَّمَ delivered a sermon in which he aroused their enthusiasm for Jihaad and charged them to prepare for battle.

The moment the sincere devotees, the dear lovers, the earnest worshippers and those who were keen to meet Allah Ta'ala heard this, it was as though a new spark of life was infused within their souls and they deduced that now the time had finally arrived for their liberation from the 'jail' of this world.

خرم آن روز کزیں منزل ویران بردم

راحت جان طلبم و زپے جانان بردم

Blessed be the day when I am to depart from this desolate place; When I will be at ease in front of my beloved.

Rasulullah's صَلَّى اللَّهُ عَلَيْهِ وَسَلَّمَ Preparation and Donning the Armour

Following the performance of 'Asr Salaah, Rasulullah صَلَّى اللَّهُ عَلَيْهِ وَسَلَّمَ went into his room accompanied by Saahibain (his two closest companions who would accompany him in this world, in the realm of Barzakh, on the field of resurrection, at the fountain of Kawthar and in Jannah – Abu Bakr رَضِيَ اللَّهُ عَنْهُ and 'Umar رَضِيَ اللَّهُ عَنْهُ.)

Rasulullah صَلَّى اللَّهُ عَلَيْهِ وَسَلَّمَ had not emerged from the room as yet when S'ad bin Mu'aaz رَضِيَ اللَّهُ عَنْهُ and Usaid bin Hudhair رَضِيَ اللَّهُ عَنْهُ addressed the people and said: "You compelled Rasulullah صَلَّى اللَّهُ عَلَيْهِ وَسَلَّمَ to go out of the city and engage the enemy whereas divine revelation of Allah Ta'ala continues to descend upon him. Perhaps it would be most appropriate to leave this decision solely up to him." In the meantime, Rasulullah صَلَّى اللَّهُ عَلَيْهِ وَسَلَّمَ emerged clad in two suits of armour. Startled, the Sahaabah رَضِيَ اللَّهُ عَنْهُمْ said: "O Rasulullah صَلَّى اللَّهُ عَلَيْهِ وَسَلَّمَ! We slipped up by insisting on a proposal that was entirely against your blessed opinion. This was undeniably inappropriate and unseemly for us. Please do whatever you deem fit."

To this Rasulullah صَلَّى اللَّهُ عَلَيْهِ وَسَلَّمَ replied: "It is not permissible for a Nabi to arm himself in preparation for war and subsequently remove his armour without engaging the enemy of Allah in war. Now I urge you to take the name of Allah and set forth and do as I command you to do. And remember if you adopt resoluteness and patience, you will certainly enjoy divine assistance and victory."

Rasulullah's صَلَّى اللَّهُ عَلَيْهِ وَسَلَّمَ Departure and Inspection of his Forces

On Friday, the eleventh of Shawwaal, after 'Asr Salaah, Rasulullah صَلَّى اللَّهُ عَلَيْهِ وَسَلَّمَ set out from Madinah in the company of one thousand men. Rasulullah صَلَّى اللَّهُ عَلَيْهِ وَسَلَّمَ was mounted on a horse with S'ad bin Mu'aaz رَضِيَ اللَّهُ عَنْهُ and S'ad bin 'Ubaadah رَضِيَ اللَّهُ عَنْهُ in full armour walking ahead of him whilst the rest of the Muslims were walking to his right and left.

As he reached the outskirts of Madinah at a place called Shaykhayn, Rasulullah ﷺ made a careful inspection of the army. The very young amongst them were sent back home. Some of these boys who were sent back were:

1. Usaamah bin Zaid رضي الله عنه
2. Zaid bin Thaabit رضي الله عنه
3. Abu Sa'eed Khudri رضي الله عنه
4. 'Abdullah bin 'Umar رضي الله عنه
5. Usaid bin Zuhair رضي الله عنه
6. 'Iraabah bin Aws رضي الله عنه
7. Baraa bin 'Aazib رضي الله عنه
8. Zaid bin Arqam رضي الله عنه

Imaam Shaafi'ee رحمه الله says: "Seventeen young Sahaabah رضي الله عنهم, all of whom were fourteen years of age, were presented to Rasulullah ﷺ. Rasulullah ﷺ declared them to be immature and sent them back home. A year later, when they were fifteen, he permitted them to join the ranks of the warriors."

Raafi' bin Khadeej رضي الله عنه was also amongst these youngsters who were presented to Rasulullah ﷺ. He was smart enough to stand on the tips of his feet to appear far taller than his age. Rasulullah ﷺ permitted him to join the army. It is also said that he was a well-skilled archer.

Samurah bin Jundub رضي الله عنه was one of the children who was refused by Rasulullah ﷺ. With an expression of deep sorrow, he lamented before his stepfather, Muri bin Sinaan رضي الله عنه: "O father! Raafi' (who is my contemporary) is permitted to join the army whilst I get left behind? I am far stronger than him and I am certain that I will overpower him in wrestling."

Muri bin Sinaan رضي الله عنه went up to Rasulullah ﷺ and submitted: "O Rasulullah! You allowed Raafi' to participate and sent my son Samurah back whereas Samurah will surely be able to wrestle him to the ground."

Rasulullah ﷺ then called on both the youngsters to match their capabilities in wrestling. When Samurah prevailed, Rasulullah ﷺ permitted him as well.

Young and old, child or adult, every single one of them was intoxicated with the spirit of self-sacrifice. Well before they were actually martyred, they were martyred by the sword of submission.

Chapter 15

Disengagement and Return of the Hypocrites

As Rasulullah ﷺ got closer to Uhud, the chief of the hypocrites, 'Abdullah bin Ubayy bin Salool, who came with a group of three hundred decided to turn back saying: "You disregarded my advice. Why should we now throw ourselves into danger needlessly? This is certainly not a war. If we believed this to be war, we would have unquestionably joined you."

In regards to such people, the following verses were revealed:

$$وَلِيَعْلَمَ الَّذِينَ نَافَقُوا ۚ وَقِيلَ لَهُمْ تَعَالَوْا قَاتِلُوا فِي سَبِيلِ اللَّهِ أَوِ ادْفَعُوا ۖ قَالُوا لَوْ نَعْلَمُ قِتَالًا لَاتَّبَعْنَاكُمْ ۗ هُمْ لِلْكُفْرِ يَوْمَئِذٍ أَقْرَبُ مِنْهُمْ لِلْإِيمَانِ ۚ يَقُولُونَ بِأَفْوَاهِهِمْ مَا لَيْسَ فِي قُلُوبِهِمْ ۗ وَاللَّهُ أَعْلَمُ بِمَا يَكْتُمُونَ$$

"And that He may test the hypocrites, it was said to them: 'Come, fight in the path of Allah or (at least) defend (yourselves)'. They replied: 'Had we known that fighting would take place, we would certainly have followed you.' They were that day, closer to disbelief than to faith, saying with their mouths that which was not in their hearts. And Allah is most knowledgeable of that which they conceal."

[Surah Aal-'Imraan verse 167]

Subsequently only seven hundred Sahaabah ؓ were left with Rasulullah ﷺ, of which only one hundred were dressed in body armour. The whole army had just two horses; one for Rasulullah ﷺ and the other belonged to Abu Burdah bin Niyaar Haarisi ؓ.

The Banu Salmah of the Khazraj tribe and the Banu Haarisah of the Aws tribe also got afraid and like 'Abdullah bin Ubayy, were a bit reluctant to forge ahead in battle. They were almost on the point of deciding to turn back but divine guidance intervened and they did not return. Both these tribes were commanding the two outer flanks of the Muslim army.

In regards to these people, the following verse was revealed:

$$إِذْ هَمَّتْ طَائِفَتَانِ مِنْكُمْ أَنْ تَفْشَلَا وَاللَّهُ وَلِيُّهُمَا ۗ وَعَلَى اللَّهِ فَلْيَتَوَكَّلِ الْمُؤْمِنُونَ$$

"Remember when two groups from amongst you almost lost heart but Allah is their Wali (protector and supporter) and upon Allah should the believers place their trust." [Surah Aal-'Imraan verse 122]

Whilst Rasulullah ﷺ was in Shaykhayn, the sun had set and Hadhrat Bilal ؓ called out the Azaan. Rasulullah ﷺ performed his Maghrib Salaah here and spent the night here as well. Muhammad bin Maslamah ؓ kept guard all night long. Periodically he would go on a round of patrol and return to Rasulullah's ﷺ tent where he would stand sentry.

Towards the latter part of the night, Rasulullah ﷺ set off and as he drew closer to Uhud, the time for Fajr Salaah set in. Rasulullah ﷺ instructed Hadhrat Bilal رضي الله عنه to call out the Azaan. Hadhrat Bilal رضي الله عنه called out the Azaan followed by the Iqaamah. Thereafter, Rasulullah ﷺ led his Sahaabah رضي الله عنهم in Salaah.

Drawing up the Battle Lines

Subsequent to the performance of his Salaah, Rasulullah ﷺ directed his attention towards the army. Facing Madinah with Uhud behind him, Rasulullah ﷺ drew up the battle lines. These columns of saintly souls who prior to this were standing humbly before Allah Ta'ala were now standing to sacrifice their lives in His path of Jihaad.

Baraa bin 'Aazib رضي الله عنه narrates: "Rasulullah ﷺ positioned a division of fifty archers at the back of Mount Uhud to prevent any attack by the Quraysh from this direction. He appointed 'Abdullah bin Jubair رضي الله عنه as their commander and sternly warned them: "Do not move from this point even if you notice us prevailing over the disbelievers and even if you catch sight of the disbelievers overpowering us, do not ever abandon your positions and do not come to assist us."

Rasulullah ﷺ forewarned them: "Even if you catch sight of us being picked apart by birds, then too do not move from this position. Remain here and protect us from the rear and even if you witness us being massacred, do not leave your positions to assist us. If you happen to see us gathering the war booty, then too stay where you are and do not dare join us."

Condition of the Quraysh Army

The Quraysh army had already reached the environs of Madinah on Wednesday and set up camp at the foot of Mount Uhud. They numbered a daunting force of three thousand strong including seven hundred armour-clad warriors. They had two hundred horses and three thousand camels. Accompanying them were the wives of the noblemen of Makkah, who roused the fighting spirit of the warriors with the recitation of provocative poetry. This is the behaviour expected of the hedonistic and shaytaanic miscreants. Allah Ta'ala forbid!

Some of these women were:

1. Hindah bint 'Utbah – wife of Abu Sufyaan and Hadhrat Mu'aawiyah's mother.
2. Umme Hakeem bint Haaris bin Hishaam – wife of 'Ikramah bin Abu Jahal.

3. Faatimah bint Waleed – wife of Haaris bin Hishaam.
4. Barzah bint Mas'ood – wife of Safwaan bin Umayyah.
5. Raytah bint Shaybah – wife of 'Amr bin 'Aas.
6. Salafah bint S'ad – wife of Talhah bin Abi Talhah Jumahi.
7. Khannas bint Maalik – mother of Mus'ab bin 'Umayr ﷺ.
8. 'Amrah bint 'Alqamah.

'Allaamah Zarqaani says: "Besides Khannas and 'Amrah, the rest of these women later embraced Islam."

The Quraysh appointed Khaalid bin Waleed as a commander of the right flank, 'Ikramah bin Abi Jahal as commander of the left flank, Safwaan bin Umayyah or 'Amr bin 'Aas as commander of the infantry and 'Abdullah bin Abi Rabi'ah as commander of the archers. All five officers later embraced Islam.

Rasulullah ﷺ Addressing the Troops

As the opposing parties drew their battle lines, Rasulullah ﷺ, grasping a sword in his hand, addressed the Sahaabah ﷺ and asked:

من يأخذ هذا السيف بحقه

"Who will take this sword with its due right?"

On hearing this, a number of hands reached out to acquire this noble boon but Rasulullah ﷺ held back. In the meantime, Abu Dujaanah ﷺ stepped ahead and asked: "What is the right of this sword, O Rasulullah!" Rasulullah ﷺ replied: "The right of this sword is that it be used to strike the enemies of Allah until they are overwhelmed."

According to another narration, Rasulullah ﷺ said: "The right of this sword is that it is not to be used to kill a Muslim and that a person does not take flight when engaging the disbelievers with this sword."

Abu Dujaanah ﷺ said: "O Rasulullah ﷺ! I will take this sword with its due right." In other words, "I will endeavour to fulfil its right." Rasulullah ﷺ promptly handed over the sword to Abu Dujaanah ﷺ.

In all probability, on the basis of divine revelation, Rasulullah ﷺ ascertained that nobody but Abu Dujaanah ﷺ would fulfil the right of this sword. This is why he surrendered it to Abu Dujaanah ﷺ specifically. And Allah Ta'ala knows best.

Note: Abu Dujaanah ﷺ was a gallant, dauntless and brave warrior. During the heat of battle, he would take on a distinctive parade and be overwhelmed with an extraordinary degree of arduous passion. Whilst engaging the enemy, he would don his red 'Imaamah (turban) and stride with a charming grace. Perhaps this is why Rasulullah ﷺ handed the sword over to him as evidenced by his future skills as a warrior.

The Launch of the Battle and the Killing of the Leading Qurayshi Contenders

From the side of the Quraysh, the first person to stride onto the battlefield was Abu 'Aamir who was the leader of the Aws tribe (of Madinah) during the pre-Islamic times of ignorance and due to his devoutness and religiousness, was famously known as Raahib (the pope). When the glow of Islam radiated in Madinah, he was unable to stomach this appealing sight and he left Madinah to settle down in Makkah. Instead of Raahib, Rasulullah ﷺ named him Faasiq (criminal).

This Faasiq came to Makkah and inflamed the Quraysh to take up arms against Rasulullah ﷺ and he himself joined the Quraysh in this campaign of Uhud. He led them to believe that when the people of Aws catch sight of him, they would willingly desert Rasulullah ﷺ and join forces with him.

The first contestant:

In the frontline of Uhud, this same Abu 'Aamir, stepped out as the first challenger and as he swaggered onto the battlefield, he bellowed:

يا معشر الاوس انا ابو عامر

"O people of Aws! I am Abu 'Aamir."

May Allah Ta'ala cool the eyes of the Aws tribe, who promptly responded:

لا انعم الله بك عينا يا فاسق

"O Faasiq! May Allah never cool your eyes."

On hearing this mortifying response, Abu 'Aamir rapidly retreated, unsuccessful in his endeavours and exclaimed: "After I left them, my people have turned for the worse."

The second contestant:

He was followed onto the battlefield by the flag-bearer of the disbelievers, Talhah bin Abi Talhah and with an air of arrogance, he challenged:

"O companions of Muhammad! You believe that Allah Ta'ala would promptly despatch us into hell with the aid of your swords whilst He would swiftly admit you with the aid of our swords into paradise. So, is there anyone from amongst you who would like to be swiftly admitted into paradise with my sword or whose sword would promptly despatch me to hell?"

On hearing this, Hadhrat Ali رضي الله عنه strode forth and engaged him in a swordfight. Hadhrat Ali رضي الله عنه delivered a slicing blow to his leg and he fell face down to the ground exposing his Satar (privates). Overcome with shame, Hadhrat Ali رضي الله عنه stepped back. Rasulullah صلى الله عليه وسلم asked: "O Ali! What made you withdraw?" He replied: "At the uncovering of his Satar, I was overcome with shame."

Hadhrat Ali رضي الله عنه then smote him on his head so severely that his head split into two.

This delighted Rasulullah صلى الله عليه وسلم and he cheered by exclaiming: "Allahu Akbar!" The Muslims also chanted exclamations of Allahu Akbar!

The third contestant:

Thereafter, 'Usmaan bin Abi Talhah, grasping the flag of the disbelievers, stepped forth onto the battlefield, reciting the following inflammatory stanza:

اِنَّ عَلٰى اَهْلِ اللِّوَاءِ حَقًّا   اَنْ تُخْضَبَ الصَّعْدَةُ او تَنْدَقَّا

"It is an obligation upon the flag-bearer to ensure that his spear is tinted with the blood of the enemy or it breaks into pieces."

In response, Hadhrat Hamzah رضي الله عنه strode up and attacked him, severing both his arms at the shoulders. The flag fell and in an instant he was no more.

The fourth contestant:

Thereafter, the flag was taken up by Abu S'ad bin Abi Talhah. S'ad bin Abi Waqqaas رضي الله عنه discharged an arrow towards him. It pierced his neck with such force that his tongue was pushed out of his mouth. S'ad bin Abi Waqqaas رضي الله عنه then promptly finished him off.

The fifth contestant:

Thereafter the flag was taken up by Musaf'i bin Talhah bin Abi Talhah. With just one blow, Hadhrat 'Aasim bin Saabit رضي الله عنه put him to death.

The sixth contestant:

The flag was then hoisted by Haaris bin Talhah bin Abi Talhah. He too was finished off with just one blow by Hadhrat 'Aasim bin Saabit رضي الله عنه. Some historians say that he was killed by Hadhrat Zubair رضي الله عنه.

The seventh contestant:

Kilaab bin Talhah bin Abi Talhah then stepped out with the flag. Hadhrat Zubair رضي الله عنه stepped ahead and did away with him.

The eighth contestant:

Thereafter the flag was taken up by Julaas bin Talhah bin Abi Talhah. The moment he stepped out, Hadhrat Talhah رضي الله عنه finished him off.

The ninth contestant:

The flag was then taken up by Artaat Shurahbil. Hadhrat Ali رضي الله عنه swiftly eliminated him.

The tenth contestant:

Shuraih bin Qaariz then took up the flag and strode out. He too was instantaneously finished off. The killer of Shuraih could not be ascertained.

The eleventh contestant:

Therafter, their slave by the name of Suwaab stepped out holding the flag. Either Hadhrat S'ad bin Abi Waqqaas رضي الله عنه or Hadhrat Hamzah رضي الله عنه or Hadhrat Ali رضي الله عنه – according to conflicting narrations – finished him off too.

In this manner, twenty-two chieftains of the Quraysh were eliminated.

The Valour of Abu Dujaanah رضي الله عنه

Abu Dujaanah رضي الله عنه, to whom Rasulullah ﷺ conferred his blessed sword, was a dauntless and gallant warrior. Firstly, he produced a red 'Imaamah (turban) and tied it onto his head. He then paraded onto the battlefield reciting the following stanzas:

$$\text{اَنَا الَّذِىْ عَاهَدَنِىْ خَلِيْلِىْ} \quad \text{وَنَحْنُ بِالسَّفْحِ لَدَى النَّخِيْلِ}$$

"I am the one from whom my Khalil (beloved whose love has penetrated every fibre of my being, i.e. Rasulullah ﷺ) had taken a pledge whilst we were at the foot of the mountain close to the date orchard.

$$\text{اَنْ لَّا اَقُوْمَ الدَّهْرَ فِى الْكُيُوْلِ} \quad \text{اَضْرِبُ بِسَيْفِ اللهِ وَالرَّسُوْلِ}$$

The pledge was that I would never stand within the ranks of the rear and I would continue engaging the enemy with the sword of Allah and His Rasool."

When Rasulullah ﷺ caught sight of Abu Dujaanah رضي الله عنه swaggering in this manner he commented: "Allah abhors such a gait except on such occasions."

In other words, when engaging the enemy, this (pride) is for the sake of Allah Ta'ala and His Rasool ﷺ and not for selfish reasons of pride and arrogance.

Tearing through the ranks of the enemy, whoever Abu Dujaanah رضي الله عنه came across would fall dead to the ground. He ploughed ahead until Hindah, the wife of Abu Sufyaan, confronted him. Abu Dujaanah رضي الله عنه raised his sword to strike her but restrained himself thinking that it was downright unbecoming of to him to use Rasulullah's ﷺ sword against a woman.

According to another narration, when Abu Dujaanah رضي الله عنه drew close to Hindah, she screeched for help but nobody came to her assistance. Abu Dujaanah رضي الله عنه says: "At that time I felt it rather indecent to test the sword of Rasulullah ﷺ on a vulnerable and helpless woman."

Valour and Martyrdom of Hadhrat Hamzah رضي الله عنه

The dauntless array of attacks launched by Hadhrat Hamzah رضي الله عنه subdued the disbelievers into a state of overwhelming panic. The instant he raised his sword upon anyone, the next instant his body would fall to the ground.

Wahshi bin Harb was the slave of Jubair bin Mut'im. During the battle of Badr, Jubair's uncle Tu'aymah bin 'Adi was slain by Hadhrat Hamzah رضي الله عنه. Jubair was heartbroken at the death of his uncle. Jubair promised Wahshi that if he killed Hamzah in revenge for his uncle, he would set him free. When the Quraysh set out for the battle of Uhud, Wahshi also accompanied them.

As the opposing parties formed their ranks at Uhud and the battle got underway, Sib'a bin 'Abdul-'Uzza swaggered onto the battlefield yelling: "Is there anyone who dares to challenge me?"

Heading up towards him, Hadhrat Hamzah رضي الله عنه replied: "O Sib'a! O son of the woman who specialises in female circumcision! How dare you brazenly defy

Allah and His Rasool?" Saying this, Hadhrat Hamzah رَضِىَ اللهُ عَنْهُ attacked him with his sword and in just a single thrust, he promptly despatched him to his death.

Meanwhile, Wahshi hid himself behind a boulder lying in ambush for Hadhrat Hamzah رَضِىَ اللهُ عَنْهُ. The moment Hadhrat Hamzah رَضِىَ اللهُ عَنْهُ passed by, he struck him on his back with such force that his spear penetrated through his abdomen emerging at his navel. Hadhrat Hamzah رَضِىَ اللهُ عَنْهُ managed tottering a few steps but eventually succumbed to his injury and 'drank from the cup of martyrdom'.

Wahshi relates: "When I reached Makkah, I was set free (as promised). I accompanied the Quraysh with the sole objective of assassinating Hadhrat Hamzah رَضِىَ اللهُ عَنْهُ. I had absolutely no intention to take part in the actual battle".

He further relates: "After I killed Hamzah, I detached myself from the army and sat down away from the fighting because I had no other intention. I joined them purely with the intention of securing my freedom by assassinating Hamzah رَضِىَ اللهُ عَنْهُ."

Note: Following the conquest of Makkah, Wahshi accompanied the delegation of Taaif to Madinah with the intention of embracing Islam. When the people caught sight of him, they exclaimed: "O Rasulullah! This is Wahshi." In other words, this is the killer of your beloved uncle.

To this, Rasulullah ﷺ replied:

دعوه فلاسلام رجل واحد احب الى من قتل الف كافر

"Let him be because the Islam of just one person is more dear to me than the elimination of a thousand disbelievers."

Thereafter, Rasulullah ﷺ requested Wahshi to give an account of the assassination of Hadhrat Hamzah رَضِىَ اللهُ عَنْهُ. With extreme shame and intense embarrassment, in fulfillment of the command of Rasulullah ﷺ, he narrated the incident of his assassination of Hadhrat Hamzah رَضِىَ اللهُ عَنْهُ. Rasulullah ﷺ then accepted his Islam but added: "If possible, avoid appearing before me because the death of my uncle is revived whenever I lay eyes on you."

Since Wahshi رَضِىَ اللهُ عَنْهُ had no intention of harassing Rasulullah ﷺ, he would sit behind him (or at the back). Wahshi رَضِىَ اللهُ عَنْهُ was ceaselessly concerned about making amends. In compensation for his assassination of Hadhrat Hamzah رَضِىَ اللهُ عَنْهُ, with the same spear he despatched to Jahannam Musaylamah Kazzaab (the impostor) who claimed prophethood after the death of Rasulullah ﷺ.

Just as he had martyred Hadhrat Hamzah رَضِىَ اللهُ عَنْهُ by impaling his navel, similarly, he killed Musaylamah Kazzaab also by stabbing him through his navel. In this manner, for killing the best of people, he made amends by slaying the worst of people.

People would ask him, "Are you the one who killed Hamzah?" He would reply:

نعم والحمد لله الذى اكرمه بيدى ولم يهنى بيده

"Yes, and praise be to Allah Who has honoured Hamzah with martyrdom at my hands without humiliating me at his hands."

In other words, if Wahshi رَضِىَ اللّٰهُ عَنْهُ was killed by Hadhrat Hamzah رَضِىَ اللّٰهُ عَنْهُ, he would have died in a state if kufr (disbelief) and there is no humiliation worse than kufr.

Wahshi رَضِىَ اللّٰهُ عَنْهُ further relates: "Thereafter Rasulullah ﷺ said: 'O Wahshi! Go! Proceed to fight in the path of Allah just as you used to fight to hinder others from the path of Allah.'"

Martyrdom of Hanzalah, Ghaseelul-Malaa'ikah رَضِىَ اللّٰهُ عَنْهُ

Hadhrat Hanzalah رَضِىَ اللّٰهُ عَنْهُ also accompanied Rasulullah ﷺ on this campaign.

Abu Sufyaan and Hadhrat Hanzalah رَضِىَ اللّٰهُ عَنْهُ clashed with one another in a fierce swordfight. Hadhrat Hanzalah sprang forward to strike Abu Sufyaan but Shaddaad bin Aws fatally attacked him from the rear rendering him a Shaheed.

On this occasion, Rasulullah ﷺ remarked: "I witnessed the angels bathing Hanzalah رَضِىَ اللّٰهُ عَنْهُ with pure hail water from silver goblets."

Upon enquiry from his wife, it was learnt that he had set out for Jihaad in the state of Janaabat and he was martyred in this state.

The wife of Hadhrat Hanzalah رَضِىَ اللّٰهُ عَنْهُ saw a dream the night preceding his martydom that a door had opened from the heavens and Hadhrat Hanzalah رَضِىَ اللّٰهُ عَنْهُ had entered there. As soon as he entered, the door closed. His wife understood from this dream that Hanzalah رَضِىَ اللّٰهُ عَنْهُ was about to leave this world.

On the termination of the battle, water was seen dripping down from his body. This is why he was eminently known as Ghaseelul-Malaa'ikah (the one bathed by the angels).

Since Hanzalah's رَضِىَ اللّٰهُ عَنْهُ father Abu 'Aamir was fighting against Rasulullah ﷺ, Hadhrat Hanzalah رَضِىَ اللّٰهُ عَنْهُ sought Rasulullah's ﷺ permission to assassinate his own father but Rasulullah ﷺ prohibited him.

These dauntless assaults and valiant attacks of the Muslims brought the Qurayshi resistance to their knees on the battlefield leaving them turning their backs and scurrying about for cover. Struck with chilling anxiety, the ladies also fled towards the mountains whilst the Muslims busied themselves in amassing the war-booty.

Muslims Archers Abandoning Positions and the Reversal of the War-Scales

When the group of archers who were appointed to guard the rear mountain pass noticed the victory of the Muslims and their subsequent amassing of the war booty, they also decided to abandon their positions and dash forth. Their Ameer 'Abdullah bin Jubair ﺭﺿﻰﺍﻟﻠﻪﻋﻨﻪ repeatedly pleaded with them not to abandon their positions and reminded them about Rasulullah's ﺻﻠﻰﺍﻟﻠﻪﻋﻠﻴﻪﻭﺳﻠﻢ emphatic order about not leaving their positions under any circumstances whatsoever. However, these people refused to take heed and they deserted their positions and proceeded to collect the booty.

Martyrdom of 'Abdullah bin Jubair ﺭﺿﻰﺍﻟﻠﻪﻋﻨﻪ and His Ten Companions

Thus only 'Abdullah bin Jubair ﺭﺿﻰﺍﻟﻠﻪﻋﻨﻪ and ten companions were left at this tactical position. Since the Muslims refused to comply with the wishes of Rasulullah ﺻﻠﻰﺍﻟﻠﻪﻋﻠﻴﻪﻭﺳﻠﻢ, the victory swiftly turned into defeat. When Khaalid bin Waleed, who was with the right flank of the Mushrikeen, caught sight of the vulnerable pass, he attacked from the rear. This attack rendered 'Abdullah bin Jubair ﺭﺿﻰﺍﻟﻠﻪﻋﻨﻪ and ten of his companions as martyrs.

Martyrdom of Mus'ab bin 'Umair ﺭﺿﻰﺍﻟﻠﻪﻋﻨﻪ

This surprisingly sudden and unexpected attack by the disbelievers left the ranks of the Muslims in bewilderment and the enemy managed to draw threateningly close to Rasulullah ﺻﻠﻰﺍﻟﻠﻪﻋﻠﻴﻪﻭﺳﻠﻢ.

The flag-bearer of the Muslims, Mus'ab bin 'Umair ﺭﺿﻰﺍﻟﻠﻪﻋﻨﻪ was standing close to Rasulullah ﺻﻠﻰﺍﻟﻠﻪﻋﻠﻴﻪﻭﺳﻠﻢ. He valiantly tackled the disbelievers in the defence of Rasulullah ﺻﻠﻰﺍﻟﻠﻪﻋﻠﻴﻪﻭﺳﻠﻢ until he himself was martyred. Thereafter, Rasulullah ﺻﻠﻰﺍﻟﻠﻪﻋﻠﻴﻪﻭﺳﻠﻢ consigned the flag to Hadhrat Ali ﺭﺿﻰﺍﻟﻠﻪﻋﻨﻪ.

Since Mus'ab bin 'Umair ﺭﺿﻰﺍﻟﻠﻪﻋﻨﻪ closely resembled Rasulullah ﺻﻠﻰﺍﻟﻠﻪﻋﻠﻴﻪﻭﺳﻠﻢ, a certain shaytaan circulated a rumour that Rasulullah ﺻﻠﻰﺍﻟﻠﻪﻋﻠﻴﻪﻭﺳﻠﻢ, the target of the disbelievers, was martyred. Immediately, a gloomy mood of bewilderment and apprehension spread throughout the Muslim ranks. The moment they heard this harrowing news, they lost their senses and fell into a state of panic. In this state of panic, they were unable to differentiate between friend and foe and they started attacking one another.

Huzaifah's Father is Erroneously Martyred by the Muslims

Hadhrat Huzaifah's ﷠ father Yamaan ﷠ was also caught up in this state of chaos. From a distance, Huzaifah ﷠ caught sight of his father coming under attack from the Muslims. He yelled at them: "O servants of Allah! That is my father." But who could have heard him in this state of utter chaos and they eventually killed him. When the Muslims learnt that they erroneously killed Huzaifah's ﷠ father, they were dreadfully ashamed and in a tone of downright remorse said: "By Allah, we failed to recognise him."

Hadhrat Huzaifah ﷠ remarked:

يَغْفِرُ اللهُ لَكُمْ ، وَهُوَ اَرْحَمُ الرَّاحِمِيْنَ

"May Allah forgive you. He is the most merciful of the merciful."

Rasulullah ﷺ offered to pay him the Diyat (blood money) in compensation but Hadhrat Huzaifah ﷠ declined to accept it. This further enhanced Huzaifah's ﷠ esteem in the eyes of Rasulullah ﷺ.

The unexpected Attack of Khaalid bin Waleed and the Unwavering Stance of Rasulullah ﷺ

Although a great many brave souls were left floundering on the battlefield following the unanticipated attack of Khaalid bin Waleed, nothing could shake the steadfastness and perseverance of Rasulullah ﷺ. How could anything agitate his steadfastness because the Nabi of Allah can never be, Allah forbid, a timid coward. The mountains may move but the messengers of Allah Ta'ala will surely stand their ground. The valour of a single messenger far outweighs the valour of the entire world of champions.

Describing this scene, Hadhrat Miqdaad ﷠ says:

فوالذى بعثه بالحق ما زلت قدمه شبرا واحد وانه لقى وجه العدو
ويفئ اليه طائفة من اصحابه مرة وتفترق مرة فربما رايته قائما
يرمى عن قوسه ويرمى بالحجر حتى انحازوا عنه

"I swear by the celestial being Who sent Rasulullah ﷺ with the truth, Rasulullah's ﷺ feet did not budge an inch in his resolute stance against the disbelievers. A group of the Sahaabah ﷢ would sometimes come to his assistance and sometimes they would disperse and quite often I witnessed

Rasulullah ﷺ discharging arrows and hurling stones at the disbelievers until the enemy melted away."

Bodyguards of Rasulullah ﷺ

During this state of turmoil, fourteen Sahaabah رضي الله عنهم stood their ground with Rasulullah ﷺ; seven from the Muhaajireen and seven from the Ansaar. They were:

Muhaajireen	Ansaar
1. Abu Bakr رضي الله عنه	1. Abu Dujaanah رضي الله عنه
2. 'Umar bin Khattaab رضي الله عنه	2. Habbaab bin Munzir رضي الله عنه
3. 'Abdur-Rahmaan bin 'Awf رضي الله عنه	3. 'Aasim bin Saabit رضي الله عنه
4. S'ad bin Abi Waqqaas رضي الله عنه	4. Haaris bin Sammah رضي الله عنه
5. Talhah رضي الله عنه	5. Suhail bin Hunaif رضي الله عنه
6. Zubair bin 'Awwam رضي الله عنه	6. S'ad bin Mu'aaz رضي الله عنه
7. Abu 'Ubaidah رضي الله عنه	7. Usaid bin Hudhair رضي الله عنه

Hadhrat Ali's رضي الله عنه name was not mentioned in the Muhaajireen because following the martyrdom of Mus'ab bin 'Umair رضي الله عنه, Rasulullah ﷺ appointed him the flag bearer of the Muslim army. He was engaged in fighting the enemy.

These fourteen gallant personalities were constantly with Rasulullah ﷺ. Occasionally when the need arose some of them would go away but swiftly return. This is why Rasulullah ﷺ was sometimes left with twelve people.

Unexpected Attack of the Quraysh against Rasulullah ﷺ and the Valiant Sacrifice of the Sahaabah رضي الله عنهم

When the Quraysh launched an attack on Rasulullah ﷺ, he invited: "Who will rid these people of me and render himself my companion in Jannah?" Hadhrat Anas رضي الله عنه says: "There were seven Ansaar with Rasulullah ﷺ and every one of them fought valiantly until, one by one, they were all rendered Shaheed."

According to the narration of Ibn Ishaaq, Rasulullah ﷺ invited:

من رجل يشري لنا نفسه

"Is there any man who is prepared to sell his life for us?"

Immediately upon hearing this, Ziyaad bin Sakan رضي الله عنه and five other Ansaar responded to this call. One after the other, each one of them demonstrated their mettle of sacrifice until they were rendered Shaheed. They bartered their lives in exchange for Jannah.

Martyrdom of Ziyaad bin Sakan رضي الله عنه

Ziyaad was blessed with an additional privilege. When he fell wounded to the ground, Rasulullah ﷺ said: "Bring him closer to me."

When his companions brought him to Rasulullah ﷺ, Ziyaad placed his cheek on the blessed foot of Rasulullah ﷺ and consigned his life over to Allah Ta'ala إنا لله وإنا إليه راجعون.

Attack of 'Utbah bin Abi Waqqaas upon Rasulullah ﷺ

Availing himself of an opportune moment, 'Utbah bin Abi Waqqaas, the brother of S'ad bin Abi Waqqaas رضي الله عنه hurled a stone upon Rasulullah ﷺ with such force that Rasulullah ﷺ lost a lower tooth and his lower lip was injured. S'ad bin Abi Waqqaas رضي الله عنه says: "I was not as eager to kill anyone else as much as I was eager to kill my brother 'Utbah bin Abi Waqqaas."

Attack of 'Abdullah bin Qumayyah upon Rasulullah ﷺ

'Abdullah bin Qumayyah, a celebrated wrestler of the Quraysh, attacked Rasulullah ﷺ with such force that two links of his armoured helmet pierced his cheek. Meanwhile, 'Abdullah bin Shihaab Zuhri hurled a stone at Rasulullah ﷺ injuring his blessed forehead. When his blessed face started bleeding, Abu Sa'eed Khudri's رضي الله عنه father Maalik bin Sinaan رضي الله عنه sucked the blood and cleaned his blessed face. Rasulullah ﷺ promised: "The fire of Jahannam will never strike you."

Abu Umaamah رضي الله عنه relates: "After inflicting this injury to Rasulullah ﷺ, Ibn Qumayyah taunted:

خذها وانا ابن قميه

'Here, take it! I am the son of Qumayyah.'"

Rasulullah ﷺ replied:

اقماك الله

"May Allah disgrace and destroy you"

Barely a few days later, Allah Ta'ala set a mountain goat over him that tore him to pieces with its horns.

Support of Hadhrat Ali ﷺ and Hadhrat Talhah ﷺ to Rasulullah ﷺ

Since Rasulullah ﷺ was also donning a pair of heavy steel armour, he fell into a hole dug by 'Abu 'Amir the Faasiq for the Muslims. Hadhrat Ali ﷺ held his hand and Hadhrat Talhah ﷺ supported his waist and only then did he manage to stand upright.

On this occasion, he remarked: "If you wish to see a living martyr walking the surface of this earth, take a look at Talhah."

Hadhrat 'Aa'ishah ﷺ narrates from her father Abu Bakr ﷺ that when two links of the armoured helmet embedded themselves into the cheeks of Rasulullah ﷺ, Hadhrat Abu 'Ubaidah bin Jarrah ﷺ gripped them with his teeth and plucked them out. He lost two of his teeth in the process.

When Rasulullah ﷺ attempted to ascend one of the peaks of the mountain, his fatigue and weakness compounded by the burden of his double armour left him helpless. Hadhrat Talhah ﷺ positioned himself in submission before Rasulullah ﷺ. Placing his foot on Talhah ﷺ, Rasulullah ﷺ managed to climb up.

Hadhrat Zubair ﷺ narrates: "On this occasion, I heard Rasulullah ﷺ declaring:

او جب طلحة

'Talhah has made Jannah compulsory for himself.'"

Qays bin Abi Haazim says: "I saw the hand of Talhah ﷺ that he used as a shield in defending of Rasulullah ﷺ on the day of Uhud. His hand was completely paralysed."

On that day Hadhrat Talhah ﷺ sustained thirty five or thirty nine wounds to his body.

Hadhrat 'Aa'ishah ﷺ narrates that whenever Abu Bakr ﷺ mentioned the battle of Uhud, he would say:

كان ذلك اليوم كله لطلحة

"That day was exclusively for Talhah."

Hadhrat Jaabir ﷺ narrates: "Whilst deflecting the attacks of the enemy, Hadhrat Talhah's ﷺ fingers were severed. Impulsively he cried out: 'Hasan (good).' Upon this Rasulullah ﷺ remarked:

لو قلت بسم الله لرفعتك الملائكة والناس ينظرون اليك، حتى تلج بك في جو السماء

'If you uttered Bismillah instead of Hasan, the angels would have raised you high up where the people would have been able to catch sight of you until they enter the atmosphere of the sky with you.'"

Hadhrat 'Aa'ishah ﷺ narrates from Hadhrat Abu Bakr ﷺ who says: "On the day of Uhud, we counted more than seventy wounds on the body of Talhah ﷺ."

Hadhrat Anas's ﷺ stepfather Hadhrat Abu Talhah ﷺ was protecting Rasulullah ﷺ with a shield. He was a master archer. On that day, he broke two or three bows. Whoever happened to pass by with a quiver of arrows, Rasulullah ﷺ would say: "Go and empty out your quiver before Abu Talhah."

Whenever Rasulullah ﷺ planned to stick his head out to check on the people, Abu Talhah ﷺ would plead with him:

بابى انت و امى لا تشرف يصبك سهم من سهام القوم نحرى دون نحرك

"May my parents be sacrificed for you, O Rasulullah ﷺ! Do not stick your head out. An arrow of the enemy may strike you. Rather it strikes my chest instead of yours."

S'ad bin Abi Waqqaas ﷺ too was a professional archer. On the day of Uhud, Rasulullah ﷺ fished out all his arrows from his quiver and placed them before S'ad ﷺ and said:

ارم فداك ابى وامى

"Go on, shoot the arrows. May my parents be sacrificed for you."

Hadhrat Ali ؓ narrates: "I have not heard Rasulullah ﷺ saying 'may my parents be sacrificed for you' for anyone other than S'ad bin Abi Waqqaas ؓ."

On the day of Uhud, Hadhrat S'ad ؓ discharged one thousand arrows.

The Gallant Sacrifice of Abu Dujaanah ؓ

Abu Dujaanah ؓ positioned himself before Rasulullah ﷺ as a human shield with his back facing the enemy. Scores of arrows landed on his back but for fear of an arrow wounding Rasulullah ﷺ, Abu Dujaanah ؓ did not budge an inch.

Rasulullah ﷺ Lamenting over the Disbelievers

Hadhrat Anas ؓ narrates: "On the day of Uhud, Rasulullah ﷺ would continue wiping the blood off his blessed face and lament in the following words: 'How can a people who stained the face of their Nabi with blood ever be successful whilst the Nabi is merely inviting them towards their Lord?'"

Rasulullah ﷺ Cursing Some of the Qurayshi Chieftains

Hadhrat Saalim ؓ narrates that Rasulullah ﷺ cursed Safwaan bin Umayyah, Suhail bin 'Amr and Haaris bin Hishaam. Upon this, Allah Ta'ala revealed the following verse:

$$\text{لَيْسَ لَكَ مِنَ الْاَمْرِ شَىْءٌ اَوْ يَتُوْبَ عَلَيْهِمْ اَوْ يُعَذِّبَهُمْ فَاِنَّهُمْ ظٰلِمُوْنَ}$$

"The decision is not for you to make (O Muhammad, but for Allah alone). He may pardon them or He may punish them because they are sinners."
[Surah Aal-'Imraan verse 128]

Hafiz 'Asqalaani ؒ says: "All three of them embraced Islam at the conquest of Makkah. Perhaps this is why Allah Ta'ala forbade Rasulullah ﷺ cursing them and revealed the aforementioned verse."

'Abdullah bin Mas'ood ؓ says: "I can still distinctly visualise the scene where Rasulullah ﷺ was busy wiping the blood off his face and pleading with Allah:

$$\text{رَبِّ اغْفِرْ لِقَوْمِىْ فَاِنَّهُمْ لَا يَعْلَمُوْنَ}$$

"O my Lord! Forgive my people because they do not know."

Spurred by his extreme affection and compassion, Rasulullah ﷺ used the words 'they do not know' in his dua. In other words, 'my people are unaware and naïve'. He didn't say 'my people are ignorant'.

Although ignorance is no excuse especially after witnessing clear proofs, Rasulullah ﷺ, who was an embodiment of compassion and mercy, apologised before the most Merciful on their behalf, citing their ignorance. Perhaps, he thought, Allah Ta'ala would free them from the web of kufr and disbelief and admit them into the circle of Islam and peace. Perhaps Allah Ta'ala would make them drink the 'wine' of Ikhlaas (sincerity and devotion) and intoxicate them with His celestial love to such an extent that the despicable nature of this world and the honour of the hereafter becomes visible to them. Perhaps they will be set free from the prison of kufr and transgression and released forever into the sheltered splendour of Imaan, Ikhlaas and Ihsaan never to depart from there again.

Qataadah bin Nu'maan ﷺ Loses an Eye during the Battle

Qataadah bin Nu'maan ﷺ narrates: "On the day of Uhud, I positioned myself right in front of Rasulullah's ﷺ face and directed my face towards the enemy so that my face may bear the brunt of the arrows instead of the blessed face of Rasulullah ﷺ. One of the last arrows of the enemy landed with such force on my face that my eyeball popped out. Holding it in my hand, I turned towards Rasulullah ﷺ. When he caught sight of my eye, his eyes welled up with tears and he made dua for me: 'O Allah! Just as Qataadah protected the face of your Nabi, protect his face and restore his eye to a condition better and sharper than what it was.' Saying this, Rasulullah ﷺ took the eyeball and replaced it into its socket. Instantaneously, my eyesight was restored. In fact, my eyesight turned out to be better and sharper than what it originally was."

According to another narration, Qataadah ﷺ held the eyeball in his hand and appeared before Rasulullah ﷺ, who said: "If you exercise patience, you will be rewarded with Jannah and if you wish I will replace your eyeball in its original position and make dua for you." Qataadah ﷺ replied: "O Rasulullah! I have a wife whom I love dearly. I fear that if I am left with one eye she may find it revolting and she may develop feelings of dislike and hatred towards me."

Taking hold of the eye, Rasulullah ﷺ replaced it into its socket and made the following dua: "O Allah! Grant him beauty and handsomeness."

Rumour of Rasulullah's ﷺ Martyrdom

When a false rumour of Rasulullah's ﷺ assassination started making its rounds, some Muslims lost courage. Despondently they said: "Since Rasulullah ﷺ is martyred, what is the need for fighting now?"

To this, Hadhrat Anas's ؓ paternal uncle countered: "O people! Muhammad ﷺ may have been killed but the Lord of Muhammad ﷺ has not been killed. Continue fighting for whatever cause you had been fighting previously and sacrifice your lives for the same. What would you stay alive and do after the demise of Rasulullah ﷺ?"

Saying this, he pitched himself in the ranks of the enemy and fought them until he was martyred.

Martyrdom of Anas bin Nadr ؓ

Hadhrat Anas ؓ narrates: "My paternal uncle Anas bin Nadr ؓ was profoundly distressed for failing to take part in the battle of Badr. Once, he mentioned to Rasulullah ﷺ: 'O Rasulullah! How lamentable that I could not participate in the foremost battle of Islam against the disbelievers. If Allah Ta'ala grants me the ability to participate in another Jihaad in the future, Allah will witness my gallant efforts and my heroic spirit of sacrifice.'"

During the battle of Uhud, when some people fled in defeat, Anas bin Nadr ؓ submitted before Allah: "O Allah! I beg your forgiveness from what some of the Muslims have done – fleeing from the battlefield - and I isolate myself from what the disbelievers have done."

Saying this, he advanced towards the enemy with a sword in his hand. When he caught sight of S'ad bin Mu'aaz ؓ before him, he said:

اين يا سعد انى اجد ريح الجنة دون احد

"Where to O S'ad?! I perceive the fragrance of Jannah beyond Uhud."

"Ah! I can smell the fragrance of Jannah emanating from the mountain of Uhud." Hadhrat Anas ؓ strode forth and engaged the enemy until he was martyred. More than eighty wounds inflicted by swords and arrows were found on his body. In his regard, the following verse was revealed:

مِنَ الْمُؤْمِنِيْنَ رِجَالٌ صَدَقُوْا مَا عَاهَدُوا اللهَ عَلَيْهِ

"Amongst the believers are men who have been true to their covenant with Allah."
[Surah Ahzaab verse 23]

The chief reason for the anguish facing the Muslims on this occasion was that they were unable to catch sight of Rasulullah ﷺ. The first person to recognise Rasulullah ﷺ during this upheaval was K'ab bin Maalik ؓ. Rasulullah ﷺ was wearing a helmet that was concealing his blessed face. K'ab ؓ says: "I recognised Rasulullah ﷺ from his radiant eyes. The moment I caught sight of him, I yelled: 'O Muslims! Glad tidings for you. There is Rasulullah ﷺ over there.'" Raising his hand to his face, Rasulullah ﷺ signalled him to maintain silence. Although Rasulullah ﷺ forbade him to mention this a second time, their hearts and minds were focused in that direction. This is why, following the single cheerful announcement of K'ab ؓ, a few Muslims dashed off towards Rasulullah ﷺ like moths to a flame. K'ab ؓ says: "Thereafter Rasulullah ﷺ gave me his armour to wear whilst he wore my armour. Thinking that I am Rasulullah ﷺ, the enemy started letting loose a torrent of arrows upon me. I sustained more than twenty wounds on this occasion."

As a few Muslims gathered around Rasulullah ﷺ, he set off for the mountain pass. Amongst others, accompanying him were Abu Bakr, 'Umar, Ali, Talhah and Haaris bin Simmah ؓ. Rasulullah ﷺ attempted to climb the mountain but due to weakness, exhaustion and the weight of the double armour, he was unable to climb up. This is why Hadhrat Talhah ؓ sat down before him. Placing his foot on Talhah ؓ, Rasulullah ﷺ clambered over.

Killing of Ubayy bin Khalaf

In the meantime, Ubayy bin Khalaf came galloping on his horse, a horse that he fed and fattened with the sole intention of sitting astride it and killing Rasulullah ﷺ.

When Rasulullah ﷺ got wind of his intentions, he at once said: "Insha Allah, I will kill him."

As he drew closer to the Muslims, the Sahaabah ؓ sought Rasulullah's ﷺ permission to finish him off. Rasulullah ﷺ said:

"Leave him. Allow him to get closer."

As he came up to them, Rasulullah ﷺ took a spear from Haaris bin Simmah ؓ and inflicted a slight spear-jab to his neck. He started shrieking at the top of his voice and returned to his people bellowing: "By Allah! Muhammad has killed me."

His people attempted to console him saying: "It is nothing but a slight prick. It is not such a serious wound that you have to scream like this." Ubayy retorted: "Don't you know? Muhammad himself told me in Makkah: 'I will kill you'. Only my heart understands the severity of this 'prick'. By Allah! If this prick were to be distributed amongst the inhabitants of Hijaaz, just this one prick would be sufficient for their destruction."

Ubayy continued bellowing like this until he reached a place called Sarif where he died.

Hadhrat Ali رضي الله عنه and Hadhrat Faatimah رضي الله عنها bathe the wounds of Rasulullah ﷺ

When Rasulullah ﷺ reached the valley, the battle had ended. He sat down whilst Hadhrat Ali رضي الله عنه brought some water and cleaned the blood off his blessed face. He also poured some water over his head. Rasulullah ﷺ then performed wudhu and led the Salaah whilst seated. The Sahaabah رضي الله عنهم also performed their Salaah whilst seated behind Rasulullah ﷺ.

Mutilating the Corpses of the Muslims

During the battle, the disbelievers started mutilating the bodies of the Muslims. They severed the noses and ears. They ripped open their bellies and lopped off their private parts. Even the womenfolk joined the men in this gruesome task.

Hindah, whose father was killed at the hands of Hadhrat Hamzah رضي الله عنه in the battle of Badr, mutilated the body of Hadhrat Hamzah رضي الله عنه. She cut his stomach open and hacked off a piece of his liver. She then tried to swallow it but since it refused to go down her throat, she spat it out.

Elated by this satisfying moment, she removed all her jewellery and handed it over to Wahshi.

She also made a necklace out of the severed ears and noses of the Muslims and hung it around her neck.

Abu Sufyaan's Taunts and Hadhrat 'Umar's رضي الله عنه reply

When the Quraysh elected to leave the battlefield, Abu Sufyaan ascended the mountain and yelled: "Is Muhammad alive amongst you?"

Rasulullah ﷺ asked his companions to refrain from responding to his provoking taunts. Abu Sufyaan yelled out thrice but each time he was greeted with absolute silence. He then called out: "Is the son of Abu Quhaafah (Abu Bakr رضي الله عنه) alive amongst you?" Rasulullah ﷺ again asked the Sahaabah رضي الله عنهم to remain silent. Repeating this question three times, he kept quiet. A little while later, he asked: "Is 'Umar bin Khattaab alive?" He repeated this thrice but this statement also failed to evoke a response. He gleefully shrieked out to his cohorts: "As for that lot, they have been killed. If they were alive they would have surely responded."

Chapter 15

However, Hadhrat 'Umar رضى الله عنه was unable to maintain his patience any longer and he screamed:

كذبت والله يا عدو الله ابقى الله عليك ما يحزنك

"By Allah! You are lying, O enemy of Allah! Allah has set aside something for you that would bring grief and anguish to you."

Thereafter, taking the name of a national deity, Abu Sufyaan yelled:

اُعْلُ هُبَل اُعْلُ هُبَل

"Rise, O Hubal! May your religion thrive, O Hubal."

In response, Rasulullah صلى الله عليه وسلم asked Hadhrat 'Umar رضى الله عنه to say:

اَللهُ اَعْلىٰ وَاَجَلُّ

"Allah is the most exalted and elevated."

Abu Sufyaan retorted:

ان لنا العزى ولا عزى لكم

"We have 'Uzza (name of a deity) whilst you have no 'Uzza." (In other words you have no 'Izzah, honour.)

Rasulullah صلى الله عليه وسلم instructed Hadhrat 'Umar رضى الله عنه to reply:

اَللهُ مولانا ولا مولى لكم

"Allah is our Mawlaa (Lord, master) whilst you have no Mawlaa."

In other words, honour lies only in one's association with Allah. Association with 'Uzza has no honour but dishonour.

Abu Sufyaan said:

يوم بيوم بدر والحرب سجال

"This day is in response to the day of Badr. War has its ups and downs."

Hadhrat 'Umar رضى الله عنه responded:

لا سواء قتلانا فى الجنة وقتلاكم فى النار

"We can never be the same because our casualties are in Jannah whilst your victims are in Jahannam."

Since Abu Sufyaan's statement 'war has its ups and downs' was true, this statement was not responded to. Allah Ta'ala's declaration in the Qur-aan 'those are the days we rotate around people' confirms this fact.

Thereafter, Abu Sufyaan summoned Hadhrat 'Umar رضي الله عنه saying:

هلُمَّ إلَيَّ يا عمر

"O 'Umar! Come towards me."

Rasulullah صلى الله عليه وسلم asked Hadhrat 'Umar رضي الله عنه to go and see what he wants. When Hadhrat 'Umar رضي الله عنه drew closer to him, Abu Sufyaan asked:

انشدك الله يا عمرا قتلنا محمدا صلى الله عليه وسلم

"I beg you to pledge in the name of Allah, O 'Umar! Did we manage to kill Muhammad?"

Hadhrat 'Umar رضي الله عنه replied:

اللهم لا وانه ليسمع كلامك الان

"By Allah! Certainly not! He is alive and listening to you as we speak."

Abu Sufyaan commented:

انت عندى اصدق من ابن قمية و ابر

"According to me, you are more truthful than Ibn Qumayyah (the celebrated wrestler of the Quraysh who was killed by a mountain goat, as explained earlier) and you are more pious than him"

Abu Sufyaan also added:

انه قدكان فى قتلاكم مثل والله ما رضيت ولا نهيت ولا امرت

"A number of your victims were subjected to physical mutilation by our people. By Allah I swear that I am not delighted with this. I did not prevent this nor did I decree it."

As he was heading off, Abu Sufyaan cried out:

موعدكم بدر للعام القابل

"Our rendezvous is Badr in the forthcoming year."

To this Rasulullah صلى الله عليه وسلم asked a Sahaabi to reply:

نعم هو بيننا و بينك موعد انشاء الله

"Yes, this is a pledge between you and us, Insha Allah."

On the departure of the disbelievers from the battlefield, the womenfolk of the Muslims left Madinah to ascertain the conditions of the Muslims. Hadhrat Faatimah رضى الله عنها noticed blood running down the blessed face of Rasulullah ﷺ. Hadhrat Ali رضى الله عنه fetched some water in his shield and Hadhrat Faatimah رضى الله عنها bathed his wound. However the more she cleansed the wound, the more the blood trickled out. They then burnt a piece of a grass-mat and filled its ash into the wound. This helped in stopping the blood.

Martyrdom of S'ad bin Rab'i رضى الله عنه

Following the departure of the Quraysh, Rasulullah ﷺ instructed Zaid bin Saabit رضى الله عنه to search for the whereabouts of S'ad bin Rab'i رضى الله عنه. He instructed him thus:

ان رايته فاقرأه منى السلام وقل له يقول لك رسول الله كيف تجدك

"If you manage locating him, pass on my Salaam to him and inform him that the Prophet of Allah asks: 'What condition do you find yourself in now'?"

Hadhrat Zaid bin Saabit رضى الله عنه narrates: "I went out in search of him and located him whilst he still had some life left in him. He had sustained seventy sword and arrow wounds to his body. When I delivered Rasulullah's ﷺ message to him, S'ad رضى الله عنه replied:

"Salaam upon Rasulullah ﷺ and Salaam upon you as well. Inform Rasulullah ﷺ that at this moment I am able to perceive the fragrance of Jannah and inform my people, the Ansaar, that if Rasulullah ﷺ is inconvenienced in any way and they have one eye left (i.e. even if there is just one person left amongst them), none of their excuses will be accepted in the court of Allah."

Saying this, he breathed his last and bade farewell to this world.

According to another narration, S'ad bin Rab'i رضى الله عنه addressed Zaid bin Saabit رضى الله عنه thus:

"Inform Rasulullah ﷺ that at this time I am about to pass on. After conveying my Salaam to him, inform him that S'ad says: 'May Allah reward you with the best of rewards on our behalf and on behalf of the entire Ummah'."

According to the narration of Ibn 'Abdul-Barr رحمه الله, Ubayy bin K'ab رضي الله عنه says: "I returned to Rasulullah ﷺ and notified him of S'ad's message. He commented:

رحمه الله نصح لله ولرسوله حيا وميتا

'May Allah shower His mercy upon him. In life and in death, he was loyal and he wished well for Allah and His Rasool.'

The Search for the Body of Hadhrat Hamzah رضي الله عنه

Rasulullah ﷺ went out in search for his uncle, Hadhrat Hamzah رضي الله عنه. He found his mutilated body in the depth of the valley. His nose and ears were lobbed off. His stomach and chest were ripped apart. On catching sight of this heartrending and agonising scene, Rasulullah ﷺ was spontaneously moved to tears. He mournfully commented: "May Allah shower you with His mercy. As far as I am aware, you were exceedingly charitable and you maintained favourable family ties. If it was not for the anguish and heartache of Safiyyah[1], I would have left you like this for the vultures and beasts. They would have devoured you and on the day of judgement you would have been resurrected from their bellies."

Also standing at the same spot, Rasulullah ﷺ vowed: "By Allah I swear! If Allah grants me victory over the disbelievers, I would mutilate seventy of them in retaliation for what they have done to you."

Rasulullah ﷺ barely moved from this spot when the following verses were revealed:

وَإِنْ عَاقَبْتُمْ فَعَاقِبُوا بِمِثْلِ مَا عُوقِبْتُم بِهِ ۖ وَلَئِن صَبَرْتُمْ لَهُوَ خَيْرٌ لِّلصَّابِرِينَ ۝ وَاصْبِرْ وَمَا صَبْرُكَ إِلَّا بِاللَّهِ ۚ وَلَا تَحْزَنْ عَلَيْهِمْ وَلَا تَكُ فِي ضَيْقٍ مِّمَّا يَمْكُرُونَ ۝ إِنَّ اللَّهَ مَعَ الَّذِينَ اتَّقَوا وَّالَّذِينَ هُم مُّحْسِنُونَ ۝

"And if you retaliate then retaliate in a manner corresponding to the adversity you were afflicted with. And if you exercise patience, it is best for the patient ones. And exercise patience, your patience is only with the divine guidance of Allah, do not be grieved over them (disbelievers) and do not be distressed by what they plot. Verily, Allah is with those who have Taqwa (Allah-consciousness) and with those who perform good deeds."

---

[1] Hadhrat Safiyyah رضي الله عنها was the sister of Hadhrat Hamza رضي الله عنه.

Rasulullah ﷺ then exercised patience, paid kaffaarah (expiation) for breaking his oath and abandoned this idea (of retaliation).

Hadhrat Jaabir ؓ narrates that when Rasulullah ﷺ glimpsed at the body of Hadhrat Hamzah ؓ, he burst out crying and in a sobbing voice he declared:

سيد الشهداء عند الله يوم القيامة حمزة

"On the day of Qiyaamah, Hamzah would be the leader of all the martyrs in the sight of Allah."

This is why he was distinguished with the title of Sayyidus-Shuhadaa.

Martyrdom of 'Abdullah bin Jahsh ؓ

'Abdullah bin Jahsh ؓ was also martyred in this battle. On the day of Uhud, prior to the actual battle erupting, 'Abdullah bin Jahsh ؓ called S'ad bin Abi Waqqaas ؓ aside and very discreetly said: "Come let us sit in one corner and make dua and we will say Aameen to one another's dua.

S'ad ؓ continues: "Both of us went to a secluded corner of the field and seated ourselves. I made a dua first in the following words: "O Allah! Let today's confrontation be with such an enemy who is valiant, dauntless and plump with fury so that I may challenge him for some time and he may contend with me. Thereafter, O Allah, grant me victory over him so that I may slay him and seize his possessions."

To this, 'Abdullah bin Jahsh ؓ said: "Aameen." He then made the following dua: "O Allah! Today let me encounter an adversary who is brave, strong and furious. May I challenge him solely for Your pleasure and may he in turn fight me and subsequently kill me. May he cut off my nose and ears and when I ultimately appear before You, you can ask me: "O 'Abdullah! Where did you lose your nose and ears?" I will then submit: "In Your path and the path of Your Nabi ﷺ." And to this You will reply: "You have spoken the truth."

S'ad bin Abi Waqqaas ؓ states, "His dua was far superior to mine. In the evening we found that his nose and ears had been cut off."

S'ad bin Abi Waqqaas ؓ continues: "Allah also accepted my dua. I also killed an exceptionally powerful disbeliever and took hold of his possessions."

Sa'eed bin Musayyib ؒ says that 'Abdullah bin Jahsh ؓ made the following dua:

اللهم انى اقسم عليك ان القى العدو فيقتلونى ثم يبقروا بطنى
ويجدعوا انفى واذنى ثم تسألنى بم ذلك فاقول فيك

'O Allah! I make a pledge unto you that I confront the enemy and they kill me and cleave my stomach apart and cut off my ears and then You would ask me why this happened and I would reply: "Solely for You."

Sa'eed bin Musayyib رحمه الله says: "Just as Allah Ta'ala accepted his dua of martyrdom in this extraordinary manner, in the same vein, I confidently expect Allah to accept the second part of his dua as well, i.e. Allah's question of why this happened and his response." This is why Hadhrat 'Abdullah bin Jahsh رضي الله عنه was distinguished with the title of Mujadd'a fillah (one whose nose and ears are cut off in the path of Allah).

Martyrdom of 'Abdullah bin 'Amr bin Haraam رضي الله عنه

Hadhrat Jaabir's رضي الله عنه father, 'Abdullah bin 'Amr bin Haraam رضي الله عنه also passed away as a martyr in this battle.

Hadhrat Jaabir رضي الله عنه narrates: "My father was martyred in the battle of Uhud and the disbelievers subjected his body to dreadful mutilation. When his body was placed before Rasulullah ﷺ, I attempted to lift the cloth covering his face to take a peek but the Sahaabah رضي الله عنهم prevented me from doing so. When I attempted to raise the cloth a second time, they again prevented me, but Rasulullah ﷺ allowed me to take a look.

"When my aunt (my father's sister), Hadhrat Faatimah bint 'Amr رضي الله عنها burst out weeping, Rasulullah ﷺ remarked: "Why do you weep? The angels are constantly casting shade over him." This continued until his Janaazah (bier) was lifted."

In other words, this is not an occasion of solemn grief but an occasion of profound joy in the sense that the angels are casting shade over your brother.

Hadhrat Jaabir رضي الله عنه narrates: "Once when Rasulullah ﷺ caught sight of me, he asked in concern: 'O Jaabir! What is the matter? I notice that you are looking somewhat depressed?' I replied: 'O Rasulullah! My father was martyred in the battle of Uhud and he left behind a burden of young children and debts.'

Rasulullah ﷺ replied: 'Should I not convey a glad tiding to you?'

'Surely', I replied. 'Why not? Please do tell me.'

Rasulullah ﷺ said: 'Allah has spoken to anyone but through a veil but in the case of your father, Allah resuscitated him and spoke to him directly and said: 'O My servant! What do you desire? Present whatever wish you have before Me.' To this your father replied: 'I wish to be resuscitated and killed once more in

Your path.' Allah Ta'ala responded: 'No, this cannot happen because it has been decisively decreed that there is no return (to earth) after death.'"

'Abdullah bin 'Amr bin Haraam ﷺ says: "A few days before the battle of Badr I saw Mubashhir bin Munzir in a dream addressing me thus: 'O 'Abdullah! Soon you will be joining us.' I asked: 'Where are you?' He replied: 'In Jannah where we move about and wander as we please.' I asked: 'Were you not killed in the battle of Badr?' Mubashhir replied: 'Yes but I was resuscitated.'"

'Abdullah ﷺ says: "I narrated this dream to Rasulullah ﷺ who remarked: 'O Abu Jaabir! The interpretation of this dream is martyrdom.'"

Martyrdom of 'Amr bin Jamooh ﷺ

In the same battle, 'Abdullah bin 'Amr bin Haraam's ﷺ brother-in-law (sister's husband) 'Amr bin Jamooh ﷺ was martyred. The account of his martyrdom is also rather astounding. 'Amr bin Jamooh ﷺ was lame and this lameness on his leg was not mild but incredibly severe. He had four sons, all of whom accompanied Rasulullah ﷺ in every one of his battles. Before their departure for Uhud, he apprised them: "I am also coming with you in Jihaad." They responded: "You are excused. Allah has offered you respite. It is better if you stay here."

But where would these enthusiasts of determination ever submit to the proposals of respite? He became so restless with the enthusiasm for martyrdom that limping heavily he appeared before Rasulullah ﷺ and submitted:

والله انى لارجو ان اطأ بعرجتى هذه فى الجنة

"O Rasulullah! (My sons forbid me from joining you.) By Allah! I hope to trample the (soil of) Jannah with this lameness of mine."

Rasulullah ﷺ responded: "You have been pardoned by Allah. Jihaad is not compulsory upon you." Rasulullah ﷺ then addressed his sons saying: "What harm is there if you abstain from preventing him? Perhaps Allah Ta'ala will bless him with martyrdom."

He then set out for Jihaad where he was martyred.

Whilst setting out from Madinah, he faced the Qiblah and made the following dua:

اللهم ارزقنى الشهادة ولا تردنى الى اهلى

"O Allah! Bless me with martyrdom and do not return me to my family."

In the same battle, his son Khallaad bin 'Amr bin Jamooh ﷺ was also martyred.

'Amr bin Jamooh's wife, Hindah bint 'Amr bin Haraam رَضِىَ اللّٰهُ عَنْهَا (sister of 'Abdullah bin 'Amr bin Haraam and the aunt of Hadhrat Jaabir رَضِىَ اللّٰهُ عَنْهُ) decided to load all three bodies (the body of her brother Abdullah bin 'Amr bin Haraam, the body of her son Khallaad bin 'Amr bin Jamooh and the body of her husband 'Amr bin Jamooh) onto one camel and transport them to Madinah for burial there. However, the camel would sit down whenever it was directed towards Madinah but it would quicken its pace when directed towards Uhud.

When Hindah appeared before Rasulullah صَلَّى اللّٰهُ عَلَيْهِ وَسَلَّمَ to apprise him of this strange phenomenon, he asked: "Did 'Amr bin Jamooh make any dua whilst departing from Madinah?" "Yes", she replied and then went on to mention the aforementioned dua. Rasulullah صَلَّى اللّٰهُ عَلَيْهِ وَسَلَّمَ commented: "This is why the camel refuses to return towards Madinah."

Rasulullah صَلَّى اللّٰهُ عَلَيْهِ وَسَلَّمَ then remarked:

والذى نفسى بيده ان منكم من لو اقسم على الله لابره منهم عمرو بن الجموح ولقد رأيته يطأ بعرجة فى الجنة

"I swear by the Being in whose absolute control lies my life, verily there are some amongst you who, if they take an oath in the name of Allah Ta'ala, He would ensure that the oath is fulfilled. One of such people is 'Amr bin Jamooh. I beheld him strolling in Jannah with the same limp."

'Abdullah bin 'Amr bin Haraam رَضِىَ اللّٰهُ عَنْهُ and 'Amr bin Jamooh رَضِىَ اللّٰهُ عَنْهُ were both buried in one grave close to the mountain of Uhud.

Martyrdom of Khaysamah رَضِىَ اللّٰهُ عَنْهُ

Hadhrat Khaysamah رَضِىَ اللّٰهُ عَنْهُ (whose son S'ad was martyred whilst fighting alongside Rasulullah صَلَّى اللّٰهُ عَلَيْهِ وَسَلَّمَ in the battle of Badr) appeared before Rasulullah صَلَّى اللّٰهُ عَلَيْهِ وَسَلَّمَ and said: "O Rasulullah صَلَّى اللّٰهُ عَلَيْهِ وَسَلَّمَ! It is a pity I missed the battle of Badr. I was extremely eager to participate in that battle. In fact, I was so keen that my son S'ad and I drew lots to determine who would be blessed with this good fortune. However, this fortune was decreed for my son S'ad. His name came up in the lot and he was blessed with martyrdom whilst I was left behind.

Last night I saw my son in a dream. He was looking extremely handsome and exceptionally attractive. I saw him strolling about in the gardens and streams of Jannah. He said to me: 'O father! Why don't you join me? Both of us will live together in Jannah. Whatever promises my Lord made unto me, I found them to be absolutely true.'

"O Rasulullah صَلَّى اللّٰهُ عَلَيْهِ وَسَلَّمَ!" Hadhrat Khaysamah رَضِىَ اللّٰهُ عَنْهُ said: "I look forward to my son's company in Jannah. I am now an old man and my bones are gone weak but my heartfelt desire is to meet my Lord. Make dua that Allah Ta'ala blesses me with martyrdom and grants me the company of S'ad in Jannah."

Rasulullah ﷺ then made dua for Hadhrat Khaysamah ؓ. Allah Ta'ala accepted this dua and he was martyred in the battle of Uhud.

Insha Allah and Insha Allah again, there is a strong hope that Hadhrat Khaysamah ؓ joined his son S'ad ؓ in Jannah.

Martyrdom of Usayrim ؓ

'Amr bin Saabit who was commonly known by his title Usayrim always remained aloof from Islam. He was initially indisposed to embracing Islam. On the day of Uhud, Islam penetrated his heart and clutching a sword in his hand, he strode onto the battlefield and valiantly fought the disbelievers until he fell down wounded. When the people discovered that it was Usayrim, they were stunned and asked: "O 'Amr! What prompted you of all people to engage in this battle? Were you prompted by an earnest desire for Islam or was it due to fanatical patriotism and nationalistic zeal?"

Usayrim replied:

بل رغبة فى الاسلام فامنت بالله ورسوله فاسلمت واخذت سيفى
وقاتلت مع رسول الله صلى الله عليه وسلم حتى اصابنى ما اصابنى

"In fact my participation in this battle was prompted solely by my earnest desire for Islam. So I embraced Islam and put my faith in Allah and His Rasool and clutching a sword I fought on the side of Rasulullah ﷺ until I was afflicted with these wounds."

He barely finished uttering these words when he left this world.

انه لمن اهل الجنة

"Surely he is amongst the inhabitants of Jannah."

Abu Hurayrah ؓ would often ask: "Tell me, who was admitted into Jannah without performing a single Salaah?" It was none other than this Sahaabi ؓ.

People of Madinah Scurry to Ascertain the Well-being of Rasulullah ﷺ

Since some horrific stories about the war had reached Madinah, the men, women, children and the elderly were eager to see Rasulullah ﷺ safe and sound, more than their own relatives.

Hadhrat S'ad bin Abi Waqqaas ؓ narrates: "On his return from this battle, Rasulullah ﷺ passed by an Ansaari woman who lost her husband, brother and father in this battle. When she was informed of the martyrdom of her husband, brother and father, she said: 'No, tell me how is Rasulullah ﷺ?' The people replied: '*Alhamdulillah!* He is well.' The lady replied: 'Show me his blessed face. I will be at ease once I set eyes on him.' When the people pointed out Rasulullah ﷺ to her, she exclaimed: 'Every calamity after you is trivial and insignificant.'"

A Special Favour upon the Sincere Sahaabah ؓ during the Anxiety of Battle

When a certain shaytaan circulated a rumour of Rasulullah's ﷺ martyrdom, some Muslims, due to their basic human temperament, were thrown into a state of mental turmoil. In this state of anguish and bewilderment, their feet staggered away from the battlefield for a little while. During this period, those who were destined for martyrdom were martyred and those who were destined to break away from the field moved off. As for those who were left on the battlefield, the devout, sincere and divinely reliant amongst them were overcome with drowsiness. These people dozed off whilst standing. One of them was Abu Talhah ؓ.

Abu Talhah ؓ narrates: "A number of times my sword fell off my hands onto the ground. Each time my sword fell down I would retrieve it."

This was actually the feeling of inner tranquillity that Allah Ta'ala had bestowed upon the people of faith and this inner calm instantly dispelled the fear of the disbelievers from the hearts of the Muslims. As for the hypocrites who were ostensibly taking active part in the battle, they were in absolute fear. Their sole concern centred on saving their own lives. These unfortunate ones were not overcome with drowsiness. In this regard the following verses were revealed:

$$ثُمَّ اَنْزَلَ عَلَيْكُمْ مِّنْ بَعْدِ الْغَمِّ اَمَنَةً نُّعَاسًا يَّغْشٰى طَآئِفَةً مِّنْكُمْ ۙ وَطَآئِفَةٌ قَدْ اَهَمَّتْهُمْ اَنْفُسُهُمْ يَظُنُّوْنَ بِاللّٰهِ غَيْرَ الْحَقِّ ظَنَّ الْجَاهِلِيَّةِ ۚ$$

"Then after the distress, He sent down peace (and security) for you. Slumber overtook a party of you, while another party was concerned (solely) about themselves and they indulged in thinking wrongly of Allah, thoughts of ignorance."
[Surah Aal Imraan verse 154]

Hafiz Ibn Katheer ؒ says: "The group that was overcome with slumber was made up of the believers who were accredited with unwavering faith, steadfastness and true reliance upon Allah Ta'ala. They had firm conviction that Allah Ta'ala would certainly assist His Rasool ﷺ and He would definitely fulfill the promise He made to His Rasool ﷺ.

The second group who were merely concerned about saving themselves and they were fretful to be overcome with sleep comprised of the hypocrites. Their only concern was their own personal safety. They were deprived of the slumber of peace and tranquillity."

Shrouding and Burial of the Martyrs

In this battle seventy Sahaabah رضي الله عنهم were martyred, most of them were from the Ansaar. They were so destitute that they did not even possess sufficient cloth to shroud their dead. When Mus'ab bin 'Umair رضي الله عنه was martyred, the sheet for his burial shroud was so short that when his head was covered, his feet would be exposed and when his feet were covered his face would be exposed. Eventually, Rasulullah ﷺ advised them to cover his head with the sheet and his feet with izkhir leaves.

A similar incident is recorded about Sayyidush-Shuhadaa Hamzah رضي الله عنه.

Some of the martyrs were not favoured even with a single sheet of cloth. Some of them were shrouded in pairs with a single sheet of cloth between the two of them, and then in sets of two's and three's, they were buried in a single grave. At the time of burial, Rasulullah ﷺ would ask: "Who knows more of the Qur-aan from amongst them?" He would then place whoever was pointed out to him towards the front of the grave facing the Qiblah. The others would then be placed behind him. Rasulullah ﷺ would then remark:

انا شهيد على هؤلاء يوم القيامة

"I will bear witness in their favour on the day of Qiyaamah."

Rasulullah ﷺ also instructed them to bury these martyrs without ghusl in their same blood-spattered clothing.

Some of the Sahaabah رضي الله عنهم expressed a desire to take the bodies of their loved ones back to Madinah for burial but Rasulullah ﷺ turned them down and bade them to bury their dead where they were martyred.

Patriotic martyrdom

On the day of Uhud, a man by the name of Qazmaan fought with outstanding valour and unique devotion and single-handedly he put down seven or eight disbelievers. Eventually, he was also wounded in battle. When he was carried back home, some Sahaabah رضي الله عنهم remarked:

والله لقد ابليت اليوم يا قزمان فابشر

"Qazmaan! By Allah, today you have displayed unrivalled feats. Congratulations to you."

Qazmaan replied:

اذا ابشر فوالله ان قاتلت الا عن احساب قومى ولو لا ذلك ما قاتلت

"Why do you congratulate me? By Allah, I did not engage in battle for the pleasure of Allah and His Rasool. I fought solely in defence of my people. If it was not for this, I would not have fought."

When he was unable to bear the pangs of pain any longer, he committed suicide.

Note: Actually, this man was a hypocrite. The valiant accomplishments he displayed whilst fighting with the Muslims against the disbelievers was prompted by sentiments of patriotism and he lost his life in this condition. This is why Rasulullah ﷺ declared him to be from the dwellers of Jahannam. A martyr is he who engages in Jihaad 'to elevate the word of Allah'. He who fights and gives his life on grounds of patriotism, may be referred to as a "patriotic martyr" in current terminology but in Islam he is not referred to as a true Shaheed (martyr).

A Synopsis of the Wisdom behind the Defeat at Uhud

As per the divine assurance of Allah Ta'ala, the Muslims prevailed over the disbelievers at the beginning of the battle but when they abandoned their positions, which Rasulullah ﷺ had assigned to them and they descended down the mountain in quest of the war booty, the tide of the war rapidly altered and the imminent victory was turned into humiliating defeat. In the divine court of Allah Ta'ala, the devoted servants and the sincere lovers are taken to task for even the most apparently 'trivial' violation. In this case, Allah Ta'ala did not like His sincere and devoted servants (the Sahaabah) to infringe, even modestly, the commandments of Rasulullah ﷺ even though this infringement was induced by misunderstanding or oversight. Furthermore, for a true beloved, his eminence of love does not warrant him abandoning his commitment and scampering after the pittance of this dunya and something as pitiful as the war booty. The war booty for which the Sahaabah  abandoned their positions and rushed down the mountain was absolutely Halaal and pure for them as Allah Ta'ala declares in another verse:

فَكُلُوا مِمَّا غَنِمْتُمْ حَلَالًا طَيِّبًا

"So eat from what you have acquired as war booty Halaal (lawful) and Tayyib (pure)." [Surah Anfaal verse 69]

However, it was inappropriate for lovers of the Sahaabah's ﷺ calibre to chase after something without the permission of Allah Ta'ala even though it may be Halaal and Tayyib.

As a form of admonishment, Allah Ta'ala transformed the imminent victory of His devoted servants into a temporary defeat to warn them of pinning their hopes on anyone other than Allah Ta'ala. Although this short-lived defeat was already preordained in the knowledge of Allah Ta'ala, but amends for this defeat would be made at the conquest of Makkah and in the future, the treasures of Caesar and Chosroe would be granted to them. In short, the hearts of the devoted lovers should be cleansed of even the inclination towards the permissible things of this dunya. In this regard, Allah Ta'ala revealed the following verses:

وَلَقَدْ صَدَقَكُمُ اللّٰهُ وَعْدَهُ إِذْ تَحُسُّوْنَهُمْ بِإِذْنِهِ ۖ حَتّٰى إِذَا فَشِلْتُمْ وَتَنَازَعْتُمْ فِى الْأَمْرِ وَعَصَيْتُمْ مِّنْ بَعْدِ مَآ أَرٰكُمْ مَّا تُحِبُّوْنَ ۚ مِنْكُمْ مَّنْ يُّرِيْدُ الدُّنْيَا وَمِنْكُمْ مَّنْ يُّرِيْدُ الْاٰخِرَةَ ۚ ثُمَّ صَرَفَكُمْ عَنْهُمْ لِيَبْتَلِيَكُمْ ۚ وَلَقَدْ عَفَا عَنْكُمْ ۗ وَاللّٰهُ ذُوْ فَضْلٍ عَلَى الْمُؤْمِنِيْنَ ۝

"And Allah fulfilled His promise (of victory) to you when you were slaying them (the enemy) with His permission (and you managed to kill seven or nine disbelievers who were the flag bearers of the army) until you lost your courage and you plunged into dispute about the commandment and you disobeyed after He showed you from that (booty or victory) which you desire. Amongst you are some who desire the world and some who desire the hereafter. Then He turned you away from them (by making you flee and bringing about your defeat) so that He may test you. (In short, He changed this victory to defeat to test you and to clearly establish who is genuine and who is fake) and Allah has forgiven you (this error. Hence, to criticise any of them or even to pass judgement on any of them is impermissible.) And Allah is most gracious to the believers." [Surah Aal-'Imraan verse 152]

In these verses, Allah Ta'ala explains that the tables have suddenly turned. The army of the disbelievers who were getting a thrashing at the hands of the Muslims were now absorbed in killing the Muslims. One of the reasons for this rapid change was that some of the Sahaabah did not comply with the instructions of Rasulullah ﷺ. The result of this negligence was that due to the shortcomings of a few, the whole army had to suffer the consequences of defeat. *Inna Lillaahi wa Inna Ilayhi Raaji'un.*

However, the infinite benevolence and immeasurable compassion of Allah Ta'ala was not interrupted. In spite of the Muslims being affectionately reprimanded, Allah Ta'ala consoled them repeatedly and encouraged them not to lose hope. He has forgiven them their indiscretions. Allah Ta'ala proclaims His forgiveness in this verse, "And Allah has forgiven you and Allah is most gracious to the believers" and at the end of the Ruku, as an additional consolatory measure, Allah Ta'ala once again announces His forgiveness when He declares:

اِنَّ الَّذِيْنَ تَوَلَّوْا مِنْكُمْ يَوْمَ الْتَقَى الْجَمْعٰنِ ۙ اِنَّمَا اسْتَزَلَّهُمُ الشَّيْطٰنُ بِبَعْضِ مَا كَسَبُوْا ۚ وَلَقَدْ عَفَا اللهُ عَنْهُمْ ۗ اِنَّ اللهَ غَفُوْرٌ حَلِيْمٌ ۞

"Verily those who fled on the day both the armies confronted one another, the only reason for this was that shaytaan caused them to stumble. Verily, Allah has forgiven them. Indisputably, He is all-Forgiving, most Tolerant."
[Aal-'Imraan verse 155]

Campaign of Hamraa ul-Asad - Sunday 16th Shawwaal 3 A.H.

As the Quraysh returned from Madinah after the battle of Uhud and they camped at a place called Rawhaa, they reckoned that their mission was still unaccomplished. They reflected that since they had already killed so many of Muhammad's companions and injured so many more, they should rather return to Madinah and once and for all launch a decisive attack on them. The Muslims, they thought, were fatigued and wounded. They would not be able to weather another attack. However, Safwaan bin Umayyah suggested: "It would be best if we returned to Makkah. Muhammad's companions are currently fired by an arduous zeal and courage. Perhaps you would be unsuccessful in your next attack."

On Saturday evening, the 15th of Shawwaal, the Quraysh landed in Rawhaa. The aforementioned discussion took place the same night. The night barely passed when at the time of true dawn, the informer of Rasulullah ﷺ alerted him to this discussion. Without delay, Rasulullah ﷺ despatched Hadhrat Bilal رضي الله عنه to enjoin the people of Madinah to make preparations to depart for battle. Further, it was announced that only those who participated in the battle of Uhud may accompany them on this expedition. Following this announcement, Hadhrat Jaabir bin 'Abdullah رضي الله عنه appeared before Rasulullah ﷺ and submitted: "O Rasulullah! My father was martyred in the battle of Uhud and since I was caught up in taking care of my young sisters, I was unable to participate in the battle of Uhud. I beg you to allow me to accompany you on this expedition." Rasulullah ﷺ thus allowed him to join in.

The objective of this advance was to demonstrate to the enemy that the spirit of the Muslims was not broken. The Muslims were not weak and vulnerable. Although the Sahaabah رضي الله عنهم were seriously wounded and exhausted and they barely managed to get a single nights sleep, they promptly heeded to the call of Rasulullah ﷺ and set out for war.

Chapter 15

رشتهٔ در گردنم افگنده دوست

می برد هر جا که خاطر خواه اوست

"The true beloved has placed a rope around my neck.

He may lead me wherever He wishes. (We are utterly subservient to His commandments and wishes.)"

On Sunday the sixteenth of Shawwaal, Rasulullah ﷺ set out from Madinah and halted at a place called Hamraa ul-Asad, which is about eight to ten miles from Madinah. Whilst Rasulullah ﷺ was encamped at Hamraa ul-Asad, the leader of the Khuzaa'ah tribe, Ma'bad Khuzaa'i, appeared before Rasulullah ﷺ to offer his condolences on the defeat of the Muslims in the battle of Uhud. He also commiserated with Rasulullah ﷺ on the martyrdom of his companions at Uhud.

When Ma'bad left Rasulullah ﷺ, he proceeded to Abu Sufyaan who expressed a keen desire to launch a fresh attack on Madinah. Ma'bad remarked: "Muhammad has set out with an enormous force to fight and hound you." The moment Abu Sufyaan heard this he promptly left for Makkah.

Rasulullah ﷺ stayed for three days at Hamraa ul-Asad and left for Madinah on Friday. In this regard, the following verse was revealed:

اَلَّذِيْنَ اسْتَجَابُوْا لِلهِ وَالرَّسُوْلِ مِنْ بَعْدِ مَآ اَصَابَهُمُ الْقَرْحُ ۚ لِلَّذِيْنَ اَحْسَنُوْا مِنْهُمْ وَاتَّقَوْا اَجْرٌ عَظِيْمٌ ۚ

"Those who responded to the call of Allah and His messenger after being wounded; for such people who perform good deeds and cherish Allah-consciousness there is a great reward." [Surah Aal-'Imraan verse 172]

Chapter 16

Miscellaneous events of 3 A.H.

1. In this year, during the month of Sha'baan, Rasulullah ﷺ married Hadhrat Hafsah ﵂, the daughter of Hadhrat 'Umar ﵁.
2. In this year, on the fifteenth of Ramadhaan, Hadhrat Hasan ﵁ was born and just fifty days later, Sayyidah Faatimah ﵂ fell pregnant with Hadhrat Husain ﵁.
3. In this year, during the month of Shawwaal, the prohibition of liquor was revealed.

Sariyyah (expedition) of Abu Salamah 'Abdullah bin 'Abdul-Asad ﵁ (4 A.H.)

On the first of Muharram 4 A.H., Rasulullah ﷺ received information that the sons of Khuwaylid, Talihah and Salamah, were mobilising their people to launch an attack on Rasulullah ﷺ.

In response, Rasulullah ﷺ despatched one hundred and fifty Muhaajireen and Ansaar under the command of Abu Salamah bin 'Abdul-Asad ﵁ to fend off any attack. The moment the enemy got wind of their attack, they took flight and dispersed.

A number of camels and goats were captured, which they brought back to Madinah. This war booty was distributed amongst the participants of this battle. After deducting the one khums (one fifth) from the booty, each of them ended up with seven camels and seven goats each.

Sariyyah (expedition) of 'Abdullah bin Unais ﷺ

On Monday, the fifth of Muharram, Rasulullah ﷺ received information that Khaalid bin Sufyaan Huzali Lihyaani was diligently amassing a force to attack Rasulullah ﷺ. As a pre-emptive strike, Rasulullah ﷺ sent 'Abdullah bin Unais ﷺ to assassinate him.

'Abdullah bin Unais ﷺ met with him and with elusive tricks, when he was presented with an opportunity he killed him and grasping the severed head, he fled into a cave. A spider wove a web over the mouth of the cave. When his pursuers searched the area and they came across the spider's web covering the mouth of the cave, they returned.

In due course, Hadhrat 'Abdullah ﷺ left the cave. He would travel at night and go into hiding during the day. Thus he made his way to Madinah on the 23rd of Muharram and dumped Khaalid's head before Rasulullah ﷺ.

Rasulullah ﷺ was exceptionally delighted and presented him with a staff saying:

تَخَصَّرْ بِهَذِهِ فِى الجنة ، فان المتخصرين فى الجنة قليل

"Hold onto this staff and enter Jannah. People holding staffs and entering Jannah would number very few."

He then added: "This would be a symbol between you and I on the day of Qiyaamah."

All his life thereafter, Hadhrat 'Abdullah ﷺ took painstaking care of this staff. On his deathbed, he willed that the staff be placed with his shroud (kafan). This is exactly what happened. His wish was carried out accordingly.

This man (Khaalid bin Sufyaan) was also rude and abusive (towards Rasulullah ﷺ).

Musa bin 'Aqabah says: "People claim that even before the arrival of 'Abdullah bin Unais ﷺ, Rasulullah ﷺ had already informed the Sahaabah ﷺ of the assassination of Khaalid bin Sufyaan."

Incident of Raj'i

During the month of Safar, some members of the 'Adal and Qaarah tribes appeared before Rasulullah ﷺ and submitted: "O Rasulullah! Our people have embraced Islam. So we request you to send us some people who would impart to us the knowledge of the Qur-aan and the teachings of Islam." Rasulullah ﷺ sent ten Sahaabah ﷺ along with them. Some of these Sahaabah ﷺ were:

1. 'Aasim bin Saabit رضي الله عنه
2. Marsad bin Abi Marsad رضي الله عنه
3. 'Abdullah bin Taariq رضي الله عنه
4. Khubaib bin 'Adi رضي الله عنه
5. Zaid bin Dasinah رضي الله عنه
6. Khaalid bin Abil-Bukair رضي الله عنه
7. M'utab bin 'Ubaid رضي الله عنه, the brother of 'Abdullah bin Taariq رضي الله عنه.

Rasulullah ﷺ appointed 'Aasim bin Saabit رضي الله عنه as an Ameer over them.

When these Sahaabah رضي الله عنهم reached Raj'i, located between Makkah and 'Asfaan, these disloyal tribesmen fell foul of their promise (they made to Rasulullah ﷺ) and alerted the Banu Lihyaan tribe. Marshalling two hundred warriors, including one hundred archers, the Banu Lihyaan set out in ardent pursuit. As they drew closer, Hadhrat 'Aasim رضي الله عنه and his companions clambered up a hillock.

The Banu Lihyaan called out to the Muslims: "Come down, we promise you refuge and sanctuary." Hadhrat 'Aasim رضي الله عنه replied: "I will never resort to the sanctuary of a disbeliever."

He then made the following dua:

اَللّٰهم اخبر عَنَّا رَسُوْلَكَ

"O Allah! Inform Your Messenger of our plight."

According to another narration, Allah Ta'ala accepted the dua of Hadhrat 'Aasim رضي الله عنه and through divine revelation, He instantly enlightened Rasulullah ﷺ about their plight. Rasulullah ﷺ then notified the Sahaabah رضي الله عنهم.

One of the duas Hadhrat 'Aasim رضي الله عنه made was:

اللهم انى احمى لك اليوم دينك ، فاحم لى لحمى

"O Allah! Today I am safeguarding Your Deen. I beg you to safeguard my flesh (my body from the disbelievers)."

Thereafter Hadhrat 'Aasim رضي الله عنه, together with seven of his companions were martyred whilst engaging the enemy in combat.

On the assurance of sanctuary and safety by the disbelievers, the remaining three Sahaabah 'Abdullah bin Taariq رضي الله عنه, Zaid bin Dasinah رضي الله عنه and Khubaib bin 'Adi رضي الله عنه descended from the hillock. However, the instant they came down, the disbelievers tied up their arms and legs. To this 'Abdullah bin Taariq رضي الله عنه

remarked: "This is the foremost betrayal. You are acting treacherously right at the beginning; I wonder what the future would hold?"

Saying this, he refused to go with them. The disbelievers dragged him on the ground and killed him. His remaining two companions, Hadhrat Khubaib رضى الله عنه and Hadhrat Zaid رضى الله عنه were taken to Makkah where they were sold as slaves.

Safwaan bin Umayyah (whose father Ummayyah bin Khalaf was killed at Badr) purchased Hadhrat Zaid رضى الله عنه with the sole purpose of putting him to death in retaliation for the death of his father. Haaris bin 'Aamir was killed in Badr at the hands of Hadhrat Khubaib رضى الله عنه. Thus the sons of Haaris purchased Khubaib.

Safwaan considered any delay in the killing of his prisoner to be inappropriate. Hence, he sent Hadhrat Zaid رضى الله عنه with his slave Nastaas out of the Haram area to a place called Tan'eem to kill him. A group of the Quraysh also gathered to watch this spectacle of death. One of the spectators was Abu Sufyaan bin Harb.

As Hadhrat Zaid رضى الله عنه was brought for execution, Abu Sufyaan tauntingly asked: "O Zaid! I ask you to swear in the name of Allah, would you not be delighted to be set free and Muhammad executed in your place whilst you are relaxing comfortably in your home?"

Annoyed by this remark, Hadhrat Zaid رضى الله عنه fervently retorted: "By Allah! I will not tolerate even a thorn pricking Muhammad صلى الله عليه وسلم on his foot whilst I am relaxing at home."

To this Abu Sufyaan commented: "I have not witnessed anyone as fanatically devoted, fervently committed and ardently selfless as the companions of Muhammad are devoted to him."

Thereafter, Nastaas put Hadhrat Zaid رضى الله عنه to death.

Later on in life, Nastaas embraced Islam.

Hadhrat Khubaib رضى الله عنه, on the other hand, stayed in their detention until the end of the month of Muharram. As he was close to his date of execution, he asked Zainab bint Haaris (who later embraced Islam) for a blade to clean himself. She furnished him with a blade and got busy with her housework. Zainab relates: "A little while later I was stunned to see my son calmly sitting on his lap with a blade in his (our captive's) hand. I was somewhat alarmed at this sight."

On witnessing my distress, Hadhrat Khubaib رضى الله عنه commented: "Are you apprehensive over me killing this child? Never! Insha Allah, I will never do something like this. We folks are neither treacherous nor deceitful."

Hadhrat Zainab would frequently recall this moment and comment:

ما رأيت اسيرا قط خيرا من خبيب ، لقد رأيته يأكل من قطعة عنب وما بمكة يومئذ ثمرة وانه لموثق فى الحديد وما كان الارزق رزقه الله

"I have not come across a captive better than Khubaib. I noticed him eating from a bunch of grapes whereas there was not a piece of fresh fruit available in Makkah at

that time. And furthermore, he was fettered in shackles. He could not have brought it from anywhere. This was nothing but the sustenance of Allah provided to him."

As he was brought to Tan'eem for execution, he appealed to them to allow him to perform two Rakaats of Salaah. They permitted him and as he completed his two Rakaats, he addressed the disbelievers saying: "I did not prolong my Salaah because you may accuse me of doing so for fear of my imminent death." He then raised his hands and made the following dua:

اللّهم احصهم عددًا، واقتلهم بددا، ولا تبق منهم احدا

"O Allah, one by one kill them all and do not leave anyone behind."

He then recited the following stanzas:

لست ابالى حين اقتل مسلما   على اى شق كان لله مـصـرعى

"I am not disturbed in the least if I am killed as a Muslim, regardless of the side I fall on provided it is for Allah alone.

وذلك فى ذات الاله وان يشأ   يبارك على اوصال شلو مُمَزَّع

And this is solely for the pleasure of Allah. If He wishes, He can bless the joints of my shattered body."

Hadhrat Khubaib رضي الله عنه was then crucified and martyred. For future generations, he also instituted a tradition of two Rakaat Salaah for every person condemned to death.

Zaid bin Haarisah رضي الله عنه was also beset by a similar incident during the life of Rasulullah صلى الله عليه وسلم. On his return from Taaif, Zaid رضي الله عنه hired a mule. The owner of the mule was also with him. En route, the owner manoeuvred the mule into an eerily desolate area where a number of bodies of his previous victims were strewn about. As he was about to kill him, Zaid رضي الله عنه asked him for a respite of just two Rakaat of Salaah. The man mockingly remarked: "Well, go ahead and perform your Salaah. Those before you also performed Salaah but to no avail."

As Zaid رضي الله عنه completed his two Rakaat, the man drew closer to finish him off. The moment Hadhrat Zaid رضي الله عنه spotted his menacing presence advancing towards him, he uttered: "Yaa Arhamar-Raahimeen! (O Most Merciful of all the merciful)."

These words of Ism-e-A'zam barely left his tongue when the man heard a voice from the unseen charging: "Do not kill him." Terrified of this bewildering voice from the unseen, this man started looking about. When he detected no physical presence, he advanced once again with this evil scheme. Hadhrat Zaid رضي الله عنه again uttered: "Yaa Arhamar-Raahimeen!" Once more the man heard a threatening sound and he apprehensively withdrew. Like before, he again strode towards him and yet again, Hadhrat Zaid ﷺ uttered "Yaa Arhamar-Raahimeen!"

He barely said Yaa Arhamar-Raahimeen the third time when suddenly before him appeared a rider wielding a spear tipped with a blazing coal. This rider propelled the spear with such force that it went straight through the murderer and emerged from his back. He was dead before he fell to the ground.

Thereafter, the rider addressed Hadhrat Zaid ﷺ and said: "When you said Yaa Arhamar-Raahimeen the first time, I was on the seventh sky and when you uttered these words a second time, I was at the sky of this world and I was already before you when you uttered them the third time."

Rasulullah ﷺ said: "A person who says Yaa Arhamar-Raahimeen thrice, a divinely appointed angel responds to his entreaty by saying: 'Arhamur-Raahimeen (Allah Ta'ala) has turned His attention towards you. Lay bare your request before Him.'"

A similar incident also happened to Abu Mu'allaq Ansaari ﷺ. Ubayy bin K'ab ﷺ and Anas bin Maalik ﷺ narrate: "Amongst the companions of Rasulullah ﷺ, Abu Mu'allaq Ansaari ﷺ was an exceptionally ardent devotee and a very saintly man. He was a phenomenally Allah-conscious man. He was also a prominent businessman. He would often undertake business journeys. On one of his trade expeditions he came across a fully equipped bandit armed with a sword, spear and cutlass (short broad-bladed curved sword). The bandit demanded: 'Leave your goods here. I want to kill you.'

Abu Mu'allaq Ansaari ﷺ said: 'If wealth is what you seek, my goods are accessible to you. Why do you need to kill me also?' The bandit replied: 'No, it is only your life I desire.'

To this Abu Mu'allaq Ansaari ﷺ replied: 'Okay, at least allow me to perform my Salaah.' The bandit sarcastically remarked: 'Sure, you may perform as much Salaah as you wish.'

Abu Mu'allaq Ansaari ﷺ performed wudhu, offered Salaah and made the following dua:

يا وَدُودُ يَا ذُوالْعَرْش المجيد يا فَعَّالُ لما تريد اسالك بعزتك التى

لاترام وملكك الذى لايضام و بنورك الذى ملأ اركان عرشك ان

تكفينى شر هذ اللص يا مغيث اغثنى

'Yaa Wadudu Yaa Zul-'Arshil-Majeed. Yaa Fa'aalul-Limaa Tureed. Asaluka Bi 'Izzatikallati Laa Turaam wa Mulkikallazi Laa Yudaam wa Bi Noorikallazi Mala' Arkaana 'Arshika An Takfiyani Sharra Haazallis. Yaa Mugheeth, Aghithni.'

O The Most Loving One! O The Possessor of the exalted throne! O The One who does as He wishes! I beg of You by Your Majesty which cannot be attained, by Your Kingdom in which no soul is oppressed and by Your Light which illuminates the pillars of Your Throne to protect me from the evil of this thief! O Helper! Help me.

He said the aforementioned words thrice. In an instant he caught sight of a rider armed with a spear looming towards the bandit whom he rapidly finished off.

Abu Mu'allaq Ansaari ﷺ then gaped at the newcomer and asked: 'Who are you?' He replied: 'Allah despatched me to offer you assistance and help. I am an angel of the fourth heaven. When you recited this dua the first time, I heard knocking sounds on the doors of the heavens. When you recited it the second time, I heard the bellowing shrieks of the dwellers of the heavens. When you recited the dua for the third time, I said to myself, this is indisputably the voice of a person in distress and anguish. At that time, I requested Allah Ta'ala to appoint me as that bandit's executioner.'

The angel then added: 'Glad tidings for you. Bear in mind that the person who offers four Rakaat of Salaah after performing Wudhu and then makes the aforementioned dua, his dua is certainly accepted, whether he is in distress or not.'"

In the battle of Uhud, Hadhrat 'Aasim ﷺ killed two sons of Salaafah bint Sa'eed. Fuelled by the rage of vengeance, she vowed to drink wine in the skull of 'Aasim ﷺ. Some people of the Huzail tribe went to fetch 'Aasim's head with the aim of selling his head to Salaafah for a princely sum of money.

Salaafah announced that the person who brings 'Aasim's head will be rewarded with a handsome prize of a hundred camels.

Hadhrat 'Aasim ﷺ had already made dua previously for the safety and protection of his body. Allah Ta'ala made miraculous arrangements for the protection of his body from his enemies by posting a swarm of wasps around his body. No disbeliever dared to venture nearby. As they drew closer to his body and set eyes on this strange scene, they said: "We will return at night when the wasps disappear and then we will sever his head." However, as the night approached, a sudden flood washed his body away leaving them all furiously disappointed. Hadhrat 'Aasim ﷺ pledged to Allah Ta'ala that neither should he touch a mushrik (disbeliever) nor should a mushrik touch him.

Whenever Hadhrat 'Aasim ﷺ was mentioned in the presence of Hadhrat 'Umar ﷺ, he would comment: "Allah Ta'ala protects some of His special servants even after their death as He protected them during their lifetime."

Hadhrat Khubaib's ﷺ body was left suspended on the cross by the disbelievers of Makkah. Rasulullah ﷺ sent Hadhrat Zubair ﷺ and Hadhrat Miqdaad ﷺ from Madinah to Makkah to bring his body down. As they landed in Tan'eem, they spotted forty guards lying around the cross. Taking advantage of their negligence, they swiftly brought his body down from the cross and loaded it on their horse. Although he was hanging for forty days on the cross, his body was still fresh without any perceptible change.

When the disbelievers opened their eyes and found the body missing, they scuttled about in search of it. They eventually apprehended Hadhrat Zubair رَضِىَ اللّٰهُ عَنْهُ and Hadhrat Miqdaad رَضِىَ اللّٰهُ عَنْهُ. Hadhrat Zubair رَضِىَ اللّٰهُ عَنْهُ gently lowered the body to the ground and almost immediately the ground split open and swallowed his body. This is why, Hadhrat Khubaib رَضِىَ اللّٰهُ عَنْهُ was distinguished as Bali'ul-Ard (one swallowed by the earth).

According to another narration, when Hadhrat Khubaib رَضِىَ اللّٰهُ عَنْهُ was martyred, his face was facing the Qiblah. The moment the disbelievers attempted to turn his face away from the Qiblah, his face miraculously turned back towards the Qiblah. They attempted this repeatedly but overwhelmed they eventually left him alone.

Chapter 17

The Incident of Bi'r Ma'unah

In the same month of Safar, another momentous incident occurred. 'Aamir bin Maalik Abu Baraa appeared before Rasulullah ﷺ and offered him a gift, but Rasulullah ﷺ declined his offer. Rasulullah ﷺ then invited him to Islam but Abu Baraa neither accepted nor denied Islam but said: "If you send some of your companions towards Najd (the Arabian highlands) with the sole purpose of inviting others to Islam, I cherish a sincere hope that they will embrace Islam." Rasulullah ﷺ replied: "I am anxious about the menace these companions may face from the inhabitants of Najd." Abu Baraa replied: "I give you my word. I vouch for their safety."

Rasulullah ﷺ sent seventy Sahaabah رضي الله عنهم with him. This august group was referred to as the Qurra (the Qaaris). Rasulullah ﷺ appointed Munzir bin 'Amr Saa'idi رضي الله عنه as an Ameer over them.

This was an incredibly devout and faithful group of souls. During the day they would collect firewood, which they would sell in the evening and buy food for the Ashaab-e-Suffah. Part of the night they would spend in learning and teaching the Qur-aan and part of it in Tahajjud Salaah.

This group of saintly personages set off and landed in a place called Bi'r Ma'unah. Rasulullah ﷺ had addressed a letter to 'Aamir bin Tufail (leader of the Banu 'Aamir tribe and nephew of Abu Baraa) and handed this letter over to Haraam bin Milhaan رضي الله عنه, the uncle (mother's brother) of Hadhrat Anas رضي الله عنه.

As they landed in Bi'r Ma'unah, Haraam bin Milhaan appeared before 'Aamir bin Tufail with this blessed letter but even before 'Aamir bin Tufail could read the letter, he gestured to another person to kill him. He thrust a spear from the back that penetrated right through him. At this moment, the following words were on his tongue:

$$\text{الله اكبر! فزت و رب الكعبة}$$

"Allahu Akbar! Allah is the Greatest. I swear by the Lord of the K'abah, I am victorious."

'Aamir bin Tufail then incited his people to kill the rest of the Sahaabah رضى الله عنهم as well but owing to the protection offered by 'Aamir's uncle, Abu Baraa, the Banu 'Aamir tribe refused to support him.

When 'Aamir bin Tufail noticed their aversion to his sinister plans and he despaired of their support, he approached the Banu Sulaim tribe for help. The tribes of 'Usayyah, R'al and Zakwaan willingly responded to his call for help. Drawn together, they unjustly put all these Sahaabah رضى الله عنهم to death. Only K'ab bin Zaid Ansaari رضى الله عنه was saved. He was scarcely alive and he was left for dead. He later regained consciousness and lived for some time thereafter. He was martyred in the expedition of Khandaq (trench). Apart from him, another two Sahaabah were also spared; Munzir bin Muhammad رضى الله عنه and 'Amr bin Umayyah رضى الله عنه. These two Sahaabah were grazing the animals in the fields when this incident occurred. They were busy grazing their animals when suddenly they caught sight of a huge flock of birds in the sky. Alarmed by this sight, they figured that something was not right. As they approached their camp, they found their companions drenched in blood 'lying on beds of martyrdom'. They consulted with one another on what action to take. 'Amr bin Umayyah suggested they return to Madinah and inform Rasulullah صلى الله عليه وسلم about this. Munzir replied: "He will somehow get the news. Why should we forfeit our chance of martyrdom?"

Nonetheless, they advanced to engage the enemy in battle. Hadhrat Munzir رضى الله عنه was martyred whilst fighting and 'Amr bin Umayyah رضى الله عنه was captured.

They took 'Amr bin Umayyah رضى الله عنه to 'Aamir bin Tufail, who shaved off his hair and released him saying: "My mother vowed to emancipate a slave. In execution of this vow, I set you free."

In this expedition, Abu Bakr's رضى الله عنه emancipated slave, 'Aamir bin Fuhayrah رضى الله عنه was also martyred and his body was raised to the heavens. In this regard, 'Aamir bin Tufail asked his tribesmen:

$$\text{من الرجل منهم لما قتل رايته رفع بين السماء والارض حتى رايت السماء من دونه}$$

"Who was this man from amongst the Muslims, when he was killed I noticed his body lifted between the sky and the earth until his body disappeared within the sky?"

The people replied: "It was 'Aamir bin Fuhayrah رضى الله عنه."

According to the narration of Bukhaari, 'Aamir bin Tufail remarked:

لقد رايته بعد ما قتل رفع الى السماء حتى انى لانظر الى السماء بينه
و بين الارض ثم وضع

"After he was killed, I witnessed his body being lifted to the sky as though it was suspended between the earth and sky. Thereafter it was put back on the earth."

Jabbaar bin Salma, the killer of 'Aamir bin Fuhayrah رَضِىَاللّٰهُعَنْهُ, relates: "When I stabbed 'Aamir bin Fuhayrah with my spear, he cried out: 'I swear by the Lord of the K'abah! I have reached my goal.'

On hearing these words, I was left astounded. I thought, what goal could he have reached? When I narrated this incident to Dahhaak bin Sufyaan رَضِىَاللّٰهُعَنْهُ, he explained: 'He meant that he has reached his goal of Jannah.' On hearing this explanation, I embraced Islam."

He explains:

ودعانى ذلك ما رأيت من عامر بن فهيرة من دفعه الى السماء علوا

"What stirred me to embrace Islam is that I witnessed the body of 'Aamir bin Fuhayrah رَضِىَاللّٰهُعَنْهُ being lifted to the sky."

When Dahhaak رَضِىَاللّٰهُعَنْهُ wrote to Rasulullah ﷺ about this phenomenal incident, Rasulullah ﷺ responded by explaining:

ان الملائكة وارت جثته فى عليين

"The angels have concealed his body in the 'Illiyyeen."

According to another narration, the angels hid his body away from the disbelievers and they were unable to determine its exact location.

When Rasulullah ﷺ was notified of the massacre of his Sahaabah رَضِىَاللّٰهُعَنْهُ in this expedition, he was driven to such anguish that never in his life was he so grief-stricken. For a whole month he continued cursing these people in the Qunoot of Fajr Salaah. He then addressed the Sahaabah رَضِىَاللّٰهُعَنْهُ saying: "Your friends and beloved companions were martyred. They requested Allah Ta'ala to inform me that they have met their Lord and that they are pleased with Him and He is pleased with them."

Battle of Banu Nazeer - Rabi'ul-Awwal 4 A.H.

As 'Amr bin Umayyah Damari رَضِىَاللّٰهُعَنْهُ (one of the survivors of the expedition of Bi'r Ma'unah) was returning to Madinah, he came across two disbelievers from the

Banu 'Aamir tribe who joined him on his journey. When they reached a place called Qanaat, they took shelter in one of the orchards. When these two disbelievers fell off to sleep, 'Amr bin Umayyah Damiri reflected that the leader of their tribe 'Aamir bin Tufail killed seventy Muslims. It was presently inconceivable to avenge the deaths of all of them. Why don't I avenge the deaths of some of them?, he thought. On this presumption, he killed both of them whereas Rasulullah ﷺ had a peace agreement with this tribe, of which 'Amr bin Umayyah Damiri had absolutely no knowledge of.

When he reached Madinah and notified Rasulullah ﷺ about his actions, Rasulullah ﷺ remarked: "We had a peace agreement with them. We ought to pay the blood money for both of them." Rasulullah ﷺ then remitted their blood money to their tribe.

Since the Banu Nazeer tribe was also an ally of the Banu 'Aamir, in terms of the peace treaty, part of the blood money was payable by the Banu Nazeer. To solicit some assistance in payment of this blood money, Rasulullah ﷺ decided to approach the Banu Nazeer. He set off in the company of, amongst others, Abu Bakr, 'Umar, 'Usmaan, Zubair, Talhah, 'Abdur-Rahmaan bin 'Awf, S'ad bin Mu'aaz, Usaid bin Hudhair and S'ad bin 'Ubaadah رضى الله عنهم.

Rasulullah ﷺ seated himself in the shade of a wall. Outwardly, the Banu Nazeer received Rasulullah ﷺ with an impressive display of courtesy and pledged to assist in the payment of the blood money but secretly they proposed to post someone on top of the roof and roll a heavy boulder onto his head and get rid of him once and for all.

However, Sallaam bin Mishkam warned his tribesmen: "No! Do not ever do that. By Allah, his Lord would surely inform him of your malicious intentions. Furthermore, this is tantamount to a violation of our peace treaty with him."

No sooner had they proposed this than Jibraa'eel عليه السلام brought down divine revelation enlightening Rasulullah ﷺ about their wicked intentions. Rasulullah ﷺ swiftly got up and headed off towards Madinah. Rasulullah ﷺ got up as though he was getting up for some temporary need. This is why the Sahaabah رضى الله عنهم continued sitting where they were. When the Jews learnt of Rasulullah's ﷺ departure, they were pitched into a cauldron of simmering despair. One of their Jewish tribesmen, Kinaanah bin Huwayraa remarked: "Don't you know why Muhammad got up from there? By Allah, he was promptly informed about your treachery. By Allah, he is a messenger of Allah."

When Rasulullah ﷺ was delayed in his return, the Sahaabah رضى الله عنهم also got up and went out in search of him towards Madinah. Rasulullah ﷺ updated them about the betrayal of the Jews and issued a directive to attack the Banu Nazeer.

Appointing 'Abdullah ibn Ummi Maktum ﷺ as an Ameer over Madinah, Rasulullah ﷺ set off for the Banu Nazeer and laid siege to them. The Banu Nazeer quickly darted into their fortresses and shut the doors. On the one hand they were conceited with their 'impregnable' and secure fortresses and on the other hand, their arrogance was given a boost when 'Abdullah bin Ubayy and the other hypocrites assured them that they could count on their support. However, none of them dared to confront the Muslims.

Furthermore, the Banu Nazeer engaged in subsequent acts of blatant treachery. They sent a message to Rasulullah ﷺ requesting him to come with three people for a discussion with three of their rabbis. They assured Rasulullah ﷺ that if these rabbis embrace Islam all of them would promptly follow suit. However, privately they advised these three rabbis that just before they are to have discussions with Rasulullah ﷺ, they should hide daggers within their clothing and at the first opportunity they should do away with him.

Long before these people came for a discussion, Rasulullah ﷺ was notified of their brazen deceitfulness.

In short, the repeated acts of treachery and betrayal of the Banu Nazeer compelled Rasulullah ﷺ to issue a directive of launching an attack against them. The siege lasted for fifteen days. Rasulullah ﷺ also ordered their palms and orchards to be set on fire. Eventually, utterly grieved and facing huge losses, they begged for clemency.

Rasulullah ﷺ responded by saying: "You have ten days to empty out your homes. You may take your wives, families and children wherever you wish. With the exception of your weapons, you may also carry away as much goods as your camels and conveyances can bear. You have unrestrained permission to take away as much as you wish."

Driven by greed, they even removed the doors and doorframes of their houses and where possible, lugged them away on their camels. In this manner, they were banished from Madinah. Most of them sought refuge in Khaybar whilst some of them settled down in Syria. Their leaders, Huyayy bin Akhtab, Kinaanah bin Rab'i and Sallaam bin Abil-Haqeeq were also amongst those who decided to settle down in Khaybar.

Rasulullah ﷺ then distributed their remaining goods amongst the Muhaajireen to lessen the burden from the shoulders of the Ansaar although the Ansaar, due to their sincerity and selflessness, did not regard this as a burden but as a source of coolness to their eyes and a balm to their hearts. Nonetheless, Rasulullah ﷺ summoned the Ansaar and formally addressed them. In this address, after praising Allah Ta'ala he paid tribute to the sacrifices of the Ansaar and their good conduct to the fellow brethren, the Muhaajireen. He then said: "O people of the Ansaar! If you wish I am prepared to distribute the wealth of the Banu Nazeer equally between you and the Muhaajireen and they will continue sharing your wealth as in the past or if you wish, I will distribute it solely amongst the Muhaajireen (and due to their subsequent independence from you) they will then vacate your homes."

S'ad bin 'Ubaadah رضي الله عنه and S'ad bin Mu'aaz رضي الله عنه, the leaders of the Ansaar submitted: "O Rasulullah ﷺ! From the depths of our hearts, we would be delighted if you distribute this wealth amongst the Muhaajireen only and despite this, they are at liberty to live in our homes and partake of our meals, as in the past."

According to another narration, the Ansaar submitted: "O Rasulullah ﷺ! You may distribute this wealth solely amongst the Muhaajireen. Moreover, it would be our pleasure if you take whatever you wish from our wealth and distribute it amongst them."

Such soothing words made Rasulullah ﷺ break out in cheerful delight and he made the following dua for them:

اللهم ارحم الانصار وابناء الانصار

"O Allah! Shower Your special compassion upon the Ansaar and the offspring of the Ansaar."

Abu Bakr رضي الله عنه remarked:

جزاكم الله خيرا يا معشر الانصار! فوالله، مامثلنا ومثلكم
الاكما قال الغنوي

"May Allah reward you favourably, O Ansaar! By Allah, the similitude between you and us can only be described in the words of the poet Ghanawi, when he says:

جزى الله عنا جعفرا حين ازلقت   بنا نعلنا فى الواطئين فزلت

ابوا ان يملون ولو ان امنا   تلاق الذي يلقون منا لملت

'May Allah reward Ja'far, when our feet slipped but he fell, this would not deter him from offering additional assistance to us. Perchance, if our own mothers were to be confronted with such a situation, they would probably be deterred.'"

Rasulullah ﷺ then distributed the entire wealth amongst the Muhaajireen and from the Ansaar, only Abu Dujaanah رضي الله عنه and Sahal bin Hunaif رضي الله عنه, due to their poverty, were awarded a share of it.

As a consequence of this expedition, only two people from the Banu Nazeer embraced Islam; Yaameen bin 'Umair رضي الله عنه and Abu Sa'eed bin Wahab رضي الله عنه. Their wealth and property were left intact. They remained in control of their property.

Surah Hashr was revealed on account of this expedition. 'Abdullah bin 'Abbaas رضى الله عنه would refer to this Surah as 'the Surah of Banu Nazeer. In this Surah, Allah Ta'ala explains the laws relating to Maal-e-Fayy (war booty) and its recipients.

Prohibition of liquor

The injunction prohibiting liquor was revealed during this expedition.

Expedition of Zaatur-Riqaa - Jumaadal-Awwal 4 A.H.

After the expedition of Banu Nazeer, from Rabi'ul-Awwal to the beginning of Jumaadal-Awwal, Rasulullah ﷺ stayed in Madinah.

During the early days of the month of Jumaadal-Awwal, Rasulullah ﷺ received information that the Banu Mahaarib and the Banu Sa'labah tribes were amassing their troops in preparation for war against Rasulullah ﷺ.

In the company of four hundred Sahaabah رضى الله عنهم, Rasulullah ﷺ set off towards Najd. When Rasulullah ﷺ landed at Najd, he met a few members of the Ghitfaan tribe but there was no occasion for all out combat. On this occasion, Rasulullah ﷺ performed Salaatul-Khawf (Salaah performed in times of fear with certain restrictions lifted) with the people.

Abu Ash'ari رضى الله عنه says: "This expedition was referred to as Zaatur-Riqaa. Riqaa means rags or patches. Due to our walking on difficult terrain, our feet became cracked and we were forced to wrap them in rags and pieces of cloth, hence the name 'the expedition of rags'."

Ibn S'ad رحمه الله, however, says: "Zaatur-Riqaa is a name of a mountain where Rasulullah ﷺ camped during this expedition. It had black, white and red signs on it."

On his return, Rasulullah ﷺ took a nap beneath a shade-bearing tree on which he had hung his sword. A disbeliever silently sneaked up to him, unsheathed Rasulullah's ﷺ sword and growled: "Tell me, who will protect you from me?" Rasulullah ﷺ calmly responded: "Allah."

Jibraa'eel عليه السلام suddenly delivered a punch to his chest. The sword fell out of his hands. Rasulullah ﷺ retrieved it and asked: "Who will protect you from me?" The man replied: "Nobody." Rasulullah ﷺ said: "Go! I have pardoned you."

This man subsequently embraced Islam and returned to his people and invited them towards Islam. A number of people embraced Islam at his behest.

This man's name was Ghawrith bin Haaris.

When he left this area, Rasulullah ﷺ then stopped over at a mountain pass. He appointed 'Ammaar bin Yaasir رضي الله عنه and 'Abbaad bin Bishr رضي الله عنه as sentinels over the pass. Amongst themselves they agreed that 'Abbaad would stand guard for the first half of the night and 'Ammaar the latter half. As per their arrangement, 'Ammaar bin Yaasir رضي الله عنه took rest whilst 'Abbaad bin Bishr رضي الله عنه devoted himself to a vigil of Ibaadat and commenced his Salaah.

A disbeliever came by and concluded that this man surely looks like the sentry for tonight's watch. He fired off an arrow that landed dead on its mark but genuine devotion to his true Master had penetrated every fibre of 'Abbaad bin Bishr's رضي الله عنه being. He was saturated in his love for his Lord and the sweetness of his faith had permeated the depths of his heart. How then, could an arrow and spearhead disturb his devotions? He continued performing his Salaah in the same serene manner. He calmly pulled out the arrow and tossed it aside. The enemy discharged a second arrow and he took that out also and flung it aside. The enemy then let loose a third arrow.

Overcome with fear of the enemy ambushing them and for fear of defeating the purpose of their appointment over the pass by Rasulullah ﷺ, he completed his Salaah and woke his friend up saying: "Get up, I am wounded." On observing him getting his companion up, the enemy bolted.

When 'Ammaar bin Yaasir رضي الله عنه got up and noticed the blood streaming down his body, he remarked: "Subhaanallah! Why did you not get me up the moment the first arrow struck you?" He replied: "I was busy reciting a certain Surah of the Qur-aan and I felt it inappropriate to cut it short. When a volley of arrows started raining down on me, I terminated my Salaah and got you up. I swear by Allah, if it was not for the instructions of Rasulullah ﷺ, my life would have terminated before the termination of my Salaah."

Expedition of the Badr - Sha'baan 4 A.H.

After his return from the expedition of Zaatur-Riqaa, Rasulullah ﷺ remained in Madinah until the end of Rajab. On his return from Uhud, Rasulullah ﷺ had promised Abu Sufyaan to meet at Badr for another encounter in the forthcoming year, Rasulullah ﷺ set out for Badr in the company of fifteen hundred Sahaabah رضي الله عنهم in the month of Sha'baan. He waited for eight long days at Badr for Abu Sufyaan but to no avail.

In the company of a number of Makkans, Abu Sufyaan had also set out for battle but when he reached Marruz-Zahraan he lost his nerve and turned back saying: "This is a year of famine and high prices and not the year of war and confrontation."

Following a wait of eight days, when Rasulullah ﷺ lost all hope of waging war against them, he returned to Madinah.

On his return from Uhud, although openly Abu Sufyaan had pledged to fight at Badr in the forthcoming year, at heart he was cowed into terror. Secretly he hoped Rasulullah ﷺ would also not make it to Badr so that he did not have to suffer further humiliation and indignity whilst holding the Muslims liable (for not making it to the meeting). A person by the name of Nu'aim bin Mas'ood was going to Madinah. Abu Sufyaan offered him some money to spread a rumour amongst the Muslims of Madinah that the Makkans were diligently assembling a massive force to root out the Muslims once and for all. Hence, it would be better for the Muslims not to advance against such a colossal army. Abu Sufyaan's objective was to intimidate the Muslims with such rumours and to dissuade them from coming out to battle.

On hearing such news, the spirit of Imaan of the Muslims was given a further boost. Chanting the words *Hasbunallah Wa N'imal-Wakeel* they set out for Badr.

Near Badr, a bazaar used to be held. For three days the Muslims engaged in trade and received substantial profits from their unexpected commercial activities. They returned to Madinah with goodness and blessings. In this regard, the following verses were revealed:

اَلَّذِيْنَ اسْتَجَابُوْا لِلّٰهِ وَالرَّسُوْلِ مِنْۢ بَعْدِ مَاۤ اَصَابَهُمُ الْقَرْحُ ۛ لِلَّذِيْنَ اَحْسَنُوْا مِنْهُمْ وَاتَّقَوْا اَجْرٌ عَظِيْمٌ ۚ اَلَّذِيْنَ قَالَ لَهُمُ النَّاسُ اِنَّ النَّاسَ قَدْ جَمَعُوْا لَكُمْ فَاخْشَوْهُمْ فَزَادَهُمْ اِيْمَانًا ۖ وَّقَالُوْا حَسْبُنَا اللّٰهُ وَنِعْمَ الْوَكِيْلُ ۚ فَانْقَلَبُوْا بِنِعْمَةٍ مِّنَ اللّٰهِ وَفَضْلٍ لَّمْ يَمْسَسْهُمْ سُوْٓءٌ ۙ وَّاتَّبَعُوْا رِضْوَانَ اللّٰهِ ۗ وَاللّٰهُ ذُوْ فَضْلٍ عَظِيْمٍ ۚ اِنَّمَا ذٰلِكُمُ الشَّيْطٰنُ يُخَوِّفُ اَوْلِيَآءَهٗ ۖ فَلَا تَخَافُوْهُمْ وَخَافُوْنِ اِنْ كُنْتُمْ مُّؤْمِنِيْنَ ۚ

"Those who responded (to the call of) Allah and His messenger after they were wounded, for those who do good amongst them and adopt taqwa, is a great reward. Those (believers) unto whom the people (hypocrites) said: 'Verily the people (the Makkans) have amassed (their forces) against you, so fear them.' but this (intimidating statement) only increased them in faith and they (Muslims) said: 'Allah alone is sufficient for us' and He is the best disposer (of all affairs).' So they returned with grace and bounty from Allah. No harm afflicted them and they pursued the pleasure of Allah. Allah is the owner of great bounty. It was shaytaan who terrified his supporters (disbelievers). So do not fear them but fear Me if you are believers." [Surah Aal-'Imraan verses 172-175]

Commentary: In this verse Allah Ta'ala refers to a rumour-monger (or propagandist) as a shaytaan when He says: 'It was shaytaan who terrified his supporters'. Allah Ta'ala described the antidote to this propaganda by exhorting the Muslims to continue with their preparations for Jihaad to the best of their abilities and to recite *Hasbunallah Wa Ni'mal-Wakeel*. In other words, place your trust firmly in Allah Ta'ala and as shaytaan is wont to do, do not spread false rumours about your enemies. Respond to lies with the truth. Allah forbid, if you were to respond to these lies with additional lies, what then is the benefit of this? Islam does not permit slander even against its enemies.

Miscellaneous Incidents of 4 A.H.

1. During Jumaadal-Awwal of this year, 'Abdullah, the son of Hadhrat 'Usmaan bin Affaan ﷺ passed away at the age of six.

2. During the month of Sha'baan of this year, Hadhrat Husain ﷺ was born.

3. In Ramadhaan of this year, Rasulullah ﷺ married Hadhrat Zainab bint Khuzaymah ﷺ Ummul-Masaakeen (mother of the destitute).

4. During Shawwaal of this year, Rasulullah ﷺ married Hadhrat Umme Salamah ﷺ.

5. In the same year Rasulullah ﷺ instructed Hadhrat Zaid bin Saabit ﷺ to learn to read and write Hebrew as he was not comfortable with the Jews reading for him.

6. According to the most acknowledged reports, Hijaab (pardah) was ordained in this year as well. Some are of the opinion that it was ordained in 3 A.H. whilst others maintain that it was prescribed in 5 A.H.

Expedition of Dawmatul Jandal

During Rabi'ul-Awwal, Rasulullah ﷺ received word that the inhabitants of Dawmatul-Jandal were preparing to launch an attack against Madinah. In the company of one thousand Sahaabah ﷺ, Rasulullah ﷺ set out for Dawmatul-Jandal on the 25th of Rabi'ul-Awwal 5 A.H. The moment they sensed the looming advent of the Muslim army, they rapidly scattered away. Without any form of physical combat, Rasulullah ﷺ returned to Madinah on the 20th of Rabi'us-Saani.

Expedition of Muraysi' or Banu Mustaliq

Rasulullah ﷺ received news that Haaris bin Abi Diraar, the leader of the Banu Mustaliq tribe had gathered a huge force and was preparing to launch an attack against the Muslims. Rasulullah ﷺ sent Buraydah bin Husaib Aslami ﷺ to confirm the accuracy of this intelligence. When Buraydah ﷺ returned and confirmed the truth of this report, Rasulullah ﷺ instructed the Sahaabah رضي الله عنهم to make preparations for battle.

The Sahaabah رضي الله عنهم were battle-ready within moments of this prophetic command. They set out with thirty horses. Of these, twenty belonged to the Ansaar whilst the remaining ten to the Muhaajireen.

On this occasion, driven by the prospective allure of abundant booty, a large group of hypocrites, who had never joined a single expedition before this, also accompanied them.

Rasulullah ﷺ appointed Zaid bin Haarisah رضي الله عنه as his representative in Madinah and from the Azwaaj (pure wives) he took along Hadhrat 'Aa'ishah رضي الله عنها and Hadhrat Umme Salamah رضي الله عنها with him. On Monday the 2nd of Sha'baan they set forth.

With lightning speed they launched an attack on the enemy forces catching them by total surprise. As the Muslim army was on the verge of launching an attack, the kuffaar were obliviously engaged in watering their animals. They were unable to withstand this sudden assault. Ten men were promptly despatched to their deaths. The remaining men, women, children and the elderly were taken as prisoners and their wealth taken as spoils of war. The Muslims seized two thousand camels and five thousand goats. Two hundred families were captured as prisoners. Amongst these prisoners was Juwayriyyah, the daughter of Haaris bin Abi Diraar, the leader of the Banu Mustaliq. When the spoils of war were distributed amongst the Mujaahideen, Juwayriyyah fell into the lot of Saabit bin Qays رضي الله عنه. He made her a Mukaatabah. In other words, he guaranteed her emancipation on the payment of a certain sum of money.

Juwayriyyah رضي الله عنها appeared before Rasulullah ﷺ and submitted: "O Rasulullah! You are well aware that I am Juwayriyyah, the daughter of the leader of the Banu Mustaliq tribe, Haaris bin Abi Diraar. The conditions of my capture are not unknown to you. During the distribution, I fell into the lot of Saabit bin Qays and he has made me a Mukaatabah. I now stand before you appealing for your assistance in paying off this Kitaabah."

Rasulullah ﷺ replied: "I suggest something far more superior than that. If you wish, I will pay on your behalf the Kitaabah that is due and I will set you free and take you in marriage." Hadhrat Juwayriyyah رضي الله عنها replied: "This will be most pleasing to me."

From the very outset Hadhrat Juwayriyyah رضي الله عنها wanted to be set free. Coincidentally, her father Haaris also appeared before Rasulullah ﷺ and submitted: "I am the chieftain of the Banu Mustaliq tribe. My daughter cannot live as a bondswoman. I implore you to set her free." Rasulullah ﷺ replied: "Would it not be more appropriate if this was left to the will and desire of Juwayriyyah herself?" Haaris went to Juwayriyyah رضي الله عنها and said: "Rasulullah

ﷺ has left the matter entirely in your hands." To this Juwayriyyah رضي الله عنها replied: "I choose Allah and His Rasool ﷺ."

'Abdullah bin Ziyaad رضي الله عنه narrates: "Hadhrat Juwayriyyah's رضي الله عنها father Haaris bin Abi Diraar took along a number of camels as ransom and set out for Madinah to secure the release of his daughter. Amongst them were two exceptionally fine camels, which he concealed on one of the mountain passes en route. When he reached Madinah, he appeared before Rasulullah ﷺ and presented his camels saying: "O Muhammad ﷺ! You captured my daughter. Take these camels as ransom for her release." Rasulullah ﷺ remarked: "Where are those camels that you concealed at so and so mountain pass?" Haaris exclaimed: "I testify that you are indeed the messenger of Allah. Nobody but Allah had any knowledge about those camels. Only Allah could have alerted you about those camels."

In short, Rasulullah ﷺ set Hadhrat Juwayriyyah رضي الله عنها free and took her in marriage. When the Sahaabah رضي الله عنهم learnt of this, they set every single captive of the Banu Mustaliq free because this tribe was now the in-laws of Rasulullah ﷺ. Ummul-Mumineen Hadhrat 'Aa'ishah Siddeeqah bint Siddeeq رضي الله عنها says: "I have not come across any woman who proved herself to be more beneficial to her people than Juwayriyyah. In just one day, one hundred families were set free because of her."

Since a huge number of hypocrites also accompanied the Muslims on this journey, they revealed their fondness for anarchy and mischief at every turn. At one of the water holes en route, a scuffle broke out between a Muhaajir and an Ansaari. The Muhaajir kicked the Ansaari and bellowed: "O Muhaajireen!" and the Ansaari also roared in response: "O Ansaar!" calling unto their respective tribes for assistance.

When Rasulullah ﷺ heard this commotion, he demanded: "What are these yells of ignorance (Jaahiliyyah)?" The people replied: "A Muhaajir kicked an Ansaari." Rasulullah ﷺ remarked:

$$دَعُوْهَا فَاِنَّهَا مُنْتِنَةٌ$$

"Abandon this because it stinks."

The leader of the hypocrites, 'Abdullah bin Ubayy exploited this ideal opportunity to wag his tongue. Scornfully he remarked: "These people (the immigrant Muhaajireen) have swamped us. By Allah! When we return to Madinah, the noble amongst us will expel the dishonourable."

When Rasulullah ﷺ heard of this rude utterance, Hadhrat 'Umar رضي الله عنه pleaded: "O Rasulullah! Allow me to smite the neck of this hypocrite." Rasulullah ﷺ replied: "No, leave him alone. (People would not understand the reality of the situation) and they would assume that Muhammad kills his companions."

Note: 'Abdullah bin Ubayy was not one of the companions of Rasulullah ﷺ. In fact he was a sworn bitter enemy of Rasulullah ﷺ. However, outwardly he bore a resemblance to the companions of Rasulullah ﷺ. Verbally he claimed to be from the companions. This is why Rasulullah ﷺ refrained from executing him. A resemblance to the sincere Sahaabah رضي الله عنهم saved his life. A resemblance to the pious, even though based on hypocrisy, is not devoid of benefit.

Note: It appears from Rasulullah's ﷺ warning:

دَعُوْهَا فَاِنَّهَا مُنْتِنَةٌ

"Abandon this because it stinks"

Good and pure things are fragrant whilst bad and evil things emit an odour and the external perception of this fragrance or odour can only be perceived by the Ambiyaa عليهم السلام and their faithful heirs.

وعن جابر رضى الله تعالى عنه قال: كنا مع النبى صلى الله عليه وسلم فارتقت ريح منتنة ، فقال رسول الله صلى الله عليه وسلم اتدرون ما هذه الريح؟ هذه ريح الذين يغتابون المؤمنين .

Hadhrat Jaabir رضي الله عنه reports: "We were with Rasulullah ﷺ when a whiff of a disgusting odour blew. On perceiving this stench, Rasulullah ﷺ commented: 'Do you know what this odour is? This is the stench emanating from the mouths of those who are talking ill of the Muslims.'"

It is evident from this Hadith that Rasulullah ﷺ and the Sahaabah رضي الله عنهم perceived the stench of the sin of backbiting but the Sahaabah رضي الله عنهم only came to know of the underlying cause of this stench after Rasulullah ﷺ notified them about it.

A similar incident occurred as they returned close to Madinah, as reported in Muslim by Hadhrat Jaabir رضي الله عنه: "Whilst we were returning from this expedition (of Banu Mustaliq) and as we drew closer to Madinah we were suddenly assailed by a foul gust of wind. Upon this Rasulullah ﷺ remarked: 'This foul-smelling wind is blowing due to the death of a hypocrite." When we reached Madinah, we learnt that a senior hypocrite had just died.'"

It is quite strange to note that 'Abdullah bin Ubayy, was a bitter enemy of Islam and the leader of the hypocrites but his son, also named 'Abdullah, was a sincere and committed Muslim. In reality he was an 'Abdullah (the slave of Allah) whilst his father was 'Abdullah by name only. When 'Abdullah, the son, heard his father's disrespectful words 'the noble amongst us will expel the dishonourable', he immediately stood up, grabbed hold of his father and demanded: "By Allah! I will never allow you to enter Madinah until you declare that you are dishonourable whilst Rasulullah ﷺ is noble." The moment his father admitted this, he released him.

When they returned to Madinah, 'Abdullah ؓ appeared before Rasulullah ﷺ and submitted: "O Rasulullah ﷺ! I heard that you are about to issue an execution order against my father. If you permit, I am prepared to behead my father and place his head before you. I fear that if you had to charge someone else to execute him, I may be overcome with anger and murder the executioner himself. In this manner, I may turn out to be guilty of murdering another Muslim."

Rasulullah ﷺ prevented him from taking the life of his father and directed him to treat his father with graciousness and politeness.

Incident of Slander

The episode of slander against Ummul-Mumineen Hadhrat 'Aa'ishah ؓ also occurred on their return from this expedition.

On this expedition, Hadhrat 'Aa'ishah ؓ also accompanied Rasulullah ﷺ. Since the injunction of Hijaab (pardah) was already revealed, Hadhrat 'Aa'ishah ؓ was carried on a hawdaj (camel carriage). She would be made to mount and dismount the camel with the hawdaj being carried up or down. The hawdaj itself was fully concealed with a curtain suspended over its sides.

As they drew closer to Madinah, they set up camp at a certain place. When the army was instructed to depart, Hadhrat 'Aa'ishah ؓ was gone to answer the call of nature at a secluded spot far away from the people. As she was returning, her necklace of pearls broke and scattered to the ground. She got delayed in searching and retrieving them.

The army was about to depart. The curtains of the hawdaj were drawn and on the inference that Hadhrat 'Aa'ishah ؓ was seated within the carriage, the carriage-bearers hoisted the carriage and mounted it onto the camel in preparation for departure. The women at that time were generally thin and Hadhrat 'Aa'ishah ؓ, due to her young age, was even more slender in built. This is why the carriage-bearers had no hint of the carriage being lighter than usual.

She only found her necklace (beads or pearls) after the army departed and by the time she returned to camp, there was not a soul to be seen. Reasoning that when Rasulullah ﷺ does not find her at the next halt, he would surely send someone to search for her at this very spot, she decided to remain where she was.

She covered herself with a sheet and lay down. A little while later she fell fast asleep.

Safwaan bin Mu'attal Sulami ﷺ, who was appointed to retrieve any valuables accidentally dropped by the travellers, passed by. The instant he laid eyes on her, he recognised her. He had seen Hadhrat 'Aa'ishah ﷺ before the laws of Hijaab were revealed.

At once, he recited *Inna Lillahi wa Inna Ilayhi Raaji'oon*. On hearing this unexpected sound, Hadhrat 'Aa'ishah ﷺ was awakened. She promptly covered her face with her sheet.

Hadhrat 'Aa'ishah ﷺ narrates:

والله ما كلمنى كلمة ولا سمعت منه كلمة غير استرجاعه

"By Allah, he did not speak to me at all nor did he utter a single word except his expression of lament (with the words Inna Lillahi wa Inna Ilayhi Raaji'oon)."

Perhaps, Hadhrat Safwaan ﷺ uttered these words loudly to alert Hadhrat 'Aa'ishah ﷺ of his presence and to ensure that there was no opportunity of further dialogue. No conversation whatsoever occured between the two.

Hadhrat Safwaan ﷺ guided the camel close to Hadhrat 'Aa'ishah ﷺ and made it sit down. He steered the camel before her whilst he himself moved away. Hadhrat 'Aa'ishah ﷺ mounted the camel and taking hold of the reins, Hadhrat Safwaan ﷺ set off. In this manner, they continued their journey until they caught up with the rest of the army.

It was in the middle of the afternoon when they arrived. The moment 'Abdullah bin Ubayy and his cohorts of hypocrites caught sight of them, they plunged into a frenzy of absurd accusations and insulting allegations. Those who were doomed to destruction were destroyed.

When they reached Madinah, Hadhrat 'Aa'ishah ﷺ fell ill. She was in poor health for a whole month. The scandalmongers and mischief-makers were engrossed in this malicious gossiping whilst she, on the other hand, had absolutely no knowledge whatsoever about the slanderous statements that were flying around regarding her. However, she was dreadfully perturbed by the relative aloofness of Rasulullah ﷺ and the unexplained withering of his affection and love for her as he was wont to display in her previous bouts of illness. She was obviously agitated by the fact that Rasulullah ﷺ came home, inquired about her health from others and walked out. "Why does he not enquire from me directly?" she mused. This detachment further aggravated her anguish and pain.

Hadhrat 'Aa'ishah ﷺ relates: "One night Umme Mistah and I went out to the field to relieve ourselves. (It was the custom amongst the Arabs of the past not to erect toilets within the homes due to the odorous smell etc.) On the way, Umme Mistah spoke ill of her son. Hadhrat 'Aa'ishah ﷺ countered: "How can you speak ill of a man who participated in the battle of Badr?" Astonished by her trusting response, Umme Mistah said: "O you naïve girl! Have you not heard the story making its rounds?" "What stories?" she asked in alarm.

When Umme Mistah related the entire incident to her, Hadhrat 'Aa'ishah's رضى الله عنها health took a turn for the worse.

The moment this false allegation fell onto her ears, she was seized by a shuddering fever brought on by this horrifying news.

Without even relieving herself, she returned home. Hadhrat 'Aa'ishah رضى الله عنها narrates: "When Rasulullah ﷺ came home, I requested him to allow me to visit my parents. I actually wanted to make further enquiries about this incident from my parents. Rasulullah ﷺ permitted me to visit my parents.

"When I came to my parent's home, I asked my mother: 'Mother! Do you know what the people are saying about me?' She replied: 'Daughter! Do not be distressed. It is an accepted norm in the world that a woman who is beautiful and morally upright and she enjoys a lofty status in the affections of her husband, jealous women are bound to haunt her with their destructive tricks.' I replied: '*Subhaanallah*! Is this rumour really making its rounds amongst the people?' I then asked: 'Does father know about this rumour?' She replied in the affirmative. She then related: "I said: 'May Allah forgive you, mother. This malicious rumour is making its rounds amongst the people and you did not even mention it once to me!' Whimpering these words, my eyes welled up in tears and I emitted a few shrieks of agony.'

"My father Abu Bakr رضى الله عنه was busy reciting the Holy Qur-aan in the upper section of the house. When he heard me shriek, he came down and asked my mother what was happening. Mother replied: 'She ('Aa'ishah) is now aware of the situation and she now knows about the rumours.' On hearing this, Abu Bakr رضى الله عنه started weeping.

"I, on the other hand, was gripped with such a bout of shivering that my mother Umme Rumaan had to wrap me with whatever available clothing she had in the house. I cried all night long. Not a moment passed without teary eyes until morning greeted us in this state of tormenting anxiety."

Since there was a delay in the revelation of Wahi (divine revelation), Rasulullah ﷺ consulted Hadhrat Ali رضى الله عنه and Hadhrat Usaamah رضى الله عنه on this matter. Hadhrat Usaamah رضى الله عنه declared: "O Rasulullah ﷺ! These are members of your family who are befitting to your lofty status and to the rank of prophethood. There is absolutely no question about their chastity and purity. The purity and chastity of your family members is more conspicuous than the blazing sun. There is absolutely no need to consult us on this matter. And if you really want my opinion, I will submit by saying: 'As far as we know, we know nothing but good about all the pure wives."

Hadhrat Ali رضى الله عنه, on noticing the anguish and sorrow of Rasulullah ﷺ, submitted:

$$\text{يا رسول الله! لم يضيق الله عليك والنساء سواها كثير وان تسأل الجارية تصدقك}$$

"O Rasulullah ﷺ! Allah Ta'ala did not fetter you with any restriction. There are many other women besides her. If you ask the slave girl, she will tell you the truth."

In other words, you are under no obligation. Separation is within your control but before you do anything, why don't you ascertain the facts from the slave girl of the house? She will be able to give you a factual report (because the maids and slaves of the house are more aware of the intimate matters of the household than the menfolk).

Rasulullah ﷺ called for Bareerah and asked:

$$\text{اتشهدين انى رسول الله؟ قالت: نعم. قال: فانى سائلك عن شىء فلا تكتمينه. قال: نعم قال: هل رايت من عائشة ما تكرهينه؟ قالت: لا}$$

"Do you testify that I am the messenger of Allah?" She replied: "Yes!" He said: "I intend to ask you something. Don't hide anything from me (because Allah will surely disclose it to me by means of divine revelation)." When she gave her assurance, Rasulullah ﷺ asked: "Did you ever notice anything about 'Aa'ishah that you found despicable?" She replied: "Never!"

Rasulullah ﷺ asked Bareerah:

$$\text{اى بريره! هل رايت من شىء يريبك}$$

"O Bareerah! Did you ever catch sight of anything that gave you cause for concern or suspicion?"

Bareerah replied:

$$\text{لا! والذى بعثك بالحق، ان رايت عنها امرا اغمصه عليها سوى انها جارية حديثة السن تنام عن عجين اهلها فتأتى الداجن فتاكله}$$

"Never, I swear by the Being who has sent you with the truth! I have not observed 'Aa'ishah engaged in anything that is objectionable or punishable. Yes, she is after all a young girl. She kneads her dough and dozes off to sleep and a kid goat would come and eat it up."

In other words, she is naïve and neglectful of simple things like her dough and dhal. How can she ever be acquainted with the cunning and scheming ways of the world?

On hearing this comforting response from Bareerah رضي الله عنها, Rasulullah ﷺ went to the Masjid, ascended the mimbar and delivered a Khutbah wherein he praised Allah Ta'ala and said:

يا معشر المسلمين! من يعذرني من رجل قد بلغني اذاه في اهل بيتي؟ فوالله، ما علمت على اهلي الا خيرا ولقد ذكروا رجلا ما علمت عليه الا خيرا

"O Muslims! Who will assist me in challenging that man who has caused me untold anguish in regards to my family? By Allah! I have not noticed anything but chastity and purity in the members of my family. As for the man whom they accuse (of this sin), I do not know of anything but good about him."

On hearing these words, the chief of the Aws tribe, Hadhrat S'ad bin Mu'aaz رضي الله عنه stood up and submitted: "O Rasulullah ﷺ! I am ready to offer you any form of assistance. If this man (the accuser) is of the Aws tribe, we would surely behead him ourselves and if he is from our brothers' tribe, the Khazraj, then too we would not hesitate in killing him if you command us to do so.

S'ad bin 'Ubaadah رضي الله عنه, the chief of the Khazraj tribe, inferred that S'ad bin Mu'aaz رضي الله عنه was making a veiled reference to them, as though he was hinting that the accusers and slanderers were from the Khazraj tribe. This implied reference drove him into a spell of uninhibited fervour. He addressed S'ad bin Mu'aaz رضي الله عنه and boomed: "Never, by Allah! You will never be able to kill him." (In other words, if he is a member of our tribe, we will take the privilege of executing him.)

S'ad bin Mu'aaz's رضي الله عنه cousin (father's brother's son) Usaid bin Hudhair رضي الله عنه addressed S'ad bin 'Ubaadah رضي الله عنه and said: "You are wrong! If Rasulullah ﷺ has to charge us to behead him we will definitely behead him ourselves, whether he is of the Khazraj tribe or any other tribe for that matter. Nobody will dare stop us. And are you a hypocrite that you are speaking in defence of the hypocrites?"

In this manner, the argument intensified as though both tribes were on the verge of exchanging blows. Rasulullah ﷺ descended the mimbar and calmed both parties down.

Hadhrat 'Aa'ishah رضي الله عنها relates: "This day also passed in unrestrained sobbing. My tears did not stop flowing for a single moment. The night also passed in this state of emotional agony. I was overwhelmed with such heartache that my parents imagined that my 'liver was sure to split in grief'.

In the morning, my parents came and sat close to me whilst I was busy sobbing away in distress. In the interim, an Ansaari woman also came and joined me in crying. We were obliviously weeping away when Rasulullah ﷺ unexpectedly came into the house. He offered Salaam and seated himself close to me. From the time these rumours were making their rounds, he had never sat so close to me. A whole month had passed in anticipation of the revelation of Wahi (divine revelation).

After taking a seat, Rasulullah ﷺ praised Allah Ta'ala and addressing me, he said:

اما بعد! يا عائشة فانه بلغني عنك كذا وكذا فان كنت بريئة فسيبرئك الله، وان كنت الممت بذنب فاستغفري الله و توبي اليه، فان العبد اذا اعترف بذنبه ثم تاب الى الله تاب الله عليه

'O 'Aa'ishah! Such and such news about you has reached me. If you are innocent, Allah will certainly declare your innocence, and if you have perpetrated a sin, seek the forgiveness of Allah and beg His pardon because if a servant confesses to his perpetration of a sin and begs the forgiveness of Allah, Allah will surely forgive him.'

Hadhrat 'Aa'ishah ﷺ narrates: "When Rasulullah ﷺ terminated his discourse, my tears stopped flowing. I could not even shed a single tear. I told my father: 'Why do you not respond to Rasulullah ﷺ on my behalf?' He replied: 'I am at a loss. I have no idea what to say to him.' I repeated the same request to my mother, who replied in the same vein. Thereafter, I took the bold step of replying myself and declared: 'Allah is well aware of my innocence but this rumour has been so deeply rooted into your hearts that if I assert my innocence – and Allah Ta'ala is well aware of my innocence – you will not believe me. On the contrary, hypothetically speaking, if I confess to this sin you will believe me whereas Allah Ta'ala Himself knows I am totally innocent.'

Sobbing in anguish, I cried out: 'By Allah! I will never repent from the sin they attribute towards me. I will simply utter what Yusuf's ﷺ father expressed before his sons:

'So patience is most fitting and it is Allah alone whose assistance can be sought against (the rumour) you attribute (to me).'"

She relates: "Saying this, I lay down on my bed. At that time I was utterly certain that Allah Ta'ala would clear me of this sin but I had absolutely no idea that Allah Ta'ala would declare my innocence by the revelation of divine verses that would be perpetually recited."

According to another narration, she says: "I had absolutely no idea that verses of the Qur-aan would be revealed about me, verses that would be recited in the Masjids and in the Salaahs.

Yes, I had merely hoped that Rasulullah ﷺ would be shown my innocence through a dream etc. In this manner, I anticipated that Allah Ta'ala would clear me of this rumour."

Revelation of the Verses of Exoneration

(In favour of the Maryam of this Ummah, the pure and most dear wife of Rasulullah ﷺ, Ummul-Mumineen Hadhrat 'Aa'ishah Siddeeqah bint Siddeeq, may Allah Ta'ala be pleased with her, her parents and those who believe in her innocence and may the curse of Allah Ta'ala strike those who doubt her chastity and purity.)

Rasulullah ﷺ barely moved from his place when suddenly the signs of divine revelation appeared on his face. In spite of the severe cold, droplets of perspiration like pearls started dripping down his blessed forehead.

Hadhrat 'Aa'ishah رضي الله عنها relates:

فاما انا فوالله ما فزعت قد عرفت أنّى بريئة، وان الله غير ظالمى،

واما ابواى فما سرى عن رسول الله صلى الله عليه وسلم حتى ظننت

لتخرجن انفسهما خوفاً من ان ياتى من الله تحقيق ما يقول الناس

"As for myself, I was not perturbed in the least because I was confident of my innocence and that Allah Ta'ala would not be unjust to me. As for my parents, they were so devastated by anxiety that I thought they would perish in fear of a verse about to be revealed corroborating these rumours."

Abu Bakr's رضي الله عنه state of anxiety was such that sometimes he would look towards me and sometimes he would cast his glance towards Rasulullah ﷺ. When he would direct his gaze towards Rasulullah ﷺ, he would be terrified and wonder what type of divine commandment was being revealed from the sky, a commandment that was bound to endure up to the day of Qiyaamah. However, when he would peer in my direction and witness my serene composure, he would cherish some hope (of my exoneration).

The entire household was seized with this apprehension between hope and fear when the divine revelation came to an end and Rasulullah's ﷺ blessed face was bright with delight and joy. Wiping his blessed forehead with his blessed hand, he turned towards 'Aa'ishah رضي الله عنها and the first words he uttered were:

Chapter 17

ابشرى يا عائشة! فقد انزل الله براء تك

"Congratulations, O 'Aa'ishah! Allah Ta'ala has revealed your innocence."

To this my mother remarked: "Stand up, O 'Aa'ishah! Express your appreciation to Rasulullah ﷺ." I replied: "By Allah! I will never express my gratitude to anyone other than Allah Ta'ala Who has declared my innocence."

Thereafter, Rasulullah ﷺ informed those present that Allah Ta'ala had revealed the following verses:

اِنَّ الَّذِيْنَ جَآءُوْ بِالْاِفْكِ عُصْبَةٌ مِّنْكُمْ ۚ لَا تَحْسَبُوْهُ شَرًّا لَّكُمْ ۚ بَلْ هُوَ خَيْرٌ لَّكُمْ ۚ لِكُلِّ امْرِئٍ مِّنْهُمْ مَّا اكْتَسَبَ مِنَ الْاِثْمِ ۚ وَالَّذِيْ تَوَلّٰى كِبْرَهٗ مِنْهُمْ لَهٗ عَذَابٌ عَظِيْمٌ ۝ لَوْ لَاۤ اِذْ سَمِعْتُمُوْهُ ظَنَّ الْمُؤْمِنُوْنَ وَالْمُؤْمِنٰتُ بِاَنْفُسِهِمْ خَيْرًا ۙ وَّقَالُوْا هٰذَاۤ اِفْكٌ مُّبِيْنٌ ۝ لَوْ لَا جَآءُوْ عَلَيْهِ بِاَرْبَعَةِ شُهَدَآءَ ۚ فَاِذْ لَمْ يَاْتُوْا بِالشُّهَدَآءِ فَاُولٰٓئِكَ عِنْدَ اللّٰهِ هُمُ الْكٰذِبُوْنَ ۝ وَلَوْلَا فَضْلُ اللّٰهِ عَلَيْكُمْ وَرَحْمَتُهٗ فِي الدُّنْيَا وَالْاٰخِرَةِ لَمَسَّكُمْ فِيْ مَاۤ اَفَضْتُمْ فِيْهِ عَذَابٌ عَظِيْمٌ ۝ اِذْ تَلَقَّوْنَهٗ بِاَلْسِنَتِكُمْ وَتَقُوْلُوْنَ بِاَفْوَاهِكُمْ مَّا لَيْسَ لَكُمْ بِهٖ عِلْمٌ وَّتَحْسَبُوْنَهٗ هَيِّنًا ۖ وَّهُوَ عِنْدَ اللّٰهِ عَظِيْمٌ ۝ وَلَوْ لَاۤ اِذْ سَمِعْتُمُوْهُ قُلْتُمْ مَّا يَكُوْنُ لَنَاۤ اَنْ نَّتَكَلَّمَ بِهٰذَا ۖ سُبْحٰنَكَ هٰذَا بُهْتَانٌ عَظِيْمٌ ۝ يَعِظُكُمُ اللّٰهُ اَنْ تَعُوْدُوْا لِمِثْلِهٖۤ اَبَدًا اِنْ كُنْتُمْ مُّؤْمِنِيْنَ ۝ وَيُبَيِّنُ اللّٰهُ لَكُمُ الْاٰيٰتِ ۚ وَاللّٰهُ عَلِيْمٌ حَكِيْمٌ ۝ اِنَّ الَّذِيْنَ يُحِبُّوْنَ اَنْ تَشِيْعَ الْفَاحِشَةُ فِي الَّذِيْنَ اٰمَنُوْا لَهُمْ عَذَابٌ اَلِيْمٌ ۙ فِي الدُّنْيَا وَالْاٰخِرَةِ ۚ وَاللّٰهُ يَعْلَمُ وَاَنْتُمْ لَا تَعْلَمُوْنَ ۝ وَلَوْلَا فَضْلُ اللّٰهِ عَلَيْكُمْ وَرَحْمَتُهٗ وَاَنَّ اللّٰهَ رَءُوْفٌ رَّحِيْمٌ ۝

"Verily those who brought forth a slander are a group from amongst you. Do not regard it as bad for you but it is good for you. For each of them is the extent he has earned of the sin. And as for him who has earned a greater share of the sin from amongst them, for him will be a great punishment. Why then, did not the believing men and women, when you heard it (the slander), think good of their own people and say: 'This (charge) is an obvious slander.' Why did they not produce four witnesses upon this? Since they (the slanderers) have not produced four witnesses, then by Allah they are liars. Had it not been for the grace and mercy of Allah over you in this world and the hereafter, a great punishment would have befallen you for what you had spoken, when you were propagating it with your tongues and uttering with your mouths that of which you have no knowledge. You regard it as something trivial whereas it is critical by Allah. When you heard this (slander) why did you not say: It is not appropriate for us to speak like this, 'Subhaanak (glory be

to You), this is a blatant slander.' Allah warns you not to repeat the likes of this forever, if you are (truly) believers. And Allah clearly explains the Aayaat (proofs, verses) to you and Allah is all-knowing, all-wise. Verily those who like evil (like adultery etc) to spread amongst the believers, for them is a painful punishment in this world and the hereafter. And Allah knows and you know not. And had it not been for the grace and mercy of Allah upon you, (Allah would have swiftly taken you to task), Allah is most affectionate, most merciful." [Surah Noor]

When Rasulullah ﷺ completed the recitation of these verses, Hadhrat Abu Bakr رضى الله عنه, on hearing the verses confirming the purity and chastity of his beloved daughter, stood up and kissed his innocent and virtuous daughter on her forehead. She asked: "Father! Why did you not consider me innocent before this?"

Hadhrat Abu Bakr رضى الله عنه, who was imbued with truthfulness in every fibre of his being, who was a mountain of honesty and could not be moved by the most dreadful tragedies, offered a reply that is fit to be inscribed on the tablets of the hearts:

اَىُّ سَمَآءٍ تُظِلُّنِى وَاَىُّ اَرْضٍ تُقِلُّنِىْ اِذَا قُلْتُ مَالَمْ اَعْلَمْ

"Which sky will provide me with shelter and which earth will bear me if I have to utter something I have no knowledge of?"

Thereafter Rasulullah ﷺ left Hadhrat Abu Bakr's رضى الله عنه house and proceeded to the Masjid where he delivered a sermon and recited the ten verses affirming the innocence of Hadhrat 'Aa'ishah رضى الله عنها.

The chief perpetrators of this gossip mongering were principally the hypocrites. *Alhamdulillah*, none of the Muslims except a few were implicated in this slander. The few who fell into this trap of the hypocrites due to their naivety and gullibility were:

Mistah bin Asaasah رضى الله عنه, Hassaan bin Saabit رضى الله عنه and Hamnah bint Jahsh رضى الله عنها. Each of them were sentenced to eighty lashes, the punishment for slander as imposed by the Islamic penal code and each one of them also repented from their sin. According to the more reputable reports, 'Abdullah bin Ubayy was not punished because he was, after all a hypocrite and not a Muslim but according to other narrations, he was also subjected to eighty lashes. And Allah Ta'ala knows best.

Mistah رضى الله عنه was the maternal cousin of Hadhrat Abu Bakr رضى الله عنه, his mother's sister's son. Due to his poverty, Hadhrat Abu Bakr رضى الله عنه would see to his financial needs but when Mistah رضى الله عنه entangled himself in this episode, Hadhrat Abu Bakr رضى الله عنه vowed never to spend on him again. Upon this, Allah Ta'ala revealed the following verse:

$$\text{وَ لَا يَأْتَلِ أُولُوا الْفَضْلِ مِنْكُمْ وَ السَّعَةِ اَنْ يُؤْتُوْا أُولِى الْقُرْبٰى وَ الْمَسٰكِيْنَ وَ الْمُهٰجِرِيْنَ فِىْ سَبِيْلِ اللّٰهِ ۪ وَلْيَعْفُوْا وَلْيَصْفَحُوْا ؕ اَلَا تُحِبُّوْنَ اَنْ يَّغْفِرَ اللّٰهُ لَكُمْ ؕ وَاللّٰهُ غَفُوْرٌ رَّحِيْمٌ ۝}$$

"And let not those who have been blessed with grace and wealth swear not to provide (any assistance) to the kinsmen, the destitute and those who migrated in Allah's path. Let them pardon and forgive. Do you not love that Allah forgives you? And Allah is forgiving, merciful." [Surah Noor verse 22]

When Rasulullah ﷺ recited this verse to Hadhrat Abu Bakr رضي الله عنه, he submitted:

$$\text{بلى! والله، انى لأحب ان يغفر الله لى}$$

"Of course, I want Allah to pardon me."

He then continued providing financial assistance to Mistah رضي الله عنه and swore: "By Allah! I will never cease helping Mistah." Compared to previous times, he now doubled his financial assistance to him.

Revelation of Tayammum

According to some narrations, in their return from this expedition, Hadhrat 'Aa'ishah رضي الله عنها lost her necklace and dawn broke whilst the caravan was searching for it. There was no water in this area. The verses of Tayammum were revealed and the Sahaabah رضي الله عنهم performed their Fajr Salaah with Tayammum. The Sahaabah رضي الله عنهم were so overcome with joy that Usaid bin Hudhair رضي الله عنه, swept with elation, remarked: "O family of Abu Bakr! This is not the first of your blessings. In fact, due to your barakah (blessings and good fortune), a number of concessions in divine commandments have already been revealed."

According to other research scholars, the verses of Tayammum were not revealed in this campaign of Banu Mustalaq but they were revealed on another journey subsequent to the campaign of Banu Mustalaq. This is evident from the narration of M'ujam Tabraani wherein Hadhrat 'Aa'ishah رضي الله عنها narrates: "On one occasion I lost my necklace and the slanderers said what they said. Subsequent to this, I once travelled with Rasulullah ﷺ on another journey in which I lost my necklace a second time. Everyone was forced to halt in search of the necklace." Hadhrat Abu Bakr رضي الله عنه reproachfully remarked to Hadhrat 'Aa'ishah رضي الله عنها: "Daughter, on every journey it seems you are becoming a nuisance to the people."

At that very moment the verses of Tayammum were revealed wherein Allah Ta'ala permitted us to make Tayammum and perform Salaah in the absence of water."

Hadhrat Abu Bakr ؓ was overjoyed with the revelation of the concession of Tayammum and addressing Hadhrat 'Aa'ishah ؓ, he cheerily commented: "You are surely blessed! You are surely blessed! You are surely blessed!"

Chapter 18

Battle of Khandaq (Trench) or Ahzaab (Confederates) - Shawwaal 5 A.H.

The battle of Khandaq took place in the year 5 A.H. On their return from the battle of Uhud, Abu Sufyaan made a threatening statement to the Muslims warning them that he would fight them the following year. Saying this he returned to Makkah. In the following year, as the time to carry out his threat drew closer, he left Makkah but returned en route citing reasons of drought and the inappropriateness of war etc. A year later, he attempted to launch an attack against Madinah with a force of ten thousand men. This expedition is referred to as the expedition of Khandaq or the expedition of Ahzaab.

The key factor behind this expedition was that following the banishment of Banu Nazeer, Huyayy bin Akhtab went to Makkah and incited the Quraysh to take up arms against Rasulullah ﷺ. Meanwhile Kinaanah bin Rab'i approached the Banu Ghitfaan tribe and persuaded them too to go into battle against Rasulullah ﷺ. Kinaanah tempted them to agree by offering them half the produce of the palm trees of Khaybar annually. On hearing this pledge, 'Uyaynah bin Hisn Fazaari (their chief) swiftly agreed. The Quraysh, on the other hand, were raging to fight from the beginning (so there was no need to entice them any further).

This is how Abu Sufyaan, with a force of ten thousand strong, set out towards Madinah to defeat the Muslims once and for all.

When Rasulullah ﷺ heard of their departure from Makkah, he consulted the Sahaabah ؓ. Hadhrat Salmaan Faarsi ؓ proposed the digging of trenches around the city. He argued that it would be somewhat gruelling to fight them on the open field. Fighting them from the protection of the trenches would be more appropriate. This proposal appealed to all the Sahaabah ؓ.

Rasulullah ﷺ himself set its boundaries, drew lines and assigned ten people per ten yards for the digging of the trenches.

The trenches were dug so deep that they encountered the moisture of the soil. The trenches were completed in six days.

Rasulullah ﷺ also physically joined the Sahaabah رضي الله عنهم in digging the trenches. He struck the very first pick to the ground with his blessed hands and the following words were on his blessed tongue:

بسم الله وبه بَدِيْنَا وَلَوْ عَبَدْنَا غَيْرَه شَقِيْنَا

"Bismillah, we commence in the name of Allah. If we devoted to anyone other than Him, we would surely be doomed to an ill fate.

حَبَّذَا رَبًّا وحَبَّذا دِيْنًا

Oh, what a wonderful Lord He is and what a magnificent religion we have!"

It was during the midst of winter. Icy cold winds were blowing and they were starving for a few days but the devoted Muhaajireen and Ansaar were enthusiastically engaged in digging the trenches. Whilst occupied in shifting mounds of sand, they would chant the following words:

نحن الذين بايعوا محمّدا   على الجهاد ما بقينا ابدا

"We are those who pledged on the hands of Muhammad (and we have sold our lives to Allah for Rasulullah ﷺ) that we would continue fighting in Jihaad as long as we have life within us."

In response to these words, Rasulullah ﷺ would chant:

اللهم لا عيش الاعيش الاخرة   فاغفر للانصار والمهاجره

"O Allah! There is really no life but the life of the hereafter. So forgive the Ansaar and the Muhaajireen."

At times he would chant:

اللهم انه لا خير الاخير الاخره   فبارك فى الانصار والمهاجره

"O Allah! There is no goodness but the goodness of the hereafter. So bestow Your blessings upon the Ansaar and the Muhaajireen."

Baraa bin 'Aazib رضي الله عنه narrates: "On the day of the trench, Rasulullah ﷺ himself was engaged in carrying the sand of the trenches to such an extent that his blessed stomach turned grimy with dust. Whilst carrying the sand, he would chant the following words:

وَاللَّهِ، لَوْ لَا اللَّهُ مَا اهْتَدَيْنَا   وَلَا تَصَدَّقْنَا، وَلَا صَلَّيْنَا

By Allah! If it was not for the divine guidance of Allah, we would not have been guided, neither would we have performed our Salaah nor disbursed charity.

فَأَنْزِلَنْ سَكِينَةً عَلَيْنَا   وَثَبِّتِ الْأَقْدَامَ إِنْ لَاقَيْنَا

O Allah! Shower us with tranquillity and keep us steadfast when we are confronted with the enemy.

إِنَّ الْأُلَى قَدْ بَغَوْا عَلَيْنَا   إِذَا أَرَادُوا فِتْنَةً أَبَيْنَا

They have been vindictive to us. If they wish to ensnare us into any temptation, we will flatly refuse." (At the end of this stanza are the words Abaynaa, Abaynaa (we will refuse, we will refuse).

Whilst Rasulullah ﷺ was singing these stanzas, as he came to the end, he would repeatedly recite in a loud tone: "Abaynaa Abaynaa Abaynaa..."

Hadhrat Jaabir ؓ narrates: "Whilst digging the trenches, we were confronted by a huge boulder. When we raised this issue with Rasulullah ﷺ, he replied: 'Wait, I will go down into the trench myself.' Due to severe hunger, Rasulullah ﷺ had tied a stone to his abdomen. We also had not tasted anything for three days. Rasulullah ﷺ gripped the pickaxe with his blessed hands and landed a single blow to the boulder turning it to a mound of sand."

According to the narration cited in Nasai, when Rasulullah ﷺ landed the first blow with the pickaxe, a third of the boulder shattered and he remarked: "Allahu Akbar! I have been awarded the keys of the kingdom of Syria. By Allah! At this moment, I can see the red palaces of Syria." When Rasulullah ﷺ struck the boulder a second time, another third broke off and he remarked: "Allahu Akbar! I have been awarded the keys to Persia. By Allah! At this moment I can perceive with my very eyes the white palace of Madaain." When Rasulullah ﷺ struck the boulder a third time, the rest of it shattered and he said: "Allahu Akbar! I have been awarded the keys to Yemen. By Allah, from where I am standing, I can clearly see the doors of Sanaa'."

According to another narration, when Rasulullah ﷺ struck the boulder the first time, a bolt of lightning flashed in the sky illuminated the palaces of Syria. To this Rasulullah ﷺ remarked: "Allahu Akbar!" This Takbeer was then also echoed by the Sahaabah ؓ. Thereafter, Rasulullah ﷺ said: "Jibraa'eel Ameen just informed me that my Ummah is destined to conquer all those cities."

The Muslims barely completed the digging of the trenches when the ten-thousand-strong well-equipped army of the Quraysh landed on the outskirts of Madinah. They set up base near Mount Uhud. With a force of three thousand Sahaabah رضي الله عنهم, Rasulullah ﷺ set out to confront them and set up camp near Mount Sil'a. The trenches were separating both the armies. Rasulullah ﷺ directed all women and children to be secured in one of the fortresses.

Until that moment, the Banu Qurayzah were still neutral. However, the leader of the Banu Nazeer tribe, Huyayy bin Akhtab tried every possible means to win them over as allies against the Muslims. Huyayy bin Akhtab, the leader of the Banu Nazeer tribe personally went to K'ab bin Asad, the leader of the Banu Qurayzah tribe, who had already signed a peace agreement with Rasulullah ﷺ. The moment K'ab caught sight of Huyayy coming, he slammed the fortress door shut. Huyayy shouted: "Open the door. (I wish to speak to you)." K'ab responded:

ويحك يا حيي! انك امرء مشئوم، وانى قد عاهدت محمدا فلست بنا

قضى ما بينى وبينه فانى لم ار منه الا صدقا ووفاء

"Shame on you, O Huyayy! You are certainly an ill-fated man. I have already entered into a pact with Muhammad and I will definitely not violate this agreement because I have not witnessed anything from him but truthfulness, honesty and execution of his promises."

Huyayy, not wanting to be put down any further, pleaded: "Allow me to present before you something that would guarantee you eternal honour. I have brought the forces of Quraysh and Ghitfaan right up to your doorstep. All of us have pledged never to budge an inch until Muhammad and his companions are utterly annihilated."

K'ab replied: "By Allah! You always bring humiliation and shame in your wake. I will never ever breach the accord with Muhammad. I haven't witnessed anything from him but truthfulness, honesty and execution of his promises."

However, Huyayy was not a person to be easily swayed. He persisted in his efforts to influence K'ab until K'ab ultimately agreed to break his commitment with Rasulullah ﷺ.

When Rasulullah ﷺ was informed of their treachery, he sent S'ad bin Mu'aaz رضي الله عنه, S'ad bin 'Ubaadah رضي الله عنه and 'Abdullah bin Rawaahah رضي الله عنه to make further investigations. He also advised them: "If this news proves to be correct, return and inform me in such ambiguous terms that the ordinary person would not be able to grasp its meaning and if this news proves to be incorrect, there is no problem in revealing it publicly."

When this group went to K'ab bin Asad and reminded him about their mutual agreement, he retorted: "What agreement? What pact? And who is Muhammad? I do not ever remember making a pact with him."

When this group returned to Rasulullah ﷺ, they merely said: "'Adal and Qaarah." In other words, just as the tribes of 'Adal and Qaarah acted treacherously with Ashaab-e-Raj'i (Hadhrat Khubaib ؓ and his companions), similarly, these Jews are also guilty of treachery.

Rasulullah ﷺ was immensely disheartened over their betrayal and treachery. Now the Muslims were surrounded by the disbelievers from all sides. Outside enemies resembling a swarm of locusts were camped right before them whilst enemies from within the siege, like the Banu Qurayzah, also linked up with them. In short, the Muslims were facing harrowing odds and to top this, the nights were bitterly cold and they were starving for a number of days.

Allah Ta'ala describes this scenario in Surah Ahzaab in the following words:

$$\text{اِذْ جَآءُوْكُمْ مِنْ فَوْقِكُمْ وَ مِنْ اَسْفَلَ مِنْكُمْ وَ اِذْ زَاغَتِ الْاَبْصَارُ وَ بَلَغَتِ الْقُلُوْبُ الْحَنَاجِرَ وَ تَظُنُّوْنَ بِاللهِ الظُّنُوْنَا ۞ هُنَالِكَ ابْتُلِيَ الْمُؤْمِنُوْنَ وَ زُلْزِلُوْا زِلْزَالًا شَدِيْدًا ۞}$$

"Remember when the enemy came upon you from above and from beneath you, and when the eyes were dazzled (with fright) and the hearts reached the throats (in horror) and you started harbouring a number (of ill thoughts) about Allah. There, the believers were tested and were powerfully shaken." [Surah Ahzaab verses 10-11]

This was a trial for the Muslims. Sincerity and hypocrisy were being screened on the 'scales of trials'. These scales separated the genuine from the bogus. Alarmed by the current events, the hypocrites launched into all forms of lame excuses. Some of them said: "O Rasulullah! Due to the low walls, our houses are not safe. The safety of our wives and children is crucial. So we appeal to you to allow us to leave."

The Holy Qur-aan describes this thus:

$$\text{يَقُوْلُوْنَ اِنَّ بُيُوْتَنَا عَوْرَةٌ وَمَا هِيَ بِعَوْرَةٍ اِنْ يُّرِيْدُوْنَ اِلَّا فِرَارًا ۞}$$

"They (the hypocrites) say: 'Our homes lie exposed (to the enemy).' But they are not exposed. They merely wish to flee. (This is why they are offering lame excuses.)"
[Surah Ahzaab verse 13]

Allah Ta'ala describes the Muslims, whose hearts were infused with sincerity and true faith, thus:

$$\text{وَلَمَّا رَاَ الْمُؤْمِنُوْنَ الْاَحْزَابَ قَالُوْا هٰذَا مَا وَعَدَنَا اللهُ وَ رَسُوْلُهٗ وَ صَدَقَ اللهُ وَ رَسُوْلُهٗ وَمَا زَادَهُمْ اِلَّا اِيْمَانًا وَّ تَسْلِيْمًا ۞}$$

"When the believers caught sight of the confederates (Ahzaab), they said: 'This is what Allah and His Messenger had promised us and Allah and His Messenger had

spoken the truth'. And this only enhanced their faith and submission." [Surah Ahzaab verse 22]

Nonetheless, the Jews as well as the hypocrites acted treacherously and deceptively on this expedition. The Muslims were thus wedged in on all sides by the enemy on the outside and an enemy within. Due to the frustrating difficulties of the siege, Rasulullah ﷺ thought that perhaps the Muslims, driven by natural human nature, would be thrown into a cauldron of panic and anxiety. This is why Rasulullah ﷺ proposed that a peace treaty be fostered with 'Uyaynah bin Hisn and Haaris bin 'Awf (both leaders of the Ghitfaan tribes) by offering them a third of the produce of the palm orchards of Madinah. This proposal, Rasulullah ﷺ deduced, would drive them away from supporting Abu Sufyaan and also somewhat relieve the current siege. Subsequently, Rasulullah ﷺ expressed this idea before S'ad bin Mu'aaz ؓ and S'ad bin 'Ubaadah ؓ. They replied: "O Rasulullah ﷺ! Did Allah Ta'ala command you to do this? If yes, it would only be our pleasure to execute this divine commandment or are you proposing this merely out of affection and compassion for us?" Rasulullah ﷺ replied: "This is not a divine commandment of Allah. This is merely a suggestion on my part with your best interests at heart. All the Arabs have united their forces against you and they are 'raining down arrows onto you from a single bow'. With the strategy I have in mind, I wish to undermine their united stance and chip away at their cohesive strength."

S'ad bin Mu'aaz ؓ submitted: "O Rasulullah ﷺ! When all of us were disbelievers, we worshipped idols. We had no idea whatsoever about Allah Ta'ala. Even at that time none of them had the guts to take a single bunch of dates from us except as a guest or by purchasing it from us. And now when Allah Ta'ala has blessed us with this incomparable gift of Hidaayat (divine guidance) and honoured us with Islam we must surrender our wealth to them? This is impossible! By Allah! We have no need to relinquish our wealth to these people. By Allah! We will present them with nothing but the sword. They may do as they deem fit."

Hadhrat S'ad bin Mu'aaz ؓ then took hold of Rasulullah's ﷺ blessed hand and rubbed out the entire text of the proposed peace agreement that was written down in this respect.

Two weeks passed like this without any actual combat. During these two weeks, both sides merely engaged in lobbing arrows at one another. At length, a few mounted warriors of the Quraysh; 'Amr bin 'Abduwudd, 'Ikramah bin Abi Jahal, Hubairah bin Abi Wahab, Diraar bin Khattaab and Nawfal bin 'Abdullah, stepped out to engage the Muslims. When they reached the trenches, they remarked: "By Allah! We've never had such deceptive tactics amongst the Arabs before this."

One section of the trench was a bit narrow. They managed to breach this weak spot, scaled over and challengingly roused the Muslims to step out for hand-to-hand combat. Amr bin 'Abduwudd, who had dropped down wounded in the battle of Badr, was encased in a full-body armour covering him from head to toe. In a menacing tone, he hailed: "Is there anyone who dares to take me on?" In response to this challenge, the lion of Allah, Hadhrat Ali ﷺ stepped forth and said: "O 'Amr! I call you unto Allah and His Rasool. I invite you towards Islam." 'Amr disdainfully replied: "I have no need for such things." Hadhrat Ali ﷺ said: "Okay, I now invite you to fight with me." 'Amr replied: "You are still a youngster. Send me someone elder than you. I hate killing someone as young as you." Hadhrat Ali ﷺ replied: "But I would love to kill you." This drove him into a blind rage. He dismounted his horse and marched up to Hadhrat Ali ﷺ. At once, he attacked Hadhrat Ali ﷺ with his sword. He managed to deflect the strike with his shield but was slightly wounded on his forehead. Hadhrat Ali ﷺ then launched an attack on him and finished him off for good.

Hadhrat Ali ﷺ yelled out the Takbeer of Allahu Akbar! This was a sign to the Muslims of his triumph over his enemy.

Nawfal bin 'Abdullah advanced with the sole intention of assassinating Rasulullah ﷺ. He was mounted on a horse. He attempted to leap across the trench but he fell into it and broke his neck. The disbelievers tendered ten thousand Dirhams to Rasulullah ﷺ in exchange of Nawfal's body but Rasulullah ﷺ responded: "He was filthy and the diyat (blood money) offered is also filthy. Allah's curse is upon him and his blood money. We have absolutely no need for his ten thousand nor for his body for that matter." Rasulullah ﷺ then relinquished his body without any form of exchange.

S'ad bin Mu'aaz ﷺ was struck on his jugular by an arrow. He then made the following dua:

O Allah! If this battle with the Quraysh is bound to last (for some time) then make me last also accordingly because I have no yearning greater than fighting the people who subjected Your Messenger to such hardship, falsified him and evicted him from the safe Haram. O Allah! If this is the end of the war, make this injury a source of my martyrdom and do not take my life away until I am able to cool my eyes with the humiliation of the Banu Qurayzah."

This was one of the fiercest days of the battle. Most of the day passed in encountering and launching arrows and rocks. In this turbulence, Rasulullah ﷺ missed four Salaahs.

Rasulullah ﷺ had secured the women and children in one of the forts. The fort was in close proximity to the locality of one of the Jewish tribes. Hadhrat Safiyyah ﷺ, Rasulullah's ﷺ father's sister was also confined to the fort. Hadhrat Hassaan ﷺ was appointed to keep guard over the fort. Hadhrat Safiyyah ﷺ caught sight of a Jew wandering about the fort. She feared that he may be a spy or he may be engaged in some wicked activity. She addressed

Hadhrat Hassaan ؓ: "Go out and kill him. He should not divulge any information about us to the enemy." He replied: "Don't you know? I am not appointed for that purpose and I am incapable of doing such a thing." Hadhrat Safiyyah ؓ then decided to take matters into her own hands; she got hold of a tent peg and struck the jew with such force that his head cracked open. She told Hassaan ؓ: "He is a man and I am a woman. So I cannot touch him. Go and take off his weapons." Hadhrat Hassaan ؓ replied: "I have no need for his weapons and goods."

During the course of the siege, one of the chieftains of the Ghitfaan tribe, Nu'aim bin Mas'ood Ashja'i appeared in the presence of Rasulullah ﷺ and submitted: "O Rasulullah! I have embraced Islam and I believe in you. My people are ignorant about my accepting Islam. Subject to your approval, I wish to embark on a strategy that would eliminate this blockade." Rasulullah ﷺ replied: "Sure. You are a man of great experience. If such a manoeuvre is possible, go for it because after all 'war is deception'."

Subsequently, Nu'aim ؓ initiated such a deceptive strategy in motion that rent the alliance between the Banu Qurayzah and the Quraysh. This forced the Banu Qurayzah to withdraw all forms of support they offered to the Quraysh.

Following the deaths of 'Amr bin Abduwudd and Nawfal, the remaining Qurayshi warriors (who had managed to breach the trench) made a hasty retreat in defeat.

Abu Sa'eed Khudri ؓ narrates: "Citing the strain and harshness of this siege, we pleaded with Rasulullah ﷺ to make dua for us. Rasulullah ﷺ replied: "Make the following dua:

$$\text{اللهم استر عوراتنا وآمن روعاتنا}$$

"O Allah! Conceal our shortcomings and eliminate the source of our fear."

Rasulullah ﷺ also made the following dua:

$$\text{اللهم منزل الكتاب، ومجري السحاب، وهازم الاحزاب اهزمهم وانصرنا عليهم}$$

"O Allah! The revealer of the divine book, the driver of the clouds, the vanquisher of the confederates! Defeat them and shower us with Your divine assistance."

Allah Ta'ala accepted this dua of Rasulullah ﷺ. He subjected the Quraysh and Ghitfaan to such a violent wind that uprooted their tents. The tent-ropes snapped. Cauldrons and other utensils overturned. A steady stream of sand and grit blowing into the eyes, threw the entire army of the disbelievers into utter confusion and absolute disorder. In this regard Allah Ta'ala revealed the following verse:

$$\text{يَا أَيُّهَا الَّذِينَ آمَنُوا اذْكُرُوا نِعْمَةَ اللهِ عَلَيْكُمْ إِذْ جَاءَتْكُمْ جُنُودٌ فَأَرْسَلْنَا عَلَيْهِمْ رِيحًا وَجُنُودًا لَمْ تَرَوْهَا ۚ وَكَانَ اللهُ بِمَا تَعْمَلُونَ بَصِيرًا}$$

"O you who believe! Remember the favour of Allah upon you when a number of armies came to you. So We despatched upon them (the disbelievers) a wind and such forces, which you were unable to perceive (i.e. angels). And Allah is vigilant over your actions." [Surah Ahzaab verse 9]

In this verse, the phrase 'forces, which you were unable to perceive' refers to the angels who infused terror and anxiety into the hearts of the disbelievers whilst fortifying the hearts of the Muslims. In this manner, a ten-thousand-strong force of the disbelievers fled in abject disarray. As Allah Ta'ala says:

$$\text{وَرَدَّ اللهُ الَّذِينَ كَفَرُوا بِغَيْظِهِمْ لَمْ يَنَالُوا خَيْرًا ۚ وَكَفَى اللهُ الْمُؤْمِنِينَ الْقِتَالَ ۚ وَكَانَ اللهُ قَوِيًّا عَزِيزًا}$$

"Despite the rage of the disbelievers, Allah drove them back. They gained no good (booty). Allah sufficed for the believers in the fighting (by sending a wind and angels against the disbelievers). And Allah is strong and mighty."
[Surah Ahzaab verse 25]

Huzaifah bin Yamaan رَضِىَ اللهُ عَنْهُ narrates: "Rasulullah صَلَّى اللهُ عَلَيْهِ وَسَلَّمَ instructed me to gather some information about the Quraysh. I submitted: "I fear being captured by the enemy." Rasulullah صَلَّى اللهُ عَلَيْهِ وَسَلَّمَ replied: "Never! You will never be captured." Rasulullah صَلَّى اللهُ عَلَيْهِ وَسَلَّمَ then made the following dua for me:

$$\text{اللهم احفظه من بين يديه، ومن خلفه، وعن يمينه، وعن شماله، ومن فوقه، ومن تحته}$$

"O Allah! Protect him from his front, from behind him, from his right, from his left, from above and from beneath him."

Due to this dua of Rasulullah صَلَّى اللهُ عَلَيْهِ وَسَلَّمَ, all my anxieties faded away and with a sense of elation I set off. As I was leaving, Rasulullah صَلَّى اللهُ عَلَيْهِ وَسَلَّمَ cautioned: "Huzaifah! Avoid doing anything unwarranted."

When I crept into their camp, the wind was blustering so fiercely that nothing was motionless and the night was so dark that nothing was visible. As I drew closer to them, I heard Abu Sufyaan muttering: "O people of the Quraysh! This is not a place to stick around. Our animals have perished, Banu Qurayzah have abandoned us and this wind has hurled us all into a state of utter confusion. Moving about and even sitting here is almost unbearable. It is best for us to return without delay." Saying this, Abu Sufyaan mounted his camel.

Huzaifah رضي الله عنه narrates: "At that instant I thought of shooting an arrow at him but the words of Rasulullah ﷺ came to mind that, 'Huzaifah! Avoid doing anything unwarranted'. I then returned to our base."

As the Quraysh started retreating, Rasulullah ﷺ remarked:

الآن نغز وهم ولا يغزونا، نحن نسير اليهم

"Now we will attack them and they will not attack us. We will now advance and launch an offensive against them."

In other words, the forces of kufr have become so weak that they lack the nerve to take offensive action against Islam, with Islam merely taking a defensive stance. On the contrary, now Islam has turned into such a powerful force that it will launch offensive strikes against the forces of kufr instead of just taking defensive measures against them.

Note: Those who argue against the concept of offensive Jihaad in Islam should read the aforementioned Hadith of Bukhaari very attentively.

Early the next morning Rasulullah ﷺ made preparation to return to Madinah and the following words were on his blessed tongue:

لَا اِلٰهَ اِلَّا اللهُ وَحْدَهُ لَا شَرِيْكَ لَهُ لَهُ الْمُلْكُ وَلَهُ الْحَمْدُ وَهُوَ عَلٰى كُلِّ شَيْءٍ قَدِيْرٌ، اٰئِبُوْنَ تَائِبُوْنَ عَابِدُوْنَ سَاجِدُوْنَ لِرَبِّنَا حَامِدُوْنَ، صَدَقَ اللهُ وَعْدَهُ، وَ نَصَرَ عَبْدَهُ، وَهَزَمَ الْأَحْزَابَ وَحْدَهُ

"There is none worthy of worship but Allah. He has no partner. To Him belongs all supremacy and praise and He has absolute control over everything. We have returned, we are repentant, we are prostrate before our Lord and we praise Him Alone. Allah has fulfilled His promise, assisted His servant and vanquished the confederates all Alone."

The siege lasted for fifteen days.

In this expedition, the disbelievers lost three men; Nawfal bin 'Abdullah, 'Amr bin Abduwudd and Maniyyah bin 'Ubaid whilst six people died as martyrs from the Muslims. They were:

1. S'ad bin Mu'aaz رضي الله عنه
2. Anas bin Uwais رضي الله عنه
3. 'Abdullah bin Sahal رضي الله عنه

4. Tufail bin Nu'maan ؓ

5. S'alabah bin 'Anamah ؓ

6. K'ab bin Zaid ؓ

Hafiz Dimyaati includes a further two names to this list:

7. Qays bin Zaid ؓ

8. 'Abdullah bin Abi Khaalid ؓ

Expedition of Banu Qurayzah

Rasulullah ﷺ returned a little while after Fajr from the expedition of the trench. He as well as the Muslims undid their armour and removed their weapons. As the time of Zuhr Salaah drew closer, Jibraa'eel ؑ appeared before Rasulullah ﷺ mounted on a mule and donning a turban. He asked: "Did you take off your armour and weapons already?" When Rasulullah ﷺ replied in the affirmative, Jibraa'eel ؑ said: "The angels have neither put down their arms as yet nor have they returned (from the battle). Allah Ta'ala commands you to proceed towards Banu Qurayzah. I am also on my way to Banu Qurayzah to jolt them."

Hadhrat Anas ؓ narrates: "A peace treaty existed between Rasulullah ﷺ and the Banu Qurayzah. When the Quraysh turned up with a ten thousand strong force to launch an attack on Madinah, the Banu Qurayzah violated the terms of this treaty and joined the Quraysh. When Allah Ta'ala defeated the confederates (the Quraysh and their allies), the Banu Qurayzah scurried into their fortresses and took cover. Jibraa'eel ؑ, in the company of a significant number of other angels, appeared before Rasulullah ﷺ and submitted: 'O Rasulullah ﷺ! Set off for the Banu Qurayzah without any delay.' Rasulullah ﷺ responded: 'My companions are still exhausted.' Jibraa'eel ؑ replied: 'Do not worry about this. Immediately proceed towards the Banu Qurayzah. I am on my way to jolt them.' Saying this, Jibraa'eel ؑ, accompanied by a great number of angels, proceeded towards the Banu Qurayzah. The whole of Banu Ghanam road was clouded with dust (caused by the movement of the angels)."

Hadhrat Anas ؓ says: "I can still visualise the dust that was raised by the mount of Jibraa'eel ؑ on Banu Ghanam road."

Nonetheless, when Jibraa'eel ؑ departed, Rasulullah ﷺ instructed the Sahaabah ؓ: "None of you should perform his 'Asr Salaah but in Banu Qurayzah."

When the time for 'Asr Salaah set in, en route to Banu Qurayzah, a difference of opinion erupted amongst the Sahaabah ﷺ. Some of them insisted that they would perform their 'Asr Salaah only when they reach Banu Qurayzah whilst the others maintained that they would read it enroute as they argued that this was not the objective of Rasulullah ﷺ. (They maintained that the aim of Rasulullah ﷺ was not that the Salaah be disregarded altogether but his aim was to persuade them to make haste in reaching Banu Qurayzah.) When Rasulullah ﷺ was informed of this conflict, he did not express disapproval towards any of the two parties because both parties had good intentions.

Thereafter Rasulullah ﷺ despatched Hadhrat Ali ﷺ with the battle-ensign of Islam. As Hadhrat Ali ﷺ landed there, he was greeted with a whole community of enraged Jews openly hurling abuse and foul language against Rasulullah ﷺ (and this in itself is an unpardonable sin).

Thereafter Rasulullah ﷺ set out himself and laid siege to the Banu Qurayzah. This siege continued for twenty-five long days. During this time, their leader, K'ab bin Asad assembled the people of his tribe and addressed them thus: "I wish to propose three options before you. One of these three options would assure your deliverance from this ordeal.

فوالله، لقد تبين لكم انه لنبى مرسل وانه للذى تجدونه فى كتابكم

فتامنون على دمائكم واموالكم وابناءكم ونساءكم

The first option is that you embrace Islam and believe in this man (Muhammad Rasulullah ﷺ) because it has become quite obvious to you that this man is truly a divine Messenger and this is the same man whose attributes you find written in the Torah. If you embrace Islam, you will be able to protect your lives, your possessions, your children and your wives."

The Banu Qurayzah retorted: "Never! We will by no means consent to this proposal. We will never renounce our faith."

K'ab said: "Fine, if you do not wish to adopt this proposal, my second proposal is that you kill your wives and children thereby liberating yourselves of any concern for their safety. Take your swords and fight gallantly and courageously against Muhammad (Rasulullah ﷺ). If you are unsuccessful in your conflict with Muhammad (Rasulullah ﷺ), you would not suffer any heartache in regards to your wives and children and if you are triumphant, women are aplenty and you will also be able to produce children through them."

The Banu Qurayzah replied: "If we kill our wives and children without any justifiable cause, what pleasure would life have to offer after that?"

K'ab responded: "Okay, if you do not agree to this, I have a final proposal to make. Tonight is the Sabbath (Saturday). In all probability Muhammad and his companions would be laid-back today under the notion that since this is a sacred day to the Jews, the Jews wouldn't be able to launch an attack against them. Why don't you avail yourselves of this negligent attitude of the Muslims and launch a sudden offensive against them tonight?"

The Banu Qurayzah replied: "O K'ab! You very well know that our forefathers were transformed into apes and pigs for desecrating this holy day. So how dare you make such a proposal?"

Nonetheless, the Banu Qurayzah rebuffed every one of K'ab's proposals.

The Banu Qurayzah enjoyed an alliance with Abu Lubaabah bin 'Abdul-Munzir رضي الله عنه. This is why they reasoned that perhaps Abu Lubaabah رضي الله عنه would be able to offer them some assistance in these trying times. So they requested Rasulullah صلى الله عليه وسلم to send Abu Lubaabah رضي الله عنه to them to seek his advice and counsel. Rasulullah صلى الله عليه وسلم permitted him to go to them. As he landed there, they all congregated around him. The moment their women and children caught sight of him, they burst out crying. On seeing this pitiable sight, Abu Lubaabah رضي الله عنه was overwhelmed with sympathy for them. They asked him: "Should we accept Rasulullah's صلى الله عليه وسلم instructions and succumb to his verdict?" Abu Lubaabah رضي الله عنه replied: "Yes, that is the best option." Whilst saying this he ran a finger across his neck alerting them to Rasulullah's صلى الله عليه وسلم decision to slaughter them.

Abu Lubaabah رضي الله عنه barely rose from his seat when he realised his folly. He severely castigated himself for betraying the trust of Allah Ta'ala and His Rasool صلى الله عليه وسلم. From there he went directly to the Masjid and tied himself up to a pillar. He swore an oath: "I will never move from this place until Allah pardons my sin." He also vowed that he would never set foot in Banu Qurayzah ever again and added: "I will never set my eyes upon the locality in which I was guilty of betraying Allah and His Rasool صلى الله عليه وسلم."

When Rasulullah صلى الله عليه وسلم learnt of this, he remarked: "If he came directly to me, I would have sought forgiveness on his behalf but since he has already done what he has done, I will not release him from his bonds until Allah Himself pardons him."

Ultimately, the Banu Qurayzah were compelled to surrender to whatever decision Rasulullah صلى الله عليه وسلم had in store for them.

Just as the Khazraj tribe were allies of the Banu Nazeer, similarly, the Aws tribe were allies of the Banu Qurayzah. This is why the people of Aws pleaded with Rasulullah صلى الله عليه وسلم and beseeched: "O Rasulullah صلى الله عليه وسلم! Just as you dealt with the people of Banu Nazeer on the request of their allies, the Khazraj, we the Aws, implore you to deal with our allies, the Banu Qurayzah in a like manner." Rasulullah صلى الله عليه وسلم replied: "Would you not be pleased if a man from amongst yourselves makes a decision in this regard?" "Surely," they replied, "we would be pleased with the decision made by S'ad bin Mu'aaz رضي الله عنه."

When Hadhrat S'ad bin Mu'aaz رضي الله عنه was wounded in the battle of Khandaq (the trench), Rasulullah ﷺ erected a tent for him in the Masjid so that he could visit him often. Rasulullah ﷺ sent someone to fetch him. He mounted a donkey and as he drew closer, Rasulullah ﷺ said: "Stand up in honour of your leader."

When he dismounted and sat down comfortably, Rasulullah ﷺ said: "In regards to the Banu Qurayzah, these people have consigned the decision-making over to you."

S'ad bin Mu'aaz رضي الله عنه replied: "My decision is as follows: their combatants i.e. their men should be executed and their women and children taken as slaves. Furthermore, all their wealth and possessions should be distributed amongst the Muslims." To this, Rasulullah ﷺ remarked: "Certainly you have passed judgement according to the divine commandment of Allah Ta'ala."

Thereafter, Hadhrat S'ad رضي الله عنه made the following dua:

"O Allah! You are well aware that nothing is dearer to me than waging Jihaad against the people who falsified Your Messenger and banished him from the Haram. O Allah! It appears to me that You have now terminated war between us and them.

So if we are still destined to go to war with the Quraysh, keep me alive to wage Jihaad against them in Your path and if You have decreed an end to fighting with them, cause this wound to gush forth and make it a source of my martyrdom."

He barely completed this dua when his wound gushed forth and he passed away. *Inna Lillaahi Wa Inna Ilayhi Raaji'oon*

Hadhrat Jaabir رضي الله عنه narrates that he heard Rasulullah ﷺ saying: "The throne of Allah shuddered at the death of S'ad bin Mu'aaz." According to another narration, all the doors of the heavens were thrown open for him, and the angels of the skies were delighted with the ascension of his soul.

Seventy thousand angels, who had never before descended from the skies, participated in his Janaazah Salaah. In regards to this incident, an Ansaari composed the following stanza:

وما اهتز عرش الله من موت هالك

سمعنا به الا للسعد ابی عمرو

"We have not heard of the throne of Allah shudder upon the death of anyone, except for the death of Abu 'Amr S'ad bin Mu'aaz."

It is said that his grave would emit the fragrance of musk. And Allah Ta'ala knows best.

Ultimately, all members of the Banu Qurayzah clan were captured and brought back to Madinah. They were detained in an Ansaari lady's house. A number of trenches were dug in the vicinity of the market place. Thereafter, the (male) prisoners would be brought out of this house in sets of two and four, escorted to these trenches and beheaded. Huyayy bin Akhtab and the chieftain of the Banu Qurayzah, K'ab bin Asad were also executed. When Huyayy bin Akhtab (the man who influenced K'ab bin Asad the chieftain of the Banu Qurayzah to betray Rasulullah ﷺ and breach the peace agreement) was brought before Rasulullah ﷺ, Huyayy cast his gaze towards Rasulullah ﷺ and said: "By Allah, I do not condemn myself for harbouring enmity against you but the truth of the matter is that he whom Allah refrains from assisting will never get assistance from anyone else."

Saying this, he then directed his gaze towards his people and remarked: "O people! This is not a problem. The divine punishment Allah had decreed for the Bani Israa'eel and the suffering He had predestined for them has come to pass."

Saying this, Huyayy sat down and he was then put to the sword.

None of the women were executed except one woman whose crime was that she dropped a millstone from an upper story thereby martyring Khallaad bin Suwaid ؓ. Her name was Bunaanah. She was the wife of Hakam Qurazi.

The executed numbered four hundred whilst the remaining captives of women and children were sent to Najd and Syria to be sold as slaves. The proceeds from this sale was used to purchase horses and arms. The goods and possession seized from the Banu Qurayzah were distributed amongst the Muslims.

Allah Ta'ala describes the incident of Banu Qurayzah in the following words:

$$\text{وَ اَنْزَلَ الَّذِيْنَ ظَاهَرُوْهُمْ مِنْ اَهْلِ الْكِتٰبِ مِنْ صَيَاصِيْهِمْ وَ قَذَفَ فِيْ قُلُوْبِهِمُ الرُّعْبَ فَرِيْقًا تَقْتُلُوْنَ وَتَأْسِرُوْنَ فَرِيْقًا ۞ وَ اَوْرَثَكُمْ اَرْضَهُمْ وَ دِيَارَهُمْ وَ اَمْوَالَهُمْ وَ اَرْضًا لَّمْ تَطَئُوْهَا وَ كَانَ اللهُ عَلٰى كُلِّ شَيْءٍ قَدِيْرًا ۞}$$

"And those of the people of the book who assisted them (the disbelievers), Allah brought them down from their forts and cast terror into their hearts (so that) a group of them you killed and a group of them you took as captives. And Allah made you heirs to their lands and houses, and their riches and a land that you had not trodden before. And Allah has absolute power over everything."
[Surah Ahzaab verses 26-27]

Note: This judgement of Hadhrat S'ad bin Mu'aaz ؓ against the Banu Qurayzah was actually in line with the divine statute laid down by the Torah (old testament) and in which they (the Jews of the Banu Qurayzah) firmly believed.

Meanwhile, Abu Lubaabah ؓ who was tied to the pillar of the Masjid used to be released only for Salaah and for answering the call of nature. He refused to eat and drink and declared: "I will not budge until I either die or Allah Ta'ala accepts my repentance." At the hour of dawn, on the sixth day of his self-imposed punishment, divine pardon was revealed in his favour. At that time, Rasulullah ﷺ was in the house of Umme Salamah رضي الله عنها. With the consent of Rasulullah ﷺ, Hadhrat Umme Salamah رضي الله عنها passed on the good news to him and offered her congratulations. When the Muslims dashed over to unravel his knots, he said: "Hang on, I swore an oath that as long as Rasulullah ﷺ does not untie me with his blessed hands, I will remain tied up." When Rasulullah ﷺ appeared for Fajr Salaah, he undid his knots and released him with his own blessed hands.

In regards to Hadhrat Abu Lubaabah رضي الله عنه, Allah Ta'ala revealed the following verse:

$$\text{يَا أَيُّهَا الَّذِينَ آمَنُوا لَا تَخُونُوا اللَّهَ وَالرَّسُولَ وَتَخُونُوا أَمَانَاتِكُمْ وَأَنْتُمْ تَعْلَمُونَ}$$

"O you who believe! Do not betray Allah and His Messenger nor knowingly betray your Amaanaat (things entrusted to you)." [Surah Anfaal verse 27]

His divine pardon was revealed in the following verses:

$$\text{وَآخَرُونَ اعْتَرَفُوا بِذُنُوبِهِمْ خَلَطُوا عَمَلًا صَالِحًا وَآخَرَ سَيِّئًا عَسَى اللَّهُ أَنْ يَتُوبَ عَلَيْهِمْ إِنَّ اللَّهَ غَفُورٌ رَحِيمٌ}$$

"And there are others who confess their sins, they have mixed a good deed with another that is evil. Perhaps Allah will forgive them. Allah is all-forgiving, most merciful." [Surah Taubah verse 102]

Abu Lubaabah رضي الله عنه remained tied to the pillar of the Masjid for twenty days (as per another narration). When this verse was revealed, Rasulullah ﷺ went to the Masjid, conveyed the good news to him and unravelled his knots with his own blessed hands.

Rasulullah's ﷺ Nikah with Hadhrat Zaynab رضي الله عنها

During the same year, i.e. 5 A.H. Rasulullah ﷺ married Hadhrat Zaynab bint Jahsh رضي الله عنها. A detailed account of Rasulullah's ﷺ Nikah with Hadhrat Zaynab رضي الله عنها will appear in the chapter of "Azwaaj-e-Mutahharaat" (the pure wives of Rasulullah ﷺ), Insha Allah.

Revelation of Hijaab

It was during the Walimah of Hadhrat Zaynab رضي الله عنها that the verses of Hijaab were revealed. Allah Ta'ala decrees: "And if you have to ask them (the women) for anything, ask them from behind the hijaab (screen)." This is a verse of Surah Ahzaab and this verse is referred to as the verse of hijaab. In other words, a woman is prohibited to appear before anyone she is permitted to marry.

Expedition of Muhammad bin Maslamah Ansaari ﷺ towards Qurta - 10th Muharram 6 A.H.

On the 10th of Muharram 6 A.H., Rasulullah ﷺ despatched thirty mounted warriors under the command of Muhammad bin Maslamah Ansaari ﷺ towards Qurta. Following a successful attack, ten men of the enemy were killed and the rest of them dispersed. One hundred and fifty camels and three thousand goats were seized as booty. Driving this sizeable booty before them, they reached Madinah after nineteen days on the 29th of Muharram and presented it to Rasulullah ﷺ. After drawing out the khums (one fifth), Rasulullah ﷺ distributed the remainder amongst the Mujaahideen. For purposes of distribution, one camel was equated with ten goats.

Islam of Sumaamah bin Usaal

Hadhrat Abu Hurayrah ﷺ narrates that they captured Sumaamah bin Usaal, the chieftain of the Banu Hanifah tribe and brought him before Rasulullah ﷺ. Rasulullah ﷺ ordered that he be tied to one of the pillars of the Masjid (so that he may witness first hand the spectacle of the Salaah of the Muslims and their humility in the court of Allah Ta'ala. Such a spectacle used to induce people to remember Allah Ta'ala and enabled them to engender an inclination for the hereafter within their hearts. Their spiritual illumination and divine purity would cleanse the spiritual darkness of the hearts).

When Rasulullah ﷺ passed Sumaamah bin Usaal, he asked him: "O Sumaamah! What thoughts do you entertain of me?" Sumaamah replied: "I only harbour good thoughts of you.

ان تقتل تقتل ذا دم وان تنعم تنعم على شاكر وان كنت تريد المال فسل منه ما شئت

"If you execute me you will be executing a person who deserves it, if you extend your kindness towards me you will be extending it to one who is grateful and if it is wealth you desire, ask whatever you wish."

On hearing this, Rasulullah ﷺ remained silent and went away. On the second day, when Rasulullah ﷺ passed by, he asked: "O Sumaamah! What thoughts do you entertain of me?" Sumaamah, sensing the compassionate tone of Rasulullah ﷺ, avoided the first and second sentences and merely replied:

ان تنعم تنعم على شاكر

"If you extend your munificence towards me you will be extending it to one who is grateful."

On hearing this, once again Rasulullah ﷺ remained silent and went away.

On the third day, Rasulullah ﷺ put the same question to him but Sumaamah simply said: "I entertain the same thoughts as I had mentioned to you previously." Today, Sumaamah did not even mention: "If you extend your kindness towards me you will be extending it to one who is grateful." He consigned his fate to the excellent character and boundless affection of Rasulullah ﷺ.

Rasulullah ﷺ addressed the Sahaabah ؓ saying: "Untie the bonds of Sumaamah."

Rasulullah ﷺ then addressed Sumaamah himself and said:

قد عفوت عنك يا ثمامة واعتقتك

"O Sumaamah! I have pardoned you and set you free."

The moment he was released, Sumaamah headed off to a palm-orchard situated near the Masjid. He took a bath there and after returning to the Masjid, he declared: *"I testify that there is none worthy of worship but Allah and I bear witness that Muhammad is His Messenger."*

He then turned towards Rasulullah ﷺ and said: "O Muhammad! Before this, there was nothing more disgusting to me in this world than your face but today there is nothing more appealing and dear to me in this world than your face. Before this, your Deen (religion) was the most revolting to me and today your Deen is most precious to me. Before this, your city was the most repellent to me but today your city is the most cherished city. I was on my way to perform Umrah when I was accosted by your mounted warriors. What is your instruction now?" Rasulullah ﷺ directed him to continue on his journey to perform Umrah and issued him with glad tidings. (In other words, 'go ahead and perform Umrah. You will be safe; nobody will harm you.)

When Sumaamah landed in Makkah, a disbeliever reproached him: "Sumaamah, you have become an apostate by renouncing your Deen." Sumaamah replied: "Never! I have become a Muslim with Rasulullah ﷺ." In other words, I have not become an apostate. Kufr and shirk (disbelief and polytheism) are certainly not any elements of Deen. They are unfounded and futile ideologies. In fact, I have become a submissive servant of Allah Ta'ala and I have submitted myself over to Him.

Sumaamah رضي الله عنه then added: "I will never return to your fictitious religion and remember that the wheat you were importing from Yamaamah, you will not receive a grain of it until Rasulullah صلى الله عليه وسلم approves."

When Sumaamah reached Yamaamah, he imposed a grain blockade on Makkah and cut off all food supplies to them. The Quraysh were forced to write to Rasulullah صلى الله عليه وسلم pleading with him: "You command maintenance of favourable family ties. We are after all, your family. We beg you to write to Sumaamah and instruct him to resume supply of our food grains." Rasulullah صلى الله عليه وسلم wrote a note to Sumaamah رضي الله عنه instructing him not to interrupt the grain supplies from Yamaamah.

Masalah: It is Mustahab for a person who embraces Islam to take a bath.

Sumaamah bin Usaal رضي الله عنه was from amongst the eminent Sahaabah رضي الله عنهم. When the people of Yamaamah turned apostate after the demise of Rasulullah صلى الله عليه وسلم and joined Musaylamah the fraud, Sumaamah رضي الله عنه recited the following verses before his people:

حٰمٓ ۚ تَنْزِيْلُ الْكِتٰبِ مِنَ اللّٰهِ الْعَزِيْزِ الْعَلِيْمِ ۙ غَافِرِ الذَّنْۢبِ وَ قَابِلِ التَّوْبِ شَدِيْدِ الْعِقَابِ ۙ ذِى الطَّوْلِ ۚ لَاۤ اِلٰهَ اِلَّا هُوَ ۚ

"Bismillahir-Rahmaanir-Raheem. Haa Meem! The revelation of the book is from Allah, the Almighty, all-Knowing. He is the forgiver of sin and the acceptor of repentance, He is severe in punishment and provider of (favours). There is none worthy of worship besides Him." [Surah Ghaafir verses 1-3]

He then declared: "Goodness! Why are you not fair? What parallel can there ever be between this incomparable divine word and the meaningless nonsense of Musaylamah?"

These truthful words immersed in the sincerity of Sumaamah رضي الله عنه had a profound effect on his audience. Three thousand of Musaylamah's adherents deserted him and re-entered the fold of Islam.

Hadhrat Sumaamah رضي الله عنه made painstaking efforts in preventing them from joining Musaylamah. He addressed them saying:

اياكم وامرا مظلما لانور فيه وانه لشقاء كتبه الله عزوجل على من اخذ به منكم وبلاء على من لم ياخذ منكم يا بنى حنيفة

"O people! Beware of this sinister evil in which there is absolutely no light. Certainly this is wretchedness predestined by Allah Ta'ala upon those who have

accepted it and it is a test for those who have not. O Banu Hanifah! Bear this advice in mind."

However, when Hadhrat Sumaamah رَضِيَ اللّٰهُ عَنْهُ realised that his words were falling on deaf ears and people were still flocking to Musaylamah, the fraud, he addressed the Muslims who were with him saying: "By Allah! I will never reside in this city. I see that Allah Ta'ala has inflicted these people with a divine fitnah (tribulation). Those who wish to depart with me may do so."

Saying this, Hadhrat Sumaamah رَضِيَ اللّٰهُ عَنْهُ set out with a group of Muslims and joined 'Alaa bin Hadrami رَضِيَ اللّٰهُ عَنْهُ.

In this regards, Hadhrat Sumaamah رَضِيَ اللّٰهُ عَنْهُ composed the following stanzas:

دعانا الى ترك الديانة والهدى   مسيلمة الكذاب اذ جاء يسجع

"He (Musaylamah) beckoned us to abandon religion and divine guidance as he was busy engaged in saying couplets in rythemic form.

فيا عجبا من معشر قد تتابعوا   له فى سبيل الغىّ والغىّ اشنع

How weird are those who chose a path of deviation by following him whereas deviation in itself is appalling."

Expedition of Bani Lihyaan - Rabi'ul-Awwal 6 A.H.

With the aim of avenging the deaths of 'Aasim bin Saabit, Khubaib bin 'Adi and other martyrs of Raj'i, Rasulullah ﷺ set out himself in the company of two hundred mounted warriors on the 1st of Rabi'ul-Awwal 6 A.H. The moment the Banu Lihyaan heard of Rasulullah's ﷺ imminent arrival, they scurried away and took refuge in the mountains. Rasulullah ﷺ camped here for one or two days. He also despatched a few raiding parties (in pursuit of the Banu Lihyaan). One of these incursions was made up of ten men under the command of Hadhrat Abu Bakr رَضِيَ اللّٰهُ عَنْهُ.

Rasulullah ﷺ returned from this expedition without any form of fighting or physical combat. As he was returning, the following words were on his blessed tongue:

آئبون تائبون عابدون لربنا حامدون اعوذ بالله من وعثاء السفر
وكآبة المنقلب وسوء المنظر فى الاهل والمال

"We are returning, we are repenting, we are devoted to our Lord and sing our praises to Him. We seek the refuge of Allah from the difficulties of the journey, from

a distressing return and from an unpleasant sight in regards to our family and wealth."

Expedition of Zi Qarad - Rabi'ul-Awwal 6 A.H.

Zi Qarad is the name of a water spring situated in the environs of Ghitfaan. This was the grazing land of Rasulullah's ﷺ camels. 'Uyaynah bin Hisn Fazaari, in the company of forty mounted horsemen, launched a raid on this meadow and fled after seizing all the camels. Abu Zarr's son, who was appointed to guard the camels, was killed in this raid and Abu Zarr's رضي الله عنه wife was kidnapped.

The instant Salamah bin Akw'a رضي الله عنه discovered what had transpired, he promptly set out in pursuit. He swiftly climbed atop a hillock and bellowed: "Yaa Sabaahaa!" thrice. This rousing cry reverberated throughout the city of Madinah. Salamah bin Akw'a رضي الله عنه was an expert archer. As he tracked them, he came upon them near a water spring. He continued showering them with volleys of arrows whilst chanting:

انا ابن الاكوع   واليوم يوم الرضَّع

"I am the son of Akw'a, this day will determine who drank the milk of a noble woman or a contemptible woman."

He continued shadowing them in this manner until he released all the camels and he also managed to seize thirty Yemeni sheets.

Meanwhile, after the departure of Salamah bin Akw'a رضي الله عنه, Rasulullah ﷺ set out himself in the company of five hundred or seven hundred men and travelling at top speed they landed at that location. Some mounted warriors were already despatched by Rasulullah ﷺ even before the rest of them departed. This small mounted band engaged the enemy the moment they landed there. Two of the disbelievers were killed; Mas'adah bin Hakamah who was killed by Abu Qataadah رضي الله عنه and Abaan bin 'Umar who was killed by 'Ukkaashah bin Mihsan رضي الله عنه. The Muslims suffered just one casualty; Muhriz bin Nadlah رضي الله عنه, whose title was Akhram. He was martyred by 'Abdur-Rahmaan bin 'Uyaynah.

Salamah bin Akw'a رضي الله عنه appeared before Rasulullah ﷺ and submitted: "O Rasulullah ﷺ! I was in hot pursuit of the enemy. I have just returned from so and so place where I left them thirsty. If I have a hundred men, I will be able to capture each one of them to the last man." Rasulullah ﷺ remarked:

يا ابن الاكوع! ملكت فاسجح

"O Ibnul-Akw'a! When you gain authority, be compassionate."

The disbelievers took flight in defeat. Rasulullah ﷺ stayed the night and day at that location and he performed Salaatul-Khawf there as well. After five days, he returned to Madinah.

Expedition of 'Ukkaashah bin Mihsan ؓ towards Ghamr

In the same month, Rabi'ul-Awwal, Rasulullah ﷺ sent forty men under the command of 'Ukkaashah bin Mihsan ؓ towards Ghamr. However, the moment the enemy got wind of their imminent arrival, they dispersed. When the Muslim unit landed there, they found no sign of anyone. They sent Shuj'a bin Wahab ؓ to scout about for them. He did not come across any sign of their animals. However, following a diligent search, he managed to catch one of the kuffaar. He steered him back to camp where he owned up to the whereabouts of the animals. The Muslims launched a raid on that area and seized two hundred camels as war booty.

Expedition of Muhammad Bin Maslamah ؓ towards Zil-Qassah

During the month of Rabi'ul-Aakhir 6 A.H., Rasulullah ﷺ sent ten men under the command of Muhammad bin Maslamah ؓ towards Zil-Qassah to confront the forces of Banu S'alabah and Banu 'Uwaal tribes. They reached at night and fell into an exhausted sleep the moment they landed there. Meanwhile, the enemy who was hiding in the mountains launched a menacing attack on the Muslims. One hundred men launched a nighttime attack upon the Muslims as they slept and ruthlessly murdered every one of them. Only Muhammad bin Maslamah ؓ was saved. He was wounded in the attack but left for dead. Another Muslim who happened to pass by, chanced upon him, picked him up and carried him back to Madinah.

Expedition of Abu 'Ubaidah bin Jarrah ؓ towards Zil-Qassah

To avenge their deaths, Rasulullah ﷺ sent forty men under the command of Abu 'Ubaidah bin Jarrah ؓ towards Zil-Qassah. They launched a successful attack on the disbelievers, who fled in defeat. Abu 'Ubaidah ؓ seized their livestock and returned to Madinah. This expedition is referred to as 'the second expedition of Zil-Qassah.

Expedition of Jamum

During the same month, Rabi'ul-Aakhir 6 A.H., Rasulullah ﷺ sent Hadhrat Zaid bin Haarisah رضي الله عنه towards Jamum – about four miles from Madinah – to engage the Banu Sulaim in battle. They only came across a lone woman who directed them to the other members of the tribe. He returned to Madinah after two days with a few captives, some camels and a small number of goats.

Expedition of 'Is

Rasulullah ﷺ got wind of a Qurayshi trade caravan returning with goods from Syria. The moment he received this intelligence, he despatched one hundred and seventy men under the command of Zaid bin Haarisah رضي الله عنه towards a place called 'Is.

This place falls on a journey of four days from Madinah Munawwarah. It is situated on the coast and the Qurayshi trade caravans would routinely pass this area.

The Muslims (who were perhaps waiting in ambush) captured all the travellers of this caravan. They also seized all their goods and possessions and returned with their booty to Madinah. Rasulullah's ﷺ son-in-law, Abul-'Aas bin Rab'i was also amongst the captives. Rasulullah's ﷺ daughter Hadhrat Zaynab رضي الله عنها offered him sanctuary. So Rasulullah ﷺ also guaranteed his personal safety and returned his goods and possessions.

Hadhrat Abul-'Aas's return and his acceptance of Islam was discussed in detail under the chapter of the battle of Badr.

Expedition of Tarif

Tarif is the name of a water spring approximately thirty-six miles from Madinah Munawwarah. Primarily to punish the Banu S'alabah tribe, Rasulullah ﷺ sent fifteen men under the command of Zaid bin Haarisah رضي الله عنه towards this water spring. However, the enemy fled by the time they got there. Zaid bin Haarisah رضي الله عنه seized a few camels and goats and returned to Madinah.

Expedition of Hasma

Hadhrat Dihyaa Kalbi رضي الله عنه was sent to the emperor of Rome with a letter of Rasulullah ﷺ. Whilst he was on his return bearing expensive gifts and royal presents, as he was passing Hasma, Hunaid Juzaami and a few members of the Juzaam tribe waylaid him. They seized all his goods and possessions leaving him with just one old tattered sheet. When Rifa'ah bin Zaid Juzaami (who had already embraced Islam) heard of this, he, accompanied by a few other Muslims, went up to Hunaid and retrieved all the usurped goods and returned them to Hadhrat Dihyaa Kalbi رضي الله عنه.

When Hadhrat Dihyaa Kalbi رضي الله عنه retuned to Madinah and informed Rasulullah ﷺ about what transpired, Rasulullah ﷺ despatched five hundred Sahaabah رضي الله عنهم towards Hasma under the command of Zaid bin Haarisah رضي الله عنه.

These Mujaahideen would travel at night and go into hiding during the day. The instant they landed there, they caught them unawares and launched a deadly attack on them. Hunaid and his son were killed. Five hundred women and children were taken captive. They also managed to seize five hundred camels and one thousand goats.

Since the kinsfolk of Rifa'ah bin Zaid رضي الله عنه, who had also embraced Islam, were also living amongst the disbelievers, some of their children and women were also erroneously captured by the Muslims. When Rifa'ah bin Zaid رضي الله عنه complained of this to Rasulullah ﷺ, he sent Hadhrat Ali رضي الله عنه with him with instructions to Zaid bin Haarisah رضي الله عنه to release all the prisoners and to return all their goods and possessions forthwith. In fact, he even instructed him to return seemingly trivial possessions like saddlecloths and saddles.

Expedition of Waadiul-Quraa

During the month of Rajab, Rasulullah ﷺ sent Hadhrat Zaid bin Haarisah رضي الله عنه towards Waadiul-Quraa to punish the Banu Fazaarah tribe. A few Muslims were martyred and Hadhrat Zaid bin Haarisah رضي الله عنه was wounded in this expedition.

Expedition of Dawmatul Jandal

Hadhrat 'Abdullah bin 'Umar رضي الله عنه relates: "Rasulullah ﷺ was sitting in the Masjid with ten of his companions; Abu Bakr, 'Umar, 'Usmaan, Ali, 'Abdur-Rahmaan bin 'Awf, 'Abdullah bin Mas'ood, Mu'aaz bin Jabal, Huzaifah bin Yamaan, Abu Sa'eed Khudri and I was the tenth person. Whilst we were sitting with Rasulullah ﷺ, a young Ansaari appeared before Rasulullah ﷺ and asked:

يا رسول الله! اى المؤمنين افضل

"O Rasulullah ﷺ! Who is the best Muslim?"

Rasulullah ﷺ replied:

احسنهم اخلاقا

"The best amongst the Muslims is he who has the best character."

He then asked:

فاى المؤمنين اكيس

"Who is the most intelligent amongst the Muslims?"

Rasulullah ﷺ replied:

اكثرهم للموت ذكرا واكثرهم استعدادا له قبل ان ينزل به، اولئك هم الاكياس

"The most intelligent amongst them is he who remembers death most frequently and the one who prepares for it the most before it strikes him. Such people are the most intelligent."

The Ansaari youth remained silent after this. Rasulullah ﷺ then addressed his companions and said:

"There are five practises that are awfully deadly. May Allah protect you from them and may He save you from setting eyes on them. They are:

1. The nation in which immodesty and shamelessness becomes rife is struck with plagues and such diseases that were never heard of before.

2. The nation that cheats in weight and measure is afflicted with drought and calamities and a cruel ruler is set upon them.

3. The nation that refrains from paying its Zakaat, rainfall is withheld from them. If it were not for the animals, they would have been totally deprived of rainfall.

4. The nation that betrays the trust of Allah and His Rasool ﷺ, Allah Ta'ala imposes the supremacy of foreign enemies over them and they (the foreign enemies) seize whatever they possess.

5. And when the leaders and rulers pass judgement in contrast to Qur-aanic law and they become arrogant and transgress, Allah Ta'ala brings about disunity and dissension amongst them."

Rasulullah ﷺ then instructed Hadhrat 'Abdur-Rahmaan bin 'Awf ؓ saying: "I will be sending you on a mission either today or tomorrow. Be prepared." The following day, just after (the Fajr Salaah), Rasulullah ﷺ summoned

'Abdur-Rahmaan bin 'Awf ﷺ and seated him right in front of him. He then proceeded to tie a black 'Imaamah over his head with his blessed hands leaving a four-finger-length of its tail hanging out at the back. Rasulullah ﷺ instructed him: 'Ibn 'Awf! Always tie your 'Imaamah like this. It looks exceptionally pleasant like this.'

Rasulullah ﷺ then asked Bilal ﷺ to bring a flag and hand it over to 'Abdur-Rahmaan bin 'Awf ﷺ. Rasulullah ﷺ thereafter recited the praises of Allah Ta'ala, recited Durood upon himself and addressed 'Abdur-Rahmaan bin 'Awf ﷺ thus: 'Take this flag and wage Jihaad in the path of Allah. Engage those who are guilty of kufr with Allah. Do not be treacherous nor deceptive. Do not mutilate the ears and nose etc. of the dead. Do not kill children. This is the covenant of Allah and the Sunnah of His Messenger.'"

Thereafter Rasulullah ﷺ commanded him to proceed to Dawmatul-Jandal with a force of seven hundred Mujaahideen. He also advised him: "If they accept your invitation and embrace Islam, do not hesitate to marry the daughter of their chief."

Hadhrat 'Abdur-Rahmaan bin 'Awf ﷺ headed off towards Dawmatul-Jandal and invited them to embrace Islam. For three successive days, he persistently invited them towards Islam. On the third day, the chief of Dawmatul-Jandal, Isb'a bin 'Umar, who was a Christian, embraced Islam and a number of others also entered the fold of Islam with him. As per the prophecy of Rasulullah ﷺ, 'Abdur-Rahmaan bin 'Awf ﷺ married the chief Isb'a's daughter, Tumaadir. 'Abdur-Rahmaan bin 'Awf ﷺ returned with her to Madinah Munawwarah. Abu Salamah bin 'Abdur-Rahmaan, who was one of the most prominent Taabi'een and a Hafiz of Hadith, was born of this union.

Expedition of Fidak

Rasulullah ﷺ received information that Banu S'ad bin Bakr had assembled a force near Fidak to assist the Jews of Khaybar. Rasulullah ﷺ despatched a hundred men under the command of Hadhrat Ali ﷺ towards Fidak. En route, they chanced upon a man and following a little intimidation he revealed that he was a spy for Banu S'ad. The Muslims offered him protection and asked him about the whereabouts of Banu S'ad. He provided the correct information and accordingly, they launched an attack on the area. However, the Banu S'ad managed to escape but the Muslims returned with a booty of five hundred camels and two thousand goats.

Chapter 18

Expedition of Umme Qirfah

Umme Qirfah is the title of a woman whose name was Faatimah bint Rabi'ah. She was the chief of the Banu Fazaarah tribe. Once, on his way to Syria, Hadhrat Zaid bin Haarisah رضي الله عنه happened to pass by with trade goods. The people of Banu Fazaarah beat him up, wounded him and snatched all his goods.

Zaid رضي الله عنه managed to make his way back to Madinah. In retaliation, Rasulullah ﷺ sent a force under the command of Zaid رضي الله عنه towards these people and they returned triumphant.

Expedition of 'Abdullah bin Rawaahah رضي الله عنه

Subsequent to the assassination of Abu Raaf'i, the Jews appointed Usair bin Rizaam as their leader. Without further ado, he launched into frantic preparations to attack Rasulullah ﷺ. Furthermore, he incited the Banu Ghitfaan and other tribes also to wage war against Rasulullah ﷺ. When Rasulullah ﷺ got wind of this, he sent 'Abdullah bin Rawaahah رضي الله عنه and three other men to investigate. 'Abdullah bin Rawaahah رضي الله عنه returned to say that the news was indeed accurate. Rasulullah ﷺ then sent thirty men with 'Abdullah bin Rawaahah رضي الله عنه to call them to a meeting to discuss these issues directly with them.

Usair bin Rizaam, their leader, (accepted this invitation and) also decided to set out in the company of thirty men (to meet Rasulullah ﷺ). All sixty of them, thirty Muslims and thirty Jews, set out with two people sharing a camel; one Muslim and one Jew. Somewhere along the way, the Jews developed some wicked ideas. Usair bin Rizaam and 'Abdullah bin Unais رضي الله عنه were seated on one camel. On two occasions, Usair stealthily attempted to strike 'Abdullah with a sword but each time 'Abdullah was alerted and he overlooked it. When Usair attempted to strike him a third time, it triggered a war between both sides. All the Jews were killed. Only one of them managed to escape unharmed. None of the Muslims were killed. Only 'Abdullah bin Unais رضي الله عنه was slightly injured.

When this group returned to Madinah, Rasulullah ﷺ remarked:

$$ قد نجاكم الله من القوم الظالمين $$

"Allah Ta'ala protected you from the oppressive nation."

Rasulullah ﷺ then applied his blessed saliva over 'Abdullah's wound and it healed instantly. He also passed his hands over his face and made dua for him.

Expedition of Kurz bin Jaabir Fihari towards 'Uraniyyeen

A few members of the 'Ukkal and 'Uraynah tribes turned up at Madinah and exposed their Islam. A few days later, they pleaded before Rasulullah ﷺ: "We are livestock farmers. Until now, we lived on milk. We are not in the habit of eating grains. The climate of Madinah is not suitable for our health. For this reason, if you permit us to live on the outskirts of the city amongst the camels of charity and allow us to consume their milk, it would be better for us."

Rasulullah ﷺ accommodated this request. The camels of charity were housed in the meadows on the outskirts of the city. Rasulullah ﷺ allowed them to stay there and to consume their milk. In a few days, these tribesmen recovered their good health and became robust and healthy. This is when wickedness took hold of them and they renounced Islam. They also murdered the herdsman of Rasulullah ﷺ and mutilated his body by cutting off his hands, legs and nose and gouging out his eyes. They also poked thorns into his eye sockets. Following this evil deed, they seized all the camels and took flight.

In Shawwaal 6 A.H. Rasulullah ﷺ despatched Kurz bin Jaabir Fihari رضى الله عنه with about twenty men in pursuit of these wicked tribesmen. They were captured to the last man. Rasulullah ﷺ decreed that they be subject to Qisaas (retaliatory punishment). They were executed in exactly the same manner as they had murdered the herdsman. However, hereafter it was decreed that any criminal, regardless of the heinousness of his crime, would not be punished in this manner. Thus, mutilation of even the most bitter enemy of Islam has been prohibited outright. So if a disbeliever murders a Muslim and disfigures his body, the disbeliever will be executed in retaliation but he will not be mutilated.

Expedition of 'Amr bin Umayyah Damri رضى الله عنه

One day, in front of a huge gathering of the Quraysh, Abu Sufyaan bin Harb challenged them saying: "Is there not anyone from amongst you who dares to assassinate Muhammad? He is not protected by a bodyguard and he walks around freely in the marketplace."

A Bedouin arose and proclaimed: "I am a professional in such exploits. If you assist me in this venture, I undertake to fulfill this assignment." Abu Sufyaan provided him with a camel and some money together with a pledge to offer his unreserved assistance.

This Bedouin, dagger in hand, set out towards Madinah Munawwarah. At that moment Rasulullah ﷺ was in the Masjid of Banu 'Abdil-Ash-hal. When Rasulullah ﷺ set eyes on him approaching, he observed: "This man comes with an evil intention."

Usaid bin Hudhair رَضِىَاللهُعَنْهُ sprang up and seized the Bedouin's hand. The dagger that he had concealed within his clothes clattered to the ground. Rasulullah صَلَّىاللهُعَلَيْهِوَسَلَّم asked him: "Tell me the truth, what brings you here?" He replied: "If I am promised safety, I will disclose my intentions." Rasulullah صَلَّىاللهُعَلَيْهِوَسَلَّم pledged: "Go ahead, you have my protection." The Bedouin then went on to give a detailed account of what transpired. Rasulullah صَلَّىاللهُعَلَيْهِوَسَلَّم released him and pardoned him. When this Bedouin witnessed this incomparable conduct, he was drawn to embrace Islam and remarked:

يا محمد! والله ما كنت ما افرق الرجال فما هو الا ان رايتك فذهب عقلى، وضعفت نفسى ثم اطلعت على ما هممت به مما لم يعلم احد فعرفت انك ممنوع، وانك على حق، وان حزب ابى سفيان حزب الشيطان فجعل رسول الله صلى الله عليه وسلم يتبسم

"O Muhammad! I am not a person who is scared of other men but the moment I laid eyes upon you, I lost my senses and became faint-hearted. Furthermore, you ascertained my evil intentions without anyone else knowing about it. From this I realised that you are safe and secure and you are certainly on the path of truth and beyond doubt the group of Abu Sufyaan is an assembly of shayaateen."

On hearing this, Rasulullah صَلَّىاللهُعَلَيْهِوَسَلَّم started smiling.

This Bedouin stayed for a few days in the company of Rasulullah صَلَّىاللهُعَلَيْهِوَسَلَّم. He then sought Rasulullah's صَلَّىاللهُعَلَيْهِوَسَلَّم permission and left. What happened to him thereafter, nobody knows.

Thereafter, Rasulullah صَلَّىاللهُعَلَيْهِوَسَلَّم sent 'Amr bin Umayyah Damri رَضِىَاللهُعَنْهُ and Salamah bin Aslam Ansaari رَضِىَاللهُعَنْهُ to Makkah with instructions to assassinate Abu Sufyaan if the opportunity presented itself.

When these two people reached Makkah, they decided to enter the Baitullah and perform Tawaaf first. The moment they entered the Haram, Abu Sufyaan spied them and bellowed: "Look! This is 'Amr bin Umayyah. He certainly comes with designs of evil."

During the pre-Islamic days of ignorance, 'Amr bin Umayyah رَضِىَاللهُعَنْهُ was notoriously known as shaytaan (the devil). The people of Makkah, terrified by the potential of 'Amr bin Umayyah to cause harm to them, amassed a bit of money and presented it to him.

'Amr رَضِىَاللهُعَنْهُ said to his companion: "Presently, the assassination of Abu Sufyaan seems unlikely. It is better if we save our lives and flee now."

On their return, they killed 'Abdullah bin Maalik Taymi. Further on, they came across a one-eyed man of the Banu Dayl tribe who was lying down reciting the following couplet:

وَلَسْتُ بِمُسْلِمٍ مَا دُمْتُ حَيًّا   وَلَسْتُ أَدِيْنُ دِين المسلمينا

"I will never embrace Islam as long as I live,

I will never take up the religion of the Muslims."

'Amr bin Umayyah رضي الله عنه delivered a blow to this man and finished him off.

As they were returning, they came across two Qurayshi spies whom the Quraysh sent to spy on the conditions of Rasulullah ﷺ. They killed one of them and the other was brought before Rasulullah ﷺ. 'Amr رضي الله عنه relates: "I gave a detailed account of our expedition to Rasulullah ﷺ. On completion of my narrative, Rasulullah's ﷺ face lit up with a smile."

Chapter 19

'Umratul-Hudaybiyyah – 1ˢᵗ Zul-Q'adah 6 A.H.

Hudaybiyyah is actually the name of a well. A village that lies adjacent to this well became known with this name as well. This village lies approximately nine miles from Makkah. Muhib Tabri says that most of the Hudaybiyyah area lies within the *Haram* whilst the balance lies in the *Hill* area.

Rasulullah ﷺ saw a dream in which he witnessed himself and a few of his companions entering Makkah with absolute peace. They performed Umrah and some of the companions shaved their heads whilst the others had cut their hair.

The moment they heard of this dream, the flicker of enthusiasm that was now dormant, flared up in their hearts and the anticipation of a visit to Baitullah made them restless with fervent excitement.

On Monday 1st Zul-Q'adah 6 A.H. Rasulullah ﷺ set out from Madinah Munawwarah towards Makkah Mu'azzamah with the intention of Umrah. Approximately fifteen hundred Muhaajireen and Ansaar accompanied Rasulullah ﷺ on this journey. When they reached Zul-Hulayfah they necklaced their camels, made Ish'aar and donned their Ihraams. Rasulullah ﷺ despatched Busr bin Sufyaan ؓ to spy on the conditions of the Quraysh. Since Rasulullah ﷺ had absolutely no intention of armed combat, they did not carry any sort of arms and military equipment. They merely carried a few basic arms normally carried by a traveller which were securely sheathed in their scabbards.

When Rasulullah ﷺ landed at Ghadir Ashtaat, his informant reported to him that the Quraysh had started amassing their forces the moment they heard of Rasulullah's ﷺ departure. He also reported that this time round, the Quraysh were hell-bent on fighting and they committed themselves to refuse Rasulullah ﷺ entry into Makkah.

Furthermore, Rasulullah ﷺ learnt that Khaalid bin Waleed, in the company of two hundred mounted soldiers, had already landed in a place called

Ghameem, as part of the vanguard. The moment Rasulullah ﷺ heard of this development, he turned away from this route and taking another route towards Makkah, landed at Hudaybiyyah. From this point on, as Rasulullah ﷺ attempted to steer his camel towards Makkah, the camel sat down. The people shouted out: "Hal! Hal!" in an attempt to rouse it and they tried every possible trick to get it to stand, but it remained inflexibly seated. Some people remarked: "Qaswa has become wayward and stubborn!" Rasulullah ﷺ rejoined: "This is not its habit but actually Allah Ta'ala has prevented it from progressing any further."

Thereafter, Rasulullah ﷺ said: "I swear by the Being in whose control lies my soul, whatever the Quraysh demand of me which contributes to the reverence of the Sha'aair (salient features) of Islam, I am fully prepared to accept."

Saying this, Rasulullah ﷺ tapped the camel with his whip. At once she got up in compliance with his direction. From here Rasulullah ﷺ proceeded towards the edge of Hudaybiyyah and set up camp there. It was a blistering hot summers' day. The Sahaabah رضي الله عنهم were suffering from severe thirst and there was an acute shortage of water. Whatever water was available in the nearby well had long since been drawn out. When the Sahaabah رضي الله عنهم brought the lack of water to the attention of Rasulullah ﷺ, he extracted an arrow from his quiver and instructed them to erect it within the well. The moment the arrow was placed into the well, so much of water started gushing forth that the entire army was satiated.

Once he set up camp in Hudaybiyyah, Rasulullah ﷺ mounted Khirash bin Umayyah Khuzaa'i رضي الله عنه on a camel and despatched him to the citizens of Makkah alerting them to the fact that the Muslims arrived in Makkah purely to visit the Baitullah and not to engage in any sort of confrontation.

When Khirash رضي الله عنه landed in Makkah and conveyed the message of Rasulullah ﷺ, they slaughtered his camel and had it not been for the last minute intervention of some of the people, they would have killed him too. Hadhrat Khirash رضي الله عنه escaped with his life, returned to Rasulullah ﷺ and related the whole incident to him.

Rasulullah ﷺ then decided to send Hadhrat 'Umar رضي الله عنه with this message to the citizens of Makkah. However, Hadhrat 'Umar رضي الله عنه excused himself saying: "O Rasulullah ﷺ! You are well aware of how incensed the people of Makkah are with me. They harbour vicious enmity for me. Not a single member of my clan resides in Makkah and nobody will be able to mediate on my behalf. If you send 'Usmaan, who has relatives in Makkah, it would be far more appropriate." Rasulullah ﷺ was satisfied with this proposal. He summoned Hadhrat 'Usmaan رضي الله عنه and instructed him: "Convey our message (of our intentions) to the people of Makkah and also convey glad tidings to those Muslims who are unable to expose their Islam that they should not panic, soon Allah Ta'ala will grant the Muslims victory and render His Deen dominant."

Under the protection of his relative Abaan bin Sa'eed, Hadhrat 'Usmaan رضي الله عنه entered Makkah where he communicated the message of Rasulullah ﷺ to the citizens of Makkah and issued glad tidings to the weak Muslims.

When Hadhrat 'Usmaan رضي الله عنه conveyed Rasulullah's ﷺ message to the chieftains of Makkah, they responded: "This year he (Rasulullah ﷺ) would certainly not be allowed to enter Makkah. Yes, if you ('Usmaan) wish to perform Tawaaf on your own, you may do so." Hadhrat 'Usmaan رضي الله عنه said: "I will definitely not perform Tawaaf without Rasulullah ﷺ."

On hearing this, the Quraysh remained silent but detained Hadhrat 'Usmaan رضي الله عنه.

Whilst Hadhrat 'Usmaan رضي الله عنه was being detained here in Makkah, in Hudaybiyyah a rumour broke out that the Quraysh had murdered 'Usmaan رضي الله عنه.

Bay'atur-Ridwaan

When Rasulullah ﷺ heard of this, he was incredibly distressed and declared: "I will not leave from here until I avenge his death."

Saying this, Rasulullah ﷺ started taking Bay'at (pledge of allegiance) right there under the acacia tree in whose shade he was sitting. This pledge of allegiance was to the effect that they would fight the disbelievers as long as they had life within their bodies. They pledged to die rather than take flight.

The first person to take this pledge was Abu Sinaan Asadi رضي الله عنه. Hadhrat 'Abdullah bin 'Umar رضي الله عنه narrates that when Rasulullah ﷺ summoned the people to take a pledge, the first person to appear before Rasulullah ﷺ was Abu Sinaan Asadi رضي الله عنه. He submitted: "O Rasulullah ﷺ! Extend your hand so that I may take a pledge." Rasulullah ﷺ asked: "On what would you like to take this pledge?" He replied: "On whatever is within my heart." Rasulullah ﷺ asked: "And what is within your heart?" He replied: "O Rasulullah ﷺ! Entrenched within my heart is that I continue brandishing my sword (against the enemy) until Allah Ta'ala grants you victory or until I am killed in His path." Rasulullah ﷺ then accepted his pledge of allegiance and everyone else also followed with a similar pledge.

Hadhrat Salamah bin Akw'a رضي الله عنه took this pledge thrice; once at the beginning, once in the middle and once at the end.

When Rasulullah ﷺ concluded this pledge, he placed his left hand over his right hand and said: "This pledge is on behalf of 'Usmaan."

The right hand was on behalf of himself whilst his left hand represented the hand of 'Usmaan رضي الله عنه. Whenever Hadhrat 'Usmaan رضي الله عنه would narrate this incident, he would remark: "Rasulullah's ﷺ left hand was far superior than my right hand."

This Bay'at (pledge of allegiance) is referred to as Bay'tur-Ridwaan, which Allah Ta'ala refers to in Surah Fatah in the following words:

لَقَدْ رَضِيَ اللّٰهُ عَنِ الْمُؤْمِنِيْنَ اِذْ يُبَايِعُوْنَكَ تَحْتَ الشَّجَرَةِ فَعَلِمَ مَا فِيْ قُلُوْبِهِمْ فَاَنْزَلَ السَّكِيْنَةَ عَلَيْهِمْ وَ اَثَابَهُمْ فَتْحًا قَرِيْبًا ۞ وَ مَغَانِمَ كَثِيْرَةً يَّاْخُذُوْنَهَا ۖ وَ كَانَ اللّٰهُ عَزِيْزًا حَكِيْمًا ۞

"Indeed, Allah was pleased with the believers when they offered you their pledge of allegiance under the tree. So Allah is aware of what is within their hearts (their love and devotion for Rasulullah ﷺ). So he sent down tranquillity upon them and rewarded them with an imminent victory and abundant spoils of war that they would capture. And Allah is all-mighty, all-wise." [Surah Fatah verses 18-19]

Nonetheless, it later emerged that the news of Hadhrat 'Usmaan's ؓ murder was false. When the Quraysh learnt of this pledge, they became terrified and awestruck. As a result they swiftly embarked on conveying a series of messages of a truce.

Although the Banu Khuzaa'ah tribe had not as yet embraced Islam, they always remained well-wishing and friendly allies of Rasulullah ﷺ. They would frequently update Rasulullah ﷺ on the schemes hatched by the Quraysh of Makkah. The leader of the Banu Khuzaa'ah tribe, Budail bin Waraqa, together with a few of his tribesmen appeared before Rasulullah ﷺ and reported: "The Quraysh have amassed a huge force on the outskirts of Hudaybiyyah near the big water-springs to ensure that you do not enter Makkah. They also have a number of milking camels with them." (In other words, they plan to camp there for an extended period of time. They will eat, drink and entrench themselves to fight.)

Rasulullah ﷺ said: "We have not come here to fight. We have come with the sole purpose of performing Umrah. War has diminished the strength of the Quraysh. If they wish, I am prepared to fix a time limit for a cease-fire. Within that time, we will not interfere with one another. They should leave the Arabs and me alone. If, by the grace of Allah, I am triumphant, you (the Quraysh) are invited to enter this Deen and currently you will be given a few days of grace, and, hypothetically speaking, if the Arabs (non-Muslims) are triumphant then your objective is accomplished. However, let me emphasise, Allah Ta'ala will definitely ensure that His Deen is triumphant. The divine promise that He has made in regards to the dominance, ascendancy and assistance of this Deen, that promise will surely be fulfilled. If the Quraysh refuse to accept this, I swear by the Being in whose control lies my soul, I will certainly wage Jihaad against them until my neck is severed from my body."

Budail then took leave from Rasulullah ﷺ and proceeded to the Quraysh informing them: "I have just heard a proposal from that man. If you wish I will present it before you?" The foolish from amongst them blurted: "We have no need for him. We do not want to listen to what he has to say." However, the level-headed amongst them said: "Sure, why not? Tell us what he has to say."

Budail said: "You people are hasty. Muhammad has not come here to fight but to perform Umrah. He extends a hand of peace before you." The Quraysh replied: "Unquestionably he has not come with the intention of fighting but whatever the case may be, he will not be allowed to enter Makkah."

'Urwah bin Mas'ood stood up and addressed them saying: "O people! Am I not like a father unto you and are you not like my children unto me?" "Surely," they replied, "why not?" 'Urwah then asked: "Do you entertain any wicked thoughts about me?" They replied: "Absolutely not!" To this 'Urwah finally submitted: "This man (Muhammad Rasulullah ﷺ) has made a proposal in your own interests and in your own favour. I personally feel that we should accept his proposal. Why don't you permit me to meet with him (Rasulullah ﷺ) and consult with him directly on his proposals?" The people accepted.

When 'Urwah appeared before Rasulullah ﷺ, he put forward the same proposals that he had put forward to Budail. 'Urwah said: "O Muhammad! Have you ever heard of anyone destroying his own nation? Furthermore, if the tables were to be turned the other way (i.e. if the Quraysh were to be triumphant) I foresee the diverse types of people who are currently with you, abandoning you and taking flight."

Hadhrat Abu Bakr رضي الله عنه who was seated behind Rasulullah ﷺ, retorted: "What? Can we ever abandon Rasulullah ﷺ and take flight?"

'Urwah asked: "Who is this man?" When the people replied that it was Abu Bakr, 'Urwah remarked: "I swear by Allah, had it not been for your favour towards me – which I haven't as yet paid back – I would have definitely responded to you."

Saying this, he continued talking to Rasulullah ﷺ. Whenever he mentioned something, he would stroke the beard of Rasulullah ﷺ."

Mughirah bin Shu'bah رضي الله عنه ('Urwah's brother's son) who was standing wielding a sword behind Rasulullah ﷺ, couldn't bear this boldness of his uncle in front of Rasulullah ﷺ. He instantly demanded: "Withdraw your hand from the beard of Rasulullah ﷺ. It doesn't behove a Mushrik (disbeliever) to touch the blessed beard of Rasulullah ﷺ."

Since Mughirah رضي الله عنه was clad in full armour, 'Urwah was unable to recognise him. Raging with fury, he asked: "Who is this?" Rasulullah ﷺ replied: "This is your nephew Mughirah bin Shu'bah." When he recognised him, 'Urwah yelled: "O you deceiver! Did I not contain your deception and the dissension that you had caused in the past?"

Before Mughirah embraced Islam, he once travelled with a few of his companions to Muqawqis, the emperor of Egypt. Compared to Mughirah, the emperor presented his companions with far superior gifts than himself. This threw Mughirah into profound sorrow. On their return, they camped at a certain spot where all his companions guzzled huge quantities of wine and fell into a drunken stupor. Availing himself of this opportunity, Mughirah killed all of them and fled with their goods. He then appeared before Rasulullah ﷺ and embraced Islam. Rasulullah ﷺ remarked: "I sanction you embracing Islam but as for the goods, I want nothing to do with it because it was acquired with dishonesty and deceit."

'Urwah, his uncle, paid the blood money of those killed and somehow managed to contain the situation.

Nonetheless, during his meeting with Rasulullah ﷺ, 'Urwah witnessed such fervent devotion and zealous attachment of the Sahaabah رضي الله عنهم to Rasulullah ﷺ which he had never witnessed anywhere else before. He noticed firsthand that whenever Rasulullah ﷺ issued a command, each one of his companions would rival one another to be the first to carry it out. Whenever saliva or sputum was discharged from his blessed mouth, the companions would not allow it to fall to the ground. They would promptly catch it with their hands and rub it on to their faces. When he performed wudhu, they would not let his used-water fall to the ground. They would avidly jostle one another to grab hold of it as though a fight was about to break out. A hair would barely fall off his blessed body when they would rush forward to retrieve it. When he spoke, a pin-drop silence would descend upon them as though each one of them had turned into an ear. Nobody dared to raise his gaze.

It was as though this spectacle was a physical response to the evil thoughts 'Urwah had at the beginning regarding the devoted adherents of Rasulullah ﷺ - that if the Quraysh were to triumph, these people would abandon Rasulullah ﷺ and take flight. The astounding scene of such ardent enthusiasm, passionate devotion and enthusiastic loyalty that the Sahaabah رضي الله عنهم displayed for Rasulullah ﷺ was a sufficient enough answer for 'Urwah's evil thoughts against the Sahaabah رضي الله عنهم. How can those who cherish such fanatical attachment and such fervent love ever abandon Rasulullah ﷺ and take flight?

When 'Urwah returned from Rasulullah ﷺ back to the Quraysh, he said to them: "O people! By Allah! I have been to the courts of Caesar, Chosroes, Negus and other majestic rulers but I swear by Allah that I have never witnessed such an astounding scenario of such dedicated love and zealous honour."

(Such a scenario was never witnessed before Rasulullah ﷺ nor is it possible after him. He was after all, the seal of all the Prophets. This astounding scenario of ardent love and zealous devotion had terminated upon Rasulullah ﷺ.)

According to another narration, 'Urwah said: "O people! I have witnessed numerous kings and rulers but I have not caught sight of anyone like Muhammad. He does not seem like a king to me."

Although 'Urwah did not mention this frankly, but he intimated that this was not the condition of kings but that of the divine Messengers.

On hearing this account of 'Urwah, the leader of the Habash (the Abyssinians) Hulais bin 'Alqamah Kinaani said: "Why don't you allow me to meet him (Rasulullah ﷺ) and return?"

As Rasulullah ﷺ caught sight of Hulais approaching from far off, he said: "Make the Qurbaani animals stand because this man is one of those who holds Qurbaani animals in high esteem." When Hulais caught sight of these Qurbaani animals standing, he returned even before he reached Rasulullah ﷺ and said to the Quraysh: "I swear by the Lord of the K'abah! These people have come here with the sole purpose of performing Umrah. They can never be prevented from the Baitullah (the house of Allah)."

The Quraysh responded: "Sit down! You are but a desert Bedouin. You do not understand." This statement threw Hulais into a furious rage. He shot back: "O people of Quraysh! Did we not make a pact between us that we would not prevent anyone from the Baitullah if he comes solely with the intention of visiting the Baitullah? I swear by the Being in whose control lies Hulais' life, if you prevent Muhammad from visiting the Baitullah, I promise to summarily withdraw from you with all the Abyssinians as well." The Quraysh replied: "There is no need to get offended. Let us deliberate over the situation and we will decide what action to take."

A little later, Mikraz bin Hafs got up from the gathering and said: "I will go to him (Muhammad Rasulullah ﷺ)."

When Rasulullah ﷺ noticed Mikraz coming, he commented: "This is an evil man." During their stay in Hudaybiyyah, Mikraz, with fifty other men, wanted to launch a night attack on the Muslims. The Sahaabah ؓ managed to apprehend them and foiled this attack but Mikraz escaped. In reference to this incident, Rasulullah ﷺ mentioned that this was an evil man.

Whilst Mikraz was busy talking to Rasulullah ﷺ, Suhail bin 'Amr appeared before Rasulullah ﷺ on behalf of the Quraysh to discuss details of a peace accord.

When Rasulullah ﷺ saw Suhail coming, he remarked to the Sahaabah ؓ: "*Qad Sahula Lakum min Amrikum* (Your problem has been slightly eased)."

Rasulullah ﷺ then added: "The Quraysh are now inclined towards a peace accord. They sent this person to discuss peace with us."

Rasulullah ﷺ and Suhail had a lengthy discussion about a peace accord and the conditions of a peace treaty. Following a verbal agreement over the conditions of the peace treaty, Rasulullah ﷺ instructed Hadhrat Ali ؓ to reduce the accord to writing. He instructed him to write *Bismillahir-Rahmaanir-Raheem* at the head of the document.

In accordance with ancient tradition, at the head of the document, the Arabs used to start off with the words *Bismika-Allaahumma*. This is why Suhail said: "I do not know what newfangled idea this *Bismillahir-Rahmaanir-Raheem* is all about. Just write *Bismika-Allaahumma* as per our ancient tradition." Rasulullah ﷺ said: "Fine, write that down then."

Rasulullah ﷺ then instructed Hadhrat Ali ؓ to write the following:

هذا ما قاضى عليه محمد رسول الله

"These are the conditions upon which Muhammad, the Messenger of Allah, has concluded a peace accord."

To this, Suhail remarked: "If we regarded you as the Messenger of Allah, we would neither have prevented you from the Baitullah nor would we have fought with you. Instead of 'Muhammad, the Messenger of Allah', write: Muhammad, the son of 'Abdullah."

Rasulullah ﷺ responded: "By Allah! I am the Messenger of Allah regardless of you falsifying me."

He then instructed Hadhrat Ali ؓ to erase this and write his name as Suhail desired. Hadhrat Ali ؓ submitted: "O Rasulullah ﷺ! I will by no means erase your name." Rasulullah ﷺ said: "Okay, then show me where the words 'the Messenger of Allah' appears. I will erase them myself." Once Hadhrat Ali ؓ pointed it out to him, Rasulullah ﷺ erased the words with his own hand and directed Hadhrat Ali ؓ to write 'Muhammad, the son of 'Abdullah'.

The conditions of the peace accord were as follows:

Terms of the Treaty of Hudaybiyyah

1. All hostilities will cease for the next ten years.

2. Any member of the Quraysh who flees to Madinah without the permission of his master or guardian will be returned even though he is a Muslim.

3. Any Muslim who flees to Makkah from Madinah will not be returned to the Muslims.

4. During this period, none of the parties will raise a sword against the other and neither will they engage in any form of treachery and betrayal.

5. This year Muhammad ﷺ will return to Madinah without performing Umrah. He will not be allowed to enter Makkah this year. He will be allowed to enter Makkah next year for a period of three days only. He should return after performing Umrah. The Muslims will not be allowed to enter Makkah with any weapons but their swords provided the swords are well-sheathed.

6. The other tribes of the Peninsula have the option to ally themselves to whichever party they wish.

Subsequently, the Banu Khuzaa'ah tribe affiliated themselves with Rasulullah ﷺ whilst the Banu Bakr joined the Quraysh.

Whilst this treaty was being put to paper, Suhail's son, Abu Jandal, escaped from captivity and appeared before Rasulullah ﷺ whilst still in leg shackles. He had already embraced Islam before this and the disbelievers of Makkah were subjecting him to indescribable atrocities. The moment Suhail saw him, he gleefully remarked: "Well, well. This is the first person to be returned as per the terms of our treaty."

Rasulullah ﷺ appealed: "Well, the treaty has not been concluded as yet." In other words, the treaty is only binding once the treaty is written out completely and the signatures affixed to it.

Rasulullah ﷺ pleaded with Suhail repeatedly to hand over Abu Jandal رضي الله عنه to the Muslims but Suhail was adamant. Ultimately, Rasulullah ﷺ surrendered him to Suhail.

The disbelievers of Makkah were subjecting him to unimaginable agony. This is why Abu Jandal, in a grief-laden voice, addressed the Muslims: "What a pity, O Muslims! I am being surrendered to the disbelievers?"

On hearing this, Rasulullah ﷺ pacified Abu Jandal by saying:

يا ابا جندل! اصبر واحتسب فانا لا نغدر وان الله جاعل لك فرجا و مخرجا

"O Abu Jandal! Exercise patience and pin your hopes on Allah, as we do not like to violate the terms of the treaty. However, be rest assured that Allah Ta'ala will surely come up with a strategy to relieve you of your difficulties."

However, his return to the disbelievers was intolerable to the Muslims in general. Hadhrat 'Umar رضي الله عنه was unable to restrain himself and stated: "O Rasulullah ﷺ! Are you not the true Messenger of Allah?" "Surely!" replied Rasulullah ﷺ. Hadhrat 'Umar رضي الله عنه asked: "Are we not on the true path whilst they are wandering on the pathways of deviation?" Rasulullah ﷺ replied: "No doubt about it." Hadhrat 'Umar رضي الله عنه in amazement asked: "Then why do we have to tolerate this humiliation?" Rasulullah ﷺ replied: "I am the Rasool and true Messenger of Allah Ta'ala. I am not willing to breach His commandments. He is my helper and supporter."

Hadhrat 'Umar رضي الله عنه then asked: "Okay, but did you not promise us that we would perform Tawaaf of the Baitullah?" Rasulullah ﷺ replied: "When did I promise that we will perform Tawaaf this year?"

Hadhrat 'Umar رضي الله عنه then went to Hadhrat Abu Bakr رضي الله عنه and had the same conversation with him as well. Abu Bakr رضي الله عنه gave him exactly the same response, word for word as offered by Rasulullah ﷺ.

Hadhrat 'Umar رضي الله عنه says: "Following this episode, I was incredibly ashamed of my actions. In compensation for this misbehaviour, I performed numerous Salaahs, observed a great number of fasts, disbursed a lot of charity and freed many slaves."

گفتگوئے عاشقاں درکار رب

جوش عشقست نہ ترک ادب

"In the work of Allah, the words of the lovers are incited by the fervour of their love. And this (apparently rude) behaviour is certainly not disrespect and cheekiness."

Hadhrat Anas رضي الله عنه relates that the Sahaabah رضي الله عنهم asked: "O Rasulullah ﷺ! How can such a condition of this treaty ever be tolerable? How can we support a condition that stipulates that a person who flees from us Muslims and joins the disbelievers will not be returned to us?"

Rasulullah ﷺ replied: "Yes, if anyone of us joins them, we do not need him. Allah Ta'ala has hurled such a person far away from His divine mercy. As for the person who flees from them and comes to us, although, as per our terms of the treaty, he will be returned to them, there is absolutely nothing to be terrified of. Shortly, Allah Ta'ala will bring about some scheme to ease him of this difficulty." (Furthermore, Alhamdulillah we have not been confronted with a situation where a Muslim took flight from Madinah to Makkah.)

Nonetheless, the treaty was concluded on these terms and both parties affixed their signatures to the document.

On finalisation of this treaty, Rasulullah ﷺ instructed the Sahaabah رضي الله عنهم to slaughter their animals and shave off the hair of their heads. However, the Sahaabah رضي الله عنهم were so disillusioned and distressed by the terms of this treaty that in spite of Rasulullah ﷺ repeating his instructions thrice, not one of them attempted to carry it out.

When Rasulullah ﷺ saw this, he approached Umme Salamah رضي الله عنها and mournfully related to her this state of affairs. She advised: "O Rasulullah ﷺ! This treaty is dreadfully challenging to the Muslims. This is why they are so dejected and distressed that they are unable to execute your instructions. Do not say anything to anyone. You personally go outside, slaughter your Qurbaani animal and shave off your hair. Inevitably the people are bound to follow suit."

Subsequently, this is exactly what happened. The moment Rasulullah ﷺ began to slaughter his Qurbaani animals, all the Sahaabah رضي الله عنهم followed suit.

May Allah Ta'ala reward Umme Salamah رضي الله عنها abundantly. Her brilliant discretion in this matter solved the predicament that Rasulullah ﷺ found himself in.

Following a stay of about two weeks in Hudaybiyyah, Rasulullah ﷺ set out for his return to Madinah. Whilst he was between Makkah and Madinah, Surah Fatah (victory) was revealed.

Rasulullah ﷺ assembled all the Sahaabah رضي الله عنهم and recited the entire Surah before them. The Sahaabah رضي الله عنهم considered this treaty to be a form of defeat for them but Allah Ta'ala referred to it as a conspicuous victory. Bewildered by this declaration, they asked in surprise: "O Rasulullah ﷺ! Is this really a victory?" Rasulullah ﷺ replied: "I swear by the Being in Whose absolute control lies my soul, this is undoubtedly a great victory."

Imaam Zuhri رحمه الله says: "This was such an outstanding victory that never before were they blessed with such a victory. Previously, due to their mutual conflict they were unable to mingle with the others but now with the peace treaty all conflicts had ceased and relative peace established. Previously those who were unable to expose their status of Islam were now able to practice Islam freely. Their mutual hatred and tension had decreased somewhat. They were able to speak openly with one another. They were afforded the opportunity to discuss and debate issues of Islam. Many of them heard the Qur-aan for the first time and this induced such a huge multitude of people to embrace Islam that many more people embraced Islam during the relatively short period from the treaty of Hudaybiyyah to the conquest of Makkah than from the very inception of prophethood right up to that time." Islam is the fountainhead of outstanding character, a mine of perfect actions and a personification of goodness but the Sahaabah رضي الله عنهم were living examples of these virtues, actions and character. Until now, the enemies' eyes of hostility, malice and disgust prevented them from perceiving this.

Now when the veils of hostility and disgust were lifted due to the peace treaty, the alluring prospects of Islam started drawing them towards it.

"The glow on the forehead of a pious man,
how can it be concealed from the sight of a perceptive person?"

Before the treaty, the disbelievers of Makkah were befitting of the verse "and they are unable to perceive". This is why the noor of Islam and the Muslims was unknown to them. With the blessings of the peace treaty, when this hostility and enmity was eliminated, they turned out to be perceptive and now they were able to make out the noor on the foreheads of those treading the right path.

A little while after Rasulullah ﷺ reached Madinah, Abu Basir رضى الله عنه escaped from the clutches of the disbelievers of Makkah and turned up in Madinah. The Quraysh promptly despatched two men to Rasulullah ﷺ demanding that he be handed over to them. As per the terms of the treaty, Rasulullah ﷺ handed Abu Basir رضى الله عنه to them and addressed Abu Basir رضى الله عنه saying: "I am bound by the terms of the treaty. I cannot contravene the terms of the peace accord. It is best if you return." Taken aback, Abu Basir رضى الله عنه asked: "Are you returning me to the disbelievers who aim to change my religion and who subject me to all kinds of distress?"

Rasulullah ﷺ pacified him by saying: "Exercise patience and place your hopes upon Allah Ta'ala. Soon Allah Ta'ala will devise some means to relieve you of this difficulty."

Nonetheless, these two people took Abu Basir رضى الله عنه in their custody and set out. En route, they stopped over at Zul-Hulayfah to take a small rest and eat some dates that they carried with them. Abu Basir رضى الله عنه said to one of them: "Your sword seems extraordinarily beautiful." Taking the sword out of its sheath, the man bragged: "I swear by Allah that this is a remarkably beautiful sword. I have put it to the test on numerous occasions." Abu Basir رضى الله عنه asked: "May I have a look at it?" The instant the man offered it to Abu Basir رضى الله عنه, he snatched it from him and finished him off in a single blow. On seeing what befell his friend, the other man promptly took flight and headed to Madinah where he appeared before Rasulullah ﷺ and submitted: "O Rasulullah ﷺ! My companion has been killed and now it's my turn."

A little later, when Abu Basir رضى الله عنه turned up before Rasulullah ﷺ, he said: "O Rasulullah ﷺ! Allah Ta'ala has fulfilled your end of the treaty. You had already handed me over to them and now Allah Ta'ala has released me from their clutches. O Rasulullah ﷺ! You are well aware that if I had to return to Makkah, these people would constrain me to abandon my faith in Islam. I had done whatever I had done solely for this reason. There is no treaty between me and them."

To this Rasulullah ﷺ replied: "This man is an instigator of war if he has any comrades with him."

Abu Basir رضى الله عنه figured from this that if he had to linger here any longer he would be handed back to the non-Muslims. This is why he quickly left Madinah and settled in a region along the coast through which the Qurayshi caravans would pass during their travels to Syria.

When the downtrodden and helpless Muslims of Makkah learnt of this, they stealthily started trickling in to Abu Basir's hideout. Suhail bin 'Amr's son, Abu

Jandal رضي الله عنه also turned up there. In this manner, a group of seventy men landed there. Whenever a Qurayshi caravan happened to pass by, they would harass them and they would feed off the booty if they happened to get their hands on it.

The Quraysh, annoyed by the turn of events, sent some people over to Rasulullah صلى الله عليه وسلم and begged him in the name of Allah and their blood relationship to call Abu Basir and his group back to Madinah. They also promised not to interfere if anyone of the people of Makkah happened to embrace Islam and flee to Madinah.

Rasulullah صلى الله عليه وسلم then wrote a letter to Abu Basir رضي الله عنه. However, the letter reached Abu Basir رضي الله عنه as he was departing from this world. The letter was handed over to him. As he began reading this letter, his delight had no bounds. He continued reading whilst enhancing his joy at the same time until he surrendered his soul whilst the blessed letter was resting on his chest. According to another narration, he passed away with the letter clutched in his hand.

Abu Jandal رضي الله عنه prepared and shrouded Abu Basir's رضي الله عنه body and buried him there. He erected a Masjid nearby as well. Thereafter, Abu Jandal رضي الله عنه, together with his companions set off for Madinah.

When Suhail bin 'Amr heard of this murder perpetrated by Abu Basir رضي الله عنه, he sought to demand his blood money from Rasulullah صلى الله عليه وسلم since the victim was Suhail's kinsman. However, Abu Sufyaan put him off by saying: "You cannot demand his blood money from Muhammad (Rasulullah صلى الله عليه وسلم) because he fulfilled his end of the treaty by surrendering Abu Basir to your messengers. Abu Basir did not kill your messenger on the bidding of Muhammad (Rasulullah صلى الله عليه وسلم) but he killed him on his own accord. Furthermore, you cannot claim his blood money from the kinsfolk of Abu Basir either because they do not adhere to the same faith."

Following this treaty with the Makkans, any Muslim male who fled from Makkah to Madinah was sent back to Makkah by Rasulullah صلى الله عليه وسلم as per the terms of the treaty. Some time later, a few women also migrated from Makkah to Madinah. The Makkans insisted that they also be returned as per the terms of the treaty. However, through divine revelation, Allah Ta'ala prevented Rasulullah صلى الله عليه وسلم from sending the ladies back explaining that this condition was confined to the males only. Women were not included in the terms of the treaty. According to some narrations, the actual words of the treaty read as follows: "No Rajul (man) will flee to you from amongst us but he will be returned." Obviously the word Rajul explicitly referred to men only. How could women be included in this?

The disbelievers of Makkah wanted to include the women in this treaty as well but Allah Ta'ala forbade it. The following verse was revealed in regard to this incident:

يَٰٓأَيُّهَا ٱلَّذِينَ ءَامَنُوٓا۟ إِذَا جَآءَكُمُ ٱلْمُؤْمِنَٰتُ مُهَٰجِرَٰتٍ فَٱمْتَحِنُوهُنَّ ۖ ٱللَّهُ أَعْلَمُ بِإِيمَٰنِهِنَّ ۖ فَإِنْ عَلِمْتُمُوهُنَّ مُؤْمِنَٰتٍ فَلَا تَرْجِعُوهُنَّ إِلَى ٱلْكُفَّارِ ۖ لَا هُنَّ حِلٌّ لَّهُمْ وَلَا هُمْ يَحِلُّونَ لَهُنَّ ۖ وَءَاتُوهُم مَّآ أَنفَقُوا۟ ۚ وَلَا جُنَاحَ عَلَيْكُمْ أَن تَنكِحُوهُنَّ إِذَآ ءَاتَيْتُمُوهُنَّ أُجُورَهُنَّ ۚ وَلَا تُمْسِكُوا۟ بِعِصَمِ ٱلْكَوَافِرِ وَسْـَٔلُوا۟ مَآ أَنفَقْتُمْ وَلْيَسْـَٔلُوا۟ مَآ أَنفَقُوا۟ ۚ ذَٰلِكُمْ حُكْمُ ٱللَّهِ ۖ يَحْكُمُ بَيْنَكُمْ ۚ وَٱللَّهُ عَلِيمٌ حَكِيمٌ ۝ وَإِن فَاتَكُمْ شَىْءٌ مِّنْ أَزْوَٰجِكُمْ إِلَى ٱلْكُفَّارِ فَعَاقَبْتُمْ فَـَٔاتُوا۟ ٱلَّذِينَ ذَهَبَتْ أَزْوَٰجُهُم مِّثْلَ مَآ أَنفَقُوا۟ ۚ وَٱتَّقُوا۟ ٱللَّهَ ٱلَّذِىٓ أَنتُم بِهِۦ مُؤْمِنُونَ ۝

"O you who believe! When believing women come to you as emigrants, examine them - Allah knows best of their faith. Then if you ascertain that they are really true believers then do not send them back to the disbelievers. They are not lawful for the disbelievers nor are the disbelievers lawful for them. And give the disbelievers whatever they have spent. And there is no sin upon you if you marry them by paying them their Mahr. Likewise, do not hold back the bond of the disbelieving women (do not hold them back as wives) and ask the disbelievers (to return) what you had spent on (these wives) and let them (the disbelievers) ask back for what they had spent. That is the judgement of Allah, He passes judgment between you. And Allah is all-knowing, all-wise.

"And if any of your wives have gone from you to the disbelievers (as apostates) and you (after going out in war) acquired booty, then pay from that to those whose wives have gone, the equivalent of what they had spent (in Mahr). And be ever-conscious of Allah in Whom you believe." [Surah Mumtahinah verses 10-11]

Thereafter the disbelievers remained silent and did not repeat their demands for the return of the women.

Chapter 20

International Efforts to Spread Islam - Letters to World Leaders

Allah Ta'ala refers to the treaty of Hudaybiyyah as a *Fatahum Mubeen* (clear victory) and a source of tranquillity and comfort. This was no doubt, a clear victory and a source of immense tranquillity and comfort because the word Fatah literally means to unlock or to open something that is closed. Due to the mutual fighting of the Arabs, the doors of invitation towards Islam were closed. This treaty threw open this door. Now the time had come to spread the word of Allah to all His servants and to give an open invitation to the people of the world to this magnificent tablecloth of Islam where everyone could share in the divinely delights this religion had to offer.

Those who accepted the divine invitation of Allah Ta'ala and seated themselves at the tablecloth of Islam, discovered that there was not even a particle of salt from every variety of outstanding character, exceptional manners, unmatched virtues and excellent behaviour that was not represented on this tablecloth of Islam. What a clean and pure tablecloth that there was not even an iota of any sort of physical or spiritual evil on this tablecloth. They washed their hands off the dunya and taking the name of Allah and His Rasool ﷺ, they commenced eating from these spiritual culinary delights. They barely consumed two morsels when rapidly the tongue relished the savour of Islam and the sweetness of Imaan and they realised that this was really the nourishment for the soul. The soul can thrive only with such nourishment. It is impossible for the soul to survive with the consumption of the filth of kufr and shirk (disbelief and polytheism).

Nonetheless, on his return from Hudaybiyyah, in Zul-Hijjah 6 A.H., Rasulullah ﷺ decided to send letters of invitation to the kings of the world. He assembled the Sahaabah ﷺ and addressed them thus:

"O People! I have been commissioned to the whole universe as an embodiment of mercy. Convey this message to the world and Allah will shower His mercy upon you. Do not fall into dispute like the disciples of 'Isa عَلَيْهِ السَّلَام. When they were instructed to journey to a close by area, they would gladly proceed but when instructed to travel to a far-off area, they would sit down on the ground as though burdened by an unbearable weight."

In the most gruelling of trials that tested their devotion, loyalty and selflessness, at every opportunity, the Sahaabah رَضِىَ اللّٰهُ عَنْهُم had acquired the loftiest certificate of success and they were crowned with medals of the highest accolades. So how could they ever faulter at this instance? With heart and soul they were enthusiastically willing to carry out Rasulullah's صَلَّى اللّٰهُ عَلَيْهِ وَسَلَّم instructions.

Nonetheless, they also advised him saying: "O Rasulullah صَلَّى اللّٰهُ عَلَيْهِ وَسَلَّم! The kings and rulers of this world do not regard a letter without an official seal affixed to it as reliable. In fact, they would not even bother to glance at it."

Abiding by the Mashwarah (advice) of the Sahaabah رَضِىَ اللّٰهُ عَنْهُم, Rasulullah صَلَّى اللّٰهُ عَلَيْهِ وَسَلَّم had a seal made in the shape of a ring. The spherical band itself as well as the seal were made of silver but it was crafted in the Abyssinian style. The words "Muhammad Rasool Allah" were inscribed on the seal as follows: Muhammad was right at the bottom with the word Allah on the top and Rasool in between.

Rasulullah صَلَّى اللّٰهُ عَلَيْهِ وَسَلَّم then despatched letters to the various rulers of the world inviting them to the truth and informing them that they would be squarely liable for the deviation of their community.

All the scholars are unanimous that they were sent after the treaty of Hudaybiyyah but before the conquest of Makkah. In other words, this progression of letters continued within these two historical events. And Allah Ta'ala knows best.

(1) Letter to the Emperor of Rome

بِسْمِ اللّٰهِ الرَّحْمٰنِ الرَّحِيْمِ

من محمد عبدالله و رسوله الى هرقل عظيم الروم. سلام على من اتبع الهدى اما بعد! فانى ادعوك بدعاية الاسلام، اَسْلِم تَسْلَم يوتك الله اجرك مرتين فان توليت فان عليك اثم اليريسين. و يا اهل الكتاب تعالوا الى كلمة سواء بيننا و بينكم ان لا نعبد الا الله ولا نشرك به

شيئا ولا يتخذ بعضنا بعضا اربابا من دون الله فان تولوا فقولوا
اشهدوا بانا مسلمون

"Bismillahir-Rahmaanir-Raheem

From Muhammad, the slave of Allah, to Hiraql (Heraclius), the head of Rome. Salaam upon those who adhere to divine guidance.

I invite you with the phrase that will bring you closer to Islam (the phrase of Kalimah Tayyibah.) Embrace Islam and you will be safe and Allah will reward you twofold. (In the Holy Qur-aan, Allah Ta'ala assures the people of the book a twofold reward for embracing Islam.) So if you turn down this invitation, the sin of the entire populace will be on your shoulders. 'O people of the scripture! Come to such a word that, between us, is an acknowledged fact; that we do not worship anyone but Allah and we do not ascribe partners unto Him and that none of us will take others as lords besides Allah. Then if they turn away, say: 'Bear witness that we are Muslims.'"

Handing this letter over to Hadhrat Dihyaa Kalbi رَضِيَ اللّٰهُ عَنْهُ, Rasulullah صَلَّى اللّٰهُ عَلَيْهِ وَسَلَّمَ sent him off to the emperor of Rome. At that instant, the emperor had just arrived in Baitul-Maqdis on foot from Hims in demonstration of his gratitude over the defeat of the Persians. Hadhrat Dihyaa Kalbi رَضِيَ اللّٰهُ عَنْهُ landed in Baitul-Maqdis in Muharram 7 A.H. and through the auspices of the governor of Busra, he availed himself in the royal court of the Roman emperor where he presented the letter.

Before handing over the letter, he delivered a short sermon.

Hadhrat Dihyaa's رَضِيَ اللّٰهُ عَنْهُ Sermon in the Emperor's court

"O Roman emperor! The personage who appointed me as his emissary is far superior than you are, and the divine Being who elected him as His Messenger is the most superior and elevated. So I urge you to listen to whatever I have to say with humility and I implore you to answer my questions with utmost sincerity. If you fail to listen with humility you will not be able to duly understand and if you lack sincerity in your answers, your response will not be impartial and just."

The emperor replied: "Okay, go on."

Hadhrat Dihyaa رَضِيَ اللّٰهُ عَنْهُ continued: "You are well aware that Hadhrat Maseeh bin Maryam عَلَيْهِ السَّلَام used to offer Salaah?"

"Yes, without doubt he used to perform Salaah," replied the emperor.

Hadhrat Dihyaa رَضِيَ اللّٰهُ عَنْهُ said: "I invite you unto the Being to Whom Hadhrat Maseeh عَلَيْهِ السَّلَام offered his Salaah, before Whom he would bow his forehead, the Being Who created Hadhrat Maseeh in the womb of his mother and the Being who created all the heavens and the earths. Thereafter, I invite you to the unlettered Messenger about whom Hadhrat Musa عَلَيْهِ السَّلَام and Hadhrat 'Isa عَلَيْهِ السَّلَام issued glad tidings. Besides, you are adequately acquainted with these facts. If you accept this invitation you will be successful in this world as well as the hereafter otherwise your hereafter will prove disastrous for you and not only that, you will have partners in this world (challenging your kingship and laying claim to your power). Be rest assured that you have only one Lord Who wields absolute power to crush the agnostics and bear in mind that He continues changing His fortunes."

Taking the letter of Rasulullah ﷺ from Hadhrat Dihyaa رَضِيَ اللهُ عَنْهُ, the emperor placed it on his head and his eyes and respectfully kissed it. He then opened it and after perusing it he remarked: "I will ponder over it and respond to it by tomorrow."

He then bade his servants to summon to court anyone they come across locally who hailed from the same family as Rasulullah ﷺ, as he wanted to make further enquiries from them. Coincidentally, Abu Sufyaan, with a group of other Qurayshis, was on a business expedition in Shaam. He was camped at Ghazzah. Abu Sufyaan had not yet embraced Islam. The emperor's messenger fetched him from Ghazzah and presented him before the royal court. With grand pomp and splendour, the court was convened. All the Roman noblemen, clergy, monks and other leading figures were in attendance.

The emperor first addressed the Arabs saying: "Amongst you who is the closest relative to this man who claims to be a Prophet?" Abu Sufyaan replied: "I am the closest to him." The emperor directed: "You come and sit close to me." He then charged the others to sit behind Abu Sufyaan. The emperor addressed the others and said: "I am going to ask him a few questions. If he speaks a lie, you should point it out."

Abu Sufyaan says: "If I did not have the fear of these people falsifying me, I would have certainly perverted the truth."

Thereafter the following conversation took place between Abu Sufyaan and the emperor:

Emperor: How is his family lineage amongst you?

Abu Sufyaan: He is a man of a noble lineage. Nobody else is favoured with such an illustrious ancestry.

Emperor: Were there any kings amongst his ancestors?

Abu Sufyaan: No.

Emperor: Did you ever find him speaking lies before he laid this claim to prohethood?

Abu Sufyaan: No.

Emperor: What class of people do his followers belong to; the rich and mighty or the poor and weak?

Abu Sufyaan: Most of them are poor and weak.

Emperor: Are his adherents increasing day-by-day or decreasing?

Abu Sufyaan: They are increasing day by day.

Emperor: Is there anyone who entered this Deen and renounced it out of aversion for it?

Abu Sufyaan: No.

Emperor: Does he ever go against his word?

Abu Sufyaan: Never! Up to this day he has not breached his word. However, nowadays we have a truce enforced between us. I have no idea if he has breached the terms of this truce during the interim. (Abu Sufyaan later commented: "Besides this one sentence, I was unable to sneak in anything else, but by Allah, the emperor did not take any heed of this statement of mine.")

Emperor: Did you ever engage him in battle?

Abu Sufyaan: Yes.

Emperor: How was the fighting between you?

Abu Sufyaan: Sometimes he would be dominant and sometimes we would prevail.

Emperor: What does he instruct you to do?

Abu Sufyaan: He commands us to worship Allah and to abstain from ascribing any partners unto Him. He commanded us to immediately forsake all our ancestral customs of shirk and kufr perpetrated by our forefathers. He also instructs us to perform Salaah and pay Zakaat and to adhere to truthfulness, chastity and favourable family ties.

Addressing his interpreter, the emperor said: "Inform our guest that I first asked him about this Messenger's family lineage and you replied that he is a man of a noble and illustrious lineage. Undoubtedly, all the Prophets hail from families that are very noble and illustrious. I then asked you if there were any kings amongst his ancestors and you replied in the negative. If there were any kings amongst his forefathers I would have assumed that this man is merely attempting to retrieve his family's lost kingship. I then asked you if he ever spoke a lie and you denied this. I inferred from this that how is it possible for a man who does not speak lies about people but, Allah forbid, he attributes falsehood to Allah? When I enquired from you who his followers are, you replied that the bulk of his adherents are weak and poor. I then asked you if his followers are increasing or decreasing day by day. You replied that they are increasing. Without doubt, this is the true condition of Imaan. Its adherents increase day by day until it reaches a level of perfection. I then asked you if anyone who adopted this religion subsequently renounced it out of resentment or revulsion and you replied in the negative. This is the status of Imaan. Once its sweetness and delight penetrates the hearts, it cannot under any circumstances be extracted. I then asked if he ever breached his word and you replied in the negative. Indisputably, this is the condition of the true Prophets. They do not ever go against their word. I then asked you about the hostilities between you and you replied that at times you are dominant and at times he is. Undoubtedly, in the initial stages, this is how the divine scheme of Allah Ta'ala works. Sometimes He makes them victorious and at times they are bound to suffer defeat. This is to put his follower's sincerity and devotion to the test. However, ultimately they are guaranteed victory and dominance. I then enquired from you about his instructions to you. You replied that he commands you to worship Allah alone without ascribing any partner unto Him. He prevents you from idol-worship and he instructs you to observe Salaah, pay Zakaat and adhere to truthfulness, chastity, etc.

If whatever you say is really true, then no doubt this man is the divine Messenger. Soon he will govern this land under my feet. I knew that the emergence of a Messenger was imminent but I had no idea that he would emerge from you (the Arabs). I cherish a profound desire to meet him. If I ever happen to be in his presence, I would wash his feet (in esteem)."

The emperor then read out the blessed letter to the entire gathering of people.

He barely managed to read the letter to the people when all hell broke loose. Chaotic bellows of disapproval were heard from every corner of the imperial court.

Abu Sufyaan relates: "At that instant we were all swiftly ushered out of court. Once we landed on the outside, I remarked (to my fellow countrymen): 'It is astonishing, even the emperor of the Roman Empire is terrified of him (Rasulullah ﷺ).' On that day I was genuinely led to believe that the Deen of Rasulullah ﷺ is set to prevail over all others, until Allah Ta'ala bestowed me with divine guidance to embrace Islam."

Imaam Zuhri رحمه الله says: "During the reign of 'Abdul Malik bin Marwaan, a leading Christian priest by the name of Ibn Natur who was present in the imperial court at the time of this incident related: 'Subsequent to this court episode, the Emperor wrote a letter to the high priest of Rumiyyah enquiring about Rasulullah ﷺ. The name of this priest was Daghatir Rumi and he was well versed with the divine scriptures.

Once the Emperor despatched his letter to the priest, he left Baitul-Muqaddas for Hims (Homs). The Emperor was still in Hims when he received a reply from the priest saying: 'This is the very same Prophet we have been eagerly awaiting. This is the Messenger about whom 'Isa عليه السلام issued glad tidings. I believe in him and I will abide by him. There is no doubt about him being a Prophet. You should also believe in him and consent to adhere to him.'"

On receiving this advice, the Emperor convened a massive court in which he assembled all the patriarchs of Rome. He then sealed off the court by closing all the doors. Whilst seated in one of the upper galleries, the Emperor addressed the entire court thus:

يا معشر الروم! انى قد جمعتكم لخير: انه قد اتانى كتاب هذا الرجل يدعونى الى دينه وانه والله لنبى الذى كنا نتظره ونجده فى كتبنا فهلموا فلنتبع ولنصدقه فتسلم لنا دنيانا واخرتنا

"O Romans! I have assembled you here for a great good. I have received a letter from this man inviting me towards his religion. By Allah! This is the Prophet whom we were enthusiastically awaiting and whom we find mentioned in our scriptures. So come, let us follow him and believe in him. In this manner, both, this world as well as our hereafter will be secured."

The moment the Roman Patriarchs heard this, they started bellowing in protest and scuttled to the doors only to find them locked. The emperor summoned them back to their seats and remarked: "I just wanted to put all of you to the test. I am exceptionally delighted over your staunchness in faith."

On hearing this, all of them were gripped with ecstasy and they fell to their knees in prostration before the emperor.

A little later, the emperor summoned Hadhrat Dihyaa Kalbi رَضِىَ اللّٰهُ عَنْهُ in private and explained: "I swear by Allah and declare that your friend is without doubt a divine Messenger. However, I am terrified of my people assassinating me. If it were not for this anxiety, I would certainly adhere to him. Go to Daghatir, the archbishop of Rome. He is an exceptionally learned man. His knowledge of these affairs is far superior to mine. Furthermore, he commands more reverence and admiration amongst the Romans than I do. Go to him and give him an account of this divine Messenger."

Hadhrat Dihyaa Kalbi رَضِىَ اللّٰهُ عَنْهُ went to Daghatir and gave him a detailed account of Rasulullah صَلَّى اللّٰهُ عَلَيْهِ وَسَلَّم. Daghatir responded by declaring: "By Allah! He is a divine Messenger. We have encountered his characteristics, conditions and attributes in our divine scriptures."

Saying this, he withdrew into his quarters, removed the black robes he was wearing and changed into white robes. Wielding a staff, he then proceeded to the church where he addressed the people thus:

يا معشر الروم! انه قدجاء نا كتاب من احمد يدعونا فيه الى الله عزوجل وانى اشهد ان لا اله الا الله وان احمد عبده و رسوله

"O Romans! A letter has come to us from Ahmad in which he invites us towards Allah, the Almighty. I hereby declare and testify that there is none worthy of worship besides Allah and Ahmad is His slave and messenger."

The instant the people heard this declaration they fell onto him and beat him to death. Hadhrat Dihyaa رَضِىَ اللّٰهُ عَنْهُ returned to the emperor and recounted whatever he witnessed. The emperor responded: "I also harbour the same fear. I am terrified of them treating me in the same manner."

The Roman emperor told Hadhrat Dihyaa رَضِىَ اللّٰهُ عَنْهُ: "I am well aware and do recognise him to be the true Prophet, as pronounced by archbishop Daghatir but if I were to publicly admit this, I will be dispossessed of my kingship and my people will assassinate me."

However, the emperor failed to take heed of the statement of Rasulullah ﷺ mentioned in the letter:

"Embrace Islam and you will be secure."

Had he embraced Islam, he would have secured this world as well as the hereafter.

With great reverence, the Emperor concealed this blessed letter of Rasulullah ﷺ in a box made out of gold. Ameer Saifud-Deen Mansuri narrates: "King Mansur once sent me with certain instructions to King Maghrib. On account of some petition, he sent me to King Faranj who was a descendant of Caesar, the Roman emperor. As I was about to return, he insisted that I wait. He enticed me by revealing: 'If you wait I will show you something magnificent and rare.' I waited until he called for a chest embellished with ingots of gold. He extracted a golden box from it and opened it. The box contained a letter wrapped in silk. Most of the words had faded away. The King pointed out: 'This is the letter of your Prophet addressed to my grandfather, the Caesar. It is in my possession as part of his legacy. My grandfather made a bequest warning us: 'As long as this letter remains safe, your empire will remain safe. This is why we take such great pains to protect, preserve and revere this letter and conceal it from the Christians.'"

(2) Letter to Chosroe Parvez, emperor of Persia

بِسْمِ اللهِ الرَّحْمٰنِ الرَّحِيْمِ

من محمد رسول الله الى كسرى عظيم فارس، سلام على من اتبع الهدى، وامن بالله ورسوله وشهد ان لا اله الا الله وحده لا شريك له وان محمدا عبده و رسوله. ادعوك بدعاية الله عزوجل فانى انا رسول الله الى الناس كلهم لا نذر من كان حيا ويحق القول على الكافرين، اسلم تسلم فان توليت فعليك اثم المجوس

"Bismillahir-Rahmaanir-Raheem

From Muhammad, the Messenger of Allah to Chosroe, the head of Persia. Salaam upon those who adhere to divine guidance, believe in Allah and His Messenger and testify that there is none worthy of worship except Allah, Who is alone and has no partner and they testify that Muhammad is His slave and Messenger. With the divine instruction of Allah, I extend to you an invitation towards the religion of which I am the Messenger to all the peoples of the world so that I may warn those whose hearts are alive and that the word of Allah be implemented against the disbelievers. Embrace Islam and you will be safe. If you decline this invitation, the sin of all the Zoroastrians will be on your shoulders."

Rasulullah ﷺ despatched this letter with 'Abdullah bin Huzaafah Sahmi رضي الله عنه. The moment Chosroe's glance fell onto this letter, he flew into a wild rage. He tore the letter to pieces and shrieked: "This man has the audacity to write a letter like this? He is inviting me to embrace Islam whereas he is my slave."

'Abdullah bin Huzaafah Sahmi رضي الله عنه returned and gave Rasulullah ﷺ a detailed report on what transpired. Rasulullah ﷺ commented: "Chosroe's country has fallen to bits and pieces."

On reading the letter, Chosroe wrote to Baazaan, the governor of Yemen to send two powerful men to apprehend this man who had written this letter to him. He instructed Baazaan to arrest him and deliver him to the imperial court.

Baazaan promptly sent two men with a letter addressed to Rasulullah ﷺ. When these two men appeared with Baazaan's letter before Rasulullah ﷺ, they were so overwhelmed with the awe of Rasulullah ﷺ that they started trembling. Shivering with anxiety, they presented the letter to Rasulullah ﷺ. On hearing the letter read out to him, Rasulullah ﷺ smiled and invited both of them to embrace Islam and asked them to return the following day. When they returned to Rasulullah ﷺ the following day, he reported: "Last night at a certain time, Allah Ta'ala enabled Sherwayh to prevail over his father, Chosroe. Sherwayh executed his father Chosroe."

This incident occurred on Tuesday the tenth of Jumaadal-Ula 7 A.H.

Rasulullah ﷺ charged both of them to return to Baazaan and give him an account of what happened. He also added: "Also inform Baazaan that my religion and my supremacy will reach as far afield as the empire of Chosroe had reached."

On hearing this, Baazaan remarked: "These surely do seem like the words of a prophet. If this information is true then I swear by Allah that this man is a divine Messenger."

Subsequently, this information proved to be correct. Baazaan, together with his kinsfolk, companions and near and dear ones, all embraced Islam. He also informed Rasulullah ﷺ of him embracing Islam.

(3) Letter to Negus, the Emperor of Abyssinia

بِسْمِ اللهِ الرَّحْمٰنِ الرَّحِيْمِ

من محمد رسول الله الى النجاشى ملك الحبشه سلام عليك، اما بعد فانى احمد اليك الله الذى لا اله الا هو الملك، القدوس، السلام، المؤمن، المهيمن، واشهد ان عيسىٰ بن مريم روح الله وكلمته القاها الى مريم البتول الطيبة الحصينة فحملت بعيسىٰ فخلقه الله من روحه ونفخه كما خلق ادم بيده. وانى ادعوك الى الله وحده لا شريك له والموالاة على طاعته وان تتبعنى وتؤمن بالذى جاءنى فانى رسول الله وانى ادعوك وجنودك الى الله تعالى فقد بلغت ونصحت فاقبلوا نصيحتى. والسلام على من اتبع الهدى

"Bismillahir-Rahmaanir-Raheem

From Muhammad, the slave of Allah, to Negus, the emperor of Abyssinia. Salaam unto you. I glorify before you the Allah besides Whom there is none worthy of worship. He is the absolute sovereign, the glorified, free from all defects, provider of security and protector of everyone. I hereby testify that 'Isa, the son of Maryam is the Rooh of Allah and His word which He had transmitted into Maryam the chaste virgin. She fell pregnant with 'Isa. Allah created him from His soul like He created Aadam with His hand. I hereby invite you towards Allah Who is all alone and He has no partner. I also invite you to worship Him eternally and that you pursue and believe in what I have brought (i.e. the Holy Qur-aan). Surely I am the Messenger of Allah and I invite you and your entire army towards Allah Ta'ala. I have conveyed the message and offered my advice. I urge you to accept my advice. And Salaam upon those who adhere to divine guidance."

Rasulullah ﷺ despatched Hadhrat 'Amr bin Umayyah Damiri ؓ with this letter. 'Amr bin Umayyah ؓ handed this letter over to the emperor and addressed him thus: "O Ashamah! I wish to tell you something. I hope you will listen attentively. We trust you and entertain good thoughts about you. Whenever we anticipated goodness from you we always acquired it. We were never confronted with fear and anxiety in your dominion of peace and safety.

The bible, which according to your own admission, is a reliable source of evidence, will be an impartial witness between you and me and its testimony cannot be rejected. It is such a judge and adjudicator that would not go beyond the limits of justice. If you do not accept this invitation, then you will be to this unlettered Messenger like the Jews were to 'Isa ﷺ. Rasulullah ﷺ has despatched his messengers to the other rulers of the world as well but compared to the others, we cherish higher expectations of you."

Negus' Response

I hereby testify and swear that he is the same unlettered Prophet who has been awaited by the people of the scripture. Just as Musa ﷺ issued glad tidings of 'Isa ﷺ by referring to him as the rider of the donkey, similarly, he had issued glad tidings of Muhammad ﷺ by referring to him as the rider of the camel. I have such firm faith in his Prophethood that even after viewing him firsthand, it would not make an iota of difference in the conviction of my faith."

Negus then accepted the blessed letter of Rasulullah ﷺ, placed it over his eyes in reverence, descended from his throne and sat down on the ground. He then embraced Islam and bore testimony to the truth. Thereafter, he dictated a reply to Rasulullah's ﷺ letter.

Negus' Reply to Rasulullah's ﷺ Letter

بِسْمِ اللهِ الرَّحْمٰنِ الرَّحِيْمِ

الی محمد رسول الله من النجاشی الاصحم بن ابجز، سلام علیک یا نبی الله! و رحمة الله و برکاته احمد الله الذی لا اله الا هو الذی هدانی للاسلام. اما بعد! فقد بلغنی کتابک یا رسول الله! فما ذکرت من امر عیسی فورب السماء والارض، ان عیسیٰ ما یزید علی ما ذکرت ثُغروفاً، انه کما قلت، وقد عرفنا ما بعثت به إلینا وقد قرینا ابن عمک واصحابه فاشهد انک رسول الله صادقا مصدقا، وقد بایعتک وبایعت ابن عمک، واسلمت علی یدیه لله رب العالمین، وقد بعثت

$$\text{اليك بابنى ارها ابن الاصحم بن الابجز فانى لا املك الانفسى وان}$$
$$\text{شئت ان اتيك فعلت يا رسول! فانى اشهد ان ما تقول حق. والسلام}$$
$$\text{عليك يا رسول الله !}$$

"Bismillahir-Rahmaanir-Raheem

To Muhammad Rasulullah ﷺ from Negus Asham bin Abjaz.

Salaam, and the mercy and the blessings of Allah upon you O Prophet of Allah! I glorify Allah besides Whom there is none worthy of worship and I praise Him for guiding me towards Islam.

Your letter has reached me, O Prophet of Allah! Whatever you mentioned about 'Isa عَلَيْهِ السَّلَام, I swear by the Lord of the sky and the earth that 'Isa عَلَيْهِ السَّلَام is nothing more than that. We have recognised (and acknowledged) the religion with which you have been sent to us.

We have entertained your cousin and his companions (whilst they were here and obtained firsthand information from them about Islam etc.)

So I bear testimony that you are the truthful and credible Messenger. I have pledged my allegiance on your hands and the hands of your cousin and I had embraced Islam upon his hands for Allah, the Lord of the worlds.

I am sending my son Arhaa bin Asham to you. I have control over myself only. O Rasulullah ﷺ! If you wish I will present myself in person before you. I hereby testify that whatever you say is absolutely true.

Salaam upon you, O Rasulullah ﷺ!"

Negus despatched his son in the company of sixty other Abyssinians to Rasulullah ﷺ. However, the ship they were travelling in sank en route (drowning all passengers on board).

This is the same Negus towards whom the Muslims migrated in the fifth year of prophethood. His name was Ashamah. He embraced Islam at the hands of Hadhrat Ja'far رَضِيَ اللهُ عَنْهُ and he passed away in Rajab 9 A.H. Rasulullah ﷺ informed the Sahaabah رَضِيَ اللهُ عَنْهُم of his death on the very day that he passed away. Rasulullah ﷺ, together with the Sahaabah رَضِيَ اللهُ عَنْهُم performed his 'absent' Janaazah Salaah in the Eid-Gaah.

Another ruler, also referred to as Negus, succeeded him. Rasulullah ﷺ wrote to him also inviting him to embrace Islam. The letter reads as follows:

من النبي محمد صلى الله عليه وسلم الى النجاشى الاصحم عظيم الحبشة، سلام على من اتبع الهدى وامن بالله ورسوله وشهد ان لا اله الا الله وحده لا شريك له، لم يتخذ صاحبة ولا ولدا وان محمدا عبده ورسوله ادعوك بدعاية الله فانى انا رسوله، فاسلم تسلم، يا اهل الكتاب تعالوا الى كلمة سواء بيننا و بينكم ان لا نعبد الا الله ولا نشرك به شيئا ولا يتخذ بعضنا بعضا اربابا من دون الله فان تولوا فقولوا اشهدوا بأنا مسلمون، فان ابيت فعليك اثم النصارى من قومك

"From the divine Messenger Muhammad ﷺ to Negus Asham, the ruler of Abyssinia. Salaam upon those who adhere to divine guidance, believe in Allah and His Messenger, testify that there is none worthy of worship except Allah Who is all alone, He has no partner and He has not taken a wife or son and that Muhammad is His slave and Messenger.

I invite you with the invitation of Allah as I am His Messenger. Embrace Islam and you will be safe.

'O people of the scripture! Come to such a word that, between us, is an acknowledged fact; that we do not worship anyone but Allah, we do not ascribe partners unto Him and that none of us will take others as lords besides Allah. Then if they turn away, say: 'Bear witness that we are Muslims.'

If you (O Negus!) decline this invitation, the sin of all the Christians of your nation will fall on your shoulders."

The Islam of this Negus could neither be established nor could his first name be ascertained. Ibn Kaseer رحمه الله says: "This Negus is different to the Negus who embraced Islam at the hands of Hadhrat Ja'far رضى الله عنه."

(4) Letter to Muqawqis, Governor of Egypt and Alexandria

بِسْمِ اللهِ الرَّحْمٰنِ الرَّحِيْمِ

من محمد عبدالله و رسوله الى المقوقس عظيم القبط، سلام على من اتبع الهدى اما بعد! فانى ادعوك بدعاية الاسلام اسلم تسلم يوتك الله اجرك مرتين فان توليت فعليك اثم القبط. يا اهل الكتاب تعالوا الى كلمة سواء بيننا و بينكم ان لا نعبد الا الله ولا نشرك به شيئا ولا يتخد بعضنا اربابا من دون الله، فان تولوا فقولوا اشهد وا بانا مسلمون

"Bismillahir-Rahmaanir-Raheem

From Muhammad, the slave and Messenger of Allah, to Muqawqis, the head of the Coptics. Salaam upon those who adhere to divine guidance.

I invite you with the invitation of Islam. Embrace Islam and you will be safe and Allah will reward you twofold. (In the Holy Qur-aan, Allah Ta'ala assures the people of the book a twofold reward for embracing Islam.) So if you turn down this invitation, the sin of all the Copts will be on your shoulders. 'O people of the scripture! Come to such a word that, between us, is an acknowledged fact; that we do not worship anyone but Allah, we do not ascribe partners unto Him and that none of us will take others as lords besides Allah. Then if they turn away, say: 'Bear witness that we are Muslims.'"

Affixing his official seal to this letter, Rasulullah ﷺ sent Haatib bin Abi Balta'ah رضي الله عنه with it to the governor of Egypt. On reaching there he was informed that the governor was in Alexandria. He then set out for Alexandria, where he found the governor seated on a terrace overlooking the sea. From the bottom, Haatib رضي الله عنه pointed towards the letter. The governor bade him to join him at the top. Haatib رضي الله عنه went up and presented the blessed letter to him. He received the letter with great reverence and respectfully read through it.

Hadhrat Haatib رضي الله عنه narrates: "Thereafter the governor of Alexandria accommodated me as a special guest in one of the imperial quarters. One day, he convened all the patriarchs and leaders and sent for me. He said: 'I wish to ask you a few questions. Deliberate before you respond.' Haatib رضي الله عنه replied: 'Fine.'"

Muqawqis, the governor, asked: "Is the person from whom you brought this letter, not a divine Messenger?"

Haatib رَضِىَاللهُعَنْهُ replied: "Off course! He is the Messenger of Allah."

Muqawqis said: "If he really is a divine Messenger, then why did he not curse his people and supplicate for their destruction when they banished him from Makkah?"

Haatib رَضِىَاللهُعَنْهُ countered: "Do you bear witness that 'Isa the son of Maryam عَلَيْهِالسَّلَام was a divine Messenger?" "No doubt," replied Muqawqis, "he was a Messenger of Allah."

Haatib رَضِىَاللهُعَنْهُ remarked: "Since he was the Messenger of Allah then why did he not curse his enemies when they conspired to crucify him? Why did he not make dua to Allah Ta'ala to destroy them? In due course, Allah Ta'ala raised him up close to Him."

To this Muqawqis commented: "You are wise and you have come before a wise person."

Lecture of Haatib رَضِىَاللهُعَنْهُ in the Court of Muqawqis

On hearing this sensible response from Haatib رَضِىَاللهُعَنْهُ, the governor was unable to offer any further comment and remained silent. Thereafter, Haatib رَضِىَاللهُعَنْهُ addressed the governor and said: "You are well aware of a man who once passed through this very country of Egypt and professed that he is the highest lord. Allah Ta'ala seized, punished and destroyed him. You should take a lesson from this. It should not be such that others take lesson from you (your punishment). There is a religion far superior to your religion and that is the religion of Islam, which Allah Ta'ala had promised to overshadow all other religions. All other religions will be rendered insignificant before this religion. Allah Ta'ala has commissioned this Prophet to invite the people to this religion. In this regard, the Quraysh proved to be most challenging, the Jews most hostile and the Christians the closest. By Allah! The glad tidings of Hadhrat 'Isa عَلَيْهِالسَّلَام issued by Hadhrat Musa عَلَيْهِالسَّلَام are precisely the same as the glad tidings issued by Hadhrat 'Isa عَلَيْهِالسَّلَام in favour of Muhammad Rasulullah صَلَّىاللهُعَلَيْهِوَسَلَّم. There is no distinction between the two (cases of glad tidings). As for inviting you towards the Holy Qur-aan, it is exactly the same as you inviting the people of the Towrah (Jews) towards the Injeel (new testament).

A nation who comes across a divine Messenger, that nation becomes the Ummah of this Messenger. They are now compelled to adhere to this Messenger. You, O governor, are also amongst those who have come across a divine Messenger. We are not prohibiting you from Christianity but rather, we are commanding you to adhere to the directive of Hadhrat Maseeh ('Isa) عَلَيْهِالسَّلَام."

Response of the Governor

Muqawqis, the governor replied: "I have pondered over this Prophet at length and found that he commands righteousness and prohibits from evil. He does not enjoin detestable things and does not forbid goodness. He is neither a sorcerer nor is he astray. He is neither a soothsayer nor is he a liar. I have come across distinct signs of Prophethood in him such as his news of the unseen. Nonetheless, allow me to deliberate upon this further."

He thereafter concealed this blessed letter in an ivory box and instructed his treasurer to keep it safely.

Subsequent to this, he called for his scribe and bade him to write a reply to Rasulullah's ﷺ letter in Arabic.

Muqawqis, Reply to Rasulullah's ﷺ Letter

بِسْمِ اللهِ الرَّحْمٰنِ الرَّحِيْمِ

الى محمد بن عبدالله من المقوقس عظيم القبط سلام عليك.
اما بعد! فقد قرات كتابك، و فهمت ما ذكرت فيه وما تدعو
اليه وقد علمت ان نبيا قد بقي، وكنت اظن ان يخرج من الشام
وقد اكرمت رسولك، و بعثته اليك بجاريتين لهما من القبط
مكان عظيم وكسرة واهديت اليك بغلة لتركبها والسلام

"Bismillahir-Rahmaanir-Raheem

To Muhammad bin 'Abdullah, from Muqawqis the head of the Copts.

Salaam upon you. I have read your letter and understood what you mentioned therein in regards to your invitation (towards Islam etc.).

I was certain that a final Messenger is yet to come but I was under the impression that he would hail from Shaam.

Nonetheless, I have received your Messenger with great respect. As a gift to you, I am sending with him two slave girls, a few sets of clothing and a mule for your conveyance. Wassalaam."

The name of one these slave girls was Maariyah Qibtiyyah (the Copt). She was included in the Haram (harem) of Rasulullah ﷺ. Rasulullah's ﷺ son, Ibraaheem رضى الله عنه, was born from her. The name of the other slave girl was Shireen and she was awarded to Hassaan bin Saabit رضى الله عنه. The name of the mule was Duldul.

Muqawqis received the ambassador of Rasulullah ﷺ with profound reverence and displayed great esteem towards his blessed letter and although he acknowledged that Rasulullah ﷺ was the final Messenger about whom the previous Prophets issued glad tidings, he did not embrace Islam. He remained committed to Christianity.

When Haatib bin Abi Balta'ah رضى الله عنه returned to Rasulullah ﷺ and related the whole incident, Rasulullah ﷺ commented: "Kingdom and kingship prevented him from embracing Islam but his kingdom will not last forever."

In accordance with this prophecy, the Muslims conquered Egypt in the Caliphate of Hadhrat 'Umar رضى الله عنه.

Muqawqis had already gleaned quite a bit of information about Rasulullah ﷺ from Mughirah bin Shu'bah رضى الله عنه. Before embracing Islam, Hadhrat Mughirah bin Shu'bah رضى الله عنه, accompanied by a few members of the Banu Maalik clan, happened to appear before Muqawqis. This is when he managed to get a good deal of information about Rasulullah ﷺ and his current circumstances.

Upon Muqawqis enquiring from them about the conditions of Rasulullah ﷺ, Mughirah bin Shu'bah رضى الله عنه replied: "This man has come to us with an entirely new-fangled religion which is totally different to our ancestral beliefs and in conflict to the faith of the governor as well.

Muqawqis: What is the reaction of his people with him?

Mughirah: Most of the youth have adhered to him whilst the elderly have opposed him. A number of battles have been fought between the two rival armies. At times they triumph and at times their rivals are victorious.

Muqawqis: What does he invite you to?

Mughirah: He instructs us to worship one Allah Alone without ascribing any partners unto Him. He commands us to renounce the idols our ancestors were worshipping. He also bids us to perform Salaah and pay Zakaat.

Muqawqis: Is there any time set for Salaah and any amount fixed for Zakaat?

Mughirah: They perform five Salaahs during the day and night, and half a Mithqaal (app 4 grams) Zakaat is levied upon twenty Mithqaals i.e. two and half percent Zakaat is payable.

Muqawqis: What does he do with the Zakaat he collects?

Mughirah: He distributes it amongst the poor and destitute. Besides this, he enjoins the maintenance of favourable family ties and the honouring of one's word.

He prohibits adultery, interest and alcohol, and he does not consume animals slaughtered upon the name of any being other than Allah.

Muqawqis: Without doubt, this man is a divine Messenger. He has been commissioned as a Prophet to all the people of the world. Hadhrat 'Isa علیہ السلام also enjoined the same commandments. Before him, all the Ambiyaa علیہم السلام also prescribed the same teachings. Ultimately, he will prevail until there will be nobody to challenge him and the range of his religion will expand to the furthest corners of the globe.

Mughirah: Even if the whole world were to put their faith in him, we would not embrace Islam.

Muqawqis: You people are foolish and stupid. Tell me, what is his lineage like?

Mughirah: He is a man of outstanding and impeccable lineage.

Muqawqis: The Ambiyaa علیہم السلام always hail from the most eminent and noble families. Tell me about his truthfulness and honesty.

Mughirah: It is due to his truthfulness and honesty that all of Arabia refers to him as Al-Ameen (the trustworthy).

Muqawqis: Ponder over this; how is it possible for a person to stick to the truth when he deals with his fellow humans but he attributes falsehood to Allah? Also, tell me, what are his followers like?

Mughirah: His followers are made up of the youth.

Muqawqis: Before him, most of the followers of the Ambiyaa علیہم السلام were the youth.

Thereafter Muqawqis asked: "What is the attitude of the Jews of Yasrib (Madinah) towards him? They are, after all, people of the Taurah."

Mughirah: They opposed him. Consequently, he killed some of them, some of them he imprisoned and some of them he expelled from their homes.

To this, Muqawqis commented: "The Jews are a painfully jealous nation. They are resentful about him being chosen as the final Messenger otherwise they, like ourselves, are well-aware of his status."

Mughirah relates: "Upon termination of our discussion with him, we exited the palace and I thought to myself: 'Even the non-Arab rulers of the world are attesting to his Prophethood whereas they are far away from him. We, on the other hand, are his relatives and neighbours and yet we have not entered his religion even though he came right to our doors to invite us.' This really cast a profound impression upon my heart. I stayed over in Alexandria for some time and not a single church remained that I did not visit and not a single clergyman remained from whom I did not enquire about the attributes and circumstances of Rasulullah صلى الله عليه وسلم. I persisted with my enquiries until I visited their archbishop who was an eminent worshipper and celebrated ascetic. People would bring their ill to him to make dua for them. I asked him: 'Is there any divine messenger left to be commissioned?' He replied:

نعم! هو آخر الانبياء ليس بينه وبين عيسى بن مريم احد، وهو نبي مرسل وقد امرنا عيسى باتباعه وهو النبي الامى العربي اسمه احمد ليس بالطويل ولا بيض ولا بالآدم، يعض شعره ويلبس ما غلظ من الثياب ويجتزئ بما لقى من الطعام، سيفه على عاتقه ولا يبالى بمن لاق يباشر القتال بنفسه ومعه اصحابه يفدونه بانفسهم، هم له اشد حبا من اولادهم يخرج من ارض حرم ويأتى الى حرم يهاجر الى ارض سباخ ونخل يدين بدين ابراهيم عليه السلام

'Yes. He (Rasulullah ﷺ) is the final Messenger. There is no Messenger between him and 'Isa عليه السلام. He is a divine Messenger. 'Isa عليه السلام instructed us to comply with him. He is an unlettered Arabian Prophet. His name is Ahmad. He is neither very tall nor short but in between, of a moderate height. He has a tinge of redness within his eyes. He is neither very fair nor very brown. He will have substantial hair (on his head and beard). He will wear coarse clothing. He will be content with whatever food is available to him. His sword will be over his neck and he will not be troubled by whoever opposes him. He will take active part in battle. With him will be his companions who will enthusiastically give their lives for him. They will cherish him more than their own children. He will appear in the Haram of Makkah and emigrate to a land of brackish water and abundant date-palms. He will adhere to the faith of Ibraaheem عليه السلام.'"

Mughirah relates: "I then asked him: 'Provide me with more details about him.' The archbishop replied: 'He will wear an Izaar (lungi or lower garment). He will wash his limbs (make Wudhu). All the divine Messengers before him were commissioned exclusively for their own people but this Prophet has been commissioned for every nation of the world. The entire earth is a Masjid and source of purity for him. Wherever Salaah time finds him and water is not available, he will perform Tayammum and offer his Salaah. He will not be restricted to a temple or church like the Bani Israa'eel. Their Salaah was not valid except in a specific place of worship.'"

Mughirah says: "I listened attentively to whatever he said and committed it to memory. I subsequently returned to Madinah, appeared before Rasulullah ﷺ and embraced Islam."

Letter to Munzir bin Sawa, Governor of Bahrain

Rasulullah ﷺ composed a letter of invitation towards Islam to Munzir bin Sawa and sent it with 'Alaa bin Hadrami رضي الله عنه.

'Alaa bin Hadrami رضي الله عنه narrates: "When I reached Munzir with the blessed letter of Rasulullah ﷺ, I addressed him saying:

'O Munzir! In worldly affairs you are regarded as very intelligent and astute. Do not become foolish and naive in terms of the hereafter. This religion of fire-worship (Zoroastrianism) is the most immoral religion around. It neither contains the nobility of the Arabs nor the knowledge of the people of the scriptures. The adherents of this religion marry such women (sisters etc.), the mere mention of which is unspeakably shameful. They consume such things that are disgusting to people of sound disposition. They worship the fire of this world whereas in the hereafter, the same fire will devour them. O Munzir! You are not foolish and naive. Reflect over this and ponder over it at length. The being who does not speak lies ever, why do you hesitate in believing in Him? Why are you suspicious of His integrity? The being who never engages in treachery, why are you sceptical of regarding Him as honest? The being who does not act contrary to His word, what misgivings do you harbour about His reliability? If Rasulullah's ﷺ blessed being is like this —and indisputably it is so — then unquestionably he is the divine Messenger of Allah Ta'ala. He is such a Messenger that if he enjoins something, no intelligent person will dare say, 'if only he did not enjoin this,' if he prohibits something, no sensible person will dare say, 'if only he did not prevent this', if he grants relief from something up to a certain degree, no rational person would say, 'why did he not offer greater relief' or if he imposes a certain punishment, he would not demand a reduction or alleviation in it. The reason for this is that every single word, action, order and injunction of Rasulullah ﷺ is in perfect harmony to the aspirations and inclinations of every person of sound intellect.'"

Response of Munzir bin Sawa

Munzir responded: "The religion that I adhere to, I have pondered over it extensively and found it to be exclusively focused upon this materialistic world and not upon the hereafter. When I deliberated over your religion, I found it to be advantageous to both this world as well as the hereafter. So what prevents me from accepting this religion? Its acceptance promises to deliver the aspirations of life and the comforts of death. Until now I was appalled by those who embrace this religion of Islam but now I am outraged by those who refute this true religion."

Chapter 20

Munzir bin Sawa's Response to Rasulullah's ﷺ Letter

Munzir bin Sawa embraced Islam and replied to Rasulullah's ﷺ letter thus:

اما بعد يا رسول الله! فانى قرأت كتابك على اهل البحرين فمنهم من احب الاسلام واعجبه و دخل فيه ومنهم من كرهه وبارضى يهود و مجوس فاحدث الى فى ذلك امرك

"O Rasulullah! I read out your letter to the people of Bahrain. Some of them are fond of Islam. They found it incredibly appealing and entered its fold. However, some of them are unwilling to accept Islam. Furthermore, there are a number of Jews and Zorastrians residing in our country. I eagerly await your judgement in regards to these people."

Rasulullah ﷺ forwarded the following reply:

بِسْمِ اللهِ الرَّحْمٰنِ الرَّحِيْمِ

من محمد رسول الله الى المنذر بن ساوى، سلام عليك، فانى احمد اليك الله الذى لا اله الا هو واشهد ان محمدا رسول الله اما بعد! فانى اذكرك الله عزوجل فانه من ينصح فانما ينصح لنفسه وانه من يطع رسلى ويتبع امرهم فقد اطاعنى ومن نصح لهم فقد نصح لى وان رسلى قد اثنوا عليك خيرا. وانى قد شفعتك فى قومك فاترك للمسلمين ما اسلموا عليك وعفوت عن اهل الذنوب فاقبل منهم وانك مهما تصلح فلن نعزلك عن عملك ومن اقام على يهوديته او مجوسيته فعليه الجزية

"Bismillahir-Rahmaanir-Raheem

From Muhammad Rasulullah to Munzir bin Sawa. Salaam upon you.

I present before you praises of the Lord besides Whom there is none worthy of worship and hereby testify that Muhammad is the Rasool (Messenger) of Allah.

I hereby remind you about Allah Ta'ala because he who acts in good faith towards Allah Ta'ala, he is actually doing good to himself.

He who obeys and complies with my Messengers has in reality been obedient to me. He who acts in good faith towards them has acted in good faith towards me. My messengers have expressed profound praise for you.

I have accepted your intercession on behalf of your people. Leave in the hands of the Muslims the possessions they embraced Islam upon. I have forgiven the errant amongst them. So accept their Islam or their repentance. As long as you remain committed to acting in good faith, I will not remove you. He who wishes to hold fast to his Judaism or to his Zorastrianism, Jizyah (tax) will be imposed upon him."

(6) Letter to the Ruler of Amman

بِسْمِ اللهِ الرَّحْمٰنِ الرَّحِيْمِ

من محمد بن عبدالله ورسوله الى جيفرو عبد ابنى الجلندى، سلام على من اتبع الهدى اما بعد! فانى ادعوكما بدعاية الاسلام اسلما تسلما فانى رسول الله الى الناس كافة لانذر من كان حيا و يحق القول على الكافرين وانكما ان اقررتما بالاسلام وليتكما وان ابيتما ان تقرا بالاسلام فان ملككما زائل عنكما و خيلى تحل بساحتكما وتظهر نبوتى على ملككما

"Bismillahir-Rahmaanir-Raheem

From Muhammad, the slave of Allah and His Messenger to Jayfar and 'Abd, the two sons of Julandi.

Salaam upon those who adhere to divine guidance.

I invite both of you with the invitation of Islam. Embrace Islam and you will be safe. I am the divine Messenger of Allah sent to all the peoples of the world so that I may warn the living of the punishment of Allah and so that the proof may be established against the disbelievers. If you embrace Islam you will be retained (as leaders of your country) otherwise bear in mind that you will soon be unseated from your kingdom, my cavalry will march right up to your entrance hall and my Prophethood will prevail over every religion of your kingdom."

In 8 A.H. in the month of Zul-Q'adah, Rasulullah ﷺ sent 'Amr bin 'Aas ؓ with this letter to the two sons of Julandi; 'Abd and Jayfar. Hadhrat 'Amr bin 'Aas ؓ narrates: "Bearing this blessed letter I landed in 'Ammaan where I first met with 'Abd. He was an exceptionally forbearing, tolerant and good-natured person. I explained to him that I am the messenger of Rasulullah ﷺ and that Rasulullah ﷺ instructed me to present this letter to him and his brother. 'Abd said: "My elder brother Jayfar is the supreme ruler. I will arrange an imperial audience for you with him. You should present this letter to him."

Thereafter, 'Abd asked me: "What did you come to invite us to?"

'Amr bin 'Aas ؓ: Worship one Allah Alone, renounce idol worship and testify that Muhammad ﷺ is the slave and Messenger of Allah.

'Abd: O 'Amr bin 'Aas! You are the son of an eminent chieftain of your tribe. Tell me, what was the reaction of your father to this religion? We will adopt whatever he has settled on.

'Amr bin 'Aas ؓ: My father passed away without Imaan upon Rasulullah ﷺ. It is my fervent wish that if only he embraced Islam and believed in Rasulullah ﷺ. For a lengthy period of time I too held onto his beliefs until Allah Ta'ala divinely guided me towards Islam.

'Abd: When did you embrace Islam?

'Amr bin 'Aas ؓ: I embraced Islam just a few days ago.

'Abd: Where did you accept Islam?

'Amr bin 'Aas ؓ: At the hands of Negus, the Emperor of Abyssinia and Negus himself also embraced Islam.

'Abd: What was the attitude of his people towards him subsequent to him embracing Islam?

'Amr bin 'Aas ؓ: As before, they retained him as their monarch and followed him.

'Abd: What was the reaction of the clergy?

'Amr bin 'Aas ؓ: All of them yielded to him.

'Abd: O 'Amr! Think very carefully before you speak because there is no habit as offensive as telling lies. There is nothing more humiliating for a man than lies.

'Amr bin 'Aas ؓ: Never! I certainly did not speak a lie, and speaking lies is not permissible even in our religion.

'Abd: I wonder if Hiraql, the Emperor of Rome is aware of Negus embracing Islam.

'Amr bin 'Aas ؓ: The Emperor is well aware of Negus embracing Islam.

'Abd: How do you know about that?

'Amr bin 'Aas ؓ: Negus was paying his taxes to the Roman Emperor but subsequent to him embracing Islam, Negus declined to pay any form of tax to him. He also declared: "I swear by Allah, if the Roman Emperor has to demand even one Dirham (in tax) I will certainly not pay it to him."

When the Emperor heard of this emphatic declaration, he remained silent. On noticing this bewildering silence, the Emperor's brother, Nayaaq howled in rage: "What? Will you let this slave of yours, Negus go unpunished even though he refuses to pay tax and renounces your religion for another one?" The Emperor replied: "Negus is free to choose whichever religion he fancies. He has opted for this particular religion and he has all the right to do so. I swear by Allah that if it was not for the fear of my kingdom, I would have also followed suit and embraced this particular religion."

'Abd (stunned by the turn of events) said: O 'Amr what are you saying?

'Amr bin 'Aas ؓ: By Allah! I am speaking the truth.

'Abd: Okay, tell me what does your Prophet command you to do and what does he restrain you from?

'Amr bin 'Aas ؓ: He commands us to obey Allah Ta'ala and restrains us from His disobedience. He instructs us to carry out good deeds and to maintain favourable family ties, and he prohibits us from cruelty, transgression, adultery, drinking alcohol, idol and cross-worship.

'Abd: What a pleasant invitation and what wonderful counsel. If only my brother were to concur with me then both of us could present ourselves before Rasulullah ﷺ and embrace Islam at his hands. However, it may be possible that my brother's concern for kingship will largely contribute to his reluctance (to embrace this faith).

'Amr bin 'Aas ؓ: If he embraces Islam, Rasulullah ﷺ will leave your brother's imperial status unchanged and he will instruct him to collect charity from the rich of the community and redistribute it amongst their poor and destitute.

'Abd: That is splendid! Tell me, how much and how is this form of charity levied?

Hadhrat Amr bin 'Aas ؓ relates: "I explained to him in detail how much of Zakaat is levied on gold and silver and to what extent it is imposed on camels and goats etc. Thereafter, 'Abd presented me before his brother Jayfar. I presented him with the sealed letter of Rasulullah ﷺ. He took the letter from me, broke the seal open and read through it. After asking me to take a seat, he enquired a bit about the conditions of the Quraysh etc. Following one or two days of reflection, he also demonstrated his inclination towards Islam. Both brothers collectively proclaimed their Islamic status and a number of people also embraced Islam with them. Jizyah (tax) was imposed on those who failed to embrace Islam."

'Allaamah Suhayli رَحْمَةُاللّٰه writes that 'Amr bin 'Aas رَضِىَاللّٰهُعَنْهُ addressed Julandi (their father) and said: "O Julandi! Although you are far away from us, you are not far away from Allah Ta'ala. The Being Who created you all alone without any partner, worship Him Alone, and the being who is not a partner to Allah Ta'ala in your creation, do not make him a partner in the worship of Allah Ta'ala. Bear in mind that the Supreme Being who gave you life will indisputably give you death too, and the Being who started off your very conception will soon call you back unto Him. So I urge you to reflect very carefully upon this unlettered Messenger who has presented to us the goodness and success of this world as well as the hereafter. If he demands any form of compensation from you, withhold it and if you perceive a hint of hedonistic pursuits (Nafsaani amusements) in any of his words or actions, you may abandon him. I then exhort you to ponder over the religion he has presented to us. Is this divine religion similar to the self-contrived laws designed by people? If Rasulullah's صَلَّىاللّٰهُعَلَيْهِوَسَلَّم religion is similar to man-made religions of today, then tell me, which religion is it similar to? If his religion is not akin to any of the man-made religions of today, then be aware that this religion is the divine religion from Allah Ta'ala. So accept this religion and implement whatever it commands you to do and beware of everything it warns you of."

To this Julandi replied: "I have exhaustively contemplated over this unlettered Prophet and found that without a doubt he does not enjoin anything good but he is the first to implement it and he does not prohibit anything evil but he is the first to abstain from it. When he triumphs over his enemies, he does not gloat in vanity and when he is defeated he does not become agitated. He fulfils his promises and honours his word. I hereby testify that he is, indisputably, a divine messenger."

He then recited the following poems:

اتانی عمرو بالتی لیس بعدها   من الحق شئ والنصیح نصیح

"Amr (bin 'Aas رَضِىَاللّٰهُعَنْهُ) appeared before me with that after which there is no other truth and the faithful adviser has offered his good counsel.

فیا عمرو قد اسلمت لله جهرة   ینادی بها فی الوادیین فصیح

O 'Amr! I openly declare that I have embraced Islam solely for the pleasure of Allah and a crier may proclaim this in the valleys (of our country)."

(7) Letter to the Chief of Yamaamah, Huzah bin Ali

بِسْمِ اللهِ الرَّحْمٰنِ الرَّحِيْمِ

من محمد رسول الله الى هوذة ابن على، سلام على من اتبع الهدى، واعلم ان دينى سيظهر الى منتهى الخف والحافر فاسلم تسلم واجعل لك ما تحت يديك

"Bismillahir-Rahmaanir-Raheem

From Muhammad, the Messenger of Allah, to Huzah bin Ali. Salaam upon those who adhere to divine guidance.

Bear in mind that my religion will reach wherever camels and horses can tread. Embrace Islam and you will be safe and I will allow you to retain custody over your domain."

Rasulullah ﷺ handed this letter over to Salit bin 'Amr ﷛ and sent him off to Huzah. Huzah read this blessed letter and entertained Salit ﷛ with royal honour and high esteem.

Salit ﷛ addressed Huzah saying:

"O Huzah! Decaying and putrefying bones have appointed you as a leader. In reality, a leader is he who is adorned with Imaan and secures a provision of Taqwa (Allah-consciousness). I wish to command you to execute something that is most eminent and I wish to prohibit you from something that is most despicable; I command you to worship Allah Alone and I prohibit you from worshipping shaytaan. If you accept this, all your aspirations will be realised and you will be safe from anxiety. However, if you refuse, then the dreadful scene of Qiyaamah (doomsday) will lift this veil that exists between you and us."

Huzah replied: "Give me a bit of time and allow me to ponder over this."

Subsequently, he responded to the blessed letter of Rasulullah ﷺ as follows:

ما احسن ما تدعو اليه واجمله والعرب تهاب مكانى فاجعل الى بعض الامر اتبعك

"What you are calling to is so magnificent and brilliant. The Arabs are awed over my status and authority. So allow me some authority and I will submit before you."

As he was leaving with this reply, Huzah offered Hadhrat Salit ﷺ some gifts that included some fine cloth produced in Hajar.

When he reached Madinah and narrated the incident to Rasulullah ﷺ, he remarked: "By Allah! Even if he has to request for a single span of land I will refuse. He and his country both are destroyed."

On his return from the conquest of Makkah, Jibraa'eel عَلَيْهِ السَّلَام informed Rasulullah ﷺ about the death of Huzah. He in turn conveyed this information to the Sahaabah ﷺ and added: "Soon a liar, who will lay claim to prophethood will emerge in Yamaamah and he will be assassinated after my demise." This is exactly what happened.

(8) Letter to the Ruler of Damascus Haaris Ghassaani

بِسْمِ اللهِ الرَّحْمٰنِ الرَّحِيْمِ

من محمد رسول الله الى الحارث بن ابى شمر، سلام على من اتبع الهدى وامن بالله وصدق فانى ادعوك الى ان تؤمن بالله وحده لا شريك له، يبقى مُلكك

"Bismillahir-Rahmaanir-Raheem

From Muhammad, the Messenger of Allah, to Haaris bin Abi Shamr.

Salaam upon those who adhere to divine guidance, believe in Allah and affirm the divine commandments of Allah.

I hereby invite you to believe in one Allah Who has no partner. If you affirm your faith in this your sovereignty will remain intact."

Bearing this blessed letter, Shuj'a bin Wahhaab Asadi ﷺ landed in Damascus. At that moment, the governor Haaris Ghassaani, was frantically engaged in making preparations for hosting Caesar, the Roman Emperor. As a token of gratitude of his victory over the Persian Empire, Caesar had then just arrived at Baitul-Muqaddas (Jerusalem) walking barefoot all the way from Hims (Homs). So a number of days passed by without Shuj'a bin Wahhaab Asadi ﷺ securing a meeting with Haaris Ghassaani, the governor.

Shuj'a bin Wahhaab Asadi ﷺ relates: "I mentioned to the doorkeeper of Haaris's court: 'I am a messenger of Rasulullah ﷺ and I wish to meet the governor.' The doorkeeper replied: 'The governor will make an appearance in a few days time. You will be able to meet him then.'

The doorkeeper actually hailed from Rome and his name was Murri. He started asking me questions about Rasulullah ﷺ. As I continued describing to him the specifics of Rasulullah ﷺ he continued weeping. On being informed about the conditions of Rasulullah ﷺ, he commented: 'I have read the Injeel (bible) and I have come across his (Rasulullah's ﷺ) name and attributes in it. I hereby declare my faith in him and testify that he is the true messenger of Allah. I fear that Haaris the governor will execute me (for declaring my beliefs).'

Nonetheless, the doorkeeper treated me with great respect and went out of his way in entertaining me as his guest."

Finally Haaris made his appearance in the royal court. Wearing the imperial crown on his head, he sat down in attendance. Hadhrat Shuj'a ؓ was then given permission to enter the royal court. Hadhrat Shuj'a ؓ presented the letter to him. On reading the letter, Haaris turned red in anger and hurling the letter aside he roared in rage: "Who is this man who threatens to usurp my country from me? I will pre-empt him and march against him."

He then commanded that his horses be equipped in preparation for battle. He also sent a letter describing the current events to the Roman emperor. The emperor replied: "Hold your horses and put off your plans."

On receiving the reply of the Emperor, Haaris summoned Hadhrat Shuj'a ؓ and asked him when he intended to return home. He replied that he planned to leave the following day. Haaris ordered that he be awarded one hundred Mithqaals of gold as a gift.

Hadhrat Shuj'a ؓ relates: "The doorkeeper also presented something as a gift and asked me to convey his Salaam to Rasulullah ﷺ. I returned to Madinah and recounted the entire incident before Rasulullah ﷺ who remarked: "His country is destroyed." I then conveyed the Salaam of Murri the doorkeeper and also informed Rasulullah ﷺ about what he said. Rasulullah ﷺ replied: "He has spoken the truth."

Chapter 21

The Battle of Khaybar 7 A.H.

وَعَدَكُمُ اللهُ مَغَانِمَ كَثِيْرَةً تَأْخُذُوْنَهَا فَعَجَّلَ لَكُمْ هٰذِهِ

"Allah has promised you abundant spoils (of war) which you will attain and He has hastened for you this (booty of Khaybar)." [Surah Fatah 20]

As he was returning from Hudaybiyyah, Surah Fatah was revealed upon Rasulullah ﷺ. In this Surah Allah Ta'ala assured the Muslims in general and the people of the pledge in particular that they will be triumphant in a number of battles and they will capture enormous spoils of war. As an immediate reward for this pledge that they had taken, Allah Ta'ala had bestowed upon them victory over Khaybar and the conquest of Makkah, which they had not as yet acquired, but would acquire soon. In future they would surmount a number of victories, the knowledge of which only Allah Ta'ala has. In this verse 'He has hastened for you this' the reference is to the conquest of Khaybar. Similarly, in the previous verse, 'And He rewarded them with a near victory.' This near victory refers to the conquest of Khaybar.

Rasulullah ﷺ returned from Hudaybiyyah to Madinah where he remained for Zul-Hijjah and the beginning of Muharram. During this period, Rasulullah ﷺ was commanded to launch an attack against Khaybar where the treacherous Jews resided who had betrayed the Muslims by inciting the disbelievers of Makkah against them in the battle of Khandaq (trench). Allah Ta'ala also informed Rasulullah ﷺ that upon hearing of the imminent conquest of Khaybar, the hypocrites too would eagerly implore him to allow them to accompany him on this expedition. Allah Ta'ala commanded Rasulullah ﷺ: "Never! These people should never accompany you on this journey." The following verse was revealed in this regard:

$$\text{سَيَقُولُ الْمُخَلَّفُونَ إِذَا انْطَلَقْتُمْ إِلٰى مَغَانِمَ لِتَأْخُذُوهَا ذَرُوْنَا نَتَّبِعْكُمْ ۚ يُرِيْدُوْنَ اَنْ يُّبَدِّلُوْا كَلٰمَ اللّٰهِ ۚ قُلْ لَّنْ تَتَّبِعُوْنَا كَذٰلِكُمْ قَالَ اللّٰهُ مِنْ قَبْلُ ۚ فَسَيَقُوْلُوْنَ بَلْ تَحْسُدُوْنَنَا ۚ بَلْ كَانُوْا لَا يَفْقَهُوْنَ إِلَّا قَلِيْلًا ۝}$$

"Those who lagged behind (in the expedition of Hudaybiyyah) will say when you set forth to seize the spoils (of Khaybar): 'Allow us to follow you.' They wish to alter the word (and promise) of Allah. Say: 'You will never ever be able to follow us, Allah has decreed this beforehand.' Then they will say: 'Nay, you are jealous of us (and you do not wish to include us in the spoils of war, whereas such a notion is ridiculous. The hearts of the Sahaabah ﷺ were absolutely devoid of jealousy and greed.)' But these people (the critics) do not understand except very little."
[Surah Fatah verse 15]

Those great personalities before whom the contents of the whole world were not even equal to the wing of a mosquito, the mere thought of them harbouring jealousy is the ultimate in stupidity and foolishness.

Following a short stay in Madinah Munawwarah, Rasulullah ﷺ set out for Khaybar with fourteen hundred infantry and two hundred cavalry towards the end of Muharram 7 A.H. From the pure wives, Hadhrat Umme Salamah ﷺ accompanied him on this expedition.

Salamah bin Akw'a ﷺ relates: "On the night we set out for Khaybar in the company of Rasulullah ﷺ, the celebrated poet 'Aamir bin Akw'a ﷺ was ahead of us reciting the following pieces of rhyming poetry:

$$\text{اَللّٰهُمَّ لَوْلَا اَنْتَ مَا اهْتَدَيْنَا ۚ وَلَا تَصَدَّقْنَا وَلَا صَلَّيْنَا}$$

"O Allah! If it were not for You we would not have been divinely guided, neither would we have distributed alms nor performed a single Salaah.

$$\text{فَاغْفِرْ فِدَاءً لَّكَ مَا اتَّقَيْنَا ۚ وَاَلْقِيَنْ سَكِيْنَةً عَلَيْنَا}$$

We are sacrificed upon You, O Allah! Forgive us for shunning aside Your commandments and blanket us with Your special tranquillity (so that the hearts may be consoled and comforted and all forms of distress and anguish is eliminated from the heart).

$$\text{وَثَبِّتِ الْاَقْدَامَ اِنْ لَّا قَيْنَا ۚ اِنَّا اِذَا صِيْحَ بِنَا اَتَيْنَا}$$

Grant us steadfastness when we confront the enemy. When we are summoned to war we are swift to respond to the call of Jihaad.

$$\text{وَبِالصِّيَاحِ عَوَّلُوا عَلَيْنَا}$$

And with this cry of war they are wailing in lament.

$$\text{اِنَّ الَّذِيْنَ قَدْ بَغَوْا عَلَيْنَا ۚ اِذَا اَرَادُوْا فِتْنَةً اَبَيْنَا}$$

Those who have transgressed against us, if they elect to ensnare us with the temptations of disbelief and polytheism, we will certainly not budge.

$$\text{وَنَحْنُ عَنْ فَضْلِكَ مَا اسْتَغْنَيْنَا}$$

And we, O our Lord, are not independent of Your grace and favour."

Rasulullah ﷺ asked: "Who is this reciting this rhyming poetry." When the people informed him that it was 'Aamir bin Akw'a, he commented: "May Allah shower him with His special mercy." According to the narration of Musnad Ahmad, Rasulullah ﷺ said: "May Allah forgive him." Whenever Rasulullah ﷺ made an exclusive dua of forgiveness in favour of someone, that person would soon die as a martyr. This is why Hadhrat 'Umar رضي الله عنه pleaded: "Jannah is compulsory for him. If only you allowed us to take advantage of 'Aamir's bravery and valour for a few more days."

En route to Khaybar, as Rasulullah ﷺ reached a hillock, the Sahaabah رضي الله عنهم raised their voices in saying the Takbeer (of Allahu Akbar). To this Rasulullah ﷺ commented: "Have pity upon yourselves. You are not calling out to a Being Who is deaf or absent. You are addressing a Being Who is close by and omnipresent. (So you do not have to shout like this.)"

Hadhrat Abu Musa Ash'ari رضي الله عنه relates: "I was close to the camel of Rasulullah ﷺ when he heard me reciting Laa Hawla wa laa Quwwata Illaa Billah. He called: 'O 'Abdullah bin Qays!' I promptly responded: 'I am at your service O Rasulullah!' Rasulullah ﷺ asked: 'Should I not reveal to you the treasures of Jannah?' I replied: 'May my parents be sacrificed for you, surely, why not O Rasulullah!' Rasulullah ﷺ revealed: 'Laa Hawla wa laa Quwwata Illaa Billah.' In other words, these words are the treasures of Jannah."

Since Rasulullah ﷺ was aware that the Jews of the Ghitfaan tribe had amassed a combat-ready force to assist the Jews of Khaybar, he camped at a place called Raj'i situated between Khaybar and Ghitfaan. He did this to instil a bit of awe within the Jews of Ghitfaan so that they do not rush to the aid of the Jews of Khaybar. Consequently, when the Jews of Ghitfaan heard that they themselves were in danger, they turned back swiftly.

As they drew closer to Khaybar, Rasulullah ﷺ bade the Sahaabah رضي الله عنهم to hold on and he made the following dua:

اللهم رب السموت وما اظللن: ورب الارضين وما اقللن، ورب الشياطين وما اضللن، ورب الرياح وما اذرين، فانا نسألك خير هذه القرية وخير اهلها وخير ما فيها و نعوذ بك من شرها وشر اهلها و شر ما فيها. اقدموا بسم الله

"O Allah, the Lord of the skies and the Lord of whatever they shelter, O Lord of the earths and Lord of whatever they bear, O Lord of the Shayaateen and Lord of whatever misguidance they had perpetrated, Lord of the winds and Lord of whatever they disperse! We beg of You for the best of this locality and the best of its inhabitants and the best of whatever is within it and we seek Your refuge from its evils, from the evils of its inhabitants and the evils within it."

Saying this dua, Rasulullah ﷺ directed the Sahaabah ؓ: "Advance in the name of Allah!"

It was a noble habit of Rasulullah ﷺ to recite this dua on entering a locality.

Hadhrat Anas ؓ narrates: "Rasulullah ﷺ reached Khaybar at night. It was his gracious habit not to launch an offensive at night. He would wait until the morning. If he heard the Azaan, he would not attack otherwise he would launch an attack. In keeping with this noble Sunnah, even at Khaybar, Rasulullah ﷺ waited for the Azaan of Fajr. When he failed to hear the Azaan of Fajr, he made preparations to attack. The moment dawn broke out, the Jews, clutching their picks and shovels, set out to work (on their fields). As they laid eyes on the invading army, they exclaimed in horror: "Muhammad and the Khamis. (Muhammad and his whole army is here)."

Khamis is derived from the word Khams that literally means five. Since the army is made up of five divisions, the army as a unit is referred to as Khamis. The arrangement of the army is as follows: the vanguard, the right wing, the left wing, the mainstay and finally the rear guard.

On catching sight of these people, Rasulullah ﷺ raised his hands in dua:

الله اكبر! خربت خيبر انا اذا نزلنا بساحة قوم فساء صباح المنذرين

"Allah is great. Khaybar is devastated. Verily when we descend in the courtyard (in the midst) of a nation then dreadful is the morning of those who had been warned."

The moment the Jews got wind of Rasulullah ﷺ, they retreated into their fortresses with their wives and children. Rasulullah ﷺ launched successive attacks against these fortresses and conquered them one after the other.

These fortresses were as follows:

(1) Naʿim Fort

The first fort that the Muslims conquered in this battle was Naʿim Fort. Mahmud bin Maslamah رضي الله عنه was standing at the foot of the fort when the Jews dropped a millstone onto him, thus rendering him a martyr.

(2) Qamus Fort

Following their triumph over Naʿim fort, the Qamus fort was conquered. This was one of the most fortified forts of Khaybar. When the Muslims laid siege to this fort, Rasulullah ﷺ was unable to personally proceed to the battlefield as he was suffering from a severe migraine. Thus he offered the battle-ensign to Hadhrat Abu Bakr Siddeeq رضي الله عنه. In spite of his unwavering efforts, he was unable to conquer the fort and he returned. The following day, Rasulullah ﷺ handed over the ensign to Hadhrat ʿUmar رضي الله عنه and sent him off to battle. He too fought with unyielding determination but he too returned without overcoming the fort.

On that day Rasulullah ﷺ revealed: "Tomorrow I will hand over this flag to a person who loves Allah and His Rasool and Allah and His Rasool also love him and at his hands this fort will be conquered."

Every person was eagerly waiting to see who is blessed with this boon. They passed the whole night in enthusiastic anticipation and vibrant zeal. The next morning Rasulullah ﷺ summoned Hadhrat Ali رضي الله عنه. At that time he was suffering from an infection of the eyes. Rasulullah ﷺ applied his blessed saliva to his eyes and recited a dua. Without delay he was cured as though nothing had afflicted his eyes. Rasulullah ﷺ handed over the flag to him saying: "Before engaging them in battle, invite them towards Islam. Enlighten them about the divine rights of Allah. I swear by Allah, if Allah guides just one person through you, it is far better for you than red camels." Holding the standard aloft, Hadhrat Ali رضي الله عنه set out and eventually the fort was conquered at his hands.

One of the most celebrated heroes of the Jews, Murahhib, strutted out onto the battlefield and pompously recited the following rhyme:

قد علمت خيبر اني مرحب   شاك السلاح بطل مجرب

"The citizens of Khaybar are well aware that I am Murahhib, bristling in arms, heroic and a veteran (of war)."

In response, Hadhrat 'Aamir bin Akw'a رضي الله عنه stepped out to challenge him whilst reciting the following rhyme:

قد علمت خيبراني عامر   شاكي السلاح بطل مغامر

"The citizens of Khaybar are well aware that I am 'Aamir, bristling in arms, heroic and reckless."

Hadhrat 'Aamir رضي الله عنه was about to strike him on his leg when the sword twisted back onto his own knee causing a fatal wound. He subsequently passed away at Khaybar.

Hadhrat Salamah bin Akw'a رضي الله عنه (his brother) narrates: "On our return from this battle, Rasulullah صلى الله عليه وسلم noticed that I was awfully disheartened and when he enquired the reason, I replied: 'O Rasulullah! People are claiming that all 'Aamir's good deeds are in vain because he died with his own sword.' Rasulullah صلى الله عليه وسلم remarked: 'Whoever said this is mistaken. He was an outstanding warrior.' Thereafter, gesturing with his two fingers, Rasulullah صلى الله عليه وسلم said: 'He will get a twofold reward.' Rasulullah صلى الله عليه وسلم said that he is a martyr and he also performed his Janaazah Salaah. "

Following this tragic incident with 'Aamir رضي الله عنه, Hadhrat Ali رضي الله عنه strode out onto the battlefield and in response to Murahhib's bragging poetry, Hadhrat Ali رضي الله عنه responded with the following couplet as he appeared to take him on:

اَنَا الذي سَمَّتْنِي أُمِّي حيدره   كَلَيْثِ غَاباتٍ كريهِ المنظره

"I am the man who was named Haydar (lion) by his mother. I am as terrifying as the predatory lions of the jungles."

As Hadhrat Ali رضي الله عنه was busy reciting these verses, he struck Murahhib with such a lethal blow of the sword that split his head into two. Subsequently, the fort was captured.

Thereafter, Murahhib's brother Yaasir decided to step forth onto the battlefield. From this end, Hadhrat Zubair رضي الله عنه stepped out and promptly finished him off.

This fort was conquered at the hands of Hadhrat Ali رضي الله عنه after a siege of twenty days. Apart from the war booty, a number of people were taken captive. Amongst the captives was Hadhrat Safiyyah bint Huyayy bin Akhtab رضي الله عنها, the daughter of the chief of Banu Nazeer and the wife of Kinaanah bin Rab'i.

Hadhrat Safiyyah رضي الله عنها and her two cousins (father's brother's daughters) were captured from this Qamus fort. Further details will be discussed later. Hadhrat Safiyyah's husband's name was Kinaanah bin Rab'i who was also killed in this battle.

(3) S'ab bin Mu'aaz Fort

Following the Muslims victory over the Qamus fort, the S'ab bin Mu'aaz fort was conquered. A huge supply of grain, fat and other consumables were stockpiled within this fort. All this fell into the hands of the Muslims.

The Muslims suffered an acute shortage of provisions and they requested Rasulullah ﷺ to make dua for them. The day after he made dua for them, S'ab bin Mu'aaz fort was conquered. This netted the Muslims an abundance of essential provisions providing them with much needed support in their campaign.

On the same day, Rasulullah ﷺ witnessed a number of fires burning all around him. When he enquired about this, the people informed him that they were cooking meat. "What type of meat is it?" he asked. They replied: "It is the flesh of domesticated asses." Rasulullah ﷺ remarked: "It is Najis (unclean). Dispose of it and break the utensils as well." Someone enquired: "O Rasulullah! If we just dispose of the flesh but wash the utensils (and use them), will this be permitted?" He replied: "Okay, wash the utensils (and use them)."

(4) Qullah Fort

Thereafter the Jews sought refuge in Qullah fort. This was also a well-fortified and well-protected fort. It was built right on the peak of a mountain, hence the name Qullah fort. The word Qullah literally means 'mountain-top or summit'. This fort was subsequently referred to as Zubair Fort because it fell into the share of Hadhrat Zubair ؓ when the spoils of war were distributed amongst the Muslims.

For three days Rasulullah ﷺ laid siege to this fort. In an unanticipated turn of good fortune, a Jew appeared before Rasulullah ﷺ and said: "O Abul-Qaasim! Even if you had to isolate these people for a whole month it would not affect them in the least. They have water springs flowing beneath them. They come out at night, fill up their containers and quickly retreat into the fort. If you cut off their water supply, you will be able to succeed."

Rasulullah ﷺ managed to cut off their water supply. They were forced to emerge from the fort. A fierce battle ensued in which ten Jews were killed and a few Muslims were also martyred but the fort was conquered.

This Qullah Fort was the last fort to be conquered in the area of Natat. Thereafter Rasulullah ﷺ pressed on to the forts of Shaqq. Following an intense battle, the first fort to fall in this area was the fort of Ubayy. The Muslims occupied the fort. Thereafter, Rasulullah ﷺ advanced to the other forts of the area.

(5) Watih and Salalim

Subsequent to his success on the aforementioned fort, Rasulullah ﷺ pushed ahead to the other forts of the area. Only when all the other forts were occupied, Rasulullah ﷺ finally proceeded to Watih and Salalim. Some narrations mention the Kaytabah fort as well. The Muslims now occupied all the other forts. These two forts were left. The Jews applied all their energies to these last two remaining forts. The Jews, fleeing from the surrounding areas, all sought refuge in these forts. Following a siege of fourteen days, the Jews were desperately driven to plead for a truce. Rasulullah ﷺ accepted their plea. The Jews appointed Ibn Abul-Haqiq as their spokesperson to discuss the terms of the truce. Ultimately, Rasulullah ﷺ spared them on condition that they immediately vacate the area and go into exile and that they leave behind their gold, silver, arms and other implements of war. He also warned them not to conceal anything and carry it away. He also cautioned them that if they violate any of these conditions, Allah and His Rasool were free of any responsibility.

However, in spite of their pledge and assurance, the Jews failed to refrain from their mischief. They somehow managed to hide away a leather bag belonging to Huyayy bin Akhtab. This bag contained all their jewellery. Rasulullah ﷺ summoned Kinaanah bin Rab'i and asked him about the bag. He replied that it was used up in the battles. Rasulullah ﷺ remarked: "Not much time has passed and the value of that wealth was enormous." Rasulullah ﷺ warned them: "If this bag happens to turn up, none of you will be safe." Saying this, Rasulullah ﷺ instructed an Ansaari to go to a certain tree in a certain area and dig out this bag from its roots. The Sahaabi went and unearthed this bag. The value of its contents was about ten thousand Dinaars (gold coins). These people were executed for this crime. One of the culprits was the husband of Hadhrat Safiyyah رضى الله عنها, Kinaanah bin Rab'i bin Abil-Haqiq.

Moreover, Kinaanah was also guilty of the murder of the brother of Muhammad bin Maslamah, Mahmud bin Maslamah, who was killed in this very battle. For this reason Rasulullah ﷺ handed over Kinaanah to Muhammad bin Maslamah رضى الله عنه so that he may execute Kinaanah in revenge of the death of his brother.

Conquest of Fadak

When the Jews of Fadak learnt that the Jews of Khaybar surrendered and entered into a truce with the aforementioned conditions, they too sent a message to Rasulullah ﷺ pleading with him to spare their lives and in exchange they offered to leave behind all their wealth and go into voluntary exile. Rasulullah ﷺ accepted this offer. The terms of this treaty were discussed through the representation of Muhayyasah bin Mas'ood. Since Fadak was taken over without any military intervention or offensive, neither the cavalry nor the infantry was required. The entire area of Fadak was left to the absolute control and 'right of use' of Rasulullah ﷺ. Unlike Khaybar, these lands were not distributed amongst the Mujaahideen.

Note: In this campaign, either fourteen or fifteen Muslims were martyred and ninety-three disbelievers were killed. Following this successful campaign, when the spoils of war and captives were drawn together, Hadhrat Safiyyah bint Huyayy bin Akhtab رضي الله عنها was also amongst them. She had just recently married Kinaanah bin Rab'i.

Huyayy bin Akhtab was a descendant of Hadhrat Haroon عليه السلام. As the captives were being escorted after the battle, Hadhrat Dihyaa رضي الله عنه submitted: "O Rasulullah! Grant me a slave girl." Rasulullah ﷺ replied: "You have a choice. Select whichever slave girl you fancy." Hadhrat Dihyaa رضي الله عنه chose Hadhrat Safiyyah رضي الله عنها. To this the Sahaabah رضي الله عنهم remarked: "O Rasulullah! This is the daughter of their leader. She is most appropriate for you." Hence Rasulullah ﷺ repossessed her and granted him Hadhrat Safiyyah's cousin in exchange of her. Thereafter, Rasulullah ﷺ set Hadhrat Safiyyah رضي الله عنها free and married her.

A detailed account of Hadhrat Safiyyah's nikah will be mentioned under the chapter dealing with the Azwaaj Mutahharaat (pure wives of Rasulullah ﷺ). Just as Rasulullah ﷺ conducted himself with Hadhrat Juwayriyyah رضي الله عنها in the expedition of Banu Mustalaq in keeping with her family honour and nobility, similarly, on this occasion, in keeping with Hadhrat Safiyyah's رضي الله عنها noble lineage and the fact that she was a descendant of Hadhrat Haroon عليه السلام, Rasulullah ﷺ set her free and married her.

An Attempt to Poison Rasulullah ﷺ

After the conquest of Khaybar, Rasulullah ﷺ stayed on for a few days more at Khaybar. During this period, Zaynab bint Haaris, the wife of Salaam bin Mushkim, presented to Rasulullah ﷺ a gift of a grilled goat seeped in deadly poison. The moment he tasted it, Rasulullah ﷺ held his hand back. However, Bishr bin Baraa bin M'arur رضي الله عنه, who was seated with Rasulullah ﷺ, consumed part of it. Rasulullah ﷺ cautioned: "Hold it. This goat is steeped in poison."

Rasulullah ﷺ summoned Zaynab and asked her the reason for this heinous deed. She confessed: "Yes, the meat was poisoned because if you are truly a divine Messenger, Allah Ta'ala would surely notify you about it and if you are a false Messenger then the people would be released from you."

Since Rasulullah ﷺ never sought revenge for any loss or injury caused to his personal self, he released her. However, when Bishr bin Baraa bin M'arur رضي الله عنه passed away with this poison, Rasulullah ﷺ handed her over to Bishr's heirs. They executed her in retaliation for the murder of Bishr.

Mukhaabarah – Sharecropping

When the lands of Khaybar were conquered and the lands fell into the lot of Allah, His Rasool ﷺ and the Muslims, Rasulullah ﷺ intended to banish the Jews from Khaybar (as per their agreement). However, the Jews begged Rasulullah ﷺ to allow them to stay on condition that they would cultivate the land and pay half the harvest to Rasulullah ﷺ. Rasulullah ﷺ accepted this condition but also added:

نقركم على ذلك ماشئنا

"We will allow you to stay on as long as we wish."

Since such a sharecropping agreement was concluded for the very first time in Khaybar, such sharecropping agreements are referred to as Mukhaabarah.

Whenever the occasion for harvest and distribution drew close, Rasulullah ﷺ would send Hadhrat 'Abdullah bin Rawaahah رضي الله عنه to determine an estimate of the crops.

Hadhrat 'Abdullah bin Rawaahah رضي الله عنه would divide the entire harvest into two equal parts and invite them to take whichever one of the two parts they preferred. On witnessing this level of fairness, the Jews would say: "It is due to this level of justice and fairness that the skies and earth are still standing." In another narration it is mentioned that Hadhrat 'Abdullah bin Rawaahah رضي الله عنه would reply:

يا معشر اليهود! انتم ابغض الخلق الى قتلتم انبياء الله وكذبتم على الله وليس يحملني بغضى اياكم ان احيف عليكم

"O Jews! You are the most despicable of Allah's creation in my eyes because you murdered a number of Prophets and attributed falsehood unto Allah. However, this revulsion that I harbour for you would never drive me to be unfair to you."

The Arrival of Abu Hurayrah ﷺ

Hadhrat Abu Hurayrah ﷺ and a few of his companions appeared before Rasulullah ﷺ after the conquest of Khaybar. However, Rasulullah ﷺ did not allocate a share for them from the war booty.

Return of the Orchards of the Ansaar

When the Muhaajireen migrated to Madinah in the early days, the Ansaar, forever eager to provide assistance, temporarily offered some of their lands and orchards to the Muhaajireen in a bid to provide a source of mutual benefit to both, the donor as well as the donee.

However, following their triumph at Khaybar, the Muhaajireen were now rendered self-reliant. Therefore they returned these lands and orchards to their respective owners. Hadhrat Anas's ﷺ mother, Hadhrat Umme Sulaim ﷺ had also awarded Rasulullah ﷺ the benefits of a few trees. Rasulullah ﷺ assigned these trees to his wet nurse Umme Ayman ﷺ who was also the mother of Hadhrat Usaamah bin Zaid ﷺ.

When the Muhaajireen returned the trees of the Ansaar, Hadhrat Umme Sulaim ﷺ also requested the return of her trees from Rasulullah ﷺ. These trees were already assigned to Hadhrat Umme Ayman ﷺ. Rasulullah ﷺ asked Umme Ayman ﷺ to return these trees of Umme Sulaim ﷺ. She refused and strapping a cloth to Anas's ﷺ neck, she tugged the cloth and said: "By Allah! I will never return these trees."

Since Umme Ayman ﷺ was the wet nurse of Rasulullah ﷺ and also a slave girl of his father, Rasulullah ﷺ did not wish to disappoint Umme Ayman ﷺ in any way. Rasulullah ﷺ said: "O Umme Ayman! Return these trees and take some other trees in exchange." Rasulullah ﷺ continued exhorting her in this manner but she only agreed to return these trees when Rasulullah ﷺ promised to give her ten trees from his personal property in exchange of each one of these trees. In view of her rights of upbringing and nurturing, Rasulullah ﷺ conducted himself in this indulgent manner with her.

Prohibitions at Khaybar

At Khaybar, Rasulullah ﷺ issued a few prohibitions. These included:

1. Prohibition of the meat of domesticated donkeys.
2. Rasulullah ﷺ forbade the sale of any share of the war booty before its actual distribution.
3. He forbade the use of (raw) garlic and
4. He endorsed the consumption of horseflesh. (The Ulama hold conflicting opinions on this issue.)

Return of the Emigrants from Abyssinia

When the emigrants, who migrated from Makkah to Abyssinia, learnt that Rasulullah ﷺ had left Makkah and migrated to Madinah Munawwarah, most of them also left Abyssinia for Madinah Munawwarah. Hadhrat 'Abdullah bin Mas'ood ؓ arrived in Madinah just when Rasulullah ﷺ was making frantic preparation for the expedition of Badr.

Hadhrat Ja'far ؓ and his fifteen companions turned up in Madinah on the day Khaybar was conquered. Rasulullah ﷺ embraced Ja'far ؓ and kissed him on his cheek. He then remarked: "I wonder what gives me more joy; the conquest of Khaybar or the arrival of Ja'far."

Abu Musa Ash'ari ؓ (who was also one of Ja'far's ؓ companions) narrates: "We turned up before Rasulullah ﷺ just as he had conquered Khaybar. He awarded us a share of the spoils of Khaybar as well. Apart from us, those who did not participate in the campaign of Khaybar were not awarded any share of the booty."

Conquest of Wadil-Quraa and Tayma

After Khaybar, Rasulullah ﷺ proceeded to Wadil-Quraa. Following a four-day siege, it fell to the Muslims. On this occasion, Rasulullah's ﷺ slave, Mid'am was fatally struck by a stray arrow whilst he was busy taking down the camel-carriage of Rasulullah ﷺ. The people commented: "May his martyrdom be blessed." Rasulullah ﷺ retorted: "Never! By Allah! The sheet he usurped from the war booty will turn to fire and burn him." When another man heard of this, he appeared before Rasulullah ﷺ with a shoelace. Rasulullah

ﷺ remarked: "Even a shoelace (acquired dishonestly) is of the fire of Jahannam."

When the people of Tayma heard of the fall of Wadil-Quraa, they surrendered and signed a peace treaty with Rasulullah ﷺ promising to pay Jizyah.

Return Journey and the incident of Laylatut-T'aris

Thereafter Rasulullah ﷺ returned to Madinah Munawwarah. On his way, Rasulullah ﷺ dismounted to rest in one of the valleys during the latter part of the night. Coincidentally, not one of their eyes opened until the sun had already turned bright in the sky. Rasulullah ﷺ was the first to awaken and in a state of utter unease, he got to his feet, roused the Sahaabah رضي الله عنهم and ordered them to head off from this valley without delay because of the overpowering influence of shaytaan there.

They moved out of the valley and alighted at a spot further on. Rasulullah ﷺ directed Hadhrat Bilal رضي الله عنه to call out the Azaan. After performing wudhu, Rasulullah ﷺ and the Sahaabah رضي الله عنهم offered two Rakaat of Fajr Sunnats. Thereafter, Hadhrat Bilal رضي الله عنه called out the Iqaamah and the Qadhaa Salaah of Fajr was performed with Jamaat.

Consummation of Marriage with Umme Habibah رضي الله عنها

During the same year, Hadhrat Umme Habibah رضي الله عنها, the daughter of Abu Sufyaan, returned from Abyssinia to Madinah Munawwarah. Rasulullah ﷺ married her through the good offices of Negus, the emperor of Abyssinia. Further details of this Nikah will, Insha Allah, be discussed in the chapter dealing with the pure wives of Rasulullah ﷺ.

'Umratul-Qadaa – Zul Q'adah 7 A.H.

According to the terms of the Hudaybiyyah truce, the Muslims would return home that year without performing Umrah and the Quraysh had pledged to allow them to perform Umrah the forthcoming year provided they return home within three days. This is why, upon observing the crescent of Zul Q'adah, Rasulullah ﷺ instructed the Sahaabah رضي الله عنهم to set out to perform Qadaa of this Umrah which the disbelievers had blocked them from performing at Hudaybiyyah. He also added that none of those who participated at Hudaybiyyah should be left out. Thus, apart from those who had been martyred or passed on in the interim, not one of the participants of Hudaybiyyah remained behind.

Thus, in the company of two thousand people, Rasulullah ﷺ set out for Makkah Mukarramah. Seventy sacrificial camels also accompanied Rasulullah ﷺ on this journey. On reaching Zul-Hulayfah, Rasulullah ﷺ and the Sahaabah رضی اللہ عنہم entered the Musjid in the state of Ihraam. Thereafter, chanting Labbayk, they set out towards Makkah. As a precautionary measure, they carried their weapons with them but since one of the conditions of the treaty of Hudaybiyyah was that they would come unarmed, they left their weapons in the valley of Yaajuj, which is approximately eight miles from Makkah Mukarramah. Rasulullah ﷺ also left behind a contingent of two hundred men to guard these weapons. Saying the Talbiyah, Rasulullah ﷺ, in the company of his beloved companions advanced towards the Haram.

During this period, Hadhrat 'Abdullah bin Rawaahah رضی اللہ عنہ, clutching the bridle of Rasulullah's ﷺ camel Qaswaa, was striding ahead whilst reciting the following couplets:

خلّوا بنی الکفار عن سبیله   قَدْ اَنْزَلَ الرَّحْمٰنِ فِیْ تَنْزِیْلِهٖ

"O children of disbelievers! Get out of his (Rasulullah ﷺ's) way. Allah Ta'ala had commanded in His book that

بان خیر القتل فی سبیله   نحن قتلناکم علی تاویله کَمَا قَتَلْنَاکُمْ عَلٰی تَنْزِیْلِهٖ

the supreme form of death is martyrdom in His path. We engaged you in battle because you refused to adhere to His divine commandment just as we engaged you in battle for refusing to believe in the divine scripture of Allah."

'Abdullah bin Rawaahah رضی اللہ عنہ also added the following words:

الیوم نـضربکم علی تنزیله   ضَرْبًا یزیل الهام عن مقیله

"Today, in accordance with His divine command, we will smite you with such force that would sever your head from your body.

ویذهل الخلیل عن خلیله   یا رب انی مؤمن بقیله

And it would make a friend negligent of his friend. O Allah! I earnestly believe in his statements."

According to Ibn Ishaaq's رحمہ اللہ narration, he said:

یارب انی مؤمن بقیله   انی رایت الحق فی قبوله

'O Allah! I earnestly believe in his statements and I regard its acceptance as the sole truth."

Upon the recitation of this poetry, 'Umar ؓ chided: "O Ibn Rawaahah! You have the audacity to recite poetry in the presence of Rasulullah ﷺ and in the very precincts of the Haram of Allah?" To this, Rasulullah ﷺ commented: "O 'Umar! Let it go. These poetical statements are more punishing to the disbelievers than letting loose a volley of arrows upon them."

According to Ibn S'ad's ؒ narration, Rasulullah ﷺ remarked: "O 'Umar! I am listening to what he says." He then instructed 'Abdullah bin Rawaahah ؓ to recite the following:

لَا اِلٰهَ اِلَّا اللهُ وَحْدَهُ، نَصَرَ عَبْدَهُ وَاَعَزَّ جُنْدَهُ، وَهزَمَ الْاَحْزَابَ وَحْدَهُ

"There is none worthy of worship besides Allah Who is alone. He assisted His servant, He honoured His army and defeated the confederates all alone."

The Sahaabah ؓ also joined 'Abdullah bin Rawaahah ؓ in reciting this sentence. In this imposing manner, they entered Makkah, performed Tawaaf, made Sa'ee between Safa and Marwah, slaughtered their animals and became Halaal from their Ihraam. Thereafter, Rasulullah ﷺ directed some of them to return to the valley of Yaajuj (where the weapons were kept) and to relieve those who were assigned to protect these weapons so that they may come and perform Tawaaf and Sa'ee. Saying this, Rasulullah ﷺ entered the K'abah and remained therein until Zuhr. As per Rasulullah's ﷺ instructions, Hadhrat Bilal ؓ called out the Zuhr Azaan on the roof of the K'abah.

Although the Quraysh, as per the terms of the truce, consented to Rasulullah ﷺ performing Tawaaf but due to their intense fury and acute jealousy they were unable to withstand this spectacle. This is why the leaders of Quraysh and their noblemen left Makkah Mukarramah and retreated to the mountains.

Nikah with Maymunah ؓ

Rasulullah ﷺ stayed on for three days at Makkah and married Hadhrat Maymunah bint Haaris ؓ. On the expiry of the three days, the Quraysh sent a delegation to Rasulullah ﷺ reminding him that his time was up and he should leave. Rasulullah ﷺ said: "If you allow me a bit more time, I would arrange a Walimah feast for Maymunah bint Haaris here in Makkah." With heartless enmity they retorted: "We do not need your feast and Walimah here. Just get out of here."

Rasulullah ﷺ instructed the Sahaabah ؓ to leave without delay. Rasulullah ﷺ left his slave Abu Raaf'i with Hadhrat Maymoonah ؓ. He brought her to a place called Sarif where Rasulullah ﷺ consummated the marriage. He then departed and arrived at Madinah in the month of Zul-Hijjah. Allah Ta'ala revealed the following verse on this occasion:

$$\text{لَقَدْ صَدَقَ اللهُ رَسُولَهُ الرُّءْيَا بِالْحَقِّ ۚ لَتَدْخُلُنَّ الْمَسْجِدَ الْحَرَامَ اِنْ شَآءَ اللهُ اٰمِنِيْنَ ۙ مُحَلِّقِيْنَ رُءُوْسَكُمْ وَمُقَصِّرِيْنَ ۙ لَا تَخَافُوْنَ ۚ فَعَلِمَ مَا لَمْ تَعْلَمُوْا فَجَعَلَ مِنْ دُوْنِ ذٰلِكَ فَتْحًا قَرِيْبًا}$$

"Indeed Allah has fulfilled the true vision (dream) of His Messenger. You will enter Masjidul-Haraam, if Allah wills, safe, (some) of you with shaved heads and (some) of you with your hair cut short, having no fear. He (Allah) knows what you do not know and besides that, He granted a near victory." [Surah Fatah verse 27]

As Rasulullah ﷺ was leaving Makkah on the completion of 'Umratul-Qadhaa, the young daughter of Hadhrat Hamzah ؓ ran behind him shouting: "Uncle! Uncle!" Immediately, Hadhrat Ali ؓ lifted her up (onto his camel). Now a dispute broke out between Hadhrat Ali, Hadhrat Ja'far and Hadhrat Zaid bin Haarisah. Each one of them aspired to take her into his care. Hadhrat Ali ؓ declared: "This is the daughter of my uncle (she is my cousin) and I have already picked her up." Hadhrat Ja'far ؓ argued: "She is the daughter of my uncle too and moreover, her maternal aunt is married to me." Hadhrat Zaid ؓ said: "She is the daughter of my brother in Deen (religious brother)."

Ultimately, Rasulullah ﷺ passed judgement that the young girl should live with her maternal aunt and proclaimed: "The maternal aunt (mother's sister) is like the mother."

Expedition of Akhram bin Abil 'Awjaa - Zul-Hijjah 7 A.H.

During the month of Zul-Hijjah, Rasulullah ﷺ sent Akhram ؓ with fifty men to the tribe of Banu Sulaim with the sole purpose of inviting them towards Islam. The Banu Sulaim retorted: "We do not need your Islam." They then released a volley of arrows on this small group of Muslims killing them to the last man. Only Akhram ؓ managed to survive. Taking him for dead, they left him alone. Due to his serious injuries, he was on the verge of death. He somehow managed to survive and returned to Madinah on the first of Safar.

Expedition of Ghaalib bin 'Abdullah Laysi رضي الله عنه - Safar 8 A.H.

During the month of Safar 8 A.H., Rasulullah ﷺ sent Hadhrat Ghaalib bin 'Abdullah Laysi رضي الله عنه with a group of men towards a place called Kadid to attack the Banu Maluh tribe. The Sahaabah رضي الله عنهم reached there and launched a nighttime attack against them. Seizing their camels, the Sahaabah رضي الله عنهم started retreating towards Madinah. However a force of the Banu Maluh tribe gave chase and as they were hot on the heels of the Muslims, Allah Ta'ala brought about such torrential rain that filled the valley between the Muslims and disbelievers. As a result, the disbelievers were unable to get through and the Muslims reached Madinah safe and sound.

Other expeditions

Between the expeditions of Khaybar and Muta, Rasulullah ﷺ had despatched a number of small contingents on other military campaigns. *Alhamdulillah*, they all returned victorious.

Islam of Khaalid bin Waleed رضي الله عنه, 'Usmaan bin Talhah رضي الله عنه and 'Amr bin 'Aas رضي الله عنه

During this time, the legendary commander-in-chief of Islam Khaalid bin Waleed رضي الله عنه and the celebrated intellectual of the Arabs, 'Amr bin 'Aas رضي الله عنه embraced Islam. There is a difference of opinion as far as their actual date of embracing Islam is concerned. Some maintain that they embraced Islam in the month of Safar 8 A.H whilst others say it was after the expedition of Khaybar in 7 A.H.

Khaalid bin Waleed رضي الله عنه narrates: "When Allah Ta'ala desired my welfare, He infused the love of Islam into the fibres of my heart. Out of the blue I was assailed by the thought that whenever I joined the ranks of the Quraysh in any encounter against Rasulullah ﷺ and returned home, my heart would chide and admonish me: 'All of your efforts and undertakings are miserably hopeless and ineffective and surely Muhammad ﷺ is bound to be triumphant.' Consequently, on the occasion of the treaty of Hudaybiyyah, I was amongst the cavalry of the disbelievers of Makkah. I caught sight of Rasulullah ﷺ in 'Asfaan leading the Sahaabah رضي الله عنهم in Salaatul-Khawf (Salaah performed under threat from the enemy). I proposed to attack Rasulullah ﷺ whilst he was engaged in Salaah but Rasulullah ﷺ was apprised of my intentions and I was rendered incapable of launching an attack against him. At that instance, I realised that this man is divinely protected and shielded by Allah Ta'ala and that he is guarded by unseen forces. I thus returned empty-handed.

When Rasulullah ﷺ formed a pact with the Quraysh and returned to Madinah, my heart was assailed with the conviction that the power and supremacy of the Quraysh is now exhausted. The emperor of Abyssinia, Negus, has also become the adherent of Rasulullah ﷺ and his companions are living in Abyssinia in peace and tranquillity. Now the only option open to me is to seek asylum with Hiraql, the Roman emperor, and convert to Judaism or Christianity once I get there. I reasoned that I might as well live a defective life under the 'Ajmis (non-Arabs). I also thought that I would hang on for a few more days in my native land and see what is divulged from the unseen. I was hesitating between this when Rasulullah ﷺ came to Makkah Mukarramah the following year to perform 'Umratul-Qadaa. I fled Makkah and went into hiding. When Rasulullah ﷺ completed his Umrah, my brother Waleed bin Waleed, who was with Rasulullah ﷺ, searched for me but to no avail. My brother subsequently wrote a letter to me as follows:

'Bismillahir-Rahmaanir-Raheem. I have not witnessed anything as strange as your aversion towards a religion as pure as Islam whereas you are a man of celebrated intellectual abilities. For anyone to remain oblivious to the goodness of a faith like Islam is awfully weird. Rasulullah ﷺ asked about you. He enquired from me: 'Where is Khaalid?' I replied: 'Allah Ta'ala will bring him soon.' Rasulullah ﷺ commented: 'It is astounding that a man of renowned intelligence like him would be ignorant of a pure religion like Islam.' Rasulullah ﷺ further added: 'If Khaalid assists the true religion (of Islam) and joins the ranks of the Muslims and combats the forces of evil, it would be far better for him and we would give preference to him over others.' So my dear brother! Avail yourself of the lost opportunities because it is still possible to redress all that you have lost.'"

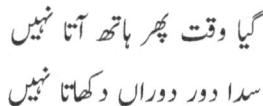

"Time and tide waits for no man."

Hadhrat Khaalid ؓ relates: "When my brother's letter reached me, it fuelled my enthusiasm towards Islam and I developed a keen sense of excitement and fervour towards Hijrah (migration to Madinah Munawwarah). Moreover, whatever Rasulullah ﷺ commented in my regard, added to my happiness and joy. During this period, I saw a dream; I was in a dreadfully cramped city afflicted by drought. I abandoned this drought-stricken cramped city and fled to a lush and spacious country. I thought to myself that this is a special dream shown to me to admonish me.

I went to Makkah and made preparations to travel to Madinah Munawwarah. For this journey, I wanted at least one other travelling companion. I met with Safwaan bin Umayyah and remarked: 'Don't you see that Muhammad ﷺ has gained dominance over the Arabs and non-Arabs alike? If we go to Muhammad ﷺ and conform to him, it would be far better for us. Muhammad's honour would be our honour.' Safwaan vehemently rejected this and retorted: 'If on the whole earth not a single person remains to be followed except Muhammad ﷺ, then too I would not follow him.' I said to myself: 'This man has lost a father and brother in the battle of Badr therefore I cannot pin my hopes on him.'

Thereafter I met with 'Ikramah bin Abi Jahal and I made the same proposal to him that I made to Safwaan. 'Ikramah retorted in the same manner as Safwaan and refused to accompany me. I returned home and whilst I was busy preparing the camel, I thought: 'Why don't I meet with 'Usmaan bin Talhah, he is a faithful friend of mine?' However, I recalled the killing of his father and grandfather (at Badr) and this cast me into a state of indecision. I was now undecided as to whether I should approach him or not. Finally, I reflected that there is absolutely no harm in me having a word with him and I made up my mind to go to him at that very moment. Subsequently, I met with 'Usmaan bin Talhah and put forward the same proposal that I had put forward to Safwaan. 'Usmaan bin Talhah consented to my proposition and added: 'I will also come to Madinah. Meet me at a place called Yaajuj. If you happen to reach there first, wait for me and I will wait for you if I happen to get there before you.'"

Khaalid bin Waleed رضي الله عنه relates: "On the appointed day, I also set out for Madinah and as planned, I met 'Usmaan bin Talhah at Yaajuj. Early the next morning, both of us set out for Madinah. When we reached a place called Haddah, we met 'Amr bin 'Aas who was also on his way to Madinah to embrace Islam. On catching sight of us, 'Amr bin 'Aas saluted us warmly and we also returned his salutations and asked: 'Where are you off to?' He replied: 'To enter the fold of Islam and to adhere to Muhammad.' We responded: 'We have also come out for the same reason.'"

Khaalid bin Waleed رضي الله عنه continues: "In this manner, the three of us got together and travelled towards Madinah. When we reached Harrah (just on the outskirts of Madinah), we made our camels sit down (to rest). Someone conveyed the news of our arrival to Rasulullah ﷺ who became extremely overjoyed. Rasulullah ﷺ remarked: 'Makkah has expelled the pieces of its liver (its darlings).'"

Khaalid رضي الله عنه relates: "I put on fine clothing and set out to meet Rasulullah ﷺ. On the way, I met my brother who cried: 'Come quickly, Rasulullah ﷺ has already heard of your arrival. He was elated to hear of you coming and he eagerly awaits you.' Very swiftly, we made our way to Rasulullah ﷺ. When he laid his eyes on me, Rasulullah ﷺ broke out in a smile.

I said: '*Assalaamu 'Alayka, Yaa Rasoolallah!*' He replied to my greeting with great delight. I then submitted:

اشهد ان لا اله الا الله وان محمدا رسول الله

'I bear witness that there is none worthy of worship besides Allah and Muhammad is the divine Messenger of Allah.'

To this, Rasulullah ﷺ replied: 'Come close.' He then commented as follows:

الحمد لله الذى هداك قد كنت ارى لك عقلا رجوت ان لا يسلمك إلا الى خير

'All praise is due to that Divine Being Who guided you towards Islam. I used to think that you are a man of intellect and I would always hope that this intellect would guide you towards goodness.'

Hadhrat Khaalid رضي الله عنه narrates: "I said: 'O Rasulullah ﷺ! You used to also witness me participating in wars against you and against the truth (and I am awfully ashamed and terribly remorseful of this). I therefore beg you to make dua that Allah Ta'ala forgives all my sins.' Rasulullah ﷺ replied:

الاسلام يهدم ما كان قبله

'Embracing Islam obliterates everything that precedes it.'

I once again made the same request to Rasulullah ﷺ, whereupon he made the following dua for me:

اللهم اغفر لخالد بن الوليد ما اوضع فيه من صد عن سبيل الله

'O Allah! Forgive all the sins of Khaalid bin Waleed which he had perpetrated in hampering (people) from the path of Allah.'"

Hadhrat Khaalid رضي الله عنه relates: "After me, 'Usmaan bin Talhah and 'Amr bin 'Aas went forward and took the pledge of allegiance at the blessed hand of Rasulullah ﷺ."

'Amr bin 'Aas رضي الله عنه narrates: "Following our appearance before Rasulullah ﷺ, Khaalid bin Waleed رضي الله عنه took the pledge of allegiance first followed by 'Usmaan bin Talhah رضي الله عنه and then I went forward to take this allegiance. However, at that time my condition was such:

By Allah! I somehow managed to sit in the presence of Rasulullah ﷺ but I was unable to raise my eyes towards him out of embarrassment and remorse.

Eventually, I completed the pledge of allegiance at the blessed hands of Rasulullah ﷺ and added: 'I make this pledge on condition that my past sins be forgiven.' 'Amr says: "At that moment, I just did not recall to ask forgiveness for my future sins as well. I only remembered my past sins."

Nonetheless, to this Rasulullah ﷺ replied: 'Islam eliminates all the sins perpetrated before Islam in a state of kufr. Likewise, Hijrah too eradicates all sins preceding it.'"

'Amr bin 'Aas ؓ says: "I swear by the Being Who does not perish that from the time we accepted Islam, whenever a military campaign came up, Rasulullah ﷺ did not treat anyone else as our equals."

'Amr bin 'Aas ؓ narrates: "Khaalid, 'Usmaan and I appeared before Rasulullah ﷺ in the opening days of the month of Safar 8 A.H. and embraced Islam."

Chapter 22

Expedition of Muta - Jumaadal-Ula 8 A.H.

Muta is the name of a place in the the region of Balqa. When Rasulullah ﷺ issued written invitations to Islam to the kings and rulers of the world, he also wrote to Shurahbeel bin 'Amr Ghassaani. Shurahbeel was the viceroy of the Levant on behalf of Qaysar, the Roman emperor. When Hadhrat Haaris bin 'Umair ؓ reached Muta with Rasulullah's ﷺ letter, Shurahbeel got him killed. For this reason, Rasulullah ﷺ despatched a three-thousand-strong force towards Muta in the month of Jumaadul-Ula 8 A.H.

Rasulullah ﷺ appointed Zaid bin Haarisah ؓ as the Ameer (leader) of the army and added: "If Zaid ؓ is killed, Ja'far bin Abi Taalib ؓ will be the leader of the army and if Ja'far ؓ is killed, 'Abdullah bin Rawaahah ؓ will be the leader and if 'Abdullah ؓ is killed too, the Muslims may appoint as Ameer anyone they deem suitable."

This is why this campaign is referred to as the expedition of the 'army of the leaders'.

Rasulullah ﷺ entrusted a white flag to Zaid bin Haarisah ؓ and instructed: "Go to the area in which Haaris bin 'Umair was martyred and invite the local inhabitants towards Islam. If they accept this invitation well and good otherwise seek the divine assistance of Allah and engage them in Jihaad."

Rasulullah ﷺ accompanied this army right up to Saniyatul-Wadaa to bid them farewell. At Saniyatul-Wadaa, Rasulullah ﷺ halted a little while and offered the following words of advice to the army: "At all times, bear in mind Taqwa (Allah-consciousness) and righteousness. Always wish well for your companions. Wage Jihaad in the path of Allah with the name of Allah against those who disbelieve in Allah. Do not fall into deception nor be guilty of a breach of trust. Do not ever kill a child, woman or elderly person."

As Rasulullah ﷺ was bidding the leaders of this expedition farewell, Hadhrat 'Abdullah bin Rawaahah رضي الله عنه burst out crying. When asked what made him weep, he replied:

اما والله، ما بي حب الدنيا ولا صبابة بكم ولكني سمعت رسول الله صلى الله عليه وسلم يقرأ آية من كتاب الله عزوجل (وان منكم الا واردها كان على ربك حتما مقضيا) فلست ادري كيف لى بالصدر بعد الورود

"Behold! I swear by Allah, it is neither my love for this world nor my fondness for you that makes me weep but it is because I heard Rasulullah ﷺ recite the following Qur-aanic verse: 'There is none of you but he would pass over hell and this has been decisively declared by your Lord.' So I do not know how I will return after passing over hell."

As the army was on the point of departing, the Muslims called out to them in dua: "May Allah Ta'ala bring you back safe and victorious." To this, Hadhrat 'Abdullah bin Rawaahah رضي الله عنه replied in the following couplets:

لكنني اسأل الرحمن مغفرة وَضَرْبَةً ذَاتَ فَرْغٍ تَقْذِفُ الزَّبَدا

"I do not aspire to return but I beg the forgiveness of Allah and I hope for a deep sword-wound that froths.

او طَعْنَةً بِيَدَيْ حَرَّانَ مُجْهِزَةً بِحَرْبَةٍ تُنْفِذُ الْأَحْشَاءَ الْكَبِدَا

or I wish for a wound inflicted by a razor-sharp spear or an arrow that penetrates right through my intestines and liver.

يَا أَرْشَدَ اللهُ مِنْ غَازٍ وَقَدْ رَشَدَا حتى يقال اذا مروا على جدثي

(I wish to be wounded) to such an extent that when people pass my grave, they may applaud me and say: 'Ah! Bravo! What a brilliant warrior, what a success he made of his life.'"

As the army was on the verge of leaving, Hadhrat 'Abdullah bin Rawaahah رضي الله عنه came close to Rasulullah ﷺ and recited the following couplets:

انت الرسول فمن يُحرَمْ نوافِلَه وَالوَجَه مِنهُ فَقَد أَزرى بِه القَدَرُ

"You are the divine Messenger. He who is deprived of your blessings and deprived of beholding your blessed countenance, destiny has disgraced him."

فَثَبَّتَ اللّهُ ما اتاكَ مِن حَسَنٍ تَثبيتَ مُوسى وَ نَصرًا كَالّذى نُصِروُا

May Allah Ta'ala grant you steadfastness and perseverance like Musa عَلَيْهِ السَّلَام in all the good He has bestowed upon you and may He extend divine assistance towards you like He did for the previous Prophets.

انّى تَفَرَّستُ فيكَ الخَيرَ نَافِلَةً فِراسةً خَالَفَت فيكَ الذى نَظَروا

I have perceived your goodness to be more than ever and this perception of mine contradicts the perception of the disbelievers."

To this Rasulullah صَلَّى اللَّهُ عَلَيْهِ وَسَلَّمَ responded:

وانت فثبتك الله يا ابن رواحه

"And you too, O Ibn Rawaahah! May Allah Ta'ala grant you steadfastness too."

When Shurahbeel heard of the departure of this army, he amassed more than one hundred thousand troops to fight against the Muslims. To lend support to Shurahbeel, the Roman emperor, Heraclius, himself landed at Balqa with another hundred thousand troops. When the Muslims landed at Ma'an, they heard that a huge army of two hundred thousand soldiers awaited the three thousand Muslims at Balqa. The Mulsim army camped over for two nights at Ma'an whilst deliberating about what to do and the way forward. One group suggested that Rasulullah صَلَّى اللَّهُ عَلَيْهِ وَسَلَّمَ be informed about this and that the Muslims should await his instructions and reinforcements. To this Hadhrat 'Abdullah bin Rawaahah رَضِيَ اللَّهُ عَنْهُ commented:

يا قوم! والله، ان التى تكرهون للتى خرجتم اياها تطلبون الشهادة
وما نقاتل الناس بعدد ولا قوة ولا كثرة، ما نقاتلهم الا بهذا الدين
الذى اكرمنا الله به فانطلقوا فانما هى احد الحسنيين، اما ظهور واما
شهادة

"O people! I swear by Allah that what you seem to abhor is exactly the same martyrdom you set out to achieve. We neither fight the disbelievers on the basis of power nor on the strength of numbers. Our fighting is solely on the basis of this

Deen that Allah has honoured us with. So get up and advance because you will attain either one of two good things; either you will be triumphant over the disbelievers or you will gain martyrdom."

To this, the people replied: "By Allah! Ibn Rawaahah has spoken the truth."

Saying this, this committed and devoted group of three thousand men advanced towards Muta to engage an army of two-hundred-thousand-strong enemies of Allah Ta'ala.

As they landed on the battlefield of Muta and both armies confronted one another, Hadhrat Zaid bin Haarisah رضى الله عنه, holding the banner of Islam aloft, stepped out to fight the enemy. He continued fighting valiantly until he was martyred. Thereafter, Hadhrat Ja'far رضى الله عنه, mounted on a horse, stepped out with the flag in his hand. When he was completely encircled by the enemy and his horse was wounded, he dismounted and cut off his horse's fetlocks (legs) and taking a courageous stance against the enemies of Allah Ta'ala, he continued fighting them.

Note: He cut off the legs of the horse so that the enemies do not derive any benefit from it.

As he was engaging the enemy, he would go on reciting the following couplets:

يا حبذ الجنة واقتِرَابُها   طَيّبةً وَبَارِدًا شَرَابُها

"How magnificent and pure is Jannah and its environs! And how cool is its water!

والرومُ رومٌ قددنا عذابها   كافرةٌ بعيدةٌ أَنْسَابُها

As for the Romans, their divine chastisement has drawn close. They are disbelievers and their lineage is distant from ours. (In other words, they do not enjoy any family relationship with us.)

عليّ إذ لا قَيْتُها ضِرَابُها

When they confront me, I am obliged to strike them."

As he was fighting, his right hand was chopped off. He then held the flag with his left hand. When the enemy lopped off his left hand too, he took the flag to his bosom until he too was martyred. In compensation, Allah Ta'ala bestowed him with a pair of wings with which he soars with the angels in Jannah.

'Abdullah bin 'Umar رضى الله عنه narrates that when Hadhrat Ja'far's رضى الله عنه body was located, he had more than ninety arrow and sword wounds on his body and every one of them was at the front of his body. He had not a single wound on the back of his body.

After the martyrdom of Hadhrat Ja'far رضى الله عنه, Hadhrat 'Abdullah bin Rawaahah رضى الله عنه assumed control of the flag and advanced towards the enemy. He was mounted on a horse. For a few moments, he was stricken with misgivings of his Nafs. He addressed his Nafs and recited the following couplets:

$$\text{اَقْسَمْتُ يَا نَفْسُ لَتَنْزِلِنَّهْ ۞ كَارِهَةً أَوْ لَتُطَاوِ عَنَّهْ}$$

"O Nafs! I swear that you will dismount from the horse and engage the enemies of Allah whether you like it or not.

$$\text{اِنْ اَجْلَبَ الناسُ وشَدُّوا الرِّنَّهْ ۞ مَالِي اراكِ تَكْرَهِيْنَ الجَنَّه}$$

If the people are screaming and lamenting, (let them do so). Why is it that I observe you harbouring an aversion towards Jannah? (In other words, why are you not advancing speedily? The fact that you are faltering in going forward is an indication of your aversion towards Jannah. He said this merely to censure himself.)

$$\text{قَدْ طَالمَا قَدْ كُنْتِ مُطْمَئِنَّهْ ۞ هَلْ اَنْتِ اِلَّا نُطْفَةٌ فِي شَنَّهْ}$$

You (O Nafs!) were always at ease. What happened to you now? You were nothing but a droplet of spermatic fluid in the uterus. (You are wavering just for this insignificant droplet?)

$$\text{يَا نَفْسُ اِلَّا تُقْتَلِي تَمُوْتِي ۞ هذَا حِمَامُ الموتِ قَدْ صَلِيْت}$$

O Nafs! Even if you are not killed today, you are inescapably going to die one day. This is the inevitable destiny of the process of death.

$$\text{وَمَا تَمَنَّيْتِ فَقَدْ أُعْطِيْت ۞ اِنْ تَفْعَلِيْ فِعْلَهُمَا هُدِيْت}$$

What you had desired is now available to you (and that is the opportunity of martyrdom in the path of Allah). If you accomplish the feats of those two people (Zaid رضي الله عنه and Ja'far رضي الله عنه), then you will be well-guided."

Saying this, he alighted from his horse. His cousin (father's brother's son) offered him a meat-bone saying: "Why don't you suck on this. Get some energy to fight. You are starving for a number of days now."

Ibn Rawaahaha رضي الله عنه took the bone and he sucked on it just once and threw it aside exclaiming: "O Nafs! People are engaged in Jihaad and you are busy with worldly pursuits." He then took hold of his sword and advanced onto the battlefield. He continued fighting gallantly until he was martyred and the banner of Islam fell from his hand. At once, Saabit bin Akhram رضي الله عنه took hold of the banner and addressed the Muslims thus: "O Muslims! Appoint an Ameer over you." The people responded: "You are our Ameer. We are pleased with you as our Ameer." Saabit رضي الله عنه commented: "I am incompetent in this field." Saying this, he thrust the flag into the hands of Khaalid bin Waleed رضي الله عنه and remarked: "You are well-acquainted with the art of war."

Khaalid bin Waleed رضي الله عنه was a bit reluctant to accept the post of Ameer but all the Muslims unanimously agreed to this appointment. Clutching the banner of Islam, Hadhrat Khaalid bin Waleed رضي الله عنه advanced against the enemy and with great courage and dynamic dauntlessness, he fought the enemies of Allah.

Hadhrat Khaalid bin Waleed رضي الله عنه himself narrates: "In the battle of Muta whilst engaging the enemy, nine swords were broken at my hands. Only a single Yemeni sword remained in my hands."

On the second day of the battle, Hadhrat Khaalid رضي الله عنه altered the plan of battle. He changed the vanguard with the rear guard whilst switching the right flank with the left flank. On noticing this modification in the ranks, the enemy was struck with fear. They assumed that more reinforcements arrived to bolster the Muslims.

Ibn S'ad Abu 'Aamir رضي الله عنه narrates: "When Khaalid bin Waleed رضي الله عنه launched an attack against the Roman forces, he crushed them so severely that never before have I witnessed such an astounding defeat. The Muslims were able to swipe their swords wherever they wished to."

They also came into possession of some spoils of war. Following the crushing defeat of the Romans, Hadhrat Khaalid bin Waleed رضي الله عنه did not deem it appropriate to pursue them any further and together with his relatively small group of men, he returned to Madinah Munawwarah.

In this battle, twelve Muslims were martyred. They are:

1. Zaid bin Haarisah رضي الله عنه
2. Ja'far bin Abi Taalib رضي الله عنه
3. 'Abdullah bin Rawaahah رضي الله عنه
4. Mas'ood bin Aws رضي الله عنه
5. Wahab bin S'ad رضي الله عنه
6. 'Abbaad bin Qays رضي الله عنه
7. Haaris bin Nu'maan رضي الله عنه
8. Suraaqah bin 'Umar رضي الله عنه
9. Abu Kulaib bin 'Amr رضي الله عنه
10. Jaabir bin 'Amr رضي الله عنه
11. 'Amr bin S'ad bin Haaris رضي الله عنه
12. 'Aamir bin S'ad bin Haaris رضي الله عنه

As these warriors of Islam were being martyred on the battlefield of Muta, Allah Ta'ala, in His absolute power, made it possible for Rasulullah ﷺ to witness these events unfolding on the battlefield of Shaam whilst he was sitting in Madinah Munawwarah. All intervening veils between him and the battlefield were raised. Rasulullah ﷺ assembled the Sahaabah ﷺ by announcing: "As-Salaatu Jaami'ah". When the Sahaabah ﷺ were assembled, Rasulullah ﷺ ascended the mimbar and the battlefield was laid bare before him. He said: "Zaid has taken the flag of Islam in his hand and he fought the disbelievers until he was martyred and he entered Jannah. After Zaid, Ja'far took the flag and he also fought the enemies of Allah valiantly until he was martyred and he too entered Jannah. He is now soaring with the angels in Jannah with the aid of his two wings."

"Thereafter 'Abdullah bin Rawaahah snapped up the flag."

Saying this, Rasulullah ﷺ observed silence and for some time this silence continued. On noticing this, the Ansaar were beset with apprehension and signs of anxiety became apparent on their faces. They guessed that perhaps 'Abdullah bin Rawaahah ﷺ did something unseemly which led to Rasulullah's ﷺ silence.

Following a short silence, Rasulullah ﷺ continued: "Now 'Abdullah bin Rawaahah ﷺ has also engaged the disbelievers. He also fought gallantly until he was martyred. All three of them were raised into Jannah and all three are relaxing on golden thrones. However, I noticed that the throne of 'Abdullah bin Rawaahah ﷺ is unsteady and shaking. When I enquired the reason for this, I was informed that 'Abdullah bin Rawaahah ﷺ was overcome with reluctance before he engaged the enemy. Only after this slight hesitancy did he step ahead and fight whilst his companions, Zaid and Ja'far engaged the enemy without a trace of reluctance." Another narration describes this thus: "Thereafter the banner was taken up by 'Abdullah bin Rawaahah. He was martyred and he entered Jannah with a bit of resistance (or hesitancy)." This caused the Ansaar a great deal of sorrow. One of them asked: "What is the reason for this?" Rasulullah ﷺ replied: "When 'Abdullah was wounded on the battlefield, (due to innate human disposition) he became a bit sluggish but he promptly admonished himself, valiantly advanced against the enemy, became a martyr and entered Jannah." This statement of Rasulullah ﷺ did away with the anguish of the Ansaar.

Whilst Rasulullah ﷺ was describing this scene of the battlefield, his eyes were brimming with tears. He then added: "After them, a 'sword of the swords of Allah' (Khaalid bin Waleed) has taken hold of the flag of Islam. He fought until Allah Ta'ala granted the Muslims victory."

According to another narration, Rasulullah ﷺ said:

اللهم انه سيف من سيوفك فانت تنصره، فمن يومئذ سمى سيف الله

"O Allah! He (Khaalid) is a sword from amongst Your swords. You alone can assist him." From that day onwards, he was called Saifullah (the sword of Allah).

When Hadhrat Abu Bakr ؓ assigned Hadhrat Khaalid ؓ to fight the renegades, as he was handing over the banner of leadership to Khaalid ؓ, he commented:

انى سمعت رسول الله صلى الله عليه وسلم يقول: نعم عبدالله واخو العشيرة خالد بن الوليد سيف من سيوف الله! سله الله على الكفار

"I heard Rasulullah ﷺ say: 'What a pleasant servant of Allah and what an amiable brother of the tribe is Khaalid bin Waleed, a sword from the swords of Allah. Allah Ta'ala has unsheathed him against the disbelievers.'"

After narrating this sorrowful incident, Rasulullah ﷺ proceeded to the house of Hadhrat Ja'far ؓ. He called his children and as Rasulullah ﷺ was patting them with his blessed hands over their heads, his eyes were flowing with tears. Hadhrat Ja'far's ؓ wife, Hadhrat Asma bint 'Umais ؓ realised that something was amiss. She enquired: "O Rasulullah ﷺ! May my parents be sacrificed for you. Why are you crying? Have you heard something about Ja'far ؓ and his companions?" Rasulullah ﷺ replied: "Yes, today he was martyred."

Hadhrat Asma bint 'Umais ؓ relates: "The moment I heard this distressing news, a piercing shriek escaped my lips. A number of women gathered around me (to comfort and console me)."

Rasulullah ﷺ then returned to his house and asked his family to prepare meals for the household of Ja'far ؓ as they were afflicted with grief. This incident had a profound effect on Rasulullah ﷺ as well. Saddened by this heartbreaking incident, Rasulullah ﷺ stayed for three days in the Masjid.

On their return from Muta, as Hadhrat Khaalid bin Waleed ؓ and his companions neared Madinah, Rasulullah ﷺ and the Muslims came out to give them a warm welcome.

Expedition of 'Amr bin 'Aas ؓ towards Zaatus-Salaasil

In the month of Jumadas-Saaniyah 8 A.H., Rasulullah ﷺ received intelligence that a group of assailants of the Banu Quda'ah tribe planned to launch an attack on Madinah Munawwarah. To nip them in the bud, Rasulullah ﷺ sent 'Amr bin 'Aas ؓ to Zaatus-Salaasil. This area is located about ten Manzils from Madinah Munawwarah. Rasulullah ﷺ despatched three hundred foot soldiers and thirty mounted warriors with him. As they drew closer to this area, they ascertained that the disbelievers had massed a colossal force ready to engage the Muslims. The Muslims decided to hold back temporarily. Hadhrat 'Amr bin 'Aas ؓ sent Raaf'i bin Makith ؓ to Rasulullah ﷺ appealing for more reinforcements. Rasulullah ﷺ despatched Abu 'Ubaidah bin Jarrah ؓ with a contingent of two hundred warriors that included Hadhrat 'Abu Bakr ؓ and Hadhrat 'Umar ؓ. As this venerable group was departing, Rasulullah ﷺ strongly advised them to meet up with Abu 'Ubaidah bin Jarrah ؓ and he also stressed the need for unity, harmony and abstention from dissension.

When Abu 'Ubaidah ؓ landed there and the time for Salaah drew closer, he decided to lead the Salaah. 'Amr bin 'Aas ؓ cautioned him saying: "I am the Ameer (leader) of this army whilst you have come just to assist us." To this Abu 'Ubaidah ؓ replied: "You are the Ameer of your group whilst I am the Ameer of my group."

Afterwards Hadhrat Abu 'Ubaidah ؓ said: "As we were setting forth from Madinah, the parting instruction Rasulullah ﷺ offered me was: 'Obey one another and refrain from disunity and dissension.' So I will comply with you even though you refuse to go along with me."

In this manner, Abu 'Ubaidah ؓ consented to the leadership and Imaamat of 'Amr bin 'Aas ؓ. Hadhrat 'Amr bin 'Aas ؓ would lead the Salaah and Hadhrat Abu 'Ubaidah ؓ would join the ranks of the followers.

In due course, all of them gathered their forces and launched an attack against Banu Quda'ah. The disbelievers fled in awe and dispersed in panic. The Sahaabah ؓ sent Hadhrat 'Awf bin Maalik Ashja'i ؓ to Madinah with the good news of their victory.

Following this victory, Hadhrat 'Amr bin 'Aas ؓ stayed there for a few more days and continued sending his horsemen in different directions. They would capture some goats and camels which the Muslims would cook and consume.

During the course of this expedition, Hadhrat 'Amr bin 'Aas ؓ experienced a wet dream. Due to the intensity of the cold, he did not perform Ghusl but led the Fajar Salaah with Tayammum. When this was related to Rasulullah ﷺ, he enquired: "O 'Amr! You led your companions in Salaah in the state of Janaabah?" Hadhrat 'Amr bin 'Aas ؓ replied: "O Rasulullah ﷺ! I feared for my life and Allah Ta'ala also commands: 'Do not kill yourselves, verily Allah is exceptionally affectionate unto you." Rasulullah ﷺ merely smiled at this and did not comment further.

Note: Khaalid bin Waleed ؓ and 'Amr bin 'Aas ؓ embraced Islam at the same time. The expedition of Muta occurred after their entry into Islam and in this expedition Khaalid bin Waleed ﷺ was appointed as Ameer. Following the battle of Muta, the expedition of Zaatus-Salaasil took place in which 'Amr bin 'Aas ﷺ was appointed as Ameer.

Expedition of Abu 'Ubaidah ﷺ towards Siful-Bahr (the coastline)

Thereafter in the month of Rajab 8 A.H. Rasulullah ﷺ appointed Hadhrat Abu 'Ubaidah bin Jarrah ﷺ as Ameer over three hundred men and sent them towards Siful-Bahr (the Arabian coastline) to attack the Juhaynah tribe. Hadhrat 'Umar bin Khattaab ﷺ and Hadhrat Jaabir bin 'Abdullah ﷺ were also in this army. As this army was setting off, Rasulullah ﷺ presented them with a bag of dates as provisions for the road. After these dates were depleted, they sustained themselves by sucking on date seeds and drinking water. In due course, when the date pips also ran out, they would shake the leaves off the trees, soak them in water and eat them. This is why this expedition was also called the expedition of Khabt. The literal meaning of Khabt is to shake leaves off a tree. Due to the Sahaabah ﷺ eating these leaves, they developed painful cuts on their lips and sores in their mouths.

One day, when they finally made it to the coast and frantic with hunger, they were suddenly confronted with a miraculous gift from the unseen. The sea threw out such a huge fish that the whole army continued eating from it for eighteen days. The Sahaabah ﷺ relate that on consuming the fish, they became healthy and fit once again. The fish was an Ambar (a sperm whale). Thereafter, Hadhrat 'Abu 'Ubaidah ﷺ took one of its ribs and erected it on the ground. He then asked one of the tallest men to ride the tallest camel beneath this rib. This rider managed to pass under this rib comfortably without his head even touching the rib.

The Sahaabah ﷺ narrate: "When we returned to Madinah Munawwarah and related this incident to Rasulullah ﷺ, he commented: 'This was the sustenance of Allah Ta'ala which He has provided for you. If you have any of its meat left over, share it with us.' Subsequently, its meat was presented to Rasulullah ﷺ and he partook of it." During this expedition, no opportunity for actual combat arose. The Muslim army returned to Madinah without physically engaging the enemy. Note: The sustenance that comes directly from Allah Ta'ala without any human intervention is considered a very blessed sustenance. Due to its blessed nature and purity, Rasulullah ﷺ requested and partook from the fish.

رَبِّ اِنِّىْ لِمَآ اَنْزَلْتَ اِلَىَّ مِنْ خَيْرٍ فَقِيْرٌ

"O my Rabb! (said Musa ؑ) I am in desperate need for whatever you send forth towards me."

Chapter 23

The Conquest of Makkah - Ramadhaan 8 A.H.

At the time when the peace treaty was signed at Hudaybiyah between Rasulullah ﷺ and the Quraysh, then in accordance with the conditions that were written down, the different tribes were given the choice of joining either of the two parties (of the peace treaty). Consequently, the Banu Bakr joined the Quraysh while the Banu Khuzaa'ah joined Rasulullah ﷺ. Both these tribes were at each other's throats since pre-Islamic times. The reason for this was that Maalik ibn 'Abbaad Hadrami went into the lands of the Banu Khuzaa'ah with his trading goods. The Banu Khuzaa'ah killed him and stole all his wealth and possessions. When the Banu Bakr got the opportunity, they killed a member of the Banu Khuzaa'ah tribe in exchange for Maalik Hadrami. In retaliation for this one person, the Banu Khuzaa'ah then killed three members of the Banu Bakr tribe. The three were leaders by the names of Dhuwayb, Sulami and Kulsoom. They were killed in the plains of 'Arafaat, very close to the boundaries of the Haram (the sanctified sanctuary of Makkah).

This killing and counter killing continued from pre-Islamic times till the advent of Islam. With the advent of Islam, it stopped because the people were more occupied with Islamic affairs.

On account of a limited peace treaty that was signed in Hudaybiyyah, the two groups now felt safe from each other and fearless of each other. The Banu Bakr now found the opportunity to give vent to their enmity. Naufal ibn Mu'aawiyah from the Banu Bakr together with his friends attacked the Khuzaa'ah. It was at night when members of the latter tribe had stopped over at an oasis by the name of Watir where they had been sleeping.

Safwaan ibn Umayyah, Shaybah ibn 'Usmaan, Suhayl ibn 'Amr, Huwatib ibn 'Abdul-'Uzza and Makraz ibn Hafs who were all from the Quraysh secretly assisted the Banu Bakr. The Khuzaa'ah fled and sought refuge in the Haram. However, they too were not spared.

The Quraysh helped the Banu Bakr in every way possible. They supplied them with weapons and men as well. People from the Khuzaa'ah sought refuge in Makkah in the house of Budayl ibn Warqaa' Khuzaa'i. However, the Banu Bakr and the Quraysh leaders got into the houses, killed them and stole their belongings. They continued thinking that Rasulullah ﷺ would not come to know of this offense. The next morning, the Quraysh regretted their actions and realised that they went against the peace treaty and that, through an error on their part, they broke their promises which they made with Rasulullah ﷺ at Hudaybiyah.

'Amr ibn Saalim Khuzaa'i went to Madinah with a delegation of 40 people and presented himself to Rasulullah ﷺ who was in the Masjid at that time. 'Amr ibn Saalim stood up and announced:

يَا رَبِّ إِنِّي نَاشِدٌ مُحَمَّدًا   حِلْفَ أَبِينَا وَأَبِيهِ الْأَتْلَدَا

"O Sustainer! I have come to remind Muhammad (ﷺ) of the old agreement that was made between my father and his father, 'Abdul Muttalib."

In pre-Islamic times, the Khuzaa'ah were the confederates of 'Abdul Muttalib. He was thus making reference to this fact that just as we are your confederates (at present), our forefathers were the confederates of your forefathers.

إِنَّ قُرَيْشًا أَخْلَفُوكَ الْمَوْعِدَا   وَنَقَضُوا مِيثَاقَكَ المُؤكدا

"The Quraysh have certainly went against your agreement. And they have broken your strong agreement and promise.

هُمْ بَيَّتُونَا بِالْوَتِيرِ هُجَّدًا   وَقَتَلُونَا رُكَّعًا وَسُجَّدًا

They attacked us at the Watir oasis while we were asleep at night. They killed us while we were bowing and prostrating (in Salaah)."

Some of them had become Muslims although 'Amr himself was not a Muslim.

وجعلوا لي في كداءٍ رُصَّدًا   وَزَعَمُوا أَنْ لَسْتُ أَدْعُو أحدا

"They placed some people to ambush us at the place called Kida'. They assumed that I will not summon anyone to come to my assistance.

وَهُمْ أَذَلُّ وَأَقَلُّ عَدَدًا   قد كنتم ولدًا وكنا والدا

They are despicable and also very few in number. "We are like a father and you are like our child."

$$ \text{وَوَالِدًا كُنَّا وكُنْتَ الْوَلَدَا ثَمَّتَ أَسْلَمْنَا وَلَمْ نَنْزِعْ يَدَا} $$

This is because the mother of 'Abd Manaaf was from the Khuzaa'ah tribe. In like manner, the mother of Qusayy, Faatimah bint Sa'd, was also from the Khuzaa'ah tribe. "Based on this relationship, it is necessary for you to help and assist us. Apart from this, we have always remained obedient and loyal to you. We never disobeyed you at any time. It is therefore hoped that you will help those who are loyal and faithful to you."

$$ \text{فانصر ايّدك الله نصرًا اعْتَدَا وَادْعُ عِبَادَ الله يأتوا مَدَدًا} $$

"You should therefore help us immediately, Allah Ta'ala will help you. Order the special servants of Allah (your Companions) so that they will certainly come to our assistance as well."

According to another narration, the following words were said:

$$ \text{فانصر ايّدك الله نصرًا اعْتَدَا} $$

"O Messenger of Allah! Come to our immediate assistance, Allah Ta'ala will help you

$$ \text{فِيْهِمْ رسول الله قد تَجَرَّدَا إِن سِيْمَ خَسْفًا وَجْهَةَ تَرَبَّدَا} $$

When the servants of Allah come to our assistance, the Messenger of Allah should certainly be among them, he who is prepared to fight the wrongdoers."

In other words, do not suffice with merely sending a group of fighters. Rather, he should personally join the army. If the wrong doers try to disgrace you in any way, may your blessed face take on a glowing expression out of self-honour."

'Abdullah ibn 'Umar ؓ narrates that after hearing all these incidents, Rasulullah ﷺ said: "You shall certainly be helped, O 'Amr ibn Saalim!" Another Hadith states that he said: "May I not be helped if I do not come to your help." Rasulullah ﷺ then asked him: "Were all the members of the Banu Bakr tribe involved in this?" He replied: "No. It was only the Banu Nufaasah and their leader, Naufal." Rasulullah ﷺ promised to help and assist him. This delegation then returned. Rasulullah ﷺ sent a delegate to the Quraysh in Makkah and asked him to convey the following message: "You may choose one of the following three options:

1. The blood money be paid for those who were killed from the Banu Khuzaa'ah.

2. The Banu Nufaasah be removed from the pact and covenant.

3. Announce that the peace treaty of Hudaybiyah is now cancelled."

When the delegate conveyed this message, Qurtah ibn 'Amr replied on behalf of the Quraysh: "We will not pay the blood money to the Banu Khuzaa'ah, the Banu Nufaasah will not be removed from the pact, but we are prepared to cancel the treaty of Hudaybiyah." However, when the delegate returned, the Quraysh regretted this. They immediately sent Abu Sufyaan to Madinah in order to renew the treaty and to increase the period of the treaty.

Abu Sufyaan leaves Makkah in order to renew the peace treaty

Abu Sufyaan left Makkah and headed towards Madinah in order to renew the peace treaty. Rasulullah ﷺ informed the companions that Abu Sufyaan was coming from Makkah in order to increase the period of the treaty and to further strengthen it. Abu Sufyaan left Makkah and when he reached a place called 'Asfaan, he met Budayl ibn Warqaa' Khuzaa'i. Abu Sufyaan asked him as to where he was coming from. He replied that he was coming from this nearby valley. On saying this, Budayl continued towards Makkah. It was then that Abu Sufyaan thought that this Budayl is certainly returning from Madinah. He therefore went to the spot where Budayl's camel had been sitting. He broke the dung of the camel and saw date seeds in it. On seeing this, he said: "By Allah! Budayl is certainly coming from Madinah. These seeds are from the dates of Madinah." On reaching Madinah, Abu Sufyaan went straight to the house of his daughter, Ummul-Mu'mineen Umme Habibah ﷺ. He said to her: "O my daughter! You have folded up the sitting mat. Do you consider the mat not worthy of me or am I not worthy of it?" She replied: "This is the bed of Rasulullah ﷺ. A disbeliever who is impure and filthy with the filth of polytheism cannot sit on it." Abu Sufyaan shouted out saying: "O my daughter! By Allah, you have fallen into evil in my absence." She replied: "Not into evil. Rather, I have come out of the darkness of disbelief and went into the light and guidance of Islam. I am surprised at you that despite being one of the leaders of the Quraysh, you worship stones that can neither hear nor see."

Abu Sufyaan got up and proceeded to the Masjid. He presented himself before Rasulullah ﷺ and said: "I have come on behalf of the Quraysh in order to renew the peace treaty and to increase the period of the treaty." Rasulullah ﷺ did not give any reply. When he got no answer from Rasulullah ﷺ, he went to Abu Bakr ﷺ and asked him to intercede on his behalf. He replied: "I cannot do anything in this regard." He then went to 'Umar ibn al-Khattaab ﷺ and asked him to intercede on his behalf. 'Umar ﷺ replied: "Allah is the greatest! If I do not find a single person in the entire world to join me, I am prepared to go out and wage Jihaad all by myself." On hearing this, he went to Ali ﷺ who was sitting with his wife, Faatimah ﷺ and his son, Hasan

ﷺ. He addressed Ali ﷺ saying: "O father of Hasan! You are the closest relative to me. I have come with an urgent need. I cannot go back unsuccessful. You should therefore intercede on my behalf before Rasulullah ﷺ." Ali ﷺ replied: "I swear by Allah that Rasulullah ﷺ has already made a decision in this regard. It is now impossible for anyone to say anything." On hearing this, he addressed Faatimah ﷺ saying: "O daughter of Muhammad! If you order this child (Hasan ﷺ) to announce that I have given refuge to the Quraysh, he will forever be recognised as a leader of the Arabs." She replied: "First of all, he is very young (giving refuge is the responsibility of adults). Secondly, who can give refuge against the pleasure of Rasulullah ﷺ?" Abu Sufyaan addressed Ali ﷺ saying: "The matter has become very serious. Now show me a way out." He replied: "I cannot think of anything except that if you think it beneficial and of help, you may do it. Go into the Masjid and announce: 'I have come to renew the peace treaty of Hudaybiyah, to further strengthen it and to increase the period of the treaty.' After saying this, go back to your city." Abu Sufyaan left, went to the Masjid and made this announcement in a loud voice: "I am renewing the peace treaty and increasing the period of the treaty." On saying this, he returned to Makkah.

On reaching Makkah and relating the entire story to the Quraysh, they asked him: "Did Muhammad accept this announcement of yours?" He replied: "No." The Quraysh said: "How can you feel pleased and satisfied without having gained the permission and agreement of Muhammad? You have merely come back with something useless – which is not difficult to break. By Allah, Ali mocked you (when he told you what to do). You have neither come with any news about the peace treaty, whereby we could feel at ease, nor have you come with any news of war whereby we could make preparations."

When Abu Sufyaan left (Madinah), Rasulullah ﷺ ordered the Sahaabah ﷺ to secretly make preparations for the journey to Makkah and to get ready their weapons of war. He emphasised that this should be kept a secret, it should not be announced. He also sent a message to the surrounding tribes to make preparations.

The story of Haatib ibn Abi Balta'ah ﷺ

During this period, Haatib ibn Abi Balta'ah ﷺ wrote a letter to the people of Makkah informing them that Rasulullah ﷺ was making preparations for Makkah. He secretly sent this letter with a woman going to Makkah. Allah Ta'ala informed Rasulullah ﷺ of this through divine inspiration. He therefore sent Ali ﷺ, Zubayr ﷺ and Miqdaad ﷺ instructing them to continue travelling till they reach a place called Raudah Khaakh where they would find a woman riding a camel. She will have a letter written by Haatib ibn Abi Balta'ah

ﷺ addressed to the people of Makkah. They should bring it back to Madinah. They relate: "We reached this place, found a woman there, made the camel sit down and we searched her. However, we did not find the letter. We said to ourselves: 'By Allah! Rasulullah ﷺ can never be wrong.' We said to the woman: 'It would be better if you hand over the letter to us. If not, we will strip you naked and take the letter from you.' The woman then removed the letter from her hair and handed it over to us. We returned with it to Rasulullah ﷺ. He summoned Haatib ibn Abi Balta'ah ﷺ and asked him for an explanation. He replied: 'O Rasulullah ﷺ! Do not hasten in punishing me. I have no family ties with the Quraysh. I merely have a pact with them. My family is at present in Makkah. They have no protectors nor helpers there. On the other hand, the Muhaajireen whose families are there have other relatives living there as well. Their families are thereby protected. I therefore thought that since I have no family ties with the Quraysh, I should do them a favour whereby they would protect my family. I take an oath in the name of Allah that I did not do this out of apostasy nor have I chosen disbelief after having embraced Islam. My only reason was what I just mentioned.'"

On hearing his account, Rasulullah ﷺ said:

$$\text{أَمَا إِنَّهُ قَدْ صَدَقَكُمْ}$$

"Listen! He has surely spoken the truth to you."

'Umar ﷺ said: "O Rasulullah ﷺ! Permit me to chop off the neck of this hypocrite." Rasulullah ﷺ replied:

$$\text{إنه قد شهد بدراً وما يدريك لعل الله اطلع على أهل بدر فقال}$$
$$\text{اعملوا ما شئتم فقد غفرت لكم}$$

"He participated in the battle of Badr. Perhaps Allah Ta'ala addressed the participants of Badr, saying: 'Do whatever you wish, for I have forgiven you.'"

On hearing this, 'Umar's ﷺ eyes were filled with tears and he said: "Allah Ta'ala and His Messenger ﷺ know best."

The subject matter of Haatib's ﷺ letter

The subject matter of Haatib's ﷺ letter also shows that his purpose of writing it was not based on hypocrisy. This was the letter:

أما بعد! يا معشر قريش فإن رسول الله صلى الله عليه وسلم جاءكم بجيش كالليل يسير كالسيل فوالله لو جاءكم وحده لنصره الله وانجز له وعده فانظروا لأنفسكم والسلام

"O Quraysh! Rasulullah ﷺ is going to come to you with a terrifying army like the night, which will flow like a flood. By Allah, if Rasulullah ﷺ comes all alone to you, Allah Ta'ala will help him and fulfil His promise of victory. (In other words, his success is not dependent on an army). You should therefore think about your consequences. Wassalaam."

The subject matter of this letter clearly supports his excuse which he had given previously: "I have written a letter that will not harm Allah and His Messenger ﷺ."

Another narration states that the subject matter of the letter was as follows:

إن محمدا قد نفر فإما إليكم وإما إلى غيركم فعليكم الحذر

"Surely Muhammad ﷺ is going to leave for war. (It is not known to whom), either to you or to someone else. You should therefore beware."

Allah Ta'ala revealed the following verse in connection to this incident of Haatib رضى الله عنه:

يَاۤ اَيُّهَا الَّذِيۡنَ اٰمَنُوۡا لَا تَتَّخِذُوۡا عَدُوِّىۡ وَ عَدُوَّكُمۡ اَوۡلِيَآءَ تُلۡقُوۡنَ اِلَيۡهِمۡ بِالۡمَوَدَّةِ

"O believers! Do not take My enemies and your enemies as friends. You convey to them the message of friendship..."[Surah al-Mumtahinah, verse 1]

In this verse, Allah Ta'ala explains the injunctions concerning ties of friendship with the unbelievers.

Departure from Madinah

On the 10th of Ramadhaan, Rasulullah ﷺ together with a group of 10 000 Companions left Madinah after the Asr Salaah with the intention of conquering Makkah. From among his wives, Umme Salamah رضى الله عنها and Maymunah رضى الله عنها accompanied him.

When he reached Zul Hulayfah or Juhfah, he met 'Abbaas ؓ and his family who left Makkah with the intention of emigrating to Madinah. Acting on the instruction of Rasulullah ﷺ, he sent his possessions to Madinah, joined the Muslim army and headed towards Makkah in order to wage Jihaad. He had embraced Islam before but had been concealing his Islam from the Quraysh. Rasulullah ﷺ said to him: "O 'Abbaas! This is your last emigration just as my prophet-hood is the last prophet-hood." 'Abbaas ؓ had remained in Makkah under the instruction of Rasulullah ﷺ so that while living there, he could convey information about the Quraysh to Rasulullah ﷺ.

While 'Abbaas ؓ was living in Makkah, he had sought permission from Rasulullah ﷺ to emigrate. Rasulullah ﷺ wrote to him saying: "O my uncle! You should remain in your place. Allah Ta'ala will complete emigration with you just as He completed prophet-hood with me."

Abu Sufyaan ibn Haaris and 'Abdullah ibn Abi Umayyah were at a place called Abwa'. They left Makkah for Madinah with the intention of embracing Islam. Apart from Abu Sufyaan ibn Haaris ibn 'Abd al-Muttalib being the cousin of Rasulullah ﷺ, he was also his foster brother. He was also breast-fed by Halimah Sa'diyyah ؓ. He was a friend of Rasulullah ﷺ before prophet-hood and was always in his company. However, when Rasulullah ﷺ became a Prophet, he became his enemy. He sang poetry disgracing Rasulullah ﷺ. These lines of poetry were responded to by Hassaan ibn Saabit ؓ. Abu Sufyaan's son, Ja'far, was also with him.

'Abdullah ibn Abi Umayyah was also the cousin of Rasulullah ﷺ. He was the son of Rasulullah's ﷺ aunt, 'Aatikah bint 'Abdul-Muttalib. He was also a very bitter opponent of Rasulullah ﷺ. They both wanted to meet Rasulullah ﷺ but because they had inflicted untold suffering on him, he turned away from them and did not permit them to meet him. Umme Salamah ؓ interceded on their behalf and said: "O Rasulullah ﷺ! One is your uncle's son and the other is your aunt's son." He replied: "I have no need to meet them. My uncle's son humiliated me. As for my aunt's son, he is the one who had said to me while I was in Makkah: 'By Allah! I will never believe in you till you get a ladder going up to the heavens and I see you climbing up with my very own eyes, and then you come down with a mandate from above, and that four angels come down with you and bear testimony that Allah has appointed you as His Messenger. Even then, I do not think that I will believe in you.'"

Umme Salamah ؓ replied: "O Rasulullah! It is hoped of your noble character that both your cousins will not be deprived of your favour. When your mercy and pardon is so wide-spread, why should these two be deprived?"

On the other side, Abu Sufyaan said: "If you do not permit me entry in your court, I will take my son, Ja'far, to a desert and die there out of hunger and thirst."

On hearing the intercession of Umme Salamah رضى الله عنها and the remorse of these two, Rasulullah ﷺ permitted them to meet him. The moment they entered, they embraced Islam and joined the Muslims heading towards Makkah.

Hadhrat Ali رضى الله عنه advised Abu Sufyaan to stand before the blessed countenance of Rasulullah ﷺ and to say the words that the brothers of Yusuf عليه السلام had said in the presence of Yusuf عليه السلام:

$$\text{قَالُوْا تَاللّٰهِ لَقَدْ اٰثَرَكَ اللّٰهُ عَلَيْنَا وَ اِنْ كُنَّا لَخٰطِئِيْنَ ﴿٩١﴾}$$

"We take an oath by Allah that Allah has certainly given you superiority over us. And surely we are in error." [Surah Yusuf, verse 91]

Hadhrat Ali رضى الله عنه advised Abu Sufyaan to approach Rasulullah ﷺ from the front so that the humility of his illustrious countenance would come as a barrier between him and his reprimand. This is what happened and the mercy to the worlds ﷺ and the embodiment of modesty ﷺ uttered these words in reply:

$$\text{قَالَ لَا تَثْرِيْبَ عَلَيْكُمُ الْيَوْمَ ۗ يَغْفِرُ اللّٰهُ لَكُمْ ۖ وَهُوَ اَرْحَمُ الرّٰحِمِيْنَ}$$

"There is no reproach on you today. May Allah forgive you, and He is the most merciful of those who show mercy."[Surah Yusuf, verse 92]

Abu Sufyaan's رضى الله عنه repentance was accepted, and in accordance with the prophetic teaching "Islam wipes out all that was committed before embracing Islam", his heart became so purified that no filth whatsoever remained in it. The qualities of Imaan, righteousness, sincerity and conviction were pounded into fine bits and filled into his heart in such a manner that no dust or atom of unbelief could reach into his heart. From that very time he joined Rasulullah ﷺ in order to sacrifice his life for the cause of Allah Ta'ala and His Messenger ﷺ.

It is said that as long as Rasulullah ﷺ remained in their midst, Abu Sufyaan رضى الله عنه did not look at him directly in the face out of modesty. Rasulullah ﷺ used to give him the glad tidings of Jannah. May Allah be pleased with him.

Abu Sufyaan رضى الله عنه also said a few lines of poetry as a way of seeking forgiveness for his past crimes.

$$\text{لعمرك إنى يوم أحمل راية   لتغلب خيل اللاّتِ خَيْلَ مُحَمَّدِ}$$

كالمدلج الحيران أظلم ليله   فهذا أوانى حين أُهدى واهتدى

"By your life! The day when I carried the flag so that the army of Laat may overpower the army of Muhammad. Then on that day I was like a person who is walking agitatedly and perturbed in a dark night. Now the time has come that I am given guidance (by Allah Ta'ala) and I am following this guidance."

After 'Abdullah ibn Abi Umayyah رضى الله عنه embraced Islam, his condition became such that due to modesty, he was unable to look at Rasulullah صلى الله عليه وسلم directly in the face.

Stopping over at Marruz-Zahraan

Rasulullah صلى الله عليه وسلم then left Kadid and reached Marruz-Zahraan at Isha time. On reaching there, he got off and ordered that each person should light a fire outside his tent. This was an old Arab custom. Rasulullah صلى الله عليه وسلم ordered the Muslims to do so accordingly. Due to their breaking the treaty, the Quraysh were on their guard as to when Rasulullah صلى الله عليه وسلم would attack them. Abu Sufyaan, Budayl ibn Warqaa' and Hakeem ibn Hizam therefore set forth from Makkah in order to obtain whatever information they could. When they came close to Marruz-Zahraan, they saw the army there and became concerned. Abu Sufyaan asked: "What fires are these?" Budayl replied: "These are the fires of the Banu Khuzaa'ah." Abu Sufyaan replied: "How can the Banu Khuzaa'ah have such a large army? They are very small in number."

The moment the night watchmen of Rasulullah صلى الله عليه وسلم saw these three people, they apprehended them. They asked them as to who they were, and they replied that Rasulullah صلى الله عليه وسلم and his companions were among them. While they were still conversing, 'Abbaas رضى الله عنه was on the donkey of Rasulullah صلى الله عليه وسلم moving about. He recognised the voice of Abu Sufyaan رضى الله عنه and said: "How sorrowful for you, O Abu Sufyaan! This is the army of Rasulullah صلى الله عليه وسلم. By Allah, if he is victorious over you, he will chop off your neck. It would be better for the Quraysh if you seek peace from him and agree to obey him." Abu Sufyaan رضى الله عنه says: "On hearing this voice, I turned in that direction until I found 'Abbaas رضى الله عنه. I said to him: 'O Abu al-Fadl! May my parents be sacrificed for you. How can I save myself and what is the way out?'" 'Abbaas رضى الله عنه replied: "Climb onto this donkey with me. I will take you to Rasulullah صلى الله عليه وسلم in order to seek asylum for you." 'Abbaas رضى الله عنه took him and left while showing him around the Muslim army.

When they passed by 'Umar رضى الله عنه and the latter saw him, he jumped up and said: "This is Abu Sufyaan, the enemy of Allah Ta'ala and His Messenger

ﷺ. All praise is due to Allah that he has fallen into my hands without any peace agreement." 'Umar ؓ was on foot while 'Abbaas ؓ and Abu Sufyaan were moving swiftly on the donkey. 'Umar ؓ unsheathed his sword and ran behind them. He reached Rasulullah ﷺ and said: "O Rasulullah! Abu Sufyaan, the enemy of Allah Ta'ala and His Messenger ﷺ, has fallen into my hands without any peace agreement. Permit me to kill him." 'Abbaas ؓ said: "O Rasulullah ﷺ! I have given him asylum."

'Umar ؓ remained standing with his sword and made the same request several times. He was waiting for a sign from Rasulullah ﷺ to carry out what he wanted. 'Abbaas ؓ said: "O 'Umar! Wait a bit. If he was from the Banu 'Adiyy tribe you would not have been so hasty in wanting to kill him. Because he is from the Banu 'Abdu Manaaf, you are so persistent in wanting to kill him." 'Umar ؓ replied: "O 'Abbaas! I take an oath by Allah Ta'ala that I was more happy with your embracing Islam than even that of my own father, Khattaab. Had my father embraced Islam, I would not have experienced the happiness that I experienced when you embraced Islam. This is because I knew very well that Rasulullah ﷺ would be more happy with your Islam than the Islam of Khattaab. This is the high position in which I hold you. However, you can think whatever you wish of me."

Rasulullah ﷺ ordered 'Abbaas ؓ to take Abu Sufyaan to his tent and to bring him back the next morning. Abu Sufyaan remained in the tent the entire night while Hakeem ibn Hizaam and Budayl ibn Warqaa' presented themselves before Rasulullah ﷺ and embraced Islam. Rasulullah ﷺ remained with them for some time asking them about the present conditions in Makkah. After embracing Islam, they both returned to Makkah in order to inform the people of Makkah of Rasulullah's ﷺ arrival.

Abu Sufyaan embraces Islam

The following morning, 'Abbaas ؓ took Abu Sufyaan to Rasulullah ﷺ. He addressed Abu Sufyaan saying: "O Abu Sufyaan! Has the time not come for you to believe that there is none worthy of worship except Allah?" He replied: "May my parents be sacrificed for you. You are extremely forbearing, kind and one who maintains family ties. I take an oath by Allah that had there been any deity apart from Him, he would have benefited us today and I would have sought his help against you." Rasulullah ﷺ said: "O Abu Sufyaan! Has the time not come that you recognise me as the Messenger of Allah?" He replied: "May my parents be sacrificed for you. You are extremely forbearing, kind and one who maintains family ties. You are still showing your kindness. Despite my enmity towards you,

you are still showing your kindness to me. I have a slight doubt with regard to you being a Prophet or not."

After 'Abbaas ؓ explained to him, Abu Sufyaan ؓ embraced Islam. After this, 'Abbaas ؓ said: "O Messenger of Allah! Abu Sufyaan is from among the leaders of Makkah. He likes position. Therefore give him something that would be a source of honour, nobility and distinction for him." Rasulullah ﷺ replied: "Certainly, make this announcement that whoever enters the house of Abu Sufyaan ؓ will be safe." Abu Sufyaan ؓ said: "O Messenger of Allah! How will all the people fit in my house?" Rasulullah ﷺ replied: "Whoever enters the Sacred Masjid will also be safe." Abu Sufyaan ؓ said: "O Messenger of Allah! Even the Masjid will not be sufficient." Rasulullah ﷺ replied: "Okay, whoever enters his house and keeps his door shut will also be safe." Abu Sufyaan ؓ replied: "Yes, there is much leniency and expansion in this."

When Rasulullah ﷺ began preparations to depart from Marruz-Zahraan, he ordered 'Abbaas ؓ to take Abu Sufyaan ؓ to the mountain pass so that he would be able to see the Muslim army in full view. Consequently, when the different tribes began passing him in groups after groups, he was left astounded and said to 'Abbaas ؓ: "The kingdom of your nephew has really grown." 'Abbaas ؓ replied: "This is not kingship. Rather, it is prophet-hood."

As each tribe used to pass by, Abu Sufyaan ؓ would ask as to who that particular tribe was. Khaalid ibn Waleed ؓ was the first to pass by with an army of 900 to 1000. After him, various tribes passed by. Eventually, the group of Rasulullah ﷺ, embellished with inner and outer power passed by with a fully armed group of the Muhaajireen and Ansaar. The flag of the Muhaajireen was carried by Zubayr ؓ while that of the Ansaar was carried by Sa'd ibn 'Ubaadah ؓ. When the latter passed by and saw Abu Sufyaan ؓ, he was overtaken by zeal and shouted out:

اليوم يوم الملحمة اليوم تستحل الكعبة

"Today is the day of fighting. Today, fighting and killing in the Ka'bah will be lawful."

On hearing this, Abu Sufyaan ؓ became alarmed and asked about the identity of these people. Hadhrat 'Abbaas ؓ replied that it comprised of the Muhaajireen and Ansaar together with Rasulullah ﷺ.

When Rasulullah ﷺ passed by, Abu Sufyaan ؓ asked: "O Rasulullah ﷺ! Have you ordered Sa'd ibn 'Ubaadah ؓ to kill your people?" He then quoted the words that Sa'd ؓ had uttered and said: "O Rasulullah ﷺ! I ask you in the name of Allah and our family ties, for you are the one who is most cognisant of maintaining family ties." Rasulullah ﷺ replied:

يا أبا سفيان اليوم يوم المرحمة يعز الله فيه قريشا

"O Abu Sufyaan! Today is the day of mercy, in which Allah will honour the Quraysh."

Rasulullah ﷺ said:

كذب سعد ولكن هذا يوم يعظم الله فيه الكعبة ويوم تكسى فيه الكعبة

"Sa'd is wrong. Today is the day in which Allah Ta'ala will honour the Ka'bah and the Ka'bah will be given a covering."

Rasulullah ﷺ then ordered that the flag be taken from Sa'd ibn 'Ubaadah رضي الله عنه and be given to his son, Qays.

When Rasulullah ﷺ was passing by, a Qurayshi woman said the following lines of poetry:

يَا نبى الهدى إِلَيكَ لجا حُّ قريش   وَلا تحسين الجآء حين

ضاقت عَلَيهِمْ سعة الأرض   وعاداهم إله السمآء إن

سعدا يريد قاصمة الظهر   بأهل الحجون والبطحاء

"O Prophet of guidance! The Quraysh have sought refuge in you when this is not the time to seek refuge. This is the time when the wide earth constricted upon them and Allah (the lord of the heavens) became their enemy. Surely Sa'd wants to break the back of the people of Hajun and Batha' (places in Makkah)."

Abu Sufyaan رضي الله عنه then left Rasulullah ﷺ and hastened towards Makkah. On reaching there, he made the following announcement: "Muhammad is coming with an army. It is my opinion that there is no one who can fight against him. Embrace Islam and you will remain in peace. The person who enters the Sacred Masjid will be safe. The person who enters my house will be safe. The person who shuts himself in his house or surrenders his weapons will be safe." His wife, Hindah, caught him by his moustache and announced: "O Banu Kinaanah! This old man has become mad and stupid. He does not even know what he is saying." She uttered many other abusive words to him. Many people gathered around them.

Abu Sufyaan ؓ said to them: "Such utterances will not help in any way. O people! Don't be deluded by this woman."

"There is no one who can fight Muhammad ﷺ. The person who enters the Sacred Masjid is safe. The person who enters my house is also safe." The people replied: "O foolish one! How many people can fit into your house?" Abu Sufyaan replied: "The person who shuts himself in his house is also safe."

Abu Sufyaan ؓ addressed his wife saying: "It is best that you also embrace Islam or else you will be killed. Go into your house and shut your door. I am speaking the truth." On hearing all this, the people began rushing to the Sacred Masjid while others ran towards their homes.

Entry into Makkah

Rasulullah ﷺ then entered Makkah from the direction of Kada'. On entering Makkah, he fully showed his respect and honour to the Ka'bah. He entered with humility, with his head bowing down. He did not enter haughtily like kings. 'Abdullah ibn Mughaffal ؓ narrates: "I saw Rasulullah ﷺ on the day of the conquest of Makkah. He was sitting on his camel and reciting Surah al-Fatah in a beautiful tone."

At the time of this great conquest, together with Rasulullah ﷺ being extremely happy and in high spirits, the effects of humility, modesty and tranquillity were also visible on his face. He was sitting on his camel. His head was lowered out of humility to such an extent that his blessed beard was touching the saddle. His servant, Usaamah ibn Zaid ؓ was sitting with him.

Anas ؓ narrates that when Rasulullah ﷺ entered Makkah as a conqueror, all the people were looking at him but he had his face lowered out of humility.

Abu Sa'eed Khudri ؓ narrates that on the day of the conquest of Makkah, Rasulullah ﷺ said: "This is the day which Allah Ta'ala had promised me." He then recited Surah Nasr.

Rasulullah ﷺ was thinking over the fact that there was a time when he had to emigrate from this city in a state of weakness and poverty. He had left all alone without the knowledge of the enemy. Now the time has come that through the help and assistance of Allah Ta'ala, he is entering the same city with much power and authority as a conqueror. This is the bounty of Allah Ta'ala which He bestows to whomever He wills.

It is for this reason that Rasulullah's ﷺ head was lowered and placed on the saddle – prostrating before Allah Ta'ala out of gratitude. Out of his extreme happiness, he was reciting Surah Fatah and Surah Nasr in a very beautiful and melodious tone. In so doing, he was saying that this clear victory, help, power and authority are all solely the blessings of Allah Ta'ala. Truth has triumphed and falsehood was defeated. The light of Islam and Imaan glittered while the darkness of disbelief was removed. The sacred land (of Makkah) was purified from the filth of disbelief and polytheism.

Rasulullah ﷺ passed through the place of Kada' and entered from the upper section of Makkah. He ordered Khaalid ibn Waleed ؓ to enter from Kuda' – the lower section of Makkah, and Zubayr ؓ to enter from Kada' – the upper section of Makkah. He emphasised on both of them not to commence any fighting. They should only fight the person who attacks them first. He then entered Makkah with much respect and reverence.

When he entered Makkah, he first went to the house of Umme Hani bint Abi Taalib ؓ. He took a bath and offered eight Rakaats of Salaah – this was the time of chasht – mid-morning.

Umme Hani ؓ said to Rasulullah ﷺ: "O Messenger of Allah! Two relatives of my husband have fled and sought refuge in my house. I have given them refuge. However, my brother, Ali ؓ wants to kill them." Rasulullah ﷺ replied: "I give refuge to those whom Umme Hani ؓ has given refuge to. Ali should not kill those two people."

On completing his Salaah, Rasulullah ﷺ went to Shi'b Abi Taalib, a place where his tent was pitched. The Sahaabah ؓ had asked Rasulullah ﷺ a day before he could enter Makkah as to where he would stay. He replied: "At the place where the Quraysh and Kinaanah had confined the Banu Haashim and the Banu al-Muttalib when they had made a mutual agreement and promise that they would sever all business dealings, marriage, etc. with the Banu Haashim and the Banu Muttalib as long as they do not hand over Muhammad (ﷺ) to them." This place is known as Shi'b Abi Taalib.

Abu Hurayrah ؓ narrates that Rasulullah ﷺ summoned the Ansaar and informed them that the Quraysh have rallied some gangsters against them. They should therefore confine them to the orchards (outskirts) and keep them there.

Safwaan ibn Umayyah, 'Ikramah ibn Abi Jahal and Suhayl ibn 'Amr gathered some gangsters at a place called Khandamah in order to fight the Muslims. A clash ensued between them and Khaalid ibn Waleed ؓ. Two Muslims, Khunays ibn Khaalid ibn Rabi'ah ؓ and Kurz ibn Jaabir Fihri ؓ, were martyred. Twelve or thirteen people from the disbelievers were killed. The remainder all fled.

When Khaalid ibn Waleed ؓ entered from the lower section of Makkah, the Banu Bakr, Banu Haaris ibn 'Abd Manaat, some people from the Hudhayl tribe and some gangsters from the Quraysh were gathered there to fight the Muslims. As soon as Khaalid ؓ reached there, they gave out the battle cry. However, they were unable to defend themselves. They were defeated and fled. About 20 from the Banu Bakr were killed while three or four were killed from the Hudhayl tribe. The remainder were left at a loss. Some of them concealed themselves in their houses while others went to the mountain tops. Abu Sufyaan ﷺ made the announcement: "The person who shuts himself in his house is safe. The person who abstains from fighting is safe." When Rasulullah ﷺ saw the glitter of swords, he summoned Khaalid ibn Waleed ﷺ and asked him about what was transpiring for he had prohibited him from fighting. He replied: "O Messenger of Allah! I did not start the fight. I abstained from fighting, but I was forced to do so when they attacked us." Rasulullah ﷺ replied: "There is good in whatever Allah Ta'ala has destined."

Peace was established thereafter. People were guaranteed safety and they were now at rest. When the conquest was completed, Rasulullah ﷺ entered the Sacred Masjid.

Entering the Sacred Masjid

After the victory, Rasulullah ﷺ entered the Sacred Masjid and made Tawaaf of the Ka'bah. 'Abdullah ibn 'Umar ﷺ narrates that when Rasulullah ﷺ entered the Sacred Masjid, 360 idols were placed around the Ka'bah. Rasulullah ﷺ pointed to each one with a knife and recited the words:

جَآءَ الْحَقُّ وَ زَهَقَ الْبَاطِلُ

"The truth has come, and falsehood is defeated."

On saying this, each idol began falling one after the other.

When Rasulullah ﷺ entered the Sacred Masjid, he was on his camel. He made Tawaaf of the Ka'bah in the same condition. On completing the Tawaaf he summoned 'Usmaan ibn Talhah, took the key to the Ka'bah from him and opened it. He saw that there were statues in it. He ordered all these to be removed. When they were all removed and the inside of the Ka'bah was washed with zam zam water, he went in and offered Salaah therein.

He went to all the corners of the Ka'bah and illuminated them with the sound of Tauheed and Takbeer (saying Allah is the greatest). Bilal ﷺ and Usaamah ﷺ were with him at that time. On completing this, he opened the door and stepped outside. He saw that the Sacred Masjid was filled with people and that they were waiting for him to address them regarding the criminals and enemies. This was the 20th of Ramadhaan. He was standing at the door of the Ka'bah with its key in his hand. He then delivered the following speech.

Rasulullah ﷺ delivers a speech from the door of the Ka'bah

لَا إِلٰهَ إِلَّا اللّٰهُ وَحْدَهُ لَا شَرِيْكَ لَهُ صَدَقَ وَعْدَهُ وَنَصَرَ عَبْدَهُ وَهَزَمَ الأَحْزَابَ وَحْدَهُ. أَلَا كُلُّ مَأْثُرَةٍ أَوْ دَمٍ أَوْ مَا يُدَّعَى فَهُوَ تَحْتَ قَدَمَيَّ هَاتَيْنِ إِلَّا سِدَانَةَ الْبَيْتِ وَسِقَايَةَ الْحَاجِّ. أَلَا وَقَتِيْلُ الْخَطَأِ شِبْهِ الْعَمْدِ بِالسَّوْطِ وَالْعَصَا فَفِيْهِ الدِّيَةُ مُغَلَّظَةٌ مِنَ الإِبِلِ أَرْبَعُوْنَ مِنْهَا فِىْ بُطُوْنِهَا أَوْلَادُهَا. يَا مَعْشَرَ قُرَيْشٍ إِنَّ اللّٰهَ قَدْ أَذْهَبَ عَنْكُمْ نَخْوَةَ الْجَاهِلِيَّةِ وَتَعْظِيْمَهَا بِالآبَاءِ. النَّاسُ مِنْ آدَمَ وَآدَمُ مِنْ تُرَابٍ ثُمَّ تَلَا هَذِهِ الْآيَةَ

﴿ يَٰٓأَيُّهَا ٱلنَّاسُ إِنَّا خَلَقْنَٰكُم مِّن ذَكَرٍۢ وَأُنثَىٰ وَجَعَلْنَٰكُمْ شُعُوبًۭا وَقَبَآئِلَ لِتَعَارَفُوٓا۟ ۚ إِنَّ أَكْرَمَكُمْ عِندَ ٱللَّهِ أَتْقَىٰكُمْ ۚ إِنَّ ٱللَّهَ عَلِيمٌ خَبِيرٌ ﴾ ثُمَّ قَالَ يَا مَعْشَرَ قُرَيْشٍ مَا تَرَوْنَ أَنِّىْ فَاعِلٌ بِكُمْ؟ قَالُوْا خَيْرًا أَخٌ كَرِيْمٌ وَابْنُ أَخٍ كَرِيْمٍ. قَالَ فَإِنِّىْ أَقُوْلُ لَكُمْ كَمَا قَالَ يُوْسُفُ لِإِخْوَتِهِ لَا تَثْرِيْبَ عَلَيْكُمُ الْيَوْمَ إِذْهَبُوْا فَأَنْتُمُ الطُّلَقَاءُ

"There is none worthy of worship but Allah. He is alone and has no partner. He made true His promise, helped His servant and defeated all the enemy groups by Himself. Listen! Every custom, be it physical or monetary, which can be claimed is now under my feet. (They are all cancelled). Except for the custodianship of the Ka'bah and providing zam zam water to the pilgrims. These customs will remain as previously. Listen! The person who is mistakenly killed by a whip or by a staff, his blood money will be 100 camels of which 40 will have to be pregnant. O group of Quraysh! Allah Ta'ala has abolished the haughtiness of the days of ignorance and pride over forefathers. All people are from Aadam عَلَيْهِ السَّلَام and Aadam عَلَيْهِ السَّلَام was created from soil. He then recited this verse: 'O people! We created you from a male and a female and made you into nations and tribes so that you may recognise each other. The most honourable among you in the sight of Allah is he who is most virtuous. Surely Allah is all-knowing, fully aware.' He then said: 'O group of Quraysh! What do you think I am going to do to you?' They replied: 'We think that

you will be good to us. You are a noble brother who is the son of a noble brother.' He said: 'I am addressing you in the same manner which Yusuf عَلَيْهِ السَّلَام addressed his brothers: 'There is no reproach on you today. Go, for you are all free.'"

The custom of pride and haughtiness over one's lineage and nobility which was prevalent among the Arabs was put to an end in this speech of Rasulullah ﷺ. The flag of Islamic equality was raised and it was demonstrated that the criterion for honour and nobility was only piety and virtue. Rasulullah ﷺ was sent as a mercy to the world for the guidance of the entire universe. His sole objective was guidance. Taking revenge from one's enemies is the trait of kings (and not true Prophets of Allah Ta'ala).

On completing his speech, Rasulullah ﷺ sat down in the Masjid. The key to the Ka'bah was in his hand. Ali رَضِيَ اللهُ عَنْهُ stood up and asked: "O Messenger of Allah! Give the key to me so that together with the responsibility of providing zam zam to the pilgrims, we will also have the honour of custodianship of the Ka'bah." This verse was then revealed:

$$\text{اِنَّ اللهَ يَأْمُرُكُمْ اَنْ تُؤَدُّوا الْاَمٰنٰتِ اِلٰٓى اَهْلِهَا}$$

"Surely Allah commands you to discharge the trusts to their recipients."
[Surah an-Nisaa', verse 58]

Rasulullah ﷺ called for 'Usmaan ibn Talhah and returned the key to him. He then said to him: "Take this key forever." In other words, it will remain in your family forever. "I am not giving it to you of my own accord. Rather, it is Allah who has given it to you. None but a tyrant and a usurper will take it away from you."

The Azaan is given at the door of the Ka'bah

When it was the time for Zuhr Salaah, Rasulullah ﷺ ordered Bilal رَضِيَ اللهُ عَنْهُ to climb the door of the Ka'bah and call out the Azaan. The Quraysh of Makkah saw this extraordinary and strange scene of the clear victory of this true religion from the mountain tops of Makkah.

The leaders of the Quraysh who could not see the humiliation of disbelief and polytheism and the honour of the true religion, hid their faces in shame. Abu Sufyaan, 'Itaab, Khaalid, Usayd, Haaris ibn Hishaam (who embraced Islam later on) and other Quraysh leaders were sitting in the courtyard of the Ka'bah. 'Itaab and Khaalid said: "Allah honoured our forefathers by taking them away from this world before they could hear this call (of the Azaan)." Haaris said: "I take an oath by Allah that if I were convinced that you are on the truth, I would certainly follow you." Abu Sufyaan said: "I am maintaining silence. If I were to utter anything, these pebbles would inform him thereof." Rasulullah ﷺ was informed of all these conversations through revelation from Allah Ta'ala. When he passed by these people he said to them: "I have been informed through revelation all that you have been speaking." He then related to them all that they had been speaking. Haaris and 'Itaab said: "We bear testimony that you are certainly the Messenger of Allah for none of us informed you of what we were conversing. (We thereby conclude that it was Allah alone who informed His Messenger of all that we were speaking.)"

After 'Itaab ibn Usayd embraced Islam, Rasulullah ﷺ appointed him as the governor of Makkah. He was 21 years old at that time. Rasulullah ﷺ stipulated that he should receive one dirham per day for his personal expenses. It was on this that 'Itaab said:

أيها الناس أجاع الله كبد من جاع على درهم

"O people! May Allah keep that liver hungry which remains hungry on one dirham."

He remained the governor of Makkah till the demise of Rasulullah ﷺ. When Abu Bakr ؓ became the caliph, he maintained him as the governor. He passed away on the same day that Abu Bakr ؓ passed away.

At the time when Bilal ؓ climbed on the door of the Ka'bah in order to call out the Azaan, Abu Mahdhurah Jumahi and a few youngsters began imitating the Azaan. Abu Mahdhurah had a very beautiful and loud voice. His imitation of the Azaan reached the ears of Rasulullah ﷺ. He summoned the entire group of youngsters and asked them as to whose voice he had heard. They all pointed towards Abu Mahdhurah. Rasulullah ﷺ asked all of them except Abu Mahdhurah to leave. The latter remained standing before Rasulullah ﷺ with the firm conviction that he would be killed. Rasulullah ﷺ ordered him to call out the Azaan. He did so with much fear. When he completed, Rasulullah ﷺ gave him a pouch in which were some dirhams. Rasulullah ﷺ then passed his blessed hands on his head, forehead, chest, heart and till his navel. He then made this dua for him: "May Allah bless you and may Allah shower His blessings on you."

Abu Mahdhurah says: "No sooner had Rasulullah ﷺ passed his hand over me, all my antagonism towards him was changed into affection. My heart was filled with love for him and I said to him: 'O Messenger of Allah! Appoint me as the muazzin of Makkah.' Rasulullah ﷺ replied: 'I appoint you as the muazzin of Makkah.' I went to 'Itaab ibn Usayd ؓ, the governor of Makkah, and informed him thereof. I then continued calling out the Azaan in accordance with the instruction of Rasulullah ﷺ.'" He remained in Makkah throughout his life and continued calling out the Azaan till his death. He passed away in 59 A.H. in Makkah.

Abu Mahdhurah ﷺ was 16 years old when he was appointed as a Muazzin and remained so till his death. When he passed away, his progeny took the responsibility of calling out the Azaan and this continued from generation to generation.

A poet says the following with regard to his Azaan:

أما ورب الكعبة المستورة   وما تلا محمد من سورة

والنغمات من أبي محذورة   لأفعلن فعلة المذكورة

"By the oath of the Ka'bah which is covered and the chapters of the Qur-aan which Muhammad ﷺ recited. By the oath of the beautiful Azaan of Abu Mahdhurah, I will certainly do such and such task."

On completing the Tawaaf, Rasulullah ﷺ went to Mt. Safa, faced the Ka'bah remained in dua and praising Allah Ta'ala for a long time. A group of Ansaar were also present. Some of them said: "Allah Ta'ala enabled Rasulullah ﷺ to conquer his city and homeland. It may well be that he will decide to remain behind and settle down in this city and not come back to Madinah." They continued speaking in this vein when they saw the effects of divine revelation on Rasulullah's ﷺ countenance. It was the habit of the Sahaabah ﷺ that when divine revelation was coming to Rasulullah ﷺ, they would not look at him. When the revelation was completed, he said: "O Ansaar! Is this what you said?" They replied: "Yes, O Messenger of Allah." He replied: "Understand this well that this can never happen. I am the servant and Messenger of Allah Ta'ala. I emigrated by the command of Allah Ta'ala. My life is your life and my death is your death." On hearing this, the Ansaar began crying and said: "O Messenger of Allah! We feared that the light which lit us will be taken away from us. We are servants who are prepared to sacrifice our lives (for Allah Ta'ala and His Messenger ﷺ) and we are prepared to give preference to others over our own selves. But we are extremely miserly when it comes to Allah Ta'ala and His Messenger ﷺ. (We are not prepared to share them with anyone else)."

باسایه ترا نمی پسندم   عشق است وهزار بد گمانی

I am in love with your being not with your shadow,
when I am infatuated with you I end up having thousands of doubts

Rasulullah ﷺ replied: "Allah Ta'ala and His Messenger consider you to be true in this regard and excuse you in this regard."

Pledge of allegiance from men and women

On completing his duas, Rasulullah ﷺ remained sitting on Mt. Safa. People gathered in order to pledge allegiance to him. Rasulullah ﷺ accepted their pledge on obedience to Allah Ta'ala and His Messenger ﷺ. From the men he took the pledge of Islam and obedience to Allah Ta'ala and His Messenger ﷺ according to each one's capability. Some Ahaadith state that from the men he took the pledge of Islam and Jihaad. When he completed taking the pledge from the men, he commenced with the women. From them, he took the pledge in matters that are enumerated in the following verse:

$$\text{يَٰٓأَيُّهَا ٱلنَّبِيُّ إِذَا جَآءَكَ ٱلْمُؤْمِنَٰتُ يُبَايِعْنَكَ عَلَىٰٓ أَن لَّا يُشْرِكْنَ بِٱللَّهِ شَيْـًٔا وَلَا يَسْرِقْنَ وَلَا يَزْنِينَ وَلَا يَقْتُلْنَ أَوْلَٰدَهُنَّ وَلَا يَأْتِينَ بِبُهْتَٰنٍ يَفْتَرِينَهُۥ بَيْنَ أَيْدِيهِنَّ وَأَرْجُلِهِنَّ وَلَا يَعْصِينَكَ فِى مَعْرُوفٍ فَبَايِعْهُنَّ وَٱسْتَغْفِرْ لَهُنَّ ٱللَّهَ ۖ إِنَّ ٱللَّهَ غَفُورٌ رَّحِيمٌ}$$

"O Prophet! If believing women come to you in order to pledge to you that they will not ascribe any partners with Allah, they will not steal, they will not commit adultery, they will not kill their children, they will not fabricate a slander between their hands and their feet, and that they will not disobey you in any good deed, then accept the pledge from them and seek forgiveness for them from Allah. Surely Allah is forgiving, merciful." [Surah Mumtahinah, Verse 12]

The bay'ah (pledge of allegiance) which Rasulullah ﷺ took from women was solely verbal. His blessed hand neither touched any strange woman, nor did he shake hands with any strange woman. Rather, he would take a pledge via a piece of cloth. In other words, he would hold one end of a piece of cloth while the woman would hold the other end.

At times, when taking a pledge from women he would ask for a cup of water and dip his blessed hand in it. He would then ask the women to dip their hands into it. They would do so and in so doing the pledge would be reinforced.

Some of the Qurayshi women who gave their pledge at that time are as follows:

1. Umme Hani bint Abi Taalib رضي الله عنها, i.e. the sister of Ali رضي الله عنه.
2. Umme Habibah bint 'Aas ibn Umayyah رضي الله عنها, the wife of 'Amr ibn 'Abd Aamiri.
3. Arwah bint Abi al-'Is رضي الله عنها, the paternal aunt of 'Itaab ibn Usayd.
4. 'Aatikah bint Abi al-'Is رضي الله عنها, the sister of Arwah.

5. Hindah bint 'Utbah رضي الله عنها, the wife of Abu Sufyaan and the mother of Mu'aawiyah رضي الله عنه.

When Hindah رضي الله عنها presented herself for the pledge, she placed a veil over her face. She was the one who had ordered Hamzah رضي الله عنه to be killed and she was the one who cut open his chest and chewed his liver. It was out of her shame and remorse that she covered her face and presented herself so that she may not be recognised. The story of her pledge is as follows:

Hindah رضي الله عنها: "O Rasulullah ﷺ! With regard to what are you taking a pledge and covenant from us?"

Rasulullah ﷺ: "To abstain from taking partners with Allah Ta'ala."

Hindah رضي الله عنها: "O Rasulullah ﷺ! You are taking a pledge from us with regard to things which you did not take from the men. Nevertheless, we accept this."

Rasulullah ﷺ: "And that you do not steal."

Hindah رضي الله عنها: "I take some things from my husband's (Abu Sufyaan) wealth. I do not know whether this is considered to be stealing or not." Abu Sufyaan رضي الله عنه was present there at that time. He said: "Whatever has passed is forgiven." Rasulullah ﷺ said: "You may take from your husband's wealth according to your basic necessities and what would be sufficient for you. This should be according to the norm whereby it will be according to your necessities and your children's necessities."

Rasulullah ﷺ: "And that you do not commit adultery."

Hindah رضي الله عنها: "What! Can a noble woman ever commit adultery?!"

Rasulullah ﷺ: "And that you do not kill your children."

Hindah رضي الله عنها: "We brought them up when they were small and you killed them on the day of Badr when they were big. So that is between you and them." On hearing this, 'Umar رضي الله عنه began laughing.

Rasulullah ﷺ: "And that you do not slander anyone."

Hindah رضي الله عنها: "By Allah, it is extremely detestable to slander anyone. And you are the one who is commanding us with righteousness and noble qualities and character."

Rasulullah ﷺ: "And that you do not disobey or refuse to comply to any good deed."

Hindah رضي الله عنها: "We did not come here even with this thought of disobeying you."

Rasulullah ﷺ asked 'Umar رضي الله عنه to take the pledge from her. After the pledge, Rasulullah ﷺ made dua for her forgiveness.

After embracing Islam, Hindah رضي الله عنها said: "O Messenger of Allah! Before embracing Islam, there was not any face that was more detestable in my sight, and

I did not harbour any enmity towards anyone more than you. But now, there is no face that is more beloved to me." Rasulullah ﷺ replied: "Your love for me will now increase."

Rasulullah's ﷺ second speech

After the conquest of Makkah, a person from the Khuzaa'ah tribe killed a disbeliever from the Huzayl tribe. When Rasulullah ﷺ heard about this, he gathered the Sahaabah ؓ, stood on Mt. Safa and delivered the following speech:

يا أيها الناس إن الله حرم مكة يوم خلق السماوات والأرض فهى حرام إلى يوم القيامة فلا يحل لامرئ يؤمن بالله واليوم الآخر أن يسفك فيها دما ولا يعضد فيها شجرة ولم تحلل لأحد كان قبلى ولا تحل لأحد يكون بعدى ولم تحلل لى إلا هذه الساعة غضبا على أهلها ألا ثم قد رجعت كحرمتها بالأمس فليبلغ الشاهد منكم الغائب فمن قال لكم إن رسول الله صلى الله عليه وسلم قاتل فيها فقولوا إن الله قد أحلها لرسوله ولم يحللها لكم يا معشر خزاعة ارفعوا أيديكم عن القتل فلقد كثر القتل لقد قتلتم قتيلا لأديته فمن قتل بعد مقامى هذا فأهله بخير النظرين إن شاءوا فدم قاتله وإن شاءوا فعقلهُ

"O people! Allah sanctified Makkah the day He created the heavens and the earth. It will therefore remain sanctified till the day of resurrection. It is therefore not lawful for a person believing in Allah Ta'ala and the last day to shed blood therein or to uproot a tree. It was never made lawful for anyone before me nor will it be lawful for anyone after me. It was only made lawful to me for this particular time because of Allah's anger on its inhabitants. It's sanctity has now returned as it had been previously. He who is present here should convey this to him who is not present. If anyone tells you that the Messenger of Allah fought and killed in Makkah, tell him that Allah Ta'ala made this lawful for him and not for you. O people of the Khuzaa'ah! Abstain from killing for too much of killing has taken place. You have *killed a person. I will now pay his blood money. Whoever kills after this, the family of the murdered person has the choice of either retaliating by killing the murderer or demanding blood money."*

Rasulullah ﷺ then gave 100 camels as blood money on behalf of the person who killed from the Khuzaa'ah tribe.

The dwellings of the Muhaajireen

The disbelievers of Makkah had taken possession of the houses, properties and estates of the Muhaajireen. When Rasulullah ﷺ completed his sermon, he was still standing at the door of the Ka'bah when Abu Ahmad ibn Jahsh stood up and tried to say something about the return of his house which, on his emigration, had been sold by Abu Sufyaan ؓ for 400 dirhams. Rasulullah ﷺ called him forward, said something softly to him and after which Abu Ahmad ibn Jahsh remained silent. Later on, when he was asked as to what Rasulullah ﷺ said to him, he replied: "Rasulullah ﷺ said to me: 'If you remain patient, it will be better for you and in return for this you will receive a house in paradise.' I said to him: 'I will remain patient.'"

Apart from him, there were other Muhaajireen who also desired that their houses be returned to them. Rasulullah ﷺ said to them: "I do not desire that the wealth which has gone for the cause of Allah Ta'ala be returned." On hearing this, the Muhaajireen remained silent and did not utter a word about the return of the houses which they left behind for the sake of Allah Ta'ala and His Messenger ﷺ. Rasulullah ﷺ himself did not even mention the house in which he was born and the house in which he married Khadijah ؓ.

After the year of amnesty

After the conquest of Makkah, Rasulullah ﷺ made the announcement of general amnesty. Rasulullah ﷺ completely forgave those who had scattered thorns in his path, those who had thrown stones at him, those who were constantly antagonistic towards him, and those who had caused his legs and feet to be covered in blood. However, there were a few who had been extremely insolent towards Rasulullah ﷺ and caused him much pain. With regard to these few, Rasulullah ﷺ ordered that they should be killed wherever they are found. This was the order of Allah Ta'ala concerning such people:

Chapter 23

$$\text{مَلْعُونِينَ ۚ أَيْنَمَا ثُقِفُوٓا۟ أُخِذُوا۟ وَقُتِّلُوا۟ تَقْتِيلًا ۝ سُنَّةَ اللهِ فِي الَّذِينَ خَلَوْا۟ مِنْ قَبْلُ ۖ وَلَنْ تَجِدَ لِسُنَّةِ اللهِ تَبْدِيلًا ۝}$$

"(They will be) cursed wherever they are found, they will be seized and put to death. Such has been the way of Allah with those who passed away. And you will not find Allah's way changing." [Surah Ahzaab, verses 61-62]

To respect and honour the Messenger of Allah Ta'ala and to help and defend him are all incumbent duties on the entire ummah. Showing disrespect to him entails disrespect to the religion of Allah Ta'ala. Allah Ta'ala says:

$$\text{إِنَّ شَانِئَكَ هُوَ الْأَبْتَرُ ۝}$$

"Surely he who hates you, he will be cut off (from every good in this world and in the hereafter)." [Surah Kauthar, verse 3]

$$\text{وَإِنْ نَكَثُوٓا۟ أَيْمَانَهُمْ مِنْ بَعْدِ عَهْدِهِمْ وَطَعَنُوا۟ فِي دِينِكُمْ فَقَاتِلُوٓا۟ أَئِمَّةَ الْكُفْرِ ۙ إِنَّهُمْ لَآ أَيْمَانَ لَهُمْ لَعَلَّهُمْ يَنْتَهُونَ ۝ أَلَا تُقَاتِلُونَ قَوْمًا نَكَثُوٓا۟ أَيْمَانَهُمْ وَهَمُّوا۟ بِإِخْرَاجِ الرَّسُولِ وَهُمْ بَدَءُوكُمْ أَوَّلَ مَرَّةٍ ۚ أَتَخْشَوْنَهُمْ ۚ فَاللهُ أَحَقُّ أَنْ تَخْشَوْهُ إِنْ كُنْتُمْ مُؤْمِنِينَ ۝}$$

"If they break their oaths after having concluded a covenant, and criticise your religion, then fight against the ringleaders of disbelief – surely their oaths are nothing – so that they may desist. What! Will you not fight against a people who break their oaths, who are intent on expelling the Messenger, and attacked you first? Do you fear them? It is Allah whom you ought to fear more, if you have Imaan." [Surah Taubah, verses 12-13]

In other words, the believers should have no hesitation whatsoever in killing those who merely intended and tried to expel the Messenger of Allah ﷺ. The believers should not fear their outward strength and material power and means. They should fear Allah Ta'ala alone. They should be prepared to sacrifice their lives and wealth in the defence of Rasulullah ﷺ.

There were about 15-16 people regarding whom Rasulullah ﷺ had issued the command that they should be killed wherever they are found. Details concerning some of them are as follows:

1. **'Abdullah ibn Khatl:** He had become a Muslim. Rasulullah ﷺ appointed him as a tax collector and sent him in order to collect zakaah. A slave and a Christian were with him on the journey. On reaching a particular point on the journey, he asked the slave to prepare some food. The slave fell asleep. When he got up, 'Abdullah saw that the food was not prepared as yet. He was overtaken by

anger and killed the slave. He then realised that Rasulullah ﷺ would certainly kill him in retaliation for killing this slave. He therefore became an apostate, went to Makkah and joined the ranks of the disbelievers. He also took the camel of zakaah with him. He used to compile poetry in disgrace of Rasulullah ﷺ and order his slave women to sing these poems. He thus committed three crimes: (1) he shed innocent blood, (2) he became an apostate, (3) he compiled poetry in disgrace of Rasulullah ﷺ. When Makkah was conquered, 'Abdullah ibn Khatl went and held on to the veils of the Ka'bah. Rasulullah ﷺ was informed of this. He replied that he should be killed at that very place. Abu Barzah Aslami and Sa'd ibn Hurayth advanced and killed him. His head was chopped off at the place between the Black Stone and the Maqaam-e-Ibraaheem.

2. and 3. **Qurtana and Quraybah**: These two were the slave women of Ibn Khatl. They used to sing poems by night and day in which they would disgrace Rasulullah ﷺ. When the disbelievers of Makkah gathered in any assembly, alcohol would be passed around and these two women would sing these poems disgracing Rasulullah ﷺ. One of these women was killed. The other made peace with Rasulullah ﷺ and embraced Islam.

4. **Saarrah**: She was a slave woman belonging to someone from the Banu Muttalib. She also used to sing poems disgracing Rasulullah ﷺ. Some are of the opinion that she was killed while others state that she embraced Islam and that she lived till the caliphate of 'Umar ؓ. She was the woman who was carrying the letter of Haatib ibn Abi Balta'ah ؓ to Makkah.

5. **Huwayrith ibn Naqid**: He was a poet who used to compose poems disgracing Rasulullah ﷺ. He therefore had to be killed. He was killed by Ali ؓ.

6. **Maqis ibn Subaabah**: He had become a Muslim. In the battle of Zi Qird, a Christian killed his brother Hishaam, after incorrectly assuming the latter to be from among the enemies. Rasulullah ﷺ ordered that blood money be paid. After accepting the blood money, Maqis killed the Christian, became an apostate and proceeded to Makkah. On the conquest of Makkah, Rasulullah ﷺ announced that it was lawful to kill him. Abdullah Laythi killed him. While Maqis was going into the market place, he was captured and killed.

7. **'Abdullah ibn Sa'd ibn Abi Surh**: Previously he was one of the scribes of Rasulullah ﷺ. He used to record divine revelation for Rasulullah ﷺ. He became an apostate and joined the disbelievers. He was the foster brother of 'Usmaan ؓ. On the conquest of Makkah, he concealed himself in order to save his life. 'Usmaan ؓ seized him and presented him before Rasulullah ﷺ who, at that time, was taking the pledge of allegiance from

the people. 'Usmaan ؓ said: "O Messenger of Allah! 'Abdullah is present here. Take the pledge of allegiance from him as well." Rasulullah ﷺ remained silent for some time. Eventually, when 'Usmaan ؓ made this request several times, Rasulullah ﷺ took the pledge from him and he embraced Islam. After his life was saved, Rasulullah ﷺ said to the Sahaabah ؓ: "There was none among you who was sharp enough – when I held back my hand from accepting 'Abdullah's pledge, one of you should have got up and killed him." Someone replied: "O Messenger of Allah! Why did you not indicate to us (through some subtle indication) at that time?" He replied: "It is not permitted for a Prophet to make subtle indications."

On this occasion, 'Abdullah ibn Abi Surh embraced Islam with sincerity and became a good practising Muslim. He was appointed as the governor of Egypt and other places during the caliphate of 'Umar ؓ and 'Usmaan ؓ. During the caliphate of 'Usmaan ؓ, the conquest of Africa in 27 or 28 A.H. was largely due to him. When the spoils of war were distributed, each person received 3000 dinars. When there was much internal strife, after the death of 'Usmaan ؓ, 'Abdullah remained aloof from the conflict. He did not give his pledge of allegiance to either Ali ؓ or to Mu'aawiyah ؓ. He passed away in 'Asqalaan towards the latter part of Mu'aawiyah's ؓ caliphate. There is a strange incident concerning his death. One morning, he got up and made this supplication:

اللهم اجعل آخر عملي الصبح

"O Allah! Make it such that my last deed is in the morning."

He performed wudhu and read the Salaah. At the end of the Salaah, he turned to his right and was about to turn to his left when his soul left his body. To Allah we belong and to Him is our return. May Allah Ta'ala be pleased with him.

8. **'Ikramah ibn Abi Jahal**: He was also from among those people whom Rasulullah ﷺ had permitted to be killed on the conquest of Makkah. 'Ikramah was the son of Abu Jahal. Like his father, he was a bitter enemy of Rasulullah ﷺ. After the conquest of Makkah, he escaped to Yemen. His wife, Ummu Hakeem bint Haaris ibn Hishaam embraced Islam. She presented herself before Rasulullah ﷺ and asked him for sanctuary for her husband. The mercy to the worlds and the embodiment of pardon, Muhammad ﷺ, immediately acceded to her request for sanctuary for the son of Abu Jahal.

'Ikramah had escaped and reached the coast of Yemen. He boarded a ship and no sooner he did so, fierce winds encompassed the ship. 'Ikramah called out to Laat and 'Uzza (two idols) for help. The people on the ship told him that Laat and 'Uzza will be of no help to him now. He should rather call out to one Allah. 'Ikramah said: "If none but Allah can come to our help when we are out at sea, then you should understand well that even on land none but Allah can come to our help." He immediately made a true promise to Allah Ta'ala by saying:

اللّٰهم لك عهد إن عافيتنى مما أنا فيه أن آتى محمدا حتى أضع يدى فى يده فلأجدنه عفوا غفورا كريما

"O Allah! I make a promise to You that if You save me from this calamity, I will certainly present myself before Muhammad (ﷺ) and place my hand in his hand. I will certainly find him to be pardoning, forgiving and kind."

In the meantime, his wife also reached there and called out:

يا ابن عم جئتك من عند أبر الناس وأوصل الناس وخير الناس لا تهلك نفسك إنى قد استأمنت لك رسول الله صلى الله عليه وسلم

"O cousin! I have come to you from the most virtuous of people, from the person who is most mindful of maintaining family ties, and from the best of people. Do not destroy yourself. I have certainly sought sanctuary for you from the Messenger of Allah."

On hearing this, 'Ikramah joined Ummu Hakeem. On the way, he desired to have conjugal relations with her. She replied: "You are still a disbeliever while I am a Muslim." 'Ikramah said: "What a great force is controlling you." On saying this, he headed towards Makkah. Before he could even reach Makkah, Rasulullah ﷺ said to the Sahaabah رضى الله عنهم:

يأتيكم عكرمة مؤمنا فلا تسبوا أباه فإن سب الميت يؤذى الحى

"'Ikramah is going to come to you as a believer. You should therefore not speak ill of his father because speaking ill of a dead person causes hurt to the one who is living."

'Ikramah came in the presence of Rasulullah ﷺ and stood before him. His wife was with him. She was veiled and stood aside. He then said to Rasulullah ﷺ: "This is my wife. She has informed me that you have given sanctuary to me." Rasulullah ﷺ replied: "She has spoken the truth. I give you sanctuary." 'Ikramah said: "What do you invite towards?" Rasulullah ﷺ replied: "You should testify that there is none worthy of worship but Allah, He is one, there is no deity apart from Him, and that I am His Messenger, and that you establish Salaah and pay the zakaah." Rasulullah ﷺ enumerated a few other things as well. 'Ikramah replied:

قد كنت لا تدعو إلا إلى الخير وأمر حسن جميل قد كنت فينا يا
رسول الله قبل أن تدعونا وأنت أصدقنا حديثا وأبرنا

"Without doubt you only invite towards good and to matters that are good and liked. O Messenger of Allah! Even before commencing this call you were the most truthful of us in speech and the most virtuous of us."

He then said: "I bear witness that there is none worthy of worship and that Muhammad ﷺ is His servant and His Messenger."

After saying this, 'Ikramah رضي الله عنه said: "I make Allah Ta'ala and all those who are present over here witness that I am a Muslim, a Mujaahid and a Muhaajir." O Messenger of Allah ﷺ! I make this request to you that you seek forgiveness for me. Rasulullah ﷺ sought forgiveness for him. He then said: "O Messenger of Allah! I take an oath in the name of Allah Ta'ala that I am now going to spend double the amount in inviting towards Allah Ta'ala as opposed to what I spent in leading others away from Allah Ta'ala, and that I am now going to fight double the amount for the cause of Allah Ta'ala as opposed to what I fought against Allah Ta'ala and His Messenger ﷺ. I am now going to go to all those places where I had stopped people from going towards Allah Ta'ala and will now invite them towards Allah Ta'ala."

When Abu Bakr رضي الله عنه dispatched an army to fight the apostates, he sent one battalion under the command of 'Ikramah رضي الله عنه. In short, he spent the rest of his life in waging Jihaad against the enemies of Allah Ta'ala and His Messenger ﷺ. He was martyred during the caliphate of Abu Bakr رضي الله عنه in the battle of Ajnadayn. His body suffered more than seventy sword and arrow wounds.

Umme Salamah رضي الله عنها narrates that on one occasion Rasulullah ﷺ saw in a dream that there was a place for Abu Jahal in paradise. When 'Ikramah رضي الله عنه embraced Islam, Rasulullah ﷺ said to Umme Salamah رضي الله عنها that this is the meaning of that dream.

After embracing Islam, 'Ikramah رضي الله عنه was such that when he used to recite the Qur-aan, he would cry profusely and fall unconscious. He would repeatedly say: "This is the speech of my Rabb, this is the speech of my Rabb."

It is narrated in one Hadeeth that on the conquest of Makkah, a Muslim was martyred at the hands of 'Ikramah رضي الله عنه. When Rasulullah ﷺ was informed of this, he began smiling and said: "The killer and the one who was killed are both in Jannah."

Rasulullah ﷺ was making reference to the fact that although 'Ikramah is a disbeliever at present, he will soon embrace Islam.

9. **Hubar ibn al-Aswad**: His crime was that he used to impose many difficulties and hardships on the Muslims. When Rasulullah's ﷺ daughter, Zaynab

رَضِيَٱللَّٰهُعَنۡهَا, who was married to Abul-'Aas ibn Rabi', was emigrating from Makkah to Madinah, then Hubar ibn al-Aswad together with some of his cronies ambushed her and struck her with a spear on account of which she fell onto a rock. She was pregnant at that time. She lost her child and she herself passed away from the illness that followed this fall.

On the conquest of Makkah, Rasulullah صَلَّىٱللَّٰهُعَلَيۡهِوَسَلَّمَ announced that it was permissible to kill him. When Rasulullah صَلَّىٱللَّٰهُعَلَيۡهِوَسَلَّمَ returned from Ji'irraanah, Hubar presented himself before Rasulullah صَلَّىٱللَّٰهُعَلَيۡهِوَسَلَّمَ. The Sahaabah رَضِيَٱللَّٰهُعَنۡهُمۡ said: "O Messenger of Allah! Here is Hubar ibn al-Aswad. Rasulullah صَلَّىٱللَّٰهُعَلَيۡهِوَسَلَّمَ replied that he saw him. One of those who were present got up to strike Hubar. Rasulullah صَلَّىٱللَّٰهُعَلَيۡهِوَسَلَّمَ indicated to him to sit down. Hubar then stood up and said:

"Peace be upon you O Prophet of Allah. I bear witness that there is none worthy of worship but Allah. I bear witness that Muhammad صَلَّىٱللَّٰهُعَلَيۡهِوَسَلَّمَ *is the Messenger of Allah. I fled from you with the intention of joining the non-Arabs. I then remembered how you benefit others, how you maintain family relations, and how you pardon those who act ignorantly towards you. O Prophet of Allah! We were disbelievers. Allah Ta'ala guided us through you and saved us from destruction. So pardon me my ignorance and whatever pain I may have caused you. I admit my evil ways and acknowledge my sins." Rasulullah* صَلَّىٱللَّٰهُعَلَيۡهِوَسَلَّمَ *replied: "I have pardoned you. Allah Ta'ala has been kind to you in that He guided you towards Islam. Embracing Islam wipes out all previous sins."*

10. **Wahshi ibn Harb**: He was the one who had murdered Hamzah رَضِيَٱللَّٰهُعَنۡهُ. Details concerning him were given under the battle of Uhud. He fled to Taa'if. He then went to Madinah, presented himself before Rasulullah صَلَّىٱللَّٰهُعَلَيۡهِوَسَلَّمَ, embraced Islam and sought forgiveness for his sins.

When Abu Bakr رَضِيَٱللَّٰهُعَنۡهُ prepared an army in order to fight Musaylamah – the impostor – Wahshi also joined this army. The dagger which he used to kill Hamzah رَضِيَٱللَّٰهُعَنۡهُ was with him. He killed Musaylamah with that very dagger. He used to say: "It was with this dagger that I killed the best of people and with it I also killed the worst of people."

11. **Ka'b ibn Zuhayr**: He was a famous poet. He used to compose poems disgracing Rasulullah صَلَّىٱللَّٰهُعَلَيۡهِوَسَلَّمَ. He was also one of those people whose killing Rasulullah صَلَّىٱللَّٰهُعَلَيۡهِوَسَلَّمَ had permitted on the conquest of Makkah. He fled from Makkah. Later on, he came to Madinah and embraced Islam. He then wrote a collection of poems in praise of Rasulullah صَلَّىٱللَّٰهُعَلَيۡهِوَسَلَّمَ. This collection is popularly known as Banaat Su'aad.

12. **Haaris ibn Talaatil**: He used to speak ill of Rasulullah صَلَّىٱللَّٰهُعَلَيۡهِوَسَلَّمَ. Ali رَضِيَٱللَّٰهُعَنۡهُ killed him on the day of the conquest of Makkah.

13. **'Abdullah ibn Zib'ari**: He was an expert in poetry. He used to compose poems disgracing and belittling Rasulullah ﷺ. Sa'd ibn Musayyib ؓ says that Rasulullah ﷺ ordered that he be killed on the day of the conquest of Makkah. He fled to Najraan. He repented later, presented himself before Rasulullah ﷺ, embraced Islam, and said the following poem in forgiveness:

يا رسول المليك إن لسانى   رَاتِقٌ مَا فَتَقْتُ إِذْ أَنَا بُورُ

آمَنَ اللحمُ والعظام بِرَبِّي   ثم قلبي الشَّهِيْدُ أَنْتَ النَّذِيْرُ

"O Messenger of Allah! My tongue will make up for that harm which I caused you during my days of destruction and deviation. My flesh and bones have brought Imaan in my Sustainer. My heart then bears testimony that you are a warner (from Allah)."

14. **Hubayrah bint Abi Wahb Makhzumi**: She was also from among those poets who used to compose poems disgracing Rasulullah ﷺ. On the conquest of Makkah, she fled to Najraan and died there as a disbeliever.

15. **Hindah bint 'Utbah**: She was the wife of Abu Sufyaan ؓ. She was the very same woman who, in the battle of Uhud, removed the liver of Hamzah ؓ and chewed it. She is also among those women whom Rasulullah ﷺ ordered to be killed on the day of the conquest of Makkah. She had caused untold misery to Rasulullah ﷺ. She presented herself before Rasulullah ﷺ, sought forgiveness and embraced Islam. She returned to her house and broke all the idols to pieces saying to them: "By Allah! It was because of you that we were in delusion."

These fifteen people were those criminals who could not have been forgiven because their crimes were extremely serious. Those who admitted their mistakes and presented themselves in repentance were granted sanctuary. Those who remained in their rebellion were killed.

We shall now relate how some of the senior and noble people from the Quraysh embraced Islam after the conquest of Makkah.

Abu Quhaafah embraces Islam

This is the incident concerning the father of Abu Bakr ؓ embracing Islam. Rasulullah ﷺ was in the Sacred Masjid when Abu Bakr ؓ brought his old father before Rasulullah ﷺ and made him sit in front of him. Rasulullah ﷺ said:

$$\text{هلا تركت الشيخ فى بيته حتى اكون انا آتيه فيه}$$

"Why did you not leave this elderly person at home so that I would have gone personally to meet him?"

Abu Bakr رضى الله عنه replied:

$$\text{يا رسول الله هو احق ان يمشى اليك من ان تمشى اليه انت}$$

"O Messenger of Allah! It is more proper that he comes to you than your going to him."

Rasulullah ﷺ then passed his blessed hand on the chest of Abu Quhaafah and made him read the kalimah. The latter embraced Islam. Due to his old age, his entire facial hair and head were white. Rasulullah ﷺ told him to dye his hair but emphasised that he should not dye it black.

When Abu Quhaafah embraced Islam, Rasulullah ﷺ congratulated Abu Bakr رضى الله عنه. Abu Bakr رضى الله عنه replied: "O Messenger of Allah! I take an oath in the name of that Being who sent you with the truth that had Abu Taalib embraced Islam, I would have been more pleased."

Safwaan ibn Umayyah embraces Islam

Safwaan ibn Umayyah was among the Qurayshi leaders. He was well known for his generosity. His family excelled in its generosity and hospitality. His father, Umayyah ibn Khalaf, was killed in the battle of Badr. On the day when Makkah was conquered, Safwaan fled to Jeddah. His cousin, 'Umayr ibn Wahb, came before Rasulullah ﷺ and asked for sanctuary in his favour. Rasulullah ﷺ gave him sanctuary and in order to demonstrate this, he gave his turban or his sheet as well. 'Umayr went to Jeddah and brought him before Rasulullah ﷺ. Safwaan said to Rasulullah ﷺ: "'Umayr tells me that you have given me sanctuary." Rasulullah ﷺ replied in the affirmative. Safwaan said: "Give me respite for two months so that I may think over the matter." Rasulullah ﷺ replied: "I give you four month's respite." He did not embrace Islam immediately. However, he accompanied Rasulullah ﷺ for the battle of Hunayn. Rasulullah ﷺ borrowed some coats of armour from him. On reaching Hunayn, he said:

$$\text{كان يربنى رجل من قريش احب الى من ان يربنى رجل من هوازن}$$

"I would prefer someone from the Quraysh seeing to me than someone from the Hawaazin."

On returning from Hunayn, Rasulullah ﷺ gave him a large number of goats. On seeing this large number, Safwaan said: "I take an oath by Allah that none but a true Prophet can be so generous." On saying this, he embraced Islam.

Suhayl ibn ʿAmr embraces Islam

He was from among the noblemen and leaders of Makkah. He was popularly known by the title of Khateeb-e-Quraysh – the orator from the Quraysh. When he came as an ambassador on behalf of the Quraysh on the occasion of Hudaybiyah and Rasulullah ﷺ saw him coming, Rasulullah ﷺ addressed the Sahaabah رضى الله عنهم and said:

قد سهل من امركم

"Your matter has now become a bit easy."

On the day of the conquest of Makkah, Suhayl sent his brother ʿAbdullah to Rasulullah ﷺ to ask him for sanctuary. Rasulullah ﷺ gave him sanctuary and addressed the Sahaabah رضى الله عنهم saying:

من لقى سهيل بن عمرو فلا يحد اليه النظر فلعمرى ان سهيلا له عقل و شرف وما مثل سهيل يجهل الاسلام

"Whoever meets Suhayl should not stare at him in anger. I take an oath on my life that Suhayl is an intelligent and noble person. A person like Suhayl cannot remain ignorant of Islam."

Suhayl did not embrace Islam immediately. He joined Rasulullah ﷺ for the battle of Hunayn and embraced Islam at a place called Jiʿirraanah. He took an oath that just as he had joined the disbelievers in waging war against the Muslims, he will now join the Muslims in waging Jihaad against the disbelievers, and that the amount of wealth he spent on the disbelievers will now be spent on the Muslims.

On one occasion, there was a crowd of people at the door of ʿUmar رضى الله عنه. People were waiting to see him. Suhayl ibn ʿAmr, Abu Sufyaan and other Qurayshi leaders were also present. When the guard was informed of this, Suhayb رضى الله عنه, Bilal رضى الله عنه and other Sahaabah رضى الله عنهم who had participated in the Battle of Badr were called inside. Suhayl, Abu Sufyaan and the other Quraysh leaders were left outside. Abu Sufyaan said: "I have not come across a day like this. Slaves are called inside while no attention is paid to us." The intelligent and wise reply that Suhayl gave is worthy of being inscribed on the hearts of people. Suhayl addressed Abu Sufyaan and the other Qurayshi leaders saying:

"O people! I take an oath by Allah that I see displeasure and anger on your faces. Instead of showing anger at others, you should be angry with your own selves. Those people were invited towards Islam and so were you. On hearing this call, they hastened towards it while you turned away and remained behind. I take an oath that the honour and virtue that these people have is far more superior than the honour of gaining entrance in this door (of 'Umar رضى الله عنه) over which you are so envious of. O people! These people have surpassed you as you can see right before your eyes. Now there is no way that you can achieve this honour and virtue. If there is any way of making up for this loss, it is only through waging Jihaad in the cause of Allah Ta'ala and laying your lives in the path of Allah Ta'ala. You should prepare for this. It is not unlikely that Allah Ta'ala will bless you with the bounty of martyrdom."

Suhayl completed his heart-rending speech, dusted himself and immediately stood up to wage Jihaad in the cause of Allah Ta'ala. He left for Syria together with his family members in order to fight the Romans. He was martyred in the battle of Yarmuk. According to some, he passed away in the 'Amwaas plague. Nevertheless, he achieved his goal. Passing away in a plague is also a death of martyrdom.

'Utbah and Mu'tab embrace Islam

When Rasulullah ﷺ entered Makkah in order to conquer it, he asked me: "Where are your two nephews, 'Utbah and Mu'tab, the two sons of Abu Jahal? I do not see them." I replied: "They have also concealed themselves with those Qurayshi leaders who concealed themselves." Rasulullah ﷺ said: "Bring them to me." In accordance with his instruction, I rode to a place called 'Urnah and brought both of them to Rasulullah ﷺ. He presented Islam to them. They both embraced Islam and pledged allegiance to him. Rasulullah ﷺ then stood up, held their hands and took them close to the door of the Ka'bah. He remained in dua for quite some time. He then returned with his face beaming with happiness. I said to him: "O Messenger of Allah! May Allah Ta'ala keep you happy forever for I see your face beaming with happiness." He replied: "I made dua to my Sustainer that He should give these two sons of my uncle, 'Utbah and Mu'tab to me. Allah Ta'ala has now given both of them to me."

Mu'aawiyah embraces Islam

Some scholars are of the opinion that Mu'aawiyah رضى الله عنه embraced Islam on the conquest of Makkah. However, the more correct opinion is that he did so on the occasion of the peace treaty of Hudaybiyah and that he concealed his Islam until the conquest of Makkah.

The Mother of the believers, Umme Habibah bint Abi Sufyaan ﷺ, was the sister of Mu'aawiyah ﷺ. A mother's brother is known as your maternal uncle. Mu'aawiyah ﷺ was thus the maternal uncle of the believers. Just as it is incumbent on a believer to love the family and close relatives of Rasulullah ﷺ, it is also incumbent to love the in-laws and other such relatives of Rasulullah ﷺ. Abu Sufyaan ﷺ was the father of his wife, Umme Habibah ﷺ. Mu'aawiyah ﷺ was her brother. To love them is an incumbent duty. It is prohibited to bear malice and enmity towards them. Whatever they may have done before embracing Islam is all forgiven. It is also prohibited to mention and enumerate all that they did before embracing Islam.

Small battalions are sent to destroy idols

After the conquest of Makkah, Rasulullah ﷺ remained in this city for about 15 days. The idols that were in the Ka'bah were destroyed and this announcement was made:

من كان يؤمن بالله واليوم الاخر فلا يدع فى بيته صنما

"Whoever believes in Allah and the last day should not have any idol in his house."

When Makkah was purified of all idols and they were all destroyed, small groups were sent to the outskirts and surrounding areas to destroy all the other idols.

'Uzza and Suwa' are destroyed

On 25 Ramadhaan 8 A.H. Khaalid ibn Waleed ﷺ was sent with a group of 30 riders to Nakhlah in order to destroy the idol by the name of 'Uzza. This place was one nights' journey from Makkah. 'Amr ibn 'Aas ﷺ was sent to destroy the idol named Suwa' which was about three miles from Makkah. When 'Amr ﷺ reached that place, the custodian of this idol asked him the reason for which he came. He replied: "I am following the orders of Rasulullah ﷺ to destroy this idol." On hearing this, the custodian said: "You will never be able to do this. The god of Suwa' will personally prevent you from doing this." 'Amr ﷺ replied: "How sad that you are still holding on to such baseless beliefs. Can this idol hear and see that it will be able to stop me?" On saying this, he struck it with one blow and reduced it to pieces. He then addressed the custodian saying: "Did you see what happened?" On seeing this, the custodian immediately embraced Islam.

Manaat is destroyed

On the 26th of Ramadhaan, Sa'd ibn Zaid Ash-hali was sent at the head of 20 riders in order to destroy the idol named Manaat which was in the town of Mushallal. In short, the entire blessed month of Ramadhaan was spent in purifying the land of Allah from the filth of disbelief and polytheism.

In the month of Shawwaal, 350 Muhaajireen and Ansaar under the command of Khaalid ibn Waleed ﷺ were sent to the Banu Juzaymah in order to invite them towards Islam. These people used to live on the banks of a lake called Ghamisa near the town of Yalamlam. Khaalid ibn Waleed ﷺ invited them towards Islam. These people, out of their excitement, could not clearly state that they had already embraced Islam. Khaalid ibn Waleed ﷺ did not consider what they said to be sufficient and therefore killed some of them and captured some of them. When he eventually went to Rasulullah ﷺ and informed him of what had happened, Rasulullah ﷺ raised his hands and said the following words two times:

$$\text{اللّٰهم إنى أبرأ إليك مما صنع خالد}$$

"O Allah! I absolve myself from what Khaalid did."

Rasulullah ﷺ then gave some money to Ali ﷺ and sent him to the Banu Juzaymah in order to pay them blood money. Ali ﷺ went and paid this money. When he was fully satisfied that he had paid every person his due, he distributed the left over money among them. When he returned to Rasulullah ﷺ, he related the entire incident to him. Rasulullah ﷺ was extremely happy with what he heard and said:

$$\text{أَصَبْتَ وَأَحْسَنْتَ}$$

"You acted correctly and you did well."

Chapter 24

The Battle of Hunayn - Shawwaal 8 A.H.

Hunayn is the name of a place between Makkah and Taa'if where the Hawaazin and Saqeef tribes lived. These tribes were very warlike by nature and very good archers. After the conquest of Makkah, it crossed the minds of these tribes that Rasulullah ﷺ might attack them. They therefore conferred with each other and decided to attack the Muslims before they could attack them. Their leader, Maalik ibn 'Auf Nasri left with an army of 20 000 in order to attack the Muslims.

Darid ibn Sammah, although being unable to move about because of his extreme old age, was still taken with because of his experience, expertise, and military skills. Moreover, they could consult with him on various matters.

Maalik ibn 'Auf emphasised upon all the soldiers that each one should bring his wife and children with so that he would fight with zeal and no one would leave his wife and children behind and flee from the battlefield. When they reached the valley of Autaas, Darid asked about the identity of this place. The people replied that it was the valley of Autaas. Darid replied that this place was extremely suitable and appropriate for battle. The ground is neither too hard, nor too soft whereby the feet would sink in. He then asked:

مالى اسمع رغاء البعير ونهاق الحمير ويعار الشاء وبكاء الصغير

"What is this that I hear the sounds of the camels, the braying of asses, the bleating of sheep and the crying of children?"

The people replied that Maalik ibn 'Auf had instructed them to bring their wives, children, animals, etc. so that the people would not flee from the battlefields. On hearing this, Darid said: "This is a serious mistake. Do those who are defeated ever take back anything? Nothing but spears and swords are of use in battle. If you are defeated, it would be a cause of disgrace and humiliation for all your families. It would be better to keep all the families behind the actual army. If we are victorious, we would all meet again. If we are defeated, our families will be safe from the attacks of the enemy."

However, due to his youthful enthusiasm, Maalik ibn 'Auf did not give due regard to this advice. Instead, he said: "I swear by Allah that I will not change my decision. This person has lost his mind due to old age. If the Hawaazin and Saqeef follow my decision, well and good. If not, I will commit suicide right now." All the people replied that they were with him.

When Rasulullah ﷺ heard of these conditions and circumstances, he sent 'Abdullah ibn Abi Hadr to establish and investigate the true situation. 'Abdullah learnt all the conditions from a distant place and returned to inform Rasulullah ﷺ of all their military preparations. After establishing all the facts, Rasulullah ﷺ also made preparations for war. He borrowed 100 coats of armour from Safwaan ibn Umayyah.

Rasulullah ﷺ left Makkah on the 8th of Shawwaal 8 A.H. with 12000 men and headed towards Hunayn. Ten thousand were those devoted followers who joined him from Madinah. Some non Muslims also joined him.

When this fully equipped army of 12000 advanced towards Hunayn, a person remarked:

لن نغلب اليوم من قلة

"Today we will not be defeated because of small numbers."

This remark, filled with pride and ostentation, was disliked by Allah Ta'ala. In this world of means, small numbers are also a cause of defeat. Therefore, on seeing this large number, some Sahaabah ؓ made this statement that they will not be defeated because of small numbers. In other words, if they are defeated on this occasion, it will not be because of small numbers. Rather it will be through the decision of Allah Ta'ala. Victory and help is from Him alone. However, Allah Ta'ala did not like this statement of theirs. And instead of victory, they first had to see the face of defeat. Allah Ta'ala says in the Holy Qur-aan:

وَيَوْمَ حُنَيْنٍ ۙ إِذْ أَعْجَبَتْكُمْ كَثْرَتُكُمْ فَلَمْ تُغْنِ عَنكُمْ شَيْئًا وَضَاقَتْ عَلَيْكُمُ الْأَرْضُ بِمَا رَحُبَتْ ثُمَّ وَلَّيْتُم مُّدْبِرِينَ ۝ ثُمَّ أَنزَلَ اللَّهُ سَكِينَتَهُ عَلَىٰ رَسُولِهِ وَعَلَى الْمُؤْمِنِينَ وَأَنزَلَ جُنُودًا لَّمْ تَرَوْهَا وَعَذَّبَ الَّذِينَ كَفَرُوا ۚ وَذَٰلِكَ جَزَاءُ الْكَافِرِينَ ۝

"And on the day of Hunayn when you prided yourselves on your large numbers, but they availed you nothing. The earth closed in upon you despite its vastness. You then turned about retreating. Allah then sent down His assurance to His Messenger and to the believers, and He sent down armies which you did not see, and He

punished the disbelievers. Such is the punishment of the rejecters."
[Surah Taubah, verses 25-26]

The Muslim army reached the valley of Hunayn on Tuesday evening. The Hawaazin and Saqeef tribes were lying in ambush. Maalik ibn 'Auf had, at the beginning, ordered them to break the sheaths of their swords and that when the Muslim army approaches, the entire army of 20 000 should attack the Muslims at once. When the Muslim army started to cross that area in the darkness of the morning, 20 000 swords suddenly attacked them. This completely scattered the Muslim army. Only 10-12 loyal and devoted companions remained next to Rasulullah ﷺ. Abu Bakr, 'Umar, Ali, 'Abbaas, Fadl ibn 'Abbaas, Usaamah ibn Zaid رضي الله عنه and a few others remained at his side. 'Abbaas رضي الله عنه was holding on to the reins of Rasulullah's ﷺ donkey while Abu Sufyaan ibn Haaris رضي الله عنه was holding on to the stirrup.

Shaybah ibn 'Usmaan ibn Abi Talhah said: "Today I will avenge my father from Muhammad." His father was killed in the battle of Uhud. When he advanced towards Rasulullah ﷺ, he immediately fell unconscious and was unable to reach him. He realised that he was prevented by Allah from reaching Rasulullah ﷺ. He embraced Islam later on.

In short, when the Hawaazin and Saqeef tribes attacked from their places of ambush and began raining down arrows on the Muslims from all sides, the Muslims lost their footing. Only the special companions of Rasulullah ﷺ remained with him. Rasulullah ﷺ announced three times: "O people! Come towards me. I am the Messenger of Allah. I am Muhammad ibn 'Abdillah."

أنا النبى لا كذب   أنا ابن عبد المطلب

I am the true Prophet. (The promises of help, victory, my protection and defence that have been made to me are certainly true. There is no possibility of going back on all this.) I am the son of 'Abdul Muttalib.

'Abbaas رضي الله عنه had a very loud voice. Rasulullah ﷺ ordered him to call out to the Muhaajireen and the Ansaar. He announced:

يا معشر الأنصار يا أصحاب السمرة

"O group of Ansaar! O those who had pledged their allegiance beneath the acacia tree."

No sooner they heard this call, they all turned and rushed towards Rasulullah ﷺ and within a few minutes they all rallied around him. Rasulullah ﷺ ordered them to attack the disbelievers. When the heavy battle commenced and heated up, Rasulullah ﷺ took a handful of soil and threw it towards the disbelievers and said:

شاهت الوجوه

"May these faces be disfigured."

It is stated in another narration of Muslim that after throwing the handful of soil, he said:

انهزموا وربّ محمد

"By the oath of the Sustainer of Muhammad, they are defeated."

There was no one to whom some of this soil did not reach. Within a moment, the enemy faltered. Many fled the battlefield while many others were captured.

On the one hand, Rasulullah ﷺ threw the handful of soil while on the other hand, the brave soldiers of Islam placed their trust solely on the help and assistance of Allah Ta'ala and attacked the enemy. Within a few moments the tables turned. Despite their strength and power, the soldiers of the Hawaazin tottered and the Muslims began capturing them. Seventy of them were killed and numerous others were captured. A huge amount of booty came into Muslim hands.

Jubayr ibn Mut'im رضى الله عنه narrates: "Even before the defeat and subjugation of the Hawaazin, I saw a black sheet descending from the sky and falling between us and our enemies. Black ants immediately came out from that sheet and spread throughout the valley. I had no doubt that they were angels. No sooner they descended, the enemy was defeated.

After the defeat, the commander of the Hawaazin and Saqeef, Maalik ibn 'Auf, fled with a group of followers and sought refuge in Taa'if. Duryad ibn Summah and others fled to Autaas and sought refuge there. Others fled to Nakhlah. Rasulullah ﷺ sent Abu 'Aamir Ash'ari رضى الله عنه, the uncle of Abu Musa Ash'ari رضى الله عنه, with a small battalion to Autaas. When the battle ensued, Durayd was killed at the hands of Rabi'ah ibn Rufay' رضى الله عنه.

Salamah ibn Durayd struck Abu 'Aamir Ash'ari رضى الله عنه with an arrow in his knee. He was consequently martyred. Abu Musa Ash'ari رضى الله عنه went forward and took up the flag of Islam. He fought with much courage and valour and killed the one who killed his uncle. Allah Ta'ala eventually gave victory to the Muslims.

At the time when Abu 'Aamir رضى الله عنه was dying, he said to his nephew: "O my nephew! Convey my Salaam to Rasulullah ﷺ and ask him to seek forgiveness for me." Abu Musa رضى الله عنه says: "I went to Rasulullah ﷺ, narrated the entire incident to him and conveyed my uncle's greeting and message. Rasulullah ﷺ immediately asked for water for wudhu, he made wudhu, raised his hands and made the following dua:

$$\text{اَللّٰهُمَّ اغْفِرْ لِعُبَيْدِ أَبِي عَامِرٍ. اَللّٰهُمَّ اجْعَلْهُ يَوْمَ الْقِيَامَةِ فَوْقَ كَثِيرٍ مِنْ خَلْقِكَ مِنَ النَّاسِ}$$

"O Allah! Forgive 'Ubayd Abi 'Aamir. O Allah! Make him above many of Your creation on the Day of Resurrection."

Abu Musa ؓ says: "I said: O Messenger of Allah! Make dua in my favour as well." Rasulullah ﷺ said:

$$\text{اَللّٰهُمَّ اغْفِرْ لِعَبْدِ اللهِ بْنِ قَيْسٍ ذَنْبَهُ وَأَدْخِلْهُ يَوْمَ الْقِيَامَةِ مُدْخَلًا كَرِيمًا}$$

"O Allah! Forgive 'Abdullah ibn Qays his sins and admit him into a noble place on the Day of Resurrection."

The siege of Taa'if

Rasulullah ﷺ issued the order that the captives and booty of Hunayn should be gathered at Ji'irraanah. He then headed towards Taa'if. Before leaving for Taa'if, he sent Tufayl ibn 'Amr Dusi and a few others to go and burn down an idol by the name of Zul Kaffayn. Tufayl ibn 'Amr joined him four days later in Taa'if. He brought a type of tank and a catapult with him.

Maalik ibn 'Auf, the commander of the Hawaazin, had reached Taa'if before Rasulullah ﷺ and locked himself in the fort that was situated there. He had stocks of grain and other edibles that would be sufficient for several years. On reaching Taa'if, Rasulullah ﷺ laid siege to this town and rained rocks onto it by using the catapult. The disbelievers placed archers on the fort who shot at the Muslims with such ferocity that many of them were wounded and 12 of them were martyred. Khaalid ibn Waleed ؓ challenged them to come forward for a hand combat but they replied that they had no need to get down from the fort because they had grain for several years. Only when all this food was used up, will they come down and fight with their swords. The Muslims sat in the tanks trying to penetrate the fort. The enemy began throwing hot steel from above. This forced the Muslims to retreat. On seeing this, Rasulullah ﷺ ordered that the orchards be chopped down. The people in the fort asked him in the name of Allah Ta'ala and their family ties that he should leave the orchards. Rasulullah ﷺ replied: "I am leaving them for the sake of Allah Ta'ala and your family ties." An announcement was then made near the wall of the fort that whichever slave comes down, he will be freed. Consequently, 12-13 slaves came down. During this time, Rasulullah ﷺ saw in a dream that a cup of milk was given to him. A fowl came and pecked at it, causing the cup to break. Rasulullah ﷺ related this dream to Abu Bakr ؓ. He replied: "It is most likely that this fort will not be conquered at present." Rasulullah ﷺ called for Naufal ibn Mu'aawiyah Daylami ؓ and asked him for his opinion in this regard. He replied: "O Messenger of Allah! The fox is in its den. If we remain, we will catch it. If we leave it, it will not cause any harm to you."

'Umar ؓ came and said: "O Prophet of Allah! You should make dua against them." Rasulullah ﷺ replied: "Allah Ta'ala did not permit me to do this." 'Umar ؓ asked: "Then what is the need for us to fight them? You ordered us to depart (for war) and while you were moving, you said:

اللّٰهم اهد ثقيفا وائت بهم

'O Allah! Guide the Saqeef and bring them as Muslims to me.'"

Consequently, this fort was automatically conquered later on. All those present embraced Islam. Their commander, Maalik ibn 'Auf himself came before Rasulullah ﷺ and embraced Islam.

The booty of Hunayn is distributed

After leaving Taa'if, Rasulullah ﷺ reached Ji'irraanah on the 5th of Zul Qa'dah. It was at this place that all the booty was gathered. The booty comprised the following: 6 000 prisoners of war, 24 000 camels, 40 000 goats and 4 000 ounces of silver. Rasulullah ﷺ remained there for more than 10 days waiting for the Hawaazin in the hope that they would come to free their relatives, children and women. However, when no one came even after 10-12 days, he began distributing the booty among the rightful recipients.

After the booty was distributed, a delegation comprising of nine people from the Hawaazin came to Rasulullah ﷺ. They embraced Islam and pledged their allegiance at the hands of Rasulullah ﷺ. They then requested that their wealth, wives and children be returned to them. Rasulullah's ﷺ foster mother, Halimah Sa'diyyah ؓ was also from this tribe. The spokesman of this tribe, Zuhayr, stood up and said: "O Messenger of Allah! Your maternal aunts, paternal aunts and those who fed you in your infancy are among these prisoners. If we had such relationships with some king or ruler, he would have been extremely kind to us. Your status is far higher than all of them. The calamity that has afflicted us is not concealed from you. Be kind to us and Allah will be kind to you." He then said the following lines:

امنن علينا رسول الله فى كرم   فإنك المرء نرجوه وننتظر

"Shower us, O Messenger of Allah, with your kindness. Surely you are a person from whom we hope and expect this kindness."

Rasulullah ﷺ replied: "I waited for you (but you did not come). The booty has now been distributed. You may choose one of the two, the prisoners or the wealth." They replied: "You have given us a choice with regard to our wealth and progeny. We choose our progeny. We will not ask you anything further regarding the camels and goats."

Rasulullah ﷺ said: "Whatever has come to my family and to the Banu Haashim and Banu Muttalib, is all yours. However, whatever has gone into the share of the other Muslims, you should stand up after the Zuhr Salaah and speak to the people. I will intercede on your behalf." Consequently, the orators from the Hawaazin delegation delivered very eloquent speeches after the Zuhr Salaah and requested the Muslims to set free their prisoners. Rasulullah ﷺ then stood up to deliver a speech. He first praised and glorified Allah Ta'ala and then said: "These brothers of yours from the Hawaazin have embraced Islam. I have given the share that came to me and my family to them. I consider it appropriate that other Muslims also return their prisoners to them. Whoever does this voluntarily and willingly, it will be better. If not, I am prepared to pay the recompense thereof later on." They all replied that they would return them voluntarily and willingly. In so doing, 6 000 prisoners were immediately freed.

From among these prisoners of war was Rasulullah's ﷺ foster sister by the name of Shima'. When the people captured her, she informed them that she was the sister of the Messenger of Allah. The people brought her before Rasulullah ﷺ in order to verify this claim. She said: "O Muhammad ﷺ! I am your sister." She then showed him the proof thereof that when he was young, he had bitten her. She then showed him the mark. Rasulullah ﷺ recognised it and welcomed her. He offered her a shawl on which to sit. Rasulullah's ﷺ eyes were filled with tears out of extreme happiness. He said to her: "If you wish, you may live with me with respect and honour. If you wish, you may return to your tribe." She replied that she would like to return to her tribe. She embraced Islam. When she was departing, Rasulullah ﷺ gave her some camels, goats, three male slaves and one female slave.

The senior Quraysh who embraced Islam on the conquest of Makkah were still weak in their faith. Imaan was not firmly embedded in their hearts as yet. In the Qur-aan they are referred to as, "those whose hearts are to be reconciled". Rasulullah ﷺ gave them a large share during the distribution of the booty. Some received 100 camels, others 200, while yet others received 300.

In short, whatever was given, was given to the noblemen from the Quraysh. The Ansaar were not given anything. It is for this reason that some youngsters from the Ansaar said: "The Messenger of Allah Ta'ala gave the Quraysh while he did not give anything to us, whereas it is our swords that are still dripping with their blood." Others said: "We are called to help during times of difficulties, but the booty is distributed amongst other people." When Rasulullah ﷺ heard this, he gathered the Ansaar and addressed them saying:

"O Ansaar! What is this that I am hearing?" The Ansaar replied: "O Messenger of Allah! None of our leading and senior people said this. Rather, it was some youngsters." Rasulullah ﷺ said: "O group of Ansaar! Were you not astray when Allah Ta'ala guided you through me? You were enemies to each other and Allah Ta'ala united you through me. You were poor and destitute, and Allah Ta'ala gave you prosperity through me." The Ansaar replied: "Whatever you said is absolutely true and correct. Without doubt, Allah Ta'ala and His Messenger have been extremely kind to us." Rasulullah ﷺ said: "You can reply to my statements by saying: 'O Muhammad! When people rejected you, it was we who believed in you. When you were without any helpers, it was we who came to your assistance. When you were without any support and base, it was we who gave you refuge. When you were poor, it was we who saw to your needs.' O group of Ansaar! Are you grieving over the fact that I gave a little wealth and a few dirhams of this world which have no real value (compared to the treasures of the hereafter) to a few people merely to reconcile their hearts towards Islam, and that I left you out because I have full confidence on your Islam, Imaan, conviction and dedication?"

Rasulullah ﷺ then said: "The Quraysh have been afflicted by the difficulties and hardships of imprisonment (in other words, in comparison to the Muslims, they were afflicted by numerous physical and monetary hardships). I therefore wish to make up for this loss by giving them something, and I wish to reconcile their hearts to Islam. In the different battles, their families and close relatives were killed or imprisoned, and they had to face various types of hardships and humiliations. Allah Ta'ala safeguarded you from all this. It is therefore appropriate to give such people from the booty in order to reconcile their hearts. On the other hand, you are believers. You are blessed with the unique and eternal wealth of Imaan and conviction. What! Are you not pleased that people take camels and goats and return to their homes while you take the Messenger of Allah with you? I take an oath by that being (Allah) in whose control is my life, that had the emigration not been something that was destined by Allah Ta'ala, I would have also been from the Ansaar. If the people follow a particular mountain pass and the Ansaar follow a different mountain pass, I will follow the mountain pass that is followed by the Ansaar. O Allah! Show Your mercy and kindness to the Ansaar and their progenies."

No sooner had Rasulullah ﷺ said this, the Ansaar began screaming out and crying to such an extent that their beards became wet. They said: "We are completely happy with this distribution that Allah Ta'ala and His Messenger ﷺ fall into our lot." The people dispersed thereafter.

Umrah Ji'irraanah

On the 8th of Zul Qa'dah, Rasulullah ﷺ left Ji'irraanah for Makkah with the intention of performing Umrah. On reaching there, he appointed 'Itaab ibn Usayd رضي الله عنه as the governor of Makkah and left Mu'aaz ibn Jabal رضي الله عنه with him for the purpose of teaching him Islam. After two months and 16 days, Rasulullah ﷺ returned to Madinah on 27 Zul Qa'dah.

The prohibition of mut'ah[2]

When Rasulullah ﷺ left Autaas for Umrah, he stood at the door of the Ka'bah, held its two sides and announced: "Mut'ah has been made unlawful till the Day of Resurrection." Since this announcement was made at night and few people were present there, everyone did not hear this announcement properly. It is for this reason that some people unwittingly committed mut'ah after this announcement as well. Rasulullah ﷺ again announced its unlawfulness during the battle of Tabuk. Later on, during the caliphate of 'Umar رضي الله عنه, some people committed mut'ah also due to lack of knowledge. On hearing about this, he stood on the mimbar and said: "The Prophet ﷺ made mut'ah unlawful. It was committed several times during his time due to lack of knowledge. He did not take anyone to task for this. The unlawfulness of mut'ah is firmly established. Now, after this announcement, if anyone commits mut'ah, I will implement the punishment of adultery on him." After this announcement of 'Umar رضي الله عنه, mut'ah came to an end.

Other incidents that took place in this year (8 A.H.)

1. Itaab ibn Usayd رضي الله عنه made the Muslims perform the Haj as was performed by the Arabs.
2. In the month of Zul Hijjah, Ibraaheem رضي الله عنه, the son of Rasulullah ﷺ was born from Maariyah Qibtiyyah رضي الله عنها.
3. Rasulullah ﷺ appointed 'Amr ibn 'Aas رضي الله عنه as a collector of zakaah and sent him towards 'Ummaan (Oman) for this purpose.
4. Rasulullah ﷺ sent Ka'b ibn 'Umayr رضي الله عنه towards Zat Ittila', a place in Syria, to invite them towards Islam. Fifteen people accompanied him. The

---

[2] Temporary marriage

people of that place killed all the Muslims except for one, who saved himself and returned to Madinah.

The appointment of governors

After the conquest of Makkah, almost the entire Arabian Peninsula came under Islamic control. A need was therefore felt for the organisation of an Islamic state. In order to establish the control of Islam, Rasulullah ﷺ appointed different governors for the different areas. Baazaan ibn Saasaan was appointed as the governor of Yemen. He was originally the governor of Yemen on behalf of Khusroes. When the latter was killed, Baazaan embraced Islam. Rasulullah ﷺ therefore maintained him as the governor of Yemen. He held this post till the day he passed away. When he passed away, his son, Shahr ibn Baazaan, was appointed as the governor of San'a, the capital of Yemen. When Shahr passed away, Khaalid ibn Sa'eed ibn 'Aas Umawi was appointed governor. Ziyaad ibn Labid Ansaari was appointed governor of Hadramaut. Abu Musa Ash'ari ؓ was appointed governor of Zabid and Mu'aaz ibn Jabal ؓ was appointed governor of the city Jand which was in Yemen. Abu Sufyaan ibn Harb ؓ was appointed governor of Najraan. His son, Yazeed was appointed governor of Timami. 'Itaab ibn Usayd ؓ was appointed governor of Makkah. Ali ؓ was appointed the judge of Yemen.

The 9th year A.H.

In the month of Muharram 9 A.H., Rasulullah ﷺ despatched zakaat collectors to different areas and tribes.

The expedition of 'Uyaynah ibn Hisn Fazaari

Rasulullah ﷺ sent Bishr ibn Sufyaan 'Adawi in order to collect zakaat. The people were prepared to pay the zakaat but the Banu Tameem created obstacles and said: "By Allah! Not a single camel will leave this place." They unsheathed their swords and were prepared to fight. On seeing this, Bishr ؓ returned. Rasulullah ﷺ therefore appointed 'Uyaynah ibn Hisn Fazaari over 50 people and sent them to a place called Suqyaa, where the Banu Tameem lived. This place is 17 miles from Juhfah. On reaching there at night, they launched an attack. Eleven men, 21 women and 30 children were captured and brought to Madinah. The Banu Tameem were forced to send a delegation of 10 people to Rasulullah ﷺ. The following personalities were also among these 10 people: 'Attaar ibn Haajib, Zibirqaan, Qays ibn 'Aasim and Aqra' ibn Haabis. When they reached

Madinah, they stood behind the rooms of Rasulullah ﷺ and called out to him: "O Muhammad! Come outside so that we may compete with you in poetry. Our praise is a source of embellishment and our criticism is a source of blemish." Rasulullah ﷺ replied: "This is the prerogative of Allah Ta'ala alone. As for me, I am neither a poet nor have I been commanded to be boastful." The following verses were revealed in this regard:

اِنَّ الَّذِيْنَ يُنَادُوْنَكَ مِنْ وَّرَآءِ الْحُجُرَاتِ اَكْثَرُهُمْ لَا يَعْقِلُوْنَ ۝ وَلَوْ اَنَّهُمْ صَبَرُوْا حَتّٰى تَخْرُجَ اِلَيْهِمْ لَكَانَ خَيْرًا لَّهُمْ ۚ وَ اللّٰهُ غَفُوْرٌ رَّحِيْمٌ ۝

"Surely those who call out to you from behind the rooms, most of them do not have intelligence. Had they remained patient until you went out to them, it would have been better for them. Allah is forgiving, merciful." [Surah Hujuraat, verse 4-5]

Rasulullah ﷺ eventually came out and performed the Zuhr Salaah. On completing the Salaah, he sat in the courtyard of the Masjid. The delegation said to him: "We have come to compete with you in self praise. Permit our poet and orator to recite." Rasulullah ﷺ replied: "He has my permission."

The speech of 'Ataarid ibn Haajib

The orator and speaker from the Banu Tameem, 'Ataarid ibn Haajib, stood up and delivered this speech:

"All praise is due to Allah who has been kind to us. It is He who made us kings and gave us plenty of wealth with which we do good. He made us the most honourable of the people of the east, the largest in number, and the most in possessions. So who among people are like us? Are we not the leaders of people and the most superior of them? Whoever wants to compete with us should enumerate the qualities that we enumerated. Had we wished, we would have said much more. However, we feel shy to say too much. And we know this very well. I am saying this at present. I challenge you to say something similar to what I said or better than what I said."

After delivering this speech, Ataarid sat down. Rasulullah ﷺ asked Saabit ibn Qays ibn Shammaas Ansaari ؓ to give a reply. Saabit ibn Qays ؓ immediately stood up and said:

"All praise is due to Allah who created the heavens and the earth and promulgated His laws therein. His knowledge encompasses everything. All that is existing is doing so solely out of His grace. It is out of His power that He made us kings and sent His best creation as a Messenger, who surpasses the entire creation in his lineage, who is the most truthful of them in speech, and the most superior in his nobility. He revealed to him a Book and made him a trust to the entire creation. He is thus the most beloved to Allah from the entire creation. He then invited the people to believe in him. The Muhaajireen from his people and his close relatives believed in him. They have the best lineage from people, they enjoy the most distinction, and they have the best deeds. Then we (the Ansaar) were the first to respond to Allah Ta'ala when the Messenger of Allah invited us. We are thus the helpers of Allah and the ministers of the Messenger of Allah Ta'ala. We wage Jihaad against the people till they believe in Allah. Whoever believes in Allah and His Messenger ﷺ, his wealth and life is safeguarded. Whoever rejects, we fight him forever for the sake of Allah. And it is very easy for us to kill him. This is what I have to say. I seek forgiveness from Allah for myself, the believing men and the believing women. Peace be upon you."

After this, Zibirqaan ibn Badr sang a poem in praise of his people. Rasulullah ﷺ asked Hassaan رضي الله عنه to give a reply to it. The latter immediately responded by saying a poem. Aqra' ibn Haabis (who was part of the Saqeef delegation) said: "I take an oath by Allah that your speaker is better than ours, and your poet is better than ours." They all then embraced Islam. Rasulullah ﷺ gave them some gifts and returned their prisoners to them.

The expedition of Waleed ibn 'Uqbah ibn Abi Mu'eet

Rasulullah ﷺ sent Waleed ibn 'Uqbah رضي الله عنه to the Bani Mustaliq tribe in order to collect the different charities. On hearing about this, these people came out very happily, and arranged themselves in military fashion in order to welcome Waleed. There had been a lengthy enmity since pre-Islamic times between Waleed's family and the Bani Mustaliq. When Waleed saw them from a distance, he assumed that because of this old enmity, these people have come out in order to fight him. Therefore, Waleed turned back there and then. He went and informed Rasulullah ﷺ that these people have become apostates and they refused to pay the zakaah. Rasulullah ﷺ became surprised at hearing this news. He was still pondering over this when this news reached the Bani Mustaliq. They immediately sent a delegation to Rasulullah ﷺ and presented the actual situation before him. The following verses were revealed:

يَا أَيُّهَا الَّذِينَ آمَنُوا إِنْ جَاءَكُمْ فَاسِقٌ بِنَبَإٍ فَتَبَيَّنُوا أَنْ تُصِيبُوا قَوْمًا بِجَهَالَةٍ فَتُصْبِحُوا عَلَىٰ مَا فَعَلْتُمْ نَادِمِينَ ۝

"O believers! If there comes to you a sinner with any information, then verify it lest you harm some people out of ignorance, and later you become remorseful over what you have done." [Surah Hujuraat, verse 6]

The expedition of 'Abdullah ibn 'Ausjah ﷺ

In Safar 9 A.H., Rasulullah ﷺ sent 'Abdullah ibn 'Ausjah ﷺ to the Bani 'Amr ibn Haarisah in order to invite them to Islam. Rasulullah ﷺ despatched him with a letter from himself. These people refused to embrace Islam. They took this letter of Rasulullah ﷺ, washed it and tied it to the bottom of a bucket. When 'Abdullah ﷺ returned to Rasulullah ﷺ and informed him of what transpired, he said: "What! Do these people have no intelligence? From that time to this time, the people of this tribe have been foolish and immature. They are devoid of intelligence and they are dumb."

The expedition of Qutbah ibn 'Aamir ﷺ

It was in the same month that Rasulullah ﷺ sent Qutbah ibn 'Aamir ﷺ at the command of 20 people to the Khash'am in order to wage Jihaad against them. Qutbah ﷺ went, fought them and defeated them. He returned with some camels, goats and prisoners. After taking out one fifth of the booty, each person received four camels, and each camel was considered to be equal to 10 goats.

The expedition of Dahhaak ibn Sufyaan ﷺ

In the month of Rabi'ul-Awwal, Rasulullah ﷺ sent Dahhaak ibn Sufyaan Kilaabi ﷺ to the Bani Kilaab to invite them to Islam. The people refused and began hurling abuses at Dahhaak ﷺ and Islam. They also prepared for war. A battle ensued and they were defeated. Dahhaak ﷺ returned very happily to Madinah with some booty.

The expedition of 'Alqamah ibn Mujazzaz Mudlaji ﷺ

Rasulullah ﷺ received information that some Abyssinians had come to Jeddah. Rasulullah ﷺ sent 'Alqamah ibn Mujazzaz ﷺ with 300 men. When these Abyssinians heard about this, they fled and disappeared. When the Muslims were returning, some of the soldiers decided to hasten so that they could reach their homes before the rest of the army. 'Alqamah ﷺ ignited a fire and ordered this group that was in a hurry to jump into the fire. Some of them were prepared to jump. 'Alqamah ﷺ said to them: "Stop, I was merely joking with you." When these people returned to Madinah, they informed Rasulullah ﷺ of what transpired. Rasulullah ﷺ said: "When anyone commands you to do something wrong, do not listen to him."

The expedition of Ali ibn Abi Taalib ﷺ

In Rabi'ul-Aakhir 9 A.H. Rasulullah ﷺ sent Ali ﷺ with 150-200 men to the Tayy tribe in order to destroy their idol by the name of Fuls. On reaching there, the Muslims attacked at night. Some people and cattle were captured. The temple in which the idol was housed was destroyed and burnt down. They also brought two swords that were in the temple. These were obtained by Haaris ibn Shamr. Among those captured was the daughter of the icon of generosity, Haatim Taa'ie. Her name was Saffaanah. On the other hand, Haatim's son, 'Adiyy ibn Haatim, fled to Syria when he heard about the approach of the Muslim army. The reason he fled to Syria was that there were many Christians there who subscribed to his beliefs. The captives were brought to Madinah and kept near the Masjid. When Rasulullah ﷺ passed by, Haatim's daughter stood up and said: "O Messenger of Allah! My father has passed away. Furthermore, the person who was seeing to me has fled. Be kind to us and Allah will be kind to you." Rasulullah ﷺ asked: "Who was the one who was seeing to you and taking care of you?" She replied: "My brother, 'Adiyy ibn Haatim." Rasulullah ﷺ said: "He is the one who fled from Allah and His Messenger? It would be better if I show kindness to you. However, do not hasten in returning. When I find some reliable person from your tribe, I will send you back to your people." Within a few days, Rasulullah ﷺ found a few people from the Tayy tribe who were going towards Syria. Due to his kindness and generosity, Rasulullah ﷺ gave her a riding animal, some provisions and some clothing, and sent her off. Saffaanah embraced Islam and expressed her gratitude to Rasulullah ﷺ with the following words:

شكرتك يد افتقرت بعد غنى ولا ملكتك يد استغنت بعد فقر وأصاب الله بمعروفك مواضعه ولا جعل لك إلى لئيم حاجة ولا سلب نعمة عن كريم إلا وجعلك سببا لردها عليه

"May Allah make that hand of yours forever grateful. That hand which became poor and empty after it had enjoyed prosperity. May that hand which became rich after being poor never gain control over you. May Allah cause your kindness to be forever found wherever it is needed. May Allah never make you in need of anything from a wretched person. May Allah never snatch away any bounty from a kind person without making you the means of returning it."

Saffaanah bid farewell to Rasulullah ﷺ and returned to Syria. On reaching there, she met her brother, 'Adiyy, and related the entire incident to him. He asked her: "What do you think I should do?" She replied:

أرى والله أن تلحق به سريعا فإن يك نبينا فالإسباق إليه فضيلة

وإن يك ملكا فلن تزال فى عز وأنت وأنت

"I take an oath by Allah that I think that you should meet him as quickly as possible. If he is a Prophet, then to run and hasten towards him is very meritorious. If he is a king, it will always be a source of honour. And you know very well."

On hearing this, 'Adiyy said: "This is a very good suggestion." He then presented himself before Rasulullah ﷺ and embraced Islam.

Ka'b ibn Zuhayr embraces Islam

It was mentioned previously that this person used to compose poetry in which he used to disgrace Rasulullah ﷺ. On the conquest of Makkah, Ka'b ibn Zuhayr and his brother, Bujayr ibn Zuhayr, fled from Makkah and went to a place called Abraq al-Ghuraab. Bujayr said to Ka'b: "You remain here while I will go, listen to Muhammad (ﷺ) and learn about his religion. If I establish his truthfulness, I will follow him. If not, I will leave it." Ka'b remained there while Bujayr went to Rasulullah ﷺ, listened to what he had to say, and immediately embraced Islam.

When Rasulullah ﷺ returned from Taa'if and reached Madinah, Bujayr wrote a letter to his brother informing him that those who used to compose poetry in order to disgrace Rasulullah ﷺ were killed on the conquest of Makkah. Those who were able to flee, fled. If you value your life, present yourself immediately before Rasulullah ﷺ. Whoever comes in repentance to him and embraces Islam, is not killed. If you are unable to do this, go to a very distant place where you could save yourself. When Ka'b learnt about this, he became angry at the fact that Bujayr embraced Islam without consulting him. He then wrote the following lines:

"O friends! Convey this message of mine to Bujayr. What is your opinion as regards to whatever I have to say? How sad, what have you done? Explain to us, if you are unable to remain on the religion of your forefathers, then what other path have you chosen? You have chosen a path which you have neither found your mother nor your father on. Nor have you found your brother on that path. If you do not act on what I say, I will not grieve. I will not say anything to you at the time of your error. The one who is trusted (Muhammad ﷺ) made you drink from a cup that removes thirst."

Bujayr did not want this incident to be concealed from Rasulullah ﷺ. He therefore showed these lines to him. Rasulullah ﷺ said: "He is correct, I am trusted from Allah's side, and I am commanded by Him." On hearing the words: "You have chosen a path which you have neither found your mother nor your father on", he said: "This is also correct. Where did he find his father and mother on this religion?"

In reply to the above lines, Bujayr wrote the following letter:

"Is there anyone who would convey this message to Ka'b? Do you have any desire to enter that religion regarding which you wrongfully reproach me, when in actual fact it is totally correct? It will convey you, not to Uzza and Laat, but to one Allah. In so doing, you will also be saved when others who believed in one Allah are saved, and you will also be safeguarded from the punishment. That is, on that day when no one will be saved and no one will be able to escape (the punishment) except he whose heart is pure (from the filth of polytheism and disbelief) and is a Muslim. So the religion of Zuhayr is nothing. And the religion of my grandfather, Abu Sulma, is prohibited to me (because I have entered the true religion of Islam)."

This letter of Bujayr had a great impact on Ka'b. He immediately wrote a poem in praise of Rasulullah ﷺ and left for Madinah. He reached Madinah and presented himself before Rasulullah ﷺ after the Fajr Salaah. He did not identify himself by his real name, and asked the following question: "O Messenger of Allah! If Ka'b ibn Zuhayr comes to you in repentance and embraces Islam, will you give him sanctity?" Rasulullah ﷺ replied in the affirmative. Ka'b said: "O Messenger of Allah! I am that sinful person. Give me your hand so that I may pledge allegiance to you." An Ansaari person stood up and said: "O Messenger of Allah! Permit me to chop off his head." Rasulullah ﷺ replied: "Let him be. He has come in repentance."

He removed a Yemeni shawl which he was wearing and gave it to Ka'b رضي الله عنه. Later on, Mu'aawiyah رضي الله عنه purchased this shawl from the progeny of Ka'b رضي الله عنه for 20 000 dirhams. This shawl remained among the caliphs for quite some time. They used to wear it on the occasions of Eid as a source of blessing. It was lost when the Tartars attacked the Islamic state.

Chapter 25

The Battle of Tabuk - Rajab 9 A.H.

The Christian Arabs had written to Heraclius, the king of Rome, that Muhammad (ﷺ) passed away and that the people were dying because of the drought that they were experiencing. It was therefore a very appropriate time to attack the Arabs. Heraclius immediately issued the order for preparations. A fully equipped army of 40 000 was prepared.

The traders of Syria frequented Madinah to sell olive oil. Rasulullah ﷺ learnt from them about this army and that the front of the army had already reached Balqa', and that Heraclius already distributed the entire year's wage to the soldiers.

On hearing all of this, Rasulullah ﷺ issued the order that preparations should be made immediately so that they could reach the border of the enemy lines and fight them. The border was Tabuk. The distant journey, the hot weather, the drought, the poverty, the lack of resources, etc. were such impediments that on hearing this order to prepare for Jihaad, the hypocrites, who claimed to be Muslims, feared that they will now be exposed. In order to save themselves, they began saying among themselves and to others as well:

"Do not go out in such heat."

One joker said: "People know that I become excited when I see beautiful women. I fear that if I were to see the beautiful women of the Romans, I would fall into temptation."

On the other hand, the sincere Muslims immediately followed the orders of Rasulullah ﷺ and began their preparations. Abu Bakr رضي الله عنه was the first person to bring all his wealth and present it before Rasulullah ﷺ. The wealth that he brought amounted to 4000 dirhams. Rasulullah ﷺ asked him: "Did you leave anything behind for your family?" He replied: "I left Allah and His Messenger for them." 'Umar ﷺ presented half of his entire wealth. 'Abdur Rahmaan ibn 'Auf ﷺ presented 200 ounces of silver. 'Aasim ibn 'Adiyy ﷺ presented 70 loads of dates.

'Usmaan ﷺ presented 300 fully laden camels and 1000 dinars. On seeing all this, Rasulullah ﷺ became extremely pleased with him. He continued passing his hands through the coins saying: "After this great deed, no deed can harm 'Usmaan. O Allah! I am pleased with 'Usmaan. You also be pleased with him."

Most of the Sahaabah ﷺ offered their help in accordance with their financial position. Despite all this, the riding animals and the provisions for the journey were not enough. A few Sahaabah ﷺ came to Rasulullah ﷺ and said to him: "O Messenger of Allah! We are totally helpless. If some arrangements for riding animals could be made, we will not be deprived of this great opportunity (of joining you on this jihaad)." Rasulullah ﷺ replied: "I have no riding animals with me." On hearing this, they went back crying. Allah Ta'ala revealed the following verse in this regard:

$$\text{وَلَا عَلَى الَّذِينَ إِذَا مَا أَتَوْكَ لِتَحْمِلَهُمْ قُلْتَ لَا أَجِدُ مَا أَحْمِلُكُمْ عَلَيْهِ تَوَلَّوْا وَأَعْيُنُهُمْ تَفِيضُ مِنَ الدَّمْعِ حَزَنًا أَلَّا يَجِدُوا مَا يُنْفِقُونَ}$$

"Nor (is there a way of reproach) against those who came to you so that you may provide them with conveyances and you said: 'I do not have anything upon which I could convey you.' They turned away, their eyes flowing with tears out of sorrow that they do not have that which they could spend." [Surah Taubah, verse 92]

When 'Abdullah ibn Mughaffal ﷺ and Abu Layla 'Abdur Rahmaan ibn Ka'b ﷺ went back crying from Rasulullah ﷺ, they met Yaameen ibn 'Amr Nadri on the way. On seeing them crying, he asked them the reason for this. They replied: "Neither does Rasulullah ﷺ have riding animals for us nor do we possess the means to prepare for the journey. We are extremely sad over the fact that we will be deprived of taking part in this battle." On hearing this, Yaameen was overcome with compassion. He immediately purchased a camel and made arrangements for the provisions for the journey.

When the Sahaabah ﷺ were ready to depart, Rasulullah ﷺ left Muhammad ibn Maslamah Ansaari ﷺ in charge and appointed him as the governer of Madinah. He also left Ali ﷺ in order to see to his family and take care of them. Ali ﷺ said to Rasulullah ﷺ: "O Messenger of Allah! You are leaving me with the women and children!" Rasulullah ﷺ replied: "Are you not pleased over the fact that you are to me just as Haroon عَلَيْهِ السَّلَام was to Musa عَلَيْهِ السَّلَام? However, there is no Prophet after me."

Rasulullah صَلَّى اللَّهُ عَلَيْهِ وَسَلَّم eventually departed from Madinah at the head of an army of 30 000 in which there were 10 000 horses.

On the way, they had to pass that place in which the punishment of Allah Ta'ala had afflicted Samud. When passing this place, Rasulullah صَلَّى اللَّهُ عَلَيْهِ وَسَلَّم was affected so greatly, that he covered his face and urged his camel to move faster. He emphasised on the Sahaabah رَضِيَ اللَّهُ عَنْهُم that no one should go to this place of wrongdoers. No one should drink water from there and no one should perform wudhu with the water of that place. They should merely pass by that place crying out to Allah Ta'ala. He ordered that those who had mistakenly taken water from there or used that water in their flour should throw that water away and feed that flour to their camels.

On reaching a place called Hijr, Rasulullah صَلَّى اللَّهُ عَلَيْهِ وَسَلَّم advised the Sahaabah رَضِيَ اللَّهُ عَنْهُم not to travel alone (they should move about in groups). Coincidentally, two persons went out alone. One of them suffered from suffocation. Rasulullah صَلَّى اللَّهُ عَلَيْهِ وَسَلَّم blew on him and he was cured. The other was carried by the winds and thrown onto the mountains of Tayy. He returned to Madinah after quite some time.

When the Muslims continued futher, there was no water. They were greatly distressed by this. Rasulullah صَلَّى اللَّهُ عَلَيْهِ وَسَلَّم made dua to Allah Ta'ala. He sent down rain which quenched everyone. When they continued on their journey, Rasulullah's صَلَّى اللَّهُ عَلَيْهِ وَسَلَّم camel got lost. A hypocrite who was with them said: "You bring to us information from the heavens (i.e. divine revelation) but you do not even know where your camel is."

Rasulullah صَلَّى اللَّهُ عَلَيْهِ وَسَلَّم replied: "I take an oath in the name of Allah Ta'ala that I have no knowledge of anything except that which Allah Ta'ala teaches me. Nonetheless now, by the inspiration of Allah Ta'ala, I have learnt that my lost camel is in such and such valley. Its bridle got caught to a branch and it therefore cannot move forward." A few Sahaabah رَضِيَ اللَّهُ عَنْهُم went and brought this camel.

About a day or so before reaching Tabuk, Rasulullah صَلَّى اللَّهُ عَلَيْهِ وَسَلَّم informed the Sahaabah رَضِيَ اللَّهُ عَنْهُم that they would reach the spring of Tabuk by mid-morning the following day. No person should use any water from that spring. When they reached that spring, water was dripping from it, drop by drop. After much toiling, they were able to gather a container of water. Rasulullah صَلَّى اللَّهُ عَلَيْهِ وَسَلَّم washed his hands and face with that water and then returned the water to the spring. No sooner he did this and it began gushing forth with water. The entire army used as much as they needed. Rasulullah صَلَّى اللَّهُ عَلَيْهِ وَسَلَّم addressed Mu'aaz ibn Jabal رَضِيَ اللَّهُ عَنْهُ saying: "If you remain alive, you will see this land green and lush with orchards." This fountain is gushing forth till today and you can hear the gushing of the water from quite a distance.

Rasulullah ﷺ remained in Tabuk for twenty days but no one came to wage battle against him. However, his coming here was not in vain. It was a source of intimidation for the enemy. The surrounding tribes came and submitted before him. The leaders from Jarba, Adhruh and Aylah came to him and agreed to make peace and pay jizyah. Rasulullah ﷺ ordered that a peace treaty be written and signed, and he gave it to them.

It was from this place that Rasulullah ﷺ despatched Khaalid ibn Waleed رضي الله عنه with 400 horsemen towards Akidar who was acting on behalf of Heraclius as the governor of Dumat al-Jandal. When he was departing, Rasulullah ﷺ said to Khaalid ibn Waleed رضي الله عنه: "You will find him hunting. Do not kill him. Rather, capture him and bring him to me. If he refuses, you may kill him." Khaalid ibn Waleed رضي الله عنه reached on a moon-lit night. It was summer. Akidar and his wife were sitting outside on the balcony of the fortress listening to some singing. Suddenly a nilgai (type of buck) came and knocked into the fortress. Akidar, his brother and a few other relatives immediately came down to hunt this animal. They mounted their horses and gave chase. They had just moved a little when Khaalid ibn Waleed رضي الله عنه reached there. Akidar's brother, Hassaan, engaged in combat with Khaalid رضي الله عنه and was killed. As for Akidar who was in chase of an animal was now himself hunted by Khaalid رضي الله عنه. The latter said to him: "I can give you refuge from being killed provided you agree to come with me to the Messenger of Allah ﷺ." Akidar agreed to this. Khaalid رضي الله عنه took him to Rasulullah ﷺ. He agreed to a peace treaty with Rasulullah ﷺ after paying him 2000 camels, 800 horses, 400 coats of armour, and 400 spears.

Masjidud Diraar

After remaining there for 20 days, Rasulullah ﷺ returned from Tabuk to Madinah. When he reached Zi Aawaan, which was about one hour from Madinah, he sent Maalik ibn Dakhshan and Ma'n ibn 'Adiyy in order to demolish and burn down Masjidud Diraar. This Masjid was built by the hypocrites so that they may use it as an assembly point to discuss matters against Rasulullah ﷺ. At the time when Rasulullah ﷺ was departing for Tabuk, the hypocrites came to him and said: "We have built a Masjid for the sick and excused people. We invite you to come and offer one Salaah in it so that it may be accepted and be blessed (by Allah)." Rasulullah ﷺ replied: "At present, I am going to Tabuk. I will decide on my return." On his return, Rasulullah ﷺ ordered the above-mentioned companions to go and destroy it. The following verses were revealed with regard to this Masjid:

$$\text{وَالَّذِيْنَ اتَّخَذُوْا مَسْجِدًا ضِرَارًا وَّكُفْرًا وَّتَفْرِيْقًا بَيْنَ الْمُؤْمِنِيْنَ وَإِرْصَادًا لِّمَنْ حَارَبَ اللهَ}$$
$$\text{وَرَسُوْلَهٗ مِنْ قَبْلُ ۚ وَلَيَحْلِفُنَّ إِنْ أَرَدْنَآ إِلَّا الْحُسْنٰى ۖ وَاللهُ يَشْهَدُ إِنَّهُمْ لَكٰذِبُوْنَ ۝ لَا تَقُمْ فِيْهِ}$$
$$\text{أَبَدًا ۚ لَمَسْجِدٌ أُسِّسَ عَلَى التَّقْوٰى مِنْ أَوَّلِ يَوْمٍ أَحَقُّ أَنْ تَقُوْمَ فِيْهِ ۚ فِيْهِ رِجَالٌ يُّحِبُّوْنَ أَنْ}$$
$$\text{يَّتَطَهَّرُوْا ۚ وَاللهُ يُحِبُّ الْمُطَّهِّرِيْنَ ۝}$$

> "Those who built a Masjid in opposition and upon disbelief, and in order to promote disunity among the Muslims, and as a lurking place for him who has been fighting against Allah and His Messenger since before. They will take oaths (saying): 'We desired only good.' Allah testifies that they are liars. Don't you ever stand in it! Surely the mosque whose foundation was laid on piety from the very first day is (more) worthy that you stand therein. In it are people who love to stay purified. And Allah loves those who stay purified." [Surah Taubah, verses 107-108]

Rasulullah ﷺ also ordered for the house of Suwaylim, a Jew, to be burnt down. The hypocrites used to gather in his house and hold meetings against Rasulullah ﷺ. Talhah رضي الله عنه and a few others went and burnt down this house.

When Rasulullah ﷺ neared Madinah, his beloved followers who were waiting to see his blessed face came out to welcome him. Out of their extreme love for him, even the womenfolk came outside. The little girls and boys were singing these lines:

$$\text{طلع البدر علينا من ثنيات الوداع}$$
$$\text{وجب الشكر علينا ما دعا لله داع}$$
$$\text{أيها المبعوث فينا جئت بالأمر المطاع}$$

> "The full moon has appeared before us from the al-Wada' mountain pass. It is incumbent on us to be grateful as long as a person invites towards Allah. O you who have been commissioned to us! You have come with a religion that has to be followed."

When Rasulullah ﷺ set his eyes on the houses of Madinah, he said: هذه طابة – this is Taabah (another name for Madinah). When he set his eyes on Mt. Uhud, he said: "This mountain loves us and we love it."

Rasulullah ﷺ entered Madinah towards the end of Sha'baan or the beginning of Ramadhaan. He first went to the Masjid-e-Nabawi and offered Salaah therein. After the Salaah, he remained seated in order to meet the people. He then went to his house in order to rest.

This was the last battle in which Rasulullah ﷺ personally took part.

Those who remained behind

When Rasulullah ﷺ left for Tabuk, the sincere and devoted believers joined him. A group of hypocrites did not join him. A few sincere believers also remained behind. They did not do so out of hypocrisy but because of some excuse.

Abu Zarr Ghifaari رضي الله عنه had a camel that was weak and thin. He felt that when this camel eats and drinks and is able to undertake such a journey, he will depart after a few days. When he lost hope in his camel recovering, he loaded his goods onto his back and began walking. In this way, he reached Tabuk all alone. On seeing him, Rasulullah ﷺ said: "May Allah shower His mercy on Abu Zarr. He is coming all alone, he will die alone and he will be raised alone." Eventually, this is what happened. He passed away all alone at a place called Rabdhah. There was no one to enshroud and bury him. Coincidentally, 'Abdullah ibn Mas'ood رضي الله عنه was returning from Kufah. He enshrouded and buried him.

Abu Khaysamah رضي الله عنه said: "Rasulullah ﷺ left for Tabuk whilst I remained in Madinah. It was extremely hot. One afternoon, my family sprinkled water around the hut and brought me cold water and food. On seeing all these (comforts) before me, my conscience pricked me and I thought to myself that this is totally unfair that Rasulullah ﷺ is in the intense heat and the hot desert winds while I am sitting here in the shade and enjoying myself in these comforts. I immediately got up, took some dates, mounted my camel and left with great speed. When I saw the army before me, Rasulullah ﷺ recognised me from a distance and said to the Sahaabah رضي الله عنهم that Abu Khaysamah is coming. I presented myself before Rasulullah ﷺ and narrated my story to him. He made dua in my favour."

The following three personalities were also among the Muslims who remained behind: Ka'b ibn Maalik رضي الله عنه, Muraarah ibnur Rabi' رضي الله عنه and Hilaal ibn Umayyah رضي الله عنه.

Imaam Bukhaari رحمه الله narrates the story of Ka'b ibn Maalik رضي الله عنه as follows. Ka'b رضي الله عنه relates, "Rasulullah ﷺ departed while I was still making preparations for the journey. I thought to myself that once I have all my goods ready, I will depart in a day or two and catch up with Rasulullah ﷺ. I delayed in this regard whilst the caravan had covered quite a distance. No one remained in Madinah except a few hypocrites and a few people who were excused (due to valid reasons). When I used to look at this, I would feel saddened. When Rasulullah ﷺ returned from Tabuk, the hypocrites went and offered false excuses to him. Rasulullah ﷺ accepted their excuses outwardly and left the condition of their hearts to Allah Ta'ala.

Ka'b ibn Maalik ؓ says: I made a firm determination that I will never remain behind from participating in a battle and then speak lies to Rasulullah ﷺ. Therefore, when Rasulullah ﷺ returned, I presented myself before him and greeted him. He turned away from me. I said: 'O Prophet of Allah! Why are you turning away from me? I take an oath by Allah that I am not a hypocrite, I am not in any doubt, nor have I renegaded from Islam.' He asked: 'Why did you remain behind?' I replied: 'O Messenger of Allah! If I was sitting before some worldly leader, I could have made up some story and saved myself from his anger. However, you are the Messenger of Allah. Even if I were to lie to appease you, it is possible that Allah Ta'ala will cause you to become angry at me. If I speak the truth to you, despite earning your anger, I hope that Allah Ta'ala will forgive me by His grace. The fact of the matter is that I have no excuse. I am at fault.' Rasulullah ﷺ said: 'This person has spoken the truth. You may wait until Allah Ta'ala reveals some order concerning you.' In a like manner Muraarah ibn Rabi' ؓ and Hilaal ibn Umayyah ؓ went to Rasulullah ﷺ and admitted their faults. Rasulullah ﷺ ordered that no one should speak to us for 50 days. Consequently, everyone stopped speaking to us. Our friends, relatives and beloved ones all seemed like strangers to us. My two friends (Muraarah and Hilaal) remained in their homes because of weakness and spent their days and nights crying. On the other hand, I was young. I used to attend the congregational Salaah. Fifty days passed in these difficult and trying circumstances. This continued to such an extent that this earth seemed constricted before us. My greatest worry was that if I were to pass away during this period, Rasulullah ﷺ and the Muslims would not even offer the Janaazah Salaah for me. After fifty days, I heard this announcement from Mt. Sila': 'O Ka'b! Take glad tidings.'

'No sooner I heard this announcement, I fell into sajdah and realised that the difficulty has now been removed. Rasulullah ﷺ had announced that our repentance had been accepted. People came from all directions in order to congratulate me and my two friends. The people were saying to me: 'May Allah's acceptance of your repentance be blessed.' When the person who gave the glad tidings came to me, I immediately removed my garment and gave it to him. I then presented myself before Rasulullah ﷺ. He was sitting in the Masjid. The moment I stepped into the Masjid, Talhah ibn 'Ubaydillah ؓ came running towards me, embraced me and congratulated me. No one else stood up. By Allah, I will never forget this act of Talhah. Rasulullah's ﷺ face was beaming like the full moon. I greeted him and he said:

أَبْشِرْ بِخَيْرِ يَوْمٍ مَرَّ عَلَيْكَ مُنْذُ وَلَدَتْكَ أُمُّكَ

'Take glad tidings with the best day that you experienced ever since your mother gave birth to you.'

Without doubt, the day on which Ka'b ibn Maalik ؓ embraced Islam was the best day in his life. However, this day was even better because it was on this day that Allah accepted his repentance. It was this acceptance that put a seal on his Imaan and his sincerity forever. The following verses were revealed:

لَقَدْ تَابَ اللهُ عَلَى النَّبِيِّ وَ الْمُهٰجِرِيْنَ وَ الْاَنْصَارِ الَّذِيْنَ اتَّبَعُوْهُ فِيْ سَاعَةِ الْعُسْرَةِ مِنْۢ بَعْدِ مَا كَادَ يَزِيْغُ قُلُوْبُ فَرِيْقٍ مِّنْهُمْ ثُمَّ تَابَ عَلَيْهِمْ ۗ اِنَّهٗ بِهِمْ رَءُوْفٌ رَّحِيْمٌ ۝ وَّ عَلَى الثَّلٰثَةِ الَّذِيْنَ خُلِّفُوْا ۗ حَتّٰۤى اِذَا ضَاقَتْ عَلَيْهِمُ الْاَرْضُ بِمَا رَحُبَتْ وَ ضَاقَتْ عَلَيْهِمْ اَنْفُسُهُمْ وَ ظَنُّوْۤا اَنْ لَّا مَلْجَاَ مِنَ اللهِ اِلَّاۤ اِلَيْهِ ۗ ثُمَّ تَابَ عَلَيْهِمْ لِيَتُوْبُوْا ۗ اِنَّ اللهَ هُوَ التَّوَّابُ الرَّحِيْمُ ۝ يٰۤاَيُّهَا الَّذِيْنَ اٰمَنُوا اتَّقُوا اللهَ وَ كُوْنُوْا مَعَ الصّٰدِقِيْنَ ۝

"Allah turned in kindness to the Prophet, and the Emigrants and the Helpers who stood by the Prophet in the hour of distress, after the hearts of a group of them were on the point of turning. He then turned again in kindness to them. Surely He is kind and merciful to them. And (He turned in kindness) to those three persons who were kept behind until the land became constricted upon them, despite its vastness, and their own lives became constricted upon them and they realised that there was no refuge from Allah except towards Him. He then turned in kindness to them so that they may return. Surely Allah alone is kind, merciful. O believers! Continually fear Allah and remain with the truthful." [Surah Taubah, verses 117-119]

I said to Rasulullah ﷺ: 'O Messenger of Allah! I intend giving all my wealth in charity in appreciation for the acceptance of my repentance.' He said: 'Don't give all, keep some for yourself.' I kept the share which I received from Khaybar and gave the rest in charity. I said to Rasulullah ﷺ: 'O Messenger of Allah! It is solely because of my truth that Allah Ta'ala saved me. In order to perfect my repentance, I will speak nothing but the truth for as long as I live.'"

Abu Bakr ؓ is appointed Ameer of Haj

In Zul Qa'dah 9 A.H. Rasulullah ﷺ appointed Abu Bakr ؓ as the Ameer of the Haj and sent him to Makkah. Three hundred people accompanied him from Madinah. He took 20 camels for sacrifice (Qurbaani) with him. The purpose of sending him was so that he could teach the people the method of performing Haj. Furthermore, he should announce the 40 verses of Surah at-Taubah which were with regard to those who broke their covenant. These verses announced that after this year, the disbelievers should not come near the Sacred Masjid. They should not circuit the Ka'bah naked. The covenant that Rasulullah ﷺ made with any group will be fulfilled. As for those with whom no covenant was made, they will be given respite for four months from the 10th of Zul Hijjah.

After Abu Bakr رضي الله عنه departed, Rasulullah ﷺ felt that these announcements concerning the maintaining and severing of the covenants should be made by someone who was from his family. The reason for this was that the Arabs only accept the statement of those who are family to the person who made the covenant. It is for this reason that Rasulullah ﷺ summoned Ali رضي الله عنه, gave him his camel, 'Adbaa', and sent him off towards Abu Bakr رضي الله عنه instructing him to announce the verses of Surah Taubah in the Haj season. From some Ahaadith it seems that the verses of Surah Taubah were revealed after Abu Bakr's رضي الله عنه departure. Therefore, Rasulullah ﷺ sent Ali رضي الله عنه later on in order to announce these verses.

When Abu Bakr رضي الله عنه heard the sounds of the camel, he thought that Rasulullah ﷺ had personally come. He stopped and waited. He then saw Ali رضي الله عنه approaching. He asked him: "Have you come as an Ameer or as my follower?" Ali رضي الله عنه replied: "I have come as your follower. I have merely come to announce the verses of Surah Taubah." Abu Bakr رضي الله عنه therefore conducted the rites of Haj and also delivered the Haj sermon. Ali رضي الله عنه merely announced the verses of Surah Taubah on the 10th of Zul Hijjah at Mina, near the Jamaratul 'Aqabah. Abu Bakr رضي الله عنه appointed a few people to help Ali رضي الله عنه so that they could take turns in making this announcement.

Consequently, these announcements were made. The people were informed that no disbeliever will be permitted to enter the Sacred Masjid. No disbeliever will be permitted to perform the Haj the following year. No one will be permitted to circuit the Ka'bah naked. The covenant that Rasulullah ﷺ made with anyone will be fulfilled according to the time that was agreed upon. Those with whom no covenant was made or no time was specified will be given a respite of four months. If he does not embrace Islam within the four months, he will be killed wherever he is found.

It is stated in one Hadith that when Ali رضي الله عنه caught up with Abu Bakr رضي الله عنه at Zul Hulayfah and informed him that Rasulullah ﷺ sent him to announce the verses of Surah Taubah, he thought that some order concerning him was revealed to Rasulullah ﷺ. He therefore returned immediately to Madinah and asked Rasulullah ﷺ about this. Rasulullah ﷺ replied: "No! You were my companion in the cave (of Mt. Thaur) and you will be my companion at the pond of Kauthar (on the day of resurrection). However, the announcement of the verses cannot be made by anyone except me or someone from my family. It is for this reason that I sent Ali."

Various incidents that took place in 9 A. H.

1. In the month of Zul Qa'dah, the leader of the hypocrites, 'Abdullah ibn Ubayy ibn Salool died. The following verse was revealed concerning him:

$$\text{وَلَا تُصَلِّ عَلَىٰ أَحَدٍ مِّنْهُم مَّاتَ أَبَدًا وَلَا تَقُمْ عَلَىٰ قَبْرِهِ ۖ إِنَّهُمْ كَفَرُوا بِاللَّهِ وَرَسُولِهِ وَمَاتُوا وَهُمْ فَاسِقُونَ}$$

"Never offer Salaah over any of them who has died, nor stand over his grave. They rejected Allah and His Messenger, and died while they were disobedient."
[Surah Taubah, verse 84]

Note: It is prohibited to attend the funeral of a disbeliever and to stand at his graveside. This is irrespective of whether the deceased is a Hindu or a Christian. This is notwithstanding the fact that the disbelief of an idol worshipper is more severe than the disbelief of a Christian or Jew.

2. Najaashi, the king of Abysinnia passed away in this year. Rasulullah ﷺ received news of his death on the very day that he passed away, via divine revelation. Rasulullah ﷺ gathered the Sahaabah ؓ and performed his Janaazah Salaah in absentia.

3. The injunction concerning the prohibition of usury (interest) was revealed in this year. Rasulullah ﷺ made a general announcement of its prohibition one year later on the occasion of the Farewell Haj.

4. The injunction concerning li'aan was revealed in this year. Details in this regard are mentioned in Surah an-Noor.

5. The verse concerning jizyah for those who did not embrace Islam but wished to live under the protection of the Islamic state was revealed in this year. Allah Ta'ala says:

$$\text{قَاتِلُوا الَّذِينَ لَا يُؤْمِنُونَ بِاللَّهِ وَلَا بِالْيَوْمِ الْآخِرِ وَلَا يُحَرِّمُونَ مَا حَرَّمَ اللَّهُ وَرَسُولُهُ وَلَا يَدِينُونَ دِينَ الْحَقِّ مِنَ الَّذِينَ أُوتُوا الْكِتَابَ حَتَّىٰ يُعْطُوا الْجِزْيَةَ عَن يَدٍ وَهُمْ صَاغِرُونَ}$$

"Fight those who do not believe in Allah, nor in the last day, and do not consider forbidden that which Allah and His Messenger have forbidden, and who do not embrace the true religion from amongst those who are the people of the Book until they pay the jizyah (exemption tax) by their own hands while being subdued."
[Surah Taubah, verse 29]

Chapter 26

The 10th year A.H. – The year of delegations

The largest tribe among the Arabs was that of the Quraysh. Its leadership was an accepted fact. No one denied the fact that the Quraysh was from the progeny of Ismaa-eel عَلَيْهِ السَّلَام. It was well known for its intelligence, insight, generosity and bravery. It was the custodian of the Sacred Masjid. However, the members of this tribe were bent on their opposition and enmity to Islam. The other Arab tribes were observing the Quraysh to see what they would do with regard to Rasulullah صَلَّى اللهُ عَلَيْهِ وَسَلَّم. The youngsters from the Quraysh had embraced Islam from the beginning and were continuing to do so. However, the seniors were still left. When Makkah was conquered and the seniors also began embracing Islam, the other Arabs tribes concluded that Islam was the true religion and that it would certainly spread throughout the world. No power would succeed in going against it. Therefore, no sooner Makkah was conquered, delegations from all directions began pouring in. Representatives and delegates from all the tribes began presenting themselves before Rasulullah صَلَّى اللهُ عَلَيْهِ وَسَلَّم. Once they learnt the truth about Islam, they would embrace Islam and promise to make an effort on the rest of their people as well. Allah Ta'ala says:

إِذَا جَآءَ نَصْرُ اللهِ وَالْفَتْحُ ۞ وَرَأَيْتَ النَّاسَ يَدْخُلُوْنَ فِيْ دِيْنِ اللهِ أَفْوَاجًا ۞ فَسَبِّحْ بِحَمْدِ رَبِّكَ وَاسْتَغْفِرْهُ ۚ إِنَّهُ كَانَ تَوَّابًا ۞

"When the help of Allah and victory comes, and you see the people entering the religion of Allah in groups, then glorify the praises of your Sustainer and seek His forgiveness. Surely He accepts repentance." [Surah Nasr]

Delegations had already started towards the end of 8 A.H. However, there was more continuity between 8 A.H. and 10 A.H. in this regard. These two years are therefore known as the years of delegations. 'Allaamah Qastalaani enumerates 35 delegations.

1. The delegation of Hawaazin

This was the first delegation that came to Rasulullah ﷺ after the conquest of Makkah. When Rasulullah ﷺ was at Ji'irraanah, a delegation of 14 people came in order to obtain the release of their wealth and prisoners. Details in this regard were given under the battle of Hunayn. Zuhayr ibn Surw Sa'di was the head of this delegation. He stood up saying: "O Messenger of Allah! Your foster aunts are also among the prisoners. Those who brought you up are also there. They are the ones who used to hold you to their bosoms (when you were a baby). Had we breast-fed Haaris Ghassaani and Nu'maan ibn Mundhir, we would have certainly hoped for some help from them during such times of difficulty. Whereas you are the best one whom we took care of. He then said the following lines:

"O Messenger of Allah! Be kind to us by virtue of your grace and mercy. Surely you are a person from whom we hope and await mercy. Be kind to the tribe whose needs have been curtailed by destiny. Its structure has become disorganised by the changes in time. O the best child that was born and chosen in the world when mankind was given all this. If your bounty and kindness does not see to them, they will be destroyed. O you whose scale of forbearance is the heaviest, and whose forbearance is clearly apparent at the time of tests and tribulations! Show kindness to us. Be kind to those women whose milk you used to drink and whose pure and flowing milk you used to fill your mouth with. Do not make us like those people whose feet slipped. Let your kindness and generosity remain with us forever. We are a noble people who do not forget anyone's kindness. We are grateful for favours that are done to us, when others show ingratitude. After this day, we will always have occasion to show gratitude. Cover those mothers, who breast fed you, with your pardon. Surely your pardon is well known. O you, on account of whose horse, other lazy horses come to life and vigour when the fires of war are ignited. We hope for such pardon from you that it completely engulfs all of them when you pardon and take recompense. Therefore forgive us. May Allah protect you from the fears of the day of resurrection and bestow you with success."

Rasulullah ﷺ said: "The share that has come to me and my family, the Banu 'Abdul Muttalib, I will give to you. As for the share that went to the rest of the Muslims, I will intercede on your behalf." Rasulullah ﷺ spoke to the rest of the Muslims and they all happily freed the prisoners. A few people delayed in this matter so Rasulullah ﷺ paid the ransom. In this way, the delegation returned with 6000 of its wives and children.

2. The delegation of Saqeef

In Ramadhaan 9 A.H. the delegation of Saqeef came to Rasulullah ﷺ to embrace Islam and pledge allegiance at his hands. This was the very Saqeef that caused Rasulullah ﷺ and the Sahaabah رضي الله عنهم severe difficulties during the siege of Taa'if. The Muslims had to return without conquering the fort of Taa'if.

When Rasulullah ﷺ abandoned the siege of Taa'if and was returning from there, someone said to him: "O Messenger of Allah! Curse them because their arrows repulsed us." Rasulullah ﷺ replied:

اَللّٰهُمَّ اهْدِ ثَقِيفًا وَائْتِ بِهِمْ مُسْلِمِيْنَ

"O Allah! Guide the Saqeef and bring them to me as Muslims."

Rasulullah's ﷺ dua was accepted. When Rasulullah ﷺ was returning from Tabuk, eight months after the martyrdom of 'Urwah ibn Mas'ood Saqafi, the Saqeef came to Madinah, embraced Islam and pledged allegiance to Rasulullah ﷺ. This delegation comprised of six people under the leadership of 'Abd Yaalil. It was either rebellion or extreme enthusiasm that they voluntarily came to Rasulullah ﷺ in order to enter the circle of Islam. The Muslims were therefore extremely happy with their arrival. Mughirah ibn Shu'bah رضي الله عنه was the first to see them approaching. When he saw them, he hastened to give Rasulullah ﷺ the good news. Abu Bakr رضي الله عنه met him on the way and when he learnt why he was so happy, he asked him permission to go and inform Rasulullah ﷺ himself. Mughirah رضي الله عنه permitted him. Abu Bakr رضي الله عنه went to Rasulullah ﷺ and gave him the glad tidings. Rasulullah ﷺ pitched a special tent in Masjid-e-Nabawi for their stay in Madinah. He did this so that they may hear the recitation of the Qur-aan and see how Salaah is offered. Khaalid ibn Sa'eed ibn 'Aas رضي الله عنه was made responsible to see to their needs. These people would never eat the food that he presented to them unless he ate thereof first. If they had anything to say to Rasulullah ﷺ, they would convey it to him via Khaalid.

They sent the following conditions to Rasulullah ﷺ:

1. They should be absolved from offering Salaah.
2. Laat (which was their senior idol) should not be broken down for three years because their women and children are greatly attached to it.
3. The idol should not be broken by their own hands.

Rasulullah ﷺ rejected the first two conditions totally and said to them:

لا خير فى دين لا صلاة فيه

"There is no good in that religion which has no Salaah."

Rasulullah ﷺ accepted the third condition. They all embraced Islam and returned to their homeland.

'Usmaan ibn Abil 'Aas was the youngest person in this delegation. He was appointed as their leader. He had the most desire to acquire knowledge of the Quraan and Islamic injunctions. Acting on the advice of Abu Bakr رضى الله عنه, Rasulullah ﷺ appointed him as the Ameer. Rasulullah ﷺ also sent Abu Sufyaan ibn Harb رضى الله عنه and Mughirah ibn Shu'bah رضى الله عنه with him in order to destroy the idol, Laat. For some reason or the other, Abu Sufyaan lagged behind. Mughirah went ahead and struck this idol. The womenfolk of the Saqeef came out bare-headed and barefoot in order to watch this scene. Mughirah broke the idol down and took all the treasures, jewellery, etc. that were in the temple. He first paid off the debts of Abu Fulayh and Qaarib ibn al-Aswad who was the son and nephew of 'Urwah ibn Mas'ood Thaqafi. The remaining wealth was presented to Rasulullah ﷺ who immediately distributed it amongst the Muslims. Rasulullah ﷺ thanked Allah Ta'ala for helping His religion and giving honour to His Messenger ﷺ. When the people of Taa'if embraced Islam after the martyrdom of 'Urwah ibn Mas'ood, Abu Fulayh and Qaarib ibnul Aswad came to Rasulullah ﷺ before the delegation of Saqeef could come to him. They both embraced Islam and said: "O Messenger of Allah! Our father's, i.e. 'Urwah and al-Aswad, debts should be paid off from the treasures that are housed in the temple of Laat." 'Urwah and al-Aswad were blood brothers. 'Urwah had embraced Islam and was martyred, as mentioned previously. Abu Fulayh was the son of 'Urwah. Al-Aswad passed away as a disbeliever. Qaarib was his son. Both of them asked for the payment of their fathers debts. Rasulullah ﷺ said: "Al-Aswad passed away as a disbeliever." Qaarib said: "O Messenger of Allah! He certainly passed away as a disbeliever. However, it is my responsibility to pay off his debts." Rasulullah ﷺ said to Abu Sufyaan: "Whatever treasures you obtain from the temple of Laat should first be used to pay off the debts of Abu Fulayh and Qaarib."

3. The delegation of Banu 'Aamir ibn Sa'sa'ah

After returning from Tabuk, the Banu 'Aamir ibn Sa'sa'ah came to Rasulullah ﷺ. 'Aamir ibn Tufayl and Arbad ibn Qays were also in this delegation. In the course of their discussions, they addressed Rasulullah ﷺ thus: "You are our master." Rasulullah ﷺ replied: "Say what is in your heart and do not let shaytaan mock at you. It is only Allah who is the master." They pretended to praise

Rasulullah ﷺ outwardly, while 'Aamir had secretly told Arbad that while he was engaging Rasulullah ﷺ in a conversation, he must unsheath his sword and kill Rasulullah ﷺ. 'Aamir started talking with Rasulullah ﷺ. He said: "O Muhammad! Make me your sincere friend." He replied: "Never – as long as you do not believe in one Allah." He asked: "What will you give me if I embrace Islam?" Rasulullah ﷺ said: "Once you embrace Islam, you will enjoy the same rights and shoulder the same responsibilities as other Muslims." 'Aamir said: "Give me power and authority after you." Rasulullah ﷺ said: "Never." He said: "You may rule over the people of the rural areas while I will rule over the towns and cities. If not, I will bring the Ghatfaan tribe and attack you. I will fill Madinah with the infantry and the cavalry." Rasulullah ﷺ said: "Allah will not give you such power." The conversation ended and when both stood up, Rasulullah ﷺ made the following dua: "O Allah! Protect me from the mischief of 'Aamir ibn Tufayl and guide his people." When he went outside, 'Aamir said to Arbad: "How sad. I waited for you but you did not even attack." Arbad replied: "Whenever I unsheathed my sword, I saw something or the other as a barrier before me. Once I saw a wall made of iron, then I saw a camel that wanted to swallow my head."

When this delegation left Rasulullah ﷺ, 'Aamir was destroyed by a plague. Since the Arabs consider it a shame to die on a bed, he asked the people to seat him on a horse. He got onto a horse and took a spear in his hand. He then said: "O angel of death, come before me." While saying this, he fell from the horse and he was buried at that very place. When the delegation reached the place of Banu 'Aamir, the people asked Arbad about the journey. He said: "His religion is worthless. By Allah, if he (Muhammad ﷺ) was in front of me now, I would have killed him with arrows." Within two days he mounted a camel and left. Lightning immediately struck him and he was conveyed to hell. Both 'Aamir and Arbad were deprived of Islam while most of the remainder of their tribe embraced Islam.

4. The delegation of 'Abd al-Qays

This was a very large tribe. They lived in Bahrain. A delegation from the tribe came to Rasulullah ﷺ on two occasions. The first delegation came before the conquest of Makkah – in 5 A.H. or even before that. There were 13-14 delegates in that delegation. When they came, Rasulullah ﷺ said to them:

مرحبا بالقوم غير خزايا ولا ندامىٰ

"Welcome to you. You will neither be disgraced nor will you have cause for remorse."

The delegation said: "O Messenger of Allah! The disbelievers from the Mudar tribe are an obstacle between us and you. We can only come to you in the sacred months in which the Arabs consider it prohibited to loot and kill. Therefore, teach us something that is so comprehensive and short, that if we do it, we will enter into paradise and to which we could also invite the rest of our tribe." Rasulullah ﷺ said: "Believe in Allah and testify that He is one, He has no partners. Establish Salaah and give zakaah. Give one fifth of the booty in the cause of Allah. And do not soak dates in four types of containers: dubba', naqeer, hantam and muzaffat."

When this delegation came to Madinah, these people jumped from their camels out of their extreme desire to see Rasulullah ﷺ. They presented themselves before him and kissed his hand. Ashaj 'Abd al-Qays Mubhami, whose name was Munzir, was also in this delegation. He was the youngest person in this delegation. He first seated all the camels and placed the goods on one side. He then removed two clean pieces of white cloth from his trunk. He wore these and presented himself before Rasulullah ﷺ. He shook hands with Rasulullah ﷺ and kissed his hand. Rasulullah ﷺ said to him: "You have two qualities in you which are liked by Allah Ta'ala and His Messenger ﷺ. One is forbearance and the other is dignity." Ashaj said: "O Messenger of Allah! Are these two qualities found naturally in me or did I go to pains in adopting them?" Rasulullah ﷺ replied: "Allah Ta'ala created you like this from birth." On hearing this, he said: "All praise is due to Allah who created me with two qualities which Allah Ta'ala and His Messenger ﷺ love."

5. The delegation of Banu Hanifah – 9 A.H.

This delegation came to Rasulullah ﷺ in 9 A.H. The notorious Musaylamah Kazzaab was also in this delegation. However, due to his pride and haughtiness, he did not meet Rasulullah ﷺ. Rasulullah ﷺ himself went to him with Saabit ibn Qays ibn Shammaas. He said to Rasulullah ﷺ: "If you give me caliphate and make me your deputy after you, I am prepared to pledge allegiance to you." Rasulullah ﷺ had a branch of the date tree in his hand at that time. He therefore said to him: "Even if you ask me for this branch, I will not give it to you. You will never be able to turn away from what Allah has destined for you. It is probably you who I have been shown in my dream. Here is Saabit ibn Qays. He will reply to you." On saying this, Rasulullah ﷺ returned from there.

Ibn 'Abbaas ؓ says: "I asked Abu Hurayrah ؓ as to what dream Rasulullah ﷺ was shown." He replied: "Rasulullah ﷺ said: 'I saw a dream in which two gold blankets were placed in my hands. I became very afraid on seeing them. In my dream I was asked to blow onto them. After blowing on them, they flew away." The interpretation of this is that there will be two imposters (claiming prophet-hood). One of them was Musaylamah and the other was Aswad 'Ansi. The latter was killed during Rasulullah's ﷺ life while Musaylamah was killed during the caliphate of Abu Bakr ؓ.

$$\text{فَقُطِعَ دَابِرُ الْقَوْمِ الَّذِيْنَ ظَلَمُوْا وَالْحَمْدُ لِلهِ رَبِّ الْعَلَمِيْنَ}$$

"The power of those who wronged themselves was severed. And all praise is due to Allah, the Sustainer of the worlds."

In 10 A.H. Musaylamah wrote the following letter to Rasulullah ﷺ:

من مسيلمة رسول الله إلى محمد رسول الله أما بعد فإني قد أشركت معك في الأمر وإن لنا نصف الأرض ولقريش نصفها ولكن قريشا لا ينصفون والسلام

"From Musaylamah, the messenger of Allah, to Muhammad the Messenger of Allah. I have been made a partner in the religion. Half the land will be for us and the other half for the Quraysh. However, the Quraysh are not just. Wassalaam."

Rasulullah ﷺ sent the following reply:

بسم الله الرحمن الرحيم. من محمد رسول الله إلى مسيلمة الكذاب. أما بعد فالسلام على من اتبع الهدى. فإن الأرض لله يورثها من يشاء من عباده والعاقبة للمتقين

"In the name of Allah, the beneficent, the merciful. From Muhammad, the Messenger of Allah, to Musaylamah, the imposter. Peace be on he who follows guidance. The land belongs to Allah. He gives it in inheritance to whomever He wills from His servants. The good outcome is for those who fear (Allah)."

This incident took place on Rasulullah's ﷺ return from the Farewell Haj.

6. The delegation of Tayy

The delegation from the Tayy tribe comprised of 15 delegates. Their leader was Zaid al-Khayl. Rasulullah ﷺ presented Islam to them and they all readily and gladly accepted. Rasulullah ﷺ changed the leader's name to Zaid al-Khayr and said to him: "Of all the Arabs whose praises I heard, I found them to be less than the praises that were showered on them. However, you are an exception."

7. The delegation of Kindah

Kindah is the name of a tribe from Yemen. A delegation of 80 came to Rasulullah ﷺ in 10 A.H. Their leader was Ash'ath ibn Qays. When they came to Rasulullah ﷺ, they were wearing gowns that were bordered with silk. Rasulullah ﷺ asked them: "Are you not Muslims?" They replied: "Why not? We are certainly Muslims." Rasulullah ﷺ asked: "Then what is this silk around your necks?" They immediately took off these garments and discarded them.

8. The delegation of Ash'ariyyin

The Ash'ariyyin was a very noble and large tribe from Yemen which was attributed to their forefather, Ash'ar. The reason why he was given this name was that when he was born he had a lot of hair on his body. The word Ash'ar means having a lot of hair. Abu Musa Ash'ari رضى الله عنه was from this tribe. When this delegation departed from Yemen, they sang this line with much enthusiasm:

غدا نلقى الأحبه محمدا وحزبه

"Tomorrow we will meet with our beloved ones, Muhammad ﷺ and his group of followers."

On the other end, Rasulullah ﷺ informed his Sahaabah رضى الله عنهم that a group of people who are very soft hearted are going to come. When the Ash'ariyyin reached Madinah, Rasulullah ﷺ addressed the Sahaabah رضى الله عنهم saying: The people of Yemen have come. They are very soft hearted people. (In other words, they are free from hard-heartedness. They readily accept the truth. They are not so hard that any admonition and wise words do not affect them). It is for this reason that Imaan is Yemeni and wisdom is also Yemeni. (In other words, the result of their soft heartednes is that their hearts are store-houses of Imaan and recognition (of Allah) and fountains of knowledge and wisdom.)

How true these words of Rasulullah ﷺ are! It is soft-heartedness alone that is the fountain of all good. Hard-heartedness is the root of all evil.

Because the people of Yemen used to tend to sheep and goats, he said that peace, tranquillity, dignity and humility are qualities that are found in people who tend to sheep and goats. As for pride and haughtiness, these are qualities that are found in people who tend to camels. Rasulullah ﷺ was referring to the disbelievers.

The delegates said to Rasulullah ﷺ: "O Messenger of Allah! We have come to gain a deep understanding of Islam and to learn about the beginning of the creation of the universe." Rasulullah ﷺ said: "First of all, there was Allah.

There was nothing apart from Him. His throne was on water. (In other words, the commencement of the universe was with water and the throne. Water was created first and then the throne). The heavens and the earth were then created. Everything was recorded in the Preserved Tablet."

9. The delegation of Azd

The delegation of the Azd tribe came to Rasulullah ﷺ and embraced Islam. This delegation had 15 delegates, among whom was Surad ibn 'Abdullah Azdi. Rasulullah ﷺ appointed him as their leader and ordered him to wage Jihaad against the disbelievers that lived around them. He took a group of Muslims and laid siege to a town called Jarsh. The siege lasted for one month with no victory. He therefore turned to leave. The residents of Jarsh assumed that his turning away was his defeat. They therefore gave chase to him. When the Muslims reached the Mt. Shakr, they turned around and attacked the people of Jarsh. They were thus defeated.

In the meantime, the people of Jarsh had sent two representatives to Madinah. Rasulullah ﷺ informed them of the defeat at Mt. Shakr on the very day that it took place. When these representatives returned home and gave all the details to them, a delegation went to Madinah and embraced Islam.

10. The delegation of Banu Haaris

The Banu Haaris was a respectable family of Najraan. It was either in Rabi'ul-Aakhir or Jumaadal-Ula 10. A.H. that Rasulullah ﷺ sent Khaalid ibn Waleed رضي الله عنه to invite them towards Islam for three days. If they do not embrace Islam within this period, he should wage Jihaad against them. When Khaalid رضي الله عنه went there, they embraced Islam immediately. He also sent others to the surrounding areas in order to invite the people towards Islam. The people of these areas embraced Islam willingly. Khaalid رضي الله عنه sent a letter to Rasulullah ﷺ giving him this good news. Rasulullah ﷺ replied, instructing him to return with a delegation from there. Khaalid رضي الله عنه took a delegation to Madinah. Qays ibn Husayn, Yazeed ibn Mihjal and Shaddaad ibn 'Abdullah were also among the delegates. When these people presented themselves before Rasulullah ﷺ, he asked:

من هؤلاء القوم الذين كأنهم رجال الهند

"Who are these people who look like Indians?"

They replied: "We are the Banu Haaris. We bear witness that you are the Messenger of Allah and that there is none worthy of worship besides Allah."

These people were a very brave nation and were always victorious over their adversaries. Rasulullah ﷺ therefore asked them the basis for their victories and successes. They replied: "We always remain united – we never differ with each other. We are not envious of each other. We do not go on the offensive. We remain patient during times of difficulty and hardship." Rasulullah ﷺ said: "You are correct." He then appointed Qays ibn Husayn as their Ameer and sent 'Amr ibn Hazm رضي الله عنه to collect the charities from them. Rasulullah ﷺ had the injunctions of zakaah and other charities written down and sent with him.

This delegation returned to its people in Shawwaal or Zul Qa'dah. Within four months after their return, Rasulullah ﷺ departed from this world.

11. The delegation of Hamdaan

The Hamdaan is a big tribe of Yemen. Rasulullah ﷺ sent Khaalid ibn Waleed رضي الله عنه to them to invite them towards Islam. He remained doing so for six months but no one embraced Islam. Rasulullah ﷺ sent Ali رضي الله عنه with a letter and told him to ask Khaalid رضي الله عنه to return. Ali رضي الله عنه went there, gathered everyone, and read the letter to them. He invited them to Islam and they all accepted in one day. Ali رضي الله عنه wrote a letter to Rasulullah ﷺ and informed him of this. Rasulullah ﷺ immediately fell into sajdah and thanked Allah Ta'ala. Out of extreme happiness, he repeatedly said: "Peace be on the Hamdaan."

This incident took place in 8 A.H. when Rasulullah ﷺ was returning from Taa'if. A year later, a delegation of Hamdaan came to meet Rasulullah ﷺ. When they arrived, they were wearing the embossed shawls of Yemen, the turbans of Aden and riding on beautiful camels. They conversed with Rasulullah ﷺ in a very beautiful and eloquent manner. He acceded to whatever requests they made and gave them a letter and appointed Maalib ibn Namt, who was one of the delegates, as their leader. Hasan ibn Ya'qoob Hamdaani says that this delegation had 120 delegates.

12. The delegation of Muzaynah

In 5 A.H. 400 people from the Muzaynah tribe came to Rasulullah ﷺ and embraced Islam. When they were departing, they said to Rasulullah ﷺ that they had no provisions for the journey and that he should give them some. He ordered 'Umar رضي الله عنه to give some provisions to them. He replied that he had very little dates and that they will not be sufficient for these people. Rasulullah ﷺ said: "Go and give them some provisions." 'Umar رضي الله عنه took them to his home and each one took as much dates as he needed. At the end, there was not a single date less in his sack of dates.

Kaseer ibn 'Abdillah al-Muzani ﷺ narrates from his father who narrates from his grandfather that the Muzaynah tribe was the first to present itself before Rasulullah ﷺ.

13. The delegation of Daus

About 70-80 delegates from this tribe came to Rasulullah ﷺ in 7 A.H. after the battle of Khaybar. Details in this regard were given under the incident concerning Tufayl ibn 'Umar Dausi's ﷺ acceptance of Islam.

14. The delegation of Christians from Najraan

Najraan was the name of a large city in Yemen. There were 73 districts and villages that were under it. Najraan ibn Zaid was the first person to come and settle in this place. The city was therefore named after him. Ukhdud, a place that is mentioned in Surah al-Burooj was a district that fell under Najraan.

In 9 A.H., a delegation of 60 delegates from the Christians of Najraan came to Madinah. Fourteen of these delegates were their noblemen and leaders. 'Abdul Maseeh was their leader while Ayham acted as their minister, consultant and organiser. Their chief bishop was Abu Haarisah ibn 'Alqamah. He was originally from the Arab tribe of Bakr ibn Waa'il. He became a Christian. The kings of Rome respected him greatly because of his knowledge, virtue, religious capabilities and fortitude. They had given him many properties. He was also appointed as the head of the church.

This delegation came to Madinah with much pomp and show. Rasulullah ﷺ settled them into the Masjid-e-Nabawi. The Asr Salaah had just been performed. When the time for their prayer came, they wanted to perform it. The Sahaabah ﷺ stopped them, but Rasulullah ﷺ said to them that they may offer their Salaah. They turned towards the east and did so.

In the course of their stay, various matters were discussed. First of all, a discussion concerning the "divinity" of 'Isa ﷺ and his being the "son of God" commenced.

The Christian delegation: "If 'Isa ﷺ is not the son of God, then who is his father?"

Rasulullah ﷺ: "You know very well that the son looks like his father."

The Christian delegation: "Of course. This is always the case."

We can thus conclude that if 'Isa ﷺ is the son of God, he would have been similar to and looked like Allah, whereas we know for a fact that there is absolutely nothing that is similar to Him. Allah Ta'ala says in the Qur-aan: "There is nothing similar to Him." "There is no one equal to Him."

Rasulullah ﷺ: "Do you not know that our Allah is 'forever living, He will never die'? And that 'Isa عَلَيْهِ السَّلَام is to die?"

The Christian Delegation: "Without doubt, this is correct."

Rasulullah ﷺ: "Are you aware of the fact that our Allah is the maintainer of everything, the protector and overseer of the entire universe, and the sustainer of all. Does 'Isa عَلَيْهِ السَّلَام possess any of these qualities?"

The Christian Delegation: "No."

Rasulullah ﷺ: "Are you aware of the fact that nothing in the heavens and the earth is concealed from Allah? Does 'Isa عَلَيْهِ السَّلَام know anything more than that which Allah taught him?"

The Christian Delegation: "No."

Rasulullah ﷺ: "You know fully well that Allah Ta'ala created 'Isa عَلَيْهِ السَّلَام in the womb of his mother as He willed. You also know for a fact that Allah neither eats nor drinks, nor does He need to relieve Himself."

The Christian Delegation: "Yes, without a doubt."

Rasulullah ﷺ: "You know very well that Maryam رَضِيَ اللهُ عَنْهَا fell pregnant with 'Isa عَلَيْهِ السَّلَام like normal women. She gave birth to him just like normal women do. She then fed him just as normal babies are fed. He used to eat and drink, and also relieve himself."

The Christian Delegation: "Without doubt, this is how it was."

Rasulullah ﷺ: "Then how did he become a God?"

In other words, he who was created and formed in the womb of a woman, who was in need of nourishment after birth, and who was in need of relieving himself – how can such a person be God?

The truth became obvious on the Christian delegation of Najraan. However they persisted in refusing to follow the truth. Allah Ta'ala revealed the following verses:

الٓمٓ ۝ اللّٰهُ لَآ اِلٰهَ اِلَّا هُوَ ۙ الْحَيُّ الْقَيُّوْمُ ۝ نَزَّلَ عَلَيْكَ الْكِتٰبَ بِالْحَقِّ مُصَدِّقًا لِّمَا بَيْنَ يَدَيْهِ وَاَنْزَلَ التَّوْرٰىةَ وَالْاِنْجِيْلَ ۝ مِنْ قَبْلُ هُدًى لِّلنَّاسِ وَاَنْزَلَ الْفُرْقَانَ ۚ اِنَّ الَّذِيْنَ كَفَرُوْا بِاٰيٰتِ اللّٰهِ لَهُمْ عَذَابٌ شَدِيْدٌ ۗ وَاللّٰهُ عَزِيْزٌ ذُو انْتِقَامٍ ۝ اِنَّ اللّٰهَ لَا يَخْفٰى عَلَيْهِ شَيْءٌ فِي الْاَرْضِ وَلَا فِي السَّمَآءِ ۝ هُوَ الَّذِيْ يُصَوِّرُكُمْ فِي الْاَرْحَامِ كَيْفَ يَشَآءُ ۚ لَآ اِلٰهَ اِلَّا هُوَ الْعَزِيْزُ الْحَكِيْمُ ۝

"Alif Laam Meem. Allah! there is no God other than Him, the living, the sustainer of all. He sent down to you the true Book. It confirms the previous books, and He sent down the Taurah and the Injeel prior to this Book, for the guidance of people. And He sent down the criteria. Surely those who rejected the verses of Allah, for them is a severe punishment. And Allah is mighty, taker of revenge. Nothing is concealed from Allah in the earth nor in the heaven. It is He who fashions you in the womb of the mother as He wills. There is no worship for anyone other than Him. He is mighty, wise." [Surah Aal 'Imraan, verses 1-6]

Rasulullah ﷺ presented Islam to the Christians of Najraan. They replied: "We were already on Islam." He asked them: "How can your Islam be valid when you believe that Allah has a son, you worship the cross, and you consume pork?" They said: "You claim that 'Isa عليه السلام is a servant of Allah. Have you ever heard or seen anyone being born like him?" The following verse was revealed:

إِنَّ مَثَلَ عِيسَىٰ عِندَ ٱللَّهِ كَمَثَلِ ءَادَمَ ۖ خَلَقَهُۥ مِن تُرَابٍ ثُمَّ قَالَ لَهُۥ كُن فَيَكُونُ ۝ ٱلْحَقُّ مِن رَّبِّكَ فَلَا تَكُن مِّنَ ٱلْمُمْتَرِينَ ۝ فَمَنْ حَآجَّكَ فِيهِ مِنۢ بَعْدِ مَا جَآءَكَ مِنَ ٱلْعِلْمِ فَقُلْ تَعَالَوْا۟ نَدْعُ أَبْنَآءَنَا وَأَبْنَآءَكُمْ وَنِسَآءَنَا وَنِسَآءَكُمْ وَأَنفُسَنَا وَأَنفُسَكُمْ ثُمَّ نَبْتَهِلْ فَنَجْعَل لَّعْنَتَ ٱللَّهِ عَلَى ٱلْكَٰذِبِينَ

"Surely the similitude of 'Isa in the sight of Allah is like that of Aadam - He created him from dust and then said to him: "Be!" and he became. The truth is that which your Sustainer says, so you do not be of the doubters. Thereafter, whoever disputes with you about this story (of 'Isa) after the true facts have come to you, then you should say: "Come! Let us call our sons and your sons, and our women and your women, and ourselves and yourselves; then let us all earnestly pray and invoke the curse of Allah on those who are liars." [Surah Aal 'Imraan, verses 59-61]

Mubaahalah (invoking curses)

After the revelation of these verses, Rasulullah ﷺ got ready for the Mubaahalah. The following day he appeared with Hasan رضي الله عنه, Husayn رضي الله عنه, Faatimah رضي الله عنها and Ali رضي الله عنه. On seeing these illuminated and blessed faces, the Christians were over-awed and asked Rasulullah ﷺ for a respite so that they could confer with each other. They would return to Rasulullah ﷺ thereafter. They therefore went aside and began conferring with each other. Ayham said to the bishop, 'Abdul Maseeh: "By Allah, you know very well that this person is a Prophet sent by Allah. If you were to engage in Mubaahalah with him, you will be totally destroyed. By Allah, I am seeing such blessed faces (referring to the family of Rasulullah ﷺ) that if they were to ask the mountains to move, they will move from their places. By Allah, you have clearly recognised his prophet-hood. Whatever he said about 'Isa عَلَيْهِ الْسَلَامْ is the absolute truth. By Allah, whoever engaged in a Mubaahalah with a Prophet never succeeded. Therefore, do not destroy yourself by engaging in a Mubaahalah with him. If you really want to remain on your religion, make peace with him and return."

They eventually retracted from the Mubaahalah and agreed to pay the jizyah on an annual basis. Rasulullah ﷺ said: "I take an oath in the name of that being in whose control is my life, the punishment (of Allah) was already hovering over the people of Najraan. Had they engaged in the Mubaahalah, they would have been transformed into monkeys and swines. Their entire valley would have turned into a fire and rained upon them. All the people of Najraan would have been destroyed. No birds would have even remained on the trees."

The following day, Rasulullah ﷺ ordered a peace treaty to be written. The essence of this treaty was:

1. The people of Najraan will have to give 2000 garments annually. 1000 in the month of Rajab and 1000 in the month of Safar. The value of each one will have to be 40 dirhams.

2. The envoy that is sent by Rasulullah ﷺ to them will have to be accommodated by them for one month.

3. If there are any hostilities or uprisings in Yemen, the people of Najraan will have to lend 30 coats of armour, 30 horses, 30 camels. These will be returned to them later on. If any of these items are lost or destroyed, the Muslims will pay for them.

4. Allah Ta'ala and His Messenger ﷺ are responsible for the protection of their lives and belongings. Their wealth, their possessions, their properties, their rights, their religion, their covenants, their priests, their families and those who follow them – nothing will be changed or altered. There will be no demands for blood money for what had passed. No army will enter their land.

5. If anyone demands any right from them, justice will be meted out to both parties.

6. The person who devours interest does not fall under this responsibility.

7. If a person commits an act of transgression and oppression, someone else will not be taken to task. (Rather, the actual perpetrator will be taken to task).

This is the guarantee of Allah Ta'ala and His Messenger ﷺ as long as they remain steadfast on all these conditions. This peace treaty was signed by Abu Sufyaan ibn Harb, Ghaylaan ibn 'Amr, Maalik ibn 'Auf, Aqra' ibn Haabis and Mughirah ibn Shu'bah.

This delegation then took this peace treaty and made preparations to return. When they were departing, they asked Rasulullah ﷺ to send a trustworthy person with them so that he could take the goods that were agreed upon in the treaty. Rasulullah ﷺ said to to them that he will send an extremely trustworthy person with them. He then ordered Abu 'Ubaydah ibn Jarrah رضي الله عنه to go with them. He was given the title of Ameenu Haazihil ummah – the trustworthy person of this ummah.

These people then departed for Najraan. When they were on the last stage of their journey, the priests and noblemen of Najraan came out to welcome them. The delegation handed the treaty to their chief priest and he became engrossed in reading it. In the meantime, the donkey on which Abu Haarisah was sitting, slipped and fell. His cousin, Kurz ibn 'Alqamah, cursed and said: "May that wretched one be destroyed." He was actually cursing Rasulullah ﷺ. Abu Haarisah said: "You are the wretched one. By Allah, he is a Messenger of Allah. He is the same person whose glad tidings are given in the Injeel and the Taurah." Kurz asked: "Then why do you not bring Imaan?" Abu Haarisah replied: "The kings will take back all the wealth that they gave us." Kurz said: "By Allah, I am turning around and I will only free my camel in Madinah (i.e. I will not stop till I reach Madinah)." He then headed towards Madinah with much enthusiasm. He was repeating these lines while going towards Madinah:

إليك تعدو قلقا وضينها   معتركا فى بطنها جنينا   مخالفا دين النصارى دينها

"This camel is hastening towards you (O Muhammad!). It's young (that is in its belly) is bridged. It is moving about in it's womb (because my camel is moving so swiftly). It's religion is now opposed to the religion of the Christians."

He then presented himself before Rasulullah ﷺ and embraced Islam. He remained in his company and was martyred in a battle. A few days later, Ayham and 'Abdul Maseeh also came to Madinah and embraced Islam. Rasulullah ﷺ accommodated both of them in the house of Abu Ayyub Ansaari رضي الله عنه.

15. Farwah ibn 'Amr Juzaami

Farwah ibn 'Amr Juzaami was the governor of Syria on behalf of the Roman king. When Rasulullah ﷺ sent him a letter inviting him towards Islam, he embraced Islam. He sent an envoy with some gifts to Rasulullah ﷺ. When the Romans heard that he embraced Islam, they ordered that he be hanged. When he was about to be hanged, he said the following lines:

بلغ سراة المسلمين بأنني   سلم لربي أعظمى ومقامى

"Convey this message to the leader of the Muslims that my bones and my place of stay have all submitted before my Sustainer."

16. Dimam ibn Sa'labah comes to Madinah

In 9 A.H. Dimam ibn Sa'labah came to Rasulullah ﷺ on behalf of the Banu Sa'd. He tied his camel near the door of the Masjid, entered and called out: "Who is Muhammad?" Rasulullah ﷺ was leaning against something in his assembly at that time. The Sahaabah رضي الله عنهم said: "This blessed person who is leaning down." The person said: "O son of 'Abdul Muttalib!" Rasulullah ﷺ said: "I have heard your call." He said: "I wish to ask you a few questions. I will be stern and strict in my questions. You should therefore not become angry." Rasulullah ﷺ: "You may ask whatever you like." He said: "I take an oath in the name of Allah and ask you, did He really send you as a Messenger to all people?" Rasulullah ﷺ replied: "Yes. O Allah! You are witness to this." The person then asked the following questions separately: "Did Allah command you to offer five times Salaah in a day? Did He order you to fast in one month of the year? Did He order you to take zakaah and other charities from the rich and distribute them among the poor?" Rasulullah ﷺ replied to all these questions: "Yes. O Allah! You be witness to this."

This person said: "I believe in everything that you have brought from Allah. I am an envoy on behalf of my people. My name is Dimam ibn Sa'labah. I take an oath in the name of that Being who sent you with the truth that I will not add or subtract what you just said to me." Rasulullah ﷺ said: "If this person is true to his word, he will certainly enter Jannah."

Note: It is learnt from this Hadith that it is permitted for an Aalim or respectable person to sit in an assembly while lying down and leaning against something.

When Dimam left Rasulullah ﷺ and returned to his people, he gathered all of them and delivered a speech to them. The first words that he uttered were: "Laat and 'Uzza are extremely evil." When the people heard this they said to him: "O Dimam! Do not utter such words. You might become mad and a leper." He replied: "How sad and sorrowful. By Allah, Laat and 'Uzza can neither harm you nor benefit you in any way. Allah Ta'ala sent a Messenger and revealed a Book to him which freed you from these fabrications. I bear witness that there is none worthy of worship besides Allah Ta'ala and that Muhammad ﷺ is the Messenger of Allah. I have learnt these injunctions from him." By the evening, all the members of this tribe embraced Islam. 'Umar رضي الله عنه and Ibn 'Abbaas رضي الله عنهما used to say: "We have not come across an envoy and delegate of a tribe who was better than Dimam ibn Sa'labah رضي الله عنه."

17. The delegation of Taariq ibn 'Abdillah Muhaaribi and the Bani Muhaarib

Taariq ibn 'Abdullah says: "I was in the market of Zul Majaaz when I saw a person saying:

ايها الناس قولوا لا اله الا الله تفلحوا

'O people! Say that there is none worthy of worship except Allah and you will find success.'

I saw another person behind him, throwing stones and saying:

يا ايها الناس انه كذاب فلا تصدقوه

'O people! He is a liar. Do not believe him.'

I asked: 'Who is this person?' Some people replied: 'He is from the Banu Haashim who claims that he is the Messenger of Allah, and the person who is throwing stones at him is his uncle, Abu Lahab.'"

Taariq ibn 'Abdullah says: "When the people began embracing Islam and Rasulullah ﷺ emigrated to Madinah, we left Zubdah and went to Madinah in order to buy dates from there. When we were near Madinah, we were planning to stop over at an orchard. A person wearing two old shawls approached us, greeted us and asked us where we were coming from. We replied that we were coming from Zubdah. He asked us where we were going. We replied that we were going to Madinah. He asked us for the reason and we said, 'to purchase dates.' We had a red camel with us. He asked us if we would give him this camel in exchange for a certain amount of dates. We agreed to this. He also agreed to the price and did not attempt to bargain over the price. He took the camel and proceeded. We began speaking among ourselves and said: 'How could we have given our camel to a person whom we do not even know and without even obtaining its value (of dates) as yet?' One of the women who was sitting in the haudaj said: 'I have seen the face of that person. By Allah, his face is like a piece of the 14th moon. It is not the face of a liar and treacherous person. Do not worry, I guarantee the price.' We were still busy in this conversation when another person came and said: 'I am the messenger of Rasulullah ﷺ. He has given these dates. You may eat from there and weigh them.' We ate to our fill and then weighed them. We found them to be exact. The following day we entered Madinah. Rasulullah ﷺ was standing on the mimbar and delivering a sermon (it was probably a Friday). We heard these words from him:

$$\text{تصدقوا فان اليد العليا خير من اليد السفلى امك واباك اختك}$$
$$\text{واخاك وادناك ادناك}$$

"Give in charity. Surely the upper hand is better than the lower hand. Be particular about giving to your mother, your father, your sister, your brother and your near relatives."

18. The delegation of Tujib

The Tujib is a branch of the Kindah tribe of Yemen. Thirteen people from Tujib came to Rasulullah ﷺ with the wealth of sadaqaat. Rasulullah ﷺ asked them to take it back and to distribute it among the poor of that area. They replied that they actually brought the remainder after distributing among the poor. Abu Bakr رضي الله عنه said: "O Messenger of Allah! Till now, no delegation like the Tujib has come to you." Rasulullah ﷺ said: "Without doubt, guidance is in the hand of Allah. When Allah Ta'ala wills good for anyone, he opens his chest for Imaan. These people asked several questions to Rasulullah ﷺ. He had them written for them and emphasised upon Bilal رضي الله عنه to be very hospitable to them.

A few days later, they requested permission to leave. Rasulullah ﷺ asked them the reason for their hurry. They replied: "O Messenger of Allah! Our hearts desire that the blessings that we gained by seeing your illuminated countenance and the benefits that we acquired from your company should also be conveyed to our people." Rasulullah ﷺ bid farewell to them after giving them some gifts. When they were departing, he asked them if anyone of them was left behind. They replied that one youngster, whom they had appointed to take care of the goods, was left behind. Rasulullah ﷺ asked them to call him. He came and said: "O Messenger of Allah! You have fulfilled the needs of my people. Now I have one request." Rasulullah ﷺ asked him: "What is it?" He replied: "The only reason why I left home and came to you is that you may make dua on my behalf to Allah Ta'ala that He forgives me, that He showers His mercy on me, and that He makes me rich of heart." Rasulullah ﷺ made this dua:

$$\text{اَللّٰهُمَّ اغْفِرْ لَهُ وَارْحَمْهُ وَاجْعَلْ غِنَاهُ فِىْ قَلْبِهٖ}$$

"O Allah, forgive him, have mercy on him, and make him rich in his heart."

In 10 A.H. some people of this tribe came for Haj. When Rasulullah ﷺ met them in Mina, he asked them about the youngster. They replied: "O Messenger of Allah! The condition of his piety and contentment is amazing. We have not come across anyone more pious and content than him. Irrespective of how much wealth is distributed before him, he does not even look at it. When some people of Yemen began reneging from Islam, this youngster addressed them in such a manner that everyone remained steadfast on Islam and no one turned away. When Abu Bakr رَضِيَ اللَّهُ عَنْهُ became the caliph, he would periodically inquire from the people about this youngster. When he heard of this incident (of how he addressed the people and how they remained steadfast on Islam), he sent a message to Ziyaad ibn Waleed to be particularly considerate towards this youngster.

19. The delegation of Huzaym

When this delegation reached Masjid-e-Nabawi, Rasulullah ﷺ was busy in a Janaazah Salaah. These people sat down on one side. When Rasulullah ﷺ was over, he called them and asked them: "Are you not Muslims?" They replied that they were Muslims. He asked them: "Then why did you not join the Janaazah Salaah of your fellow Muslim brother?" They replied: "We did not know whether it was permissible for us to join in since we have not pledged our allegiance to you as yet." He replied: "You become Muslims wherever you may be (once you embrace Islam, you are Muslims, there is no need to wait to pledge allegiance to me)."

Later, the people pledged allegiance to Rasulullah ﷺ and were departing. They had left a youngster to take care of their possessions. He called these people back. This youngster came forward and pledged allegiance to Rasulullah ﷺ. These people said: "O Messenger of Allah! He is the youngest amongst us and he is our servant." Rasulullah ﷺ said:

اصغر القوم خادمهم بارك الله عليك

"The youngest person is the servant of the people. May Allah shower you with His blessings."

By the blessing of this dua, this youngster became the most knowledgeable of the Qur-aan from this tribe. Rasulullah ﷺ eventually appointed him as their leader and Imaam. Rasulullah ﷺ instructed Bilal رَضِيَ اللَّهُ عَنْهُ to give these people some gifts. When they returned to their homes, the entire tribe embraced Islam.

20. The delegation of Bani Fazaarah

On Rasulullah's ﷺ return from Tabuk, about 14 people from the Bani Fazaarah came to Rasulullah ﷺ. He asked them about their land. They replied that they were suffering from a severe drought which was causing much destruction. He made dua for rain for them.

21. The delegation of Bani Asd – 9 A.H.

Ten people from this tribe came to Rasulullah ﷺ. He was sitting in the Masjid at that time. They greeted him and one of them said: "O Messenger of Allah! We bear witness that Allah is one, He has no partner, and that you are His Messenger. We have come to you without your calling us." The following verse was revealed:

$$يَمُنُّوْنَ عَلَيْكَ اَنْ اَسْلَمُوْا ۭ قُلْ لَّا تَمُنُّوْا عَلَيَّ اِسْلَامَكُمْ ۚ بَلِ اللّٰهُ يَمُنُّ عَلَيْكُمْ اَنْ هَدٰىكُمْ لِلْاِيْمَانِ اِنْ كُنْتُمْ صٰدِقِيْنَ ۝$$

"They consider it a favour to you that they have embraced Islam. Say: 'Do not consider your Islam a favour to me. Rather, Allah has done you a favour by guiding you to the path of Imaan, if you are saying the truth.'" [Surah Hujuraat, verse 17]

These people then asked Rasulullah ﷺ about fortune telling. Rasulullah ﷺ prohibited them from this.

22. The delegation of Bahraa'

Thirteen people from the Bahraa' tribe of Yemen came to Rasulullah ﷺ. They stayed at the house of Miqdaad ibn Aswad ؓ. Before their arrival, Miqdaad ؓ prepared a special dish for them (prepared with dates and cheese). When these guests arrived, he presented it to them. They all ate to their fill. Miqdaad ؓ sent the remainder to Rasulullah ﷺ with his slave-woman, Sidrah. Rasulullah ﷺ ate thereof and also gave his entire family. He then returned the bowl in which it had come. As long as the guests remained, they continued eating twice a day from that bowl. One day, one of the guests asked in surprise: "O Miqdaad! We heard that the people of Madinah eat very simple food, yet you are providing us with such delicious food everyday which we cannot eat daily at our homes?" Miqdaad ؓ replied: "All this is through the blessed hand of Rasulullah ﷺ." He then informed them of the Barakah in the bowl (i.e. through the blessing of Rasulullah ﷺ). These people's Imaan and conviction increased even more. They remained in Madinah for a few days, learning the injunctions and tenets of Islam. They then returned to their homes. When they were departing, Rasulullah ﷺ gave them some gifts and provisions for the journey.

23. The delegation of 'Udhrah

This is a tribe of Yemen. Twelve people from this tribe came to Rasulullah ﷺ in Safar, 9 A.H. They asked him: "What do you invite towards?" Rasulullah ﷺ replied: "That you worship Allah, who is one and has no partner, and that you bear testimony that I am the Messenger of Allah to the entire mankind." The people then inquired about the compulsory acts of Islam and Rasulullah ﷺ informed them thereof. They then said: "We bear testimony that there is none worthy of worship beside Allah and that you are certainly Allah's Messenger. You invited us and we accepted. We are your helpers and supporters with all our heart. O Messenger of Allah! We go to Syria for our business. That is where Heraclius is. Has any revelation in this regard been sent to you?" Rasulullah ﷺ replied: "Syria will be conquered soon and Heraclius will flee." Rasulullah ﷺ then prohibited them from going to fortune tellers and from eating their sacrificial animals. They departed after a few days. Rasulullah ﷺ gave them some gifts on their departure.

24. The delegation of Baliyy

In Rabi'ul-Awwal 9 A.H. a delegation of Baliyy came to Rasulullah ﷺ and embraced Islam. Rasulullah ﷺ said to them:

الحمد لله الذى هداكم للاسلام فكل من مات على غير الاسلام فهو فى النار

"All praise is due to Allah who guided you towards Islam. Anyone who dies on a religion other than Islam shall enter the hell fire."

The head of the delegation, Abu ad-Dabib, said: "O Messenger of Allah! I like entertaining guests. Is there any reward for me in this?" Rasulullah ﷺ replied: "Yes. There is reward in this as well. When you show kindness to anyone, whether he is rich or poor, it is recorded as a charity in your favour." He asked: "O Messenger of Allah! What is the limit of entertaining a guest?" Rasulullah ﷺ replied: "Three days. Thereafter it is charity. It is not permitted for a guest to cause discomfort to the host." These people left after three days. Rasulullah ﷺ gave them provisions for the journey when they were departing.

25. The delegation of Bani Murrah

After Tabuk, a delegation of 13 members from the Bani Murrah came to Rasulullah ﷺ in 9 A.H. Haaris ibn 'Auf was the leader of this delegation. They said to Rasulullah ﷺ: "O Messenger of Allah! We are from your people. We are from the progeny of Lu'ayy ibn Ghaalib." Rasulullah ﷺ smiled and inquired about their land. They replied that there was much destruction because of the severe drought. He immediately made dua for rain. When they returned to their land, they learnt that it had rained the very day in which Rasulullah ﷺ had made dua for rain. The entire land had become green and lush. When they were leaving, Rasulullah ﷺ gave 10 ounces of silver to each of them and 12 ounces to their leader.

26. The delegation of Khaulaan

In Sha'baan 10 A.H. ten people from the Yemeni tribe of Khaulaan came to Rasulullah ﷺ and said: "O Messenger of Allah! We believe in Allah and in His Messenger. Allah and His Messenger have been very kind to us. We have travelled a great distance because of our desire to meet you." Rasulullah ﷺ replied: "This journey of yours has not been in vain. You are rewarded for every step that you took. The person who comes to visit me in Madinah will be under my protection on the Day of Resurrection." Rasulullah ﷺ then inquired of them about their idol, 'Amm Anas. They replied that through the guidance of Rasulullah ﷺ and his teachings, they found a far better alternative, and that no one besides a few old men and old women bother about it. They added that on their return, Insha Allah, no traces of it will be left.

Rasulullah ﷺ taught them the compulsory injunctions of Islam and advised them to fulfil their promises, fulfil their trusts, see to the needs of neighbours, and to abstain from oppressing anyone. When they were departing, he gave them 12 ounces of silver. The first thing they did when they returned was that they destroyed that idol.

27. The delegation of Muhaarib

The people of this tribe were very stern and rough. When Rasulullah ﷺ used to invite the Arab tribes in Makkah during the days of Haj, these people used to treat him very harshly. Ten members of this tribe came to Rasulullah ﷺ in 10 A.H. and embraced Islam. One of them said to Rasulullah ﷺ: "O Messenger of Allah! From my friends, there was not anyone who was more severe than me to you and more antagonistic towards Islam than my self. My friends have now passed away. I am the only one left. All thanks are due to Allah Ta'ala that he kept me alive till I brought Imaan in you and testified to your truthfulness." Rasulullah ﷺ replied: "The heart is in the control of Allah." The person said: "O Messenger of Allah! Make dua to Allah Ta'ala on my behalf and seek forgiveness for me that Allah forgives whatever disrespect I had shown to you." Rasulullah ﷺ replied: "Embracing Islam wipes out disbelief and all actions that were done when one was a disbeliever." These people then returned to their homes.

28. The delegation of Suda'

When Rasulullah ﷺ returned from Ji'irraanah in 8 A.H., he sent Muhaajir ibn Abi Umayyah to San'a', Ziyaad ibn Labid to Hadramaut, and Qays ibn Sa'd ibn 'Ubaadah with 400 riders towards Qanaat. Rasulullah ﷺ also instructed Qays to visit the Yemeni area of Suda'. When Ziyaad ibn Haaris Suda'i heard of this, he came himself and said: "O Messenger of Allah! Call your army back. I guarantee that my people will embrace Islam." Rasulullah ﷺ summoned Qays ibn Sa'd back. Ziyaad ibn Haaris came to Rasulullah ﷺ with a delegation of 15 people. They all embraced Islam and pledged allegiance at his hands. Rasulullah ﷺ addressed Ziyaad saying: "O Ziyaad! Your people are very obedient to you." He replied: "O Messenger of Allah! It is the kindness of Allah and His Messenger that Allah guided them to Islam." After pledging their allegiance, these people returned and Islam spread throughout the tribe. One hundred people from this tribe took part in the Farewell Haj.

29. The delegation of Ghassaan

In Ramadhaan 10 A.H. three people from this tribe came to Rasulullah ﷺ and embraced Islam. They said that they were not sure as to whether their people would follow suit or not. When they were departing, Rasulullah ﷺ gave them gifts and provisions for the journey. Since their people hadn't embraced Islam, they concealed their beliefs. Two of them passed away. The third person met Abu 'Ubaydah ؓ in the battle of Yarmuk and informed him of his Islam. Abu 'Ubaydah ؓ showed much respect to him.

30. The delegation of Salaamaan

A delegation of seven people from this tribe came to Rasulullah ﷺ in Shawwaal 10 A.H. and embraced Islam. They complained of a drought. Rasulullah ﷺ raised his hands and made dua for them. He then gave them some gifts and provisions and bid them farewell. On reaching their homes, they learnt that it had rained there on the exact day and time when Rasulullah ﷺ had raised his hands and made dua.

31. The delegation of Bani 'Abas

Three members from this tribe came to Rasulullah ﷺ and said: "O Messenger of Allah! We have heard that Islam without emigration is not accepted. We have some wealth and cattle on which we survive. If Islam is not accepted without emigration, can there be any blessing in our wealth and cattle? Should we sell everything and emigrate to you?" Rasulullah ﷺ replied:

اتقوا الله حيث كنتم فلن يَلِتَكُمُ الله من اعمالكم شيئا

"Fear Allah wherever you may be. Allah will not reduce the rewards of your deeds in any way."

32. The delegation of Ghaamid

This is a tribe from Yemen. Ten members of this tribe came to Madinah in 10 A.H. and dismounted in Baqi'. They left a youngster to see to their goods and proceeded to Rasulullah ﷺ. He asked them: "Who did you leave with your goods?" They replied: "We left a youngster." Rasulullah ﷺ said: "A bag has been stolen." A person said: "O Messenger of Allah! That bag belonged to me." Rasulullah ﷺ said: "Don't worry, it has been found." When these people returned to their goods they learnt that the youngster had fallen asleep. When he woke up, he realised that one bag was missing. He therefore went out in search for it. He saw a person sitting at a distance. When he advanced towards him, this person ran away. On reaching the spot where that man was sitting, he found that the ground there had been dug up recently. On digging it, he found the bag there. These people said: "Without doubt, he is the Messenger of Allah." Ubayy ibn Ka'b رضى الله عنه was instructed to teach them the Qur-aan. When they were leaving, some injunctions of Islam were written and given to them. As was his habit, Rasulullah ﷺ gave them some gifts.

33. The delegation of Azd

Seven members from this tribe came to Rasulullah ﷺ. He was impressed by their appearance and mannerisms. He inquired as to who they were. They replied: "We are believers." Rasulullah ﷺ smiled and said: "There is a proof for every claim. What is the proof of your Imaan?" They said: "Fifteen characteristics:

five of which your envoys asked us to believe in, five of which your envoys asked us to practise on, and five of which we possess since pre-Islamic times."

Rasulullah ﷺ asked: "What are those which my envoys asked you to believe in?" They replied: "To believe in Allah, His angels, His Books, His Messengers, and life after death." Rasulullah ﷺ asked: "What are those which my envoys asked you to practise on?" They replied: "We should continuously say that there is none worthy of worship but Allah, we should establish Salaah, we should pay the zakaah, we should fast in the month of Ramadhaan, we should perform the Haj if we are able to."

Rasulullah ﷺ asked: "What are the five qualities which you have since pre-Islamic times?" They replied:

الشكر عند الرخاء والصبر عند البلاء والرضا بالقضاء والصدق فى مواطن اللقاء و ترك الشماتة بالاعداء فقال صلى الله عليه وسلم حكماء علماء كادوا من فقههم ان يكونوا انبياء ثم قال وانا ازيدكم خمسا فتمت لكم عشرون خصلة ان كنتم كما تقولون فلا تجمعوا مالا تاكلون ولا تبنوا مالا تسكنون ولا تنافسوا فى شىء انتم عنه غدا نائلون واتقوا الله الذى اليه ترجعون و عليه تعرضون وارغبوا فيما عليه تعرضون وارغبوا فيما عليه تقدمون وفيه تخلدون

"(1) To be grateful at times of prosperity. (2) To be patient at times of hardship. (3) To be pleased with whatever has been destined. (4) To remain steadfast when meeting the enemy. (5) To abstain from being happy when calamity afflicts the enemy." Rasulullah ﷺ said: "You are very wise and intelligent people. You are very close to being Prophets based on your intelligence." Rasulullah ﷺ then said: "I will now add five other qualities thereby completing 20. If you are as you claim, then (1) Do not horde that which you will not eat. (2) Do not build that in which you will not live. (3) Do not compete in something that you are certain to leave behind tomorrow. (4) Fear Allah to whom you are going to return and before whom you will be presented. (5) Desire that in which you are going to live forever, i.e. the hereafter."

These people went back taking along this advice of Rasulullah ﷺ. They remembered it well and practised on it.

34. The delegation of Bani al-Muntafiq

This delegation came to Rasulullah ﷺ after the Fajr Salaah. Coincidentally, Rasulullah ﷺ had gathered the Sahaabah رضي الله عنهم and gave them a lengthy talk in which he explained the resurrection, paradise, hell, etc. to them. When he completed his talk, these people went up to him, pledged allegiance to him and returned.

35. The delegation of Nakha'

This was a tribe from Yemen. Two hundred people from this tribe came to Rasulullah ﷺ in the middle of the month of Muharram, 11 A.H. A person by the name of Zuraarah ibn 'Amr was also part of this delegation. During this journey, he saw several dreams which he related to Rasulullah ﷺ who interpreted it for him. Among these dreams, he saw one in which a fire was emanating from the ground which came as a barrier between himself and his son. The fire was calling out:

لظى لظى بصير واعمى اطعموني اكلكم اهلكم ومالكم

"I am the fire, I am the fire. Give me a person who can see and a blind person to eat. I will eat you, your family and your wealth."

Rasulullah ﷺ said: "There will be a tribulation wherein people will kill their leader. The evil ones will consider themselves to be very pious. Killing believers will be more enjoyable than drinking water. If your son passes away first, you will witness this tribulation. If you pass away first, your son will witness it." Zuraarah said: "O Messenger of Allah! Make dua on my behalf that I do not have to witness this tribulation." Rasulullah ﷺ made dua in his favour. Zuraarah passed away after some time and this was followed by the tribulation of the martyrdom of 'Usmaan رضي الله عنه. Zuraarah's son had joined the ranks of the rebels. Allah Ta'ala knows best.

Islam is taught in Yemen

In 9 A.H. or 10 A.H. Rasulullah ﷺ sent Abu Musa Ash'ari رضي الله عنه and Mu'aaz ibn Jabal رضي الله عنه to the people of Yemen in order to teach them Islam. However, both were not sent to the same place. Abu Musa رضي الله عنه was sent to the eastern section of Yemen while Mu'aaz ibn Jabal رضي الله عنه was sent to the west, i.e. to Aden and the areas surrounding Jund.

Khaalid ibn Waleed's ﷺ expedition to Najraan

In Rabi'us-Saani or Jumaadal Ula 10 A.H., Rasulullah ﷺ sent Khaalid ibn Waleed ﷺ at the head of an expedition to Najraan and the surrounding areas. Rasulullah ﷺ ordered him to invite the people towards Islam for three days before fighting them. If they embrace Islam within these three days, he must accept their Islam. If they refuse to embrace Islam, he may fight against them. When Khaalid ﷺ reached Najraan and invited them towards Islam, they all responded positively. Khaalid ﷺ began teaching them the basics of Islam. He sent a letter to Rasulullah ﷺ informing him of this news. Rasulullah ﷺ sent a reply that Khaalid ﷺ should return to Madinah with a delegation from the Banu Haaris ibn Ka'b tribe. Khaalid ﷺ complied with these instructions of Rasulullah ﷺ and brought these people to Madinah. Rasulullah ﷺ hosted them with much honour. When they were departing in Zul Qa'dah 10 A.H., he appointed Qays ibn Husayn ﷺ as their leader. Rasulullah ﷺ also appointed 'Amr ibn Hazm ﷺ to teach them the injunctions and rules of Islam, to collect the taxes, etc. Rasulullah ﷺ also gave him the following letter:

> In the name of Allah, the Beneficent, the Merciful.

> This is an order from Allah and His Messenger. O you who are believers! Fulfil your covenants. This is a covenant from Muhammad, the Prophet and Messenger of Allah for 'Amr ibn Hazm when he sent him to Yemen. He commands him to fear Allah in all his affairs. Surely Allah is with those who fear and those who do good. He commands him to hold on to the truth as Allah commanded him. That he commands the people with good and gives them the glad tidings thereof.

> That he teaches the people the Qur-aan and gives them an understanding of it. That he prohibits the people from touching the Qur-aan without being in a state of purity. That he informs the people of their rights and their responsibilities. That he be lenient to them in matters of the truth and strict on them in matters of oppression. Surely Allah dislikes oppression and prohibited it. Allah says: "Listen! Allah's curse is on the oppressors." That he should give the people the glad tidings of Jannah and teach them the deeds that will convey them to Jannah. That he warns the people of the Jahannam and caution them against deeds that will convey them to the hell-fire. That he should attract the people towards him so that they may learn about Islam.

> That he teaches the people about Haj, the Sunnah and obligatory acts thereof and all that Allah ordered concerning it. That he should teach them about the Umrah as well. That he should prohibit the people from offering Salaah in a small garment

unless it is a garment whose two ends are thrown over the shoulders. That he prohibits people from wearing clothes in such a way that their private parts are exposed to the sky. That he prohibits the people from plaiting their hair by their neck. That when there is any dispute among people, they should not shout out the slogans of families, tribes, etc. Rather, they should call to one Allah and to His commands. If anyone does not call to one Allah, and instead, calls out the slogans of families and tribes, then he should be put to the sword.

That he commands the people to perform a complete Wudhu: washing their faces, their hands upto the elbows, and their feet upto the ankles and that they wipe their heads. This is the procedure as commanded by Allah (in the Qur-aan). That he orders that Salaah be performed at its correct time, and that they complete the bowing posture and prostrations properly with humility. That they offer the Fajr Salaah when it is dark, the Zuhr Salaah after mid-day, the Asr Salaah when the sun spreads its light on the earth towards sunset, the Maghrib Salaah the moment the night commences (immediately after sunset) – it should not be delayed to the extent that stars begin appearing in the sky, and the 'Isha Salaah in the first third of the night. That when the call to the Jumu'ah Salaah is made, they should hasten to it. That they should take a bath before going for the Jumu'ah Salaah.

That he takes out from the booty one fifth which is the right of Allah Ta'ala. That he collects the sadaqah from the produce of the lands belonging to Muslims. One tenth of the produce should be given as charity from lands that have been irrigated with rain water and springs. One twentieth of the produce should be given as charity from lands that have been irrigated with water from wells.

For ten camels, the charity that is due is two sheep. For 20 camels it is four sheep. For 30 cows it is one cow. For 40 sheep it is one sheep. This is the duty which Allah Ta'ala made incumbent on the believers with regard to zakaah. Whoever gives more, it will be better for him.

Whoever embraces Islam after being a Jew or a Christian and he is sincere in his Islam, then he shall enjoy the same rights and bear the same responsibilities as other believers. He who remains on his Judaism or Christianity and wishes to live under the Islamic state will have to pay the jizyah which is one dinar or its value in clothing. This is applicable to every mature person irrespective of whether the person is male or female, free person or slave. Whoever pays this shall enjoy the responsibility of Allah and His Messenger ﷺ (i.e. his life, wealth and honour will be protected). Whoever refuses to pay this jizyah is the enemy of Allah, His Messenger ﷺ and of all believers.

Allah's peace, salutations, mercy and blessings on Muhammad.

Ali's ﷺ expedition towards Yemen

In the month of Ramadhaan 10 A.H., Rasulullah ﷺ appointed Ali ﷺ at the head of 300 men and sent him towards Yemen. Rasulullah ﷺ personally tied a turban onto his head. This turban had three folds. One end of it which was an arm's length was made to hang in the front while the other end which was a span's length was made to hang at the back. Rasulullah ﷺ said to him: "You must move straight ahead, do not be diverted in any direction. On reaching there, do not attack. You should first invite them towards Islam. If they accept, do not do anything to them. By Allah, if a single person embraces Islam at your hands, it will be better for you than this world and whatever it contains." Ali ﷺ departed with 300 men and on reaching Qanaat, he stopped over there. From this place, he sent small detachments of the Sahaabah ﷺ in different directions. The Muslim army first reached the area of Mudhjij and acquired many children, women, camels and goats. All this booty was gathered at one spot. They then had to face another group (of disbelievers). Ali ﷺ invited them to Islam. They refused and instead, began flinging arrows and rocks onto the Muslims. It was only then that Ali ﷺ attacked them. Twenty of their people were killed and the remainder dispersed. After a short pause, Ali ﷺ gave chase to them. He invited them to Islam a second time. They accepted Islam for themselves and on behalf of their tribe as well. They made a promise that they will pay the zakaah which is the right of Allah Ta'ala.

Ali ﷺ gathered all the booty, took out one fifth and distributed the balance among the Mujaahideen. He appointed a person as his deputy in order to lead the army and hastened towards Makkah before his companions. Ali ﷺ had received the information that Rasulullah ﷺ had left Madinah in order to perform the Haj. He therefore left Yemen and went straight to Makkah. He joined Rasulullah ﷺ for the Farewell Haj.

Chapter 27

Hajjatul Wadaa – The Farewell Haj

The help and assistance of Allah Ta'ala came and Makkah was conquered. People embraced Islam in droves. The power of disbelief and polytheism was broken. Delegations and tribes from far and wide came to Rasulullah ﷺ, repented from their disbelief and polytheism and testified to the oneness of Allah Ta'ala and the prophet-hood of Rasulullah ﷺ with sincerity. The responsibilities of prophet-hood were fulfilled and the injunctions of Islam were taught both verbally and physically. Rasulullah ﷺ sent Abu Bakr رضي الله عنه to Makkah in 9 A.H. in order to completely wipe out all traces of jaahiliyyah.

The time now came for Rasulullah ﷺ to personally perform the Haj so that the people may know forever how the Haj is to be performed, according to the method of Ibraaheem عليه السلام and Ismaa'eel عليه السلام. The rites of Haj, from beginning to end, entailed the oneness of Allah Ta'ala. They were completely pure of words denoting polytheism and customs of the days of ignorance (Jaahiliyyah). Rasulullah ﷺ used to pay particular attention to the talbiyah so that no traces of polytheism whatsoever would remain. The talbiyah that he used to say was:

لَبَّيْكَ اللَّهُمَّ لَبَّيْكَ لَبَّيْكَ لَا شَرِيْكَ لَكَ لَبَّيْكَ إِنَّ الْحَمْدَ وَالنِّعْمَةَ لَكَ وَالْمُلْكَ لَا شَرِيْكَ لَكَ

"Here I am, O Allah! Here I am. You have no partner. Here I am. All praise, bounty and kingdom belongs to You. You have no partner."

The order that Haj is compulsory was revealed in 9 A.H. In that year, Rasulullah ﷺ appointed Abu Bakr رضي الله عنه as the Ameer of the Haj and sent him to Makkah. The Muslims performed the Haj in that year under his leadership. In Zul

Qa'dah 10 A.H. Rasulullah ﷺ made the intention of personally performing the Haj. An announcement was made in the surrounding areas that Rasulullah ﷺ is to perform the Haj that year. Rasulullah ﷺ left Madinah on 25 Zul Qa'dah 10 A.H. on a Saturday, between the Zuhr and Asr Salaah. The Muhaajireen, the Ansaar and numerous other loyal Muslims joined him. It was an assembly of 90 000 to 114 000 or even more. Rasulullah ﷺ entered Makkah on 4 Zul Hijjah on a Sunday.

Nine of Rasulullah's ﷺ wives, plus his daughter, Faatimah رضى الله عنها, accompanied him. Various other close associates and servants were with him. Ali رضى الله عنه, whom Rasulullah ﷺ had sent in the month of Ramadhaan to Yemen, met him in Makkah. Rasulullah ﷺ fulfilled the different rites of Haj and delivered a lengthy sermon on the fields of 'Arafaat. He first praised and glorified Allah Ta'ala. He then said:

The Farewell Sermon

"O people! Listen attentively to what I have to say. It is possible that I will not meet you next year. O people! Your lives, your honour and your wealth are all sacred to each other just as this day, this month, and this city are all sacred. All the matters related to jaahiliyyah are all crushed beneath my feet. All the jahili claims of blood are forgiven. I first of all forgive the Banu Huzayl for the blood of Rabi'ah ibn Haaris ibn 'Abdil Muttalib. All the interest and usury of jaahili times is written off. You may only keep the capital wealth. I first of all write off the usury of 'Abbaas ibn 'Abdul Muttalib."

Rasulullah ﷺ then explained the mutual rights of husband and wife.

"I am leaving behind such a firm thing, that if you hold on to it, you will never go astray: The Book of Allah and the Sunnah of Rasulullah. On the day of resurrection you will be asked about me. What reply will you give?" The Sahaabah رضى الله عنهم replied: "We will testify that you conveyed Allah's message to us, that you fulfilled the trust of Allah and that you desired the well-being of the ummah." Rasulullah ﷺ pointed his index finger to the sky and said three times:

اللهم اشهد

"O Allah, You be witness to this."

When Rasulullah ﷺ completed his sermon, Bilal رضى الله عنه called out the Azaan for the Zuhr Salaah. The Zuhr and Asr Salaah were both offered at one time. Rasulullah ﷺ then remained engaged in the praise, thanks, seeking forgiveness and remembrance of Allah Ta'ala. While he was busy in this, the following verse was revealed:

اَلْيَوْمَ اَكْمَلْتُ لَكُمْ دِيْنَكُمْ وَاَتْمَمْتُ عَلَيْكُمْ نِعْمَتِىْ وَرَضِيْتُ لَكُمُ الْاِسْلَامَ دِيْنًا

"Today have I perfected for you your religion and completed My favour on you, and I chose Islam as a religion for you." [Surah Maa'idah, verse 3]

On reaching Mina on the 10th of Zul Hijjah, Rasulullah ﷺ slaughtered 63 camels, equivalent to his age, with his own hands. Ali رضى الله عنه slaughtered a further 37 camels on his behalf. Rasulullah ﷺ delivered a similar sermon to the one which he delivered in 'Arafaat. He eventually made the farewell Tawaaf. When he shaved his head in Mina, he distributed his blessed hair among the Sahaabah رضى الله عنهم so that they may keep it as a source of blessing.

Because he did not get the opportunity of performing the Haj the following year, and he had alluded to this fact in his sermons in 'Arafaat and Mina, this Haj is known as the Farewell Haj in the sense that he bade farewell to his ummah. This Haj is also referred to as Hajatul Islam because it was the first Haj in Islam after it was made a compulsory duty.

The sermon at Ghadir Khum

When Rasulullah ﷺ was returning from the Haj, Buraydah Aslami رضى الله عنه made certain complaints against Ali رضى الله عنه. Rasulullah ﷺ delivered a sermon in Ghadir Khum, a place between Makkah and Madinah. The gist of the sermon was:

"I am a mortal. It is possible that a messenger from my Sustainer will call me soon and that I will accept his call." (This was a reference to the fact that his time to depart from this world had drawn near). He then emphasised the importance of having love for his family and said with regard to Ali رضى الله عنه: "The person who is my friend, Ali is also his friend." After hearing this sermon, 'Umar رضى الله عنه congratulated Ali رضى الله عنه and Buraydah رضى الله عنه also no longer harboured any ill-feeling towards Ali رضى الله عنه.

Return to Madinah

After the Farewell Haj, Rasulullah ﷺ returned to Madinah and reached there towards the end of Zul Hijjah. Within a few days, the 10th year after emigration came to an end and the 11th year commenced.

Jibraa'eel عَلَيْهِ ٱلسَّلَام comes to Rasulullah ﷺ

Some days after Rasulullah's ﷺ return from the Farewell Haj, Jibraa'eel عَلَيْهِ ٱلسَّلَام came in the form of a stranger dressed in pure white clothes. He sat right in front of Rasulullah ﷺ with great respect. He asked Rasulullah ﷺ questions with regard to Imaan, Islam, Ihsaan, the resurrection, the signs of resurrection, etc. Rasulullah ﷺ answered all these questions. When he left, Rasulullah ﷺ asked the Sahaabah رَضِىَ ٱللَّهُ عَنْهُم to go and see who this person was. When they went out, they did not see anyone. Rasulullah ﷺ said that he was Jibraa'eel عَلَيْهِ ٱلسَّلَام who had come to teach them about Islam. He added that prior to today he had always recognized him.

The military expedition of Usaamah ibn Zaid رَضِىَ ٱللَّهُ عَنْهُ

On 26 Safar 11 A.H. Rasulullah ﷺ ordered the Sahaabah رَضِىَ ٱللَّهُ عَنْهُم to prepare for war against the Romans at Ubna. This was the place where the battle of Mu'tah had taken place, and in which Usaamah's رَضِىَ ٱللَّهُ عَنْهُ father, Zaid ibn Haarisah رَضِىَ ٱللَّهُ عَنْهُ, Ja'far Tayyaar رَضِىَ ٱللَّهُ عَنْهُ, 'Abdullah ibn Rawaahah رَضِىَ ٱللَّهُ عَنْهُ and others were martyred.

This was the last military expedition and the last army prepared by Rasulullah ﷺ. He appointed Usaamah ibn Zaid رَضِىَ ٱللَّهُ عَنْهُ as the commander-in-chief of this army and ordered many other senior Sahaabah رَضِىَ ٱللَّهُ عَنْهُم from among the Muhaajireen and Ansaar to join. Rasulullah's ﷺ illness started on a Wednesday. The following day, despite being ill, he personally gave a map to 'Usaamah رَضِىَ ٱللَّهُ عَنْهُ and said to him:

اغز باسم الله وفى سبيل الله فقاتل من كفر بالله

"Wage Jihaad in the name of Allah and in the cause of Allah, and fight those who reject Allah."

Usaamah رَضِىَ ٱللَّهُ عَنْهُ gave the map to Buraydah Aslami رَضِىَ ٱللَّهُ عَنْهُ, gathered the army at Juruf, and all the senior Sahaabah رَضِىَ ٱللَّهُ عَنْهُم from among the Muhaajireen and Ansaar rushed and gathered there. 'Abbaas رَضِىَ ٱللَّهُ عَنْهُ and Ali رَضِىَ ٱللَّهُ عَنْهُ returned to Madinah in order to tend to Rasulullah ﷺ. Abu Bakr رَضِىَ ٱللَّهُ عَنْهُ and 'Umar رَضِىَ ٱللَّهُ عَنْهُ used to take permission from Usaamah رَضِىَ ٱللَّهُ عَنْهُ in order to visit Rasulullah ﷺ. On Thursday his illness intensified. He was unable to go to the Masjid for the Isha Salaah. He therefore ordered Abu Bakr رَضِىَ ٱللَّهُ عَنْهُ to lead the Salaah in his place. The army was still gathered at Juruf. This place was about 2 miles from Madinah. When Rasulullah's ﷺ health improved on Sunday and the Sahaabah رَضِىَ ٱللَّهُ عَنْهُم felt that he would recover, Usaamah رَضِىَ ٱللَّهُ عَنْهُ made a decision to proceed. He was busy making preparations when his mother Umme Ayman رضى الله عنها sent a message that Rasulullah's ﷺ health had deteriorated badly. Within a short while they heard the news that he passed away. To Allah we belong and to Him is our return.

Panic spread throughout Madinah and all the Sahaabah رضى الله عنهم returned dejectedly. Buraydah رضى الله عنه brought the map and placed it on the door to Rasulullah's ﷺ room. When Abu Bakr رضى الله عنه became the caliph, the first thing that he did was that he despatched the army of Usaamah رضى الله عنه despite protests from the other Sahaabah رضى الله عنهم. He accompanied the army till Juruf. The army then continued on its journey and returned victorious after 40 days. Usaamah رضى الله عنه fought valiantly against anyone who came before him. He also killed the person who had killed his father, Zaid ibn Haarisah رضى الله عنه. Before returning, the houses and orchards of these people were burnt down. When they returned, Abu Bakr رضى الله عنه went out of Madinah in order to welcome them. When Usaamah رضى الله عنه entered Madinah, he went into the Masjid, offered two Rakaats of Salaah as thanks and then proceeded to his house.

Chapter 28

Preparation for the journey to the hereafter

After his return from the Farewell Haj, Rasulullah ﷺ began preparations for his journey to the hereafter. He remained fully engaged in the glorification and praise of Allah Ta'ala, repenting to Him and seeking His forgiveness. The first indication of the approach of his death was the revelation of the following Surah:

إِذَا جَآءَ نَصْرُ اللّٰهِ وَالْفَتْحُ ۞ وَ رَاَيْتَ النَّاسَ يَدْخُلُوْنَ فِيْ دِيْنِ اللّٰهِ اَفْوَاجًا ۞ فَسَبِّحْ بِحَمْدِ رَبِّكَ وَ اسْتَغْفِرْهُ ؕ اِنَّهٗ كَانَ تَوَّابًا ۞

"When the help of Allah and victory come, and you see people entering the religion of Allah in large numbers, then glorify the praises of your Sustainer and seek His forgiveness, surely He is forgiving."

In other words, when the help and victory which Allah had promised have come, when the head of disbelief and polytheism has been smashed, when the flag of Tauheed has been raised, when the truth has vanquished falsehood, when people have entered the true religion in droves, when the world has received the message of Allah, and when the religion of Allah has been completed and perfected – then the purpose behind sending you to this world has been accomplished, and the responsibility that was given to you has been fulfilled. You should now prepare to return to Us. The task for which Allah sent you to this world has been completed. You should now prepare to return to that Being who sent you into this world. This fleeting world is not for you to remain in. It is more appropriate for a sanctified soul like you to remain in the company of Mala-ul-a'laa (the highest assembly) and Ar-rafeequl-a'laa (the highest companion).

Rasulullah ﷺ would therefore recite the following wherever he was – sitting, walking, going, returning, etc.

$$\text{سُبْحَانَكَ اللّٰهُمَّ رَبَّنَا وَبِحَمْدِكَ اَللّٰهُمَّ اغْفِرْ لِيْ وَتُبْ عَلَىَّ إِنَّكَ أَنْتَ التَّوَّابُ الرَّحِيْمُ}$$

"Glory to You O our Sustainer! And praise to You. O Allah! Forgive me and accept my repentance. Surely You are the one who accepts repentance, the merciful."

At times he would recite:

$$\text{سُبْحَانَ اللّٰهِ وَبِحَمْدِهِ اَسْتَغْفِرُ اللّٰهَ وَأَتُوْبُ إِلَيْهِ}$$

"Glory to Allah and praise to Him. I seek forgiveness from Allah and I turn to Him in repentance."

At times he would recite:

$$\text{سُبْحَانَكَ اللّٰهُمَّ وَبِحَمْدِكَ اَسْتَغْفِرُكَ وَأَتُوْبُ إِلَيْكَ}$$

"Glory to You O Allah, and praise to You. I seek Your forgiveness and I turn to You in repentance."

On one occasion, Rasulullah ﷺ said to Faatimah رضى الله عنها: "Jibraa'eel عليه السلام used to come to me every Ramadhaan and make one recitation of the Qur-aan with me. This year he came and made two recitations. I think that my time of departure has drawn near." Rasulullah ﷺ used to remain secluded in the Masjid in the month of Ramadhaan for 10 days every year. This year, he remained secluded for 20 days. When the verse: "Today have I perfected your religion for you..." was revealed to Rasulullah ﷺ on the occasion of the Farewell Haj, he understood the importance of it. In his sermon of the Farewell Haj, he therefore said to the people: "It is possible that I will not meet you next year and I may not be able to perform the Haj with you again." In his sermon at Ghadir Khum, he said: "I am a human, and no human has ever lived forever. It is possible that the envoy of my Sustainer will soon come to take me." On his return from the Farewell Haj, he went to Jannatul Baqi' (the graveyard of Madinah) and, after a period of eight years, offered the Janaazah Salaah for those who were martyred at Uhud and made dua for their well-being. This is what a person normally does when he is bidding farewell. He then went into the Masjid, climbed the mimbar and delivered a sermon. He addressed the people saying: "I am going before you so that I may make the necessary arrangements for you at the Haud-e-Kauthar, etc. Our meeting place will be at Haud-e-Kauthar. I can see it this very moment from where I am standing now. I have been given the keys to the treasures of this world. I do not have this fear that you will collectively fall into polytheism." In other words, I do not have this fear that the entire ummah will fall into polytheism as was the case with previous nations. "However, I fear that you will fall greedily towards this world, compete with each other to acquire it, fight with each other for it, and thereby be destroyed."

Rasulullah ﷺ falls ill

In one of the last 10 nights of Safar, Rasulullah ﷺ woke up, got his slave Abu Muhaybah up and said to him: "I have been ordered to seek forgiveness for the people of Jannatul Baqi'." When Rasulullah ﷺ returned from there, he suddenly felt ill and complained of a headache and flu.

It was a Wednesday and it was the turn of the mother of the believers, Maymunah ؓ. In this sick condition, he continued going to his other wives according to the days that were allotted to them. When his condition worsened, he sought permission from them to spend his time with Aa'ishah ؓ. He went to her room on a Monday. He passed away in her room the following week on a Monday. Rasulullah ﷺ remained ill for 13-14 days. The last week of his life was spent under the care of Aa'ishah ؓ.

It is stated in a Hadith that when Jibraa'eel عليه السلام came to Rasulullah ﷺ with Surah Nasr, he said to him: "O Jibraa'eel! This Surah gives me the news of my demise." Jibraa'eel عليه السلام said: "The after life is better for you than this world."

During his illness, Rasulullah ﷺ received the information that the following people had become apostates and were claiming prophet-hood: Aswad 'Ansi, Musaylamah and Tulayhah Asdi. He emphasised on the Sahaabah ؓ the importance of waging Jihaad against them and sent a group of Ansaar to quell the rebellion of Aswad 'Ansi. The latter was killed about a day before Rasulullah's ﷺ demise.

Aa'ishah ؓ says: "During this illness, Rasulullah ﷺ used to say that this illness was the effect of the poison that he had consumed at Khaybar." Another Hadith states that it was his noble habit that whenever he fell ill, he would recite the following Surahs: Surah Ikhlaas, Surah Falaq, Surah Naas, and then blow onto himself and pass his hands across his entire body. Aa'ishah ؓ says: "During his final illness, I used to recite these Surahs and blow onto him. However, I would pass my hands over his body as a source of blessing for me."

Faatimah ؓ cries and smiles

During this illness, Rasulullah ﷺ called for Faatimah ؓ and whispered something into her ears. She began crying. Rasulullah ﷺ again said something in her ears and she began smiling. Aa'ishah ؓ says: "After

Rasulullah ﷺ passed away, we asked her about this." She said: "Rasulullah ﷺ said to me that Jibraa'eel عَلَيْهِ السَّلَام used to recite the entire Qur-aan once every Ramadhaan, but this year he read it twice to him. He feels that he is going to pass away this year. I therefore began crying. He then said to me that from his family, I will be the first to join him. On hearing this, I smiled."

Faatimah رَضِيَ اللهُ عَنْهَا passed away six months after the demise of Rasulullah ﷺ.

Another Hadith states that Rasulullah ﷺ said to her: "You will be the leader of all the women in Jannah."

Aa'ishah رَضِيَ اللهُ عَنْهَا says: "When Rasulullah ﷺ returned from Jannatul Baqi', I had a headache. Because of the pain I was experiencing, I cried out: 'O my head!' When Rasulullah ﷺ heard this, he also cried out: 'O my head! It is possible that I will pass away in this way.'" Aa'ishah رَضِيَ اللهُ عَنْهَا says: "He then said to me: 'O Aa'ishah! If you pass away before me, of what loss will it be to me? I will make arrangements for your shroud and burial, I will offer the Janaazah Salaah for you, and seek forgiveness for you.'" Aa'ishah رَضِيَ اللهُ عَنْهَا replied: "It is as though you want me to die. If I were to depart from this world, you will bring another wife into this very house of mine on that very day." What she meant was that he will forget her and become engrossed with his other wives. On hearing this, Rasulullah ﷺ smiled thinking to himself that she is unaware that he is the one who is departing from this world and that she will remain alive after his demise.

The incident of Qirtaas

About four days before his demise, when Rasulullah's ﷺ illness intensified, he asked those who were present in the room to bring him paper, pen and ink so that he may dictate some words of advice after which the Muslims cannot go astray. On hearing this, those who were present disagreed. 'Umar رَضِيَ اللهُ عَنْهُ said to him: "You are ill, you are experiencing much pain. It is not appropriate for us to cause you trouble in such a condition. The Book of Allah is with us (which is sufficient to save us from going astray)." Some Sahaabah رَضِيَ اللهُ عَنْهُمْ agreed with 'Umar رَضِيَ اللهُ عَنْهُ while others said that the writing material should be brought and they said: "Has Rasulullah ﷺ ever said anything foolish or unintelligible during his illnesses and state of unconsciousness? Ask him; he is the Messenger and Prophet of Allah Ta'ala. His heart and tongue are protected from error. He is not like others who begin speaking nonsense when they fall ill." A Hadith states that on one occasion Rasulullah ﷺ pointed to his tongue and said: "I take an oath by that being in whose control is my life that nothing but the truth emanates from this tongue."

When those who were present began arguing and differing among themselves, Rasulullah ﷺ asked them to leave and said to them: "Leave me as I am. I am in a better condition than what you are calling me towards." Thereafter, despite the pain that he was suffering, he issued three words of advice to them:

1. The disbelievers should be expelled from the Arabian Peninsula. No disbeliever should be permitted to live there.
2. Whenever delegations come to meet them, they should present gifts when bidding farewell to them, as had been his noble practice.
3. Rasulullah ﷺ either did not mention the third advice, or the narrator forgot it.

Some are of the opinion that the third advice was any of the following: They should practise on the Qur-aan; they must send the army of Usaamah رضي الله عنه; they must not turn his grave into a place of worship and prostration; they must be particular about their Salaah; they must see to the slaves.

It is not known whether the words of advice which he gave orally were the same as those which he wanted to have written down or whether he had something else in his mind. Allah Ta'ala knows best.

Aa'ishah رضي الله عنها says that during this illness, Rasulullah ﷺ said: "I wish to talk to Abu Bakr and his son, Abdur Rahmaan. Send someone to call them so that I may give them some words of advice, make him (Abu Bakr رضي الله عنه) my successor so that no one may be able to say anything (against him) and no one may desire (this leadership once he has been appointed). I have now changed my mind and decided not to give him these words of advice. I know for a fact that Allah Ta'ala will not permit anyone else to become the caliph after me. Even the believers will not accept the caliphate of anyone besides Abu Bakr." Another Hadith has the following words:

معاذ الله ان يختلف الناس على أبي بكر

"Allah forbid that the people differ with regard to (the caliphate of) Abu Bakr."

It becomes quite clear from these Ahaadith that it was Rasulullah's ﷺ heartfelt desire that Abu Bakr رضي الله عنه should be the caliph after him. However, he left it in the hands of fate, destiny and the unanimous decision of the ummah to implement it. Fate and destiny would decide that Abu Bakr رضي الله عنه would be the caliph and his caliphate will be established by the unanimous decision of the senior Companions of Rasulullah ﷺ. All the Muslims will accept his caliphate. The words of Imaam Bukhaari رحمه الله also indicate that these words show that Rasulullah ﷺ wanted to write down the caliphate of Abu Bakr رضي الله عنه.

When this incident (of Rasulullah ﷺ asking for writing material) took place and the people began differing and arguing with each other, Rasulullah ﷺ asked them to leave because it was not appropriate to argue in his presence. The people then left.

When the people left, Rasulullah ﷺ rested till the time of Zuhr Salaah. When he felt a bit better and the intensity of his illness decreased, he asked for seven containers of water to be poured on his head and said: "Perhaps I will experience more comfort and I may give some advice to the people." Accordingly, this water was poured on him and he felt much more comfortable. He then took support from Abbaas رضي الله عنه and Ali رضي الله عنه on either side of him and went to the Masjid. He performed the Zuhr Salaah and then delivered a sermon. This was his final sermon.

Rasulullah's ﷺ final sermon

After completing the Salaah, Rasulullah ﷺ went onto the mimbar, and after praising and glorifying Allah Ta'ala, he spoke about the martyrs of Uhud. He asked for forgiveness for them. He then addressed the Muhaajireen saying: "You will be in the majority while the Ansaar will be in the minority. Look, the Ansaar gave me refuge. You must be kind to those who are good and righteous among them and you must overlook those who err among them."

He then said: "O people! Allah has given to a servant of His to choose between enjoying the bounties of this world or those of the hereafter that are with Allah. That servant has chosen to enjoy the bounties that are with Allah in the hereafter." Abu Bakr رضي الله عنه who was the most knowledgeable among the Sahaabah رضي الله عنهم immediately understood that the servant referred to was none other than Rasulullah ﷺ. He therefore began crying and said: "O Messenger of Allah! May my parents be sacrificed for you." Rasulullah ﷺ said: "Wait and remain firm." He then turned towards the Masjid and asked the people to shut all the doors of the Masjid and that only one door, that of Abu Bakr رضي الله عنه, be left open. He then said: "As regards his life, wealth, companionship and friendship, Abu Bakr رضي الله عنه is the one who is kindest to me. There isn't anyone who was kinder to me than him. I repaid all those who did favours to me, except for Abu Bakr. The reward for his favours will be given by Allah Ta'ala personally on the day of resurrection. Were I to make someone apart from Allah Ta'ala my bosom friend, I would have chosen Abu Bakr. However, he enjoys Islamic brotherhood and friendship. He surpasses everyone in this regard. There is no one equal to him in this brotherhood and friendship."

In short, Rasulullah ﷺ enumerated those merits of Abu Bakr رضي الله عنه which were not shared by anyone else. He did this so that these virtues and merits of his may be well known to the people and there may be no difference with regard to his succession after him. In order to emphasise this, Rasulullah ﷺ appointed him to the leadership (Imaamat) of the greatest of acts of worship, viz. Salaah. It was for this reason that at the time of giving Abu Bakr ؓ the pledge of allegiance, the Sahaabah ؓ said: "If Rasulullah ﷺ chose him for our Deen (leadership in Salaah) why should we not choose him for our wordly affairs (caliphate and leadership)?"

In this sermon Rasulullah ﷺ also asked that the army of Usaamah ؓ be despatched quickly. He also said: "I know that some people (referring to the hypocrites) object to the leadership of Usaamah (for this army) in the sense that why should a youngster be given leadership when there are so many other senior people present? Listen! Even before this, there were people who objected to his father's (Zaid's) leadership. By Allah! His father was qualified for that post and so is his son, Usaamah, qualified for this post. Furthermore, he is extremely beloved to me."

Rasulullah ﷺ then said: "Allah's curse befell the Jews and Christians who turned the graves of their Prophets into places of prostration." Rasulullah ﷺ wanted to warn the ummah against turning his grave into a place of prostration.

Rasulullah ﷺ said: "O people! The news has reached me that you have become fearful of the demise of your Prophet. Has any Prophet before me remained forever with his people that I should now remain forever with you? Allah Ta'ala says:

$$\text{وَمَا جَعَلْنَا لِبَشَرٍ مِّنْ قَبْلِكَ الْخُلْدَ}$$

"We did not allow any human before you to remain till eternity."

$$\text{وَمَا مُحَمَّدٌ إِلَّا رَسُولٌ قَدْ خَلَتْ مِنْ قَبْلِهِ الرُّسُلُ}$$

"Muhammad is but a Messenger. Messengers before him also passed away."

"Listen! I have to meet Allah and you also have to meet Allah. I advise all the Muslims to treat the early Muhaajireen with kindness, and I advise the early Muhaajireen to remain steadfast on the fear of Allah and good deeds. Allah Ta'ala says:

$$\text{وَالْعَصْرِ ۞ إِنَّ الْإِنْسَانَ لَفِي خُسْرٍ ۞ إِلَّا الَّذِينَ آمَنُوا وَعَمِلُوا الصَّالِحَاتِ وَتَوَاصَوْا بِالْحَقِّ وَتَوَاصَوْا بِالصَّبْرِ ۞}$$

"By the token of time, man is certainly in loss. Except those who have Imaan and did good deeds. And they advise each other in matters of truth and they advise each other to exercise patience."

"O Muslims! I advise you to treat the Ansaar well and with kindness. They are the ones who gave refuge to Islam and Imaan. They made you partners in their homes, lands, orchards and fruits. They gave preference to you over themselves despite being in need and in poverty. Allah Ta'ala says:

$$\text{وَ يُؤْثِرُوْنَ عَلٰٓى اَنْفُسِهِمْ وَلَوْ كَانَ بِهِمْ خَصَاصَةٌ}$$

"They give preference over themselves even though they themselves may be in dire circumstances."

"Listen! I am leaving before you. You will also meet me. Our meeting place will be Haud-e-Kauthar."

Rasulullah ﷺ then got off the mimbar and went to his room.

Rasulullah's ﷺ last Salaah with congregation

As long as he had the strength, Rasulullah ﷺ would come to the Masjid for Salaah and continue leading the Sahaabah ؓ in Salaah. The last Salaah which he led was the Maghrib Salaah of Thursday. He passed away four days later on a Monday. Ummul Fadl ؓ says that Rasulullah ﷺ led us in the Maghrib Salaah in which he recited Surah wal-Mursalaat. He did not lead us in any Salaah thereafter, and then he passed away. When the time for the Isha Salaah came, he asked whether the people had performed their Salaah. The reply was given to him that the people were waiting for him. He tried getting up several times but the severity of his illness would cause him to fall unconscious. He eventually said: "Order Abu Bakr to lead the Salaah on my behalf." Aa'ishah ؓ said to him: "O Messenger of Allah! Abu Bakr is very soft-hearted. If he were to stand in your place, he will be overcome by emotion and he will not be able to lead the people in Salaah. He will start crying and people will not hear his recitation. You should therefore order 'Umar to lead the Salaah." Although this is what Aa'ishah ؓ said to Rasulullah ﷺ, in her heart she felt that the person who stands in the place of Rasulullah ﷺ will consider him to be an ill omen (indicating the departure of Rasulullah ﷺ from this world). Rasulullah ﷺ therefore said to her: "You are like the women in the time of Yusuf ؑ. You verbally utter something while you have something else in your heart. Inform Abu Bakr that none but he has to lead the people in Salaah."

Rasulullah ﷺ said this to Aa'ishah ؓ three times, but each time she refused. Rasulullah ﷺ persisted and emphasised that none but Abu Bakr ؓ should lead the Salaah. Eventually, Abu Bakr ؓ began leading the people in Salaah.

On Saturday or Sunday when he felt a bit better, Rasulullah ﷺ took support of 'Abbaas ؓ and Ali ؓ and entered the Masjid. Abu Bakr ؓ was leading the Zuhr Salaah at that time. Rasulullah ﷺ sat down to the right of Abu Bakr ؓ and led the people for the remainder of the Salaah. Rasulullah ﷺ was now the Imaam and Abu Bakr ؓ began following him. The remainder of the people completed their Salaah by following the Takbeers of Abu Bakr ؓ.

This Zuhr Salaah was the last Salaah which Rasulullah ﷺ led. After this, he did not come to the Masjid at all.

On Saturday, Usaamah ؓ and other Sahaabah ؓ who were to leave for Jihaad came to meet Rasulullah ﷺ. They bid farewell to Rasulullah ﷺ and left. They left Madinah and stopped over at Juruf. They left in obedience to the instruction of Rasulullah ﷺ, but because of his illness, they did not have the heart to leave. Rasulullah's ﷺ condition worsened on Sunday. On hearing this, Usaamah ؓ came back to visit Rasulullah ﷺ. He saw that his condition was quite bad and that he was unable to speak. Usaamah ؓ bent down and kissed Rasulullah's ﷺ forehead. Rasulullah ﷺ raised both his hands towards the sky and then placed them on Usaamah ؓ. Usaamah ؓ says: "I think that Rasulullah ﷺ was making dua for me." He then returned to Juruf.

Aa'ishah ؓ says that they assumed that Rasulullah ﷺ was suffering from pleurisy. They therefore inserted some medicine into his mouth. Rasulullah ﷺ indicated to them to stop but they thought that he was merely portraying a natural dislike just as when a person is ill and shows a natural dislike for a certain medicine. Later, when his condition improved, he asked: "Did I not stop you? The punishment is that this medicine should be inserted into the mouths of all of you, apart from 'Abbaas because he did not join you in this persistence."

The day of Rasulullah's ﷺ demise

It was a Monday when Rasulullah ﷺ left this fleeting world for the eternal life of the hereafter and met with Allah Ta'ala. On the morning of this Monday he raised the curtain of his room and saw that the Sahaabah were standing in lines and offering their Fajr Salaah. On seeing the Sahaabah ؓ he smiled.

Abu Bakr ؓ intended to go back (from the spot where he was leading the Salaah). Rasulullah ﷺ indicated to him to continue. Due to his weakness, Rasulullah ﷺ could not stand up fully. He lowered the curtain of his room and went back inside.

Rasulullah's ﷺ raising the curtain and looking at the Sahaabah رضي الله عنهم was the last time that he appeared before them. And it was the final opportunity of their seeing the beauty of Rasulullah ﷺ. A poet says:

وكنت أرى كالموت من بين ساعة   فكيف ببين كان موعده الحشر

"I used to consider a single moment's separation (from him) to be death. Now what can I say about this separation after which the next meeting will only be on the Day of Resurrection?!"

When Abu Bakr رضي الله عنه completed the Fajr Salaah, he went directly to the blessed room of Rasulullah ﷺ. He said to Aa'ishah رضي الله عنها: "I see that he is enjoying peace at present, and the previous pain and discomfort seems to have improved." Abu Bakr رضي الله عنه had two wives, one of whom lived just outside Madinah. That day was the turn of the one who was living outside Madinah. He therefore sought permission from Rasulullah ﷺ in the following words: "O Prophet of Allah! I see that you have got up in a good condition this morning by the bounty and grace of Allah Ta'ala. Today is the turn of Bint Khaarijah. Can I go to her?" He replied: "Yes."

When the others heard that Rasulullah ﷺ was feeling quite well, they also returned to their homes.

Ali رضي الله عنه came out of the room, people asked him about Rasulullah's ﷺ condition. He replied that all praise is due to Allah Ta'ala that he is feeling quite well. The people were satisfied with this and therefore dispersed. 'Abbaas رضي الله عنه held Ali رضي الله عنه by the hand and said to him: "O Ali! I swear by Allah that after three days there will be another ruler and you will be his subject. By Allah, I think that Rasulullah ﷺ is going to pass away in this illness. I think we should ask him as to who should be the caliph after him. If it is one of us, we will know of it. If not, he will advise us as to who it should be." Ali رضي الله عنه replied: "It is possible that he will refuse to give it to one of us. If he does that, we will be deprived of it forever. By Allah, I will not say a single word in this regard to him."

Rasulullah ﷺ in the throes of death

The people assumed that Rasulullah's ﷺ condition had improved and they therefore dispersed. After a short while, he began experiencing the pangs of death. He placed his head in the lap of Aa'ishah رضي الله عنها and lied down. Just then, her brother, Abdur Rahmaan رضي الله عنه came in with a miswaak in his hand. Rasulullah ﷺ began looking at him. Aa'ishah رضي الله عنها asked: "O Rasulullah! Should I get a miswaak for you?" Rasulullah ﷺ nodded in the affirmative. She then asked: "Should I soften it for you?" He again nodded in the affirmative. She softened it by chewing on it and then gave it to him. Later on, Aa'ishah رضي الله عنها used to proudly express this great favour of Allah Ta'ala that He caused her saliva to mix with that of Rasulullah's ﷺ during this final hour of his, that he passed away in her room, when it was her turn, and on her shoulder.

The person who is constant in using the miswaak will automatically recite the kalimah at the time of death, while this will not be the case of the one who consumes opium.

A glass of water was kept at Rasulullah's ﷺ side. He repeatedly extended his hand towards it, dipped his hand in it and wiped his face with it. While doing this, he would say: "There is none worthy of worship but Allah. Surely there are many pangs of death." He then looked at the ceiling, raised his hands and said: "O Allah! I want to go to ar-Rafiq ul-A'laa – the highest companion." This refers to the sanctified place which is the abode of the Prophets and Messengers.

'Aa'ishah رضي الله عنها says: "I had heard Rasulullah ﷺ saying on several occasions that the soul of a Messenger is not taken until he is shown his abode in Jannah, and until he is given the choice to either remain in this world or to leave it. When he said the above words, I immediately understood that he will no longer remain with us and that he has already chosen to be in the close companionship of Allah Ta'ala. When he said:

$$\text{اَللّٰهُمَّ الرَّفِيْقَ الْأَعْلٰى}$$

"O Allah! I desire to be in the highest companionship."

His soul had traversed this realm towards the upper realm and his hands (which had been raised) fell down.

$$\text{إِنَّا لِلّٰهِ وَإِنَّا إِلَيْهِ رَاجِعُوْنَ}$$

"To Allah we belong and to Him is our return."

The date of Rasulullah's ﷺ demise

This heart-rending and soul-tearing incident which deprived this world of the blessings of prophet-hood and Messenger-ship and the illumination of divine revelation took place on a Monday afternoon, on the 12th of Rabi'ul-Awwal.

There is no difference of opinion with regard to the fact that Rasulullah ﷺ passed away in Rabi'ul-Awwal on a Monday.

However, there are various opinions with regard to the exact date of Rasulullah's ﷺ demise. The famous opinion is that it was the 12th of Rabi'ul-Awwal. Some say it was the 1st while others say it was the 2nd.

At the time of his demise, Rasulullah ﷺ was 63 years old.

The uneasiness of the Sahaabah رَضِىَاللّٰهُعَنْهُم

As soon as the news of this sign of Qiyaamah reached the ears of the Sahaabah رَضِىَاللّٰهُعَنْهُم, it was as though the resurrection had begun. The moment they received this news, they lost their senses. Panic descended on Madinah. Whoever received this news fell into bewilderment. 'Usmaan رَضِىَاللّٰهُعَنْهُ was in a state of shock. He was sitting against a wall, and due to his extreme sorrow, was unable to speak. Ali رَضِىَاللّٰهُعَنْهُ cried so profusely that he fell unconscious. The mountain of grief and pain that befell Aa'ishah رَضِىَاللّٰهُعَنْهَا and the other wives of Rasulullah ﷺ cannot even be described. 'Abbaas رَضِىَاللّٰهُعَنْهُ was also at a loss in this severe grief. 'Umar رَضِىَاللّٰهُعَنْهُ suffered the most grief and affliction. He unsheathed his sword, stood up and announced in a loud voice: "The hypocrites assume that Rasulullah ﷺ has passed away. He certainly has not passed away. Rather he is gone to his Sustainer just as Musa عَلَيْهِالسَّلَام went to Allah Ta'ala on Mt. Sinai and then returned. By Allah, Rasulullah ﷺ will certainly come back in a similar manner and then completely uproot the hypocrites." 'Umar رَضِىَاللّٰهُعَنْهُ was in a state of fervour, with his sword unsheathed. No one had the courage to tell him that Rasulullah ﷺ had indeed passed away.

Abu Bakr رَضِىَاللّٰهُعَنْهُ was not present at the time when Rasulullah ﷺ had passed away. When he heard this heart-rending news, he immediately mounted his horse and came to Madinah. He dismounted at the entrance of Masjid-e-Nabawi and advanced towards Rasulullah's ﷺ room very dejectedly. He asked Aa'ishah رَضِىَاللّٰهُعَنْهَا for permission and entered. Rasulullah ﷺ was on his bed with all his wives sitting around him. When Abu Bakr رَضِىَاللّٰهُعَنْهُ entered, all of them, except Aa'ishah رَضِىَاللّٰهُعَنْهَا, covered their faces. Abu Bakr رَضِىَاللّٰهُعَنْهُ removed the sheet from Rasulullah's ﷺ face, kissed his blessed forehead, and cried out saying:

وا نبياه واخليلاه وصفياه

"O the Prophet of Allah! O the friend of Allah! O the chosen one of Allah!"

Abu Bakr رَضِىَاللّٰهُعَنْهُ said this three times.

He then said: "May my parents be sacrificed for you. By Allah, He will not cause you to taste death twice. The death that was prescribed for you has come to you." On saying this, he came out of the room and saw that 'Umar رَضِىَاللّٰهُعَنْهُ was in a highly emotional state. Abu Bakr رَضِىَاللّٰهُعَنْهُ said: "Rasulullah ﷺ has passed away. O 'Umar! Have you not heard these words of Allah Ta'ala:

(إِنَّكَ مَيِّتٌ وَإِنَّهُمْ مَيِّتُونَ وَمَا جَعَلْنَا لِبَشَرٍ مِنْ قَبْلِكَ الْخُلْدَ)

'You shall certainly die and they shall certainly die (as well). We did not permit eternity for any human since before.'"

The people then left the assembly of 'Umar ﷺ and congregated around Abu Bakr ﷺ.

Abu Bakr's ﷺ sermon

Abu Bakr ﷺ went towards the mimbar, announced in a loud voice that everyone should remain silent and be seated. When they were all seated, he praised and glorified Allah Ta'ala and then delivered the following sermon:

"Whoever among you had been worshipping Allah, then surely Allah is alive and does not die. Whoever among you had been worshipping Muhammad ﷺ, then Muhammad ﷺ has certainly passed on. Allah Ta'ala says: 'Muhammad is but a Messenger. Messengers before him passed away. If he dies or is killed, are you going to turn back on your heels? Whoever turns back on his heels will never harm Allah in any way. Allah shall certainly reward the grateful ones.' Allah Ta'ala addressed Muhammad ﷺ: 'You shall certainly die and they shall certainly die (as well).' Allah Ta'ala says: 'Everything is going to come to an end except the essence of Allah. To Him belongs absolute authority and it is to Him that you will be returned.' Allah Ta'ala says: 'Everything that is on earth is to die. It is only the countenance of your Sustainer, the possessor of might and honour, that will remain.' Allah Ta'ala says: 'Every soul shall taste death. You shall receive your recompense in full on the day of resurrection.'

Surely Allah Ta'ala caused Muhammad ﷺ to live until such a time that he established the religion of Allah, clearly explained the injunctions of Allah, conveyed the message of Allah, and strove in the cause of Allah. Allah Ta'ala then caused him to pass away in a manner that he left you on a clear path. Now whoever goes astray and is destroyed will do so after the truth had been laid bare to him. He whose Sustainer is Allah, let him know that Allah is alive and does not die. He who had been worshipping Muhammad ﷺ and considering him to be a deity, let him know that his deity has died. Fear Allah then, O people, hold on firmly to your religion, and place your trust on your Sustainer. Surely the religion of Allah shall remain and the promise of Allah will be fulfilled. Allah shall certainly help the one who helps Him, and He shall give honour to His religion. The Book of Allah is with us. It is a light and a cure. It was through this Book that Allah guided Muhammad ﷺ. It contains the lawful and unlawful matters of Allah. By Allah, we are not bothered in the least by the one who attacks us. The swords of Allah are unsheathed; we have not laid them down. We will wage Jihaad against those who fight against us just as we had joined the Messenger of Allah ﷺ in waging Jihaad. The opponents should therefore beware and blame none but themselves."

No sooner had Abu Bakr ﷺ delivered these words, the Sahaabah ﷺ came out of their stupor and the veils of absentmindedness were raised. They were all convinced that Rasulullah ﷺ had indeed passed away. It seemed as if they had never heard these verses of the Qur-aan before. They all began reciting these verses.

It is stated in one narration that when Abu Bakr ﷺ received the news of Rasulullah's ﷺ demise, he immediately left his house at Sunh and proceeded towards Madinah. He approached crying, gasping for breath and panting. He entered the room of Rasulullah ﷺ in that very condition while sending salutations to Rasulullah ﷺ. Despite this grief and sorrow, he was fully conscious and did not lose his senses in the least.

He exposed the blessed face of Rasulullah ﷺ and kissed his forehead. He continued crying and continued saying: "May my parents be sacrificed for you. You remained pure both in life and in death. By your demise, the chain of prophethood and divine revelation have both come to an end. Both of these never came to an end with the demise of any other Prophet. You are beyond description and in no need of this crying. You are unique in that your being is such that others can take consolation from your death. You benefited all of us to the extent that we all became equal before you. Were it not for the fact that your death was by your choice (Allah had given you the choice to choose between this world and the hereafter) we would all have sacrificed our lives for your life. Were it not for the fact that you had prohibited us from excessive crying, we would have exhausted all the tears of our eyes. However, there are two things which we cannot remove and wipe out: (1) the sorrow of being separated from you, (2) our bodies becoming thin because of our sorrow. These are two things that are inseparable. O Allah! Convey this condition of ours (to our Prophet). And O Muhammad ﷺ! Mention us by your Sustainer. We hope that you will remember us."

"Had you not filled our hearts with peace and tranquillity by remaining in your company, we would never have been able to bear the loss of this separation."

Abu Bakr ﷺ then left the room and addressed the people.

The remainder of Abu Bakr's ﷺ sermon

اَشْهَدُ اَنْ لاَّ اِلٰهَ اِلاَّ اللهُ وَحْدَهُ وَصَدَقَ وَعْدَهُ وَنَصَرَ عَبْدَهُ وَغَلَبَ الْاَحْزَابَ وَحْدَهُ فَلِلّٰهِ الْحَمْدُ وَحْدَهُ واشهد ان محمدا عبده ورسوله وخاتم انبياء ه واشهد ان الكتاب كما نزل وان الدين كما شرع وان الحديث كما حدث وان القول كما قال وان الله هو الحق المبين

"I testify that there is none worthy of worship except Allah, He is one. He fulfilled His promise, helped His servant, and vanquished the enemies single-handedly. So all praise belongs to Allah alone."

"I testify that Muhammad ﷺ is His servant, His Messenger and the seal of His Prophets. I testify that the Book (Qur-aan) is exactly as it was revealed, that the religion (Islam) is exactly as He propagated, that the Hadith is exactly as he (Muhammad ﷺ) related, that the words are exactly as he (Muhammad ﷺ) said, and that Allah is the truth, the expounder of the truth."

"O Allah! Send salutations to Muhammad, Your servant, Messenger, Prophet, beloved, entrusted one, the best of Your creation, the choicest of Your creation – with the best salutations that You ever sent to any of Your creations. O Allah! Cause Your salutations, Your protection, Your mercy, and Your blessings to descend on the leader of the Messengers, the seal of Prophets, and the leader of the righteous, Muhammad – the guide towards good, the leader of good, and the Messenger of mercy. O Allah! Make him even closer (to You), make his evidence greater, honour his position, and convey him to the Maqaam-e-Mahmud (the place of intercession) regarding which all the past and future generations will desire. Enable us to benefit from his Maqaam-e-Mahmud on the day of resurrection. Shower us with Your mercy in this world and in the hereafter as compensation for him. Convey him to the highest stages of Jannah. O Allah! Send salutations to Muhammad and the family of Muhammad, and bless Muhammad and the family of Muhammad just as You sent salutations and blessings on Ibraaheem and the family of Ibraaheem, surely You alone are praiseworthy, majestic."

ثم قال ايها الناس من كان يعبد محمدا فان محمدا قد مات ومن كان يعبدالله فان الله حى لا يموت و ان الله قد تقدم لـكم فى امره فلا تدعوه جزعا وان الله تبارك و تعالى قد اختار لنبيه عليه السلام ما عنده على ما عند كـم وقبضه الى ثوابه وخلف فيكـم كتابه وسنة نبيه فمن اخذبهما عرف ومن فرق بينهما انكـر. يَاَيُّهَا الَّذِيْنَ امنوا كُوْنُوْا قَوَّامِين بالقسط ولا يشغلنكـم الشيطان بموت نبيكـم ولا

يفتنكم عن دينكم وعاجلوا الشيطان بالخير وتعجزوه ولا
تستنظروه فيلحق بكم ويفتنكم

He then said: "O people! He who was worshipping Muhammad ﷺ should know that Muhammad ﷺ has passed away. He who was worshipping Allah should know that Allah is alive, He does not die. Allah had already alluded to his (Muhammad's ﷺ) passing away. There is therefore no need to become distressed. Allah Ta'ala chose His Prophet ﷺ to be with Him than to be with you and He took him to His honourable abode. He left behind His Book and the Sunnah of His Prophet with you. He who holds on firmly to both of them has truly recognised the truth. He who separates the two (e.g. by believing in one and not in the other) has not recognised the truth. O you who are believers! Be the upholders of justice. Do not allow shaytaan to keep you preoccupied with the death of your Prophet. Do not allow him to move you away from your religion. Hasten towards good before shaytaan can tempt you. Frustrate his efforts by hastening towards good. Do not give him any time to come to you and tempt you."

When he completed his sermon, he said: "O 'Umar! Is it true what I heard about you, that you were standing at the door of the Prophet ﷺ and saying: 'By that being in whose control is the life of 'Umar, the Prophet of Allah has not died'? Do you not remember what Rasulullah ﷺ said on such and such day? And that Allah Ta'ala said in His Book: 'You are to die and they are also to die.'" 'Umar ؓ said: "By Allah, it was as though I had never heard this verse before. This was because of the calamity that afflicted us (i.e. because we were so overcome by grief over the demise of Rasulullah ﷺ). I testify that the Book is exactly as it was revealed, the Hadith is as he related, and that Allah is alive, He does not die. To Allah we belong and to Him is our return. Salutations of Allah Ta'ala on His Messenger. We hope that we will be rewarded by Allah for this calamity."

Chapter 29

The Ansaar gather at Saqeefah Bani Saa'idah

After this tragic incident took place, Abu Bakr ؓ learnt that the Ansaar gathered at Saqeefah Bani Saa'idah to discuss the successor to Rasulullah ﷺ. The Muhaajireen asked Abu Bakr ؓ to present himself there as well. Abu Bakr ؓ, 'Umar ؓ and some of the Muhaajireen all proceeded there.

Hadhrat Abu Bakr ؓ and Hadhrat 'Umar ؓ feared that the people might become hasty and pledge their allegiance to just anyone which could become a cause of disunity later on. When this matter was sorted out and Abu Bakr ؓ was unanimously chosen as the caliph and successor to Rasulullah ﷺ, the Muslims began preparations for the enshrouding and burial of Rasulullah ﷺ. This meeting at the Saqeefah took place on Monday evening. The tragic news of Rasulullah's ﷺ demise was announced around mid-day, after which Abu Bakr ؓ came from his house in Sunh and delivered his sermon. At some time in the evening the gathering at Saqeefah took place.

The family of Rasulullah ﷺ were gathered in his room. When Abu Bakr ؓ and 'Umar ؓ heard about the gathering of the Ansaar in the Saqeefah, they proceeded there. They knew that since Rasulullah ﷺ has passed away, the coming down of divine revelation has terminated, and Rasulullah ﷺ had been continually warning of impending trials and tribulations. In the present circumstances, no forms of rebellion, division and disunity should take place which would completely turn the organisation of Islam upside down. This would cause the 23 year effort of Rasulullah ﷺ to be reduced to disarray, and the body of Islam to become disunited and scattered. This would make it difficult to bring it back together again.

Abu Bakr ؓ went to the Saqeefah in order to resolve the matter of succession. However, no one knew that Allah Ta'ala had already destined that he would be the very one to succeed Rasulullah ﷺ. He was forced into accepting this position. He tried his utmost to delay this matter. But in his presence, the people looked up to no one else. Abu Bakr رضي الله عنه did not even imagine that he would be appointed as the caliph of Islam. He went solely to prevent any disunity. He did not know that this position of caliph will be placed on his head.

$$\text{ذَٰلِكَ فَضْلُ اللهِ يُؤْتِيهِ مَنْ يَشَاءُ}$$

"This is the virtue from Allah which He bestows on whomever He wills."

The burial arrangements

After pledging their allegiance to Abu Bakr رضي الله عنه, the people began the burial arrangements. When they intended bathing Rasulullah ﷺ, the question of whether his clothes should be removed or not arose. The people were suddenly put into a daze and they heard an unseen voice saying that the Messenger's ﷺ clothes should not be removed. He should be bathed in his clothes. He was thus given a bath with his clothes on and then they were removed (for the shroud).

Ali رضي الله عنه was giving the bath, 'Abbaas رضي الله عنه and his two sons, Fadl رضي الله عنهما and Qathm رضي الله عنه, were changing the position of Rasulullah ﷺ, while Usaamah رضي الله عنه and Shuqraan رضي الله عنه were pouring the water.

After the bath, Rasulullah ﷺ was enshrouded in three lengths of cloth which did not contain a shirt and turban. The clothes in which he was bathed were removed.

The question then arose as to where he should be buried. Abu Bakr رضي الله عنه said: "I heard Rasulullah ﷺ saying that the Messenger is buried in the very place where he passes away."

Rasulullah's ﷺ bed was therefore moved from its spot and his grave was dug there. However, there was a difference with regard to the type of grave that should be dug. The Muhaajireen said that the type that is dug in Makkah should be dug, viz. a standard grave with an indentation on one side where the body is tucked in. The Ansaar said that the Madinah type of grave should be dug, viz. a standard grave with a trench at the center of the bottom of the grave. Abu 'Ubaydah رضي الله عنه and Abu Talhah رضي الله عنه were knowledgeable in digging each of these graves respectively. It was therefore decided to call both of them. The one who reaches first will dig the type of grave that he is an expert at. Abu Talhah رضي الله عنه reached first and so a trench type of grave was dug.

The Janaazah Salaah

When they completed the burial arrangements on Monday, the blessed body of Rasulullah ﷺ was placed in front of his grave. Group after group would come into the room and offer the Janaazah Salaah individually. No one was the Imaam for this Salaah. Each person came, offered his Salaah and left.

The people asked Abu Bakr ﷺ as to whether the Janaazah Salaah for Rasulullah ﷺ should be read. He replied in the affirmative. They asked him the procedure. He said that one group at a time should go into the room, say the Takbeer (Allah is the greatest), and after sending Durood and reciting the prescribed dua, he should return. Everyone should offer the Salaah in this way.

Abu Bakr ﷺ and 'Umar ﷺ also entered the room of Rasulullah ﷺ with a group, stood before the body of Rasulullah ﷺ and read the following:

السلام عليك أيها النبي ورحمة الله اللّهم إنا نشهد أنه قد بلغ ما أنزل إليه ونصح لأمته وجاهد فى سبيل الله حتى أعز الله دينه وتمت كلمته فاجعلنا يا إلهنا ممن يتبع القول الذى أنزل معه واجمع بيننا وبينه حتى يعرفنا ونعرفه فإنه كان بالمؤمنين رؤفا رحيما لا نبتغى بالإيمان بدلا ولا نشترى به ثمنا

"Peace and mercy of Allah be on you O Prophet! O Allah! We testify that he conveyed whatever was revealed to him. He advised his followers and fought in the cause of Allah until Allah elevated His religion and fulfilled His promise. O Allah! Make us among those who follow the revelation that was sent to him and join us with him so that we may recognize each other. Surely he was kind and merciful to the believers. We do not desire anything in exchange for Imaan and we will not sell it for any price."

The people who were present said *Aameen* to this dua. When the men completed, the women went in. They were then followed by the children.

When Rasulullah ﷺ was on his death bed, he summoned his family members. They asked: "O Messenger of Allah! Who should perform your Janaazah Salaah?" He replied: "When you are over with my burial arrangements, you should all leave my room for a little while. Jibraa'eel عليه السلام will be the first one to offer the Janaazah Salaah. He will be followed by Mikaa'eel عليه السلام, Israafeel عليه السلام, the angel of death, and then the remaining angels. Thereafter, you should all come in groups and send durood to me."

Allah Ta'ala says the following with regard to Rasulullah ﷺ:

﴿إِنَّ اللهَ وَمَلٰٓئِكَتَهُ يُصَلُّوْنَ عَلَى النَّبِيِّ ۚ يَآ اَيُّهَا الَّذِيْنَ اٰمَنُوْا صَلُّوْا عَلَيْهِ وَ سَلِّمُوْا تَسْلِيْمًا﴾

"Surely Allah and His angels send salutations on the Messenger. O you who believe! Send salutations and peace on him."

This verse commands each believer to send individual Durood to him. Just as it was incumbent to send Durood without any Imaam and without any congregation when he was alive, so too after his demise, Durood is to be sent without any Imaam and without any congregation.

30 000 people offered the Janaazah Salaah for Rasulullah ﷺ.

Burial

Rasulullah ﷺ passed away on a Monday afternoon. It was the same time as when he had emigrated from Makkah and entered Madinah. The majority of scholars are of the opinion that he was buried on Wednesday. Others are of the opinion that he was buried on Tuesday.

Ali رضي الله عنه, 'Abbaas رضي الله عنه and his two sons, Fadl رضي الله عنه and Qasam رضي الله عنه, lowered Rasulullah ﷺ into his grave. When they completed the burial, the grave was heaped in the shape of a camel's hump. Water was then sprinkled on it.

After completing the burial, the Sahaabah رضي الله عنهم returned to their homes, sad and dejected. They continued reciting:

إِنَّا لِلّٰهِ وَإِنَّا إِلَيْهِ رَاجِعُوْنَ

"To Allah we belong and to Him is our return."

Chapter 30

Saqeefah Bani Saa'idah and the pledge of allegiance

Rasulullah ﷺ departed from the fleeting world to the eternal life of the hereafter on a Monday afternoon. On hearing this news, the Sahaabah ؓ were left in a stupor. Some of them felt that he had not died as yet. This was based on their extreme love for him and not due to misunderstanding. On hearing this news, Abu Bakr ؓ came very sadly and dejectedly into Madinah and consoled the Sahaabah ؓ.

On that evening, someone came and informed Abu Bakr ؓ that the Ansaar had gathered in the Saqeefah Bani Saa'idah and that they want to pledge their allegiance to Sa'd ibn Abi 'Ubaadah ؓ. Some Ansaar were also suggesting that one leader should be from them and another from the Quraysh. Some of the Ansaar felt that they were eligible for the caliphate because they had helped the religion, gave refuge to Rasulullah ﷺ and joined him in waging Jihaad against the enemies of Allah Ta'ala. Some of the other Ansaar objected to this. The discussions in this regard continued. This news gradually reached Abu Bakr ؓ and 'Umar ؓ. They both went to Saqeefah Bani Saa'idah together with Abu 'Ubaydah ibnul-Jarrah ؓ in order to control the situation just in case problems break out. They met 'Aasim ibn 'Adiyy and 'Uwaym ibn Saa'idah on the way. These two tried to stop them from proceeding, but they continued and rushed to where the Ansaar were meeting. Mutual discussions then ensued.

When they reached the Saqeefah Bani Saa'idah, Sa'd ibn 'Ubaadah ؓ was already present. He was sitting down with a blanket around him. He was ill but the Ansaar brought him to the meeting so that they could appoint him as the leader.

The speech of Sa'd ibn 'Ubaadah رضي الله عنه

Sa'd ibn 'Ubaadah رضي الله عنه stood up and after praising and glorifying Allah Ta'ala, he delivered the following speech:

اما بعد! فنحن الانصار وكتيبة الاسلام وانتم يا معشر قريش رهط بيننا وقد دفت الينا دافة من قومكم فاذا هم يريدون ان يغصبونا الامر

"We are the Ansaar - the helpers of Islam and the army of Islam. And you, Quraysh, are a small group among us (i.e. we are in the majority while you are in the minority). A small group of your people came and sought refuge with us. Now they want to snatch away our right to the caliphate."

Another narration states that Sa'd ibn 'Ubaadah رضي الله عنه said the following in his speech:

"O group of Ansaar! You surpassed others (in embracing Islam) and enjoy a virtue that no other Arabs enjoy. Muhammad صلى الله عليه وسلم lived among his own people for over 10 years, inviting them, but only a few believed in him. They were so few that they were unable to defend him, to give honour to his religion nor to stop the oppression of an enemy. When Allah decided to give you virtue, He conveyed the means of honour to you and blessed you with Imaan in Him and in His Messenger صلى الله عليه وسلم. He gave you the ability to defend His Messenger صلى الله عليه وسلم and his Companions, and to wage Jihaad against his enemies. You were the firmest against his enemies until the Arabs submitted to the order of Allah Ta'ala willingly and unwillingly. Even those who lived far away were vanquished and submitted before him. The Arabs became obedient to His Messenger صلى الله عليه وسلم through your swords. Allah Ta'ala then caused him to leave this world in a state that he was pleased and delighted with you. You should take up this position (of caliphate) because it is your right and no one else's."

Those who were present liked this speech tremendously and they all expressed their agreement. Discussions in this regard ensued and the Muhaajireen raised their objection by saying: "We are the first Companions of Rasulullah صلى الله عليه وسلم. We were the first ones to believe in him and we belong to his tribe. We emigrated with him, leaving behind our families, relatives, homeland and everything else and came here." The Ansaar said: "We should rather have two leaders, one from the Muhaajireen and one from the Ansaar. Both of them should take up the responsibility of the caliphate and work together for the general good." On hearing

Chapter 30

this, Sa'd ibn 'Ubaadah رضي الله عنه said: "This would entail the first weakness (in Islam)."

'Umar رضي الله عنه wanted to say something but Abu Bakr رضي الله عنه asked him to remain silent. Since he did not want to displease Abu Bakr رضي الله عنه, he sat down. Abu Bakr رضي الله عنه then delivered the following speech:

Abu Bakr's رضي الله عنه speech

Abu Bakr رضي الله عنه stood up, and after praising and glorifying Allah Ta'ala, delivered the following speech:

"Allah sent a Messenger among us who would watch over the ummah so that they may worship Allah alone. Previously, they used to worship many idols made of rock and wood. It was difficult for the Arabs to leave the religion of their forefathers. Allah thus gave special inspiration to the early emigrants (Muhaajireen) from his people to believe him, to support him, to remain patient over the severe hardships that were imposed by his people, and their rejection of him. All the people were against him and his supporters. Despite their small number, they were not intimidated by their opponents and they did not abandon him. So they were the first people on earth to worship Allah and to believe in Allah and the Messenger. They are the Messenger's associates and family. They are more eligible for this caliphate than others. None but a wrongdoer can dispute with them in this matter. As for you, O Ansaar! None can deny your virtue in religion nor your early acceptance of Islam. Allah was pleased with you as the helpers of His religion and His Messenger, and He promulgated the emigration towards you. After the early emigrants, you enjoy the highest status. We are therefore the leaders while you are the ministers. Your counsel will be sought and no matter will be decided without consulting with you."

Another narration states that Abu Bakr رضي الله عنه gave the following reply to the Ansaar:

ما ذكرتم من خير فانتم اهل وما تعرف العرب هذا الامر الا لهذا الحى من قريش هم اوسط العرب نسبا ودارا

"Your merits which you enumerated are certainly found in you. However, the Arabs will not recognise the caliphate for anyone but the Quraysh because they are considered to be the most superior in their lineage and their place of residence (Makkah).''

What Abu Bakr رضي الله عنه meant by this was that a caliph should be from a people whose leadership and genealogical honour are widely accepted so that people may unanimously accept this leadership and that they do not consider it beneath them to follow and obey him. As long as any type of honour, virtue and merit is not accepted, people are not ready for any type of obedience. Instead, they consider him to be low and contemptible. Abu Bakr رضي الله عنه wanted to show to them that the virtue and merit of the Quraysh was accepted by all the Arabs. They do not look up to the Aus and Khazraj with any real honour and respect. Therefore, if anyone from the Ansaar was appointed as the leader, the Arab tribes will not be prepared to follow and obey him. The general masses of the country will not unanimously accept his leadership. The most important aspect concerning the caliphate and leadership is that the people must accept the leader, and they must be united and unanimous about his leadership.

Another narration states that Abu Bakr رضي الله عنه addressed the Ansaar saying:

يا معشر الانصار انا والله ما ننكر فضلكم ولا بلائكم فى الاسلام ولا حقكم الواجب علينا ولكن قد عرفتم ان هذا الحى من قريش بمنزلة من العرب فليس بها غيرهم وان العرب لن تجتمع الا على رجل منهم فنحن الامراء وانتم الوزراء فاتقوا الله ولا تصدعوا الاسلام ولا تكونوا اول من احدث فى الاسلام الا وقد رضيت لكم احد هذين الرجلين لى. اى لعمر ولا بى عبيدة فايهما بايعتم فهو لكم ثقة

"O group of Ansaar! I take an oath by Allah that we do not deny your virtue and your sacrifices in Islam, nor your incumbent right over us. But you know that the Quraysh hold a certain position among the Arabs which is not shared by anyone else. The Arabs will never rally around anyone but someone from them. We shall therefore be the leaders and you will be the ministers. Fear Allah, then, and do not be the first ones to split Islam and do not be the first ones to introduce innovations in Islam. It is my opinion that one of these two men are appropriate for the leadership, 'Umar and Abu 'Ubaydah. Which ever of the two you pledge allegiance to will be worthy of your trust and confidence."

After this speech of Abu Bakr رضي الله عنه, Khabbaab ibnul-Munzir ibn Jamooh رضي الله عنه stood up and said that it would be appropriate to appoint one leader from the Ansaar and one from the Muhaajireen. Abu Bakr رضي الله عنه replied that Rasulullah صلى الله عليه وسلم said that the leaders should be from the Quraysh.

Abu Bakr ﷺ replied:

"It is not permissible for the Muslims to have two leaders. If this were to happen, their orders and commands would differ, the unity of the Muslims will be scattered and they will differ with each other. When this happens, the Sunnah will be abandoned, innovations will come to the fore, and rebellion will increase. There is no good for anyone in this. This matter of caliphate will remain among the Quraysh as long as they obey Allah and they remain steadfast on His commands. This Hadith has reached you or you have heard it from Rasulullah ﷺ: 'Do not differ, or else you will become cowardly and your power will dissolve. Remain patient for Allah is with the patient ones.' So we shall be the leaders and you the ministers. You are our brothers in Islam and our helpers and supporters in it."

'Umar ﷺ said: "How sad! Can there be two swords in one sheath!? Can a woman have two husbands!?" In other words, one country cannot have two rulers. 'Umar's ﷺ reply was a rational reply while that of Abu Bakr ﷺ was a traditional reply – he quoted a clear statement of Rasulullah ﷺ. Basheer ibn Sa'd Ansaari said: "I have also heard this Hadith from Rasulullah ﷺ." Other Ansaar and Muhaajireen also affirmed this Hadith. Khabbaab ibnul-Mundhir ﷺ and other Ansaar who were persistent on having a caliph from the Ansaar also changed their opinions after hearing this Hadith. The noise and clamour with regard to the matter of caliphate all subsided and everyone remained silent.

Zaid ibn Saabit ﷺ, the scribe of Rasulullah ﷺ, said: "Rasulullah ﷺ was from the Muhaajireen. His caliph should therefore be from the Muhaajireen. Just as we had been the helpers and supporters of Rasulullah ﷺ, we shall remain the helpers and supporters of Rasulullah's ﷺ deputy." He then held the hand of Abu Bakr ﷺ and said: "This is your caliph, pledge allegiance to him."

Sa'd ibn 'Ubaadah's ﷺ acknowledgement

Abu Bakr ﷺ and 'Umar ﷺ went to (the Saqeefah Bani Saa'idah) and spoke to the Ansaar. Abu Bakr ﷺ addressed them and enumerated all the virtues and merits of the Ansaar. He said to them: 'You know that Rasulullah ﷺ said that if the people were to choose to travel through a particular valley while the Ansaar chose another valley, he would travel through the valley chosen by the Ansaar. And you know very well, O Sa'd, that on one occasion you were sitting in the assembly of Rasulullah ﷺ when he said: 'The Quraysh should be in charge of this matter of caliphate. The good among them follow the good people while the evil ones among them follow the evil people.' Sa'd said to him: 'You have spoken the truth. We are the ministers while you are the leaders.'"

This narration explicitly states that Abu Bakr ﷺ addressed Sa'd ibn 'Ubaadah ﷺ by taking an oath in the name of Allah Ta'ala that he was present when Rasulullah ﷺ said that the Quraysh should be in charge of this matter. Sa'd ﷺ replied by saying: "You have spoken the truth." It is for this reason that Ibn Katheer رحمه الله has a special chapter titled: "Sa'd ibn 'Ubaadah's testimony to the authenticity of what Abu Bakr ﷺ said at the meeting in the Saqeefah."

'Abdullah ibn Mas'ood ﷺ narrates that when the Ansaar proposed that there should be one leader from them and one from the Muhaajireen, 'Umar ﷺ said: "O group of Ansaar! You know that Rasulullah ﷺ ordered that Abu Bakr ﷺ should lead the people in Salaah. Now who among you would like to go ahead of Abu Bakr ﷺ?" The Ansaar replied: "We seek refuge in Allah from trying to go ahead of Abu Bakr ﷺ."

What he meant by this is that Rasulullah ﷺ specifically emphasised and insisted that Abu Bakr ﷺ should lead the people in Salaah and to take his place. This was a clear proof that Rasulullah ﷺ considered Abu Bakr ﷺ to be the most preferable for nomination as Khalifah.

A Hadith of Shamaa'il Tirmizi states that when the Ansaar suggested that there should be one leader from them and one from the Muhaajireen, 'Umar ﷺ enumerated three qualities of Abu Bakr ﷺ and asked the assembly if anyone else possessed these three qualities:

- Allah Ta'ala referred to Abu Bakr ﷺ as one of the two (Abu Bakr ﷺ and Rasulullah ﷺ) who were in the cave. (ثاني اثنين إذ هما في الغار)

- Allah Ta'ala referred to Abu Bakr ﷺ as being the close companion of Rasulullah ﷺ. (إذ يقول لصاحبه لا تحزن)

- Allah Ta'ala referred to His being with them (Rasulullah ﷺ and Abu Bakr ﷺ). (إن الله معنا)

It should be borne in mind that Allah's companionship and knowledge is with everyone and encompasses everyone. Yet, He specifically mentions His presence in the above verse.

These three qualities of Abu Bakr ﷺ are established from the Qur-aan. This demonstrates his pre-eminence and that he alone is eligible for the caliphate.

Abu Bakr ﷺ then addressed the assembly and said to the people: "'Umar and Abu 'Ubaydah are both present here. Choose whichever of the two you want as your leader." 'Umar ﷺ and Abu 'Ubaydah ﷺ both said: "We take an oath by Allah that it is impossible for us to take the reigns of caliphate in your presence. You are the most superior among all the Muhaajireen. Salaah is a pillar of Islam and the most superior fundamental of the religion of Islam – Rasulullah ﷺ appointed you to lead the people in Salaah and made you stand in his place. O Abu Bakr! Give us your hand and we will pledge allegiance to you."

A Hadith states that Abu Bakr رضي الله عنه addressed 'Umar رضي الله عنه saying: "O 'Umar! Extend your hand so that I may pledge allegiance to you." 'Umar رضي الله عنه replied: "You are better than me." Abu Bakr رضي الله عنه replied: "You are stronger than me." 'Umar رضي الله عنه eventually said: "My strength will be with you together with your superiority." In other words, the superior person (Abu Bakr رضي الله عنه) will be the leader and the stronger person ('Umar رضي الله عنه) will be his minister.

'Umar رضي الله عنه then asked Abu Bakr رضي الله عنه to extend his hand so that he could pledge his allegiance to him. When 'Umar رضي الله عنه and Abu 'Ubaydah رضي الله عنه were about to extend their hands to Abu Bakr رضي الله عنه, Basheer ibn Sa'd Ansaari رضي الله عنه hastened forward and pledged his allegiance to Abu Bakr رضي الله عنه. 'Umar رضي الله عنه and Abu 'Ubaydah رضي الله عنه then followed suit.

The general pledge after the special pledge

Abu Bakr رضي الله عنه was chosen as the caliph after the unanimous decision of the Muhaajireen and Ansaar. The assembly came to an end after the pledge of allegiance. This took place on the evening of the Monday on which Rasulullah ﷺ passed away. In other words, this special pledge took place on the evening of the 12th of Rabi'ul-Awwal 11 A.H. The general pledge took place the following day, Tuesday, in the Masjid-e-Nabawi on the mimbar.

After the pledge at the Saqeefah, the people gathered the following day in the Masjid-e-Nabawi. All the senior Sahaabah رضي الله عنهم, Muhaajireen and Ansaar were present. 'Umar رضي الله عنه first stood up and delivered a short but comprehensive speech. Abu Bakr رضي الله عنه remained seated silently.

'Umar رضي الله عنه delivers a speech before the general pledge

'Umar رضي الله عنه said: "I hoped that Rasulullah ﷺ would pass away after all of us. Since he has passed away, if Allah Ta'ala wills, there will be no void in the religion because Allah Ta'ala placed a guiding light (the Qur-aan) in your midst. This is the means for your guidance. After Rasulullah ﷺ, Abu Bakr رضي الله عنه is present amongst you. He is the companion of Rasulullah ﷺ in the cave and the second of the two. He is Rasulullah's ﷺ special friend and companion. From all the Muslims, he alone is eligible to take the reigns of authority in all matters. O Muslims! Get up and pledge allegiance at his hands."

A Hadith states that 'Umar ؓ asked: "O Muslims! Who is there apart from Abu Bakr regarding whom Allah Ta'ala said: 'The second of the two when they were in the cave'? And who is there apart from Abu Bakr regarding whom Allah Ta'ala referred to as the companion of Rasulullah ﷺ? 'When he said to his companion.' And who is there apart from Abu Bakr regarding whom Allah said: 'Surely Allah is with us.'? In short, there was no one beneath the heavens and on the surface of the earth who shared these excellent qualities with Abu Bakr ؓ. How then, can there be anyone to share with him the eligibility of becoming caliph? You should understand well that the person regarding whom Allah Ta'ala said: 'The second of the two', is a unique person – he has no second. You should therefore go to him and pledge allegiance at his hands. His hands come after those of Rasulullah ﷺ."

When 'Umar ؓ completed his speech, he asked Abu Bakr ؓ to ascend the mimbar. Abu Bakr ؓ hesitated, but 'Umar ؓ urged him on. Abu Bakr ؓ eventually climbed the mimbar and the general body of Muslims pledged their allegiance to him.

Abu Bakr's ؓ first speech after the general pledge

After 'Umar ؓ urged Abu Bakr ؓ to climb the mimbar, he did so but he sat on a step lower than that on which Rasulullah ﷺ used to sit. He then took the pledge of allegiance from the general body of Muslims. He then addressed the assembly as follows:

"O people! I have been made your leader despite not being the best of you. If I do good, help me. If I do anything wrong, correct me. Honesty is an act of trustworthiness while dishonesty is an act of treachery. The weak among you is strong in my sight till I remove his complaint, if Allah Ta'ala wills. The strong among you is weak in my sight till I take the dues from him, if Allah Ta'ala wills. When a people abandons Jihaad in the cause of Allah, He disgraces them. When immorality becomes rife in a people, Allah Ta'ala encompasses them with calamities. Obey me as long as I obey Allah Ta'ala and His Messenger ﷺ. If I disobey Allah Ta'ala and His Messenger ﷺ, you do not have to obey me. You may now stand up for the Salaah. May Allah have mercy on you."

Abdur Rahman ibn Auf ؓ narrates: "Abu Bakr delivered a speech and said: 'I take an oath by Allah that I never desired leadership – neither by day nor by night. I was neither inclined towards it nor did I ask Allah for it in secrecy or in public. However, I feared disunity. I find no solace in leadership. I have been shouldered with a very serious matter. I neither have the strength nor the power to bear it except by the strength and support of Allah Ta'ala.'"

The following is related in Kanzul Ummaal: Abu Bakr رضي الله عنه delivered a speech and said:

"O people! If you think that I took your caliphate out of desire for it or out of the desire to be above you and the Muslims, then I take an oath by that Being in whose control is my life, that I neither took it out of desire for it nor out of the desire to be above you and the Muslims. I neither longed for it in secrecy nor in public. I have been shouldered with a serious matter. I do not have the strength to bear it unless Allah Ta'ala helps me. It was my wish that it should have been given to any other companion of Rasulullah صلى الله عليه وسلم who would deal with justice. I am now returning it to you and the pledge that you gave me is terminated. Give this caliphate to whomever you wish, I am just an ordinary person amongst you."

Ali's رضي الله عنه pledge of allegiance

When all the people pledged their allegiance, Abu Bakr رضي الله عنه looked at the assembly and did not see Ali رضي الله عنه and Zubayr رضي الله عنه. He said: "I do not see Ali and Zubayr. Call them as well." Some people from the Ansaar got up and went to call them. Abu Bakr رضي الله عنه addressed them saying: "O cousin and son-in-law of Rasulullah! Do you wish to cause disunity among the Muslims?" He posed the same question to Zubayr رضي الله عنه as well. They both replied: "O caliph of Rasulullah! Do not rebuke us. We do not wish to cause disunity among the Muslims." Ali رضي الله عنه and Zubayr رضي الله عنه said:

"We are not angry except for the fact that we were left out of the consultation. We consider Abu Bakr رضي الله عنه to be the most eligible for the caliphate. He was the companion (of Rasulullah صلى الله عليه وسلم) in the cave. We acknowledge his merit and distinction. The Messenger of Allah صلى الله عليه وسلم had ordered him to lead the people in Salaah while he was alive."

Another narration states that they said: "He (Rasulullah صلى الله عليه وسلم) was pleased with him (Abu Bakr رضي الله عنه) for our spiritual affairs, so why shouldn't we be pleased with him for our worldly affairs?"

On saying this, both of them pledged their allegiance to Abu Bakr رضي الله عنه.

Abu Bakr رضي الله عنه excused Ali رضي الله عنه and Zubayr رضي الله عنه and said to them: "I take an oath by Allah that I did not have the least desire for leadership. Neither did I have any inclination towards it in my heart, nor did I ask Allah for it in secrecy or in public. However, I feared that if I delayed the matter till your arrival, there would be some rebellion."

After the demise of Faatimah رضي الله عنها, Ali رضي الله عنه sent a message to Abu Bakr رضي الله عنه to visit him at his house but that he should not bring anyone else with him.

This was a reference to 'Umar ؓ because he was quite strict while Abu Bakr ؓ was lenient. When 'Umar ؓ heard about this, he said to Abu Bakr ؓ: "By Allah, you should not go alone." Abu Bakr ؓ replied: "By Allah, I will certainly go. I do not expect him to do anything to me." When Abu Bakr ؓ went there, Ali ؓ praised and glorified Allah Ta'ala and then said:

"We are fully aware of your virtue and merit and whatever Allah Ta'ala bestowed to you. We are not envious of the good and honour which Allah bestowed to you (i.e. the caliphate). However, our complaint is that the caliphate was decided upon without consulting us. We felt that because of our closeness to Rasulullah ﷺ, we should have also been consulted." Ali ؓ continued speaking in this vein until tears began flowing from Abu Bakr's ؓ eyes.

When Abu Bakr ؓ began speaking, he said:

"I take an oath by that Being in whose control is my life that the family ties of Rasulullah ﷺ are more beloved to me than my own family ties. As for the dispute that took place between me and you with regard to the wealth of Fadak, I did not display any shortcoming in doing good and what was best and I did not abandon the way of Rasulullah ﷺ in this regard in the least. (I distributed this wealth as Rasulullah ﷺ would have done)."

Ali ؓ said to Abu Bakr ؓ: "I make a promise that I will present myself in the afternoon in order to pledge my allegiance to you."

After performing the Zuhr Salaah, Abu Bakr ؓ climbed the mimbar and spoke about the matter concerning Ali ؓ, his delay in pledging allegiance and his reason for it. He then sought forgiveness from Allah Ta'ala and came down. Ali ؓ then stood up and spoke about the merits and rights of Abu Bakr ؓ. He stated that what he did was not out of envy towards Abu Bakr ؓ nor rejection of the bounty (caliphate) which Allah bestowed him with. His only complaint was that he was not consulted when he should have been. The Muslims became very pleased with what they heard and said: "You have spoken well."

In the light of all these Ahaadith it becomes absolutely clear that Ali ؓ had no doubt whatsoever as regards the superiority and eligibility of Abu Bakr ؓ for the caliphate, nor did he harbour any jealousy or envy towards his caliphate. He pledged his allegiance to Abu Bakr ؓ happily and readily. His complaint that he had against Abu Bakr ؓ was actually based on his love for him. A person does not have complaints for outsiders. In fact, this Hadith shows that Ali's ؓ heart was filled with love for Abu Bakr ؓ and that he had no doubt whatsoever concerning the superiority of Abu Bakr رضي الله عنه. Distancing himself from the pledge was in no way because of jealousy and envy. Rather it was an affectionate and sincere complaint, and he did it out of his gracefulness. It was not a real objection or protest.

Abu Bakr رضي الله عنه did not go to the Saqeefah to become the caliph. Rather, he went to clear the misunderstanding between the Muhaajireen and the Ansaar. Even when he reached there, he did not ask the people to pledge allegiance to him. Rather, those who were present pledged their unanimous allegiance to him of their own accord. Had he not accepted the pledge under such circumstances, it would have probably resulted in rebellion. In such volatile and unstable circumstances, it is not appropriate to ask why he did not call such and such person and why he did not consult such and such person. When Abu Bakr رضي الله عنه explained these reasons to Ali رضي الله عنه, all his complaints were removed and he pledged his allegiance to Abu Bakr رضي الله عنه with his heart and life.

Abu Bakr's رضي الله عنه intention to give up the caliphate

Abu Bakr رضي الله عنه had accepted the caliphate because he feared disunity and also because the people had insisted that he accept it. However, it pained him for having accepted this heavy responsibility. He therefore remained sad and dejected in his house. When 'Umar رضي الله عنه went to Abu Bakr رضي الله عنه, he rebuked 'Umar رضي الله عنه and complained to him by saying: "You are the one who placed me in this serious position. It is very difficult to pass judgement among the people." 'Umar رضي الله عنه consoled him by saying: "Have you not heard the words of Rasulullah صلى الله عليه وسلم that when a ruler or judge uses all his faculties and abilities to pass judgement, then when he passes his judgement, he will receive a single reward if he is wrong in his judgement and a double reward if he is correct." On hearing this, Abu Bakr رضي الله عنه felt a bit easier.

It is stated in one Hadith that after the pledge of allegiance, Abu Bakr رضي الله عنه remained in his house for three days. When he used to come to the Masjid, he would climb the mimbar and say:

"O people! I am returning your pledge, so pledge your allegiance to whomever you like." On each occasion, Ali رضي الله عنه would stand up and say: "By Allah, we will neither remove you nor will we take back our pledge. Who can remove you when it was Rasulullah صلى الله عليه وسلم who put you forward?"

An interesting incident

When Rasulullah صلى الله عليه وسلم passed away, 'Amr ibn Aas رضي الله عنه was either in Bahrain or 'Ammaan. The news reached him that the people (Muslims of Madinah) rallied around Abu Bakr ؓ and appointed him caliph. The people of that place (Bahrain or 'Ammaan) asked 'Amr ibn Aas ؓ: "Who is this person around whom the people rallied. Is he the son of your Prophet?" He replied: "No." They asked: "Is he his brother?" He replied: "No." They asked: "Is he his closest relative?" He replied: "No." They asked: "Then who is he (that the people unanimously elected him)?" He replied: "They appointed the best person amongst them and made him their leader." The people said: "They will continue experiencing good as long as they continue in this manner."

Chapter 31

The Pure Wives of Rasulullah ﷺ

The wives of Rasulullah ﷺ are the mothers to the believers in the honour and respect that they deserve. Allah Ta'ala says:

$$\text{يٰنِسَآءَ النَّبِيِّ لَسْتُنَّ كَاَحَدٍ مِّنَ النِّسَآءِ اِنِ اتَّقَيْتُنَّ فَلَا تَخْضَعْنَ بِالْقَوْلِ فَيَطْمَعَ الَّذِىْ فِىْ قَلْبِهٖ مَرَضٌ وَّ قُلْنَ قَوْلًا مَّعْرُوْفًا ۚ وَقَرْنَ فِىْ بُيُوْتِكُنَّ وَلَا تَبَرَّجْنَ تَبَرُّجَ الْجَاهِلِيَّةِ الْاُوْلٰى وَ اَقِمْنَ الصَّلٰوةَ وَ اٰتِيْنَ الزَّكٰوةَ وَ اَطِعْنَ اللّٰهَ وَ رَسُوْلَهٗ ۚ اِنَّمَا يُرِيْدُ اللّٰهُ لِيُذْهِبَ عَنْكُمُ الرِّجْسَ اَهْلَ الْبَيْتِ وَ يُطَهِّرَكُمْ تَطْهِيْرًا ۚ وَاذْكُرْنَ مَا يُتْلٰى فِىْ بُيُوْتِكُنَّ مِنْ اٰيٰتِ اللّٰهِ وَ الْحِكْمَةِ ۚ اِنَّ اللّٰهَ كَانَ لَطِيْفًا خَبِيْرًا}$$

> "O wives of the Prophet! You are not like any of the other women provided you fear (Allah). Therefore do not be too soft in speech lest he in whose heart is a disease should be moved with desire. But speak in an honourable manner. Remain in your homes and do not display yourselves as was the custom of displaying in the former days of ignorance. Establish the Salaah and continue giving the zakaah, and remain in the obedience of Allah and His Messenger. Allah only wants to remove loathsome things from you, O family of the Prophet, and to completely purify you. Remember what is recited in your homes of Allah's words and of wisdom. Surely Allah knows the subtleties, all-aware." [Surah Ahzaab, verses 32-34]

Since they have been given this title of Mothers of the believers, it is absolutely prohibited to marry them after the demise of Rasulullah ﷺ. Allah Ta'ala says:

وَمَا كَانَ لَكُمْ أَنْ تُؤْذُوا رَسُولَ اللّٰهِ وَلَآ أَنْ تَنْكِحُوٓا أَزْوَاجَهٗ مِنْۢ بَعْدِهٖٓ أَبَدًا ۚ إِنَّ ذٰلِكُمْ كَانَ عِنْدَ اللّٰهِ عَظِيْمًا ۞ اِنْ تُبْدُوْا شَيْـًٔا اَوْ تُخْفُوْهُ فَاِنَّ اللّٰهَ كَانَ بِكُلِّ شَيْءٍ عَلِيْمًا ۞

"It does not behove you to hurt the Messenger of Allah, nor to ever marry his wives after him. Surely this act of yours is a major sin in the sight of Allah. If you say anything openly or conceal it, Allah has knowledge of everything."

[Surah Ahzaab, verses 53-54]

Any self-respecting and self-honouring person will feel hurt to imagine his wife going to someone else after he has departed from this world. Can there be anyone more self-respecting and self-honouring in this entire world than Rasulullah ﷺ? Moreover, since they have been given the title of "Mothers of the believers", it is against their lofty status and position to enter into any other marriage. To marry your father's wife is both rationally and traditionally despicable. Allah Ta'ala says:

وَلَا تَنْكِحُوْا مَا نَكَحَ اٰبَآؤُكُمْ مِّنَ النِّسَآءِ اِلَّا مَا قَدْ سَلَفَ ۚ اِنَّهٗ كَانَ فَاحِشَةً وَّمَقْتًا ۚ وَسَآءَ سَبِيْلًا ۞

"Do not marry the women whom your fathers had married, except what has already passed. This is an indecency, and a disgusting act, and an evil way."

[Surah Nisaa', verse 22]

The number of Rasulullah's ﷺ wives and the order in which he married them

Rasulullah ﷺ had 11 wives, two of whom had passed away in his very life: Khadijah رضى الله عنها and Zaynab bint Khuzaymah رضى الله عنها. Rasulullah ﷺ had nine wives at the time of his demise.

Abu Sa'eed Khudri رضى الله عنه narrates that Rasulullah ﷺ said: "I did not marry any of my wives nor did I get any of my daughters married except by revelation from my Rabb which was brought to me by Jibraa'eel عليه السلام."

Ummul-Mu'mineen Khadijah رضى الله عنها

Khadijah رضى الله عنها is unanimously accepted as the first wife of Rasulullah ﷺ. She is also unanimously accepted as the first Muslim – no male or female preceded her in embracing Islam. She was from the Quraysh tribe. Her father's name was Khuwaylid and her mother's name was Faatimah bint Zaa'idah. Her lineage is as follows: Khadijah bint Khuwaylid ibn Asd ibn 'Abd al-'Uzza ibn Qusayy. Her lineage meets with that of Rasulullah ﷺ at Qusayy.

Since she was free from the customs and habits of jaahiliyyah, she was popularly referred to as Taahirah (the pure one) even before Rasulullah's ﷺ commission as a Prophet.

Her first marriage was with Abu Haalah ibn Zuraarah Tameemi. From this marriage, she had two sons by the name of Hind and Haalah. Both these children embraced Islam and are therefore Sahaabah ؓ. Hind ibn Abi Haalah ؓ was very eloquent in his speech. The detailed Hadith with regard to the physical description of Rasulullah ﷺ is by and large narrated by him.

When Abu Haalah passed away, Khadijah ؓ married 'Ateeq ibn 'Aa'idh Makhzumi from whom she had a daughter by the name of Hind. She also embraced Islam and is blessed with being among the Sahaabiyaat. However, there are no Ahaadith narrated from her. After some time, 'Ateeq also passed away and Khadijah ؓ remained a widow.

Nafisah bint Munibah narrates that Khadijah ؓ was a very noble and wealthy woman. When she became a widow, every nobleman from the Quraysh desired to marry her. However, when Rasulullah ﷺ went on a trade journey with her goods and returned with immense profits, she became inclined towards him. She sent a message to him asking him what was stopping him from getting married. Rasulullah ﷺ replied: "I do not possess anything." She asked him: "If this concern of yours is taken care of, and you are invited towards a woman who has wealth, beauty and compatibility, then do you still have any excuse?" Rasulullah ﷺ asked: "Who is that woman?" She replied: "Khadijah." Rasulullah ﷺ accepted this proposal.

The actual reason is that the closer the time for Rasulullah's ﷺ commission as a Prophet came, the more miracles of his prophet-hood were demonstrated. This used to happen through the statements of the 'Ulama' of the Taurah and Injeel, by the statements of astrologers, or through unseen voices. When any scholar of the Taurah or Injeel set eyes on him, he would immediately say: "This young man is going to be the final Prophet whose glad tidings were given by Musa عليه السلام and 'Isa عليه السلام."

Khadijah ؓ had full knowledge of these incidents. She had heard from her slave, Maysarah, the incidents that took place with Rasulullah ﷺ on the journey to Syria and the story of a monk. She had heard about Buhayra, the monk. Her cousin, Waraqah ibn Naufal, was an eminent scholar of the Taurah and Injeel. He was awaiting the dawn of the last Prophet. Bearing in mind all these incidents, Khadijah's ؓ heart desired to marry Rasulullah ﷺ. Coincidentally, an incident occurred that in one of the festivals of Jaahiliyyah, the women of Makkah gathered. Khadijah ؓ was also among them. She suddenly saw a person appearing and announcing in a loud voice:

"There is going to be a Prophet in your city. His name will be Ahmad. Whoever among you can become his wife should do so. On hearing this, all the women pelted him with stones, except Khadijah. She remained silent."

Khadijah's ﷺ heart was already filled with hopes and desires of having this wonderful opportunity of being his wife. After hearing this announcement, the fire of her hopes began burning even more.

When her slave, Maysarah, returned from the journey to Syria and related the incidents that took place, and also the conversation with Nastoora, the monk, she said: "If what the Jewish astrologer said is true, then it can be no one but him (Muhammad ﷺ)."

We learn from this that the women's assembly at that festival took place before the return of Maysarah. Khadijah ﷺ was not merely given the name Taahirah by chance, rather it was from Allah Ta'ala that He instilled this name in the minds of the people so that her purity and chastity may become well known. This is similar to Rasulullah ﷺ being given the title of Ameen – the trustworthy, so that his trustworthiness and credibility may be an accepted fact, and no one may have any reason to doubt. It is for such occasions that it is said that the utterances of people should be considered to be the kettle-drum of Allah Ta'ala. Khadijah ﷺ was the Maryam ﷺ of her time. She therefore received a special share of the purity and chastity of Maryam ﷺ, when Allah Ta'ala says in the Qur-aan:

$$وَطَهَّرَكِ وَاصْطَفَاكِ عَلٰى نِسَاءِ الْعٰلَمِيْنَ$$

"He purified you and chose you over the women of the worlds."

Khadijah ﷺ got a share of this and was given the name Taahirah. It is now obvious that such a pure and chaste woman will naturally be inclined towards a person who is pure and chaste. Allah Ta'ala correctly said, and who can be more correct than Him? Allah Ta'ala says:

$$الطَّيِّبٰتُ لِلطَّيِّبِيْنَ وَ الطَّيِّبُوْنَ لِلطَّيِّبٰتِ$$

"The pure females are for the pure males, and the pure males are for the pure females."

Everyone is aware that prophet-hood and Messenger-ship is not any kingship. It has nothing to do with the luxuries and comforts of this world. There is no way that dirhams and dinaars can remain in the house of a Prophet, unless it remains for a little while in wait for a person asking a loan. Weeks and months go by without the fire-place being lit. Nights pass without any light being lit. It is also a known fact that the love for wealth, riches, comforts, luxuries, jewellery, etc. are in the nature of women. Despite this and despite the fact that all the noblemen and wealthy people of Makkah desired to marry Khadijah ﷺ, she inclined towards Muhammad ﷺ. This is clear proof of her purity and chastity. From this, we can also gauge the high understanding and foresight of Khadijah ﷺ. To desire the marriage of a Prophet and a Messenger is not the work of an ordinary mind. It is only deep intelligence and foresight that can prepare one for such a desire. Intelligence demands that in order to enter into a marriage with a Prophet, the woman must be prepared to wash her hands off from this world. She must be prepared to cover herself with the blankets of poverty. The desire to marry a Prophet is synonymous to desiring poverty. It is synonymous to inviting difficulties and hardships.

Khadijah ﷺ fully considered all these factors and understood everything fully well and then made the first move of proposing to Rasulullah ﷺ. In so doing, she dashed all the hopes of the noblemen of Makkah. How could that blessed lady who had already resolved to shun the world ever bother to look at the slaves of this world? When she had no concern for wealth, why should she have any concern for the wealthy? How could the wealth and prosperity of a prosperous person ever incline this woman toward him? This noble woman who is prepared to sacrifice her own wealth for the cause of Allah Ta'ala!

Rasulullah ﷺ consulted his kind uncle, Abu Taalib, and accepted her proposal. Her father Khuwaylid, had already passed away. However, her uncle 'Umar ibn Asad, was alive at that time and he attended the marriage.

On the appointed date, Abu Taalib together with other members of the family including Hamzah, went to the house of Khadijah ﷺ and the marriage rites were performed. Abu Taalib read the marriage sermon and the dowry was set at 500 dirhams.

Khadijah ﷺ was 40 years old at that time while Rasulullah ﷺ was 25 years old. Waraqah ibn Naufal was also present for the marriage. When Abu Taalib completed his sermon, Waraqah ibn Naufal delivered a short speech.

Some Traditions state that after the offer and acceptance of the proposal, Khadijah ﷺ had a cow slaughtered; food was cooked and fed to the guests.

The initial stage of Khadijah's ﷺ hope and wish was fulfilled. The destination (i.e. Rasulullah's ﷺ commission as a Prophet) was still at a distance. The discomfort and unease at waiting for this remained with her. On one occasion, Rasulullah ﷺ went to Khadijah ﷺ. On seeing him, she immediately embraced him and hugged him to her bosom. She then said:

"May my father and mother be sacrificed for you. I am not doing this for any ulterior motive. Rather it is my wish that you will be the Prophet who is soon to be commissioned. If you are commissioned, you may remember my right and position. You should also make dua for me to the God who will commission you. Rasulullah ﷺ said: 'I take an oath by Allah that if I am made that Prophet, I will never

forget the kindness you showed to me, and if someone else is made a Prophet, you should understand that the God for whom you are doing this will never let your deeds go to waste.'"

Zubayr ibn Bakkaar narrates that Khadijah رضي الله عنها used to go repeatedly to Waraqah ibn Naufal and inquire about Rasulullah ﷺ. He would reply:

ما أراه إلا نبى هذه الأمة الذى بشر به موسى وعيسى

"I am sure that he is the Prophet of this nation whose glad tidings Musa and 'Isa gave."

A Hadith states that on one occasion, Khadijah رضي الله عنها went to Waraqah and related something about Rasulullah ﷺ to him. In reply, Waraqah said a poem. A part of it is as follows:

هذه خديجة تأتينى لأخبرها وما لنا بخفى الغيب من خبر

بأن أحمد يأتيه فيخبره جبريل أنك مبعوث إلى البشر

"This Khadijah comes to me again and again so that I may inform her, but I do not have knowledge of the unseen that Jibraa'eel عليه السلام will come to Ahmad and inform him saying: 'You are commissioned (as a Prophet) to mankind.'"

فقلت علىَّ الذى ترجين ينجزه لك إلا له فرجى الخير وانتظرى

"I said to her: It is not far fetched to assume that what you are hoping for, Allah will certainly cause it to take place. You should therefore place your hopes in Allah and remain waiting."

Children

It was from Khadijah رضي الله عنها that Rasulullah's ﷺ four daughters were born: Zaynab رضي الله عنها, Ruqayyah رضي الله عنها, Umme Kulsoom رضي الله عنها and Faatimah رضي الله عنها. Two sons were also born from her. Details in this regard will be given in the next chapter, Insha Allah. The sons passed away at a very young age. However, the daughters lived, grew up and also married.

Demise

As long as Khadijah رضي الله عنها remained alive, Rasulullah ﷺ did not enter into any other marriage. She passed away 10 years after prophet-hood in Makkah (or three years before the emigration to Madinah). She was buried in Hajun. Rasulullah ﷺ personally lowered her into her grave. The Janaazah Salaah was not prescribed at that time. She remained in the marriage of Rasulullah ﷺ for 25 years. She passed away at the age of 65.

إِنَّا لِلّٰهِ وَإِنَّا إِلَيْهِ رَاجِعُوْنَ

"To Allah we belong and to Him is our return."

Virtues and merits

Abu Hurayrah رضى الله عنه narrates that on one occasion, Jibraa'eel عليه السلام came to Rasulullah ﷺ and said: "O Messenger of Allah! This Khadijah is about to bring some food to you. When she does so, convey her Rabb's Salaams (greetings of peace) to her and my Salaams to her as well. Give her glad tidings of a palace in Jannah. This palace will be made of a single pearl. There will be no noise in this palace nor any hardships and difficulties."

On hearing the above, Khadijah رضى الله عنها said:

"Surely Allah Ta'ala is As-Salaam (the giver of peace) Himself. Peace be on Jibraa'eel, the mercy of Allah and His blessings also." Ibnus Sunni adds from another chain of narrators: *"And peace be on all those who hear this Salaam, except for shaytaan."*

For Allah Ta'ala to convey His Salaam to someone is a virtue and merit that is enjoyed by none other than Khadijah رضى الله عنها. No one shares with her in this merit.

The 'Ulama are unanimous that the most superior women are the following three: Khadijah رضى الله عنها, Faatimah رضى الله عنها and Aa'ishah رضى الله عنها.

Ummul-Mu'mineen Saudah bint Zam'ah رضى الله عنها

A few days after the death of Khadijah رضى الله عنها, Saudah رضى الله عنها came into the marriage of Rasulullah ﷺ. She was also from the noblewomen of the Quraysh. Her lineage is Saudah bint Zam'ah ibn Qays ibn 'Abd Shams ibn 'Abdud ibn Nasr ibn Maalik ibn Hasl ibn 'Aamir ibn Lu'ayy.

On reaching Lu'ayy ibn Ghaalib, her lineage meets with that of Rasulullah ﷺ. Her mother's name was Shamus bint Qays ibn 'Amr ibn Zaid. She was from the Ansaar and the Banu Najjaar tribe. She embraced Islam at the beginning. Her first marriage was with her cousin, Sukraan ibn 'Amr. When the Sahaabah رضى الله عنهم went on the second emigration to Abyssinia, Saudah رضى الله عنها and her husband, Sukraan also migrated. When they were returning to Makkah, Sukraan passed away. They had one son by the name of 'Abdur Rahmaan. He also embraced Islam and was martyred in the battle of Jalula.

Rasulullah ﷺ was extremely grief-stricken by the death of Khadijah رضي الله عنها. Khaulah bint Hakeem رضي الله عنها came to him one day and said to him: "O Messenger of Allah! I see you grief-stricken by the absence of Khadijah." He replied: "Yes, she was the one who took care of all the children and saw to the running of the house." Khaulah رضي الله عنها asked: "Should I not send a proposal on your behalf?" Rasulullah ﷺ replied: "It is the appropriate thing to do. Women are more suited for such a task. Where do you intend sending a proposal?" Khaulah رضي الله عنها replied: "If you desire a virgin wife, then you could marry the daughter of the most beloved person to you, Aa'ishah, the daughter of Abu Bakr. And if you desire a widow, Saudah bint Zam'ah is available. She brought Imaan in you and follows you." Rasulullah ﷺ said: "Send a proposal to both places." Khaulah رضي الله عنها first went to Saudah and said to her: "Rasulullah ﷺ sent me with his proposal." She replied: "I have no reason to say no, but you should speak to my father. Greet him in the jaahili way." Khaulah رضي الله عنها says: "I went to him and greeted him by saying: 'Good morning'. He asked: 'Who is this?' I replied: 'I am Khaulah.' He welcomed me and asked: 'What is the reason for your visit?' She replied: 'I have come to you with the proposal of Muhammad ibn 'Abdullah ibn 'Abd al-Muttalib for your daughter.' On hearing this, he said: 'Without doubt he is a noble and suitable person. But I do not know what Saudah has to say about this.' I said: 'She is also ready.' Rasulullah ﷺ thereafter went and the marriage was solemnised."

When 'Abdullah ibn Zam'ah, the brother of Saudah رضي الله عنها heard about this marriage, he placed dust on his head (to display his disapproval). Later when he embraced Islam, he regretted this action of his. Whenever he thought about this, he would say: "I was extremely immature on that day when I placed dust on my head on hearing of my sister's marriage to Rasulullah ﷺ."

Since the marriage of Saudah رضي الله عنها and Aa'ishah رضي الله عنها took place at almost the same time, the historians differ as to which marriage took place first. The correct and preferred opinion is that Saudah's رضي الله عنها marriage took place first. The dowry was fixed at 400 dirhams.

On one occasion, Rasulullah ﷺ intended divorcing Saudah رضي الله عنها. She said to Rasulullah ﷺ: "O Rasulullah ﷺ! Keep me in your marriage. It is my desire that I be raised among your wives on the day of Qiyaamah. Since I am aged, I will give my turn to Aa'ishah." Rasulullah ﷺ accepted this. It is learnt from some Ahaadith that he had already divorced her and revoked the divorce later on. Allah Ta'ala knows best.

Saudah رضي الله عنها was tall and quite heavily built. She had a humorous nature and used to make Rasulullah ﷺ laugh at times. She passed away in Zul Hijjah 23 A.H. towards the end of the caliphate of 'Umar رضي الله عنه.

Ummul-Mu'mineen Aa'ishah Siddeeqah رضي الله عنها

'Aa'ishah رضي الله عنها is the daughter of Abu Bakr رضي الله عنه. Her mother's name was Zaynab with the title of Umme Rumaan. Aa'ishah رضي الله عنها did not have any children of her own. However, she was given the title of Umme 'Abdillah due to her nephew, 'Abdullah ibn Zubayr رضي الله عنه. Rasulullah ﷺ married her after or with Saudah رضي الله عنها in Shawwaal 10 A.H.

Khawlah bint Hakeem رضي الله عنها conveyed the proposal on behalf of Rasulullah ﷺ. Abu Bakr رضي الله عنه said: "Mut'im ibn 'Adiyy had sent a proposal for his son, Jubayr, which I have already accepted." Abu Bakr رضي الله عنه was a person who never went back on his promise. On saying this, he immediately went to the house of Mut'im and asked him: "What have you decided about the marriage?" Mut'im's wife was also present. He therefore addressed her asking: "What is your opinion in this regard?" She replied: "If my son were to marry your daughter, I have this strong feeling that he will abandon his religion, give up the religion of his forefathers and embrace your religion." Abu Bakr رضي الله عنه turned to Mut'im and asked him: "What do you have to say?" He replied: "You have already heard what my wife has to say." The tone in which Mut'im and his wife spoke to him was a clear indication to him that he no longer had to fulfil his promise. He returned to his house and informed Khaulah رضي الله عنها saying: "I accept Rasulullah's ﷺ proposal. He may come whenever he pleases." Rasulullah ﷺ went over, the marriage was solemnised and the dowry was set at 400 dirhams.

The marriage took place three years before the emigration to Madinah in the month of Shawwaal in the 10th year of prophet-hood. Aa'ishah رضي الله عنها was six years old at that time. The marriage was consummated seven or eight months after the emigration, also in the month of Shawwaal. She was nine years and a few months old at that time. She remained in the marriage of Rasulullah ﷺ for nine years. She was 18 years old when Rasulullah ﷺ passed away. She remained alive for another 48 years and passed away in 57 A.H. in Madinah. In accordance with her request, she was buried at night in Jannatul Baqi' (the graveyard of Madinah).

Aa'ishah رضي الله عنها was 66 years old at the time of her death. Abu Hurayrah رضي الله عنه performed the Janaazah Salaah. Qaasim ibn Muhammad, 'Abdullah ibn 'Abdur-Rahmaan, 'Abdullah ibn Abi 'Ateeq, 'Urwah ibn Zubayr and 'Abdullah ibn Zubayr lowered her in her grave. (They were all her nephews).

We had related the Hadith of Abu Sa'eed Khudri ﷺ that Rasulullah ﷺ did not marry any woman without first receiving divine revelation from Allah Ta'ala via Jibraa'eel ﷺ. This also happened in the case of Aa'ishah ﷺ. Abdullah ibn 'Umar ﷺ narrates that Rasulullah ﷺ said: "Jibraa'eel ﷺ came to me and informed me that Allah Ta'ala has performed my marriage to Aa'ishah, the daughter of Abu Bakr. I was also shown an image of Aa'ishah, informing me that this is my wife."

Aa'ishah ﷺ was the daughter of Abu Bakr ﷺ. She acquired a special share of his understanding, insight, intelligence and trustworthiness. Umme Rumaan was her mother. Rasulullah ﷺ said about her: "The person who wants to see the Huris of Jannah, should look at Umme Rumaan."

It was therefore the divine will of Allah Ta'ala that the daughter of Rasulullah's ﷺ most beloved companion be given to him in marriage and placed under his training from a very young age. At such an age, the heart was absolutely clean and pure. No falsehood was ever depicted on it. Her age was one of innocence. At the same time, there was no falsehood or deception from the father and mother. In fact, the father enjoys the title of Siddeeq (one who perpetually treads the truth), he is the envy of the angels, he enjoys the constant companionship of Allah Ta'ala. The mother is like a Huri of Jannah. On such a clear and pure tablet, whatever mark of the knowledge of prophet-hood is made on it will be so firmly embedded and so productive that it will never be wiped out.

Consequently, she acquired such in-depth and wide-ranging knowledge in a period of nine years, that after the demise of Rasulullah ﷺ, whenever the senior Sahaabah ﷺ encountered any problems in understanding certain matters, they would consult with Aa'ishah ﷺ. Her knowledge, her expertise in jurisprudence and her knowledge of history were all accepted during the era of the Sahaabah ﷺ. This was to such an extent that it has been said that one quarter of the injuctions of the Shari'ah have been narrated by her alone.

Abu Musa Ash'ari ﷺ says that whenever the Sahaabah ﷺ encountered any problem in understanding any matter, they would consult Aa'ishah ﷺ and they would certainly find a solution with her.

Knowledge

Imaam Zuhri ﷺ says that if the knowledge of Aa'ishah ﷺ was compared with that of the rest of the wives of Rasulullah ﷺ and all the other women of Islam, the knowledge of Aa'ishah ﷺ would surpass the rest.

Her eloquence in speech was such that Mu'aawiyah ﷺ says: "I have not come across any speaker more eloquent than Aa'ishah."

She had deep knowledge of Arabic history and incidents. She knew many poems by heart. When she had to say something, she would almost certainly quote a poem in support of that.

Abstinence

The above were a few examples of her knowledge. The following is an example of her abstinence. The fountain of all merits and virtues is two things: knowledge and abstinence. Abstinence refers to severing ties with this world. Just as love for this world is the root of all evil, abstinence from this world is the root of all good. O Allah, make us abstinent in this world and bestow us the desire for the hereafter. An example of her abstinence is as follows:

Umme Durrah used to frequent the house of Aa'ishah ﵂. Umme Durrah narrates: On one occasion, 'Abdullah ibn Zubayr ﵁ sent two bundles of money to Aa'ishah ﵂. The money amounted to approximately 180 000 dirhams. Aa'ishah ﵂ immediately began distributing this money. By the evening, she did not have a single dirham left. She was fasting. When the sun set, she asked her servant to present some food. She brought some bread and olive oil. Umme Durrah said to her: "Had you bought some meat for one dirham, it would have been good for you." Aa'ishah ﵂ replied: "Had you reminded me (when I had the money) I would have bought it."

'Urwah ﵁ says: "I saw Aa'ishah ﵂ distributing 70 000 dirhams at a time while she was wearing patched clothes."

It was based on these qualities and merits that Rasulullah ﷺ loved her the most. Had he loved her solely because she was his only virgin wife, he would have certainly forgotten Khadijah ﵂. However, he used to constantly think of Khadijah ﵂ and make mention of her. When he used to slaughter any animal, he would certainly seek out the friends of Khadijah ﵂ and send some meat to them. He did not marry any other woman as long as she was alive. On the other hand, he married eight women while married to Aa'ishah ﵂. Allah forbid, if Rasulullah ﷺ was marrying merely to fulfil his desires, he would never have married widows. Umm Salamah ﵂ and Safiyyah ﵂ were more beautiful than Aa'ishah ﵂. Rasulullah's ﷺ object in entering into several marriages was to teach the ummah the injunctions and rulings that are related to women which may be easily conveyed by his wives. What were the pure wives of Rasulullah ﷺ? They were actually students of a women's school. The men were taught in Masjid-e-Nabawi while the pure wives were taught at the house of Rasulullah ﷺ. These wives were to become teachers of the ummah later on. Each one of them acquired knowledge in accordance with her capability. However, Aa'ishah ﵂ surpassed all of them in her knowledge and merits. This is the bounty of Allah Ta'ala which He gives to whoever He wills. It is for this reason that she is considered to be the best woman after Faatimah رضى الله عنها and Khadijah رضى الله عنها.

These qualities and merits were naturally placed in the temperament of Aa'ishah رضى الله عنها by Allah Ta'ala. Allah Ta'ala then commanded His Messenger صلى الله عليه وسلم to take her into his marriage so that those natural qualities and merits may come to the fore by staying with him and remaining under his tutelage. In this way, the world may benefit from her knowledge. Eventually, this is what happened – that the senior Sahaabah رضى الله عنهم benefited from her knowledge.

'Umar رضى الله عنه, 'Abdullah ibn 'Umar رضى الله عنه, Abu Hurayrah رضى الله عنه, Abu Musa Ash'ari رضى الله عنه, 'Abdullah ibn 'Abbaas رضى الله عنه and other senior Sahaabah رضى الله عنهم narrated from Aa'ishah رضى الله عنها. Senior Taabi'een like Sa'eed ibn Musayyib, 'Amr ibn Maymun, 'Alqamah ibn Qays, Masruq, 'Abdullah ibn Hakeem, Aswad ibn Yazeed, Abu Salamah ibn 'Abd ar-Rahmaan and others were her students.

Merits and virtues

1. Aa'ishah رضى الله عنها narrates: "One day, Rasulullah صلى الله عليه وسلم said to me: 'O Aa'ishah! Here is Jibraa'eel عليه السلام, he conveys Salaam to you.' I replied: 'Peace be on him, and also the mercy and blessings of Allah be on him.' I then said: 'O Rasulullah صلى الله عليه وسلم! You can see him while I cannot.'"

2. Abu Musa Ash'ari رضى الله عنه narrates that Rasulullah صلى الله عليه وسلم said: "There are many men who reached great heights. However, from among the women, it is only Maryam bint 'Imraan and Aasiyah, the wife of Fir'aun, that have reached great heights, and the merit of Aa'ishah over all other women is like *Sareed* (meat and broth) over all other food."

3. Aa'ishah رضى الله عنها says: "I have been bestowed with certain qualities from Allah Ta'ala. No woman apart from Maryam رضى الله عنها has been bestowed with these qualities. By Allah, I am not saying this out of pride. I am merely enumerating the bounties and favours of Allah Ta'ala. They are:

    - Rasulullah صلى الله عليه وسلم did not marry any virgin woman apart from me.
    - Before the marriage, the angels came down with an image of myself and showed it to Rasulullah صلى الله عليه وسلم saying: 'This is your wife. Allah orders you to marry her.'
    - Rasulullah صلى الله عليه وسلم used to love me the most.
    - I am the daughter of the person who was most beloved to Rasulullah صلى الله عليه وسلم, i.e, Abu Bakr رضى الله عنه.

- Several verses in the Qur-aan were revealed proving my innocence. I was created pure and unadulterated. I am living with a pure and unadulterated person (Rasulullah ﷺ), and Allah Ta'ala promised my forgiveness and noble sustenance.

- I saw Jibraa'eel علیه السلام. None of the other wives of Rasulullah ﷺ saw Jibraa'eel علیه السلام.

- Jibraa'eel علیه السلام would come with divine revelation to Rasulullah ﷺ while I was lying down with Rasulullah ﷺ under the same sheet. Jibraa'eel علیه السلام did not come like this to any of the other wives.

- I had two nights and two days with Rasulullah ﷺ while the other wives had one night and one day. (Aa'ishah رضی اللہ عنہا had one night and one day, which was her right. Later on, Saudah رضی اللہ عنہا gave her her turn because Saudah رضی اللہ عنہا had become old).

- When Rasulullah ﷺ passed away, his head was in my lap.

- He was buried in my room.

Ummul-Mu'mineen Hafsah bint Umar رضی اللہ عنہا

Hafsah رضی اللہ عنہا is the daughter of 'Umar ibn Khattaab رضی اللہ عنہ. Her mother's name is Zaynab bint Maz'oon رضی اللہ عنہا. Hafsah رضی اللہ عنہا was born five years before prophethood at the time when the Quraysh were busy renovating the Ka'bah. Her first marriage was with Khunays ibn Hudhaafah Sahmi. She emigrated with her husband to Madinah. He passed away after the Battle of Badr.

When Hafsah رضی اللہ عنہا was widowed, 'Umar رضی اللہ عنہ went to 'Usmaan رضی اللہ عنہ and said: "If you wish, I will get Hafsah married to you." 'Usmaan رضی اللہ عنہ replied: "I will think about the matter and inform you." When I met him later on, 'Usmaan رضی اللہ عنہ excused himself and said that he does not intend marrying her. 'Umar رضی اللہ عنہ says: "I then went to Abu Bakr رضی اللہ عنہ and said to him: 'If you wish, I will get Hafsah married to you.'" Abu Bakr رضی اللہ عنہ remained silent and did not give any reply. I was quite grieved by his response. A few days later Rasulullah ﷺ proposed to her. I got Hafsah married to Rasulullah ﷺ. Abu Bakr رضی اللہ عنہ met me after that and said: 'O 'Umar! You are probably angry with me. The reason why I did not give you any reply was that I knew that Rasulullah ﷺ was intending to propose to her. I therefore remained silent and did not feel it appropriate to reveal Rasulullah's ﷺ secret. Had Rasulullah ﷺ not proposed to her, I would have certainly accepted your offer."

The preferred opinion is that Rasulullah ﷺ married Hafsah رضي الله عنها in 3 A.H.

On one occasion, Rasulullah ﷺ divorced Hafsah رضي الله عنها. Jibraa'eel عليه السلام came down with the divine instruction saying:

ارجع حفصة فإنها صوامة قوامة وإنها زوجتك فى الجنة

"Take back Hafsah for she fasts a lot, prays a lot and she is your wife in Jannah."

Hafsah رضي الله عنها passed away in Madinah in Sha'baan 45 A.H. during the caliphate of Mu'aawiyah رضي الله عنه. Marwaan ibn Hakam performed the Janaazah Salaah. She was 60 years old at the time of her death.

Ummul-Mu'mineen Zaynab bint Khuzaymah رضي الله عنها

Her name was Zaynab, but because she was extremely generous even before Islam, she was given the title Ummul-Masaakeen – the mother of the poor. Her father's name was Khuzaymah ibnul-Haaris Hilaali. Her first marriage was with 'Abdullah ibn Jahsh رضي الله عنه. He was martyred in 3 A.H. in the battle of Uhud. On the expiry of her 'iddah, Rasulullah ﷺ proposed to her. The dowry was set at 500 dirhams. Two or three months after the marriage, she passed away. Rasulullah ﷺ personally performed the Janaazah Salaah and she was buried in Jannatul Baqi'. She was 30 years old at the time of her death.

Ummul-Mu'mineen Umme Salamah bint Abi Umayyah رضي الله عنها

Umme Salamah was her title while her name was Hind. She was the daughter of Abu Umayyah Qurashi Makhzumi. Her mother's name was 'Aatikah bint 'Aamir ibn Rabi'ah. Her first marriage was with her cousin, Abu Salamah ibn 'Abd al-Asad Makhzumi. She embraced Islam together with her husband and also undertook the first emigration to Abyssinia with him. On returning from there, she emigrated to Madinah.

Abu Salamah رضي الله عنه participated in the battles of Badr and Uhud. In the Battle of Uhud, he injured his side. He had to treat it for about a month till it healed. In the beginning of Muharram 4 A.H., Rasulullah ﷺ sent him at the head of a small army. They returned after 29 days. On his return, his old wound resurfaced and he eventually passed away on account of it on 8 Jumaadal-Ukhraa 4 A.H.

Umme Salamah رضي الله عنها says: "One day, my husband, Abu Salamah came into the house and said to me: 'I have heard a Hadith from Rasulullah ﷺ which is more beloved to me than this world and whatever it contains. The Hadith is: 'When a person is afflicted by any calamity and he says:

$$\text{إِنَّا لِلَّهِ وَإِنَّا إِلَيْهِ رَاجِعُوْنَ}$$

'To Allah we belong and to Him is our return.'

And then reads the following dua:

$$\text{اَللّٰهُمَّ عِنْدَكَ أَحْتَسِبُ مُصِيْبَتِيْ هَذِهِ اَللّٰهُمَّ اخْلُفْنِيْ فِيْهَا بِخَيْرٍ مِّنْهَا}$$

'O Allah! It is in You that I place my hope for the reward for this calamity. O Allah! Bestow me with something better in place of it.'

Then Allah will certainly bestow him with something far better."

Umme Salamah رَضِىَ اللهُ عَنْهَا says: "I remembered this Hadith after the death of Abu Salamah رَضِىَ اللهُ عَنْهُ. When I began reciting this dua, I thought to myself, how will I get someone better than Abu Salamah? However, since it was a teaching of Rasulullah ﷺ, I recited this dua. Consequently, the fruit of this dua was that after the expiry of my 'iddah, Rasulullah ﷺ proposed to me. There is nothing better than this in this world."

When Rasulullah ﷺ proposed to her, she offered the following excuses:

- I am gone very old.
- I have children. These orphans are under my care.
- I am extremely jealous by nature.

Rasulullah ﷺ replied: "I am older than you. Your children are the children of Allah and His Messenger. I will make dua to Allah Ta'ala to remove that jealousy from you."

Rasulullah ﷺ made dua for her and his dua was accepted.

Rasulullah ﷺ married her towards the end of Shawwaal 4 A.H. Anas رَضِىَ اللهُ عَنْهُ narrates that Rasulullah ﷺ gave her some goods in dowry, the value of which was 10 dirhams.

Rasulullah ﷺ also gave her a mattress which was filled with date leaves, instead of wool. He also gave her a plate, a bowl and a mill-stone.

Demise

There is much difference with regard to the date of her death. The most preferred opinion is that she passed away in 62 A.H. Umme Salamah رَضِىَ اللهُ عَنْهَا was the last to pass away from the pure wives of Rasulullah ﷺ.

Abu Hurayrah رَضِىَ اللهُ عَنْهُ performed the Janaazah Salaah. She was 84 years old at the time.

She was lowered into her grave by her two sons from her previous marriage. Their names were 'Umar and Salamah. The following two people were also there to lower her in her grave, 'Abdullah ibn 'Abdullah ibn Abi Umayyah and 'Abdullah ibn Wahb ibn Zam'ah. She was buried in Jannatul Baqi'. May Allah Ta'ala be pleased with her and may He shower His mercy on her.

Virtues and merits

The virtues, merits, beauty, understanding, insight and intelligence of Umme Salamah ﵂ were an accepted fact. At Hudaybiyah, Rasulullah ﷺ had instructed the Sahaabah ﵁ to slaughter their sacrificial animals and shave their heads. He issued this instruction three times but because they were so overtaken by sorrow, they did not pay heed. When Umme Salamah ﵂ heard about this, she said to Rasulullah ﷺ: "O Rasulullah! These Companions are overtaken by grief and sorrow by this peace treaty. Do not issue any verbal instructions. Rather, slaughter your animal and shave your head." No sooner had Rasulullah ﷺ slaughtered his animal, the Sahaabah ﵁ rushed to slaughter their own animals and then shaved their heads as well. This problem was thus solved by the advice of Umme Salamah ﵂. May Allah Ta'ala reward her.

She was extremely beautiful. Aa'ishah ﵂ says: "When Rasulullah ﷺ married her, I became extremely jealous of her because of her beauty and good looks."

Ummul-Mu'mineen Zaynab bint Jahsh ﵂

Zaynab bint Jahsh ﵂ was the daughter of Rasulullah's ﷺ paternal aunt, Umaymah bint 'Abdul Muttalib. In other words, she was his paternal cousin. Before coming into the marriage of Rasulullah ﷺ, she was married to Rasulullah's ﷺ adopted son and freed slave, Zaid ibn Haarisah ﵁. Since there was no mutual compatibility, Zaid ﵁ divorced her. Zaid ﵁ was a freed slave while Zaynab ﵂ was from a very distinguished family and the cousin of Rasulullah ﷺ. The Arabs considered it below their dignity to marry freed slaves. Therefore, when Rasulullah ﷺ proposed to Zaynab ﵂ on behalf of Zaid ﵁, Zaynab ﵂ and her brother both refused. The following verse was revealed:

﴿وَمَا كَانَ لِمُؤْمِنٍ وَّلَا مُؤْمِنَةٍ اِذَا قَضَى اللّٰهُ وَرَسُوْلُهٗ اَمْرًا اَنْ يَّكُوْنَ لَهُمُ الْخِيَرَةُ مِنْ اَمْرِهِمْ وَمَنْ يَّعْصِ اللّٰهَ وَرَسُوْلَهٗ فَقَدْ ضَلَّ ضَلٰلًا مُّبِيْنًا﴾

"It does not behove a believing male nor a believing female that when Allah and His Messenger issue an order, for them to have a choice of their own. Whoever disobeys Allah and His Messenger has certainly gone clearly astray."

The "believing male" in this verse specifically refers to 'Abdullah ibn Jahsh رضي الله عنه while the "believing female" refers to his sister, Zaynab رضي الله عنها. The verse means that it is not permitted for a believing male and female not to accept a matter that is decided by Allah Ta'ala and His Messenger صلى الله عليه وسلم.

After the revelation of this verse, they both accepted and Zaynab رضي الله عنها married Zaid رضي الله عنه in accordance with the order of Allah Ta'ala. Although the marriage took place, Zaid رضي الله عنه remained contemptible and detestable in the sight of Zaynab رضي الله عنها. There was therefore constant fighting and bickering in the house. Zaid رضي الله عنه complained regularly to Rasulullah صلى الله عليه وسلم with regard to Zaynab's رضي الله عنها lack of affection towards him and expressed his desire to leave her. Rasulullah صلى الله عليه وسلم would dissuade him from divorcing her, and say to him: "You married her because of me. If you are going to leave her now, it will cause you more disgrace, and I will feel ashamed in my own family."

When these fights and arguments were mentioned to him repeatedly, Rasulullah صلى الله عليه وسلم concluded in his heart that if Zaid divorces her, there will be no way of consoling her except by his personally marrying her. However, Rasulullah صلى الله عليه وسلم feared the bad thoughts and accusations of the ignorant ones and the hypocrites, that they would say: "He has married his son's wife and kept her in his own house." They would say this although an adopted son is certainly not considered to be one's own son. It was an old Arab custom that they considered it a great blemish to marry the wife of one's adopted son. It was the divine will of Allah Ta'ala to break this old custom by the action of Rasulullah صلى الله عليه وسلم. Allah Ta'ala informed him via divine revelation that when Zaid رضي الله عنه divorces Zaynab رضي الله عنها, she will come into his marriage. In so doing, the people will learn and realise that the injunction that is applied to the wife of one's own son is not applicable to the wife of one's adopted son.

In short, Rasulullah صلى الله عليه وسلم was informed through revelation that Zaynab رضي الله عنها will come into his marriage. However, because he was afraid of the accusations and insults of the mischief makers that he is marrying the wife of his adopted son, he did not divulge this information to anyone. He left it concealed in his heart and thought to himself that these words of Allah Ta'ala are totally true. They will certainly be realised at the appropriate time. Furthermore, Allah Ta'ala also did not order him to divulge this information at present. He therefore kept this injunction in his heart, while he continued advising Zaid رضي الله عنه not to divorce Zaynab رضي الله عنها. This is also the order of the Shari'ah that the husband should always be advised not to divorce his wife, that he should exercise patience over the lack of interest of the wife. If anyone learns, through revelation or inspiration, that this is going to happen in the future and that fate and destiny have already decided that this is going to happen, then he will have to follow the order of the Shari'ah at present. Fate and destiny will automatically bring to fruition whatever is supposed to be brought to fruition.

Eventualy, Zaid ﷺ came to Rasulullah ﷺ and said: "O Messenger of Allah! I have become totally fed up and therefore issued a divorce to Zaynab." Rasulullah ﷺ remained silent.

Anas ﷺ narrates that when the 'iddah of Zaynab ﷺ expired, Rasulullah ﷺ instructed Zaid ﷺ to go personally to Zaynab ﷺ and convey a proposal of marriage on behalf of Rasulullah ﷺ (so that it may become clear that whatever happened, happened with the approval of Zaid ﷺ). Zaid ﷺ took this proposal of Rasulullah ﷺ and went to the house of Zaynab ﷺ. He turned his back towards the door and stood there (although the order of Hijaab was not yet revealed. This was the high level of Zaid's ﷺ piety and devoutness.) He then said: "O Zaynab! Rasulullah ﷺ has sent me with his proposal of marrying you." She replied: "I cannot comment until I have consulted with Allah Ta'ala." She immediately got up, went to a corner where she used to offer her Salaah and engaged in istikhaarah.

Zaynab ﷺ did not consult any creation. She desired the counsel of Allah Ta'ala alone and asked Him for goodness because He alone is the true protector of the believers. Allah Ta'ala therefore, through His special protection, performed the marriage of Zaynab ﷺ with Rasulullah ﷺ in the heavens, in the presence of the angels. This announcement was made in the heavens. The need was to announce this on earth as well. Jibraa'eel ﷺ came down with this verse:

$$\text{فَلَمَّا قَضَىٰ زَيْدٌ مِّنْهَا وَطَرًا زَوَّجْنَٰكَهَا}$$

"When Zaid accomplished his purpose with her, We got her married to you."
[Surah Ahzaab, verse 37]

Rasulullah ﷺ then went to the house of Zaynab ﷺ and entered without seeking permission (because she was now his wife).

One Hadith states that Rasulullah ﷺ was in the house of Aa'ishah ﷺ when this verse was revealed. Rasulullah ﷺ smiled and turned towards the Sahaabah ﷺ saying, "Who is it who will go to Zaynab and give her these glad tidings." Rasulullah ﷺ recited the following verse to them:

$$\text{وَإِذْ تَقُولُ لِلَّذِىٓ أَنْعَمَ اللَّهُ عَلَيْهِ وَأَنْعَمْتَ عَلَيْهِ أَمْسِكْ عَلَيْكَ زَوْجَكَ وَاتَّقِ اللَّهَ وَتُخْفِى فِى نَفْسِكَ مَا اللَّهُ مُبْدِيهِ وَتَخْشَى النَّاسَ ۖ وَاللَّهُ أَحَقُّ أَن تَخْشَىٰهُ ۚ فَلَمَّا قَضَىٰ زَيْدٌ مِّنْهَا وَطَرًا}$$

Chapter 31

$$\text{زَوَّجْنٰكَهَا لِكَىْ لَا يَكُوْنَ عَلَى الْمُؤْمِنِيْنَ حَرَجٌ فِىْٓ اَزْوَاجِ اَدْعِيَآئِهِمْ اِذَا قَضَوْا مِنْهُنَّ وَطَرًا ۭوَكَانَ اَمْرُ اللّٰهِ مَفْعُوْلًا ۝}$$

"When you said to him upon whom Allah had shown favour and upon whom you had shown favour: 'Keep your wife to yourself and fear Allah.' And you were concealing in your heart something which Allah wants to reveal, and you were fearing the people, whereas you ought to fear Allah more. When Zaid accomplished his purpose with that woman, We gave her to you in marriage so that there may be no sin on the believers in marrying the wives of their adopted sons once they have accomplished their purpose with them. And Allah's command must be fulfilled."

[Surah Ahzaab, verse 37]

Aa'ishah رَضِىَ اللّٰهُ عَنْهَا says: "When Rasulullah صَلَّى اللّٰهُ عَلَيْهِ وَسَلَّم recited this verse, I thought to myself that first of all Zaynab is so beautiful. However, she will now further boast that Allah Ta'ala performed her marriage in the heavens."

Rasulullah صَلَّى اللّٰهُ عَلَيْهِ وَسَلَّم first sent a messenger to Zaynab رَضِىَ اللّٰهُ عَنْهَا informing her that Allah Ta'ala had revealed these verses with regard to her marriage. When this news reached her, she immediately fell into a sajdah of gratitude.

Since the divine order and revelation had reached Zaynab رَضِىَ اللّٰهُ عَنْهَا, Rasulullah صَلَّى اللّٰهُ عَلَيْهِ وَسَلَّم went into her house without seeking permission. The divine announcement of this marriage, her acceptance of it after Rasulullah صَلَّى اللّٰهُ عَلَيْهِ وَسَلَّم conveyed the message to her, her falling into sajdah and the fact that this proposal had been conveyed previously by Zaid رَضِىَ اللّٰهُ عَنْه, are all matters that are more than what actually takes place in a marriage. After entering her house, Rasulullah صَلَّى اللّٰهُ عَلَيْهِ وَسَلَّم asked her: "What is your name?" Her original name was Barrah. She therefore replied: "My name is Barrah." Rasulullah صَلَّى اللّٰهُ عَلَيْهِ وَسَلَّم decided to call her Zaynab instead.

After this incident, the hypocrites began making accusations and said: "On one hand, the Messenger says that it is unlawful to marry your son's wives, while he himself is marrying the wife of his son (daughter-in-law)." Allah Ta'ala provides the following reply to these hypocrites:

$$\text{مَا كَانَ مُحَمَّدٌ اَبَآ اَحَدٍ مِّنْ رِّجَالِكُمْ وَلٰكِنْ رَّسُوْلَ اللّٰهِ وَخَاتَمَ النَّبِيّٖنَ ۭ وَكَانَ اللّٰهُ بِكُلِّ شَىْءٍ عَلِيْمًا}$$

"Muhammad is not the father of any of your men. Rather, he is the Messenger of Allah and the seal of Prophets. And Allah is aware of everything."

[Surah Ahzaab: verse, 40]

Date of the marriage

Zaynab رَضِيَ ٱللَّهُ عَنْهَا came into the marriage of Rasulullah ﷺ in 4 A.H. while others say it was in 5 A.H. She was 35 years old at the time of her marriage. The dowry was stipulated as 400 dirhams.

Walimah

Since this marriage took place under the special supervision of Allah Ta'ala and then specific verses concerning it were revealed, Rasulullah ﷺ gave special attention to the walimah (marriage feast) for this marriage. Anas رَضِيَ ٱللَّهُ عَنْهُ says that Rasulullah ﷺ did not pay as much attention to the walimah of any wife as he paid for his marriage to Zaynab bint Jahsh رَضِيَ ٱللَّهُ عَنْهَا. He slaughtered a sheep and invited the people. He fed them meat and bread which they all ate to their fill. The people left after eating. However, three people remained seated and continued talking. Due to his extreme bashfulness, Rasulullah ﷺ did not ask them to leave. However, he got up from there so that these people will get the message (that they should leave). Rasulullah ﷺ went to the room of Aa'ishah رَضِيَ ٱللَّهُ عَنْهَا who congratulated him on the occasion of his marriage. He then went to the other wives and greeted them. In the meantime, these verses were revealed:

يَٰٓأَيُّهَا ٱلَّذِينَ ءَامَنُوا۟ لَا تَدْخُلُوا۟ بُيُوتَ ٱلنَّبِىِّ إِلَّآ أَن يُؤْذَنَ لَكُمْ إِلَىٰ طَعَامٍ غَيْرَ نَٰظِرِينَ إِنَىٰهُ وَلَٰكِنْ إِذَا دُعِيتُمْ فَٱدْخُلُوا۟ فَإِذَا طَعِمْتُمْ فَٱنتَشِرُوا۟ وَلَا مُسْتَـْٔنِسِينَ لِحَدِيثٍ إِنَّ ذَٰلِكُمْ كَانَ يُؤْذِى ٱلنَّبِىَّ فَيَسْتَحْىِۦ مِنكُمْ وَٱللَّهُ لَا يَسْتَحْىِۦ مِنَ ٱلْحَقِّ وَإِذَا سَأَلْتُمُوهُنَّ مَتَٰعًا فَسْـَٔلُوهُنَّ مِن وَرَآءِ حِجَابٍ ذَٰلِكُمْ أَطْهَرُ لِقُلُوبِكُمْ وَقُلُوبِهِنَّ

"O believers! Do not enter the houses of the Prophet except when you are permitted to a meal and not (so early as) to see its preparation. But when you are invited, then go. Once you have eaten, disperse without lingering for idle talk. Surely this would cause harm to the Prophet and he might feel shy of (asking) you (to leave). Allah is not shy of saying the truth. When you go to ask his wives anything that you need, ask them from behind a screen. In this there is great purity for your hearts and their hearts." [Surah Ahzaab, verse 53]

Virtues and merits

Zaynab رَضِيَ ٱللَّهُ عَنْهَا used to boast to the other wives of Rasulullah صَلَّى ٱللَّهُ عَلَيْهِ وَسَلَّمَ that their marriages were conducted by their relatives while her marriage was conducted by Allah Ta'ala in the seven heavens.

In reality, this was not boasting and bragging. Rather, it was expressing the bounties of Allah Ta'ala. Her extreme happiness and love for Allah Ta'ala caused her to express this bounty and favour of Allah Ta'ala. It is for this reason that Rasulullah صَلَّى ٱللَّهُ عَلَيْهِ وَسَلَّمَ would also hear her mentioning this but he would remain silent.

Zaynab رَضِيَ ٱللَّهُ عَنْهَا used to say to Rasulullah صَلَّى ٱللَّهُ عَلَيْهِ وَسَلَّمَ: "O Messenger of Allah! I have three reasons to be proud of you: (1) My grandfather and your grandfather is the same person, i.e. 'Abdul Muttalib. Another Hadith states: "I am the daughter of your paternal aunt." This also conveys the same meaning. "(2) Allah Ta'ala performed your marriage to me in the heavens. (3) Jibraa'eel عَلَيْهِ ٱلسَّلَامُ was the one who made these arrangements."

Aa'ishah رَضِيَ ٱللَّهُ عَنْهَا says: "Zaynab bint Jahsh رَضِيَ ٱللَّهُ عَنْهَا used to compare her position and my position before Rasulullah صَلَّى ٱللَّهُ عَلَيْهِ وَسَلَّمَ. I have not come across a woman more religious than Zaynab, more fearful of Allah, more truthful in speech, more concerned about maintaining relationships, and more generous in charity, more hardworking and giving the income thereof in charity and gaining the proximity of Allah Ta'ala thereby."

Piety

When the hypocrites accused Aa'ishah رَضِيَ ٱللَّهُ عَنْهَا of adultery (details of which were given previously), Zaynab's رَضِيَ ٱللَّهُ عَنْهَا sister, Hamnah bint Jahsh, in her naivety also joined this accusation. However, when Rasulullah صَلَّى ٱللَّهُ عَلَيْهِ وَسَلَّمَ asked Zaynab رَضِيَ ٱللَّهُ عَنْهَا about Aa'ishah رَضِيَ ٱللَّهُ عَنْهَا, she replied:

"O Rasulullah! I am safeguarding my ears and eyes. I take an oath by Allah I do not know anything but good about Aa'ishah."

In other words, if I have not seen something with my own eyes or heard with my own ears, how can I utter it with my tongue? My knowledge and certainty about her is nothing but good.

It is a well known fact that Aa'ishah رَضِيَ ٱللَّهُ عَنْهَا was her co-wife. She was also fully aware that Aa'ishah رَضِيَ ٱللَّهُ عَنْهَا was the most beloved wife of Rasulullah صَلَّى ٱللَّهُ عَلَيْهِ وَسَلَّمَ. Had she wanted, she could have said something that would have caused Aa'ishah's رَضِيَ ٱللَّهُ عَنْهَا status to fall in the sight of Rasulullah صَلَّى ٱللَّهُ عَلَيْهِ وَسَلَّمَ. However, her excellent piety and faithfulness did not permit her to even remain silent. Instead, she took an oath in the name of Allah Ta'ala and confined herself to just one short sentence in order to emphasise her point. Aa'ishah رَضِيَ اللَّهُ عَنْهَا herself attests to the piety and faithfulness of Zaynab رَضِيَ اللَّهُ عَنْهَا:

فعصمها الله بالورع

"Allah Ta'ala protected her (from this tribulation) on account of her piety."

Worship

Zaynab رَضِيَ اللَّهُ عَنْهَا had a special affinity with worship. She used to worship Allah Ta'ala with extreme humility and humbleness. When Zaid رَضِيَ اللَّهُ عَنْهُ conveyed Rasulullah's صَلَّى اللَّهُ عَلَيْهِ وَسَلَّمَ proposal to her, she immediately engaged in Istikhaarah Salaah.

Maymunah رَضِيَ اللَّهُ عَنْهَا narrates that on one occasion Rasulullah صَلَّى اللَّهُ عَلَيْهِ وَسَلَّمَ was distributing some booty among the Muhaajireen when Zaynab رَضِيَ اللَّهُ عَنْهَا suddenly began speaking. 'Umar رَضِيَ اللَّهُ عَنْهُ hushed her. Rasulullah صَلَّى اللَّهُ عَلَيْهِ وَسَلَّمَ said: "O 'Umar! Leave her alone, do not say anything to her, surely she is a woman who is an awwaah - extremely soft-hearted in her worship of Allah Ta'ala."

A person asked: "O Rasulullah! What is the meaning of awwaah?" Rasulullah صَلَّى اللَّهُ عَلَيْهِ وَسَلَّمَ replied: "It means a person who is very humble and unassuming." Rasulullah صَلَّى اللَّهُ عَلَيْهِ وَسَلَّمَ then recited the following verse:

﴿ وَإِنَّ إِبْرَاهِيمَ لَحَلِيمٌ أَوَّاهٌ مُنِيبٌ ﴾

"Surely Ibraaheem is forbearing, soft-hearted and constantly turning (to Allah)."

On one occasion Rasulullah صَلَّى اللَّهُ عَلَيْهِ وَسَلَّمَ was going towards his house and 'Umar رَضِيَ اللَّهُ عَنْهُ was also with him. On reaching his house, he saw Zaynab رَضِيَ اللَّهُ عَنْهَا engrossed in Salaah and dua. On seeing her like this, Rasulullah صَلَّى اللَّهُ عَلَيْهِ وَسَلَّمَ said:

إنها لأواهة

"Surely she is extremely soft-hearted."

Ummul-Mu'mineen Umme Salamah رَضِيَ اللَّهُ عَنْهَا says regarding Zaynab رَضِيَ اللَّهُ عَنْهَا:

كانت صالحة صوامة قوامة صناعا تصدق بذالك كله على المساكين

"She was a righteous woman who used to fast a lot and engage in night Salaah (Tahajjud) a lot. She used to make handicrafts and give the income of all that into charity to the poor."

Abstinence

When 'Umar رضى الله عنه sent the annual expenditure to Zaynab رضى الله عنها for the first time, she thought that the money was for all the wives of Rasulullah ﷺ and said: "May Allah forgive 'Umar, he was more capable of distributing it among all the wives (he should not have given me this responsibility)." The people who were present there said to her: "All this is for you (and not to be distributed to the other wives)." She said: "Glory be to Allah and she concealed herself from the wealth (so that she does not have to see it)."

She ordered Barzah bint Raafi' رضى الله عنها to keep that wealth aside and to cover it with a cloth. She then said: "Take out a handful of money from beneath that cloth and give it to so and so orphan. Take another handful and give it to so and so person." When that wealth was distributed and a little was left, Barzah رضى الله عنها said to her: "May Allah forgive you, we also have some right over that wealth." Zaynab رضى الله عنها replied: "Okay, you may take whatever is beneath that cloth." Barzah رضى الله عنها says: "When I lifted that cloth, I saw that there were 85 dirhams left." When all the wealth was distributed, she raised her hands and said:

اللّٰهم لا يدركنى عطاء عمر بعد عامى هذا

"O Allah! May the spending of 'Umar not find me after this year."

Consequently, Zaynab رضى الله عنها passed away within that year.

Another Hadith states that her annual stipend was 12 000 dirhams. When this amount of money from the Islamic Treasury came to her, she constantly made this dua:

اللّٰهم لا يدركنى هذا المال من قابل فإنه فتنة

"O Allah! May this wealth not come to me in the future for it is surely a trial."

On saying this, she immediately began distributing this money to her relatives and the poor and needy. When 'Umar رضى الله عنه was informed of this, he said: "It seems that Allah Ta'ala has willed good for her." He immediately sent another 1000 dirhams. He conveyed his Salaams to her and said: "You have given that 12000 dirhams in charity, you should now keep these 1000 dirhams for your personal needs." On receiving this second amount, she immediately distributed it as well.

Demise

Aa'ishah رضى الله عنها narrates that one day, Rasulullah ﷺ said to his pure wives: "The one from among you whose hands are the longest will be the first to join me (after my demise)." Rasulullah ﷺ was referring to generosity and big-heartedness while the pure wives took the literal meaning. Consequently, when the pure wives used to meet after the demise of Rasulullah ﷺ, they would measure each others hands to see whose hands are the longest. Zaynab رضي الله عنها was a bit short. When she was the first one to pass away, they all realised that Zaynab's رضي الله عنها hand was the longest in giving charity. She used to physically work with her hands, she used to tan leather and whatever income she derived from this, she would give it in charity.

She had even prepared her shroud (kafan) before she could pass away. Qaasim ibn Muhammad narrates that when Zaynab's رضي الله عنها death approached, she said: "I have already kept my shroud ready. 'Umar رضي الله عنه would probably send a shroud for me. You should use one shroud for me and give the other in charity." After her demise, 'Umar رضي الله عنه sent five pieces of cloth for her shroud after having applied perfume to them. She was enshrouded in the shroud that 'Umar رضي الله عنه sent while her personal shroud was given in charity by her sister Hamnah رضي الله عنها.

When Zaynab رضي الله عنها passed away, Aa'ishah رضي الله عنها said:

لقد ذهبت حميدة متعبدة مفزع اليتامى والأرامل

"(How sad)! A woman who possessed praiseworthy qualities, who was an ardent worshipper of Allah Ta'ala, and who was a refuge for the orphans and widows has departed."

She passed away in 20 A.H. in Madinah. 'Umar رضي الله عنه performed her Janaazah Salaah. She was 50 or 53 years old at the time of her demise. She was 35 years old when Rasulullah ﷺ married her.

Ummul-Mu'mineen Juwayriyah bint Haaris رضي الله عنها

Juwayriyah رضي الله عنها was the daughter of Haaris ibn Diraar, the leader of the Banu Mustaliq tribe. Her first marriage was with Musaafih ibn Safwaan Mustalaqi who was killed in the battle of Muraysi'. Many women and children were captured in this battle. Juwayriyah رضي الله عنها was among the captives. Rasulullah ﷺ freed her and brought her into his marriage. Her dowry was set at 400 dirhams. Details with regard to how she came to marry Rasulullah ﷺ were given under the chapter concerning the battle of Bani Mustaliq.

She married Rasulullah ﷺ in 5 A.H. She was 20 years old at the time. She passed away in Rabi'ul-Awwal 50 A.H. She was 65 years old at the time of her demise. Marwaan ibn Hakam, who was the governor of Madinah at the time, performed her Janaazah Salaah. She was buried in the famous graveyard of Madinah, Jannatul Baqi'.

She was particularly attached to engaging herself in the worship of Allah Ta'ala. She set aside a special place in her house for her worship. She referred to this place as her Masjid. 'Abdullah ibn 'Abbaas ﷺ narrates from Juwayriyah ﷺ: "One morning, Rasulullah ﷺ came into my house while I was busy in my Masjid. He therefore went away. He returned around mid-day and found me at the same spot. He asked: 'Have you been engaging in worship from that time till now?' I replied: 'Yes.' He said to me: 'I am going to teach you some words. You should read them constantly. They are:

3 times سُبْحَانَ اللهِ عَدَدَ خَلْقِهِ

3 times سُبْحَانَ اللهِ رِضَا نَفْسِهِ

3 times سُبْحَانَ اللهِ زِنَةَ عَرْشِهِ

3 times سُبْحَانَ اللهِ مِدَادَ كَلِمَاتِهِ

Rasulullah ﷺ said to her: "I will now recite four sentences three times each. If these are weighed against all the zikr which you read from morning till now, these four will out-weigh your zikr. The sentences are:

سُبْحَانَ اللهِ وَبِحَمْدِهِ عَدَدَ خَلْقِهِ وَرِضَا نَفْسِهِ وَزِنَةَ عَرْشِهِ وَمِدَادَ كَلِمَاتِهِ

"Glory and praise to Allah equal to the number of His creation, the extent of His pleasure, the weight of His throne and the number of His words."

Ummul-Mu'mineen Umme Habibah bint Abi Sufyan ﷺ

Her name was Ramlah while Umme Habibah was her kunniyat. She was the daughter of Abu Sufyaan ibn Harb Umawi, the famous leader of the Quraysh. Her mother's name was Safiyyah bint Abil-'Aas who was the paternal aunt of 'Usmaan ﷺ. She was born 17 years before prophet-hood. Her first marriage was with 'Ubaydullah ibn Jahsh.

Umme Habibah ﷺ embraced Islam at the very beginning and so did her husband, 'Ubaydullah ibn Jahsh. They both emigrated to Abyssinia. While there, she gave birth to a daughter whom they named Habibah. She is therefore known as Umme Habibah (the mother of Habibah) and became popular by this name. While in Abyssinia, her husband, 'Ubaydullah, renounced Islam and became a Christian. However, Umme Habibah ﷺ remained steadfast on Islam.

Umme Habibah ﷺ says: "Before 'Ubaydullah could become a Christian, I saw him in a dream in which he was in a very ugly and repulsive form. I became terrified. The next morning I learnt that he became a Christian. I related this dream to him so that he may come to his senses, but he paid no attention and became totally immersed in alcohol. He eventually died in this intoxicated state. A few days later I saw a dream in which a person addressed me as 'O Mother of the

Believers.' I became nervous by this dream. No sooner I completed my 'iddah, I received Rasulullah's ﷺ proposal of marriage."

In the meantime, Rasulullah ﷺ sent 'Amr ibn Umayyah Damri to Najaashi, the king of Abyssinia, telling him that if Umme Habibah agrees to marry me, you should act as my representative and perform our marriage. You should then convey her to me. Najaashi sent his slave-woman, Barrah, to Umme Habibah ﵂ with the following message: "I have received a message from Rasulullah ﷺ that he proposes to marry you. If you accept his proposal, you should appoint a representative on your behalf." Umme Habibah ﵂ accepted the proposal and appointed Khaalid ibn Sa'ed ibn al-'Aas Umawi as her representative. When she received the good news of Rasulullah's ﷺ proposal, she removed the two bangles from her hands, anklets from her feet, and rings from her fingers, and gave them all to Barrah, who brought the good news. Najaashi then gathered Ja'far ﵁ and all the other Muslims who were in Abyssinia and performed the marriage. His marriage sermon was as follows:

الحمد لله الملك القدوس السلام المؤمن المهيمن العزيز الجبار أشهد أن لا إله إلا الله وأن محمدا عبده ورسوله وأنه الذى بشر به عيسى بن مريم صلى الله عليهما وسلم. أما بعد، فإن رسول الله صلى الله عليه وسلم كتب إلى أن أزوجه أم حبيبة بنت أبى سفيان فأجبت إلى ما دعا إليه رسول الله صلى الله عليه وسلم وقد أصدقتها أربعمائته دينار

After praising Allah Ta'ala with some of His names, Najaashi said: "I testify that there is none worthy of worship except Allah and that Muhammad ﷺ is His servant and Messenger. And that he is the Prophet regarding whom 'Isa ibn Maryam ﵇ gave glad tidings. The Messenger of Allah Ta'ala wrote to me asking me to perform his marriage to Umme Habibah bint Abi Sufyaan. I have discharged his request and given her 400 dinars as dowry."

Najaashi then handed the 400 dinars over to Khaalid ibn Sa'eed ﵁. The latter then stood up and said:

الحمد لله أحمده وأستعينه وأستغفره وأشهد أن لا إله إلا الله وحده لا شريك له وأشهد أن محمدا عبده ورسوله أرسله بالهدى ودين الحق

لیظهره علی الدین کله ولو کره المشرکون. أما بعد، فقد أجبت إلى ما دعا إلیه رسول الله صلى الله علیه وسلم وزوجته أم حبیبة بنت أبي سفیان فبارك الله لرسول الله صلى الله علیه وسلم

"All praise is due to Allah. I praise Him, seek His help and His forgiveness. I testify that there is none worthy of worship except Allah, who is one and He has no partner. I testify that Muhammad ﷺ is His servant and Messenger. He sent him with guidance and the true religion so that it may supercede all other religions even though the disbelievers may dislike it. I have discharged the request of Rasulullah ﷺ and got him married to Umme Habibah bint Abi Sufyaan. May Allah Ta'ala bless Rasulullah ﷺ."

The people who were present began getting up from the assembly. Najaashi said to them: "Please remain seated. It is the Sunnah of the Prophets that there should be a walimah (wedding feast) after the marriage." Food was thus presented to them. The people departed after having partaken of the meal.

When the dowry was conveyed to Umme Habibah رضي الله عنها, she gave 50 dinars to Barrah. Barrah took those 50 dinars and all the jewellery which Umme Habibah رضي الله عنها had given her previously and returned everything to Umme Habibah رضي الله عنها. She said to her that Najaashi had emphasised upon her not to take anything. She then said to her: "I am now a follower of Muhammad ﷺ and I have embraced the religion of Islam. The king has just today sent an order to all his wives to present to you some of the perfumes and fragrances that they have in their possession." Consequently, Barrah came the following day with various perfumes including 'oud and 'amber. Umme Habibah رضي الله عنها says: "I kept all those perfumes and took them with me when I went to Rasulullah ﷺ." Barrah said to her: "I have one request. When you go back, convey my Salaams to Rasulullah ﷺ and tell him that I have embraced his religion." Umme Habibah رضي الله عنها says: "Right till my departure from Abyssinia, Barra would come to me everyday and remind me about her request. When I went to Madinah, I informed Rasulullah ﷺ of everything that transpired while I was in Abyssinia. Rasulullah ﷺ continued smiling and eventually replied to the Salaam of Barrah and said: 'And peace be on her, and also the mercy and blessings of Allah Ta'ala.'"

Umme Habibah رضي الله عنها passed away in Madinah in 44 A.H. Some scholars say that she passed away in Damascus. However, the authentic report is that she passed away in Madinah.

Since she was born 17 years before prophet-hood, it would mean that she was 37 years old at the time of her marriage and 74 years old at the time of her death.

Aa'ishah رضى الله عنها says: "When Umme Habibah رضى الله عنها was departing from this world, she called me and said to me: 'You are fully aware of what transpires amongst co-wives. Forgive me for whatever I may have said or did. May Allah Ta'ala forgive you.' I said to her: 'Everything is forgiven. May Allah Ta'ala forgive both of us.' She said: 'O Aa'ishah! You have made me happy. May Allah Ta'ala keep you happy.' She then called for Umme Salamah رضى الله عنها and said the same thing to her."

Ummul-Mu'mineen Safiyyah bint Huyayy رضى الله عنها

Safiyyah رضى الله عنها was the daughter of Huyayy ibn Akhtab, the leader of the Banu Nazeer tribe. Huyayy was from the progeny of Haroon عليه السلام, the brother of Musa عليه السلام. Her mother's name was Darrah. Her first marriage was with Salaam ibn Mishkam Qurazi. When he divorced her, she married Kinaanah ibn Abi al-Huqayq. Kinaanah was killed in the battle of Khaybar and she was captured in this battle. Rasulullah ﷺ freed her and brought her into his marriage. Her freedom was her dowry. On proceeding from Khaybar, Rasulullah ﷺ stopped at a place called Sahbaa, which was the first stop over point from Khaybar. It was at this place that Rasulullah ﷺ consummated the marriage and also prepared a walimah.

This walimah was quite unique. A leather mat was laid down and Rasulullah ﷺ asked Anas رضى الله عنه to announce that whoever has any food should come with it. Someone brought dates, someone brought cheese, someone brought broth, someone brought ghee, etc. When all these items were brought together, everyone sat down and partook of this meal. There was no meat or bread in this walimah.

Rasulullah ﷺ remained at Sahbaa for three days during which Safiyyah رضى الله عنها remained in Hijaab. When Rasulullah ﷺ was departing from there, he personally seated Safiyyah رضى الله عنها onto the camel. He then gave her his cloak with which she covered herself so that no one would be able to see her. This was a sort of announcement that she was his wife (Ummul-Mu'mineen) and not a slave woman.

When she came into the marriage of Rasulullah ﷺ, he saw a green mark in her eyes. Rasulullah ﷺ asked her about it. She replied: "One day I was sleeping with my head on my husband's lap. I dreamt that the moon came and fell in my lap. I related this dream to my husband. He gave me a hard slap and said: 'You are desiring the king of Yasrib?'" (Referring to Rasulullah ﷺ).

When Safiyyah رضى الله عنها came to Madinah from Khaybar, she was taken to the house of Haarisah ibn Nu'maan. When the Ansaar women heard about her beauty and attractiveness, they all came to see her. Aa'ishah رضى الله عنها also came, but she covered herself in a veil so that she will not be recognized. However, Rasulullah

ﷺ recognized her. When he returned (to Aa'ishah's house) he asked her: "O Aa'ishah! What did you see?" She replied: "I saw a Jewess." Rasulullah ﷺ said: "Do not say that. She has embraced Islam and she has done so very well."

On one occasion Rasulullah ﷺ saw Safiyyah رضى الله عنها crying. When he asked her the reason for this, she replied: "Aa'ishah and Hafsah are interfering with me and claiming that they are more beloved and more honoured in your eyes than I am. Apart from being your wives, they are also related to you." Rasulullah ﷺ replied: "Why did you not say to them: 'How can you be better than me? My father is Haroon عليه السلام, my uncle is Musa عليه السلام and my husband is Muhammad ﷺ.'"

Aa'ishah رضى الله عنها says: "On one occasion I said to Rasulullah ﷺ that Safiyyah is sufficient for you, and I then described how short she was." Rasulullah ﷺ said: "You have said such a thing that if what you said were placed in the oceans, it would all become impure."

On one occasion Rasulullah ﷺ was on a journey when Safiyyah's رضى الله عنها camel fell ill. Zaynab bint Jahsh رضى الله عنها had an extra camel. Rasulullah ﷺ said to her: "If you give your extra camel to Safiyyah, it will be a good act from you." She replied: "Yes! I will give it to that Jewess!" Rasulullah ﷺ became displeased with this reply and did not go to her for two to three months.

When Rasulullah ﷺ was in his final illness, all his wives gathered around him. Safiyyah رضى الله عنها said to him: "O Prophet of Allah! It is my wish that your entire illness comes to me while you recover from your illness." On hearing this, the other wives began making signs to each other (trying to say that she was merely putting up an act). Rasulullah ﷺ saw this and said: "I take an oath by Allah that she is certainly saying the truth."

Safiyyah رضى الله عنها was a very intelligent, forbearing and virtuous woman. One of the slave women of Safiyyah رضى الله عنها went to 'Umar رضى الله عنه and said to him that Safiyyah رضى الله عنها likes Saturdays a lot and that she has very good relations with the Jews. 'Umar رضى الله عنه sent a message to her, asking her for an explanation. She replied: "Ever since Allah Ta'ala gave me Friday in place of Saturday, I never liked Saturdays. As for my good relationships with the Jews, the reason for that is that I have many relatives among them and I maintain my family ties (as is the teaching of Islam)." On hearing this, 'Umar رضى الله عنه asked the slave woman: "What made you say such a thing?" The slave woman spoke the truth and said that it was from shaytaan. Safiyyah رضى الله عنها freed this slave woman.

Sa'eed ibn Musayyib رحمه الله relates that when Safiyyah رضى الله عنها came to Madinah, she had gold earings on her. She gave some of the gold from there to Faatimah رضى الله عنها and some to a few other women.

Glory to Allah! No sooner she became the wife of Rasulullah ﷺ, the love for this world disappeared from her heart. She passed away in Ramadhaan 50 A.H. and is buried in Jannatul Baqi'.

Ummul Mu'mineen Maymoonah bint Haaris رضي الله عنها

Her name is Maymoonah, her father's name is Haaris and her mother's name is Hind. Rasulullah ﷺ married her in Zul Qa'dah 7 A.H. at the time when Rasulullah ﷺ went to Makkah to perform 'umratul qadaa'. Ibn Sa'd رحمه الله says that this was his last wife. He did not marry any woman after her. She was previously married to Abu Rahm ibn 'Abdul 'Uzza. When he passed away, she married Rasulullah ﷺ. The dowry was set at 500 dirhams.

Ibn 'Abbaas رضي الله عنه says that when Rasulullah ﷺ proposed to her, she appointed 'Abbaas رضي الله عنه as her representative, who consequently got her married to Rasulullah ﷺ.

There are conflicting narrations as to whether he was in ihraam or not at the time of marrying her. Imaam Bukhaari رحمه الله says that the preferred opinion is that he was in ihraam. On leaving Makkah, Rasulullah ﷺ stopped at a place called Sarif and consummated the marriage there.

It is gauged from some traditions that the marriage and the consummation both took place at Sarif. It was also at this place that she passed away in 51 A.H. She was also buried at this place. The Janaazah Salaah was performed by 'Abdullah ibn 'Abbaas رضي الله عنه. She was lowered in the grave by 'Abdullah ibn 'Abbaas رضي الله عنه, Yazeed ibn Asamm, 'Abdullah ibn Shaddaad and 'Ubaydullah Khaulaani. The first three were her nephews while the fourth was an orphan who was brought up by her.

The above are the eleven women whom Rasulullah ﷺ married. They are given the title of Ummahaatul Mu'mineen – the Mothers of the Believers. There were other women whom Rasulullah ﷺ married but divorced before the marriage could be consummated. They were Asma' bint Nu'maan, Jauniyah and 'Amrah bint Yazeed Kilaabiyyah.

Slave women

Rasulullah ﷺ had four slave women, two of whom are well known.

Maariyah Qibtiyyah رضي الله عنها: She was his Umm walad (mother of his child). Rasulullah's ﷺ son, Ibraaheem, was born from her. Muqawqis, the ruler of Alexandria, had sent Maariyah رضي الله عنها as a gift to Rasulullah ﷺ. She passed away in 16 A.H. during the caliphate of 'Umar ﷺ and was buried in Jannatul Baqi'.

Rayhaanah bint Sham'un ﷺ: She was either from the Banu Qurayzah or Banu Nazeer. She was brought as a captive and remained as Rasulullah's ﷺ slave woman. She passed away after the Farewell Haj in 10 A.H. and was buried in Jannatul Baqi'. Another opinion is that Rasulullah ﷺ freed her and married her. Allah Ta'ala knows best.

Nafisah ﷺ: She was originally the slave woman of Zaynab bint Jahsh ﷺ. When relating the life of Safiyyah ﷺ, we mentioned that Rasulullah ﷺ got angry with Zaynab ﷺ because of what she said about Safiyyah ﷺ, and that Rasulullah ﷺ did not go to Zaynab ﷺ for two to three months. When Rasulullah ﷺ forgave her, she gave this slave woman of hers to Rasulullah ﷺ as a way of expressing her joy to Rasulullah ﷺ.

Rasulullah's ﷺ children

There are different opinions with regard to the number of Rasulullah's ﷺ children. The more accepted and reliable opinion is that he had three sons and four daughters.

They were Qaasim, 'Abdullah (who was also known as Tayyib and Taahir) and Ibraaheem. The daughters were Zaynab, Ruqayyah, Umme Kulsoom and Faatimah. There is no difference with regard to the daughters – there were four, they all grew up, got married, embraced Islam and emigrated. There is also no difference with regard to Ibraaheem. He was born from Maariyah Qibtiyyah ﷺ and passed away when still a child.

Apart from Ibraaheem, all the other children were born from Khadijah ﷺ. Rasulullah ﷺ had no children from any of the other wives. All the sons that were born from Khadijah ﷺ passed away in infancy. There is therefore a difference of opinion in their number. The scholars of biography in general, are of the opinion that two sons were born from Khadijah ﷺ – Qaasim and 'Abdullah. 'Abdullah was also referred to as Tayyib and Taahir.

Qaasim ﷺ

He was the first of Rasulullah's ﷺ children and passed away before Rasulullah ﷺ attained prophet-hood. He passed away when he was just two years old. Some scholars are of the opinion that he reached an age of understanding and then passed away. Rasulullah ﷺ is given the title of Abul Qaasim (father of Qaasim) because of this son of his.

Zaynab رضى الله عنها

She is unanimously considered to be Rasulullah's ﷺ eldest daughter. She was born 10 years before prophet-hood. She embraced Islam and emigrated after the battle of Badr. She was married to her maternal cousin, Abul-'Aas ibn Rabi'. Details concerning her emigration were given under the discussion of the captives of Badr. She passed away at the beginning of the 8th year after emigration. She left behind two children, a son by the name of Ali and a daughter by the name of Umaamah.

There are different traditions with regard to her son, Ali. It is popularly believed that he reached the age of understanding and passed away while his father was still alive. Another opinion is that he was martyred in the battle of Yarmuk.

Rasulullah ﷺ loved his granddaughter Umaamah dearly and she was very attached to him. At times she used to climb on Rasulullah's ﷺ back while he was in Salaah. Rasulullah ﷺ would lower her gently.

On one occasion Rasulullah ﷺ received a gold necklace as a gift. All his wives were present at that time. Umaamah was playing in a corner of the house with some sand. Rasulullah ﷺ said: "I am going to give this necklace to my most beloved family member." All those who were present thought that Aa'ishah رضى الله عنها will receive it. However, Rasulullah ﷺ called Umaamah, wiped her eyes with his blessed hands and then placed that necklace around her neck.

When Faatimah رضى الله عنها passed away, Ali رضى الله عنه married Umaamah. Before Ali رضى الله عنه could be martyred, he wrote a bequest to Mughirah ibn Naufal that he should marry Umaamah. Some scholars say that from this marriage between Mughirah and Umaamah, a son by the name of Yahyaa was born. Other scholars say that Umaamah had no children. She passed away while still married to Mughirah.

Ruqayyah رضى الله عنها

Ruqayyah رضى الله عنها and Umme Kulsoom رضى الله عنها – these two daughters of Rasulullah ﷺ were married to two sons of Abu Lahab, namely, 'Utbah and 'Utaybah, respectively. Both these daughters were married to these two sons of Abu Lahab, but the marriages were not consummated as yet. When the Surah Lahab was revealed, Abu Lahab summoned his two sons and said to them: "If you do not divorce the daughters of Muhammad, it will be Haraam for you to stay in my house." Both the sons obeyed their father and divorced their respective wives before the consummation of the marriages.

Rasulullah ﷺ got Ruqayyah رضي الله عنها married to 'Usmaan رضي الله عنه. When he emigrated to Abyssinia, Ruqayyah رضي الله عنها also accompanied him. Rasulullah ﷺ did not receive any news from them for quite some time. After some time, a woman came and informed him that she met both of them in Abyssinia. On hearing this news, Rasulullah ﷺ said: "May Allah be with both of them. 'Usmaan is the first person after Lut عليه السلام to have emigrated with his wife and family."

While they were in Abyssinia, a son by the name of 'Abdullah was born to them. He passed away when he was six years old.

When Rasulullah ﷺ was departing for the battle of Badr, Ruqayyah رضي الله عنها was ill at that time. 'Usmaan رضي الله عنه could therefore not participate in the battle of Badr. He was busy tending to his wife. She passed away on the very day when Zaid ibn Haarisah رضي الله عنه came into Madinah to give the good news of the Muslims' victory over the Quraysh of Makkah.

Usaamah ibn Zaid رضي الله عنه also did not take part in the battle of Badr because of Ruqayyah's رضي الله عنها illness. He was busy making the burial arrangements when he heard the Takbeer (someone saying Allah is the greatest). 'Usmaan رضي الله عنه asked him: "O Usaamah! What is this?" When they looked, they saw Zaid ibn Haarisah رضي الله عنه riding Rasulullah's ﷺ camel and coming with the news that the disbelievers were defeated. Ruqayyah رضي الله عنها was 20 years old when she passed away.

Umme Kulsoom رضي الله عنها

She was popularly known by this title. It seems that this was her name as well. She does not seem to be known by any other name. After the death of her sister Ruqayyah رضي الله عنها, she married 'Usmaan رضي الله عنه in Rabi'ul-Awwal 3 A.H. She remained with him for six years. They had no children. She passed away in Sha'baan 9 A.H. Rasulullah ﷺ performed the Janaazah Salaah. She was lowered into the grave by Ali رضي الله عنه, Fadl ibn 'Abbaas رضي الله عنه and Usaamah ibn Zaid رضي الله عنه. Rasulullah ﷺ was sitting by her grave side and tears were flowing from his eyes.

Umme Kulsoom رضي الله عنها was first married to the son of Abu Lahab, 'Utaybah (as mentioned previously). He divorced her on the instruction of his father. The other brother, 'Utbah, had also divorced Ruqayyah رضي الله عنها. 'Utaybah did not suffice with just issuing a divorce. He went to Rasulullah ﷺ and said: "I reject your religion. I have divorced your daughter. She does not like me and I do not like her." He then attacked Rasulullah ﷺ and tore the long robe that Rasulullah ﷺ was wearing. Rasulullah ﷺ cursed him and made the following dua: "O Allah! Impose one of Your animals over him." On one occasion a Qurayshi trade caravan travelling towards Syria stopped over at a place called Zarqaa'. Abu Lahab and 'Utaybah were both in this caravan. At night, a lion came, scanned the faces of all those who were part of the caravan and sniffed them. When it reached 'Utaybah, it immediately mauled his head. 'Utaybah died there and then. The lion disappeared and could not be found.

When Umme Kulsoom رضي الله عنها passed away, Rasulullah ﷺ said: "If I had ten daughters, I would have given them one after the other in the marriage of 'Usmaan."

Faatimah رضي الله عنها

Her name is Faatimah and she has two titles: Zahraa' and Batool. The word Batool comes in the meaning of cut-off or severed. She is referred to by this name because her merits and virtues were such that she surpassed the other women of this world and was thereby cut-off from them. Another meaning could be that she was cut-off from everything and everyone apart from Allah Ta'ala. She was referred to as Zahraa' because of her internal beauty, splendour and purity.

She was the youngest of Rasulullah's ﷺ daughters while Zaynab رضي الله عنها was the eldest. Zaynab رضي الله عنها was followed by Ruqayyah رضي الله عنها, followed by Umme Kulsoom رضي الله عنها and then Faatimah رضي الله عنها.

She was married to Ali رضي الله عنه in 2 A.H. Based on the first opinion of her date of birth, she was 15 years and five and half months old at the time of her marriage. There is a difference of opinion as to how old Ali رضي الله عنه was when he embraced Islam. One opinion is that he was eight years old while the other opinion is that he was 10 years old. Based on the first opinion, he was 21 years and five months old at the time of his marriage. Based on the second opinion, he was 24 years and one and half months old at the time of his marriage.

She had five children, three boys and two girls: Hasan, Husayn, Muhsin, Umme Kulsoom and Zaynab. Rasulullah's ﷺ lineage did not continue from any of his children apart from Faatimah رضي الله عنها. Muhsin passed away in his infancy. Umme Kulsoom married 'Umar رضي الله عنه but they did not get any children. Zaynab was married to 'Abdullah ibn Ja'far رضي الله عنه and they had children.

Faatimah رضي الله عنها passed away six months after the demise of Rasulullah ﷺ in Ramadhaan 11 A.H. 'Abbaas رضي الله عنه performed the Janaazah Salaah. Ali رضي الله عنه, 'Abbaas رضي الله عنه and Fadl ibn 'Abbaas رضي الله عنه lowered her in her grave.

Rasulullah ﷺ loved Faatimah رضي الله عنها the most. On many occasions Rasulullah ﷺ asked her: "O Faatimah! Does it not please you that you will be the leader of all the women of Jannah?" In one Hadith, he said to her: "You are the leader of all the women of this world, apart from Maryam." It was Rasulullah's ﷺ habit that when he left for a journey, he would meet Faatimah رضي الله عنها last and when he returned from a journey, he would meet her first.

An entire book can be dedicated to the virtues and merits of Faatimah رضي الله عنها. We have sufficed with just a few.

Ibraaheem رضي الله عنه

He is the last of Rasulullah's ﷺ children. He was born from Maariyah Qibtiyyah رضي الله عنها in Zul Hijjah 8 A.H. Rasulullah ﷺ made his 'aqeeqah on the seventh day. Two sheep were slaughtered, his head was shaved and the equivalent of the hairs weight in silver was given in charity. The hair was buried and he was named Ibraaheem. He was given to a wet-nurse on the outskirts of Madinah. Rasulullah ﷺ would occasionally go to visit him, carry him and play with him. He lived for about 15-16 months and passed away in 10 A.H. Coincidentaly, the day on which he passed away, there was a solar eclipse. It was the belief of the Arabs that when a great person passes away, the sun goes into eclipse. In order to refute this baseless belief, Rasulullah ﷺ delivered a sermon and said: "The sun and moon are from among the signs of Allah Ta'ala. They do not go into eclipse by the birth or death of anyone. Allah Ta'ala is actually frightening His servants. When you see such a phenomenon, you should offer Salaah, make dua to Allah Ta'ala and give charity."

Chapter 32

The blessed physical features of Rasulullah ﷺ

Rasulullah ﷺ was neither too tall nor too short. He was of average height. He had a large head which was in proportion to his body. He had a thick beard. His head and beard had about 25 grey hairs. His face was luminous and handsome. Whoever saw his blessed face described it to be luminous like the full moon.

His perspiration had a special fragrance. When droplets of his perspiration fell from his face, they looked like pearls. Anas ؓ says that we did not touch silk softer than the palms of Rasulullah ﷺ, and we did not smell any musk and Amber more fragrant than the fragrance that emanated from the body of Rasulullah ﷺ.

The seal of prophet-hood

The seal of prophet-hood was situated between his shoulders, closer to the right shoulder. A Hadith of Sahih Muslim states that there was a piece of red flesh similar to that of a pigeon's egg situated between Rasulullah's ﷺ two shoulders.

This seal of prophet-hood was a special sign of his prophet-hood and was mentioned in the previous divine Books and mentioned by the previous Prophets of Allah Ta'ala. The scholars of the Bani Israa'eel used to see this and recognise Rasulullah ﷺ as the last Prophet regarding whom the previous Prophets had given glad tidings, and that the seal of prophet-hood which they had mentioned was found in Rasulullah ﷺ. This seal of prophet-hood was a sort of mandate or certificate from Allah Ta'ala attesting to his prophet-hood.

'Allaamah Suhayli رحمه الله says that the seal of prophet-hood was close to the right shoulder bone. The reason for it being situated there is that it is the area from which shaytaan enters the human body. He enters from the back and whispers into man's heart. The seal of prophet-hood was placed at this spot so that the entry point of shaytaan may be sealed and no whispering of shaytaan may enter his luminous heart.

Some Ahaadith state that this seal of prophet-hood which was on Rasulullah's ﷺ back seemed to have the words Muhammad Rasulullah naturally inscribed on it.

It is narrated on the authority of Ibn 'Umar رضي الله عنه that the seal of prophet-hood was on the back of the Prophet ﷺ like a hazelnut made of flesh. In it was written with flesh, Muhammad Rasulullah.

Rasulullah's ﷺ hair would most of the time reach his ear lobes and sometimes go beyond that. He used to comb his hair and also apply surmah (antimony) to his eyes. This is despite the fact that his eyes had the natural look of having surmah.

Rasulullah's ﷺ eyes were large and wide (in proportion to his face). They were quite black. There was a very fine line of hair extending from his chest to his navel. His upper arms and feet were fleshy. When he walked, it seemed that he raised his feet with force and that he was descending from an elevated place.

His blessed body and luminous face were beautified by all external and internal beauties. Apart from smiling, Rasulullah ﷺ did not laugh with his mouth wide open. It is stated in the Hadith that he resembled Ibraaheem ؑ the most in his ways and in his appearance.

Rasulullah's ﷺ blessed beard

Rasulullah ﷺ had a thick beard. Rasulullah ﷺ did not trim it completely. However, he used to trim his moustache. He would occasionally trim those hairs of the beard that stuck out (of the normal shape of the beard) so that it does not look untidy and unkempt. The beard was a Sunnah practice of all the Prophets of Allah Ta'ala. It was never kept on the basis of national or cultural reasons as is the assumption of some deviated and immature people.

The beard is not only a Sunnah of Muhammad ﷺ and the way of Islam, rather it is a Sunnah of all the Prophets (who numbered approximately 124 000). A Hadith states that the beard is from among the Sunnah practices of all the Prophets.

The clothing of Rasulullah ﷺ

Rasulullah's ﷺ clothes used to be extremely simple and basic. He led an ascetic life. His clothes in general comprised of a sheet, a kurtah, a cloak and a shawl – many of which used to have patches. He used to like green clothes. His clothes in general were white in colour.

The sheet that he wore was a Yemeni sheet which had green and red lines on it. He used to like this sheet a lot. He prohibited men from wearing full red garments.

His hat (topi) used to stick to his head. He never wore a high hat. Abu Kabshah narrates that the hats of the Sahaabah ﷺ used to be flat. They stuck to the head and were not high. Rasulullah ﷺ was particular in wearing a hat beneath his turban. He used to say: "There is a difference between us and the disbelievers that we tie our turban above our hats."

When Rasulullah ﷺ tied his turban, one end of it would hang between his shoulders. Sometimes, he would cause it to hang to the left or to the right. Sometimes he would tie it below his chin. It is stated in a Hadith that Rasulullah ﷺ said: "During the battles of Badr and Hunayn, Allah Ta'ala sent such angels to assist me who were wearing turbans. These angels are mentioned in the Qur-aan: 'Five thousand angels on marked horses.'"

It is stated in a Hadith that Rasulullah ﷺ saw trousers being sold in the market place of Mina. On seeing the trouser, he liked it and said that it is more concealing than an izaar (lungi). Rasulullah ﷺ purchased the trouser but it is not confirmed that he wore it.

Rasulullah ﷺ liked kurtahs a lot. The opening of his kurtah used to be at the chest. At times, the buttons used to be open.

Rasulullah ﷺ used to wear leather socks and make masah (passing of wet hands) on them.

Rasulullah's ﷺ pillow was made of leather. It was filled with palm leaves. Sometimes, Rasulullah ﷺ used to sleep on a straw mat.

Rasulullah ﷺ had a silver ring which he used to wear. When Rasulullah ﷺ began writing letters to the rulers of Rome, Abyssinia, etc. he made a silver ring which had the words Muhammad, Rasool, Allah inscribed on three separate lines. The reason for making this ring was that kings did not accept any letters that did not have a seal. This ring was used as a seal.

Rasulullah ﷺ wore flat sandals which had a single layer of sole and two straps on the top. He would insert his mubaarak toes in these straps.

Rasulullah ﷺ also had a black woollen shawl which had patches on it. A black woollen shawl with patches is also a Sunnah of the Prophets of Allah Ta'ala. This was also worn by the Auliyaa (friends) of Allah Ta'ala and the pious. It is extremely sad that this Sunnah has departed from this world. A sufi is referred to as a sufi because he wears a woollen shawl in emulation of the Sunnah of the Prophets of Allah Ta'ala. He is the person who has completely divorced himself from worldly pursuits and considers the royal garb and dress to be totally insignificant in comparison to this black woollen shawl.

Ibn Mas'ood ﺭﺿﻰﺍﻟﻠﻪﻋﻨﻪ says that the Prophets used to ride donkeys, wear woollen clothes, and milk the goats. Rasulullah ﺻﻠﻰﺍﻟﻠﻪﻋﻠﻴﻪﻭﺳﻠﻢ said: "The day on which Allah spoke to Musa ﻋﻠﻴﻪﺍﻟﺴﻼﻡ, the latter was wearing a woollen shawl, a woollen hat, a woollen cloak and woollen pants. His sandals were made from the skin of a dead donkey."

Abu Bardah ibn Abi Musa Ash'ari ﺭﺿﻰﺍﻟﻠﻪﻋﻨﻪ narrates that one day Aa'ishah ﺭﺿﻰﺍﻟﻠﻪﻋﻨﻬﺎ took out a thick woollen shawl with patches on it and a thick cloak and said: "Rasulullah ﺻﻠﻰﺍﻟﻠﻪﻋﻠﻴﻪﻭﺳﻠﻢ passed away in these two garments." Aa'ishah's ﺭﺿﻰﺍﻟﻠﻪﻋﻨﻬﺎ purpose in saying this was to show Rasulullah's ﺻﻠﻰﺍﻟﻠﻪﻋﻠﻴﻪﻭﺳﻠﻢ simplicity, humility and ascetic way of life.

Allah Ta'ala addressed Rasulullah ﺻﻠﻰﺍﻟﻠﻪﻋﻠﻴﻪﻭﺳﻠﻢ in the Qur-aan as Muzzammil (one who is wrapped in garments) and Muddassir (one who is enshrouded) to show that these garments were most beloved by Allah Ta'ala.

Chapter 33

The Miracles of Nabi Muhammad ﷺ

Allah Ta'ala sent Ambiyaa and Messengers from among mankind for the guidance of mankind. He did this in order to convey His injunctions through these pious personalities, to remind man of his Creator and in order to complete His evidence against man. Allah Ta'ala says in the Qur-aan: "So that the people may not have any evidence against Allah after the Messengers." Moreover, after the message has been conveyed by the Prophets and Messengers, people will have no excuse for not obeying the commands of Allah Ta'ala.

Since the Prophets and Messengers were humans and their external forms were no different from other humans, Allah Ta'ala gave them miracles which would be proofs and evidences of their truthfulness. Allah Ta'ala says in the story of Musa عليه السلام: "These two (the staff and the luminous hand) are two proofs (of your prophet-hood) from your Sustainer." [Surah al-Qasas, verse 32]

Nabi ﷺ was also given many miracles to prove his Messenger-hood. At times voices were heard from trees and rocks which gave testimony to Rasulullah's ﷺ prophet-hood and which contained their greetings to him: "Peace be upon you O Messenger of Allah!" On one occasion, Rasulullah ﷺ summoned a tree to him. It came to him and when he asked it to return to its original place, it returned.

Miracles of barakah (blessings)

The essence of every Prophet and Messenger is a fountain of blessings and goodness. Just as Muhammad ﷺ surpasses the other Prophets in other attributes and qualities, his miracles of blessings and goodness are unsurpassed. In short, through his blessings, a small amount of food and a small quantity of water sufficed a huge army on several occasions.

1. In the battle of Khandaq, a small quantity of flour in the house of Jaabir ﷺ filled the bellies of a large number of people.

2. Abu Talhah رضى الله عنه invited Rasulullah ﷺ alone to his house and prepared food for 2-3 people. Rasulullah ﷺ fed all his companions to their satisfaction from this little food.

3. On one occasion, about 2kg of barley and the mutton of a lamb sufficed 80 people.

4. There was no water left in the well at Hudaybiyah. Rasulullah ﷺ poured the left over water of his wudhu water into it and it began flowing like a spring. One thousand five hundred people drank of that water and gave to their animals as well.

5. The spring that was at Tabuk had become dry. Rasulullah ﷺ placed his wudhu water into it. It began flowing so profusely, that thousands of people drank from it.

6. On one occasion, the entire army of Muslims was restless due to thirst. Rasulullah ﷺ took a cup which was so small that his hand could not fit into it. He placed his fingers over it and water began gushing from between his fingers. The entire army drank from that water and also performed wudhu.

7. On one occasion a cup of milk was brought to him. Rasulullah ﷺ ordered Abu Hurayrah رضى الله عنه to call all the people of Suffah. They numbered about 70-80. All of them drank to their fill from that one cup. When they all finished, the milk was still as it had been.

8. When Rasulullah ﷺ married Zaynab رضى الله عنها, then the mother of Anas رضى الله عنه, Umme Sulaym رضى الله عنها, prepared some food and sent it to Rasulullah ﷺ. Rasulullah ﷺ invited many Sahaabah رضى الله عنهم and ordered that 10 of them should sit at a time and partake of that food. Approximately 300 of them ate from that food. The balance of the food was more than what was originally prepared.

Acceptance of Duas

From among the miracles of Rasulullah ﷺ is that whatever dua he made for anyone, it was accepted. Such miracles are also referred to as Sayf al-Lisaani. In other words, whatever is uttered by the tongue, happens exactly like that without any delay. This is a sign that the person is a chosen one of Allah Ta'ala and divinely assisted. Whatever Allah Ta'ala causes that person to say, takes place exactly like that. What can be said of the forceful tongue of Rasulullah ﷺ!

Whatever he said was as if it was engraved in rock. Whatever he said about a particular person, took place exactly like that.

1. Rasulullah ﷺ made dua for Anas رضي الله عنه who was a very poor person. Through this dua, he became very wealthy.

2. 'Abdur Rahmaan ibn 'Auf رضي الله عنه became so wealthy by the dua of Rasulullah ﷺ, that he became a multi-millionaire.

3. Rasulullah ﷺ made dua for Sa'd رضي الله عنه that Allah Ta'ala should make him a person whose duas are readily accepted. This dua was accepted.

4. On the occasion of the hijrah, Suraaqah followed Rasulullah ﷺ (in order to capture him). Rasulullah ﷺ made dua that Allah Ta'ala should cause his horse to sink into the ground. No sooner he made this dua, the horse sank into the ground till its knees. When Suraaqah embraced Islam, Rasulullah ﷺ again made dua and the horse emerged immediately.

5. Rasulullah ﷺ made dua in favour of 'Abdullah ibn 'Abbaas رضي الله عنه that Allah Ta'ala should bless him with knowledge. Consequently, he became a fountain of knowledge and wisdom.

6. Rasulullah ﷺ made dua for the memory of Abu Hurayrah رضي الله عنه. Consequently, he never forgot whatever he heard thereafter.

7. Rasulullah ﷺ made dua for the guidance of Abu Hurayrah's رضي الله عنه mother. She embraced Islam soon thereafter.

8. On one occasion, Rasulullah ﷺ went to someone's house. He placed a sheet over all of them and made dua. The threshold of the door and the walls of the house said Aameen three times to his dua.

9. When the Quraysh displayed extreme opposition and antagonism towards him, he cursed them by saying: "O Allah! Inflict them with a drought." Consequently, a drought was inflicted on them.

10. Madinah experienced a drought. While Rasulullah ﷺ was delivering his sermon, a person stood up and said: "O Rasulullah! Make dua for rain." Rasulullah ﷺ raised his hand and made dua. It started to rain immediately.

Curing the sick

1. During the battle of Khaybar, Ali رضي الله عنه experienced some pain in his eyes. Rasulullah ﷺ placed some of his blessed saliva on to them and they were immediately cured. He never experience pain in his eyes again.

2. An eye of Qataadah ibn Nu'maan ﷜ fell off during Jihaad. Rasulullah ﷺ picked it up with his blessed hand and placed it back in its place. This eye sparkled and looked more appealing than the other eye (that hadn't fallen off).

3. 'Abdullah ibn 'Atik ﷜ killed Abu Raafi'. When 'Abdullah ﷜ was coming down from the steps, he fell and broke his legs. Rasulullah ﷺ passed his blessed hand over his legs and they were immediately cured as though they had not been broken.

4. While they were in the cave of Hira', a snake bit Abu Bakr ﷜. Rasulullah ﷺ placed his saliva on that spot and it was immediately cured.

5. A blind person came to Rasulullah ﷺ. Rasulullah ﷺ taught him a special dua and said to him: "After performing wudhu, offer two Rakaats of Salaah and make dua to Allah Ta'ala by using my name. Allah Ta'ala will fulfil your need." This blind person followed the advice of Rasulullah ﷺ. 'Usmaan ibn Haneef ﷜ says: "We still hadn't got up from that assembly when that blind person's eyesight was returned to him."

6. Habib ibn Abi Fudayk's father ﷜ developed white specks in his eyes and became blind. Rasulullah ﷺ recited something and blew into his eyes. His eyes were immediately cured.

7. During the Farewell Haj, a woman came to Rasulullah ﷺ with her child. She informed him that this child was dumb. Rasulullah ﷺ asked for some water, washed his hands, gargled his mouth and said: "Give this child this water to drink and sprinkle some of it on him." When the woman came the following year, her child was completely cured and could speak.

8. When Muhammad ibn Haatib ﷜ was still a child, he fell from his mother's lap into the fire and got slightly burnt. Rasulullah ﷺ placed some of his blessed saliva on him and he was completely cured.

9. Abu Hurayrah ﷜ complained to Rasulullah ﷺ about his memory – that he forgets whatever he hears from him. Rasulullah ﷺ asked him to spread out his shawl. He then placed something with both his hands onto it and asked him to place it against his chest. Abu Hurayrah ﷜ said: "I did exactly that and I never forgot anything thereafter."

10. A person came to Rasulullah ﷺ and said: "O Messenger of Allah! My brother is ill. The effects of insanity are on him." Rasulullah ﷺ asked him to bring his brother to him. When he was brought, Rasulullah ﷺ

recited several surahs of the Qur-aan and blew onto him. He was immediately cured and no traces of insanity remained on him.

There are various other incidents where Rasulullah ﷺ cured people who were ill. He cured them with his blessed saliva, by blowing on them or by passing his hand over them and they were immediately cured.

Bringing the dead to life

The noble Prophets are essentially spiritual doctors. They have been commissioned to treat the ailments of the heart and soul. However, Allah Ta'ala occasionally enables them to cure such physical ailments which doctors are unable to treat. Occasionally, He also enables them to bring back the dead so that it may be made clear that these Prophets are the chosen ones of Allah Ta'ala. Miracles of this nature were given to a large extent to 'Isa عليه السلام.

Although Allah Ta'ala blessed Muhammad ﷺ with numerous types of miracles, He also endowed him with a fair share of miracles related to curing the sick and bringing back the dead to life. Allah Ta'ala caused a group of dead people to come to life at his hands.

Imaam Qurtubi رحمه الله writes in his book, Tazkirah, that Allah Ta'ala caused a group of dead people to be revived at the hands of Muhammad ﷺ.

1. Anas رضي الله عنه narrates that a young son of an elderly old woman passed away. Everyone placed a cloth over him and covered him. The old lady was greatly disturbed and began screaming out and saying: "O Allah! You know very well that I embraced Islam solely for Your sake. I abandoned all the idols and emigrated to Your Messenger after much difficulties. O Allah! Do not give the idol worshippers the opportunity to ridicule me and do not place this unbearable burden on me." Anas رضي الله عنه says: "Rasulullah ﷺ and all of us, the people of Suffah, were present at that time. I take an oath by Allah Ta'ala that we were still present there when that boy suddenly came to life. He removed the sheet that was covering his face and took meals with us. He remained alive till after the demise of Rasulullah ﷺ. His old mother passed away in his lifetime." This child came back to life by this dua of this woman and the blessed presence of Rasulullah ﷺ.

2. Rasulullah ﷺ invited a person to Islam. He replied: "I will only embrace Islam if you bring back to life my daughter who passed away recently." Rasulullah ﷺ said: "Show me her grave." That person took him to her grave. Rasulullah ﷺ stood there and called out her name. The girl came to life and said: "Here I am and I am fortunate to be before you." Rasulullah ﷺ asked her: "Would you like to live with your parents?"

She replied: "O Rasulullah ﷺ! The companionship of Allah Ta'ala is better. And I have found the hereafter to be better than this world."

3. Aa'ishah ◌ narrates that during the Farewell Haj, Rasulullah ﷺ got off at a place called Hajoon and when he left, he was sad and crying. When he returned to me after some time, he was happy and smiling. When I asked him the reason for this, he replied: "I requested Allah Ta'ala to cause my parents to come back to life. Allah Ta'ala brought them back to life, they brought Imaan in me, and passed away again."

4. It is narrated through several narrations in the books of Hadith that when Rasulullah ﷺ was at Khaybar, a Jewish woman presented a roasted goat to Rasulullah ﷺ. She had poisoned this goat. Rasulullah ﷺ ate a little from it and the Sahaabah ◌ also did the same. Suddenly he asked the Sahaabah ◌ to stop eating and said to them: "This goat has just informed me now that it has been mixed with poison."

5. Rasulullah ﷺ used to lean against the stump of a date palm in the Masjid-e-Nabawi and deliver his sermons. Later when his mimbar was made, he began delivering his sermons from the mimbar. This stump was so overcome by grief over its separation from Rasulullah ﷺ, that it began crying out loudly. He got down from the mimbar, went to it and embraced it. It then began sobbing. Rasulullah ﷺ said: "This stump used to constantly listen to my sermon. Since it no longer listens to it, it began crying."

Chapter 34

Khasaa'is-e-Nabawi (Special Merits of Nabi ﷺ)

Khasaa'is-e-Nabawi refers to those virtues and merits which Allah Ta'ala bestowed on Muhammad ﷺ alone. Allah Ta'ala did not bestow such virtues and merits to any of the other Prophets. Rasulullah ﷺ said: "I have been given certain things which none of the other Prophets before me were given."

1. My commissioning as a Prophet was to the entire mankind. The Prophets before me used to be commissioned to their respective peoples, only while I have been commissioned to the entire world. Allah Ta'ala says:

قُلْ يَٰٓأَيُّهَا النَّاسُ اِنِّىْ رَسُوْلُ اللّٰهِ اِلَيْكُمْ جَمِيْعًا

"O people! Surely I am the Messenger of Allah to all of you."

وَمَآ اَرْسَلْنٰكَ اِلَّا كَآفَّةً لِّلنَّاسِ

"We have not sent you but to all the people."

تَبَٰرَكَ الَّذِىْ نَزَّلَ الْفُرْقَانَ عَلٰى عَبْدِهٖ لِيَكُوْنَ لِلْعٰلَمِيْنَ نَذِيْرًا

"Blessed is He who sent down the Criterion to His servant so that he may be a warner to the worlds."

2. I am the seal of Prophets. The chain of prophet-hood has ended with me. There is to be no Prophet after me. Allah Ta'ala says:

مَا كَانَ مُحَمَّدٌ اَبَآ اَحَدٍ مِّنْ رِّجَالِكُمْ وَلٰكِنْ رَّسُوْلَ اللّٰهِ وَخَاتَمَ النَّبِيّٖنَ

"Muhammad is not the father of any of your men. Rather, he is the Messenger of Allah and the seal of Prophets."

$$\text{اَلْيَوْمَ اَكْمَلْتُ لَكُمْ دِيْنَكُمْ وَاَتْمَمْتُ عَلَيْكُمْ نِعْمَتِىْ وَرَضِيْتُ لَكُمُ الْاِسْلَامَ دِيْنًا}$$

"Today have I perfected for you your religion and completed My favour on you and chose Islam as a religion for you."

3. I have been given comprehensiveness in speech. In other words, such short and comprehensive words which are few in number but whose meanings are numerous. The collection of Ahaadith is testimony to this. His Ahaadith are a collection of all true beliefs, correct deeds, noble characteristics, and all rules and injunctions related to religion and the world.

4. I have been given victory and help through my awe. Without any external causes, my enemies are intimidated by me and scared of me despite their being at a distance of a month's journey. This was divine help that caused his enemies who were as far as one month's journey to fear him and be terrified of him. Allah Ta'ala says:

$$\text{سَنُلْقِىْ فِىْ قُلُوْبِ الَّذِيْنَ كَفَرُوا الرُّعْبَ}$$

"We shall cast terror in the hearts of the unbelievers."

$$\text{وَ قَذَفَ فِىْ قُلُوْبِهِمُ الرُّعْبَ}$$

"And He cast terror in their hearts."

5. The entire earth has been made a place of sajdah for me and a pure place. In other words, my followers are permitted to offer Salaah everywhere – whether they are in the Masjid or not. I have received the permission to purify myself with pure sand. I am permitted to make tayammum everywhere. Sand has been made pure for me just like water.

6. Booty has been made lawful for me. It was not permitted to any Prophet before me.

7. My followers will be more in number than the followers of all the other Prophets. It is stated in a Hadith that on the day of Qiyaamah, all the nations of the world will cover 120 lines. From these, 80 lines will consist of my followers.

8. I have been given the Shafaa'ah al-Kubraa, the major intercession. On the day of Qiyaamah, all the early and latter nations will come to me. I will intercede for them in the court of Allah Ta'ala.

9. I will take my followers and cross the Bridge of Siraat before all the other Prophets.

10. I will enter Jannah first. Abu Bakr رضى الله عنه and 'Umar رضى الله عنه will be to my right and left sides. In Jannah, every Prophet will have a fountain. My fountain will be the widest and most brilliant.

Conclusion

This weak servant has given a very brief and short explanation of the miracles and khasaa'is of Muhammad ﷺ. The Ahaadith in this regard are well known and popular.

I now end this work, Seeratul Mustafa. I make dua to Allah Ta'ala that He decrees a good end for myself and my offspring. I pray that He enables me to enjoy the intercession of Muhammad ﷺ, to be present at his fountain of abundance, and to drink from its water. *Aameen.*[3]

وآخر دعوانا أن الحمد لله رب العالمين. والصلاة والسلام على حبيبه سيد الأولين والآخرين وعلى آله وأصحابه وعلماء أمته وأولياء زمرته أجمعين. وعلينا معهم يا أرحم الراحمين ويا أكرم الأكرمين وأجود الأجودين وخير المسئولين ويا خير المعطين. آمين يا رب العالمين .

Completed on 28 Muharram al-Haraam 1385 A.H.
Muhammad Idrees رحمه الله

---

[3] *Al-hamdulillah,* it is with the grace of Allah Ta'ala that the abridged version of the Seerat-e-Mustafa ﷺ has also been completed at the Mubaarak Raudha of Rasulullah ﷺ. May Allah Ta'ala accept this treatise and make it a means of us all attaining the closeness of Rasulullah ﷺ.

O Allah, make this book a means of the Ummah learning about our beloved Nabi Muhammad ﷺ, understand his sacrifices for Deen, practice on his beloved sunnats and strive towards the cause for which he spent his entire life.

وَ صلى الله على النبى الأمى وعلى اله وصحبه وسلم تسليما كثيرا كثيرا

OUR PUBLICATIONS
Available on Amazon

Logic for Beginners
Translation of تيسير المنطق

The Creed of Imam Tahawi
Arabic with *English* & *Farsi* translation

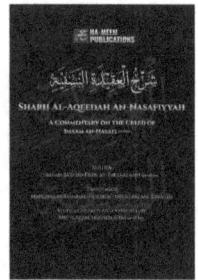

Sharh Al-Aqeedah An-Nasafiyyah
English Translation

Solving Tarkeeb
Translation of حلّ تَرْكِيْب

Arabic Tutor: Arbi Ka Mu'allim
(Volumes 1, 2, 3, 4)

From the Treasures of Arabic Morphology - من كنوز الصرف

Simplified Principles of Fiqh
Translation of آسان اصول فقہ

Miftah ul Qur'an
(Volumes 1, 2, 3, 4)

Masail Al Qudoori Made Easy
Question Answer Format (English)

Al-Hizbul A'zam
(Pocket Size)

Tajweed for Beginners

Muhammad (SAW) -
A Mercy unto mankind

Etiquettes for Teachers
آداب المعلمين

Etiquettes for Students
آداب المتعلمين

Hadhrat Mufti Mahmood Hasan
Gangohi رحمة الله عليه

Hadhrat Moulana Maseehullah
Khan Saahib Sherwaani
رحمة الله عليه

The Life and Mission of Hadhrat
Moulana Husain Ahmad Madani
رحمة الله عليه

Hadhrat Moulana Muhammad
Qaasim Nanotwi رحمة الله عليه

www.ingramcontent.com/pod-product-compliance
Lightning Source LLC
Chambersburg PA
CBHW071112080526
44587CB00013B/1319